I0456361

Bibs
Cabbages & Kings

Lady of the
House

Byrne Corbin

orn in Boston on August 21st, 1911, Elizabeth Annette Nener was the third of six children of mother Lucy and father John James Cornelius Willoughby Nener the 7th. Her gift for writing developed early and continued to grow as she developed into the 20th Century's more prolific and ambitious raconteurs of life at home, abroad, or while serving as the Town of Braintree's first female State Representative.

Written in 1929 are the following words used to describe her.... (From her Malden Girls Catholic High School Yearbook)

Rough seas, beacon lights, and a white ship gallantly plunging
over deep green and white turned waves, plunging carefully,
yet swiftly, straight way ahead! The captain at the helm, head
uplifted with sure and firms touch on the wheel, with never
a backward glance, now and then guided by the brilliant
stars overhead but ever confident and sure of herself.
This is Elizabeth!
High above she shoots through air and light
Above all low delay,
There's nothing earthly bounds her flight,
Nor shadow dims her way.

She'd burn the midnight oil, struggling into the wee hours of the morning to catch some elusive idea, possibly poetic, often weaving it about imaginary people of the world to which she has the magic key, and bringing forth some drama which leaves us in an amazing wonder at the clever head which produced it. Yet withal, Elizabeth is one of the jolliest among us, and to those who know the true friendship that is hers to possess, she can never be other than the gallant captain. The quest for intellectual advancement and the glorious principal that there is nothing more admirable than love of honor; and nothing of greater benefit to the human mind than love of knowledge.

Her mother advised her to keep a scrapbook because she would lead an interesting life. This book attempts to capture some of the more exciting and entertaining words and ideas of her 86 years on earth from the many scrapbooks she assembled.

After the death of her husband, she went back to work starting her own secretarial business in Boston in 1944 to support her two young children Richard and Gael. Three years later, she would meet and marry Edward A. Metayer and fulfill a lifelong dream by moving to the historic town of Braintree, Massachusetts where her childhood idol Abigail Adams had lived with husband John, our Second President. She admired Abigail's strong hand guiding the Adams family while husband John was away attending to affairs of the State and founding a new nation. Fascinated with this wife of the Second President and mother of the Sixth, she read everything she wrote. She delighted in her request of John as he dealt with the Declaration of Independence to "remember the ladies".

Considered to be THE most important woman in the early history of our country, the indefatigable Abigail influenced and continues to inspire with her deeds and intellectual pursuits recorded in her many letters.

Braintree's resources and historical significance drew Elizabeth to the East side of town where she began her forty years of public service living at 33 Arthur Street.

Twelve days before the death of our beloved President John F. Kennedy on November 10th, 1963, the first of many newspaper articles would be written for the Braintree Sunday News under the title of Cabbages and Kings. Typed upstairs in a little room in the corner of the house for over twenty-one years.

She had been asked by the editor of the newspaper Mr. John Donahue to write a weekly newspaper column calling it "Cabbages and Kings" from "Alice in Wonderland", for I too shall speak of many things".

"The time has come," the Walrus said,
"To talk of many things;
Of shoes - and ships - and sealing wax -
Of cabbages - and kings"

Lewis Carroll

It was just another Wednesday, - that rather pivotal day that, like an arrow, splits the week in twain, bringing one up sharply to wonder what on earth happened to Monday and Tuesday, and how on earth one can possibly tuck into Thursday and Friday all the myriad things that constitute a prelude to the magic of one's weekend. Yes, it began like any day, and yet, before the sun had set. I'd be writing a column for the Braintree Sunday News! How marvelously unpredictable is life" she wrote in her first column.

Some of the titles of the many poems she penned include....

"Aftermath" about the day after Christmas (her favorite holiday as you'll soon read), Anniversary (the first of JFK's death), Cape Cod, Back to School, April, August, Busy! Busy!, Christmas Epilogue, Christmas Thoughts, Driftwood, Farewell to February, Grandson, Holidays Ahead, Involvement, January Rivers, Let It Be Said, March, New Year Resolutions, Night Noises, Optimism, Rainy Spring, Reflections, Snowstorm, Summer, The Candidate, The Christmas Corsage, The First Robin, The Month of March, The Wig, 'Tis Spring, and What A Winter.

Stories and tales sure to entertain especially...Abraham, Advent Wreath, A Skunk At A Toy Party, Bicentennial, Birds In Their Nests, Braintree in the Fifties, Christmas Guest, Christmas Memories, Christmas on Beacon Hill, Idylls Of A King, Growing old, Jet Travel, Kennedy Compound Visit, Kindergarten, Library School, Madame Zara, Memory Lane, More From The State House, No Gentleman This!, On Grand motherhood, On Home, Rainy Weather, Spring???, Swearing In, and Wild Life are just a few of the many you'll find enlightening.

Describing....the streets of Boston as one of the rivers of Hades in Greek Mythology as being gloomy, dark, infernal and hellish across which the ferryman Charon conveyed the souls of the dead in a nether world kingdom. Why such a stygian cave on this Tuesday evening November 14th, 1965? The entire state along with New York City, Buffalo, New Hampshire and Connecticut were experiencing a Blackout!

Once for a Town Meeting in 1972 she composed a poem paying tribute to the Town Meeting Members for that vote authorizing the expenditure of a designated amount of public funds for a specific purpose.

"No one ever quite remembers to say,
Thanks Town Meeting Members for that vote
that changed our lives since last we met!
Which is why tonight I'm standing;
and these accolades I'm handing to a group whose
kindness we shall not forget."
It was just a year ago when Pilgrim Road and
Mayflower too were the sickest saddest sorriest streets in town,
I'm telling you! On all sides, the
mud was oozing; manhole covers rose on high
so that every child on bike or trike was knocked
flat as he passed them by
There were rocks and stones threatening breaking bones...
each street was a total mess!
Then we brought our problem to you good friends,
and we pleaded and......can't you guess?
The appropriation was voted - to fix up the
streets, each one...and - by the ending of summer
why the whole darned job was done!
Our roadways are now macadam;
and we've sidewalks as well, by gosh;
and the manhole covers are all in place;
and the area looks quite posh!
So -tonight we thought we'd thank you all
and take a moment to note that when it comes
to Town Meeting Members, you sure all have our vote!

She'd participate in historical town affairs by dressing in colonial costume for the Bicentennial Parade or Time Capsule Dedication.

Braintree's 350th Anniversary celebration was also a chance for her to look as lovely as ever in her beautiful ball costume gown observing Braintree's Heritage of 350 years in a meaningful and memorable way. As guest speaker for this special occasion she delivered her usual eloquent address to all in attendance dedicating the Heritage Rock on a perfect Saturday morning on the grounds in front of Town Hall and gratefully captured on film for all to see this very special lady.

The many clubs she joined or had her application for membership accepted especially Women's Clubs was amazing. As a member she would sometimes play hostess, write, direct or star in a play or drama scene. As President elected in 1954 of the Braintree Point Woman's Club she produced this poem for another President at a tribute for the Massachusetts State Federation of Women's Clubs…

She is no more; her loving heart is stilled;
The brighter better world she sought to build
No more shall know the magic of her smile,
The ease with which her friendship could beguile.
She walked in beauty; and the years were kind,
Leaving their stamp upon a brilliant mind,
Attuned to each fond hope and dream, each plan
That filled the troubled soul of mortal man…
I look back on the golden days we shared
To marvel at how totally she cared;
The warmth of the compassionate embrace
She offered to the whole human race…
Our Federation Ship of State she steered;
Ne'er from the paths of service ever veered;
Rising to high achievement and acclaim,
To add to our fair Federation fame.
She won the loving friendship of her crew.
How loath we were to bid her fond "Adieu"
As, her fair term of office wisely spent,
She then became a loved Past President!
To know this gallant lady was indeed
A privilege for those the fates decreed
Might share the golden gladness of her years,
Might know her gentle laughter, and her tears.
We'll MISS her; we'll remember with a sigh
Her tender smile when last we said "Good-bye"!
Rest well, dear kind friend, Ada, safe above;
Now sheltered 'neath the mantle of God's love.

For the Corbin and Metayer families, Gramma Metayer was a source of pride especially on January 1st, 1975. I had to rush to finish my paper route before we could leave to go into the State House to attend her inauguration. We loved seeing her raise her hand and be sworn into office as we watched enchanted by all the protocol, pomp, and circumstance. My mother, father, brothers James and Gregory, and grandfather and I witnessed the magnificent pageantry from the Gallery as she accepted her oath of office in the House Chamber.

"I, Elizabeth Metayer, do solemnly swear", the words of the oath finding a warm response within her soul and ours too! Solemn indeed, this oath, and this moment was a day to remember. A day toward which all the other days of her exciting life seem to have pointed like so many arrows.

It was climbing Mt. Everest...and crossing the Atlantic in a rowboat...and scaling the Grand Canyon wall all rolled up into one.

Elizabeth's eyes rise high, high above the Bullfinch State House dome to where the loving Father of us all can hear the prayer within her heart. Standing there within the half-moon of that most historic august circle along with 239 other legislators. The awesomeness of the task undertaken stirs their collective souls like some great surging wave.

"Dear God," she asks, "Help me to measure up; help me to justify their faith in me - those wonderful people on my team; and those wonderful people who have voted for me - help me ever to remember that this legislator's worth will e'er be measured by the deep concern she has for all the people she will serve...Help me,"

Within this hallowed place our Gramma would find her House Seat #141 among the other bright and shining historic figures found here. The spirit of freedom emanating from their faces eager to tackle the great task that lay before them, this first day of 1975.

After being defeated in 1966, Elizabeth ran again in 1974 as a candidate for Braintree's State Representative won! The official notification letter from the Secretary of the Commonwealth of her nomination at the Primaries held September 10th, 1974 as a Candidate for the Office of Representative Seventh Norfolk District under the political designation of Democrat to be voted for at the State Election, November 5th, 1974 began with the words...Dear Sir:

She was elected and served as Braintree's first female State Representative for ten years under the Golden Dome on Beacon Hill. A fact which delighted her was occupying the same seat as this illustrious American President John Adams in the House of Representatives, representing even as he did the people of Braintree. Her busy days and nights were summarized for the constituents of the town in her weekly column titled Lady of the House. One of her bills to name the bridge and the ramp leading out of the Quincy Adams MBTA station for America's second First Lady, Abigail Adams was thought to be a tawdry way to remember the wife of the nation's second president opined the great-great-great-grandson of Abigail, Thomas Boylston Adams. His comments prompted her to respond in a letter that she honestly thought he would approve. Naming the gateway to the most historic, - and indeed the loveliest part of our Commonwealth in her way of thinking Cape Cod was anything but a cheap publicity stunt. Such objections didn't faze Elizabeth who planned a festive dedication of the "gateway". It will be a great day" she said. The idea that the millions who will use the roadway over the years will raise their eyes and be reminded of a lady who played a key role in the success of her husband's political and diplomatic career. He could go off to Europe or to other parts of this country, while she managed the family farm, brought up the children, handled the finances and all the while kept up her husband's spirits by writing some of history's loveliest and most refreshing letters.

Approved by the Governor Michael Dukakis on May 8th, 1984; an Act designating the overpass in the Town of Braintree as the Abigail Adams Overpass became a reality. "It will be a great day," Elizabeth said. "One idea I've had is to put in some sort of planting in addition to a plaque or monument…You know, Abigail was the first person to bring the York rose from England to America. Maybe we'll plant some of those."

Elizabeth's contributions to the people of Braintree were acknowledged by naming the crosswalk in the heart of the town in her honor connecting Town Hall with the Town Library.

A section of this same library was also named in her honor for her many years of service, dedication and kindness to the people especially the children of Braintree. The Metayer Tower serves as a reminder in the library as does this book of the magic and wonder that books stir.

May you discover and experience the wonderful world as seen and so eloquently documented by my grandmother Elizabeth "Bibs" Metayer. Named to be included among the "Foremost Women of the Twentieth Century" in a biographical publication published in Cambridge shire, England. The goal of the publication in whose Spring 1985 edition appears her name is "to place on record a selection of the achievements and accomplishments of leading women throughout the world, in order to encourage those of future generations to endeavor to achieve their full potential."

Listed in "The Two Thousand Women Of Achievement" in 1969 as well as Who's Who in American Politics. The National Register of Prominent Americans included her in their 1970 Edition and The International Platform Association too…Formerly called the International Lyceum Association and Before that the American Lyceum Association in 1903. Started in 1826 by the most illustrious orator in the nation's history Daniel Webster who helped to found in the town of Milbury, Massachusetts the nation's first "Lyceum" which Webster tells us is "an association for debate and literary improvement, an educational organization providing inspirational lectures, concerts, entertainment etc." Perhaps the most noteworthy stimulus to the growth of Webster's "Lyceum" was the organization's effort to schedule an American lecture tour for the incomparable English author, Charles Dickens. A Boston journalist responsible for establishing America's first lecture bureau one James Redpath sought the assistance of Webster's "lyceum". Together this lecture bureau was responsible for presenting such illustrious figures as Mark Twain, Julia Ward Howe, Ralph Emerson, Henry Ward Beecher, P.T. Barnum and Josh Billings. The International Platform Association, the oldest international organization in the U.S. has included on its membership rolls a large percentage of the great names that mark our American Heritage.

Presidents Theodore and Franklin Roosevelt, Herbert Hoover, William Howard Taft, Woodrow Wilson, John F. Kennedy, Harry Truman, Lyndon Johnson and Richard Nixon.

The name of William Jennings Bryan appears in the distinguished membership records, as well as that of Carl Sandburg, Art Buchwald, Otto Preminger, Winston Churchill, "Dear Abby" Van Buren, David Brinkley, Betty Furness, and Rex Harrison along with a host of others in the fields of statesmanship, business, oratory, the theater, movies and entertainment.

People admired the accomplishments of her many years in public service and recognized her performance in the following areas....

Healthcare, the elderly, crime fighting, tax relief, child care, hazardous waste, transportation, the handicapped, women's issues, the displaced homemakers program and in 1986 received the Governor's award in addressing AIDS. When the problem of AIDS first surfaced, Elizabeth was Vice Chairman of the Healthcare Committee. A special meeting on the subject was held to which were invited the Commissioner of Public Health and various members of the medical profession to provide information on the medical dangers involved in the disease. Among the causes listed for the spread of AIDS was the infected blood donors. The Red Cross representative especially was concerned and it was revealed selling blood for liquor. "The menace was great," Elizabeth added.

Metayer asked commissioner Bailus, Jr. of the Department of Public Health how much money they would need from the state to fund this crash program and after consultation she was told $1,500,000.00.

"It was budget time and I sought to have the large amount added. I defended it on the floor of the house and won" she said. The million and a half was added and the research programs were instituted. The test is now a reality.

She joins the following historical names for the literary, scientific, or civic contributions to the Commonwealth and especially the Town of Braintree...John Adams, John Quincy Adams, Abigail Adams, Thomas Watson, Caleb Stetson, Benjamin Vinton French, John Hancock, Sylvanus Thayer, The Morrison Family, and Norton Hollis!

A town that in 1882 during a town meeting appealed to see whether the town will, by its vote or otherwise ask the Legislature to extend to women who are citizens the right to hold town office and to vote in town affairs on the same terms as male citizens. Ninety-two years later, Elizabeth in this very progressive town made history as the first female to be elected in this town office.

An ebullient woman who still found time to be a loving wife, mother, grandmother, a good neighbor, a writer, an active citizen, a champion of a cause, or someone who would greet you at the local

Capitol Supermarket with a hello and a smile. She sponsored Babe Ruth, a Girls Softball Team Metayer's Marauders and a Boys Baseball Team The Cubs. Her involvement with all these affairs never prevented her from being a grandmother to my brothers Jimmy and Greg and I and our two cousins Richard and Franklin Metayer from Mystic, CT. Staying at grandma's house up the street from Watson park was always special. I remember her tucking us in at night, but not before we said our prayers as we knelt beside the bed. Praying to God to take care of family and friends and to please make us good boys. We'd finish by saying Angel of God my guardian dear, to whom God's love commits me here, ever this day be at my side, to light and guide, to rule and guard Amen. Then we'd all climb into bed and listen as she'd tell us stories about Sammy the Squirrel, or the friendly snake seen earlier that day in the garden, or of masted sailing vessels from long ago. We'd drift off with visions of talking animals or great sea adventuress filling our dreams safe in Grandma's loving arms. We were her darlings, dears, angels, little lambs, pussycats, the cat's whiskers, or even sometimes little imps! When something startled her she would say "holy jumpin!" Even when I accidentally painted her fence the wrong color she would never utter a bad word. When I stepped on a piece of glass out by the pool that has smashed on the patio while I was watering the garden, I heard her say the same words as when I painted the fence the wrong color years before. Her and grandpa were baby-sitting us at the time and I must have knocked an ashtray off the picnic table with the hose and had not heard it hit the ground. After stepping on the jagged chunk of clear glass slicing my foot I hobbled over to the screen door and announced that I was in need of a Band-Aid and some Mercurochrome. "Jesus, Mary, and Joseph," she cried. Those were the harshest words I ever heard her utter. She told me that her mom and dad never argued, yelled, screamed or got cross. Her father only once had to punish her for spilling milk all over his desk and drafting table, soaking a new set of plans he had been working on as an engineer. With a pencil he tapped here gently once over her knuckles she said. The plans were structural drawings for the Hatch Shell Boston.

Being interested in history I asked her once where she was on that day of infamy December 7th, 1941 when the U.S. Naval Base was attacked by Japan at Pearl Harbor, she replied…

We were all together at a big family dinner at my mother's in Alston. The radio was on softly in the background. When the news suddenly flashed on we all sat in absolute horror. I remember we all started calling the enemy names. My father said….and we've been sending then scrap iron to make bullets to kill our boys".

As evidenced by her excellent attendance record, people continued to be impressed by her sensitivity to the needs of her constituents, and her knowledgeable response to the most complex business issues that faced our state. Described in the March 11th, 1982 edition of The Christian Science Monitor as, "one of the legislature's most experienced members," proving her outstanding ability by being appointed as Assistant Majority Leader in the House of Representatives. Called by one of her more politically savvy friends as a "citizen representative" meaning that she was close to the people she represented, and had no other ambition but to serve them well.

When asked to sum up her feelings about her decade of service as Braintree's State Representative, Elizabeth said, "I have loved every day of it. I have loved serving the wonderful people of Braintree on Beacon Hill; and I have loved the wonderful people I have known there, the colleagues with whom I have served; the people in our state agencies; the employees whose mission it is to smooth the paths of all of us in government; everyone in all three branches. They've been great to me. Altogether, the past ten years have represented the frosting on the decidedly beautiful cake that has been my life."

Her life as a State Representative may be better understood by reading her Lady of the House columns as she climbed the State House for ten years. This part of the book should be of particular interest to those seeking to serve in public office. Dedication speeches, resolutions, Proclamation, Bills, and testimonials are included for your review and historical significance.

Her inspirations sometimes were the very people she represented. For instance, she filed legislation at the request of Patrick Leonard, a Braintree resident, recommending that Deborah Sampson, the female soldier of the American Revolution be honored by a commemorative stamp. Not content to support her fellow countrymen indirectly and from a distance, she disguised herself as Robert Shurtliff and enlisted in the Continental forces on May 23rd, 1782 at Uxbridge, marched to West Point, and became a member of the Brigade. Her 5'8" frame and physical strength managed to keep her gender undetected until she fell victim to typhoid fever. But not before she was wounded three times suffering saber wounds and a shot of lead to the thigh. She was honorably discharged on October 25th, 1783 and with the help of Paul Revere in 1792 by then living in Canton, MA helped Sampson who moved to adjacent Sharon secure her pension as the war's only female pensioner. She was a direct descendant of Captain Myles Standish, John Alden, Governor William Bradford.

Governor Michael S. Dukakis signed a proclamation prepared by State Rep. Elizabeth N, Metayer proclaiming May 23rd as Deborah Sampson Heroine of the Commonwealth Day.

Also of important historical note in another first for women as our country developed was on February 21st, 1838 at the Massachusetts State House. Angelina Grimke spoke before the legislative Committee of the Great and General Court and presented to the legislators a petition signed by 20,000 Massachusetts women demanding the liberation of black people. She had to fight a double battle, for not only the subject of her speech, Abolition of Slavery, but also the idea of a woman Delivering it were unprecedented.

Never before had a woman dared to break through the confines of her home and attempt to reconstruct the male realm of public policy. Angelina Grimke, a Southern lady of the Charleston aristocracy, with natural uncorrupted childhood feelings of kinship and love for the slave children on her family's estate, succeeded through her appearance before the legislative committee in holding her audience spellbound and converting many borderline abolitionists despite their recalcitrant attitudes. She shared much with the slaves for whom many fought, for like blacks, women were oppressed and cut off from social political, and educational opportunities afforded only white men. The gallery crowd which has congregated to witness such a phenomenon hissed and scoffed at the "freak" whom they believed intellectually incapable of logically dealing with momentous issues of constitutional law. Termed by the media in newspapers of the day as a "Devilina," journalists conceded her great talent as an orator, which fact in itself constituted a remarkable achievement for a woman who have been denied a classical education.

Elizabeth N. Metayer also understood and recognized the uphill battle that women faced. She sought to emphasize the role of women in the economy, their accomplishments in their professions, in government, in the arts and humanities, and their roles as wives and mothers. Women have enriched our society as homemakers and community life through dedicated service as volunteers. With the growing awareness of the significant contributions women have made to the development of our Commonwealth and its social and economic life, during her lifetime, saw awards that had been called Man of the Year changed to Person of the Year due to the fact that women were now opening doors to the future through diligence, hard work, and education.

When first elected in 1974, only 16 female state representatives out of the 240 members would serve in the male dominated State House under the Dukakis administration.

A revolution in attitudes however was starting to take place among men and, more importantly, among women.

One sign of the change was across the pond in England at Wimbledon where girls were now allowed to participate after 100 years of being excluded as ball boys at this tennis tournament's most celebrated event in 1977.

A Town Meeting Member for twenty-five years, she also held the following titles…Auctioneer. author. Assistant Majority Leader Vice Chairman, Clubwoman, Candidate, Columnist, Fortune Teller, Grand Marshal, Legislator, Trustee, Founder, organizer, Honorable, Professional Book Reviewer, World Traveler, Director, guest speaker, Representative, Teacher, President, Community Leader, Philergian, Volunteer, and in 1981 the "Distinguished Citizen of the Year" by the Old Colony Council, Boy Scouts of America. In high school she belonged to the Chester-Belloc Club, Dramatics, Sports Club, and Children of Mary.

Now it's time for you to find in the following pages how Elizabeth captures the spirit of adventure and zest for learning and reading. She believed that education consists not merely in intellectual attainments; equally essential are those in the spiritual order. As you turn the pages and poems and tales unfold, may your dreams and spirits take wing. You may find yourself smiling, laughing, and dreaming with maybe a tear or two springing to your eyes.

Discover America as you journey across the U.S. and Canada on an 11,000-mile trek in a self-contained fan trailer that Elizabeth and her husband Ted traveled during the summer of 1970.

Starting in Niagara Falls they headed west and en route visited Mount Rushmore, South Dakota And the Presidential Monuments; Pennsylvania, Yellowstone National Park; Glacier National Park; Montana, Banff and Lake Louise, Alberta; the Columbia Ice Fields and Jasper National Park, California; The Grand Canyon's North Rim; Zion Canyon, Salt lake City and Dinosaur National Park Utah; Mohave Desert, Carmel and Monterey, Kentucky, New Mexico; and Amish Country. Take a 6,000-mile journey over two months' time in a travel trailer through Canada's Maritime Provinces, Quebec, Ontario, with highlights of New Brunswick. Visits to St. Andrew By the Sea and Fundy National Park where the world's largest flower pots line the rocky shore. Nova Scotia with its storied Cabot Trail; Grand Pre, the land of "Evangeline"; Annapolis Royal and Yarmouth.... Prince Edward Island and a journey about Charlottetown, a stay at Cavendish Beach and an exploration of Cornwall...

The Gaspe Peninsula with a stop at Perce, that immense rock arch far out to sea through which, at low tide, one may walk on the ocean floor to find fossils millions of years in age; a look at the outdoor ovens with their wonderful home-baked bread, the racks of cod drying in the sun...Quebec City, with the historic Chateau Frontenac towering above the magnificent fortress La Citadelle, crowning Cap Diamont; Quebec City with a look of France about it and an old-world flavor that delights the soul...Quebec City, the "Cradle of Canadian History." Montreal, old and new...and Ontario with its magnificent Parliament Buildings at Ottawa, its changing of the Guard and the rest.

European Holiday and you'll travel to the 19 countries she and husband Ted visited. Planned to take advantage of the ideal vacation weather in each country visited climate-wise, they crossed and criss crossed the European Continent and the British Isles.

In 1970, this poem appeared in the book Braintree Our Town written for the third-grade school children about the rich heritage of the town published for their use by the Philergians of Braintree.

An Indian Tale

Where boys and girls now romp and play
Indian children once held sway
Roamed the forest far and wide
Fished the silver streams beside
Tracked the deer, and trailed the bear;
Lived in wigwams everywhere
Long before the white men came
To give our Braintree-town its name
There were no streets on which to walk
And only sound of Indian talk
And Indian fun, and Indian games
And funny sounding Indian names
Not a school, nor church nor shop
Just the forest and, on top
Miles of sky that all looked down
On Indian children in our town

Elizabeth N. Metayer.

I was attending Sacred Heart School in Weymouth Landing as a third grader at the time and we were all presented with the book that I still treasure to this day. Seven months before she died while living in Pompano Beach, Florida, I asked her to autograph it for me and this is what she wrote…………..

To Byrne L. Corbin,

"Grandson extraordinaire," a beautiful human being who has brought nothing but joy into the lives of his family and especially into the life of his Grandmother.

Elizabeth N. Metayer
Nov. 10, 1997

In December of 1970 after reading "Cabbages & Kings" the Director of Travel Division for the State of South Dakota Mrs. D.J. Cline responded to the Braintree Observer and Sunday Forum by writing…

A clipping of an article of South Dakota written by you came across my desk recently. Thank you for the generous coverage, your descriptions are very picturesque and vivid. In your travels you certainly are observant and have a keen eye for details which would behoove any writer. Is "Cabbages & Kings" a regular column? If so, are the topics usually of a travel or vacation nature? Thank you again!

For thirty-six years as a grandmother to me, she gave many gifts and did many wonderful things for me. Typing reports for school projects or helping me write or assist with my homework are just some of the many written assignments she lent to me her expertise. This book is my way of returning and sharing that which was bestowed upon me as the grandson of the twentieth century's "Cabbages & Kings" and "Lady of the House."

I now bring before the public this collection of literary works presented to inspire the child in all of us.

BYRNE CORBIN
Grandson

"The time has come", the walrus said,
"To talk of many things;
of shoes-and ships-and
sealing wax-
of cabbages-and kings"

"Cabbages and Kings"

Contents

WRITTEN FOR THE SUNDAY NEWS

"The time has come", the Walrus said,
"To talk of many things;
Of shoes - and ships - and
Sealing wax -
Of cabbages - and kings"
—Lewis Carroll

It was just another Wednesday, - that rather pivotal day that, like an arrow, splits the week into twain, bringing one up sharply to wonder what on earth happened to Monday and Tuesday, and how on earth one can possibly tuck into Thursday and Friday all the myriad things that constitute a prelude to the magic of one's weekend.

Yes, it began like any day, and yet, before the sun had set, I'd be writing a column for the Braintree Sunday News! How marvelously unpredictable is life! And how exciting when one is fifty, has the leisure, and can sift into the twenty-four of one's day till the things one can do naught but dream about when one is young. You know, it's a golden age, - fifty, - and yet I remember back to when I thought quite differently!

I shall hate it when I'm fifty!
I was barely twenty-two
And the world was wide with
wonder, and the sky was
cobalt blue,
While ahead life stretched before
me like a roadway fresh with flowers…
Oh, the blessed, breathless beauty
of those twenty-two-ish hours!
I shall hate it being fifty - I shall love my life no more,
To be fifty - half a hundred -
What a dreadful, dreadful bore!

I'll just hate it when I'm fifty;
  I was almost thirty-eight,
And my roots were firm and
  Fastened, and my children tall
And straight
Brought their magic to my
  moments, and their glory to
  my days,
Oh, the wise sophistication of my
  Thirty-eight-ish ways!
I shall hate it being fifty;
  Life is fleeing far too fast,
Let me cling, please, to my
  Thirties; let me make their
  Magic last!

How I'll hate it when I'm fifty;
  I was nearly forty-three
And my children planned quite
  Gaily to go sailing off from
Me.
And I watched with apprehension
While they blithely marched
Toward life
While my daughter sought a
Husband, and my son brought
Home a wife.

Oh, how lonely and how empty
Now my days were doomed
To be,
How I faced with trepidation
Thoughts of being drab fifty!

How I love it, being fifty -
Here I'm nearly fifty-one
And my children nicely married
All my days I fill with - FUN!
I may spend their golden hours
In a spree of pure delight;
With a pen beguile the morning;
With a book beguile the night.
I could maybe run for office -
Plan a gift shop - write a
Book...
I could give this grand wide world
Of ours another brand new
Look!

Why, I love it, being fifty;
I face sixty with a zest,
For the years that followed fifty
Are decidedly the best!

Yes, it is wonderful fun being fifty. That little verse just naturally wrote itself, flowed from my pen as I stopped a moment to look back and ponder over what has lain behind and what will lie ahead. Like every other wife and mother, I've done a "job of work", and now I face the "golden years", and they are golden. The nicest thing about life is the fact that each decade of living is an exciting prelude to the next.

At twenty-two I wouldn't have had the depth, the insight, for CABBAGES AND KINGS: at thirty-eight, I wouldn't have had the time; at forty-three, I might not have had the interest; but at fifty- what FUN! Here's to being fifty - and here's to CABBAGES AND KINGS!!!

11-16-69 ABRAHAM

This is the story of a little Cedar Waxwing - the which, in case you do not know, is a tiny creature, characterized in Webster's unabridged as a "cherry bird...widely distributed over temperate North America."

This particular little "immature Cedar Waxwing" had flown against the porch of a neighbor of my friend Eleanor; and lay panting on the cold ground, his wing injured, and his obvious flight south cruelly interrupted. He was found in this helpless state by a group of neighborhood children, who immediately summoned to the scene Jay, the young son of friend Eleanor, and the neighborhood naturalist.

Jay lifted the little bird tenderly in his warm young hands, and hurried homeward "We'll have to put him in a cage," he said. "I'll get one," cried a friend. "My mother has a beautiful cage" he said, and was off like an arrow in the direction of home, to return promptly and breathlessly, cage in hand. It was a beautiful cage; just about the loveliest one anyone would, in all probability, ever behold; and, fortunately for the small boy, his mother, busy about the house, had failed to note the removal of the handsome, handcrafted creation which had been designed especially for her by an artist friend, and executed at fabulous cost...

The little Waxwing was obviously appreciative of the finer things in life, for he settled down happily in his lush new abode. A wild bird instinctively resists captivity, generally refusing food, and so bringing about his demise. Not this small fellow, however!

He hopped about the cage gaily, though awkwardly, casting a decidedly friendly eye toward the young Samaritans who clustered about him, Audubon in hand, boning up on the care and feeding of waxwings... their little friend unhesitatingly downed the Yew berries they offered him from nearby shrubs; and even the arrival of one irate, cage demanding mother, and his consequent transfer to less lofty surroundings, appeared to disturb the small bird not at all.

"You know, Jay," said sister Sheila, "He should have a name... "Yes." echoed the rest, "Jay, you should pick up a good one!" Several pairs of eyes turned expectantly toward the young conservationist, whose own glance at that precise moment, fell upon the Presidents' wastebasket in the corner of his room. "Let's call him Abraham," he said, eyeing the mournful face of good old Honest…

The group acquiesced automatically. Not one eye batted at the prospect of tacking the large name, "Abraham," on the small caged fellow. The neighborhood kids expect the unusual from Jay. Isn't his guinea pig called "Jonas," after the Jonas Perkins School? And how about "Eustis," the useless Rabbit??? And, "Thomas Jefferson Cat," originally named "Tom" for one of his ancestors, a trio of cats belonging to his friends, the Daiutes, with the intriguing names of Tom, Dick and Harry Cat. The name has seemed to fit until Tom cat began to develop unusually high-class characteristics, when Jay had seen fit to call the haughty feline by his given name of "Thomas," adding "Jefferson" for his birthplace which was Jefferson, Maine.

Incidentally, Abraham has been rescued on Tuesday; and by Wednesday he was merrily alighting on the fingers of his young friends, who found themselves hand-feeding the berries they brought his way in such quantities that a strict diet, or death from gluttony, was looming larger and larger on the horizon of their new pet…

My friend, Eleanor, meanwhile, was eyeing the situation with some misgivings. The little fellow's wing, she was quite sure, was broken, and should be set.

If Abraham succumbed while in the possession of Jay and Sheila and their young friends, he would merely find a resting place, along with innumerable other family pets, under the big tree in the back yard.

On the other hand, if we were turned over to the Trailside Museum, those in charge would know precisely what to do about the broken wing; in addition, should he succumb in captivity, as most wild birds do, they might stuff the little fellow, and include him in their bird collection.

And so off to the Trailside Museum went Eleanor and Abraham; accompanied by a group of reluctant conservationists who thus sought, mournfully, to put an end to what had been quite an adventure…

"Such a friendly little fellow." said the museum attendant. "They're not usually, you know-wild birds; of course, we'll take him."

The little immature Cedar Waxwing must have adjusted to the limelight of the Trailside Museum quite as beautifully as he had adjusted to the life in the happy habitation of my friend Eleanor…As a matter of a fact, the limelight obviously turned out to be precisely his cup of tea. For did you happen to see a merry little speckled, brownish Cedar Waxwing making like a Thespian on Major Mudd's television show a couple of weeks ago??? Well, that was none other than the pride of Eleanor's neighborhood – ABRAHAM!

The children aren't quite so lonely for their little friend these days; the star makers, you see, are comforted by the knowledge that thousands of other children will be enabled now to share their delight in the little wild creature that so happily came their way.

12-28-63 A CHRISTMAS WREATH

WRITTEN FOR THE SUNDAY NEWS

A Christmas wreath hangs gaily on my door. Its great red bow read quite simply "Noel", but there's a "Merry Christmas" woven into its holly and red berries; there's "Welcome" in its golden bells; and there's "What a proud, beautiful time of year it is!" in the shining sight of it and the sweet soft fragrance of it.

"Everywhere, everywhere, Christmas!" cries my foyer.

There's a Christmas tree in just about every room. Tiny lights twinkle like stars on one of them, and glow softly on the branches of another, and across the cool, silver sweep of the third, shafts of color toss a Christmas rainbow. Candles illumine the windows. Stockings hang expectantly by the fireplace; and Christmas bells tinkle softly from every Christmas corner.

We've "decked the halls" and decked the walls. We're intoxicated with the holiday wine of color and form and beauty. We're stringing the wonderful days of the Christmas season like jewels upon a golden chain. Christmas carols are part and parcel of our days; Christmas greetings race across the miles and back. And in a quiet corner, almost unnoticed in the splash and splendor of Christmas, there's the CRECHE!

We pause a moment, our eyes upon its simple beauty, our hearts ablaze. There's no tinsel and no glitter here, no holly, no red berries and no bows, just a rude, brown stable, but the real magnificence of

Christmas is housed within – here with the tiny figure in the manger, the little Christ, the Prince of Peace; here with the mother Mary and with Joseph and the shepherds from the hills, the Wise Men from the east. Yes, here IS Christmas!

The wreath that speaks a gentle "Noel" on door is merely saying "Happy Birthday, blessed Child!" The candles shining softly in the night bespeak a welcome to the little one for whom there was no room once in the inn. The Christmas tree, bedecked with gifts, but tells the Wise Men's story. "Peace on earth," the great, glad cry of Christmas, "Good will to men!" The angel – song is housed within our hearts; the blessed Christmas story in our souls…the blessed Christmas story…

"Now it came to pass in those days, that a decree went forth from Caesar Augustus that census of the whole world should be taken. This first census took place while Cyrinus was governor of Syria. And all were going, each to his own, to register. And Joseph also went from Galilee out of the town of Nazareth into Judea to the town of David, which is called Bethlehem—because he was of the house and family of David—to register, together with Mary his espoused wife, who was with child. And it came to pass while they were there, that the days for her to be delivered were fulfilled. And she brought forth her firstborn son, and wrapped him in swaddling clothes, and laid him in a manger, because there was no room for them in the inn. And there were shepherds in the same district living in the fields and keeping watch over their flock by night. And behold, an angel of the Lord stood by them and the glory of God shone round about them, and they fear exceedingly. And the angel said to them, "Don't not be afraid, for behold, I bring you good news of great joy which shall be to all the people; for today in the town of David a Savior has been born to you, who is Christ the Lord. And this shall be a sign to you; you will find an infant wrapped swaddling clothes and lying in a manger." And suddenly there was with the angel a multitude of the heavenly host praising and saying, "Glory to God in the highest, and on earth peace among men of good will."

St. Luke, Chapter II

Here, then is the great, beating heart of Christmas: here? Motivating force behind the glitter and the glory, here in the blessed birthday of a tiny child

Peace on earth, good will toward men
Echoes on the wind again;
"The child is born!" the ages cry
As Christmas glory lights the sky
Oh, blessed be the hearts of men
As Christmas comes our way again.
A happy and Holy Christmas to all.
Sweet Christmas…
Dear Christmas…Let us have joy this
Blessed day – and reverence – and let us for the little
Christ Child's sake, love one another.

A DAY AT THE BEACH

It's beach time, again. Spending a day at the beach is a simple matter for Ted and me these lush summer days. We may drive leisurely to our destination, lunch at a nearby spot and return home without fuss or fuddle—OR TOO MUCH FUN! 'Twasn't so in the "good old days" when we and our offspring were young. Going to the beach was a project then.

The Metayer children would awaken us in the cold gray dawn; then after an anxious scanning of skies and an interminable wait for the day to make up its mind weather-wise, we would proceed with the business at hand.

A trailer could have been pressed into the service to transport the beach paraphernalia.

There was lunch, first and foremost-enough of it to feed the troops! Experience had taught mother that the principal diversions of beaching were eating and drinking. Huge hampers and throaty thermos jugs, tinkling gaily with ice cubes, would be tucked into the yawning car trunk. (The beach, we had found, is akin to the Sahara in its thirst-inducing propensities for beach-bound children.)

There were beach blankets and towels and chaise lounges for mother and dad; and a beach umbrella, unfailingly toted in case (Heaven forbid!)

any renegade from our sun-worshipping clan might feel the ridiculous urge for shade.

Each child had a favorite toy which must accompany him; and a friend from whom he couldn't possibly be separated for a day. There were books and friends and occasionally a neighbor or two…the car invariably strained at the seams as we headed toward captivating Cape Cod…

Our day always passed in a whirl of excitement. The beach sand was bleached as white as the salt that that had originally flavored our sandwiches, so no one noticed the added seasoning; if a sandwich or two were a bit gritty to the tongue, the fact was scarcely discernible, for our younger ones appeared to swallow things whole in their haste to return to the wonderful wide water.

Ted and I would walk the beach for miles, our entourage trailing behind us, in search of shells and seaweed and fascinating objects which would perfume the neighborhood from our back porch for many days to come. (Until we surreptitiously spirited them away to the backyard incinerator Board of Health, please ignore!)

We managed to look innocently away and pretend they were anyone's but our own when the little darlings in our party splashed elderly ladies, or trailed large wet feet through a neighboring beach encampment, or landed a ball in the soft mid-section of a sleeping beachcomber; or – secure in the presence of Dad – flattened the sand battlements of an army of teenage boys with the little tolerance for the playfulness of the younger set.

And speaking of battlements, "See," we would say delightedly one to another, Ted and I, as Richard built his thrilling sand castles on our best beach towels, "he will surely be an engineer like his grandfather." (Quite as though every small boy on the beach had not created something as incredibly clever on HIS parents' favorite beach blanket.)

Mother's Day was a succession of providing small children with large lunches; of applying sun tan lotion in carload lots; of producing sweaters against cool beach breezes; and sneakers against the perils of sand dunes and rock piles; of providing band-aids for Junior's toe and aspirin for Dad's aching head; and of passing out endless supplies of dry towels and wet libations and cheerful smiles…

Dad's contribution to the day's fun consisted mainly in providing the shoulders from which every' small boy and girl for miles around dived into the sweet sea; and in patiently supporting the resolute chins of the "littlest angels" in their valiant struggle with the fine art of swimming.

There was ALWAYS – or so it seemed – a thunderstorm to climax the day and send us scurrying madly between the beach encampment and the car, toting a soggy succession of things and people, all of which having been immersed in water for hours on end, found themselves suddenly loath to be exposed to the unsolicited onslaught of mere rain.

A century would be consumed, or so it seemed, in fighting our way back to Braintree in the mad Cape traffic. A week later we'd still be brushing sand from the recesses of the family car, and decorating our insect-ridden persons with large coin dots of red mercurochrome; and sleeping right-side down to coddle a sunburn; and applying Ben-Gay liberally to Dad's outraged shoulder muscles.

Strangely enough the entire situation would have righted itself by the time the week had waned and sweet, sweet Saturday and Sunday loomed ahead – when we'd be off to the beach again…

Yes, it's different today. Ted and I may drive leisurely to the nearest, nicest motel and fall quietly into the nearest nicest chaises, then swim sweetly and serenely in the clearest, nicest pool. There's never a speck of sand in the motel dining room; and insects are definitely barred, along with pets and children, from the pleasant environs of this home away from home. So we sit side by side, and we sip tall summer drinks, and the ice tinkles and we smile and then grow silent as we remember other days at the beach…

Thank Heaven some of our grandchildren reside in Braintree…I wonder if Gregory's new red tricycle will fit in the trunk of the family car. He'll never spend Saturday at the beach without it, and the weatherman has promised a perfect summer weekend…

6-21-70 "ADVENTURE"

It was one of those soft spring evenings when to be cheering one's Little League grandsons at Watson Park was all fun!

Jim and Byrne had both played well. Their teams had won. Not that that fact would have mattered a whit to those adoring grandparents following their every move from the bleachers—but it does seem to bring a special glow of pride to the faces of small boys. And—we were warm and comfortable as we watched, a condition not usually present. One invariably has to dress for an evening of Little League along the dear old Monatiquott like one prepared for a trek to the arctic.

At any rate the games were over, and on this particular evening three grandchildren were to repair from the park directly to Grandmother's house, there to sleep in that brand-new trailer that lay parked in Grandpa's driveway. Gregory and I were to occupy the two beds in this newest possession of the Metayers; while the two older boys would curl up in the sleeping bags on the floor.

Excitement ran high; so high, in fact, that with the games over, our young men showed no Disposition to quiet down.

"Let's go ride on the swings," said Gregory, leading me toward the small children's play area at the end of the park. That which we promptly did. Rode on the swings, and swung about on the merry-go-round, and generally had a "bully" time of it.

"I know," said Jim when the three had tired of this particular form of amusement, "Let's go for a walk in the wilderness." "The wilderness?" I repeated, "Where on earth is the wilderness?" "Come follow the river all the way to Swift's Beach."

"Are you sure we can get through?" I asked doubtfully. "We won't sink in the mud, will we? And there aren't any SNAKES, are there?"

The two boys laughed merrily. "NO, of course not, Gram. Anyhow, if there were, they would only be harmless ones.

And so, we set out all four of us, Grandpa having returned to the house, with Jim and Byrne blazing the trail for small Greg and his Grandmother like we were on Safari in the African Bush. And indeed, that's just about how adventurous I felt, never having traveled these paths before.

It was along "Monahan's Path" to be sure. "Why Monahan's Path?" I asked the boys. "I don't know," said Jim. "It just IS" said Byrne.

I asked no questions when I found myself following our young guides to the top of "John's Mound" and across "Mary's Field" to "Jack's Wide Path," "Swiftee's Rocks," and finally to Swift's Beach, which was reached easily—precisely as our young guides had promised. And what a "fun" trek through the wilderness it was!

We picked long beautiful marsh grass which we dropped off at the home of a friend in the final stage of the journey.

We came upon the beached half-hull of an ancient boat, a skeleton which delighted the boys to no end. "what kind of a boat do you suppose it was, Grandma?" they asked earnestly, studying it from all angles.

Arrived at the beach. It was up the ladder-like rungs of the lifeguard's perch to the top and a wide wonderful view of the boats below—with three-year old Greg following his brothers every step of the way to his Grandmother's horror; followed by a turn about the raft, beached until the summer season should call it forth to action.

And, oh yes, the night itself in the brand-new trailer—it also went well. What a job for Grandma to curl up with her three small boys and listen to their dear innocent chatter until sleep claimed them!

Have I thought to mention lately in this column of mine what an absolute joy it is to be a GRANDMOTHER??

12-8-74   "ADVENT WREATH"

Writing a column several days in advance can sometimes throw a columnist off base…like this past week when I discovered that the lovely Advent season had begun and I had failed to preface its arrival with a column on that delightful symbol of this time of year the Advent Wreath!

So – we're a week late in sharing our thoughts on the Advent season and the Advent Wreath – but because a number of my readers asked to do just that, VOICI!

Ours was among the very few families I know who in years past featured the Advent Wreath.

Mother would dust off what must have been a ring mold, though it could have been a very large round cake pan, and place four tall HOLY CANDLES at equal distances within it, fastening them to the mold with nice little puddles of candle drippings.

Then, using what was probably scotch tape or its equivalent, she would attach a purple ribbon, long enough to gracefully drape the family dining table. Filling the mold with sand and keeping the sand moist provided a bed for the little sprigs of green she would next place within the mold…sometimes she used laurel or holly as I remember it; and sometime pine or cedar. Draping these sprigs of green so that they covered the outside of the mold and fell gracefully against a white tablecloth, we had a seasonal centerpiece of especial beauty as well as significance.

The Advent Wreath made its debut on the first Sunday in that special season when, with due ceremony, we would gather about the table and Dad would appeal to His Heavenly Father to bless those fortunate humans who had been placed within his care. (Dad was a wonderful Father and we adored him…) The lighting of the Advent candles would then begin.

On each of the evenings within the first week of Advent the YOUNGEST child lit one candle as the head of the house led his family in a special seasonal prayer which Mother must have unearthed somewhere. Mother had taught school in suburban London and brought many of the wonderful old English Christmas traditions with her here to American when she and Dad, married and with one child, had decided to head his way, happily for the Nener family.

On each evening of the second week, it was the OLDEST child who lit not one, but TWO candles within the Advent Wreath; and on the evenings of the third week, Mother was given a turn to light THREE candles before the evening meal. Father's turn came during the fourth and final week when all four candles glowed throughout the mealtime hour, serving as a bright reminder that the coming of the little Christ Child was at hand.

A pious custom and a beautiful one, I think, looking back on those days in Malden when, growing up, our thoughts were steered more in the direction of the religious significance of the Christmas season than perhaps they are today. Yes, a pious and a beautiful custom…a small but shining piece in the wondrous mosaic that for me has always been the blessed Christmas season.

There were other little traditions within the Nener family. We were encouraged to place what we called our "Saturday money," but which children today term their allowance, in a little "mite box" for the missions; and to perform acts of kindness which Mother classified as "pieces of straw to place within the manger of the Christ Child to keep him warm against the winter cold…"

Christmas was a wondrous time of year within our family; it still is…and its observance invariable began with the blessed Advent season now upon us.

Advent… "God with us."

"O KEY OF DAVID, AND SCEPTER OF THE HOUSE OF ISRAEL, WHATEVER YOU OPEN, NONE SHALL CLOSE; WHATEVER YOU CLOSE, NONE SHALL OPEN…O LIGHT FROM THE EAST, AND SPLENDOR OF LIGHT ETERNAL, YOU WHO ARE THE SUN OF JUSTICE ETERNAL, LET YOUR LIGHT SHINE FORTH…O KING OF NATIONS, FOR WHOM THE NATIONS HAVE LONGED, YOU ARE THE CORNERSTONE TO JOIN ALL NATIONS, TO BRING ALL MEN TOGETHER…"

The beautiful Liturgy of the beautiful Advent season.

A FADED CARPET

You are all grays,
And pale lavenders,
And time-worn pinks, little carpet
For you are old and faded, but-
I love you.
The petals
Of your roses are crushed
And browned at the edges, but
Their perfume
Is yet sweet, little piece
Of artistry, for
I love you.
You are
Hard beneath my feet,
And your dying colors dim
My dying eyes,
But
You are my wandered world, oh

Little, previous memory, and
I love you.

E.A. Nener
(Forty-five)

12-29-68 "AFTERMATH"

'Tis the day after Christmas, and lo! Our ménage
Looks precisely as though it withstood a barrage!
Gay gift wrappings are strewn about each tousled room,
While petite ribbon bows set the carpets abloom.

***

In every odd corner, a mountain of toys
Gives mute evidence to five normal small boys...
There are trains, quite derailed; there are cars without wheels;
And a tiny stuffed bunny that no longer squeals.

***

There's a dump truck on end, with its miniature gears,
Being solemnly turned by two small engineers.
There are books without pages; a skate san its strap;
And a bow tie that seems to have lost all its snap...

***

There's the top of pajamas; a single lone sock;
A box that once housed a toy chest with a lock;
There's the wooliest puppy, his tail in midair;
And a slipper that surely was one of a pair!

***

Jolly Santa is missing a whisker or two,
And his red tasseled cap is slightly askew;
While the angel that brightened the top of the tree,

Is as sorry a sight as an angel can be!
Christmas bells—quite de-clabbered—stand mute and unstrung;
And the stereo sags with carols unsung;
Turns a fave to our own that is slightly careworn

***

The holly that once graced the bend in the stair
Devoid of its berries, is barren and bare;
And the wreath of gay evergreens high on the door
Can boast of its utter perfection no more…

***

Sweet candles that once in the windows shone bright,
Sending soft Christmas messages forth in the night,
Having gone galley west and been caught in midair,
Sport a bulb that has known better days here and there.

***

The dining room tapers are burned to the nub;
And the white linen cloth nestles deep in the tub;
While the turkey that yesterday brought such delight
Is the saddest and sickest and sorriest sight.

***

He lies naked and numb, all his succulence gone.
(How that holiday on his platter once shone!)
And of pies and of cakes (They were baked with such care.)
Not a smidgin remains within sight anywhere.

***

Mounds of memorabilia dot each table top;
And the kitchen floor screams for the touch of a mop;
And those stockings we hung by the chimney with care
Lie in heaps on the couch, or in piles on the chair…

***

'Tis the day after Christmas; the holiday's o'er;
That dear Days of all Days lies ahead now no more.
How we cherished each link in the holiday chain
That brought Christmas—CHRIST'S BIRTHDAY—our way once
  again!

**

'Tis the day after Christmas; what joy we have known!
Now has all of the holiday magic quite flown??
There's a strange sort of silence pervading the air…
And a large let-down feeling is rife everywhere…BUT

**

Though the family ménage is a trifle awry,
Santa's winking the merriest kind of an eye;
For he knows in a twinkling all order will be,
With no sign of our chaotic holiday spree…

**

Only MOTHERS and FATHERS, serene and content;
(And a couple of GRANDPARENTS, now slightly spent!)
And five tired but happy small GRANDSONS to boast
That all days on earth, they love Christmas the most…

**

Comes the postman with the cards from recalcitrant senders…
(Along with the bills for the mates of us spenders…)
And so Christmas is over; its blessing depart;
And a new set of memories dwells in the heart.

**

But how blessed, how beauteous, His birthday has been
Time of sweet peace on earth, time of good will toward men…
May the Child in the Manger, whose birth we hold dear
Bring each one a most Holy and Happy New Year!

10-2-66 "AIN'T NATURE GRAND???"

It happened one day last week.

Sammy, which is our pet name for a little old bushy tailed squirrel that has been pipping about our place for as many years as a squirrel's life span will permit him to pip about any one place, came sailing along the walk where we were gardening, Ted and I, his cheeks puffed out with the acorns he was obviously storing up against the winter want.

He stopped, and all but nodded to us; (he's the tamest little old fellow this side of the Franklin Park Zoo); carefully removed one of the nuts, and dropped it into the ground.

He scampered away the second acorn still in his mouth, until he reached a quiet spot by the rose garden, where he stopped-didn't even bother to peer about, for he knows he's among friends in our ménage - removed the acorn; pried off the crown with his tiny sharp teeth; and then merrily buried his small brown treasure on the lawn.

It was a sight to see. The small feet dug furiously; he all but stood upon his head in the process, bushy tail in midair. He systematically covered the cache with earth, tamped it down, and returned for the second acorn, which he promptly buried just as neatly in another part of our grassy green.

"Wait until I tell you what Sammy squirrel did today," I told my grandchildren.

"How do you know it was 'Sammy' squirrel?" asked their mother.

"Goodness," I laughed, "I'd know Sammy anywhere!" And you know – I would!

He's a squirrel with a personality, this Sammy.

When Lady Jane, our terrier, was with us, he'd race across the wire above her head, and toss fat acorns down upon her as she dozed upon the summer grass.

I swear he'd look at us and laugh as back and forth she'd run beneath the wire, quivering in every muscle, and emitting a series of small, tortured sounds of annoyance from her little throat.

He's sailed along our walks for years, this little fellow - his tail a furry pennant in the wind. He's sat by us upon the patio, he's brought his young proudly to cavort about our willow tree; I know 'twas for our pure approval. At which performance, I must now admit, we wondered if, perhaps, his name just might have been Samantha…

Incidentally, his newest escapade with the acorns has knocked beautifully into the proverbial cocked hat, my previous theories about squirrels and their happy habits.

The children's favorite story is the one about the two naughty, lazy little squirrels who danced ballet on the high white wires above the garden all the summer long, while their good little brother was busily at work, tucking hordes of chestnuts and acorns and the rest into the nooks and corners of the little round hole in Ghiorse's apple tree across the way that is, presumably, their home.

"Oh, please," the lazy squirrels were forced to beg of their good little brother as the winter winds closed in. "give us some food, or we shall surely die of hunger, for we've naught to eat in all this empty world…" The which, of course, our Sammy finally did…

Quite naturally we had convinced our wide-eyed boys that from that moment on, our squirrels all would with deep industry and joy, perform an endless set of journeyings, complete with acorns and their ilk, that ever and always ended with that? place they knew as home.

Now, however, we who learn something new each day if we garden and keep our bright eyes peeled, have come to know that squirrels like Sammy and his friends bury their winter wants instead…the which is why great oaks from little acorns have been growing in our lawn for all these many years…

And all the time we thought it was the wind that bore the seeds….

2-20-72   "AMONG US DOG LOVERS"

Her name is "Scotch Mist of Wintergreen", but everyone calls her "Misty." She's a Dandie Dinmont Terrier, a decidedly rare breed of dog, "a very courageous terrier with short legs, long body, pendulous ears and a rough coat," says Webster's… "Of a breed originally on the border between Scotland and England…Its color is pepper or mustard and it is distinctive for its very full topknot of silky light-colored hair." Webster also tells us that "Dandie Dinmont" was "In Scott's 'Guy Mannering' a border farmer who owns two terriers claimed to be the progenitors of the Dandie Dinmont terriers…"

Misty must at some time or other have taken a peek at Webster's and had it go to her head.

Either that or one of her ancestors could have tipped the lady off to the fact that the distinguished Sir Walter found her breed so fascinating he recorded its doing in his novels. At any rate, Misty has more temperament than Sir Walter himself ever had; and history records that distinguished gentleman's temperament as colossal.

For instance, in most families, the humans OWN their pet; in the case of Scotch Mist of Wintergreen, however, she owns and operates the humans. Here is one Dandie Dinmont Terrier who does precisely as she pleases.

A very valuable animal (there are but a few hundred in all in these United States), even prior to the Leash Law, Misty was never allowed to run free. A special pen was built for her beneath the family sundeck; and a nice long chain run placed in such a way as to afford her ample space for pipping about the family back yard. Her actual perambulations about the neighborhood never were too frequent, however, as it must be admitted there is little or no fun in being dragged madly at the end of a leash to wherever Misty's adventurous soul leads-like up hill and down dale and around and about the family garden at fifty miles an hour.

It is understandable, therefore, that Misty would spend most of her time indoors dreaming up ways to escape parental supervision and enjoy freedom, the love of which those Scotch-English border ancestors of hers must have planted deeply in her soul. And it is equally understandable that she should select a spot on the rug just inside the front door for napping…for while the lady naps, she is ever and always on the ready. One never can tell when some unsuspecting visitor will ring the bell and one of the smaller members of the household will open the door just wide enough for a small gray streak of lightning to slip through. Consequently, cries of "Watch Misty!" "Hold the dog!" "Don't Let Misty Out!" and "Watch the dog!" vie constantly for sound with the strains of "Miss Jean" and "Sesame Street" issuing forth from the nearby Family Room. "I never go there unless I have plenty of time to spend," said one visitor recently, "for just as surely as I do, the dog escapes and I spend fifteen minutes or more in the foyer while every member of the family tears off in a different direction chasing down the escapee."

It was tough sledding for them all at first, but by now Misty's family has that chase down to a science. Some members are better at it than others needless to say; like, for instance, the head of the house. He explains his technique…as he returns triumphantly from the hunt, with Misty trotting expectantly at his heels. "I follow her at a distance," he says. "and you know, she adores HOT DOGS. So-I don't look at her, but I ask her if she wants a hot dog. If I looked at her, she would know I was trying to get her back, and she wouldn't come…So I turn my head away from her and say casually, "I am going in to have a hot dog; I wonder if Misty would like one.' just as though I really didn't care one way or another. She usually comes back in with me because she loves hot dogs and we don't give them to her normally. She likes Maple Leaf hot dogs best…"

Mother's technique goes off in another direction. "I take the car keys outside and rattle them," she says. Then I open the car door, "Misty loves to ride in the car, so I say, 'Want a ride in the car, Misty???' Sometimes I have to open and close the car door a dozen times and call her a dozen times before she decides to come. And sometimes I even have to start the car and drive it down the street before she believes me…sometimes in my pajamas and robe if it is early in the morning or at night…" You do get my point about that Dandie Dinmont Terrier owning and operating the family, I trust…

The doings of Misty bring to mind all sorts of delightful animal tales…like the latest one about Byrne Corbin, the nine-year old Metayer grandson. "Mommy," he cried excitedly one day last week, bursting open the door on his return from school (while everyone in the establishment held on to Misty's collar), "Guess what! Barry's dog had puppies while we were in school this morning. His sister came home and she FOUND them!" "How nice," said his animal-loving mother fondly, "But didn't they know she was going to have babies?" "No Mommy," said Byrne seriously, "HIS name is ED!"

Another bit about Scotch Mist of Wintergreen…She took a trip this past weekend all the way to New York State to a kennel where she is to be boarded right beside a real celebrity, her "mother" reported proudly… "a Dandie that belongs to Robert Montgomery!" "Did you get his autograph?" I asked.

Misty's mother had another spot of news. The Kennel owner has just imported from England at a cost of two thousand dollars, a Dandie from the famous Bellmead blood line, with which the pedigree of Scotch Mist of Wintergreen is liberally sprinkled…so can one really blame this charming little lady for having a spot of temperament?

9-6-64   "AMONG US GARDENERS…"

I never thought I'd ever, though I walked the earth forever, in a whirl of mad endeavor, welcome somber summer rain.

With the August heat a-falling, and the sea's soft voice a-calling to my summer plans enthralling, I'd consider it a pain

For the heavens to deliver a be-rainbowed summer river; with annoyance I would quiver as I counted up to TAIN, For I love the sun-drenched hours; I'm averse to summer showers that invade my quiet bowers and make mush of my terrain.

I invariably go under at the very thought of thunder; lightning tears my soul asunder in a paroxysm of pain;

Yet right now I'd sing their praises if the heavens roared like blazes; I'd respond with gentle phrases to the wildest storm's refrain.

For I'm tired of spending hours making simulated showers, while the man in Town Hall glowers, and grows weary with the strain

Of producing endless water for a town that simply oughter find a Great Pond's smaller daughter for a spring devoid of rain.

I quite frankly curl my toes-ies, as I view my luscious rosies, and my myriad other posies travel softly down the drain;

While my evergreens stand drooping, where they once were wild and shooping, and I know there's no recouping all the losses I'll sustain.

AND-that lawn that was my pride, sir - why, it just plain up and died sir; do you wonder that I cried, sir, as I watched it, pink with pain?

How I hate those evening hours I spend quenching thirst for flowers in my bare, bereaved bowers that will never bloom again!

I find seven to eight most boring, with my social life no-morning, and that silly water pouring from the hose I must restrain.

So, I now confess I'm cheering as the sound of rain endearing, falls at last upon my hearing in a pitter-pat refrain.

Never dreamed I'd greet each drop that came tumbling from on top, praying, "PLEASE DON'T LET IT STOP!"

4-3-66 "AMONG US GRANDPARENTS"

A most exciting experience was mine last week. Three different people, on three separate occasions said, "When are you going to write another cabbage about your grandchildren?" Now, this sort of thing happens all the time. Folks are forever saying, "I wish you would write a cabbage about the younger generation…" (If I didn't, they'd hate it; I think the younger generation is the cat's whiskers- and boy, does that expression of opinion date me…).

Or then again, "Why don't you write a cabbage about people who fail to respond to an invitation with R.S.V.P?" Or, "Good heavens, you should write a roaring little cabbage on apathy…" I invariably smile sweetly and promise a Brussels sprout or two on each small subject.

It is simple, however, to deliver the goods on my grandchildren; they make for awfully easy copy Currently their nice parents are having their first home built - here in Braintree, of course; (is there any other town??) This is quite an event in the lives of two young people in their twenties, and we are all neck-deep in the development of their very smart ménage. In fact, the contractor has grown so accustomed to finding Corbins and Metayers breathing down the backs of his workmen, that he is contemplating selling sandwiches and cold drinks at the scene.

The two young men of the family are naturally in high glee. "Did you know we're going to have a collie in our new house, Nama?" "A real live Lassie like the one on TV." This had been their cry for months. With what utter joy they had awaited the arrival of this newest addition to the family…until the evening recently when, with grandmother baby-sitting, they had been permitted to stay up a bit later than usual to watch "Daktari."

Since that memorable event, it's been a monkey, no less, our children have demanded. "A real live monkey, and we'll put a leash on Blackie and Whitey, Sharon's two kitties, and he'll pull them around," James III, told his mother excitedly the following morning.

"And I'll call him Louie," said Byrne sweetly. "Not me," announced James, "I'm going to call him Fryeburg!" "Oway, Jim," said Byrne with resignation. "We can call him Louis Fryeburg…"

"Why Fryeburg?" I asked in astonishment. James' small face furrowed. "Don't you think that is a nice name for a monkey, Grandma?" he inquired. "It's a lovely name for a monkey, darling," I said hollowly.

"And he's going to sleep with me in my bed," announced Byrne. "Uh-uh," said Jim violently "He's not sleeping in the upper bunk on top of me!" James is not the animal lover Byrne is. "If you want him to sleep with us, he's gotta sleep under the bed." "He'll catch cold," said Byrne.

James was adamant. "We'll put down blankets and a pillow for him," he said thoughtfully. "1 know," said his brother, "I'll lend him my pajamas and robe!" He would, too…

"I know we shouldn't have let them watch "Daktari," said their father. Their mother shrugged helplessly. "How could I know," she asked, "they'd demand a monkey? Wouldn't you really like a collie better?" she asked pleadingly, "a nice big, beautiful collie like Lassie, who will fetch a stick for you, and play ball…"

James appealed to me. "Gram," he said, "Can a collie lead a cross-eyed lion around on a leash?" I had to admit he could not. (In Dakarti, this feat is common practice.) "That settles it," said Byrne firmly, "We'll take the monkey…" "And call him Louis Fryeburg Corbin," added James.

His mother shuddered. We have, however, one consolation. The new house will not be ready until May, and it's amazing how short small memories can be….especially if they are not subjected to a renewal of acquaintance with "Daktari." For days after Walt Disney's recent story of the adventures of two baby raccoons, at the conclusion of which their father had informed our grandchildren that he had seen one of the tiny fellows in the vicinity of the garage, our small men had planted caches of food in every corner of the yard, and spent whole days hiding behind trees waiting for "the poor hungry baby raccoons to find their dinner."

There was another occasion when, after having delighted in a cartoon dealing with the misadventures of a most enticing small snake, our angels had been reported missing for an hour while they methodically searched the neighboring woods for a "cute little snakey like Windemere…" Ho-hum-one part of me definitely leans towards the happy hope that we shall all settle for a nice big beautiful collie like Lassie on TV-but just imagine the kind of cabbages I could write about a monkey named "Louis Fryeburg," or a snake named "Windemere…" What fun this column is…

6-17-73   "AND NOW TIS SUMMER"

A pale blue sky above the hill; a fly-hum on my windowsill;
The music of now busy bees; a warm caressing summer breeze;
A hint of gold on legs and arms; how much it lends to summer charms…
The splash of children in the pool; the lack of enthusiasm for school;
The bathing suits upon the line in sizes one to ninety-nine…
The sound of birdsong soft and sweet; the sight of little boys' bare feet;
The carpeting of summer flowers that's laid upon our backyard bowers;
The picnicking beneath the trees, quick showers on the summer breeze;
The hamburgers, hot dogs and such…(Would you BELIEVE we'd eat
*   so much???)*
The ice cream vendor's merry ring; cicadas' nighttime whispering;
The ever-awesome symphony of summer sky and sand and sea…
The gossiping with neighbors nice; the happy tinkling sound of ice;
The inchworm, feasting merrily upon the family's favorite tree;
The squirrels dancing on the wires; the pungent scent of charcoal fires;
The sound of thunder on the air; the full green leafings everywhere;
The pretty thought of summer white; those summer cottons, rainbow bright;
The sprinklers spouting on the lawn; the birds all welcoming the dawn;
The bicycles a million strong; the boats upon the river long;
Young fishermen with poles in hand; the hunt for shells upon the sand;

The Little Leaguers in the park; the nice postponement of the dark;
The lazy lounging on the chaise; contentment with a book; and, YES,
The charcoal cooking; poolside drinks; the lazy, lovely live,…Methinks
Though of each season some may boast, 'tis summer that I love the most…

8-4-65   "AND THE RAINS CAME"

It was to have been a garden party kind of luncheon. What else would one plan for a day in June, with a drought upon the land, and a group of garden-gay clubwomen on the loose?

Gay, colorful grouping of chaises lounges and trays, of lawn umbrellas and patio tables, and redwood picnic chairs, vied wildly with the scarlet and gold and rose of the flower beds, in a delightful challenge to the lawn's lush green.

Tiki lamps tossed their copper and brass against the sky, ready for a soft Hawaiian touch, or a bout with any mad marauding mosquito who dared to come their way.

A calm confident committee awaited the forty or so luncheon guests whose arrival was anticipated. The hostess was smiling and serene. A club luncheon is an event of social significance, a well-ordered affair.

THE RAIN AND THE LUNCHEON GUESTS ARRIVED SIMULTANEOUSLY!

"JUST a drop of two," murmured the hostess. "It won't amount to anything, I'm sure." Mr. Matthews must have been on his knees at that precise moment, for it let go with a veritable cloudburst! The weather, however, proved not to be the only complicating factor.

The first hint of the eventual avalanche the club luncheon was to become, came with the arrival of a lady who had made reservations for four people, and brought along ten. She was to establish a pattern that would last for the entire affair, which instead of hosting forty luncheon guests outdoors, would turn out to accommodate eighty within the rather narrow confines of the lady's house!

How does the hostess remain serene and social while dashing through a deluge with a chair under each arm, and miscellaneous collections of dripping silverware, reeking trays and soggy solubles protruding from every one of her well rounded angles?

How can she greet graciously and sprint savagely at one and the same time! It took a bit of doing and for a moment or two, it looked like our Club President might well lose her aplomb. She didn't, dug!

The guests spilled into and over every room in the house, with the single exception of the you-know-what! And still the rains and the ladies came. They numbered sixty-five strong at the end of the first thirty minutes, and it was, "Please may we be served immediately? We're on your lunch hour." or "May we take out two orders for our friends, who couldn't come?"

A few intrepid souls scanned the hectic horizon within, and retreated under one of the dripping lawn umbrellas that mushroomed over the place, and actually they were high and dry and much more comfortable than the less intrepid ones indoors.

Additional complications began to emerge as the day progressed. For instance, the twenty-seven gallons of iced tea that lay in readiness for a long, hot noon hour, lay unloved and unwanted as the temperature dropped, and hot coffee became the order of the hour…until it ran out.

With a superfluity of sprinters recovering the appurtenances from the back yard, the silverware was momentarily lost sight of, and there were a few frantic moments when one of the more resourceful committee members was detected applying a rather tired brillo pad to the summer camp silver. This crisis also passed, as the sterling popped up in the bread tray!

Trim little ash trays had adorned every table in the garden, and there was even a "Butt Bucket" the which our hostess had found in a dear little Gift Shoppe. It swayed there, and it stayed there, as did the ash trays-every man jack of them - in the rippling rain. NO SMOKING, PLEASE!

The napkins never did turn up. They were found later, in the mopping up process.

Halfway amidships, the hostess suffered an untoward household interruption.

"Mother," said her sixteen year old son apologetically, "I have to go to work at two." (His first summer job at the gas station, and is he ever important???) "Did you iron my shirt?"

She hadn't.

All in all, our Club Luncheon could be termed a HUGE success!

Isn't it the living limit, though, what can happen to the best laid plans of mice and clubwomen???

11-22-64 "ANNIVERSARY"

WRITTEN FOR THE ANNIVERSARY OF THE DEATH OF PRESIDENT KENNEDY. WRITTEN FOR THE BRAINTREE SUNDAY NEWS

He is not dead; he sleeps, serene and still,
In martyred manhood, there beneath the hill.
He once had marked the spot, and looked afar
To where a golden dome caressed a star,
Finding contentment in the hallowed place
That was to know the fairness of his face.

He is not dead; he rests awhile, to rise
And spread his golden glory from the skies.
Who will forget his elegance, his style,
The dear delightful gold of his gay smile?
His wit, his kind compassion, or the charm?
The happy heart; the boyish grin, so warm?

The lock of sandy hair that marked his brow?
His graceful gestures, still and silent now?
The tall, dear figure, coatless in the wind?
The brilliant beauty of that facile mind?
His swift, decisive step, his vital glow?
That special grace the world would come to know?

He sleeps not alone; beside him lie
Two fair and fragile forms who passed him by
With naught but whispered greetings as they fled.

His martyred blood would stain their couches red.
About him comrades rest, their battle o'er;
Their Chieftain at their side forevermore.

The snow upon his form a blanket lays,
    And the rain its murm'ring muted music plays;
The sun upon his heart is warm and sweet,
    And gentle are the flowers that cloak his feet.
By night, a million silvered stars look down
To form a prince's high, bejeweled crown.

He is not slain; his soul eternal glows
Through summer's soft caress and winter's snows,
Above his placid breast, a living flame
Ignites a world in freedom's blessed name!
High in the sheltering trees, soft zephyrs sigh,
While over the earth, a dark, despairing cry - WHY?

5-15-66   "APRIL"

The sun's tossing golden bracelets 'round the arms of tasseled trees;
    And a tantalizing note has crept within the spring-ing breeze;
And the heart that I awake with rises, laughing to the sun,
    That exploringly reminds me there's spring cleaning to be done
Oh, the greenest, gayest lawn invites the patter of my feet;
    And the robin's minuet upon the banking can't be beat;
I delight in all the velvet that I view-to my undoing-
    For it serves just to remind me of the rugs that need shampooing!
Ah, the lady bug picks daintily her way upon the glass
    Of my windows, screaming silently for Windex spray, alas!
While the pink of budding rosies makes me think of winter clothes-ies
Waiting to be tucked away e'er we greet the month of May,
I behold my friend, the garden snake, upon the stone wall curled
And remember garden hoses once again to be unfurled;

I salute the saucy squirrel's aerial act upon the tree
  And bethink me that my stole should in the furrier's vault be!
Sweet spring breezes sing a cradle song to blossoming old vines
  And I know my drapes and curtains should be swinging on the lines;
While the lawn chairs that all beckon just remind me that I reckon
  I should really be indoors, at a thousand cleaning chores...
Ah, but there's so little April, month of magic, time apart;
  Why, each year upon its advent, the singing in my heart
Can be heard above the sound of nature's symphony divine
  That peculiarly in April fills my garden, and is mine.
So-I close my big front door, and then I toss away the key;
  No spring sun's exploring fingers now my dust reveal to me;
And I stride about my garden, and salute that snoozy snake;
  Then I dash into the tool shed for a big old bamboo rake!
I am singing as the squirrel nods a greeting from the wire,
  And it's difficult to know whose soaring spirit is the higher.
I nod "Hi" to each fat rose bush, sending sproutings to the sky;
  And I pat each blooming hyacinth; "You lovely things!" say I.
With a smile I greet the pansies, peering gaily all around;
  Then I toss a lazy blanket on the lushness of the ground;
And I let the springtime's magic steal, unfettered, to my heart...
  Ah, who cares for old spring cleaning??? Come tomorrow, I shall start!

11-1-70   A SKUNK AT A TOY PARTY?

Perhaps he had had a sneak preview of the long line of stuffed animals that Marjorie Caldeira and Linda Wing intended to offer for sale at the Toy Party they were to hold at the home of Mrs. John Maitland at 424 Commercial Street in East Braintree, and decided that the real thing would be much more fun for the ladies gathered there. Or maybe he was a playboy kind of animal that just plain likes parties...

At any rate, the full grown skunk that crashed the gate at this particular affair last Monday evening not only stole the show; he CLOSED it!

It promised to be a happy kind of evening with a group of Judy Maitland's friends and neighbors gathered to do a spot of early Christmas shopping in the comfort of the family living room – which is not a bad place to shop...

A ring at the doorbell signaled the arrival of the toy ladies for whom they were waiting, and the hostess went happily to the door, opened it and dashed to the curbside car to help with the merchandise. Her guests waited expectantly for her return, complete with toys.

It was not Judy Maitland who came through the open door, however; nor was it Mrs. Maitland's toy skunk but a real skunk that nonchalantly strolled through the living room to the kitchen, then through the kitchen to the bathroom where - the evening being just a mite on the chilly side - he promptly curled up in a ball on the hot air register and went to sleep.

To be sure there were a few squeals from the ladies present as the gate crasher came their way; but for the most part his promenade had been met with a stunned silence. Pandemonium was quick to follow the closing of the bathroom door, however.

What to do with a gate crasher at a party is always a bit of a problem, however when that gate crasher is a full grown skunk, the problem becomes compounded.

The Braintree Police were called. It wasn't easy to persuade them that their informant wasn't kidding when she reported the presence of a skunk in her happy home. They arrived, however, took one look at the black and white interloper and shrugged collective shoulders. "If we shoot him, you'll have to move out," they said helplessly. "He'll go spraying!!!"

The Braintree Firefighters, who had also been summoned, arrived at just about the same conclusions as those stalwart sons of Braintree whose duty it is to "serve and protect" and in this instance, were helpless to do either.

The girls drew a blank with the Animal Rescue League, the Angell Memorial Hospital and every "Vet" in the area they managed to reach. "You've got a problem!" was the general consensus of opinion when the ladies phrased the plaintive question, "How do you get a skunk out of a party?"

The head of the house of Maitland, summoned finally from work, proved equal at last to the situation. With two brave friends who volunteered to help he erected a runway from the bathroom to the front door, utilizing the baby's playpen, chairs, tables, etc.

It wasn't easy, but he finally, by dint of prodding and poking, persuaded the uninvited guest to awaken, yawn and reluctantly amble down the runway to the great outdoors where he had obviously previously decided he did not belong.

The Maitlands, meanwhile, baby and all, had tucked themselves into the family car outside for safety's sake; as had all the ladies who had assembled to Christmas shop as well as their toy-toting salesladies.

Oh yes, the skunk DID leave at last, he did not go far, however. To the consternation of all he merely curled up in a soft ball at the bottom of the family evergreens and resumed his slumber.

The toy party had to be called off because by now it was EVERYBODY'S bedtime. It will be held next Monday evening, and Judy Maitland has assured her friends that when she dashes out to help her toy-toting associates, she will carefully close the front door behind her.

"A SNOWSTORM",

WRITTEN IN 1929 BY E.A. NENER

What a monotonous fascinating thing you are,
offspring of winter!
Millions of flurried crystal things,
Falling, falling.
From where to you flutter,
Children of winds?
Are you perhaps
Tiny drops of dew frightened from God's garden
By the great sun
That shone today,

Folding yourself as you fall
For fear of the mighty thing I call
My lamp?
Or dainty white petals shaken
From the flowery crowns
Of angels as they bow their perfumed heads
Before the King?
Some of you
Drive to the East, some go West
You make wild my eyes
Vainly following your flight
You change my love of you
To strange annoyance.
I am within,
You are without, out in the gale, but
That is where you belong.
For you are cold, you
Unconquerable bits of nothingness,
Cold
I am wearied from Looking at you.
Why must you keep on
Falling, falling, falling?
Is it because
You would like to bury my feet and me
Just to show
Your might?
If you do not stop soon your falling,
I shall hate you.
You are so weak,
I have so much strength.

E.A. Nener

AUGUST

WRITTEN FOR THE BRAINTREE SUNDAY NEWS

I'm tired to death of August…tired of wearing sleeveless dresses and contending with my tresses, the mere sight of which depresses.

I begin to loathe August mornings; one awakes 'neath blankets sticky, on a pillow damp and icky, with a mad yen for lime ricky!

By noontime, things have invariably gotten worse. How that horrid sun screams down at our 'poor defenseless town, turning everything dark brown!

Evenings are nearly as bad. With the dinner hour ahead, I could almost wish me dead, but –1 cook away instead!

I could list a hundred reasons why the nicest of all seasons, when it reaches August days, leaves me dripping in a daze.

Cleaning house drives one to madness; I am seized with sticky sadness as I fight the August dust, knowing fully that I must.

Ten or twenty times a day, wipe the wretched stuff away! Polished floors are damp and clammy, and the strangest sort of whammy.

Seems to so mark each fair lamp that it droops with spirit damp; all the curtains limply hang like they just don't give a dang;

While my roses once raised high dewy dreamings to the sky; lawns lie gasping in the sun, wishing the August days were done…

Soon, with luck, 'twill be September! Then we scarcely shall remember all the humid, hot excesses, and the drooping of our tresses.

Fair fall cleaning will erase August's hot touch from each place. Then, as sure as fate, we'll cry, 'cause summer's passed us by…

9-8-68   BACK TO SCHOOL

Every dear little boy is just jumping for joy;
Every sweet little girl is agog and awhirl!
Shaggy locks have been shorn; hands are pure pink and white;
Shoes are mirrors reflecting small faces alight…

Mother weeps as she bids a long, loving adieu
To young Tommy and Tessie and Sammy and Sue!
How she'll miss the sweet sound of their voices at play…
Ah, how dreary and empty 'twill be this FIRST DAY…

At the schoolhouse, resplendent in starch and in style
Every teacher awaits with a welcoming smile
(How she's MISSED them!!!) the darlings who'll make her
    days bright,
And fill her sweet soul with such constant delight…

While each Principal - back at his duties at last -
After months which at snail's pace reluctantly passed -
Views his charges with pride; claps his hands in sheer joy
And then glowingly greets each small girl and sweet boy…

Why, of course - THAT'S the reason! Couldn't you guess
At the whys and the wherefores of such happiness???
'Tis the FIRST DAY OF SCHOOL! One more year has begun;
And the long days of one more sweet summer are done…

Did you notice the smile on the traffic gal sweet
As she marshals her charges across the school street?
Did you stop to reflect, as you drove o'er the town
Why each "teach" is so gay, and each mom looks so DOWN???

How we'll MISS them, our DARLINGS, proud mothers all
    say…
Ah, how empty and long will be each autumn day.…
But we'll SMILE through our tears; and we'll STIFLE our PAIN;
For we know that our LOSS will be dear TEACHER'S GAIN…

3-23-75 "BICENTENNIAL"

Outdoors, Saturday was a gray old day. One had to slosh through puddles and play leapfrog over brassy little brooks to negotiate the parking lot at Braintree Town Hall...Once inside, however, that historic place was awash with its own special brand of sunshine...The clock for that afternoon had been turned back, you see...back to the historic date of March 15, 1775; and Braintree was about to take another step in its official observance of our country's Bicentennial here in the town where liberty is said to have been born.

Militiamen milled about the newly painted foyer, their muskets on the ready; and erstwhile Tory officers stood gravely by, swords in scabbards; Colonial dames were at their quilting; and a Colonial schoolmarm kept her young charges sternly in tow.

Braintree V.I.P.s, 1975 style, were pipping about in charge of the arrangements. Carl R. Johnson, III, looking every inch the character, he was to portray in "Braintree Fights for Liberty," the dramatic sketch that lay ahead - namely Selectmen Chairman Johnathan Bass, Esp. - moved importantly through the group. Otis B. Oakman, Jr., Braintree's own "Oaky," having written the script of the play, along with Joseph Darche, presented such a convincing picture of what has become a colorful Deacon Palmer that your columnist all but greeted him by that historic name. (He's been using it a bit, hither and yon, of late you know...)

Material for the play had been taken from Volume I, Braintree Town Records - 1640-1793; and we marveled at the fact that so much of America's history has been preserved for all time within our Town Hall vaults. Incidentally, credit for this important fact goes largely to former Braintree Town Clerk, Carl R. Johnson, Jr.

But - now to the program of the afternoon, "Braintree Fights..." "Attune your ears to 1775," we were asked; we did just that. As a matter of fact we not only attuned our ears to that historic date; WE WERE THERE!

An obviously hand-picked group of young Boy Scouts was on hand to help with seating arrangements. "How many in your party?" asked a darling young man of about ten, with all the poise of his dad. "One???"

A march down the center aisle; a careful perusal of seating gaps; and he was back to escort me to the very front row, where, joy of joys, I found several of my friends…

The sound of fifes…the roll of drums… "Yankee Doodle," of course; and it was "Please to begin" for this Bicentennial Committee affair. In came the Colonial dames of Braintree, quilters and wool winders and knitters all, to be followed by members of the "Dame School," teacher and pupils; the Town Clerk of 1775; the Town Moderator; the Minute Man Committee members; Covenant Committee members; and - last but by no means least - the inevitable Town Crier!

There were to be wonderful utterances in this historic Town Meeting that took place in Braintree's First Church so long ago, a Town Meeting that included in its Agenda such delightful items as "to determine if Hoggs shall run free…"

We were to hear Town Clerk Lisha Niles call for the nomination of Deacon Palmer, the seconding of that nomination by none other than John Adams, Esq. and the resounding chorus of "Ayes" (along with a couple of "Nays" from the small fry) which confirmed our Deacon's nomination. And we were to witness this delightful Town Moderator as he chaired the meeting, obviously mindful of the Town Clerk's fervent prayer for his success, "May God Be With You."

Dame Patience was to be asked by him to introduce the ladies of her quilting party by past names, (all decidedly Puritan) and by present nomenclatures (anything BUT Puritan in most instances.)

The small fry was to be quizzed on their lessons by this engaging town official whose charm was undoubtedly totally lacking in his counterpart. But to return to those historic utterances. some of them actually more HYSTERIC than historic in aspect. There was one, for instance… "Mr. Moderator…Point of Order! Point of Order!" "The Chair recognizes Mr. John Hall, JR. What is your point of order?" "Deacon, you're a good Church-going man; and I'm a good Church-going man; and I want all you folks to know that I voted AGAINST Hoggs running at large. You well know I don't keep hoggs and I don't think it's fair for other folks' hoggs to come in and eat up my vegetables…" "Mr. John Hall, you're out of order and you know it. I suggest you speak to the prescience HOGGREAVE…"

And then, on the serious side, "Fellow Townsmen, as your elected delegate to the February meeting of the Provincial Congress in Cambridge, I bring you alarming, disturbing and serious news. As you will recall, that odious and infamous Boston Port Bill went into effect on June 1, 1774... Since that time our neighboring town has undergone the most severe hardships; idle ships, grass grown wharves and starving people...Town Meetings are abolished, but WE DARE GO ON!" "It is our thinking that our Town needs a Militia to protect its farms and farmlands..." and, from the lips of His Majesty's FORMER Colonel Thayer, "On November 14th of the year past, I stood on this same platform to show my disfavor for His Majesty's unfair treatment of Colonial subjects. At that time I relinquished my commission and tendered my sword. Now, with the blessing of God, I retrieve my sword to lead those who would fight for liberty..." "It is the sworn duty of this town to protect its democratic heritage..." "Mindful of the blessings of liberty and the rights of free men..."

What fun to hear the "proper arms" that were to be handed out to that Militia and IN LIEU OF PAY TO BOOT - "to wit: One good fire lock, Bayonet and Cartouch Box, one pound of powder, twenty-four lead balls, twelve flints, and a knapsack..."

But to return to those HISTORIC utterances... "We, the People of the Town of Braintree in the Province of Massachusetts Bay are determined to do everything in our power to confirm and establish the union which so happily exists not only between the Town and Colony but between the Colonies themselves...WE...avow our allegiance to the King and ourselves...We...avow our allegiance to the King and our English brethren throughout the country. HOWEVER recent oppressive acts passed by Parliament...the deprivation of our American right of a trial by our peers..." with an "illegal trial beyond the sea..." the suspension of "the elected governments of not only Boston, but the entire Province of Massachusetts..." "We, the people of the Town of Braintree firmly agree under the sacred ties of virtue, honor and love of country to the following: FIRST, that we will not import any goods from Great Britain, Ireland or the East Indies, nor shall we import any molasses, wines, coffee or foreign indigo from the West Indies. SECOND, that we will neither import nor purchase any slave brought to America since December 1st, 1774. THIRDLY, we will cease to purchase all tea sold by the British India Tea Company…We will endeavor to improve the breed of our home-bred sheep by killing them sparingly, and by refusing to export them to the Indies…We will encourage a frugal economy… Also in the death of any relative, we will conform to the suggestions of the Continental Congress that the long-practiced tradition of GIVING SILK GLOVES AT FUNERALS BE DISCONTINUED…" Marvelous utterances…Marvelous resolves…

There were marvelous little extras as well in Saturday afternoon's delightful Bicentennial program-the kind of extras that add a spot of spice! John Bass, Esq. for instance, was to leap upon the bench with a resounding "I cast one NAY in favor of King George III in absentia!" only to send it and two companions seated upon it crashing to the floor. And there was the hilarious moment when Deacon Palmer's "timepiece," that teller of time that was to signal the ending of Town Meeting 1775, turned out to be "in absentia" along with good old King George…

The message of the Braintree Town Meeting of March 15, 1775 on Saturday came over loud and clear, nonetheless. It WAS March 15, 1775 on Saturday in dear, historic Braintree Town Hall; and a giant step had been taken toward liberty in this little old town we love. AND WE WERE THERE!

7-18-71   "BIRDS IN THEIR NESTS"

It all began with one trim little sparrow's nest we found tucked snugly into the peak of our house that April day so long ago when first we took up our abode in Braintree.

"I'll get rid of it tomorrow," Ted said matter-of-factly, "before it houses a family." "Oh, no," I said quickly, "Happy is the home where the bird nests," I added softly, looking back, way back into another April day long years before. I was a small child then, watching with dreaming eyes as a fat round robin built her nest close by our beach house.

"Happy is the home where the bird nests," mother had said, coming upon the scene. "Why does a bird nest in a HAPPY home?" "Because a bird is a creature of nature," she had replied, "and instinctively, for the protection of her young, she will choose a happy home, free of turmoil and strife and raucous noises…" "What are raucous noises?" I am sure I must have asked at this point…

But- to return to the sweet trim sparrow's nest within the peak of our new abode. It soon housed a small gray family of eggs; and then a small gray family of sparrows that chirped their cries of hunger and their cries of alarm, and tried their wings between the gable and our flowering crab, and lent a gay new enchantment to the soft spring days of the Metayers.

It might have been just a sweet summer idyll had not the word gone out! No bird-watching, yellow-bellied, sapsucker-seeking, Audobon Society family THIS ONE…sparrows, ugly ducklings of the winged world, were WELCOME at Metayers.

They came in droves. They set up housekeeping in the gutters and in the downspouts, in the crannies and in the nooks. They warred with one another for the spot with southern exposure, the peak with running water, the corner adjacent to patio and birdbath…

Each morning found the family sundeck littered with tiny, naked, wide-mouthed casualties of overcrowding; a veritable birdies' graveyard was developing under the apple tree where Gael, our youngest, insisted on burying one and all with due ceremony.

"Birds in your little nests, AGREE!" I would quote imploringly as the little feathered darlings awakened me with their tongue wars in the cool gray summer dawn when school vacation would have permitted me to slumber peacefully till nine.

"And for the RICH, they SING!" said a wag (my brother), eyeing the once shining spotless burgundy shutters - for the choice spot at the top of which they vied unceasingly with one another, with devastating results.

"Ted," I announced firmly, "We are conducting a bird sanctuary. Either they or we will have to go!" "After the eggs have hatched," (Ted is the essence of kindness.) or "as soon as the baby birds have learned to fly," he would reply firmly.

But by the time one generation of fledglings had mastered the fine art of flying, another generation was tucked snugly into each and every nest; and we were off again!

Incidentally that bit about the turmoil and raucous noises was for the birds, if you'll pardon the pun! Turmoil we had; and raucous noises??? Only the birds seemed not to mind the combination of the "rock and roll" of teen-aged Gael and her companions, Richard's stereophonic symphonies and Ted's Channel 2 television. I grew so accustomed to wearing ear plugs that the neighbors commenced articulating.

I shudder to think of the outcome of it all had not the man of the family decided about that time to have a new siding installed upon our little abode. I pretended not to notice as the burly carpenters ruthlessly eliminated our dear little house guests, one by one. Thank heaven they eliminated at the same time most of the cavities in which our feathered tenants were wont to nest.

We still maintain a few small efficiency apartments around the eaves that would delight the heart of Rachel Carson and her clan. Ours is anything but a "Silent Spring." High in the peak above the porch beside my room their summer symphony begins my day. They drink their morning nectar from the leafy cups that top the hedge. Our birdbath is their fountain; and our flower beds, with soft sweet earth, their place of play. Their nests are sporting coral streamers from a dress our child once wore; and bits of things she fashioned with slow knitting needles trail in summer's wind. Our son's old fishing line falls free; and there's a strand or two that looks like tennis racket twine; the lacing from a shoe…

"Happy is the home where the bird nests - in moderation," I tell myself each summer morning as our day begins…

11-14-65 "BLACKOUT"

Boston, on Tuesday evening, was a stygian cave.

Motorists drove along the streets with slow uncertainty, as if the absence of traffic signals and lighted lamps was more than they could conceivably contend with.

You could taste the dark. It crawled into the car through closed windows, the which you had carefully locked; to lay beside you on the inky seat; it dried in your mouth; its silence hammered in your ears; it moved with you along the coiled streets.

I know, because I crossed the great felled city at six o'clock.

It was, I decided, as though a giant squid had settled over the place, releasing an inky fluid that blended with the liquid night. The creature's eye looked into your own from a thousand shadow places. Its underside was soft and repulsive; its tentacles lay in waiting in the valleys between the great and grotesque heights of blackened buildings - they moved menacingly; they hovered…The dark was a live, pulsing, fetid force that tore at your smooth self-confidence until it made a naked coward of you.

A built-in fear of shadowy figures in dim places made of each poor pedestrian, of every know of stranded, hurt humanity, a sinister force, endowed by you with grim intent. people were gray wolves, slinking about the mountainsides the buildings made of Boston's downtown area.

I forced myself to drive across the sickened city. No light shone from the high Prudential tower no beacon on the Hancock Building's tall spiked crown, challenged the leaden sky.

As though to mock the dark, a harvest moon appeared and puffed out its cheeks, and hurled its silvered breath upon the scene. It hung there - high, haughty, unconcerned…

It had begun like any other journey, this trip to Park Square, Boston, on Tuesday evening. I'd popped last Sunday's fine, leftover roast into the oven, then tucked a pair of fat baking potatoes fore and aft, and driven off to pick up Ted, my husband.

I'd reached East Milton Square before I became aware of a subtle change in the familiar face of the Expressway. "Why," I thought, "the lights are out," and then, because I like the company of good Paul Benzaquin as I drive, I pressed the knob that sends my radio antenna skyward, and snapped on the lighted dial.

"All emergency vehicles are being lined up on the runway," a voice was saying on the air. "Another plane crash, I thought-how sad!" And then the full import struck. "Planes are circling the airport, awaiting landing instructions." I was aware suddenly of a tense excitement in the voice. "New York's airport is closed; Boston is a City in darkness; we've no idea what's behind the blackout. New York City is without lights; Buffalo is out; all of Massachusetts; New Hampshire; Connecticut. No explanation…" A sense of shock sent me upright against the car cushions.

"So it has come," I thought. "The prelude to an atomic attack." Everything I'd ever read rushed to mind. Immobilize the seats of government; paralyze transportation; disarm the cities… "People trapped in elevators, hospitals using auxiliary power to complete brain surgery; Boston Edison powerless to explain…!"

My quiet acceptance of the situation as I drove through a dark world amazed me. "I'll keep going," I thought. I'll pick up Ted; with luck, we'll make it home. Then, if there's time, we'll gather our loved ones about us. We'll face it together."

Where had I gotten these sudden reserves of strength, I wondered suddenly - I, the most devout coward of my acquaintance. On I went, over the stygian streets of Boston.

"Did you think I'd be afraid to come?" I asked of Ted. He smiled. "I knew you would," he said." Is it an attack?" I asked. "Let's hope not," he answered. With what relief I handed him the wheel…

Braintree was a Christmas toy village all lined up upon the blackest mantelpiece our eyes shall ever see. We rounded a big, dark hill and there it was! Its lights shone and twinkled as though some child's warm hand had plugged it in…a Christmas village - a warm and wondrous place.

"No one seems to know what happened, but they've ruled out a sabotage," said the voice on the air. I sighed, a long, dark, shuddering sigh, and looked upon the light that lay ahead. "The roast," I said happily, "will be done just about right."

10-27-68 "BRAINTREE GHOST"

It was one of those big duplex houses that may be found here and there in northeast Braintree.

"Let's buy it," said Mary, whose name wasn't Mary at all, to John, whose name wasn't John. "My sister Jane (name similarly fictitious) and her family can move into the other side, and we can have all sorts of fun together…JOINT babysitters…joint parties…

"Joint, as it would turn out, NOCTURNAL VISITATION - however that little fringe benefit was not to trouble the joint heads of our nice young people until considerably later. It was, however, to form the basis of this Halloween Cabbage.

I suppose it is only natural that Braintree, a very old Massachusetts town, should have a ghost or two. We just hadn't ever happened to hear of one until Mary and Jane and their families settled themselves in the big duplex house where our story begins.

"What on earth do you suppose Jane and Jim were doing, running up and down stairs last night?" asked Mary one morning at breakfast. "I didn't sleep a wink. They were at it one night last week also," she added.

"I don't know," said John. "Why don't you ask them?"

"Oh, I don't want to sound like landlady," said Mary. "After all, she IS my sister…"

EVEN as Mary was reaching this conclusion, sister Jane was registering her complaints about the self-same matter, next door. "I hate to say anything; after all they are family; but what on earth do you suppose they do over there every few nights, running up and down stairs for hours on end???"

Time wore on, with neither sister putting into her words her annoyance with the eerie nighttime footfalls that intermittently originated in the vicinity of the stairs…

As a matter of fact, neither appeared to have commented either on the other strange happenings that began to befall them - the mischievous disappearance of written babysitting instructions that, although seen clearly at one point by both the girls and their baby-sitting parent, turned up later in a discarded purse, etc., etc.

Came the day when the haunt of the big duplex house landed on her two sepulchral feet squarely in the middle of two distraught young women.

"You know, mom," said the small daughter of one of them. "I LIKE that gray-haired lady who lives in our house." Her mother regarded her steadily.

"There is no gray-haired lady living in our house, dear," she said evenly.

"Oh, yes there is," said the little girl. "She comes to see me when I'm in bed. She's nice…"

Came the crisis. "Was it you and John on the stairs? Wasn't it you and Jim? Did you put the note in the pocketbook?" etc., etc.

Two very disturbed young women awaited the return from work of their two young husbands that summer evening.

"You won't believe this, but," they began. The boys didn't… "You two have been reading too many mystery novels," they said merrily.

The spectre in the duplex must have been standing in the shadows, listening, for the next chapter in our ghost story was directly squarely at the unbelievers…

***

Let's clean out that big old attic," said one of the boys one weekend not long afterwards. "it would make an excellent place for the children to play on rainy days, and there's nothing but junk up there!" There WAS nothing but junk - the accumulation of many years of ordinary living.

"We'll start with this big old bathtub," one of the boys said. "What on earth made them save a thing like this???"

They raised the massive object high above their heads and started down the narrow attic stairs, to come suddenly to an abrupt halt…for a MURMURING had swept through all the attic in their wake; and the battered banners of bygone years began a weird discordant symphony of sound.

Tired tables stamped their small clawed feet; and chairs made scraping sounds; and bags and crates were swirled about..

"What in heaven's name?" asked the boys, looking from one to another. "It's the GHOST," said Mary.

"It's the spirit who haunts the house. She must LIVE here!" said Jane. "Put the bathtub back and see what happens," they said in chorus. Which is what the boys decided to do.

The dark din slowly faded, and the attic settled quietly under its layer of dust, to sound more.

***

The boys are beginning to wonder about this ghastly business in the big old duplex house. At least, they no longer "pooh pooh" their better halves when the subject comes up.

Meanwhile, four young people await patiently these days the next chapter in the tale of the nocturnal phenomenon they seem to have purchased along with their nice big ménage in northeast Braintree. Séance, anyone??? And just in time for Halloween!

4TH ANNUAL HISTORICAL ISSUE BRAINTREE FORUM 'BRAINTREE IN THE FIFTIES' THURSDAY, MARCH 18, 1982 "SUNSWEPT SWIFTIE'S BEACH BY DAY:"

East Braintree in the fifties was a far cry from the East Braintree we know today. One seemed to know all of one's neighbors. We were able to greet them by name at church on Sunday morning, and if a stranger should walk by as one gardened or gossiped with a friend, the question would be asked, "Now, who is that?" And if, by chance it was determined that she could be "the lady who has moved into so-and-so's house," a real attempt would be made to welcome her into the neighborhood. A friendly phone call or an invitation for coffee, and the lady would be firmly established as belonging to East Braintree.

The people of the area seemed to move in a rather regular pattern. The men marched off to work five mornings a week, parading down Quincy Avenue toward the train station at Weymouth Landing where the Old Colony Railroad was to run until 1959. Very few of the women worked. The men and women who went to business had all gotten to know one another. They took the same train each morning; and usually the same train brought them back to the Landing at day's end.

They would then either be picked up by their mates, or they would parade once again along Quincy Avenue, the men now and then slapping their rolled up newspaper against their legs as they exchanged views on the news of the day, or passed on the latest bit about their families or the families of their neighbors. Thus it was that their wives were kept rather well informed on the happenings within the area. It was kind of a closed corporation.

Gordon Road, which is now totally built up, was an unfinished roadway running through a rather dense wooded area...so dense that our children were cautioned not to walk through it alone. This area had been part of the Thomas Watson estate, and the foundations of his original building remained. They made great forts for small boys, playing cowboys and Indians, and nice houses for small girls playing the inevitable game of "house."

In winter these children coasted and skied down slopes that are now the backyards of homes Little League had not yet come into its own, and so in spring and fall a steady stream of boys all ages would head toward Watson Park to play sandlot baseball or touch football. Since girls' sports were at that time an unknown quantity in the town's recreational program, there were no softball teams such as my own "Metayer's Marauders" or other sports to occupy our young ladies. They therefore streamed down to watch the boys at play, and I really cannot recall any compelling complaints about the situations.

Scouting was extremely important. Our boys were encouraged to join the Boy Scout program, and our girls to join either Girl Scouting or Campfire Girls. Both programs were enthusiastically supported.

Invariably somewhere in Watson Park could be seen the sturdy figure of Captain Petersen, a wonderful old retired sea captain with a face lined and seamed by years upon the briny deep. He loved the children of East Braintree. In warm weather he would sit with them upon the grass and spin his seafaring yarns. The younger generation found him fascinating. He would frequently bemoan the fact that when the tide was out, his young friends were unable to swim in the saltwater river nearby.

"You should have a pool," he would say. And when he passed away and his will was read, it was found that Captain Petersen had left a considerable amount of money to build a pool at Watson Park for the children of East Braintree. The pool, incidentally, has never been built.

East Braintree was a family-oriented place.

In summer we all gravitated toward what was then Swift's Beach but which has since been renamed Smith Beach (for some reason unknown to most East Braintree residents). There weren't so many of us in the fifties. The area was not built up as it is now, and so we all seemed to know one another. Parents were friends and our children were friends. We packed lunches and stayed at the beach for hours on end, turning a nice nut brown in the summer sun. We had picnics together on holidays. The water was clean. It was a nice place to spend a warm summer day, and East Braintree regulars faithfully checked the tides and delighted in the privacy of their own little beach. It has not then been enlarged to its present size. It was purely a local beach, with no sand other than that supplied by nature.

Not only was it used by day, but of a summer evening couples with their small fry in tow might be seen strolling back again toward "Swiftie's". We might also be found strolling down Quincy Avenue in the summer dusk, greeting one another and pausing now and then to chat, perhaps to drop into a neighbor's house for coffee. Canasta was the "in" thing, and so frequently that cup of coffee might be followed by a game or two of cards.

One of our favorite winter diversions was coasting down the long hills that mark East Braintree. Mothers and dads and their children all seemed to be able to produce those big Flexible Flyers needed for the sport. We would don warm clothing and take to the hills with our sleds, taking turns as "lookouts" for the cars that were not quite so numerous in those days. The smaller children would be held tightly in the arms of mom or dad, and the older ones would be allowed to make it on their own, much to their delight. And what fun it was to sail down the hills, with the wind in our faces.

East Braintree wore a decidedly different look in those days. Where we now have the Quintree Mall there was a collection of abandoned U.S. Navy barracks, leftovers, of course, from the war years when the Fore River Shipyard had to be protected from possible enemy attack.

Streiferd's Greenhouse and Fogg Trucking occupied the area that now houses Plywood Ranch and its parking lot. WE all patronized the neighborhood florist that was located where for the past several years the 7-11 Convenient store has stood. Where Monatiquot Village now stands, there was a bleachery and a pond.

There was but one electric light plant. It was located then as it is now on Allen Street, and we spent our lives bemoaning and cleaning up after the black soot that was emitted by its boilers, to float over the area twice daily. We paid our electric bills at the local drugstore where we complained bitterly each month. This made us feel better, however it forced no one in town government to make the slightest attempt to deal with the problem.

Where Quirk Chevrolet now stands, there was a tired diner. It was perched high on a great rock which could be seen from far down the avenue.

Ours was a storefront branch library. It was located on Quincy Avenue in a block of stores enroute to Weymouth Landing, and just about everyone in East Braintree knew and loved the branch librarian. She was young and pretty. Her name was "Miss Handy," and she was a remarkable young woman indeed.

Miss Handy managed to commit to memory the preferences of most of her readers, and we could expect to get a phone call whenever she received a new book in which she thought we might be interested. The Thomas A. Watson School was the center of most neighborhood activity. The P.T.A. held card parties and other fundraisers and although we might have no children in the school we all appeared to be interested, to patronize and to help in making a success of whatever was planned. East Junior High School, the Morrison School and Elridge School were far in the future.

Where East Junior is today, there was farmland. Liberty Street, on which the Morrison and Eldridge school are located today was a narrow winding street whose greatest claim to fame lay in the fact that some of its residents remembered seeing the Sacco-Vanzetti getaway car which took that route after the South Braintree Robbery.

There was an effort during the fifties to locate propane gas storage tanks along the Monatiquot River and the vicinity of Weymouth Landing, and the entire area rose in revolt. The memory of a prior explosion at Boston Gas was still fresh in the minds of those with cracked walls and ceilings, none of which had been adequately dealt with.

Our efforts to prevent the installation were happily crowned with success, and the people of East Braintree seemed closer than ever. Much of the action had come from the Braintree Point Woman's Club. As its president I persuaded club members to join hands with the area businesses that were fighting against the menace of propane tanks. It represented a triumph for the residents when the plan was abandoned.

The Braintree Point Woman's Club drew its membership then as it does now primarily from the residents of East Braintree. It had always enjoyed a closed membership with a long waiting list. And it was in the fifties that it was decided to expand the club membership to 75 and to hold the meetings in the Braintree Yacht Club, it being no longer feasible to entertain the larger membership in the homes. We met twice monthly, and we became a force to be reckoned with should anything surface which could menace East Braintree.

The Metropolitan Yacht Club was not in existence. Where it now stands was a little-used boatyard.

There were no tennis courts in Watson Park. The Walter Delory Baseball Field had not yet been built, nor had any of the ball fields that now dot the park. Organized play had not really come into its own. Young people from the area skated on Factory Pond, and they took their B.B. guns and hiked to Pond Meadow where they "hunted" birds or squirrels.

I well remember the day when son Richard, whose "hunting" expeditions had always proved fruitless, arrived home with a limp squirrel and an air of triumph, and asked that he be permitted to cook it in the family oven…(No, he didn't eat it…)

It was during the fifties that a young local doctor began to come into his own in East Braintree.

Archie Graham Keigan had been brought up here. His mother, Ruby Keigan was known and loved. He was "one of us," to be recommended to all newcomers as a "super doctor and a super person." Doctor Keigan was all that and more, but little did we realize that this tall, slim dedicated young man to whom so many of us confidently entrusted the health of our families would in the decades to follow turn out to be East Braintree's favorite son.

The fifties seemed to mark the beginning of an era of conformity among the young, an era that has been with us ever since. We began to notice it with our girls, every single one of whom trotted off to school in brown and white saddle oxfords.

East Braintree in the fifties was a lovely place in which to live and to bring up one's family. It still is. Very special people seem to have settled here.

2-9-75   "BUSY! BUSY!"

No time to have my hair done or to shop for pretty clothes;
Thank goodness for the pantsuit that will hide my running hose;
Seems the workload for this legislator grows and grows and grows,
And where that rascal "Time" goes, golly, goodness, only knows…

No time for phoning brightly all the friends I love to know;
Now that there's a Friday "Sitting," even STORY HOUR must go!
I could use a pair of roller skates for dashing to and fro
Through the myriad State agencies, constituents in tow...

No time for social gatherings; my days are spent instead
At those great Committee Hearings where so many things are said
That affect the lives of people; or that keep out of the red
This poor troubled Massachusetts whose economy seems dead...

Or I'm off to our House "Sittings" where the State's business is done;
And although we suffer keenly on occasion, it's sure fun;
And where all the wise lawmaking has in earnest now begun...
Shall I ever get to know my revered colleagues every one???

The circles that are growing, I observe with some chagrin
Neath my eyes (though THEY'RE still shining), now come almost
    to my chin;
And I find at each week's end that it invariably has been
Six or seven hectic days since I have greeted kith and kin...

Yes, I'm madly, wildly busy - the proverbial busy bee
As I wrestle with the problems of the State's economy
Versus all the crucial needs of an oppressed humanity;
How to reconcile the whole contrives to haunt poor troubled me...

My phone now rings from morn till night! The freshening gold of
    morning light
Has barely crossed the Braintree sky-betokening the day - when I
Am off by bus and train to where my world grows every day more fair;
That wondrous place called Beacon Hill...(I still approach it
    with a thrill)...
The STATE HOUSE...'Neath its Golden Dome, WHAT JOY
    TO KNOW I'M NOW AT HOME

4-7-68   "CAN I HELP?"

Legend tells us that when the Father of all was creating this wonderful wide world of ours, there came his way one day, four angels, each one of whom brought to him a question.

The first angel, a bright eyed, inquisitive little fellow, so the story goes, asked "HOW are you doing it?"

The second, a thoughtful analytical kind of being, asked, "WHY???"

The third one, with an acquisitive gleam in his eye, said, "May I have it when you finish?" And the fourth little angel asked softly, "CAN I HELP?"

Few phrases rival, for sheer unadulterated promise, that happy combination of words, "Can I help?"

"I want to be friends with you," says the phrase. "I'd like to know you better. I think it might be fun to be associated with you in some endeavor or other. You're my kind of person. I'd like to help you...

"I believe in what you are about to do," it says, "I share your feeling of involvement with others; your concern for the things that require attention; your willingness to extend yourself...

"I agree with your obvious motivation in that which you are doing," it says; "I, too, believe it is more blessed to give of one's self than to receive. I want to join you in experiencing that wonderful warmth of heart that comes from simply doing for others.

I'm all for that little old parable about the talents," it says. "I'M NOT REALLY talented at all, in the true sense of the word; but I could probably do some things as well or better than you if I really tried. I'm good with people; and I can react beautifully in an emergency; and my family tells me I'm a good cook; and my neighbors are always coming to me for advice; and I LOVE bringing smiles to people's faces...

"I expect to have a BALL HELPING," it says, "for I've helped out a bit in my day; here and there, and really, it was FUN! Come to think of it, that's how YOU happen to be needing help. I recall the Sunday afternoon when YOU offered to help Mary Jones with the Church Social!

"She asked you to join her committee; and the next thing I knew you were PRESIDENT of the Guild. I'll bet if you hadn't been Guild President, you'd never have been asked to be President of the Woman's

Club; and if that hadn't happened, you'd never have made all those wonderful friends of yours from federated clubs across the State. And you wouldn't have gone to Conventions and meetings; and heard all those fascinating speakers, and had all those wonderful experiences about "Gosh, I never realized how many doors might just be opened to me by uttering that simple little phrase that started life all over again for you -AND NOT SO LONG AGO...

"Heavens, CAN'T I HELP?? I'm not quite sure what I can do, but I must be able to do something! Tell me - my potential new friend - HOW CAN I HELP????"

This is that time of year when club and organization Presidents everywhere are planning madly for the year that lies ahead. They simple cannot handle that task alone...

Just about every one of us belongs to some group or another; and is acquainted with one overburdened presiding officer...How's about you and I taking a leaf out of the book of that little ambitious fourth angle and asking him or her, "CAN I HELP???"

6-20-65   "CAPE COD"

The sea salutes a summer sky;
White cotton-candy clouds wave "Hi!"
The sky descends to meet the sea
In silken silence, endlessly.
The golden shore's embracing sand
Becomes a gleaming wedding band
About the finger of "the Sound"
And prayerful peace is all around.
The dawn has come to softly lay
The gilt and glory of the day,
To place a special kind of grace
Upon this rare enchanted place.
Beach roses wear their crimson smile,
And sandpipers the shore beguile.

The sea its symphony begins;
Soft breezes sound the sweet woodwinds;
The surf a thundering cello roar;
The gull-cry violins a-soar…
The tides a magic necklace toss
The jettied, Joyous beach across;
A string of beads on seaweed hung;
A seashell with its song unsung;
Limp feathers from some soaring bird;
A pebble smooth, from some unheard
Of land; dark driftwood, fresh with foam;
A strange, intoxicating poem
This day that halts with such delight
The frantic fleeing of the night…
No day is dawning anywhere
More brightly favored, or more fair!

With dash and drama-lo! the sun
Announces that the day is done.
Across the skies a swathe of rose
With wild abandon, nature throws,
A thousand subtle shades and hues
Upon the setting sun to loose;
Thence to the coffers of the sea
To hurl her gold in lavish spree…
And to bid the day a fond goodbye!
The woodwind breezes sadly sigh.

Dark night walks softly to the sea
And cloaks its depths with mystery;
A merry moon appears, to spill
Its silvered laughter on the hill.
Great wide-winged bats of clouds ride high
Upon the pearl gray of the sky
The ocean's voice has quiet grown;
The winds a lonely chanty moan;

The dunes are shadowed, dim and deep;
The woods have lain them down to sleep;
the sea gulls now no longer fly;
And stars are lanterns in the sky...
With so much blessed beauty hurled
Upon this corner of the world,
Why surely, it would seem that God
Elects to dwell upon Cape Cod!

2-25-68   "CARPENTER'S HELPER"

You've heard about the man who hid his talents under a bushel! Well, we've discovered we've been hiding one of ours for years...Our retiree of a husband turned carpenter - Do It Yourself TED - unearthed it. He now has a brand-new assistant - ME!!!

We took our first sweet steps toward employment in this exciting capacity one spring-like afternoon not long ago when we arrived home, bright and breezy, from an afternoon at club, and speedily sought out our retiree-turned-carpenter husband, who was busily engaged in effecting some needed repairs below decks.

"What an afternoon!" we trilled happily. "The speaker was excellent, and the day so nice that everyone was there. What a lovely time we had! And how did you make out, dear?" we added solicitously. "Did you have a nice productive p.m.?"

Ted looked our way with an expression which indicated clearly that in his opinion tomorrow could only be worse...

"As a matter of fact, I didn't," he said. He sighed. "I put a level on every angle of these darned shelves, and though every angle appeared to be straight, there's a full inch in difference between the top and the bottom of the thing..."

A small buzzer-left lying about from years of being involved in Girl Scout projects, or was it perhaps Woman's Club doings-went off brightly under our flowered hat... "Did you put a PLUMB LINE on it?" we asked. "Your level may be off."

Ted's expression changed instantly and he laughed aloud. "As a matter of fact, my dear," said the one member of our family who always manages to have the answer to everything, it seems, "I didn't!"

The plumb line held the answer this time, and we found our self-hired on the spot! We became-- from that day forward--the carpenter's helper!

"Please pass the hammer," says Ted, whose promotion to the rank of foreman, with one man under him, might almost appear occasionally to have gone to his head. "Now the finish nails…is the screwdriver handy? May I have the nail set? Plug in the saw; now plug out the saw and plug in the drill. Man that barge…Tote that bale…Scalpel…sutures…clamps…C Clamps…"

It has become a full-time job. As a matter of fact, my prospects for permanent employment were never better. For never did the head of a household face retirement with more happy tasks awaiting him…all for his own good naturally.

"We cannot have you spend your retirement like poor John Jones, who simply sat before the TV and deteriorated; and we cannot gad about the world all the time," we announce periodically. "Poor John Jones," we add in a sepulchral tone, "He's deteriorating permanently now. So, darling let us work…"

The amusing thing about MY participation in the Do-It-Yourself marathon at the Metayers is that I like it! It's a lark! "You know, Ted," I announced merrily one afternoon last week when after what seemed like three months of measuring and re-measuring, and mitering and re-mitering, and a handsome piece of moulding was placed securely about the stairwell, "This is FUN! I wish I had nothing to do but to help you build things every day!"

"Darling," said Ted quietly, "I've news for you. One more 'fun' job like this one, and there'll be no more building."

There are, of course, "wheels within wheels" in my new employment. I have become, for instance, a collector-of scratches, splinters, bumps and bangs. (So-Anyone can collect bone china!)

My style has consequently changed a bit. I've become more formal! I've taken to wearing shoulder length gloves, for instance, to hide the miscellaneous marks of my profession. (Eight Band-Aids on one forearm do absolutely nothing for a spring ensemble…)

And I'm growing accustomed to the amazement of mailmen, delivery boys and political candidates whose ring at my door is answered by a housewife complete with earmuffs, fur coat and high buttoned boots-our cellar being akin to the Arctic wastes these chilly days…

Yes, I'm the Carpenter's Helper…local 275 ½ of the Amalgamated Association of This and That would never approve of my salary, but then they'd not approve of the Carpenter's salary either come to think of it… And I can't think of a single fringe benefit that could be included in contract negotiations. Isn't it marvelous, then, that we LOVE our work?

12-1-63   "CHANGING THE WORLD"

On a flag-bedecked street in Texas, a short unbelievably sorrowful week ago, one man, motivated by hate, changed the world.

One single act of incredible violence set up a chain reaction that was to spread in ever widening circles until it literally enveloped the earth.

For the first time in the memory of man, Russians would weep for an American in the streets of their capital city.

In Berlin, a million candles would burn their cry of freedom and heartbreak into the black night.

In France, the autocratic ruler who could not be persuaded to parley with a President, would come to mourn a man.

The affairs of state would cease in Canada and in Panama. Tribesmen would weep in Africa, and Indian villagers would cable a grieving widow that they "loved President Kennedy so much."

The flags of the world would fly at half-staff. Dimmed would be the luster of the Irish smile; broken the reserve of the British heart; and the soul of sophisticated, materialistic America would be unashamedly washed clean in one great, unending torrent of tears.

And for the first time in the history of mortal man, a world would merge to acknowledge in one magnificent, fused symphony of prayer, the brotherhood of man and the fatherhood of God. In a thousand tongues, and in a thousand creeds, that prayer would rise with one great voice to heaven; the world would pray as one.

Thus, had one man, motivated by hate, changed the world. He did not mean it to be this way, this warped purveyor of hate, this tortured soul. He could not know in his unholy state that one man, the martyred target of his hate, motivated by love, had himself begun to change the world. He could not know that one man, motivated by love, had already sown so many seeds…motivated by love, against the brightness of which hate must ever pale to insignificance.

You, too, can change the world. You can begin by changing your world. If you have talents, give of them; if you have ideals, live them; if you have dreams, dream hard and high, and fight to make those dreams come true. If there is hate in your heart, stifle it; if there is love nourish it.

Yes, motivated by love, you can change the world; change one small corner of it, and you have begun to change the world. Peace and brotherhood and honor and idealism are not born in the halls of the mighty, in the conference rooms of kings. They begin in the heart, the home, the community; they flow directly from the families of the nation into the bloodstream of the nation.

You are young? The assassin of Dallas was a youth; the man on whom he rained his black and bitter death was in his prime.

You are old? Goodness is ageless-love as old as eternity. Yes, you can change the world. With submission of self, with justice and brotherhood your goal, with good your intent, with right your target, with love your motivation, you can change the world. You "are but one," but you "are one!"

On a flag-bedecked street in Texas, in the country of our hopes and dreams, the pendulum of life, swept by a great, grim wave of hate, swung to the farthest blackest point our grieving souls can contemplate. God willing, and with every proud American at hand, it must begin the long, slow inevitable journey back to brotherhood and reason…

Out of the discordant chaos of our tears, we seem to hear the first faint whispers of an awakened conscience. Here and there in the quiet corners of this great land of ours we find the words "rededication, rebirth, renaissance…" Souls, washed clean with tears, seem to be taking stock.

With the death of our martyred President, every American died a little; in the great hate of this assassin are the small, pet hates of every one of us.

Oh, let the eternal torch that was lighted for a martyred hero glow in your hearts and shine in your deeds. Light your one small candle from its flame. Yours need not be a great, an overwhelming contribution, but you can let your influence for good be felt in your home, in your place of business, in your community, in your nation.

Let lesser mortals stop at weeping; you who have faith in the ideals, the dreams for which America's martyr lived and died.

You who love America and humanity, you can set up your own chain reaction that will spread in ever widening circles until it, too, covers the face of the earth. You can change the world!

4-9-75   "CHESS CLUB"

No one was particularly surprised when the Metayer's Number Two Braintree grandson, Byrne Corbin, asked for a Chess Set when the matter of birthday gifts for his upcoming tenth birthday was brought up. Byrne, you see, is a student at the Sacred Heart School, and at the Sacred Heart School CHESS is definitely the "in" thing!

Approximately sixty of the rather small fry for such adult entertainment, we think - the students in grades 4 through 8 - meet every Wednesday and Thursday afternoons from two-thirty to four-thirty for a spot of CHESS. And are they ever enthusiastic about the game???

It all began when Mrs. Mary Ellen Caesar, the fourth-grade teacher at the school, observed that a number of children were arriving complete with chess sets, proposing to have a go at the game during recess periods.

Now it so happened that Robert Caesar, the attractive young teacher's husband, had taught this fascinating form of entertainment to his best girl while both were students at Stonehill College, and when the romance ended in marriage, a handsome set of Knights and Pawns and Bishops and other paraphernalia had gone along with the young couple into their brand new home. They have been avid chess players ever since.

The couple are residents of New Bedford, where in the local Holy Family High School, Bob Caesar and a friend promptly went about founding a Chess Club. He carried his hobby a step further by joining the New Bedford Chess Club; and then, his wife having joined the faculty at Sacred Heart School, our young man turned his attention toward the town of Weymouth.

Both Bob and Mary Ellen are involved up to their eyebrows in the weekly Chess Club activities at Sacred Heart, and their enthusiasm it seems has similarly affected the more than sixty members who show up every Wednesday and Thursday, appurtenances in hand, all set for an afternoon of what they obviously consider FUN with a capital "F."

The club has been going on since October of last year, and its first tournament was held on January 9. There were 35 contestants with 11 rounds; and Stephen Crawford, a sharp fifth grader, won handily. No one was particularly surprised at this; Steve has remained top scorer in the club for the past four months. He's a WHIZ, but there are many others in the group with a decided talent for this engrossing game. Two or three of the small fry reports, as a matter fact, having taught their chess-playing fathers a thing or two about the aspects of technical scoring.

Now comes the point in my writing this "Cabbage" about the Chess Club at Sacred Heart. The Caesars would like very much to line up a "match" with a team from another elementary school, so HOW ABOUT IT, BRAINTREE-ANYONE FOR CHESS??? There must be similar groups tucked away in our own progressive public-school system whose members would like to match wits with the students at Sacred Heart.

If there are, won't someone get in touch with Mrs. Caesar at the school? She will be more than happy to make the arrangements and who knows what exciting developments might follow in the wake of this experiment in interscholastic competition?

And oh yes, one last note, a note of admiration for this beautifully idealistic young couple who appear never to have heard of the time-and-a-half for overtime bit (or is it double time now???) … who with no remuneration at all-unless, of course, one counts the love and adulation of sixty kids - are willing to give of themselves so generously week after week, out of a pure unadulterated love for children…and a desire to promote the kind of hobby that will keep young minds occupied and provide a wholesome happy outlet for young mental energies...Our hats are off to the Caesars! Aren't yours? And now-how about that Chess Match, Braintree? Wouldn't some of you like to tackle their tournament winners?

CHESTER-BELLOC CLUB

PRESIDENT, ELIZABETH NENER
SECRETARY, MARY MCCARTHY

Out from the mists of erring England have come within this century of doubt and misinformation two mighty warriors, armed with superb intellect and indomitable love of truth; Gilbert K. Chesterton and Hilaire Belloc, contending in glorious battle with those sad humans whose lives are overruled by untruth.

Out from the honored walls of G.C.G.S., there come six and ten warriors, each in the land of wishes and dreams, a Chesterton; each a Belloc, armed with the love of learning, the quest for intellectual advancement, and the glorious principal: There is nothing more mighty in life than love of truth, nothing more admirable than love of honor; and nothing of greater benefit to the human mind than love of knowledge.

The Chester-Bellocs contend in glorious battle, glorious in its faculty of broadening that most intricate of mechanisms, that most perfect of masterpieces, - the human brain. For to seek the truth is to find the truth whether the subjects regard Politics, Religion, of Life, and in Debate will truth be brought to the foreground; error, detected and shunned.

"The Electoral System should be abolished, and our National Executive elected by direct vote of the people" -and the Chester-Belloc Debating Society made its debut on the field of contention. Eight sturdy warriors issued forth to battle, smiling, but with determination. One the affirmative side of the field, seeping the standards of victory before their path, came the warriors; Evelyn Finnegan, Gladys Nener, and, Beatrice Barry; and, contending in rebuttal was the Warrior, Elizabeth Nener.

Upholding the principals of the Negative side, came the noble warriors: Louise Kennally, Annette Cunningham and Helen Spiers; and in the rebuttal, Margaret Reardon, another of our sturdy group.

The battle of the day was quickly over, decisive, cleanly fought, fairly won; the battles of our year of debating our year of contending, of upholding the standards of keen, active thinking, are as quickly over. We have worked hard and loved it; we have contended, argued with the zest of true warriors and remained loyal to our lofty principals. None could do more.

CHILDREN OF MARY

PREFECT: ELIZABETH NENER
VICE PREFECT: ANNETTE CUNNINGHAM
SECRETARY-TREASURER: ELIZABETH CARROLL

There is no greater factor in molding the character of a Catholic girl than the noble privilege of being a Child of Mary. Education consists not merely in intellectual attainments; equally essential are those in the spiritual order. What better spiritual armor, what loftier Catholic ideals, what more certain fundamental truths can be given to a daughter of the church than those inculcated, in the sodality of Mary?

Weekly, the student body of our loved Sodality congregates for the purpose of giving honor and tribute to the Mother of God. The conferences given by our Reverend Director, Fr. J.J. O'Leary, D.D., have been an asset in furthering the aims of the Sodality and increasing in each student a tender love for our Mother, Mary Doubtless, when we fare forth from the portals of our Alma Mater to face the trials of the future, we shall be favored many graces and blessings merited by true devotions to Our Lady. She in turn will look down from Heaven upon her children and bless them because they have honored her.

12-26-65 "CHRISTMAS"

Behold a Virgin shall conceive and bear a son, and His name shall be called Emmanuel" -Isaias,7.

"He shall be great, and shall be called the Son of the most High, and the Lord God shall give unto Him the throne of David His father…" -Luke 1.

"Rejoice greatly, O daughter of Sion, shout for joy, O daughter of Jerusalem; behold thy King will come to thee, the Holy and Savior." -Zachary 0

"At that time there went out a decree from Caesar Augustus, that the whole world should be enrolled. This enrolling was first made by Cyrinus, the governor of Syria. And all went to be enrolled, every one into his own city. And Joseph also went up from Galilee out of the city of Nazareth, into Judea to the city of David, which is called Bethlehem: because he was of the house and family of David, to be enrolled with Mary his espoused wife, who was with child. And it came to pass, that when they were there, her days were accomplished that she should be delivered. And she brought forth her first-born Son, and wrapped Him up in swaddling clothes, and laid Him in a manger: because there was no room for them in the inn. And there were in the same country shepherds watching and keeping the night-watches over their flock. And behold an angel of the Lord stood by them, and the brightness of God shone round about them, and they feared with a great fear. And the angel said to them: Fear not; for behold I bring you good tidings of great joy, that shall be to all the people: for this day is born to you a Savior, who is Christ the Lord, in the city of David. And this shall be a sign unto you: you shall find the infant wrapped in swaddling clothes, and laid in a manger. And suddenly there was with the angel a multitude of the heavenly army, praising God, and saying: Glory to God in the highest, and on earth peace to men of good will." -Luke 2, 1-14.

A MERRY CHRISTMAS! Write the greeting in great, gay, golden letters! Cherish the happy hours. String upon a silvered chain like jewels the soft, resplendent days.

Lovingly drape the precious gift; trim it with ribbon and holly.

With the warmth of a Christmas heart, set the house ablaze.

But know, even as rose-red poinsettias blaze in golden glory; as Christmas greetings race across the miles; as carolers with song caress the starlit night - that God's own Infant presence has made the circumstance. Sweet Christmas! Dear Christmas! Let there be joy that blessed day; let there be reverence. And let us, for the little Christ Child's sake, love one the other, that we may echo the song of the angels that first Christmas morn, long centuries ago, "Glory to God in the highest, and on earth peace to men of good will." Luke 2, 1-14.

May the blessings and joys of Christmas be with you, my readers and with all those you hold dear…And to quote (or rather, to misquote) from one of my very favorite poems:

> *"Bless the four corners of your house,*
> *And be the lintel blest.*
> *And bless your hearth, and bless your board,*
> *And bless each place of rest.*
> *And bless your door that opens wide*
> *to strangers as to kin,*
> *And bless each crystal window pane*
> *That lets the sunlight in,*
> *And bless the rooftree overhead*
> *And every sturdy wall.*
> *The peace of man, the peace of God*
> *The peace of love on all."*

12-20-70 "CHRISTMAS"

And now an inconsequential journey must be interrupted in the telling because of another journey -a journey that was taken nearly two thousand years ago by a young Jewish maiden called Mary and her tender spouse, Joseph - a journey to a little town called Bethlehem, at the end of which a Child was to be born in a rough crude stable upon a lonely windswept hill, on a night that would be filled with the wonder of a shining star; and echo the song of Angels…a night that would live forever in the hearts of Christians everywhere! "Glory to God in the highest," the celestial voices from on high would sing, "And on earth Peace to men of good will." And men of good will would celebrate the blessed and beautiful Feast of Christmas from that day on...There would be the Christmas Creche, and the Christmas Carol, and the Christmas Star and the Christmas Story...

Once upon a time there was a lonely old wood cutter who, dozing by the fire in his humble cottage one Christmas eve, dreamed that the little Christ Child came within the circle of his hearth and spoke to him.

"You are lonely," said the holy Child, "but tomorrow is my special day...my birthday...and I shall share it with you. I shall be your special guest!" And the old man awoke with joy, and swept the hearth and hung gay boughs of holly from the rafters high above and brought sweet pines from out the woods to place upon the door, and spread the table with the only meager fare that he possessed, and made the copper kettle so to gleam that he was dazzled by the sight...and Christmas morning dawned...and the lonely woodcutter waited...and a knock came upon his humble door.

"Tis the Christ Child," said the old man happily, and hastened to sweep it wide in welcome; but there on the hard-white ground-cold and shivering - stood only a tattered beggar.

"May I share the warmth of your fire?" he asked. "My feet are bare and my coat is worn thin and I shiver with the snow and cold..."

"I cannot ask you to stay," said the woodcutter, "for I am expecting a special guest; but I DO have two pairs of shoes, and you may have one of them; and although my second cloak is old, it is good and warm and you are welcome to it." and he warmed the frozen feet of the poor sad beggar by his meager fire, and placed upon them his own coarse socks and his second pair of shoes; then he placed the cloak, warm and comforting, about the thin shoulders of the beggar – who went his way, blessing the woodsman for his kindness.

And the lonely woodcutter waited, and again a knock came upon his door and he swept it wide his way once more. An old crone, bent and withered with age, stood upon the snow outside. In her arms she carried a bundle of faggots. "Please let me come in and rest,' she begged, "for I've yet long miles to go and my arms indeed grow weary."

"Alas," said the woodcutter, "you cannot tarry long, for I'm awaiting a special guest. He would not mind, however," he added kindly, "if you placed your burden on the hearth for just awhile." And then as his eyes swept the poor pinched face of the ancient one, he sighed and brewed her a cup of tea, and - taking the one small cake he had set out for himself - he gave it to her. And the old crone smiled and blessed him, and went on her way...

And the hours of Christmas passed and again a knock came upon the lonely woodsman's door. He flung it wide once more! A small lost child stood there before him, his dark eyes wide and weary. "Please, sir," he said, "I beg you, take me quickly into the fork in the road by the wide mill pond, or I am sorely lost and if I reach not that one landmark, then shall I wander in the woods until the darkness falls and the wolves devour me; for my father is dead, and my mother - who is blind – can never come in search of me."

"I cannot leave my hut," said the woodcutter, "for I am expecting a special guest for Christmas. I'm sorry, child." But as the child's eyes filled with tears the heart of the lonely woodcutter melted. "I think perhaps my guest will understand and wait," he said. "Come, little one. I shall take you indeed to the fork in the road by the wide mill pond that you may find your way from there before the darkness falls and the wild wolves threaten…Nay, I shall take you to your poor blind mother…" And he raised the boy upon his shoulders high and swept with him through the deepening forest. Darkness was falling as the lonely woodcutter returned to his little cottage. "Alas," he said aloud as he opened the pine-decked door, "how foolish was I to build my hopes upon an old man's dreaming by the fire. Christmas is all but o'er and see - the little Christ Child has not come to grace my humble hearth, but then why should He come indeed to one as poor as I?"

Then out of the shadows by the fire, a soft sweet voice replied. "Thrice have I come your way this Christmas day," it said. "I was the beggar on whose feet you placed your shoes; and I was the aged one to whom you gave your one small cake; and I was the child with whom you raced across the night…"

And as the wondering woodsman watched, the flame of the firelight quickened, and a soft white light swept all the room, and the boughs of holly stirred and a fragrance was about…and then the soft sweet voice began again…

"Always at Christmas," it said, "always, but ESPECIALLY at Christmas, when the flame of charity engulfs your heart, I am there; I am with you…For I am love; and love is Christmas. Love is the one real message of Christmas…love and peace…peace and love…"

THE CHRISTMAS GUEST was one of my mother's own favorite Christmas tales. She told it to me when I had known a very few dear Christmas seasons; how I delight in remembering her joy at Christmastime as I pass along this lovely tale to you…A happy and a holy Christmas, everyone!

12-5-71   "CHRISTMAS AND GREGORY"

There are those who take a dim view of being fed Christmas music on Labor Day and Christmas trimmings with their hobgoblins on All Hallows Eve - but the Metayers aren't numbered among them. We are perhaps the most Christmas addicted family on record.

The generations - one after another - come by this fondness for the Yuletide season quite naturally, they tell me, from a columnist grandmother who managed to feed her family giant doses of Christmas spirit along with their Pabulum.

At any rate, regardless of how and why it came about, each and every member of the family loves Christmas with a purple passion - and none more passionately than four-year-old Gregory Scott Corbin, the youngest of the clan.

Greg is a frequent and wonderfully welcome visitor (Visitor??? Greg refuses to "sleep over" in the family GUEST room; "I'm NOT a GUEST," he informs us; I'm YOUR angel!") at Grandmother's where may be found his favorite stuffed dog; his pet tractor-trailer; his most scribbled in coloring book and the beat-up crayons that go with it; and - most important of all - his own personal private record player with its endless supply of CHRISTMAS recordings…the which this small lover of music delights in playing endlessly as-seated in the big chair in the T.V. room - he clutches their holiday-decorated jackets in his chubby small hands and thrills for hours on end to the music of "Rudolph the Red Nosed," "Jingle Bells," and "I'm Dreaming of a White You-Know-What…"

The season matters not a whit to Gregory. His Christmas concert goes on endlessly through the snows of winter; the surge of spring; the swish of summer and the sweep of fall - from one wonderful Christmas season to the next with no let-up other than perhaps an occasional dose of "Sound of Music" or "Mary Poppins."

And as for Gregory and CHRISTMAS TREES…The Metayer attic houses - for about eleven of the year's twelve months- (our lights go on December 8 and blaze 'til January 6) at least one tree for each and every room in the ménage. In the normal course of events, this holiday forest would be tucked away in the Christmas corner of the attic in January of each year, to be lost to sight until the next year's holiday season rolls around…A sad fate in the opinion of Gregory, and one not to be tolerated for his adored Christmas memorabilia. Consequently, each sojourn with Grandma must include a trip to the family attic for a visit with those wonderful, wonderful holiday occupants.

"Good morning, living room Christmas tree," he will say; or "Hi, dining room tree! Here is Gregory come to visit you…Wait a minute, Grandma; I didn't KISS them all yet…"

Greg paid the attic a particularly memorable visit one rainy afternoon last week. Grandfather had washed the family windows and Grandmother was merrily laundering and dispatching to the family cleaners just about every curtain and drapery in the establishment. "Why are you washing all the windows and curtains?" Greg wanted to know. "Well," said Grandma, "Christmas coming and soon we'll be putting our Christmas lights in the windows and we want everything to be shiny and clean for them, don't we?" Small Gregory beamed his approval of this exciting explanation and this wonder spot of news.

"Mom," he said immediately upon his return home, "Why don't we wash all our windows and curtains for Christmas?

"They don't need washing," said his mother; "they were washed two weeks ago."

"Well," said small Gregory, "Grandma and Grandpa washed theirs; and windows are 'sposed to be clean and shiny for the Christmas lights, you know, Grandma said so."

Mother's already clean windows did not come in for additional washing, needless to say; but what followed the suggested cleaning spree was a lovely discussion of the Yuletide season…a discussion that brought home to young Gregory the wonderful realization that Christmastime really was just around the corner and holiday decorating closer than he thought. "Grandma," he said brightly the following morning, "Will you come up to the attic with me? I want to tell the Christmas trees something. Christmas trees, you know what??? Pretty soon, it is going to be Christmas and guess what???" (Gregory was all breathless from his mad dash up the attic stairs and across to its Christmas corner.)

"You'll ALL be coming downstairs and having ornaments put on you and twinkle lights that go on and off and you'll be BEAUTIFUL! Won't that be fun??" His answer came in the high falsetto voice our Gregory adopts when indulging in fascinating conversations with his favorite stuffed toys. "Oh, goody, goody, Greg!" said the merriest sounding Yule trees on earth. "And guess what else…Grandma and Grandpa washed all the windows for you and the curtains so you'll be able to see right outdoors when the lights are on…Did you hear that, living room tree? You'll be all shiny and you'll have pretty balls hanging on all your branches; and you, guest room tree - you'll have soldiers and drums; and you, pine-cone tree, you'll be in the front hall where everyone can see you when they come in Grandma's door…" "Oh, goody, goody, Greggie; that will be wonderful!"… "There, Gram," said our own Christmas angel, tucking a chubby and somewhat grubby little paw into my own; "I told them, and did you hear how glad they were??? They must get awful lonely up there in this attic when it's not Christmastime, Gram, don't you think?

Gregory Scott's own room is already decorated for the holiday season. The little fellow was especially quiet one day last week; and mother, busy with her morning chores, experienced the feeling of apprehension that comes to all mothers of small, suddenly quiet boys. "What are you doing, Greg?" she called. "I'm decorating my room for Christmas," answered her little son promptly.

"Don't come in 'til its all finished," he added; "I want to surprise you…It's FINISHED now, Mommy; come in and see how PRETTY it looks!"

Greg's adoring mother entered her smallest son's room, and then swept him lovingly into her arms; for it was decorated for Christmas - this small boy's room-and in a manner all his own. The Christmas tree decorated cover of one of last year's Christmas card boxes (Gregory never can bear anything Christmas-y thrown away…) hung by a string from the light switch near his door; and the ladder section of his two bunk beds lay jauntily beside them, with a big red Santa Claus perched precariously on one of its rungs; and a tired little Christmas crèche, much loved, propped carefully against another.

Isn't it PRETTY, Mommy?" he asked breathlessly. "It's BEAUTIFUL, darling," she said and planted a kiss on his shining face. "Do you think the Baby Jesus will like to be put THERE?" He asked anxiously. "I put Him there so He can see the Christmas tree…'cause it's His birthday, you know…" Ah me, wonderful, wonderful Christmastime…How perfectly great to know it's lying just Ahead…

12-25-66 "CHRISTMAS BLESSINGS"

"Lift up your gates, O ye princes, and be ye lifted up, O eternal gates, and the King of glory shall enter it…"

And the day of wonder dawned upon our town, as once it did upon a place called Bethlehem long centuries ago; and we awoke to know it was the birthday of the Prince of Peace.

All the stars in heaven, it seemed, had shone with all their twinkling might, upon the night that was just passed. Their light was caught and held imprisoned in the glow of thousands of bright burning candles placed within the windows of the waiting town. Surely, we thought, as we gazed about us fondly on our lighted world, is the little Christ Child welcome in this place.

That star, we opined sagely, as above, its rays surpassing all its fellows, high it shone, could well have been the Star of Bethlehem!

The night was deep and dim. WE fancied there were shepherd's forms against the moon-outlined hills; winds were soft angels' wings and in their sighing was the angels' song of joy…

In the places of worship, solemn hush was soon to be replaced with sweet rejoicing. Chimes would ring out, and mankind would rejoice. "Glory to God in the Highest," they would cry, "and on earth peace to men of good will…"

***

Where shall we find the measure of the majesty of Christmas?

Hearths and hearts everywhere swept clean, made warm and ready. For to Christians everywhere, this is the day!

"A light shall shine upon us this day; for the Lord is born to us; and He shall be called Wonderful, God, the Prince of Peace, the Father of the world to come: of whose reign there shall be no end…This is the Lord's doing; and it is wonderful in our eyes."

What a wondrous time is Christmas! How blessed is the spirit of this season of all joy! It speaks within the deeds of passerby, the smiles of strangers.

This, a world seems to say, is the time for giving, of ourselves, our worldly goods, our kindness and our hearts. This is the time for loving, for is not the coming of the little Babe of Bethlehem the supreme act of love? This is the time for worshipping, for giving thanks; this is a friendship time…

This is the time for sending Christmas blessing o'er the miles.

This is the time for remembering kindness; for forgetting enmity; this is the children's time of dreams come true; the grownup's time of dreaming net anew…

God bless all those we love at Christmastime. God bless all those we do not love; and those we do not know; and those whom we shall never know…

***

We wish you peace at Christmastime, and in the year ahead. "God Bless Thy Year

thy coming in
thy going out
thy rest
thy traveling about
the rough
the smooth
the bright
the drear
God Bless Thy Year."

***

A Happy and a holy birthday of the Christ Child to you, one and all!
A VERY MERRY CHRISTMAS!

1-1-67   "CHRISTMAS EPILOGUE"

There's a slightly tired aspect to the tinsel and the holly;
And somehow old Santa's mien seems a smidgen less than jolly;
While about to lose their glamour, 'tis indeed quite plain to see,
Are the toys that lie in heaps beneath the drooping Christmas
    tree.
Now, the sight of old Tom turkey at the corner grocery store
Fails completely to inspire as it did in days before
Strange - those rosy red poinsettias o'er the fireplace holding sway
Suddenly, as we behold them, just don't take our breath away…
Christmas wreaths and decorations, we now handle in our stride;
How we "oh"-ed and "ah"-ed as first they burst upon our
    Christmastide!
How enchanting seemed the aspect of our special Christmas
    world.
In the days before those miles of scarlet ribbon were unfurled!
Candles shining soft and glowing in our neighbors' windows
    sweet,
Spilling gay and golden coinage on the snow-bedecked street,

We have come to take for granted; why, our hearts now barely
   sing
At the welcome they're extending to the little Infant King...
One more Christmastime is over; one more year in glory ends
With the loving of our loved ones; the remembering of friends...
Once again, we've wrestled gladness from each moment, every
   hour;
How we revel as each blessed Christmas season comes to flower
But, alas, perhaps the reason now o'er things we fail to linger
Is because we're too exhausted, gals, to even lift a finger...
Come next year, I vow, I'm starting on my Christmas at
   Thanksgiving;
Quietly and quite relaxed I shall prepare for gay gift-giving.
Pine cone wreaths and holly hallow I shall fashion in November;
And my good old Christmas cleaning I'll not leave until December.
I'll address with vim and vigor in fair June or July
Those delightful Christmas cards that, come tomorrow, I shall
   buy.
But, my gosh, if all the color of the season I remove;
With, neatly done and quite dispatched, the many chores I've
   grown to love –
What about that Christmas spirit - will it fully flood my heart
As about the tasks of Christmas I no longer have to start?
Will the blessed balm of Christmas bring its healing to my soul
As each candle, sweetly glowing, brings me nearer to the goal?
Ah, well - let's not really worry; plans are things I make galore...
Bet next Christmas will be hectic as all those that went before!

12-27-70 "CHRISTMAS IN RETROSPECT"

A sad little bell tolls in my soul with the passing of every Christmas. It's my very special, favorite season. This year, however, the tolling began even before the Great Day arrived.

I first noticed it as I wandered up and down the aisles of every department store in town, seeking a Christmas gift for the man who has everything - only to keep seeing in my mind's eye a vision of the man who has nothing.

"Tell me, darlings," I had said to the grandchildren of my heart, "What would you like for Christmas?" "Surprise me," said one, after a moment of deep thought during which I surmised that-possessing all things of consequence to small boys - he was completely at a loss for suggestions.

"A Shrink Machine!" said another, echoing the words of the last T.V. toy salesman within his memory.

"Tell me, little Pakistanian child," I found myself thinking sadly, "little Indian nomad wandering the streets of Bombay, belong to no one. "What would YOU like for Christmas?" "A crust of bread…a cup of milk…LIFE!"

That was the way it began…I found suddenly that Christmas, that special time of year when my soul has always soared skyward, was decidedly less than perfect. I knew the reason!

Life was easier and prettier, I reflected, before the days when instant communication brought instant war and instant misery into our comfortable living rooms; when the haunting faces of the Vietnamese peasant, the Pakistanian orphan, the doomed little black American of Buford County, South Carolina (if that is how you spell the place) were slightly less than real.

Now, however, they ARE real; so what, I found myself wondering dismally, can the birthday of the Prince of Peace really mean to one who has never known peace???

What significance can the natal day of Him Who is the embodiment of perfect love have for those to whom all love, concern and compassion have been forever denied?

I wandered from room to room of my warm and handsome home, endeavoring to find my customary joy in the beauty of the Christmas scene. It left me, somehow, cold.

I paused before the little Christmas Creche that holds the meaning of it all. Did I imagine it, or had the lovely smile faded from the face of the little Christ Child's figure?

I sought my myriad Christmas trees, their silver lights twinkling like a thousand stars; I could see only the coldness of a nighttime winter sky; the blue, pinched faces of the homeless…

I saw the nest of Christmas gifts beneath the tree - my own - and I bethought me of the empty hands of other grandmothers in ghettos and in war-torn lands…

Gladly would I share my Christmas gifts with any one of them, I thought. But - perfume for someone to whom soap is untold luxury? nylons for a mother, perhaps struggling against a winter wind? A clock for someone for whom time stands still? A missal for a soul whose prayer has never known response? The latest in a slide projector that will bring into a poor and blasted life the beauty of my own? Lingerie and loveliness? Femininity and frivolity? My Christmas gifts…sighed…

Is it possible, I thought, that I am growing bored with Christmas? Maybe I am growing old…And then my friend dropped by!

"Elizabeth," she said. "Thank you for your nice Christmas card. I didn't send any this year. I haven't been able to spend money on cards and stamps since Biafra. Not with half the world starving…I sent the money to care instead…"

"Annette!" I said, "You too?" I sighed. I said, "I have the strangest feeling that from here on in our Christmases are going to be different. Perhaps we're really coming of age, we Americans! I do believe that individually as well as collectively, we honestly are beginning to care…"

I spent considerably less on Christmas cards this year; and who knows - perhaps next year I'll find the courage to send only to those whose lives are far away from mine…that somewhere in a foreign land a child may find another day of life beneath a dark defoliated tree…

This is a "Cabbage" from another year - repeated by special request because it seems to have lingered within the minds of others whose quests for gifts for those who have everything have brought them also face to face with those who have nothing…

12-26-70 "CHRISTMAS MEMORIES"

Another Christmastime has come and gone…Christmastime… time for remembering, for looking back….

Christmas was such a wonderful day for the children in our home… the home of my own happy childhood. Every child found under the Christmas tree exactly what she had asked of Santa. I smile to myself as I remember a long list of questionable articles he was committed by family tradition to tote to our ménage…like knickers; and shiny rubber boots that came to the knee and enabled Sister Gladys and me to wade through every puddle between our home and school; and short hair, styled by Jordan Marsh, when bobbed hair was just coming in and the mothers of correct young ladies were fighting it every inch of the way! How wily are the young…

Christmastime in our neighborhood - on the Fellsway in Malden - was wonderful as well. There was something on every neighbor's tree for every neighbor's child - a red paper cornucopia stuffed with candy; or a chocolate Santa; or a lickin' good candy cane. We'd go from house to house "to see the tree" and receive a Christmas treat; and our own doorbell seemed to be constantly alive to other small fry.

Christmas Eve was the most exciting time of all. We'd bundle up against the cold and climb merrily into dad's big black "Hudson Super Six" and head for Fitchburg, where we always spent the day. There'd be mother and dad, and "Gaga" (which is a typically English name for a grandmother) and tiny, gentle paternal grandmother who made our home with us; and all five of the eternally chattering Nener children. Dad would have lit the nice long charcoal heater that kept our feet like toast in the back seat while the rest of our anatomy froze. We'd all rush to occupy the two small jump seats that were such fun; (and Mother would referee the argument that invariably developed over who reached what first…) and off we'd go.

Our beloved Aunt Birdie lived in Fitchburg - Mother's oldest sister, with her great warm heart and incomparable graciousness. "Why is she called 'Birdie'?" I had asked when a very young child. Her name was "Mary Ellen" and I thought that quite beautiful. "Well," Mother had said, "she was the first child in the family and her fond father delighted in watching her being fed. She would open her mouth like a small bird and her father began to call her his "little birdie'. Then later - when she grew old enough to talk and was still his adored first born, he would call as he arrived home in the evening, "Birdie, birdie, where's your nest???", and the little girl would answer with a phrase her loving father had taught her, 'In the heart that loves me best.'" and so she became "Birdie" to her father and eventually to everyone.

But - to return to our Christmas Eve journey…Oh, those wonderful, memorable Christmas Eve journeys…Invariably it would snow, and we'd sit fascinated as the gold of our car's headlights sent the tiny "snow fairies" as Mother called them, scurrying into the black night. We'd sing Christmas Carols all along the way; and finally, we'd have mounted the last big hill of our journey and Fitchburg would lie before us, its Christmas lights flung like a great necklace of jewels against the black throat of night.

Aunt Birdie's big rambling home at last - and out of the big car poured the Neners, toting their myriads of gaily-wrapped gifts. Grandmother Philips, our maternal grandmother would be there, and she'd embrace "Gaga" and they'd disappear into "Grandma's room" like two delighted schoolgirls. They'd been "best friends" in England long ago when they were young; and they were still "best friends."

Dad and Uncle Harry would trim the big fragrant tree that filled the living room with magic, Oh, the joy of those Christmas evenings, with Mother and Uncle Samuel at the piano and dad at the violin, and each of us "saying our Christmas piece" (we all "took elocution", heaven help our audiences); or singing our Christmas song…There'd be a thousand candles on the tree, it seemed - real live candles of wax in a riot color, spilling their gold profusely into the Christmas night…

Other things I remember as Christmastime comes our way another year. Mother would term each of the little kindnesses we children performed during the Christmas season a "little piece of straw for the manger of the Christ Child, to keep Him warm against the winter snow," "How cold the little Christ Child will be on Christmas morning!" she would say reprovingly to us when we had misbehaved. And how very hard the Nener children really tried to make His manger warm…

One more thing I remember - the Christmas plum pudding! It took a full day to bring to life this bit of Christmas magic. There'd be piles of raisins and piles of currants and piles of muscats; there'd be lemon peel and citron and beef suet and spices; and there'd be our annual ceremony. Each one of us in turn would stir the pudding, according to his age. Gaga would begin the ritual; and dad and mother would follow; and then the children down to the tiniest tot, into whose moist little palm mother would place the great wooden spoon.

Wonderful, strange-sounding words would issue from Mother's lips as each of us stirred the spicy mixture. They were forming a Christmas Prayer, a bit of Gaelic from her Irish ancestors. "May the blessing of God," she was saying, "descend upon our home this Christmas season and throughout the coming year." Mother's plum pudding was the highlight of our Christmas dinner. She'd pour brandy over it, and tuck a sprig of holly in its crown, and then ignite it. I always fancied I saw a Christmas angel in the soft blue flame that sent the spicy fragrance of Mother's Christmas pudding through the house.

I remember other things too - the big wax "holy candle" in the living room window. "We must light the way for the Christ Child," Mother would say; "we must let Him know there is room in our hearts and home for Him on Christmas morning."

Yes, Christmastime is for remembering, for looking back...way, way back...May the Christmas memories that I have made for those I love...my wonderful husband, my own dear children...have the warmth and wonder, the beauty and the faith of memories that always will be mine at Christmastime!

12-29-74 "CHRISTMAS ON BEACON HILL"

It was Christmastime on Beacon Hill. One knew it the moment one entered that immense front door through which so many of our distinguished citizens have passed into History. One knew it because the sound of Christmas Carols was drowning out everything including the voices of those troubled members of the Official Family who must - somewhere in the depths of the Beacon Hill scene - have been contending with the nightmares of deficit budgets and soaring service costs; of unemployment and an ailing economy; of all the ills that DO INDEED beset the State and soon will face those "legislators" who have elected to help solve them for their trusting electorate The Christmas music came from the third floor of the State House where a group of professional entertainers-engaged by Secretary of State Davoren for that purpose - was entertaining a hundred or so underprivileged youngsters.

Small hands everywhere clutched hamburgers and cold drinks; big eyes on all sides looked adoringly into those of a Santa Claus whose gifts were piled high beneath a towering tree, and a clown that would have done justice to Barnum and Bailey was dancing about merrily with one small child after another. It was a lovely scene; and people gathered about the perimeter to watch.

Your Columnist was at the State House to meet with all the other members of our newly formed Women's Legislative Caucus, in the office of the Speaker of the House, the Honorable David M. Bartley. We hoped to secure a Legislative Assistant and an Aid; and to reinforce our requests to serve on the kinds of State Committees we felt best suited our talents.

Speaker Bartley was gracious as we knew he would be. We met with him in his handsome chamber where a fire burned brightly in the huge fireplace. Our "host" pointed to it. "you see," he said, as we seated ourselves in a nice neat circle, "I too, am cooperating with the energy shortage." I found myself earnestly stressing my past involvement with the coming of the MBTA to Braintree; and appealing for an appointment to the Transportation Committee. It's a "glamour" committee, they tell me; though I can't see what could possibly be GLAMOROUS about it…

But- to return to the Speaker's Chamber. Its walls are handsomely carved; and from high above the faces of all those who have preceded him in this high office look down upon its present occupant.

"Take a look at that fellow up there," said the Speaker laughingly. "He's 19th Century, but look at his beard and those wide lapels; wouldn't he look right at home today?" We agreed that he would.

Our meeting went well, we thought; and at its conclusion we newcomers to the House were invited by the Speaker to follow him into a small room adjacent to the Chamber…A door opened; and dead ahead lay THE HOUSE OF REPRESENTATIVES itself! It is currently being renovated. Huge swathes of carpeting in royal blue and shining gold lay all about us; and there was considerable disorder. I saw none of it, however. In my mind's eye I was beholding THE HOUSE OF REPRESENTATIVES as it has looked to me for oh, so many years; and as it will look upon that day when I shall first be seated and belong…

The colorful Seal of the Commonwealth will grace the high vaulted ceiling. The names of our most distinguished Massachusetts sons will encircle the dome in a ribbon of history. A series of murals depicting "milestones on the road to freedom in Massachusetts" will adorn the walls. The lettering beneath the murals will undoubtedly as always be dimmed an faded slightly with the years; but bright and shining still will be the spirit of freedom emanating from the faces of the great historic figures found there.

The magnificent pageantry of the way we have elected to be governed will be all about us. On a dias will stand the three carved chairs, the central one of which-higher than all else, and framed by a vaulted and draped window - will be occupied by the gentleman currently serving as our guide, the Speaker of the House. His huge carved desk, and the gavel he will wield with considerable force now and then, we warrant, will add to the impressiveness of the scene.

Young uniformed pages whose duty it will be to run errands for the Legislators once the House is in session, will occupy the four chairs that lie before the desk, facing the House members. And at one of those desks that lie within the half-moon itself, the "House," your Columnist will be seated, fulfilling a dream, she never thought could come to fair fruition.

High above, and to the left will be Press Gallery; and on the same level, across the entire rear of the House, the Spectators Gallery wherein I pray that I shall find, on many occasions, some of those wonderful Braintree people who have elected me, there to watch their government at work.

The GREAT CLOCK, capped by an eagle with outstretched wings, will announce the opening hour of the session; the Stars and Stripes together with the State Flag will flank the great throne chair; the electric roll call will be primed for action; and a brand new day will dawn for this "legislator" whose great good fortune it will be to take with her to Beacon Hill the love and good wishes of oh, so many beautiful Braintree people; an, I hope, their prayers as well, that she will measure up to the awesome responsibility and privilege that is now hers...

This particular visit to Beacon Hill was not to end with a guided tour of the Speaker's Chambers. It WAS Christmastime on Beacon Hill; and so we were to find ourselves partying within offices of the Committees on Banks and Banking; and Labor and Commerce; to meet more of the wonderful people we are finding each time we visit Beacon Hill...And then we were to return to Braintree on our rapid transit lines - part of the "work force" for the first time in years; part of the crowd of that humanity that keeps our world in motion...Do you wonder that I found myself smiling broadly into the faces of passerby??? And giving up my seat in the subway??? And carrying a dear elderly lady's packages down the subway stairs??? And acting generally as though I'd come upon a pot of gold at the end of my rainbow??? I HAVE! Happy New Year, Everyone!

12-19-65 "CHRISTMAS SHOPPING"

Christmas shopping time...carols coursing on the wind; lights laughing in the night; shoppers beaming and bargaining; snowflakes spilling silver; Christmas memories tinting and tugging at the darling soul...Yes, it's Christmas shopping time, and my! what fun it is to join the gay and gallant crowd -to magically tote a parcel ten feet tall and three feet wide upon a crowded shopping aisle without the maiming of a single solitary soul, for life! To look about for something special for a darling daughter, or something absolutely mad for merry grandsons; to seek that gracious gift for dear Aunt Glad; the sweet surprise for dad, who's busy with a raft of smug surprises all his own.

What magic in the toy department-yes, and what sophistication! The natty little army tank, for instance, which once delighted tiny Byrne, must now be an atomic one; and "automatic" bowling pins will now be bought for James who from the day he crept, or so it seems, has merrily been placing ten pins in a nice, neat set of rows, for knocking down-small tongue resting on a lower lip that jutted out with comic concentration.

We poke about the shelves, and ponder. What would they like to have this year, our darling boys? Now, if one of them had been a girl, we'd buy her that nice, soft baby doll…What nice soft baby doll?

"I'm frustrated," a friend had screamed that very day. "All I wanted for my little Anne was a cuddly baby doll that she could take to bed with her and roll upon without spinal fracture. There's no such thing these days! They all wet or walk or hold long conversations. They're stuffed with mechanism and hard as rock…"

Christmas shopping-I adore it! Our entire family is addicted to gift giving, actually. The ones who marry us are flabbergasted. We exchange gifts all along the line, as far as fourteenth cousins, several times removed! The which, incidentally, serves to bring about the most delightful Christmas circumstances.

One year, for instance, a member of the clan gave to each of our men a handsome shaving bowl, complete with supplementary appurtenances-a most delightful gift, had it not been for the fact that every man in the family managed to receive a nice electric shaver that very year, the use of which rendered a shaving bowl completely useless.

"Oh, well," said every practical gal in the lot, "it's a lovely set; I'll give it to Cousin Larry for his birthday, (we also exchange birthday gifts by the thousands) or to Uncle John next year at Christmas." The which was a perfectly sound idea per se, only everyone in the family had it simultaneously, and so the saga of the perambulating shaving bowls began.

It is still going on, for it takes awhile to penetrate several layers of family; and it has become the seasonal joke "Who will wind up with the shaving bowls this year?" we ask one another merrily. One year, one of my more domestic neighbors had a bright idea for Christmas giving. "Let's all make our gifts," she said, "we'll meet once a week for coffee, and exchange ideas. It will be fun!" I settled on woolen scarves for the men on my list, and handsome skiing mittens for the children ("They're a breeze to make", said teacher). I purchased needles and yarn, and commenced to learn to knit. "For the scarves," said my neighbor, "we'll buy the finest imported woolens. You'd never be able to find anything like this in the stores," she assured me as we purchased away, "it's wonderfully warm, and so smart, and even if it does cost $100 a yard, we'll get four scarves from it…

Well, I sewed and sewed, and fringed and fringed, and knitted and knitted - and viewed with glee the finished products - as I pressed and pressed and steamed and steamed and fumed and fumed-for no two mittens were the same size. There wasn't a pair in the lot!

The scarves were even worse.

"How do like it?" I asked my brother-in-law, beaming

"Oh, it's lovely," he said gallantly.

It was months before I learned that the fine imported woolen affair reached just about to the bottom of his bright bow tie! Teacher had made a slight error in cutting. Instead of following the 60" width of the material, she had cut her four scarves from the 36" length…Oh, well…

Back to the toy department, and the lingerie; to men's wear and the subterranean world of sub- teens; to the merry merry music and the mad melee! It's Christmas shopping time again.

12-17-64 "CHRISTMASTIME AGAIN…"

Something exciting happened this past week. December arrived!

We had begun to wonder if the weatherman wasn't a mite mixed up. Lilac bushes and maple trees we're budding all over the place, with no sense at all of the seasonal fitness of things. Petunias and pansies bloomed away, and lawn mowers were still doing duty occasionally, and winter coats lay nestled in the vaults, quite unrequirell, when-my, oh my…

Down came a wild wind from the arctic; and down dipped a startled thermometer; and along came December! DECEMBER-that merry month toward which, in my book of holiday enchantment, all the other months of the year merely point like so many small and unexciting arrows…

Yes, it's December, and the wonderful Christmas season commences to whisper its way to New England.

Gay ropes of lights adorn the trim town squares of Braintree, and staid store windows have assumed a merry look.

We don a slightly tired old holiday corsage from other years, (we never can quite bear to toss that little item away, though we purchase one each year, and so we've inexhaustible supplies), and tuck a scarf about our throat against the wind the weatherman assures us lies without, and gather our grandchildren about us; and Ted and I are off to Boston Common and the Christmas Festival about which the newscasters have, as always, been enthusiastically commenting. The Christmas Festival on Boston Common, where each year, the real spirit of Christmas seems to seep sweetly with the cold caress of winter, into the human heart...

Christmas is many things, to many people, and here in this panorama of pageantry, there is something for everyone.

It's a season of light, and Boston Common is a fairyland.

The great black naked trees are wrenched quite suddenly from their winter sleep, their hearts warmed to blessed beating by a thousand lights. They toss their arms in youthful joy; they preen, and lend enchantment to the night, crowning its inky face with great, glad, tiered tiaras of red rubies, and of sapphires, or diamonds and topaz and emeralds.

Christmas Trees, afire with lights, throw triangles of flaming green or red or gold upon the dark. Against the skyline of the distant shops, lying there, mute and prostrate upon their avenue of silence, gathering strength against tomorrow's onslaught of gay Christmas shoppers, a great, grave tree of lights in deep, dark, eerie bine, rises to thrust the golden star that crowns its peak, into the heavens where stars belong.

The Common lies there in the winter night - a great, lined casket, spilling its jewels upon the gray of grass...

We find the Christmas of song and story, and Santa's reindeer, white and sweet, reach small moist muzzles for the bits of loaf sugar my grandchildren hold within their moist and mittened hands. "There is Dasher, and Dancer," sings small James, "Nama, where is Rudolph, the red nosed reindeer?"

And we find the Christmas of Santa and the big, brash Christmas stocking. Oh, the panorama of trees and toys and tots...

"Look, Nama, there's a tiny, bitty, specky army gun!" (Byrne is two, and it's sub-machine gun toy, fully four feet long).

And there's the Christmas with Christ in it. The Creche, the great, dark stable with the Holy Child; shepherds on the green, their still white sheep about them; the donkey, bearing Mary and Joseph to the place where there would be no room within the inn; the three Kings, solitary figures, journeying from afar. There's the glow of a Madonna in the trees, and the little Church from which a choir of youthful voices sends its Christmas caroling our way.

"Listen, Nama," says our smallest grandchild, to whom, along with his bigger brother of three we have been telling the blessed story of the little Christ Child, "God is singing!"

We do not dispute him. "Yes," we find ourselves saying softly, and we draw our coat about us in the winter winds, and we are silent as we walk, a family together, along the lighted path. We look above the jeweled trees to where a bright, December star is twinkling softly in sweet, understanding challenge in the night, and the peace, the joy of Christmas comes officially our way.

12-13-64 "CHRISTMAS THOUGHTS"

It just wouldn't be December if the somber, smoky skies
Didn't find a snowy teardrop in their gray December eyes;
If the tall trees failed to sport an ermine cap upon their hair,
And the world a shining silver kind of halo didn't wear.

And it wouldn't seem like Christmastime if every part of town
Wasn't showing off the jewels in the crimson of its crown;
If gay portraits of old Santa did not wink a merry eye
At the throng of mittened shoppers toting parcels, passing by.

If the chorusing of carols failed to sound upon the air;
And the Christ-like Christmas spirit were not walking everywhere;
If no tambourines sought gifts for Santa's poor; no cornets sounded;
If within the hearts of men, no blessed peace, no love abounded.

If no holly berried blithely, and no mistletoe hung high
In romantic invitation to fair lovers passing by;
If no tiny Christ Child's figure in a little manger lay
To remind a weary world of the REAL splendor of the day.

If the postman wasn't bent beneath a ton of Christmas letters
Mailed early by rembember-ers and late by fagged forgetters;
If a thousand Christmas bells upon the landscape failed to sing,
And no candles in the windows smiled warm welcome to the King.

But-three cheers!-it IS December, and the world is winter white,
And a million Christmas stars are spilling silver on the night,
And the blessed Christmas spirit is upon the earth again;
May we echo with the angels - "Peace on earth; good will to men!"

1-29-69   "CONNECTICUT IDYLL"

It was the first day of summer, and we were off-- Ted and 1- to spend the weekend in Connecticut with Richard and Dolores, our children.

"I hope we shall reach there in time for whatever plans Richard has made for us," I observed, as we tucked our bags in the car.

"Don't worry," said James, our eight-year-old would-be Meteorologist grandson. (James has always had a tremendous preoccupation with the weather), "You are going to have 15 hours and 17 minutes of daylight today. The sun rose at 5:07, and it will set at 8:24." With which pertinent bit of information, we were on our way.

Mystic, Connecticut, is a wonderful little town. Richard's latest toy, a pint-sized tractor for home use, had obviously been used to good advantage on the family lawn, which was lush and lovely. Our Connecticut grandchildren, Richard Jr., aged ten, and Franklin John, aged six, bounded to meet us, tripping as they came over "Bim", the huge Dalmatian with the long series of names and the short nickname.

Richard, as usual, had a dozen plans. We drove along winding River Road. Across the Mystic River lay the Seaport, with the great masts of its old sailing ships sharp against the summer sky. Equally sharp against the sky was the wonderful new spire of the local Baptist Church.

"They have wanted it for years; and at last they had money enough to build it," said Dolores. "Isn't it beautiful??" It was!

Mallards floated on the tiny inlets, their projeny trailing behind them in a tidy string of greens and blues; and great white swans rested gracefully on the quiet water. A lovely ride on a lovely summer evening…

Sunday was another day for adventure; and we set out early in the afternoon - our destination the Pachaug State Forest! Connecticut is a rather wonderful state, we have decided.

Many years ago, a group of far-sighted legislators engineered the purchase of large quantities of land, for the timber which grew there in abundance. The timber proved not to be particularly valuable; the land, however, WAS!

"There are perhaps 40,000 acres of it," said Richard, "and it is all reserved for recreational use." The Pachaug State Forest is a 23,000 acre parcel of this land.

We drove from Mystic to North Stonington, a dear little town incorporated in 1721; and thence past Wyassup Lake to Voluntown. Voluntown is a small village which houses in a lovely old farmhouse that COMMUNITY OF PACIFISTS that demonstrates against the launching of each new submarine that is built by General Dynamics in nearby Groton.

Not too long ago, we learned, a group of so-called "super patriots", armed with shotguns, descended on Voluntown-- their target the pacifists. The State Police had been alerted, however, and an old fashioned "Shoot Out" followed. Happily, said Richard, it was the invaders who suffered in the melee…

The LAUREL is Connecticut's State Flower, and this was Laurel Sunday. The flower was expected to reach its beautiful flowering peak. IT DID! Great banks of it lay against the hills like mounds of snow, in white and palest pink!

We thrilled to it as we drove through the local Indian Reservation, where can be found the remnants of the proud Eastern tribe of Pequot Indians. "There is Long Pond," said Richard. "We often fish there, young

Rich and I." He laughed. "We never catch anything," he said, "but the pond is so beautiful."

Pachaug State Forest at last. "Keep your eye out for deer," said our son. "Last time we were here, we saw two of them feeding - a doe, and a buck with a huge rack." We kept our eyes out, however the deer did not materialize. "If you want to get written up in my grandmother's column," said Franklin, "you had better come out right now, you deer!" They apparently had no such ambition.

The State Forest was picturesque and beautiful. Rustic handmade signs pointed the way to such delightful sounding places as Slepstone Falls, Escoheag Hill, Lowden Fall, Quinbaug Trail, Hell Hollow, Plainfield Pike and Flat Rock.

We headed for the Rhododendron Sanctuary, hoping that this would be Rhododendron Sunday as well. IT WASN'T! Great masses of this beautiful plant rose 20 to 30 feet high on all sides, their buds profuse; the great gnarled roots of them creeping about the place like huge black snakes. The sun had not yet kissed them into blooming, however.

It was fascinating to be there, nonetheless. Partridges rose at our approach; and birds sang from the great cedar and pine trees that must have witnessed the passing of painted Indian warriors, so ancient were they all.

Mossy tussocks, where the wild folk live, lay all around, their small openings challenging the curious. "Those are wild rabbit warrens," said young Richard. "And that is an opossum's house, I bet; and - look up in that tree - a SQUIRREL'S NEST!"

I saw these wondrous illustrations of nature's artistry through different eyes. I've been reading Tolkien's stories of the little folk who "inhabit a land that is called The Shire, a place between the River Brandywine and the Far Downs." And if ever there was a River Brandywine, it was the little stream that sang its way beside us; and if ever there was a Far Down...I laughed aloud.

"I'll bet HOBBITS live there," I said merrily...And so the rest of our afternoon was spent in the happy telling of the tales of these enchanting little people whose fairy footsteps I could all but find in the Rhododendron Sanctuary of the Pachaug State Forest, in beautiful Connecticut, on a weekend whose fifteen hour days were filled with happy enchantment.

5-12-90   DEDICATION SPEECH- HERITAGE ROCK

Madam Chairman and Members of the 350th Anniversary Committee…Members of the Clergy. Government officials at all levels… Ladies and Gentlemen:

How Beautiful to be back home in my beloved Braintree!

Out of long forgotten decades, one special day always has shone forth - the day I came to live in this wonderful town…1640 and the first white settlers found their way to the Hamlet of Monatiquot, a beautiful area nestled peacefully against the proud Blue Hills…and History would begin the recording of the town that was to be Braintree, of its heroes and its heroines, the courage of its people, and their undying commitment to the rights and dignity of mankind.

Two Presidents of the United States would be born here, men who would be destined to help frame the Constitution and the Bill of Rights, and to leave their stamp upon the history of our great nation-John Adams and John Quincy Adams. And through John we would come to know and to love the indomitable Abigail, his wife, who, although she was not born in Braintree, came to live here and so we claim her. I particularly claim her for it was reading about the remarkable life of Abigail Adams that drew me to this little town south of Boston from where I had always lived, north of Boston.

General Sylvanus Thayer, the builder of Fort Warren and the Father of West Point would first see the light of day in Braintree; and he would build and endow a free public library, an almost unheard of happening 120 years ago. Our recordings indicate that the idea was not very palatable to some of the town fathers, however the General would prevail, and the library would be built…And, to celebrate this achievement his supporters would hire a brass band and march to his home to serenade him.

What delightful things we read about the irascible John Adams… When Thomas Jefferson declared he would not be able to get the Declaration of Independence drafted in one week's time as Mr. Adams demanded, he is reported to have said, "My word! A whole week! A whole week! The world was created in a week." "Yes," said the droll Mr. Jefferson, "Sometime you must tell me how you did it."

And again from Mr. Adams after a hectic debate in the Continental Congress on that same Declaration of Independence, "If I come to the conclusion that one useless man is called a disgrace, two are called a law firm, and three or more become a Congress."

Oh, the impact that has been made on our Country's history by the wonderful citizens of this town that is celebrating its 350th Birthday today…

As far back as March of 1775, as we were reminded recently so delightfully by our Historical Society Presentation, Braintree "declared itself in opposition to the edicts of the crown", and formed companies of militia to defend itself. Its citizens voted favorably on a "Covenant of Liberty" for the fair redress of grievances.

Decades before the Civil War, its town meeting voted to condemn slavery…The first Dame School in the United States was established here. A progressive town from the very beginning.

American independence really began here, for it was Braintree's own John Adams who led the revolt against England's Stamp Act, and persuaded Town Meeting to accept a set of instructions to the Great and General Court in opposition to it, an action that was soon adopted, unchanged, by 40 other towns.

And let us not forget that Braintree's own John Hancock's signature was the one and only signature on that Declaration of Independence on July 4, 1776, the day of its adoption. Later, as we know, this outstanding Braintree-ite would become the first Governor of Massachusetts.

The other evening while watching a T.V. movie on the Civil War, I heard the following startling announcement: "Florida secedes from the Union!" I was momentarily stunned, and then, "Of course," I thought, "Florida was one of the southern states…" and then, "What am I doing here, I who come from the town of Braintree, the birthplace of those who helped bring into being these United States of America that the State of Florida attempted to rend asunder?

I was shocked; I was just a little ashamed; and then I remembered a certain special Braintree friend of mine who flew the Confederate flag beneath Old Glory, of course, when his little southerner grandson came to visit him…And I didn't feel quite so bad…

Well, I do live in Florida, but I'm NOT a Floridian. In my own mind I'm still and always will be a Braintree-ite.

When I turn on my T.V. and find a walkway paved with leaves of gold, I think of Braintree…a snowstorm comes into view and I can see my town robed in ermine…a pussy willow in a Florist's shop, and I'm strolling through Pond Meadow…a rose on my dining room table and I'm back on Arthur Street in my rose garden…forsythia in a picture book and it's April and Braintree is alive with GOLDENBELL…

I close my eyes and I'm back at town hall, scene of so many happy hours, with Thayer House across the street, and scattered about the town the beautiful Church buildings of all denomination…our great educational facilities…There's Sunset Lake, and Smith's Beach…and so much more…At the risk of sounding repetitive, how beautiful to be back home in my beloved Braintree…And how privileged I feel to be part of the dedication ceremony of this marker commemorating the 350th Anniversary of the founding of our town.

A town that produced heroes when men and women a cut above the rest were called for…And statesmen when they were needed to fashion a country that was to personify freedom and justice to all the countries of the world.

And beautiful people like those gathered here today to mark a shining hour in its history, its 350th Birthday…

May the loving Father of us all continue to shower His blessings upon the town of Braintree, and upon all who will ever dwell here.

Thank you, my very treasured Braintree friends, for having permitted me to share in this historic occasion with you…

9-18-66 "DEFEAT..."

Not so long ago, the defeat of Adlai Stevenson induced me to toy with a political novel. It began: "Defeat lay heavy upon his tongue, its bitter, acrid taste spreading in ever widening circles as returns came in, until his mouth became a sea of salt."

How very wrong I was about defeat - It's not that way at all, as now I know. It's a sort of singing in the heart that says, "I tried; I tried my best, but it was not to be..." The bitter acrid taste comes on the day before election when you realize the "die is cast..."

It takes courage and concern to run for public office. With this mantle, you tell yourself, you become the public servant of 40,000 people. Their cares are your cares; their problems are, in whole or in part, your problems.

Ahead of you will lie you years of pure dedication and denial. No long, leisurely vacations, without a cut-off date; no freedom from the specters of poverty and deprivation and fear; no escape from a personal intimate concern with the problems of public education, civil service, consumer protection, air and water pollution and the rest...

Yes, it takes courage and concern to seek to serve, but those you had in massive measure – that you knew.

You, single-handedly, wanted to help. You planned to implement a grave concern forth with all the problems of the state and of the age; you meant to add the light from your one tiny candle to the flame of others with a like concern; you wanted so to change so many things; and so you ran for office. But in people you would represent, there rests the choice, and those same people chose...

If you would have become a force for change; if you were destined to augment the ranks of those who truly seek to serve - then have the people lost; if all your dreams and promises were not to be fulfilled, then have the people gained; and so it goes.

Actually, even in defeat, you are a winner. You've had a rare and most unique experience. You've made an army of new friends.

Two thousand people have believed in you. Two thousand people heard your words and said, "This voice may speak with me on Beacon Hill." With what humility now, you seek to say a "thank you" to them all.

You have your moments, and you weep a tear or two, for you're a woman. You think of the legislation you might have filed and fought for, the influence you could, perhaps, have once exerted when integrity was under siege, you think of dreams that you have dreamed for all the people of your state, and then the bitter acrid taste begins to form, perhaps.

But it's a wondrous world if you're a woman...

There's that bedroom set you wanted to refinish-you'll have the time. The new baby that quite possibly could be a girl, and queen it over all the grandsons that you love...Those grandsons that you love...

Next summer, when the legislature wrestles with a thousand things, you'll be in Europe on a six- months trip...And you'll be sending cards to that terrific team of yours, those folks who wanted you to win, those friends whose hearts will be forever joined to yours in loyalty and love... the gals...Yes, it's still a wonderful world, even for the loser...And next time, we'll work even harder.

6-26-66   "DOG SHOW"

It began one day in June when daughter Gael burst in her customarily enthusiastic manner through the door.

"Mother" she said. I've found a dog!" (Gael, whose new Braintree home will be ready by August 1, plans to complete her family circle with a canine first edition.) "It's a Dandie Dinmont Terrier," she said "I found him in the dog book.

Mom, he's small and has silky fur and large eyes, and pendulous ears, and a long tail and short legs, and, mom, he has dignity and reserve, and, when aroused the Dog Book says, he will "fight to the finish, either of himself or his opponent." See, here's his picture."

I regarded the little beastie pictured before me, struggling valiantly to visualize the little dear fighting to the finish anything larger than a small mouse.

"Don't you love him, mom?" asked Gael. "Jim loves him and the boys…" "He's sweet, dear," I said.

"Mother," said Gael, They're very rare, Dandie Dinmonts, Jean says." (Jean is Gael's neighbor, and an authority on dogs. She's also the proud owner of Bonnie Belle, a show Collie, par excellence.) "And, mom, Jean says there's a Dog Show in Wellesley tomorrow and they're showing two Dandies, and she's showing Bonnie, and oh, mother, Bonnie's so beautiful she's sure to win first prize, and am just dying to see Bonnie in a show…" she paused for breath, briefly, "so, mom, will you come with us?

It was a beautiful day, and a wonderful Dog Show. There were 1,379 canine entries in various classes. "But wouldn't you know you'd be late?" Jean wailed on our arrival. "The Dandies were on first, you've missed them."

Gael all but cried. "Never mind," I said comfortingly, "we'll find them. They're here somewhere. "They can't leave the area until the Show is over," said Jean. And so, a-hunting we did go, past the booths that gaily advertised "Hi Tor Pet Uorts" and the House of Coquette, with its "Unique Togs for Dogs," and the whole bit, back to the sheltered area where the show dogs stood proudly for the final grooming by their owners.

There were Irish setters-three from one kennel alone, Scarlett and Rhett and Tara, no less. A giant-sized cage housed an English sheep dog, and a small boy, side by side. Pekinese panted, their little pink tongues pointing skyward. Afghan hounds looked down their long, aristocratic noses at the lesser breeds. Basset hounds marched mournfully about the ring, and Collies pranced like miniature blooded horses, and varied colored ribbons adorned everyone and everything,

There were quiet dogs and noisy dogs. "Keep quiet, Mollie," said a grooming attendant crossly, to a small black terrier. "How undisciplined you are. Goodness, where is your mother?"

It wasn't easy; we hadn't really the faintest idea what they looked like actually; but we found the Dandies. There were two of them, from the same Westchester County kennel. There are only 150 Dandies in the country; none in New England, we learned from the trainer. It's of Scottish ancestry, we learned.

"Sir Walter Scott mentioned the Dandie frequently in his novels," the trainer told us proudly.

"Robert Montgomery has two Dandies on his hunting preserve in upstate New York; they're from our kennel. And Lloyd Nolan has a Dandie. A wonderful dog," he added, "Quiet - you wouldn't know it was in the house, but a fine watch dog."

Gael produced the bit about fighting to the death. I winced, regarding skeptically the soft round eyes of "Tansi" which was a nickname for the unpronounceable set of cognomens that had been appended to the small show dog before us. "It's true," said the trainer, "I once saw a Dandie kill a German shepherd…"

We all fell instantly in love with Tansi, and she with us. She settled down in our arms like she was home. She had won the National Specialty of Westminister, and a dozen other shows, we learned. We may never possess a Dandie Dinmore, but we made the acquaintance of two of them that Saturday afternoon, and that is more than can be said of the average family, and that day may come…

Looking into the large blue eyes of daughter Gael as she bade farewell to the little lady, I realized that ownership of a Dandie Dinmont will be tucked very neatly into the "dreams come true" corner of her future.

It was a delightful day. The sun was warm; the rings were alive with handsome, healthy animals; the children were well behaved; the owners and trainers were friendly; the 80 Pinkerton men who were guarding the affair were alert and cooperative, too.

And, oh yes - we mustn't forget a pat on the handsome head of Bonnie Belle, our own particular pet collie. Naturally, she won first prize. She always does! Gael and Jim and the boys want one of Bonnie's puppies, also!

2-25-73   "DO-IT YOURSELF"

If you should happen to drop by Chez Matayer these days and mention the "Do It Yourself" craze, be prepared to be met with an icy stare; for, as far as the Metayers are concerned, "Do it yourself" is for the birds…Ted, you see, has just finished installing a new dining room ceiling; in the course of which nasty little job the "do it yourself" challenges he was obliged to meet, You Wouldn't Believe!

It all began when I casually announced that life would be incomplete without a brand new deal in dining room wallpaper. Well, it really began earlier than that…last April, in fact, when our darling children presented us on the occasion of our wedding anniversary with a gorgeous new dining room chandelier. "Wouldn't that have been handsome with the Chinese red wallpaper you had in that room a few years back?" someone made the mistake of asking. "Wouldn't it, though???" I found myself thinking; and the seed was planted. I would once again have a dining room with the handsome red wallpaper that always went so beautifully with my Christmas decorations and would serve to provide a splendid background for the new family chandelier…

A slight complication developed, however, when the dining room ceiling, shaken to the roots along with all the other ceilings in our ménage by the constant passage over our streets for 15 years of immense tanker-trucks enroute to the Electric Light plant, developed a huge, unsightly crack. "The ceiling will have to be replaced before we paper," Ted announced. I groaned. The memory of plasterers at work in our living room ceiling last winter was still fresh. We ate, drank and dusted plaster for months! "Couldn't we settle for one of those block ceilings?" I wanted to know. "I loathe the things and so do you, however…" And so the die was cast; the ceilings blocks were purchased and delivered, and our do-it-yourself rolled up his sleeves and went to work, nailing up a furry frame about the ceiling and preparing to search out the floor joists on which to fasten the strips across the ceilings surface. Alas! No two of them appeared to be the same distance apart. Soundings with the family hammer from one end to the ceiling's surface to the other revealed no uniformity whatsoever in the huge beams that should have been spaced accurately had not the carpenters been intoxicated, to quote my do-it-yourselfer. "I hate to tell you," he announced finally, "but the ceiling will have to come down." I groaned anew.

The thermometer was hovering around zero; and the winds were delivering a chill factor of at least a hundred below, and Ted and I were now faced with the happy task of removing the furring frame and tearing down and tossing out OPEN windows onto the floor of the sun deck a thousand tons of plaster…

The opportune arrival of a dear son-in-law with a borrowed truck solved the problem of transporting the resultant outside mess to the town dump, however the mess that remained within had by now settled upon and unsettled every inch of the igloo our usually snug residence had by now become. "Well," said an exhausted but satisfied (temporarily) husband, "at least now I can see what I am doing! How the fates that govern do-it-yourselfers must have chuckled at that one… that utterance that was made BEFORE the head of the house took a good look at the laths that now lined the ceiling's surface and ran… not the way Ted had envisioned them at all, but in a totally unsuitable direction. They will have to come down as well," he announced dismally. And so once more it was on with the winter coats and up with the windows and out onto the sundeck with the laths and up and down with the dry mops and the dust pans and the vacuum cleaners… and oh, yes, it had to be on with the family dish towels over noses and mouths to prevent the do-it-yourselfers from choking to death on the plaster dust…We're down to the bare bones now, and Ted can at least see and make allowances for the thousands of "irregularities" he keeps encountering "They must have been intoxicated, those carpenters; they COULDN'T HAVE BEEN SOBER" he keeps saying mournfully.

I'm the carpenter's helper incidentally. Ted's exasperated expression every now and then indicates that it's better to have me than no helper at all, but not much better! I'm the hander upper of the hammer, and the holder of the wood for sawing and the picker upper of the nails that fall; and the locater of the chisel and the square and the nail set and the pencil and the long-nosed pliers…Later I shall serve as the hander upper of the ceiling tiles, and the filler of the stapler with staples; and the peerer upward to ascertain the straightness of the lines; and the hander upper of the hammer and the picker upper of the staples that undoubtedly will fall; and the locater of the chisel and the square and the nail set and the long-nosed pliers…AND the cleaner upper of the sawdust and the shavings and the rest…I'm also the doer of an occasional errand for the boss, like the purchase of "a piece of blue chalk for a snap line…" (Are you sure the man will know what I mean, Ted?)

The Metayer ménage still looks like a disaster area…AND NOW COMES THE CLINCHER! I've explored every wallpaper salesroom in town, and I can't find a single thing in red to come up to that gorgeous dining room paper of long ago! The fact has me decidedly down, but it doesn't seem to bother my do-it-yourself husband one small bit…Ted says he's been seeing RED in that dining room for days, and right now he'd just as soon opt for a complete turnabout in color schemes anyhow…

4-1-73   "DO IT YOURSELF CONTINUED"

"How are you coming along with the RED dining room of yours?" people keep asking; and they're surprised at seeing me shudder before replying. That "red" dining room, you see - the subject of a recent column-continues to generate problems for the Metayers.

To begin with, I never DID manage to come up with the luscious Chinese red wallpaper I was envisioning while merrily removing all that perfectly good GREEN wall covering from the sale a Manger. Consequently, having ceased to see RED, I found myself returning to the shade we had so painstakingly removed-GREEN! Now, green wallpaper is to be found in abundance; and so it was easy to select a beautiful affair entitled "Fields of Poppies." There were lush green flocked poppies vying with gold foil ones on a handsome muted background. It was love at first sight…or at least, at one thousand one hundred and first sight (We had perused every wallpaper book in the community) "How soon can I have it?" I asked the salesman. He was obviously so relieved at the thought of getting rid of a potential customer who had worn his books to the nub that he hesitated not a moment before replying. "Today is Saturday," he said. "We'll have it for you by Monday evening!"

That Monday evening was to be a full and frustrating month in coming; as a matter of fact it has not even as yet arrived. "Fields of Poppies," we were to learn to our dismay, has become so appealing to the general public that the supply cannot keep up with the demand. "I hope you don't find it in the home of every friend you have," said daughter Gael. "Besides, I want to use it in my front hall!" At this point in time, however, I really don't care. As a matter of fact, I am secretly rather relieved. How "Fields of Poppies" could ever have been tucked into my March Agenda I cannot possibly imagine…

One drawback to the situation, however, is the look of the family dining salon. It has definitely lost its appeal. The coat of white plaster, patched hither and yon, does little or nothing for it; nor does the absence of all the furnishings that customarily add to its appearance. In addition, the family living room, housing the contents of its neighbor as well as of itself, has taken on the look of local furniture store…If we are not all handsome and habitable by Easter, I plan to fold my tents and steal silently…away, I mean.

Incidentally, with a less bulging Agenda, wallpapering IS fun for this columnist…now that she has mastered the fine arts of measuring and matching. Time was, however, when I considered the papering of the family walls a completely professional and profound undertaking, having been brought up in a family where the annual selection of new wallpaper in needed areas was made in the privacy of the home and under the watchful eye of the local paperhanger, by a Mother who planned to be thirty miles distant at the family beach house while the stuff was being hung.

It was not until we moved to Braintree more than twenty-six years ago, that I was to learn that just plain people could paper walls. I had been invited to tea at the home of a welcoming neighbor, my friend Helen. Her papers were exquisite. "I do it myself," she said proudly. "I do ALL the papering!" I was aghast. So was sister Gladys when I duly reported this astounding fact. "How CLEVER she must be!" we chorused. Came the day when we began to doubt that our paper-hanging friend had a monopoly on cleverness. "Do you think WE could do it?" we asked of one another. Came the answer: "If SHE can, WE can!" And the die was cast. The opportune departure of Gladys' husband on a hunting trip afforded us an excellent opportunity to try our wings. We selected a new paper for her living room and went to work with a will (and with every kind of papering tool an eager salesman had managed to load us down with)….

The first trip went up beautifully. "See!" we said, elated. "It's EASY!" Then came the second strip. It FAILED TO MATCH! The idea of cutting the pattern to fit did not occur to either of us. We had never in our lives watched anyone hang wallpaper. Besides, I always HAVE missed the obvious; and on this occasion, so did Glad! We were preparing to complain to the wallpaper establishment when friend Helen arrived to save the day… and to teach us the fine arts of cutting and matching and the rest. We were now off and running; and we've been papering the family walls ever since…I can't answer for Gladys, but I've managed to pull a few boners along the way to expertise in this little do-it-yourself area. There was the time when a sea of most unusually shaped and entwined green leaves graced our living room walls. "How unusual!" people were forever saying, "How DIFFERENT! What kind of leaves ARE they?" "I really don't know," I would reply smugly. "I've seen anything like them myself. They ARE unusual…" Came the day when that same friend Helen, standing pretty much on her head while attempting to retrieve an earring that had fallen under the divan saw my living room walls in a brand new light. "Bibs!" she screamed, "They're UPSIDE DOWN PALM TREES!!! Your paper - it's PALM TREES! You put it on upside down…" Oh well, I probably would not have liked it half so well had I hung the stuff correctly, I told myself. I'm really not all that fond of palm trees right side up…

4-23-67 "DO YOU BELIEVE IT'S SPRING?"

When the earth is wearing its springtime mien,
Isn't the grass supposed to be green?
When spring has laced on her ballet shoes
And danced off the premises winter's blues;
When the robin has found his way home, should he find
That those soft silken breezes were all left behind?
When the daffodils toss out their soft green arms
And the tulips start sporting those colorful charms,
Should the croci lie shivering down by the wall?
(Sure, they look like they just don't belong there at all…)
Didn't that calendar back a ways
Tick off a series of mild March days,
Then come to a point where a date quite gay
Announced Old Man Winter would stomp away???

Didn't we don a bonnet new?
And rush to find springtime's golden hue?
What happened to all of those things we planned
When we fancied that spring was upon the land?
Where are tree tassels of green and gold?
Just about this time, they should all unfold…
Why are there ice crystals on the pond?
Why that cold black lace on the hills beyond?
I just must get out in my garden neat!
Wanna don a kerchief, and tuck my feet
To where hyacinths don them a golden crown
That those soft silken breezes were all left behind?
Which they tip in glee, to the robin fair
Who is not too cold to be playing there…
Wanna sop up sunshine, and feel the touch
Of that springtime magic I love so much!
Wanna tuck away mufflers and scarves and mitts;
And try on my swimsuit to see if it fits;
And go on that diet I always take on
When I look me over at springtime's dawn.…
Wanna work for my suntan, and walk on the beach
Till I painfully burn like an overripe peach…
Aw, come on, Miss Spring-where on earth are you?
Brush the gray from your skies, and replace it with blue…

4-8-65   "DRIFTWOOD"

When all that's left of winter's roar is piles of driftwood on the shore,
I love to sit the sea beside, and watch the ebbing of the tide.
What joy to find upon the sand some trifle from a far-off land!
How sad to ponder on the spars, once wooing dim and distant stars,
That now lie prone, their timber spent, their unhappy hauteur
     bowed and bent.
Whence have you come, oh relics gray, by ocean stormings tossed
     my way?

Whisper to me of the fate so grim, that hurled you ashore on the sea's soft rim…

Were you, in distant ages past, the backbone of some towering mast

Upon the which great sails were hung; about whose base were chanteys sung?

Did you once woo the tropic breeze; charter a course through savage seas?

Have you, perhaps, known hurricane; the typhoon's savage scream of pain?

What of your Captain? Was he young; a minstrel, with his song unsung?

Was he, perhaps, a tyrant bold, the scourge of seamen, young and old?

Was he a dreamer, visions fine lighting his eyes as if by wine?

Was there a poem within his soul? Or was a golden cache his goal?

Did he his ship by starshine sail? Was he a man one dared not fail?

Ah, bits and pieces of driftwood, I would know you, if I could…

Are you the bones of some proud barque? The remnants of a Noah-boy's ark?

A raft, on which he planned to ride smooth seas across the world so wide?

Fragments of wood, I see you tossed, with saves awash, alone and lost,

And, quite unbidden, visions rise, to float before my conjuring eyes.

Were you, perhaps, a scrap of some great luxury liner, no become

Only a legend, a tale to tell of a day when the sea rang your dark death knell?

Are you from India, far away? Or from the slopes of Iceland gray?

Are you the skeleton, perchance, of some fair craft that knew romance?

The dory of bronzed fisherfolk? the stave of some great cask of oak?

What other shores have you caressed? By what strange seas were you possessed?

E'er you traversed the world, to find a field of fancy in my mind,

To lie upon a springtime morn, unloved, dismembered, and forlorn,

Tossing and turning with changing tide, prostrate your golden, gleaming pride?

Once the sea yielded to your charms; now you lie cradled in its arms…

I'm a fan of Rachel Carson's…Her astute philosophy
I espouse with fiery fervor, right from "A" on down to "Z".
With a SILENT SPRING, I'd suffer to a most mark-ed degree;
But…good gosh! each day at dawning, WHAT THOSE BIRDIES
  DO TO ME!

They sing songs beneath my windows; they have fights upon my lawn;
I keep wondering WHEN and IF they SLEEP, so early is THEIR
  dawn…
Long before the daylight threatens, they are at it! My night's gone!
From deep slumber I'm awakened; from sweet dreams I am
  withdrawn…

They're rehearsing some WILD concert…At least, that is what it seems
Must assuredly be happening as they murder all my dreams
With the trilling of sopranos; the wild altos; and great streams
Of deep bassos, most profundo, each one straining at the seams…

NOW the little darlings whisper; and then suddenly they SHOUT
In a way that makes me wonder what the ROW is all about…
From the mayhem that o'er follows, I most earnestly want OUT!
Did dear Mother call THIS "PRAYING"? Holy smokes, am I in
  doubt???

Though I love the feathered darlings; by their presence I am stirred
In a manner most delightful; I ADORE each lovely bird,
Still…at four a.m. each morning, it seems utterly absurd
That they practice not that adage to "be seen" but "not be heard!"

There won't be any lights this year to sing their song of Christmas cheer;
No candle gleams will shine to say the Heavenly Child is on His way;
And in the dark December night, no smiling silvering lovely light
Will send its glow upon the street to light the way for shoppers' feet.

No tree will deck the village green, all lighted, lovely and serene;
No tree at all…No door alight to send its greeting to the night;
No Santa Claus on rooftop high, his glowing reindeer 'gainst the sky;
No lights at all??? Not even ONE, to say that Christmas has begun???

How all forlorn each home will look…an unillustrated storybook;
An orchestra sans violin; a friend's abode with no one in;
A spring devoid of robin's calls; a winter without soft snow squalls;
A summer stripped of sunshine bold; an autumn lacking all its gold…

I find my heart is strangely sore. No window lights??? Not any more???
For years I turned them on with glee, then set out every Christmas tree
With myriad candles, all ashine. What joy come Christmastime
     was mine!
Now here it is DECEMBER and no Christmas glow may light
     the land…

The streets are all so dark and dim; no welcoming lights to shine
     for Him
Within the windows, once aglow. 'Tis Christmastime??? You'd
     never know…
The town is dark; it seems so drear… Tis like just ANY time of year…
A MERRY Christmas, people say??? There's little reason to be gay…

Yet, lo! Did not just one star's light upon that first fair Christmas
     night,
One star that shone alone on high within the dark Judean sky

Serve to lead shepherds to where He lay, the Child born on that
    Christmas day???
Did not ONE star the Wise Men guide unerringly to the Christ
    Child's side?

In truth, those stars that shine above…those manifestations of His
    love
ARE CANDLES, lovelier by far! What earthly light can match
    a star???
This energy crisis that we know may serve to curb OUR candle-glow
Yet high above the stars will still be raining glory on the hill…

And no decree can e'er impart an energy crisis to the heart.
It still may beautifully be alight, reflecting joy and shining bright;
May still be warm and all aglow that one small Child may rightly
    know
His welcome is on Christmas morn as though a million CANDLES
    shone!

And all those kindnesses we show when Christmas sets our hearts
    aglow…
Why, let's all make them twice as bright to make up for the lack
    of light!
Our good deeds let us multiply; no cry for help let pass us by;
No plea for pardon; cry of pain be sent our Christmas way in vain….

Yes, though our candles fail to gleam, yet may our light so brightly
    beam
That its great glow, when borne on high illumines the whole
    December sky!
No darkness then shall each one feel; THE GLOW OF CHRISTMAS
    WILL BE REAL
And high above, the Child will smile; this energy pinch CAN
    prove worthwhile…

1-2-66 "AN EPILOGUE TO CHRISTMAS"

Comes the week after Christmas....

Not a card remains to be written; no gracious gift cries invitingly to be wrapped; no scarlet bow beckons to be tied upon a bough...(thank Heaven!)

Every Merry Christmas has been said by telephone and telegraph and tell-everybody-we-met!

The happy holiday packets are all gone from under the tree; as a matter of fact, the tree is a bit but with a small gift for everyone. The angel's halo is a mite awry; and bits and pieces of what once were shining baubles o'er the onslaught of gay grandsons, sparkle sweetly from the folds of natty net beneath the boughs.

Grandpa's hay fever is abating, now that pine pitch has died down and needles nestle in a hundred happy heaps about the gay ménage.

The gay ménage, itself, is slowly running down.

We've commenced to disconnect the spots without, and throw the switches on the window lights within, at twelve now, 'stead of two; and we can wait till dark to set them all aglow.

We've pried the last mashed sugar plum from off the rugs.

And we've unearthed the last lean bullet shell and trim torpedo from beneath the chairs where they were fired by grandsons who appear to have no real regard at all for poor dear grandmother's pat pledge against the purchase of those violence toys this blessed Christmas. "And what do you want Santa to bring you, Franklin darling?" "A cannon that shoots fat bullets." "And you, Baby Byrne what do you want from Santa?" "A rifle - a big air rifle."

The turkey, like a great ghost ship bleached white by sea and sun, lies naked in the stuffed refrigerator.

Scales betray a crushing need for dieting, come leaner January days.

We're terribly a feared we'll hasten the demise of our Town Dump by perfect years with all the boxes, bales and crates we've stored in the garage for rubbish day.

We've toasted Merry Christmas till we're hoarse, and wished each friend so well.

We've whispered tender thanks upon the Holy Child for not one vacant chair about our festive board in yet another year. And we've congratulated Santa and those darling deer of his upon a pack well filled, a trip well taken.

A gift or two remain beneath the tree; we'll get to them come New Year's. And, oh yes - we must join Operation Gift Exchange one sunny morning soon, like everybody else, and therein lies a tale.

Cousin Mary is just about my age, but there's considerably more of her.

"What shall I give to Cousin Mary?" I've been asking me, come Christmastime, for years. The gift of lingerie, I have quite studiously avoided, for how can you buy someone you love something dainty in a size 50 or 60, without betraying the fact that deep down within, you consider her a mite outsized?

This year, I looked at the lovely things, and had a brainstorm. "Of course," I said, "I simply shall remove the size; that way, she cannot take offense." The which, I did. It's such a pretty gift; but what a pity Cousin Mary booby-trapped the subterfuge! The dear, sweet gal arrived on Christmas morning, fine and fair and fresh from what, I know to be the only diet she has ever known!

"Do exchange it for a 36," she pleaded airily, then laughed aloud. "What size is it?" she asked, "I'm sure it was designed by Omar, the Tentmaker!" I do hope I shall be able to explain to the nice salesperson, the absence of a size!

Well, anyhow - Happy New Year everybody! A kiss on both your cheeks, according to the custom of the French! May all the dreams that lie upon your soul be realized in 1966. And may the year bring peace upon its passing - peace within your heart, your home, your town, and so - your world!

12-2-73 "EPILOGUE TO THANKSGIVING DAY"

There's something special about Thanksgiving Day! Perhaps it is because upon that day in this America of ours the thoughts of most of us turn Heavenward, however briefly, in prayerful gratitude for all the blessings life has brought us...the gift of life itself; the gifts of friendship and of love; the gifts of peace and freedom. It's a day when families everywhere look lovingly one upon the other as they break Thanksgiving bread together, look now indeed with so much love as to quite beautifully warm the very heart and soul of this our land...It's a day that signals the start of the joyous Christmas season...It's a day of joy...joy for the lonely and the elderly unloved who are invariably remembered and are feasted at that special time...a day of Worship Service everywhere in all the Churches and the Temples of the land... It's a VERY SPECIAL day!

Our Thanksgiving Day was, I am certain, quite like your own. We gathered about a groaning table here in the Metayer dining room, the warm glow of the gold foil accents in our new wall coverings blending beautifully with the soft candlelight to cast a shimmering light across the faces of our loved ones. There were Ted and I, the hosts; our two beautiful children, Richard and Gael and the two beautiful people they have married, Dolores and Jim, along with the dearly loved parents of them both and the elder sister of our Dolores, her Beverly, now a member of the Sisters of Charity of St. Vincent de Paul, a beautiful young woman whom we watched grow from a delightful neighborhood child into a dedicated nurse and then an even more dedicated nun. Completing the scene was its hope for the future- the five strong handsome grandsons of the family, delightful to be in each other's company for the day and chattering like so many magpies.

The festivities were hushed as the Father of the family rose to ask a blessing upon the food that lay before us and upon those who were about to partake of it; and then our wine glasses were raised in a series of gay familiar family toasts, commencing as always with a solemn "thank you" to the loving Father of us all for the blessed and beautiful fact that once again not one sad empty chair would mar the beauty of the sweet Thanksgiving scene. Thus, has it been for eight beloved and beautiful years for the Metayers - a family completely united on Thanksgiving Day as are all families- either at daughter Gael's or at Mother's; and then together again for Christmas Day at Richard's in Connecticut!

What makes Thanksgiving Day so very special for the families of America, I asked myself as, one more fair Thanksgiving Day behind us, I went now about the house, straightening chairs and tucking dishes into the family dishwasher and leftovers by the barrel into the family fridge? What special grace does this fine day possess that we all savor it with such delight??? And then my eyes found Gael and Jim's Thanksgiving card above the family fireplace and I stopped, dust cloth in hand, to read for just about the hundredth time its proud Thanksgiving message:

"For Two Wonderful Parents," it read; "Hope Both of You Have a Happy Thanksgiving! Why God Made Parents…God knew that we each would need shelter and guidance Throughout all our growing-up years, Warmth and compassion for all our problems, and strength for our worries and fears…He saw that we all needed wisdom for living, A knowledge of heaven above, True understanding of life's deeper meanings, Examples of kindness and love, And so He made parents to stand by our side, To inspire us in every endeavor, Whose faith and devotion will last through our lives. And whose love we will cherish forever." A message of love!

And now, eyes a trifle on the misty side, I turned once more to where a gaily colored child's Thanksgiving sketch stood propped against the family T.V. The nicely drawn fruit bowl caught my admiring eye and then the printing just beneath…the work of sixth grade grandson Byrne, who had been privileged to read it for all of us Thanksgiving afternoon. It read:

"THANK YOU GOD FOR THANKSGIVING.

T-for Trees, Truth and Trust.
H-for Health, Happiness, Heaven. These are a must.
A-Thank you, God, for Animals, America and Air.
N-for Nature, Night, Neighbors who care.
K-Thank you for Kids, Knowledge and Kindness.
S-for our Saviour, Sharing, Sight without Blindness.
G-Thank you, God for Grandparents, Goodness and Giving.

1-for Intelligence, Imagination, Independence in our living.
V-for the Virgin Mary, Vision and Vacations.
1-for Infants, Irish Setters and Invitations.
N-for Nurses, our Nation and Names.
G-for Glory, Gifts and Games.
Thank you for all these things! Happy Thanksgiving!"

You know, I think that just about sums it all up for most of us! We're just plain thankful to be one more nice American family, loving and loved, celebrating one more glad Thanksgiving Day together, turning prayerful eyes Heavenward as we do so, to the loving, caring Father of us all. And yet-shouldn't we stop to count those blessings of ours a little more often, dear friends?

12-16-73 EVERYWHERE, EVERYWHERE CHRISTMAS CORSAGES!

And aren't they beautiful??? I saw my first one this year the very morning after Thanksgiving. Its wearer was sporting it like she couldn't wait another minute. It was a little bit seedy; berries had dropped off here and there, and the gay shiny leaves of yesteryear were crumpled a bit about the edges, but it was beautiful to behold!

"Look at me!" it cried. "I'm a harbinger of CHRISTMAS, and I'm echoing the joy that warms my wearer's heart because that blessed day lies just ahead…"

I saw it and I laughed with glee; I couldn't help it…I always do when first I see a Christmas corsage each year; and then I dashed right home and opened wide my Christmas drawer and trotted out a thousand of them (or so it seemed…) from other years, and shook their golden bells, and straightened ribbon bows, and then remembered other Christmases…

I never can bear to throw away a Christmas corsage when the season is spent; it's much too much like discarding a dream…

This one, for instance, was our Christmas favor that happy time when I was President of my Woman's Club; and that one a beautiful elderly lady pinned - long, long ago - upon my gown before I gave out with a Christmas program of the verses and tales that were to find their way eventually to "Cabbages and Kings."

This one was Mother's last…I found it on her coat the Christmastime she left us. It was so like Mother - beautiful, smart and expensive; I shall never discard it!

In memory, I trod the trail of Christmas corsages through the years - the red and green and holly- berry kind of long ago; the shining blue; the gold; the pale sophisticated pink.

There are those who favor one kind of another (I love them all!) just as there are those who like tall perfectly formed synthetic Christmas trees and those who prefer the just plain green and aromatic kind.

Richard, my son is very vocal in his preference for a real green tree. "Who ever heard of a synthetic Christmas tree?" he asks. "Give me a tall full tree, fresh from the Connecticut woods near my home…" (Richard and his boys visit a tree farm around Thanksgiving time each year to select their own growing tree. They are then allowed to purchase it and chop it down and carry it home for Christmas.) "I like to SMELL my fresh Christmas tree all through the house," he says. If Richard were five foot and blonde instead of six foot and dark, he would undoubtedly favor the red and green corsage with the princess pine and the holly berries that I tuck within a corner of my greens each year. Incidentally, Dolores, our dear daughter-in-law happily shares her husband's preference for things. Gael, my daughter, on the other hand, is just like her mother - she's the silver or gold type when it comes to corsages; and her idea of Christmas beauty is a great gleaming perfectly formed synthetic tree decorated with the shining blue and gold of her décor. Happily son-in-law Jim, the artist of family, shares her enthusiasm for the spotlighted dramatic effect the Corbin tree thus produces.

Dad also prefers the synthetic tree - but for different reasons entirely…having been married for years and years to a gal who trotted out the family tree on December 5th or 6th to be duly enjoyed until January 6th, and strung with a thousand happy lights all of which blazed from dusk almost until dawn, Dad had found himself listening miserably to the crackling of dry needles and eyeing the family insurance policy and kissing his loved ones a tender goodbye each time he left the house.

Actually I'm surprised he wasn't the INVENTOR of this safe and sane gadget!

Yes, there are Christmas trees and Christmas trees…and Christmas corsages and Christmas corsages…and each one beautiful in its own delightful way just because it's Christmastime and there is beauty in everything that surrounds this lovely time of year…CHRISTMASTIME, "the music" of which "is laughter" "the warmth" of which "is friendship"; and "the SPIRIT" of which "is LOVE!"

1-13-74   "FAREWELL, SANTA CLAUS!"

January 6-LITTLE CHRISTMAS- and we begin the lonely task of tucking away our Christmas till another year; of finding space within the family attic for the myriad of trees; the little crèche; the glitter and the gold; the ornaments and the tinsel…of bidding farewell to all the Christmas beauty that has made our little home a place of magic for the past four weeks.

The task seems especially lonely this year. Gregory Scott Corbin, you see, our Christmas-loving smallest grandson is growing up. He'll be seven next month…which means that now no longer will our boy be taking Grandma's hand and leading her up stairways to the attic now and then, as Christmas memories fade, to wave a greeting to the Christmas trees that sleep there; and we can expect no strains of "Jingle Bells" or "Rudolph" to lend their jolly background music to the moods of March or June or August as has been the case for oh, so many years, since Gregory first found his way around the family Hi-Fi.

Yes, Gregory, our littlest Christmas angel's growing up! He still thrills in his own small wonderful way to Christmas. His Christmas tree must dwarf all else within his room. It groans beneath the weight of countless paper chains and stars created and placed there by Gregory, as well as with an avalanche of Christmas trimmings begged from everyone and everywhere…Even "Tiffy," the family poodle and Greg's own special love, must know it's Christmastime. Tiff's probably the only doggie in existence to have her own fair pint-sized Christmas tree, decorated and glowing beside her bed.

Actually, Gregory Scott Corbin, we have decided, always will love Christmas. It's an odd thing about small boys and this special time of year. They seem to carry its enchantment right on down through the years into manhood and even beyond. Son Richard, for instance, was always a Christmas sentimentalist. He never would allow me to discard the small Christmas angel we placed atop our tree when he was ten. Each year I'd scrutinize the tired little figure and announce quite firmly, "Now really, we ought to have a grand new angel for the top of the tree." And Richard could be relied upon to say rather sheepishly but nonetheless firmly, "Gosh, Mom, this one looks all right. Let's KEEP it."

Well, we kept that tired little tinsel lady until Rich grew up and married. And he's STILL sentimental about Christmas. His family Angelabra was looking a bit seedy about the edges, Dolores, his charming wife reported this year. She tried sprucing it up, but with little or no real success; and it need new candles. I said, "Oh, well, we really don't need an Angelabra, do we fellas?" Her six-foot tall, engineering executive husband looked up from the book he was reading and grinned a bit sheepishly, "Sure we do, don't we, boys?" he said. "We ALWAYS had an Angelabra at Christmastime. Buy another one, hon…" She did!

We were amused by another tale of Christmas sentimentality that came our way this week from sister Gladys, a former Braintree-ite, now settled - most contentedly, we might add-in Maine. She had purchased a lovely artificial tree and seized the opportunity one evening when hubby Tim and son Michael were off at a meeting of the local Volunteer Fire Department (they're both members) to assemble and beautifully decorate the lovely thing. Home came the firefighters to be confronted by Glad's handiwork. "Gosh, Mom," moaned six-foot plus tall and quarter-century old son, Michael, "A FAKE Christmas tree??? Nobody in Maine EVER has a fake Christmas tree. They go out in the woods and cut their own. I'll get us one tomorrow - a REAL Christmas tree. I'll get Norman Abbott and we'll go up to his mountain (he really does own a mountain.) and we'll cut one down He knows how to cut trees down so they won't die…" The which son Michael did.

"It's squashed in the back, Mom," he said apologetically as he lowered the huge fir through the family doorway. "Some of the branches are squashed, but you can put it in a corner, can't you? Anyway, remember when we were kids, you told us the story of the little Christmas tree that stood in the forest and was smaller and not as straight as the other trees??? And every year it would say, 1 hope somebody picks ME!' but nobody ever did??? Well, I saw this tree, and you know - those squashed branches-I thought of the poor little Christmas tree and I said, 'I'll bet nobody will pick this tree!' so I did…" P.S. That REAL tree, squashed branches and all, sent the fragrance of Christmas all through the house; and when finally, it came down, his mother trimmed it with suet and set it out for the songbirds, she reports, only to have Chuckie, the big brown neighborhood dog, normally the world's fussiest eater, march straight up the street and systematically devour every last scrap of the birdies' holiday treat, bit by bit by bit.

Christmas sentiment??? It's rather general, wouldn't you say? I, personally, wouldn't exchange the few tired old Christmas tree ornaments that date way back to my long-lost childhood for the costliest and loveliest baubles on the shelves…Oh well, FAREWELL you wonderful little old season for another year! Sleep deeply, little Christmas trees in Grandma's attic and on the forest floors until we meet again next Christmastime!

3-4-73   "FAREWELL TO FEBRUARY"

So now, WHAT HAPPENED TO FEBRUARY??? 'Tis supposed to bring us snow to pile it in grim gray mountains that refuse to melt and go…

Wild winds should have blown great gales; and the temperature should have dropped; And the donning of scarves and mittens and boots should not for a moment have stopped!

Instead, we saw scarcely a snowflake; and the winds weren't wild at all;

And only on rare occasions did the thermometer choose to fall.

In the parks, our little ones gathered, coats wide open and caps all askew;

And above us, the skies were not somber and dark, but an elegant shade of bright blue.

Why, we even began eyeing gardens where - amazingly - BUDDING we find;

And, as sunshine illumined our winter-wan rooms, SPRING CLEANING was coming to mind…

We quite dismally checked last Spring's wardrobe, taking stock of the averdupois that has settled on places from kicking o'er traces and counting those calories no more! 'Tis a wonderful thing to be welcoming March, that MILD month…How far off it had seemed when a short while ago, dire predictions of snow meteorologists dismally screamed…

Winter's practically o'er when THIS month is no more; why the thought makes our very hearts sing…

All the birds will return, there'll be sunshine to burn
AND AHEAD WILL LIE GLORIOUS SPRING!

6-20-71   "FATHER'S DAY"

Hats off to Father on his day!

Always in mid-June when the sun is gay and golden and the family rose gardens reach their magnificent zenith, lavishing their precious perfume on the summer air, comes that special day when Dad, the family darling, comes into his own.

Dads come in various shapes and forms.

There's the great-outdoors type. He hitches a travel trailer to the family car and heads for the wild north woods, his brood about him. He's an authority on how to pitch a tent; and lead a singalong at the campfire; and find a whippoorwill; and track a snowshoe rabbit throughout the brush; and loose the legends of the stars. He's that all-grown-up Daniel Boone and Wild Bill Hickok he himself adventured with when but a boy…He may never have made "Eagle" in his Scouting youth, however, his wings soar high above the world of those he loves…

And then there's the INDOOR sport. He excels in tracking down, overwhelming and taking possession of the softest chaise lounge on the home front. His Northwoods know-how exists only to the degree that he can find his way (with it)…to the shadiest spot in the family back yard; and his acquaintances with things meteorological - recalled from Science I - is evidenced only by his acumen in placing his back firmly against the wind so that a sudden gust will not dislodge the Ivy League cap from its nesting place over his eyes…There's the perennial college-boy type of dad - pipe, tennis racket and all; and there's the dad of dignity and decorum, stuffy but substantial …

THEN there's the AVERAGE dad! He's the genius who fixes everything from the small squat wheels of Junior's first little red fire truck to the washing machine pump and the hopelessly stalled automobile engine of the gal next door. He's the solver of family problems; the stabilizer of family crisis; the rock on which the foundations of the clan rest. On his energy and drive, his ambition and accomplishment, will depend the kind of homes his family will inhabit, the kind of life his family will enjoy.

His son will, in all probability, grow up to be largely like him; and his daughter will look for his traits in the man to whom she will ultimately say, "I do." Mother may cook and scrub, nurse and nurture ("A mother's work is never done???) but Father is the one to whom the brood will race like so many homing pigeons when the day is done. Mother may patronize Elizabeth Arden and Oleg Cassini, but to the younger set, Father has the glamour. Incidentally, all the cosmetics in Christendom will never achieve for Mother the fresh, scrubbed look of dad as he emerges, clean-shaven, from his morning shower.

With the passing of the years, Father will become Grandfather, but that magic will merely go on. Grandmothers are grand to have around, but only until grandfathers arrive on the scene. Father's lot in life is not a particularly easy one. he's the family breadwinner in this cake- demanding era. His nine-to-five commitment sets the stern pattern of his life. His psychological know-how must embrace the judicious handling of a wife he will never quite understand; sons whose problems he has undoubtedly completely lost sight of from his distant youth; and daughters who are as complex as the combined characteristics of himself and the girl he married can have made of them. BUT THE COMPENSATIONS ARE MANY!

Father can be the pride of his wife; the companion of his sons' and the joy of his daughters' lives until another potential father - patterned pretty much after himself, so the psychologists tell us-comes along.

Yes, WE DON'T OFTEN STOP TO TELL HIM SO, BUT FATHER IS A VERY, VERY IMPORTANT GUY! We don't often stop to tell him so simply because mother is usually too busy for bouquet pinning; and the brood, in this age of regimentation and planned activity, has little time for such non-essential chatter. But we're all keenly aware of the sterling worth of the average American dad God bless him; and once a year, anyhow, we pause to tell him so!

Commercially motivated, you say, this Father's Day business??? Well, perhaps you're right. But the motivation isn't always the important angle of the things in life. It's the end result that counts; and the end result of Father's Day is a pat on the back for the wonderful American male. So-HATS OFF TO FATHER on his special day. Happy Father's Day, you Fathers!

11-26-72 "FOOTBALL SEASON"

Our own New England Patriots may be wearing lengthy faces this football season (to match those of their fans); not so their small Connecticut namesakes, the Mystic Patriots. The two Connecticut grandsons of the Metayers, Richard, Jr. and Franklin are leading lights among that group of Mystic Peewee Footballers named for our Massachusetts team. Rich plays for the Peewees and Frank for the Midgets; and Richard and his teammates have only just achieved the distinction of reaching a qualifying age for the Senior team; last year THEY were MIDGETS. This is Frank's first year as a Midget and making the team was no easy accomplishment for this handsome fun-loving boy who appears to love everything about life, especially EATING. Frank, you see, is inclined to be on the chubby side; and unfortunately (or fortunately, as the case may be) the weight limitation for Mystic's Peewee program is rigidly enforced…

The Metayers spent last Labor Day weekend with son Richard and his family, and at that point weigh-in for the Peewee football season lay dead ahead. Frank was a borderline case, weight-wise, and the entire family was alerted to the problem of his qualifying. "Frank," his father would say sternly as his young son reached for a sixth hot dog (a perfectly normal reach for Franklin, we might ad) at the family cook-out. "Remember Saturday!" (weigh-in day). "Hold it, Midget," elder brother Rich would yell loudly each time Franklin headed toward the family candy supply. "Mom," said Franklin finally, his huge brown eyes wide with a sudden consoling thought, "if I starve this week may I EAT EVERYTHING IN THE HOUSE after I get weighted in???" This is the first year young Franklin has shown any real interest in football and his parents are delighted. With his build and enthusiasm for anything he undertakes, Frank, they feel, should be a natural. Young Richard, on the other hand, has always loved the game and has proved to be quite an asset to his team. What fun it was for the Metayer grandparents to see them off to season and watch this eldest of all grandchildren perform on the football field and help bring his Mystic last Midgets to victory. "Those kids are GREAT!" Grandfather Metayer had announced proudly, and grandmother had proudly, and Grandmother had promptly agreed. "They play like college kids," he had added. Richard, Sr., himself a former college hockey player now eats, drinks and sleeps football. He is finishing his second year as President of the Peewee organization, and with Dolores, his charming wife, is neck-deep in this All-American pastime. The Mystic Patriots pattern themselves after our own New England Patriots all the way. They and their parents are often to be found in the bleachers at Foxboro; and insignia decidedly like that of the professional team was designed especially for their uniforms and equipment. Dick, Sr. is surrounded by the most dedicated and involved group of adult volunteers imaginable, a group that includes one or two college football stars of yesteryear who happen to live in the area; and the quality they try hardest to instill in their young athletes is sportsmanship.

But-to return to young Richard and the Peewees. A couple of weeks back an impassioned plea had come our way from Mystic, Conn. "Mom," a proud Mother had written, "Please pray like crazy for our Peewees! They're in first place; and if they win Sunday's game they'll have won the EASTERN DIVISION CHAMPIONSHIP and will play in the Super Bowl Game at the Coast Guard Academy on the 12th." I sometimes wonder what the good Lord thinks of some of the strange requests I find myself making of Him; but "pray like crazy" I did; and through the mail on the following Tuesday came a huge card bearing an exciting message. "MYSTIC NO. 1" it read. WE GO TO THE SUPER BOWL ON THE 12TH!" Congratulations went off to the Mystic Metayers by return mail. "We'll phone you at nine on the 12th," we said. "By that time if you've WON you should have finished celebrating; and if you've LOST and cut your collective throats, the blood should be starting to congeal."

Came nine p.m. on the evening of the 12th and an eager call to Connecticut. "Hello," said an alien voice that was barely audible above the greatest din human ears have recorded to date. "Did you WIN?" I wanted to know. "Wat a minute," said the cheery unknown, "I'll get Dick." "What in the world is happening there?" I asked when after a decidedly long pause son Richard picked up the phone. "Did you WIN? "No," said Richard almost indifferently, "But Mom, what a GAME those kids played! They were GREAT! And what good sports they were, etc., etc., etc. Wait a minute, the gang wants to say 'Hi'" at which point the loudest and merriest football cheers we have ever encountered smote our ears. They came from the cheerleading coaches and it sounded like they numbered at least a hundred. "Who in the world is there?" I asked finally.

"Oh," said Richard, "the coaches and the managers and the cheerleading coaches. We're CELEBRATING!" "Dolores," I said to our darling daughter-in-law who was next in line, "We figured that by now, win or lose, you'd be through celebrating. What in the world gives???" The Mother of the family laughed gaily. "Oh, EVERYTHING!" she said. "We'd a wonderful supper for the kids and their families and friends at the High School. There must have been 300 there. And now the gang is here and we're having a BALL!" "I'm sorry you LOST, dear," I said sympathetically. "Oh," said my second daughter, equally as airily as her mate, "It doesn't matter at all. What a GAME those kids played! And what good sports they were. Why, do you know that when it was over they could HARDLY WAIT to run across the field and congratulate the other team. They're just wonderful!" "How did our Richard play?" I asked. "Oh, beautifully, Mom." "And what was the score?" There was a slight pause and then "24 to 0," said Dolores merrily. "And gosh, Mom, WHAT A GAME IT WAS!" We keep wondering, Dad and I, what kind of celebration we'd have interrupted if Mystic Peewees had WON!

11-8-73   FOR DOG LOVERS ONLY-PLEASE"

Mamselle Tiffany of Alexander, nickname "Tiffy," the five and a half pound white toy poodle pet of the Corbin family received a package this past week. It came first class and was addressed to Miss Tiffy Corbin; and in the upper left hand corner was the sender's name - Miss Gigi Cogan. The package contained a very modish sweater in Tiffy's mother's favorite shade of blue; and it had come from Tiffy's own canine cousin, a black toy poodle, resident in Wakefield. With the sweater came a charming little note. It read: "Dear Tiffy, All cousins give each other their out-grown clothes so I am sending you this sweater which I hope you will like. It is too small for me now as I am putting on a little weight. Hope to see you soon, and we will have some fun. Your loving cousin, Gigi." The sweater had been especially made for Gigi by Bessie, a friend (very dear & not canine) of the Cogan family. Tiffy, every inch the lady, was prompt in sending her "thank you" note. It was actually a thank you CARD; and to Tiffany's way of thinking it left much to be desired. She had carefully instructed her Mother, you see, to find precisely the right kind of hallmark, one featuring two poodles, a black one and a white one. Tiffany had failed to clear the request with Hallmark, however, and so a compromise had to be reached - a compromise in the form of one small bunny rabbit and a pale gray mouse. The sentiments were satisfactory however. The card read, "Like you lots? Well, I should say! That's why I'm sending this today!" And Tiffy had added her own little personal touch to the missive. She wrote: "Dear Gigi: Everyone tells me I look like a doll in my new sweater. It is my mother's and my own favorite color. I am in total sympathy with your weight gain; I have the same problem I simply cannot tolerate that high-calorie, cereal-rich dog food and insist upon steak or lean beef, much to my Mother's disgust. I am not the athletic type and so must look well in my teeny weeny bikini (Have you, by any chance, outgrown one of these???) as I float about the family pool in my very own raft. Thank you! Thank you! Thank you! And do come soon to visit me. Love and laps, Tiffy"

Miss Corbin was cheered no end by the thought that suitable raiment had been procured for her before winter set in. It wasn't so bad between clippings, she reflected, but BRR…with the holiday season ahead and all the comings and goings and entertaining she'd be sure to be kept clipped to the veritable bone…and these mornings are getting increasingly colder… There is even the prospect of that horrid white stuff covering the ground…

Tiffany wasn't the only member of the family whose spirits had lifted at sight of the trim little package and the treasure it contained. Her grandmother, too, rejoiced. For weeks she had been trailing daughter Gael from pet shop to pet shop in search of just the right outer garment for her petite pet. "Why on earth do they have to make these sweaters in such homely colors?" Gael kept wailing "Red and green and that hideous garish blue! Can you possibly see our Tiffany in any of these things? She, who is so dainty and feminine…"

I had regarded one small white puppy who at one of those moments when Gael was posing the question had come bounding into the kitchen after a swim in the rain water that had collected on the cover of the family pool, a brisk roll in the family flower beds and a romp through the pile of leaves that awaited the arrival of the leaf picker. Dainty indeed! As a matter of fact one small set of whiskers was awash with leaf fragments; a wilted petunia clung to the waggingest tail in town and the ear that should have been snowy white in color still sported a fair-sized application of gray paint, received when Mamselle Tiffany had insisted upon reclining upon her mother's lap while daughter Gael touched up the trim on the new storage shed door. "Well," said Gael, following my gaze, "I mean USUALLY she is dainty and feminine. Today, of course, she's a dirty little beast and I shall have to give her another bath; and she should be CLIPPED again this week." "It's still a traumatic experience for her, being dropped off at the kennel to be bathed and clipped, Tiffy's ears drooped and her tail came to an abrupt halt. "Poor baby," said Gael sympathetically isn't it, Tiffy?" The dog's ears drooped even lower. "Well," said Gael, "shall we change the subject, Tiff? How about trying on the new sweater for Grandma? Aren't you glad you won't have to learn to knit after all, Mom?" she added laughingly. Grandmother laughed right along with her. She knew, however, that daughter Gael wasn't kidding when she had wailed dismally, "Why don't you KNIT like all the other grandmothers, Mom? You could make all sorts of sweaters in beautiful colors for your poor little cold grandchildren, and I wouldn't have to be planning a trip all the way to Boston to find something decent!" Well, thanks to cousin Gigi, and friend Bessie, and the U.S. Postal Service, and the failure of Canine Weight Watchers, Inc. to stem the tide of Gigi's weight gain, the problem of Tiffany Corbin's winter wonder wear has been solved. So - sink lower, you little old thermometer; and fall, you silly old white stuff - Mamselle Tiffany of Alexander and her doting Mama now couldn't care less!

1-20-74   "FOR MANY ARE COLD (BUT FEW ARE FROZEN)

Cheers for the chap who invented this year's LAYERED LOOK! He must have seen the energy crunch coming...The Metayers, these chill T.V. evenings, are wearing the layered look – IN SPADES!

It all began a few weeks back when "Our Leader" requested the conservation of the nation's energy supply by a general lowering of the family thermostat to 68 degrees. "We'll have to comply," Ted and I told one another. "It's the patriotic thing to do. Besides, think of the people with small babies, and the elderly people who are ill and won't be able to comply..." And so the family thermostats plummeted from the 78 degree heat we've been enjoying - day and night for six months of every year from time immemorial - to a noble 68. Now there are some who find 68 degrees heat comfortable; or even 65 or 60. Not the Metayers! We're the cold type; and so this new patriotic fervor was going to hit us hard!

It wasn't too difficult to bear at first. We were having a holiday heat wave, so to speak; and a nice warm sun kept obliging us by streaming through the windows DAILY; and then there are always the various housekeeping duties that can manage to keep one's blood circulating - BY DAY...The EVENINGS, however were a different dish. Sitting before the T.V. or immobilized with a good book one could feel the chill fingers of evening clutching at a house that for yars and yars had been kept so warm as to make house guests gasp for breath and shed outer garments like leaves...

So on went the family sweaters and the family long johns; and as winter began to tighten her icy grip on this little old corner of the world, the socks and the scarves, the robes and the under sweaters, the this, that and the other thing hither and yon ad infinitum. "You wouldn't look for a real WARM robe for me, would you, hon?" asked Ted one evening with a meaningful glance at the one he was wearing, a very sharp but not very warm gift from daughter Gael and her Jim. "Of course," I answered readily. I knew just what he meant. My own collection of robes - left over from last summer's hospital stay - was handsome but terribly inadequate. The search in the local emporiums for something really warm and heavy proved fruitless, however. We are just NOT geared to Arctic weather hereabouts…as yet…And so I ended by purchasing a length of the heaviest wool I could find, a length of French flannel for lining, and fashioning for my darling a robe that requires two men and a boy to lift…ankle length, incidentally, to keep his legs warm…with a matching scarf to tuck about the back of his neck. I even tried my hand at fashioning a nightcap to complete the ensemble; and I was not happy when gales of laughter and not humble appreciation on the part of my spouse greeted my presentation of the nice tasseled tidbit. The matter of MY inadequate robes came next under scrutiny as the outside temperatures dropped lower and lower and the family shivers took on new dimensions with each succeeding night. And then I remembered the nice heavy quilted padded stuffed and layered first-cousin-to-thermal robe I had purchased a few years back when we were planning a trailer trip that was to include a stay at the Columbia Ice Fields. It was still in "Fanny," the family travel trailer. I had taken it to a Mass. State Federation of Women's Clubs Convention at a Cape Cod seaside resort one spring a few years back, after a previous Convention stay had seen our gals assigned to a heatless ocean front room, with rain pelting and winds howling and the seaside temperatures doing nose dives. The robe matches our trailer slumber bags, which means that it is wildly patterned in red, yellow and blue. "That robe doesn't LOOK like you," my fellow Conventioner and friend Betty had said as I donned it lovingly before dressing for dinner. "I know," I had replied happily, "but when the frost is on the punkin it sure FEELS like me!" P.S. That particular year our room was stifling…P.P.S. I shudder when I look down, but it helps!

Well, anyhoo, we began, we and others, to receive almost daily - via the family T.V. - little hints on the prevention of frostbite to viewers… hints like wearing a hat (I affect a wig!) and placing one's cold feet in a cardboard box. We've tried them all. As a matter of fact we now have His and Her Campbell Soup cartons. I'm thinking of covering them with Contact so they'll blend with the living room décor…and setting aside a few, similarly adorned, for friends who drop in. Oh! well, as I tell myself and Ted as we sit anything BUT comfortably despite a layered look that would promptly stamp the two of us as PRIME candidates for Diet Workshop, January is a half over; and February is a short month; and in March the FLOWERS come up! So you see, already Spring can be said to be really just around the corner…Canada, meanwhile, however had better stop sending down those COLD FRONTS or I'LL wind up wearing that tasseled cap. I may even throw away my PREMARIN! A few nice warm you-know-whats now and then could prove to be a boon.…P.S. Does anyone have a pattern for a nose warmer?

7-21-69   "GARDENING"

How charming and chic are the amateur gardeners pictured so beautifully in "House and Garden" and the rest!

LARGE FLOPPY hats shade their serene brows from the sun; backless (and spotless) sun-dresses drape their gracefully kneeling figures; or perhaps it is the very newest thing in gardening attire they have affected, impeccably tailored coveralls, complete with smooth swish pockets into which to tuck the diminutive cutting shears they tote…the decorate trowel.…

HOW I ENVY EVERY SINGLE ANTISEPTIC ONE OF THEM!

I, personally, belong to that sad breed of amateur gardeners who manage to look an unmitigated MESS in the great outdoors!

Item number one- Those GLOVES they affect, complete with stenciled cuffs (gardening symbols, of course) are DARLING; and I'd LOVE to wear out forty or fifty pairs each season; only I HAVE to grub about the garden with my bare hands!

There is undoubtedly a reason for this; childhood frustration, probably. My dear mother, who felt that the cultivation of flowers should lie completely within the domain of the local florist, stoutly maintained to the end of her days that no LADY would permit her hands to be roughened, or her face to be exposed to the direct rays of the wrinkling sun, merely for the sake of indulging in the "rather vulgar" sport of gardening; or for any other reason for that matter...

Mother, with her peaches and cream English complexion, felt very strongly about the adverse effects of wind and weather. As a matter of fact, we were probably the only children at our summer resort to affect bathing suits with sleeves, and bathing caps with ruffles...

On occasion, I can see Mother's Point-Nature IS a savage! My particular pride is a rose garden that sports 49 floribundas in a neat double row-all giant-sized -AND DO THOSE SWEET-SMELLING LOVELIES HAVE THORNS!!!

Thanks to them and their roving branches, I pass the summer looking as though my daily gardening adversaries were large leopards instead of small Japanese beetles. I am perhaps the only females in captivity who spends the growing season in sports clothes and long white gloves - and if you only knew the multiplicity of wounds that lie beneath them!

GARDENING is, however, my very favorite pastime. There's a special sweet serenity to be found close to the moist brown earth. I have made my share of "boo boos" in this area, heedless to say. For instance, we purchased our home in April, and I waited impatiently for May, the entire month of which I spent weeding the vast flower beds; waiting to pounce on each alien growth the moment it reared its small green head. "I shall simply have to put a NEW LAWN in THIS area," I told myself firmly of one particular spot, "This place is absolutely full of weeds." I hied me off to the local market where I purchased Scott's best, which I promptly sowed and hosed... "Tell me," said my neighbor down the street, as June's arrival brought the world to bloom. "What do you think of your perennial garden? Isn't it absolutely fantastic??? So many varieties..."

I regarded her blankly. "My PERENNIAL garden??" I repeated. "You mean my ROSE GARDEN!" She didn't; she meant my perennial garden, every single "fantastic" occupant of which I had painfully uprooted and replaced with grass! Ah me, I do have a tendency to go overboard, anyhow, when I garden. I've moved my specimens about the place so many times that I have bewildered even myself...The peonies and iris duck for cover when they see me coming! Oh well, September is a particularly wonderful month for gardening; and this a particularly lovely day...just the right kind for mounding those rascally roses; and pruning the evergreens slightly about the edges; and stretching out in the midst of things on the family lawn chair...So I'll garden! Now, where DIDI put that darling white gardening hat I picked up at a bargain price last week??? And the apron with the cute ruffled pockets for those tiny, jeweled pruning shears I got for Christmas; and those loafers I retrieved from the family wastebasket seven year ago and am still wearing cause they're so COMFORTABLE; and that sweater with the sagging hemline; and those dear old jeans with the knees out??? It's off to the garden for your columnist! Ho Hum...Wonder if it's too early for the well-dressed amateur gardener to cut back the peonies, and pot the blooming begonias, and coax some of the geraniums indoors...

6-23-68   "GOODBYE, JOHN!"

"You will find him rather a formidable character," one of our leading citizens had said of John C. Donahue, Jr., editor and publisher of our town's brand new newspaper, The Braintree Sunday News...

It was the summer of 1963, and we had said we were on our way to visit him for the first time—as a prerequisite to establishing a brand new League of Women Voters in our town.

Visit, and, hopefully, establish rapport with the town officials, news media, etc." the State League manual had instructed us; and, as founding president of Braintree's Provisional League, we were about to do just that!

The journalistic background of the editor in question, we told the L.W.V. state officer who accompanied us, read like an entry in "Who's Who"... "What in the world brought him to BRAINTREE?" the Lincoln-ite had asked, quite as though Braintree were the unfinished end of a one-way-street. "Well," we had said, "There are rumors that he is gathering material for a BOOK! He'll find it in Braintree," we had added, laughing.

WE were to learn afterwards…when we had come to KNOW the "formidable character"; to see the sterling worth of this great and good man who was to light our town like a blazing torch for too brief a span of years…that he, also, had HAD A DREAM…the dream of establishing a first-rate weekly newspaper in a typical New England town!

He had, after very careful consideration, selected Braintree as a decidedly typical town. He wanted to light that one small candle, the one which we all dream of setting aglow!

Good government, he believed, can and must start at the grass roots level if democracy is ever to succeed; and the citizens of a town have a right to know and to decide on issues and policy makers…

But-to return to the bright summer morning on which we went to meet the gentleman in question. Accompanied by the hovering State League officer, we entered the decidedly unprepossessing office of the "Sunday News." "Mr. Donahue?" we asked, a mite timidly.

All eight feet, or so it seemed, or a rather merry male rose from behind a cluttered desk to greet us. "Yes," he said; and a slow smile began to form in the bright blue eyes with the crinkles all about them that peered through horn-rimmed glasses into our own.

It spread-that rather wonderful smile-to form long laugh-lined roadways in the broad intelligent forehead; it turned up the corners of a ridiculous small moustache, and then swept over the nicest friendliest masculine mouth we'd encountered in years…

It was obvious to the State League gal, and to this founding president as well, that the editor of the "News" was tickled to death to learn of the advent of Braintree's League of Women Voters. And why not??? we were all seeking the same goal - AN INFORMED CITIZENSHIP, THINKING ACTING AND VOTING INTELLIGENTLY…

That was the beginning - to quote the old cliché - of a beautiful friendship! For to know this man was decidedly, we learned, to like him all the way; to respond to his dedication, his integrity, his total disregard for the material; his magnificent journalistic style and terrific talent; the strange compelling force which inspired the kind of loyalty in those about him that is occasionally linked with leadership of a unique and moving brand…

That was also the beginning of CABBAGES AND KINGS, the "fun" column which it has been delighting me to produce ever since!

We'll MISS John Donahue; we'll miss his "Chris", the wondrous wife whose innate goodness matches well his own. We'll miss them all, those Donahues!

We think the "formidable character" about which we write took that small sweet weekly paper of his, and carried it to the stars! It wasn't an easy thing to do. It called for courage and for faith; for taking stands and sticking fast; for making enemies as well as friends; for even making enemies of friends…But he sure made the town we live in COME ALIVE. And he sure had the COURAGE OF HIS CONVICTIONS…and HE HAD CONVICTIONS!!! Ah, yes, we shall indeed miss good Sir John, the shining knight who sought to make a "Camelot" of Braintree! We'll think of him when elevated trains roar past; and smokestacks rise; and open meetings close their doors…The town, we feel, won't be the same without our "Keeper of the Flame!" But, nonetheless, HOW WE REJOICE THAT BRAINTREE WAS A DREAMER'S CHOICE…THE BRAINTREE STAR DECEMBER 11, 1969 GRACIOUS LADIES,

BY VIVIAN WOODLOCK

Turning her calendar to the month of December is all that Mrs. Edward Metayer needs to ignite the holiday spirit and give her an excuse to start decorating, so that she will be the first on Braintree Point to announce that 'tis the season to be jolly." Since she has been doing it for twenty-five years, it has become a tradition at "the Point" and everyone awaits her signal.

Already the Metayer home has taken on a holiday air. In every room there is a Christmas tree, variously sized from the glittering miniature picked up in London to one ceiling-high in the solarium; another, personally fashioned of pinecones in infinite variety; a memory tree with trinkets commemorating every happy occasion in a busy life; and a tree, specially trimmed for the enjoyment of five grandsons. Even now, three weeks before Christmas, the tree lights are rehearsing their blinking, and mistletoe hangs to trap the unwary. "Bibs" Metayer has never outgrown Christmas. Her enthusiasm is contagious. Ted, her husband, now retired, has become infected by this virus of happiness and lends a hand when required.

To attempt a biography of Elizabeth Metayer would require more than this space permits, but even in a brief interview one is aware that she is a person whose desires have been completely fulfilled. Ted, as well as Bibs, speak proudly of the achievement of their son, Edward, Jr., M.I.T. graduate, who is Chief Hull and Structural designer in the atomic submarine program of General Dynamics Corp. in Mystic, Conn. He married a Braintree girl, Dolores Crehan, and they have two son's Richard, 10 and Franklin,7. Gael Metayer, Mrs. James M. Corbin, Jr., of Braintree is the mother of three sons' James III, Byrne and Gregory, daily visitors to the Metayer household and the pride and joy of their grandparents, who compete for the job of baby-sitting. Gregory, 3 has inherited his grandmother's enthusiasm for Christmas decorations, rather than the small fry's usual reaction to new toys.

Always interested in art, Elizabeth Metayer is now pursuing it seriously with a teacher. Four of her canvases will be completed for Xmas gifts commissioned by her family. She delights in painting rocks being washed by raging seas (a nemesis to most painters).

The Metayer's celebrated Ted's retirement by spending six months in Europe. They "free-lanced" their tour so as not to be tied to the usual tour schedules. Only climate was their guide as they moved about in twenty-three countries, acquiring in each a silver trinket to compose an international charm bracelet. As a professional book reviewer, "Bibs" covers a wide range of subjects. Her favorite are historical novels. She is charmed by the stories of Victoria Holt and Thomas Costain, amused by Stephen Birmingham's writings; disgusted by modern smut. Recently she assisted in the promotion and publication of a textbook for third-graders sponsored by the Philergians and titled "Braintree-Our Town". Now ready for use in the Town's schools, an off-the-press celebration will be held in the Town Hall, January 5. Aside from personal pursuits, Elizabeth Metayer concerns herself on all topics of civic interest, and her vigorous campaign as effective in preventing the MBTA from bringing their equipment to roost in Braintree.

She was a Town Meeting member for 15 years, the founding President of the Braintree League of Women Voters; and a candidate for the Legislature on the Democratic ticket. Her club affiliations include: President of the Braintree Point Women's Club, President of the Second District Past President's Club of the Mass. Federation of Women's Clubs, Vice Chairman of the Division of International Affairs for the Mass Federation, and Vice Chairman of the Past Chairman's Club, also of the Mass. Federation. Her present concern as Veteran's Chairman of the Philergians is preparing the Christmas gift packages for the hospitalized women veterans at Brockton Veteran's Hospital.

Her newspaper column, "Cabbages and Kings", is widely read. Green, the color of her eyes, is "Bibs" favorite color; Chanel No. 5 and Coty's L'Aimant vie as her favorite scents; Loretta Young and Kirk Douglas are her preferred performers.

Thousands of Floribunda roses surround the Metayer garden and she gives them most of her personal time when the club season quiets down. Will they be playing second fiddle when the shiny new trailer, now parked in the rose garden, tempts its owners to hit the trail come Spring, and lure them to distant green pastures for a new chapter in the rich life in which all of their dreams have come true? Happy voyaging!

6-14-70   GRADUATION TIME

Friday, the 19th of June, and a red letter day in the lives of the fifty or so small tots who are enrolled in the Watson Park Library Pre-School Story Hour; for you see it is their Graduation Day. Some of them will receive certificates indicating the completion of a year of pre-school endeavor; while others will be presented with an honest-to-goodness real live diploma.

The latter, for whom the day will be highlighted by the wearing of mortar boards, caps, and a Graduation ceremony "par excellence," with a member of the Board of Library Trustees, no less handing out the "parchments," will go on to kindergarten.

The Story Hour children adjust much more readily, we have been told, to this first step up the ladder of education, than do those who have not had the experience of having been part of this "fun" class.

Last year's alumnae (and an alumnus or two now and then, though boys do not seem to attach themselves quite so strongly to the "teachers" as do our little girls,) visit those volunteer ladies regularly, to report their educational prowess, to exhibit outstanding schoolwork, and generally to exchange the news of the day.

Janice is an alumna from last year's class. She is also a doll. "Well." We "teachers" asked her eagerly after a week or so at the local kindergarten. "How are you doing, dear?" "Oh, fine," she said with enthusiasm. "I got to be the BEST RESTER yesterday. "Oh, how nice!" we replied politely, "And what," we asked a trifle hesitantly "does the BEST RESTER do?" "She puts her head on the desk and rests the best," said Janice happily.

"Do you like kindergarten?" she was asked. "Oh, yes," she fairly beamed. "The teacher, you know, puts your name on the board and you get to turn on the lights." Aren't they delightful, these little ones?"

Janice is especially delightful, She was recently out riding with her parents, her older brother, James, and his friend, Paul and to pass the time the children engaged in a kind of word game as they drove along. One observed an object and described it vaguely while the others attempted to identify it. It was Janice's turn at bat, and the boys were having difficulty. "I'll give you a clue," she said magnanimously.

"GREE…GREE…" "What" asked her brother's friend a shade disgustedly "is GREE?" "You know," said Janice merrily, "GREE, like in GRIEFCASE!" Well, what is a GREIFCASE?" he asked "Gosh," said the young lady equally disgustedly, "Everybody knows that, Paul. It's a little suitcase But to return to this years' Pre-School Story Hour graduation class, they have been visited by Safety Officer Bill, and warned of the perils that face our small fry during the summer months. They have been taught the importance of a library in the lives of children; and the value of books; of reading…

Their lives have been enriched by the experience of participating in this labor of love for those ladies who staff the Story Hour; ladies whose own lives have been equally enriched by this exciting "fun" task.

This is Graduation Time, this beautiful month of June. Congratulations, little Story Hour graduates!

We'll be missing you next year!

GRADUATION TIME Fifty-nine small preschoolers "graduated" from the Watson Park Branch Library Story Hour program on Friday morning. No mortarboards went skyward in celebration of the event; the mortarboards were there, however, sitting primly on small neat heads; or hanging rakishly over one bright eye; or- every now and then - sliding to the back of an energetic head or two, to be hastily pushed back into place, to the detriment of bangs and side parts and the whole bit.

Some among the group were finishing a year in Story Hour and will be back next year; at least we "teachers" hope so…to be petted; taught their letters and numbers; read to; exercised and played with and indulged for a "fun" hour by a group of volunteers, each of whom is a grandmother, with all of the grandmother's tolerance, understanding and abundant love…

For others, of course, it represented the close of a small sweet chapter in their lives as they journey off to the kindergarten that will serve as a bridge to the educational world beyond.

It was a very special occasion for them all…exciting…challenging because Mothers, Dads, Grandparents and small brothers and sisters had been invited to attend and were there in force… "fun" because a party was to follow the graduation exercises, and to small boys and girls a party is ALWAYS fun!

The diplomas-darling affairs that had been designed by Miss Constance Binns, a former librarian with a rare understanding of little ones - were to be presented to the first class by Mrs. John J. Canavan, a lady particularly beloved in Braintree and one of the town's Library Trustees; and to the second class by Branch Librarian Mrs. Sarah Nightingale, one of East Braintree's very favorite people, a brilliant Librarian who manages to be untiring in her efforts to meet everyone's literary demands.

We had planned the day carefully with a view to providing a happy occasion for everyone. Our volunteer teaching staff was on hand, as well as an additional group of ladies from the Braintree Point Woman's Club, sponsoring organization of the weekly pre-school Story Hour which represents a facet of its continuing general Federation of Women's Clubs - Sears, Roebuck & Company Community Improvement Project Contest.

The refreshment table was resplendent in daffodil yellow and white; and the lovely floral arrangement that graced it -flanked by tall candles and tiny graduation figures - had come straight from your columnist's garden. Its tea roses and snapdragons and iris and the rest seemed to whisper, "Summer has come; New England summer is here…"

Some of our Story Hour graduates wore anything BUT happy faces. "I'm going to miss you," they managed to say despite the general air of excitement that prevailed. To these dear little sentiments and to the hugs and kisses we were receiving we found ourselves responding with a tear or two. It's a rewarding experience, this directing of the weekly Story Hour at the Watson Park Library...Tears were apparently not confined to the teaching side of things. Small Heather Flynn, one of our littlest angels whom we hope to have again next year, had shed a few the previous night, so Mother and Dad had confided as they delivered their pride and joy into our waiting hands. "She didn't WANT to graduate," they said, "She wanted to KEEP COMING to Story Hour..."

With our dear Doris Canavan at the piano and "Pomp and Circumstance" in the air, the graduation festivities were to begin, with the small fry-their trim white mortarboards, at least at this stage, securely in place - marching solemnly in to take their places on the tiny chairs that awaited them. They seemed totally oblivious to the flash bulbs that went off about them; and suddenly serious about the entire affair. IT WAS obviously serious business to them...

The graduation exercises were to go off without a hitch. Small hands were to be placed solemnly over beautiful young hearts in a Salute to the Flag of the United States of America; ears were to ring with a wildly enthusiastic rendition of the "Library Laughing Song" and that perennial favorite, "Officer Bill's Safety Song", and then-THE HANDING OF A DIPLOMA TO EACH SMALL CHILD Wish all of the Mothers and Dads assembled might have had the privilege of viewing the combined innocence and beauty of the close to sixty little ones we graduated that momentous morning; wonder if they were completely aware, as well, of the extent of the love and pride that shone in their rapt attentive faces as each small sweet Sue or Tiny Tom came forward, all on cue...

We had scheduled a minimum of speeches. Mrs. Canavan was to congratulate the little ones; and Mrs. Nightingale was to invite them to "hurry and learn to write your names so that you may secure your VERY OWN library card and takeout books all by yourselves..." And representing all of the volunteer teachers to whom these little ones have endeared themselves over the many months, your columnist was to bid them a fond farewell, concluding a labor of love that each year adds a measure of enrichment to the lives of each and every one of us...And, oh yes, we were all to be presented with the most timely and thoughtful of gifts by our story hour mothers - lovely gold pins that featured one of our most inspiring and favorite friends - Jonathon Livingston Seagull! We, too, had had our moment of SOARING!

2-14-71   GRANDCHILD

It could be mere coincidence that Gregory Scott Corbin, the youngest of the Metayer grandchildren, bears a strong resemblance to the Christmas Angel illustrations in his favorite story book; on the other hand, HOW APT! For if ever there was a "Christmas" angel, it is our Greg...

The entire Metayer family, manages to FLIP over Christmas; it's traditional with us. Its tiniest member however is easily the most rabid one of all when it comes to the observance of that blessed and beautiful time of year...in December...or January, or even like now - in the middle of February. The wonderful Christmas season just seems to go on and on and on for this our littlest lad. Which is the reason why - if you should have occasion to phone the Metayer ménage these days and find yourself and your telephone partner involved in the mad effort to conduct a conversation against the jangling background music of "Jingle Bells" - played at No. 12 strength on the sound track, or "Rudolph, the Red Nosed", or even the loudest "Away in a Manger" that could possibly have been envisioned by good old Kate Smith as she cut the recording, know forthwith that young Gregory Scot Corbin is visiting Grandma.

"I'm here!" he announces merrily as he hurls open the front door and dashes from his mother's protective grasp. "All right now, Grandpa," he adds even as he is divesting himself of hat and jacket and boots and parking his inevitable shopping bag of small dog-eared and dog-chewed treasures, "Let's put Jingle Bells' on the Stereo - the FIRST Jingle Bells record! (We happen to have one or two other Christmas albums in which "Jingle Bells occurs further along the line, however, Greg can't wait for them...) Now Mother, Grandmother and Grandfather can be assured of a full hour of coffee and conversation while the family's beside the

Stereo, his huge brown eyes wide and wondering as he absorbs - quite as intently the very first time - the melodic strains of "Silent Night", so long as the Music spells Christmas…or "White Christmas" or "I Saw Mommy Kissing Santa", or indeed anything else that happens to come up on the holiday recording. The tune-after his favorite "Jingle Bells" - doesn't seem to matter a bit, just Gregory, who will be four this month, doesn't stop there, however. "Now, Grandma," he can be relied upon to say after he (and everyone else) has had his fill of Christmas caroling. "Let's go up to the attic and visit the Christmas trees! Oh, there is the BATHROOM TREE! (breathlessly) Isn't it pretty? Now show me the dining room tree…and the pine cone tree…and YOUR bedroom tree… and the tree you brought from London…and the T.V. room tree…." And each one in turn (the dismantled artificial ones in their cardboard nests) receives a loving and tender pat from the chubby (and frequently grubby) little paws of our Christmas-addicted small grandson. "It's going to be Christmas again soon, isn't it, Grandma?" he can be depended upon to ask wistfully, "After summer comes, I mean," he hastens to add, "and we go to the Cape in your trailer…" (including the which believe it or not, still stands fully decorated in the children's corner of that happy place simply because I haven't yet had the heart to really put an end to Christmas for this our little Christmas angel. "Now," he is sure to say next, "Let's go to the playroom and see OUR Christmas tree!" , This kind of thing happens every year incidentally. It was April of 1970 before the small tree in the Metayer kitchen went the way of all holiday trappings; only the way IT went was across town to a place of honor on the top shelf in Gregory Scott Corbin's boudoir…And by the way it may have looked a bit dog-eared and decrepit to others by the time July and August rolled around, but not to Gregory! He was still "oh"-ing and "ah"-ing over it, and drifting off to dreamland with it clutched in his small chubby hands night after night….There's no doubt about it- THIS LITTLE LAD LIKES CHRISTMAS!

He also likes "Sneakers", the family cat and "Misty", the Corbin dog, a Dandie Dinmont terrier which, despite its mile long pedigree and the breed's reputed distaste for small boys, returns his affection in spades. "God bless Mommy and Daddy," Greg can be depended upon to say first in his nightly prayers, but he can also be relied upon to add hastily, "and Kitty and Misty." "Whom do you love best in all the world?" is a favorite question of ours to this little one who is the light of our lives He hesitates not a moment before answering. "Kitty and Misty", he says matter-of-factly.

Greg has another love. The hundreds of slides that have been taken by his adoring grandparents on their many travels delight him to no end. "Let's see the movies," he will say. "Show me Hitler's EAGLES NEST!" or "I want to see Yellowstone Park and the Grand Tetons and you and Grandpa and the car and the trailer…" The projector and its operator may tire of trotting out tray after tray of slides, but never Gregory; he's the world's most prefect audience…

The care and training of their little brother has always been of grave importance to Jim and Byrne, the older Corbin boys - especially to Byrne whose avowed intention of becoming a Pediatrician shows all along the line. "Leave him to me," said Byrne recently when small Gregory had answered his Mother a mite boldly. "I'll take care of him. Shame on you, Gregory," he said sternly, "for speaking to Mommy like that. You don't hear your big brothers answering Mommy back, do you? You're just a BABY, that's what you are!"

Gregory, who is certain he can perform in a bigger and better way than his brothers in any area of action, reacted fiercely to this outrageous charge. "I am NOT a baby. I'm a big kid!" he said angrily, "I go to LIBRARY SCHOOL! "You wouldn't be allowed to go to Library School if they heard you answer Mommy back," said Byrne sternly. "Big boys don't ever speak like that to their good Mothers and Fathers.." We would love to be able to report that from that day forward Gregory Scott Corbin behaved angelically, however, he is, after all, a very normal (though decidedly remarkable) little boy…

Gregory is also certain, we might add at this point, that grandparents were invented solely for his entertainment. "Now what shall WE do?" he may be relied upon to ask as one by one of the various forms of grandparently entertainment are exhausted. "Shall we read SIX books?" (We read SIX books.) "Let's play cards; let's play WAR!" (Have you ever played WAR…Some people call the game EVERLASTING, and it is…) "Now I'm hungry. Grandma; shall we have some punch and a Ring Ding? And a banana? And an apple - and will you please take the skin off and cut it up into nice little pieces? And an orange - and let Grandpa fix it cause he fixes it nicely the way I like it…And a sandwich - and will you please cut the crusts off? Mommy doesn't cut the crusts off my sandwich; she says they'll give me curly hair but I don't WANT curly hair.…I wasn't the crusts cut off…Now LET'S PLAY JINGLE BELLS ON THE STEREO again…the FIRST Jingle Bells record!" And thus is goes…and don't we love it, Grandpa and I…Gregory Scott Corbin will celebrate his fourth birthday on the 20th of this month. Three…going on four…is such a wonderful age for a small boy. What shall Grandpa and I ever do when Gregory Scot Corbin, our littlest angel, is little no more???

6-16-68   GRANDCHILDREN

A LOT of wonderful people have been kind enough to say they enjoy the "Cabbages" which concern my grandchildren - which statement delights me no end and reminds me of a favorite quote of my own dear grandmother, gone these many years. "There's but one PERFECT child," she would say, "and every grandmother has it!"

We have been baby-sitting our three "perfect children" during the present illness of our daughter and we could easily produce a "Cabbage" a day on the unbelievable antics of these delightful small boys.

Their mother and I, for instance, departed for the local barber shop recently with the two oldest in tow. Despite the newer and longer hair styles, daughter Gael has remained faithful to the rapidly disappearing "Crew cut."

"It's neater and nicer" she has stated resolutely, adding, "I'll keep it short until they are old enough to protest." James, our seven-year old, is apparently "old enough"!

The barber shop was, as always, crowded and we awaited our turn at bat. Young James settled himself and proceeded in his inimitable manner to watch the hair cutting operation as intently as though he were an immediate candidate for barber college.

As the barber's small-boy victim descended from the chair, tossing back a free-flowing mane from his young eyes, James sighed. "Mom, he said sweetly, shaking his head and wrinkling a small nose," I wish I didn't have to have my hair cut…you know, all standing up in front like "Milton Munster.""

The big brown eyes were deadly serious. "I'd really rather have it like Herman Munster. No-I think I'd like it like Eddie Munster best!"

JAMES, whose thirst for knowledge and depth of thought constantly amazes us, provides the bulk of my Cabbage material today.

"Grandma," he said earnestly the other day, "You are 49 years older than I am, aren't you?"

I agreed that I was. "That means," he said, "That you will DIE 49 years before me, doesn't it?" I thought I might do just that. "Well, Gram," he said, "If your body gets buried in the cemetery and only our soul goes to Heaven…the EYES are going to stay here in the grave, aren't they?" "Yes," I said, wondering what might come next. There was long silence.

"Well, Gram," he said soberly, "if YOUR EYES get left down here in the grave…HOW WILL YOU KNOW ME when I get to heaven 49 years after you?"

I kissed the dear small wrinkled forehead of an adored little boy. "Jim Jim darling," I said, "I'll know you! I'll be up there waiting to hug you the moment you arrive, 'cause I'll have missed you so!"

Two big dark eyes looked fervently into mine. "You PROMISE, Gram?" he asked.

Yes I could indeed write a Cabbage per day about James alone. Baby brother Gregory is needless to say, the pet of the two older boys. Their pride in him and his development knows no bounds. They cheerfully part with their toys and possessions for the adorable little tyrant who accepts all the adulation in the world as his birthright.

The other day, however, one of the "slaves" betrayed an unexpected impatience with his miniscule master. We heard harsh words issuing from baby's room and tiptoed to the door. James had placed his small brother's back against the side of the dresser and was ordering him forward.

"WALK, Gregory!" he was saying sharply. "For goodness sake, little Robbie down the street is SIX WEEKS YOUNGER than you and HE walks. How do you think I feel when his brother asks me about you? Do you want everybody to call you a DUMB baby? Come on, Greg-walk for Jimmy or he won't speak to you!"

Yes indeed-a Cabbage a day could be produced on Grand children!

More About Grandchildren

"WHAT about ME, Grandma? Don't I say anything funny for your 'Cabbage'? You wrote one about Jimmy, but you didn't write anything about ME…" A tear or two seemed about to gather in the big China-blue eyes - so like his mother's- of Byrne Laurence Corbin, one year and two days his brother's junior.

"You say and do the funniest things imaginable, we told him, giving the second of our Braintree grandchildren a sound hug, "and we are planning to write our Cabbage ALL ABOUT YOU this week!" The which we now proceed to do…

Actually, it's an easy task! Byrne furnishes us with an incident per day. He's as different from brother James, incidentally, as chalk is from cheese. "BYRNE LAURENCE???" his totally masculine father had repeated, with disdainfully wrinkled nose, when Gael, our daughter, had announced her choice of names for the new boy baby.

"With a 'U' - not a 'W'," she had added. "He'll have to be a holy terror to get through life with THAT name," his father had declared. Byrne's a bit of a holy terror, but everyone's darling nonetheless…his mother's angelic face, but with a latent imp in each blue eye, waiting always to emerge…And do they ever????

TUESDAY, was a typical day. Byrne had arrived from kindergarten, complete with daily quota of papers "with everything CORRECT, Gram; can I go out to play?" all in one breath….

It had rained the night before, and the area surrounding Gael's lovely new home was - as always - a quagmire, "Well," I had said, "If you wear your BOOTS; and try not to get your feet wet. With mommy sick, you know…" "Oh, I WON'T, Gram," he had promised.

We looked through the window to see Byrne Laurence go "clomping" down the driveway a few minutes later, wearing on his incredibly tiny feet, his brother's huge boots… "Byrne," we called, "those are JIM's boots!"

"I know, grandma," he said, "but I can't find mine!" By the time we had located the missing boots in the utility room, Byrne L. had clomped right out of sight! "Oh, well," we said, "by the time Jim returns from school, it may have dried out some…" (Dreamers!)

Byrne's ulterior motive in the donning of this brother's larger and considerably higher boots soon came to light. "Grandma," called an excited young voice from the sundeck, "Come out and see what I have! SEVENTEEN FROGS! Please bring a paper bag QUICK, Gram!"

We opened the kitchen door, to have the largest, slimiest frog we had ever encountered, LAND RIGHT ON OUR HEAD! We screamed! "He won't hurt you," Byrne hastened to assure us. "That's FREDDIE! No-I think it's FRANK!"

The frog and Grandma leaped simultaneously, to land head long into chaos! For in the midst of a group of squealing boys was Byrne, his face one big grin. He clutched a dripping pail of water, from which the most enormous frogs in Braintree were leaping in all directions. They sailed through the air like giant June bugs…They plopped on fans and furnishing alike. In the middle of the muddle was Colleen, the family dog, madly pursuing all 17 of them at once.

It took the combined efforts of all of us to get the 17 denizens of the depths of the nearby brook tucked neatly into the big brown paper bag - from which, for every frog we succeeded in depositing within its soggy confines, we released six more for subsequent recapture…Oh, yes - the reason for brother Jim's high boots was apparent - Byrne had GONE FROGGING! His favorite sport…

Boots and boy were dried out, James arrived from first grade and the dinner hour approached -SO DID THE NEXT OF SMALL BYRNE'S CRISES! "Grandma," said Jim, appearing suddenly, frantically, at the backdoor. "Come quick! Byrne is up a TREE, and he CAN'T GET DOWN!"

"Ted," I screamed to Grandpa, who was peacefully reading his paper. "Get a ladder quick! Byrne is up a tree!" "Most of the time," I thought I heard him say as he calmly put down the evening news and ambled to the door - by which time, I was, of course, half-way across the backyard!

A small waving hand and a big, though distant grin, led my horrified eyes to the top of the highest tree on the place. "Hi, Gram," said a little voice "Know what??? I climbed all the way up here by myself…but I CAN'T climb down!"

Grandpa arrived finally SANS ladder, but WITH advice… "Turn around and bring your arm over the limb of the tree trunk; now let go of the limb; etc. etc. Now shinny down!" "Next time he'll know how to get down by himself," said philosophical Grandpa, returning to his paper.

WE WERE having dinner when the next episode of "Byrne's Day" came to light. "Grandma," do you know what?" he said happily, "I got HIT right on my head; HARD, with a great big piece of wood when I was up in the tree house today. A BOY threw it right at me. (NO NAME-Byrne's been taught not to carry tales.) I even CRIED!"

"Darling, I'm sorry," I said, "Why didn't you come in and let Grandma kiss it better?" Byrne plopped a huge piece of pot roast into a small sweet mouth, "Gram," he said, "MARINES don't get kissed better. When I grow up, I'm gonna be a MARINE, so I gotta practice being brave…

"Grandma," he added sweetly, the big blue eyes suddenly a gleam, "When I get to be a Marine-huh - THEN I can march in the 4th of July Parade, can't I?" I nodded agreement. He grinned happily.

"Gram," he said, "Will you come and see me march???" "You bet I will," I said, hugging him hard, "You just bet I will, Byrne Laurence…" A Cabbage a day on this young man also…

7-19-70   GRANDSON

He doesn't wear a halo; he's not equipped with wings;
But you can bet his grandma sees him sporting both those things;
To others he's perhaps a most completely normal lad
With the usual combination of the good and of the bad;
To his parents he's a problem; to his teachers he's a pest;
But to grandma, of all boys in all the world he is the best
No, he doesn't wear a halo and he never will, I bet,
But to his doting grandma, he's the biggest angel yet!

5-16-65   GREEN THUMBS

A Most exciting kind of thing
Occurred in my ménage this spring.
Geraniums I brought inside
Last fall, before they up and died,
Survived the heating system's blast,
To greet the spring in style, AT LAST!
All horticulturists agree
This represents no chore for me,
The salvaging from year to year
Of those germaniums so dear.
My neighbors do it every time;
It cannot, therefore be the clime
My friends are quick to point with pride
To plants all blossoming inside,
I seem to be the only soul
Unable to achieve the goal
Of bringing back from year to year
Those scarlet messengers of cheer.
I buy them by the gross, and then,
Next year I'm buying them again -
Now really, with great care I've tried
To tend the blooming things in- side
I've followed all directions fine
From every single friend of mine.
I've shaken out the earth quite free
And hung them upside down. You see,
They then will rally and take root,
I'm told; immediately they'll shoot
With bright new growth' quite handsomely.
THEY JUST LIE DOWN AND DIE FOR ME!
I've sprinkled plant food round each base;
With care I've sponged each soft green face;
I've watered, and they damped and died;
I haven't watered, and they dried

The story always was the same.
NOT ONE SURVIVED WHEN SUMMER CAME!
Last fall, I looked them in the eye.
My garden gems, as I passed by.
"I'll pot you all and bring you in,"
I told them gaily, with a grin,
"But really, I shan't weep with zest
If everyone of you goes west;
Quite obviously, I've not the knack
Of holding winter's ravage back."
I hunted up a giant pot
And went to work upon the lot'
I tucked them in quite merrily,
And toted them inside with glee.
I plopped my treasures in the den,
And watered when I had a yen.
No plant food ever came their way;
I gave no thought from day to day
To whether they were e'en alive;
No prayers I prayed that they'd survive
Occasionally, I'd stop, and think
To give the thirsty dears a drink.
"Tis May, the month to plant again,
The growing time of sun and rain.
The garden's call is sweet and strong.
And days are wondrous warm, and long.
I toted out my giant pot.
ALIVE AND KICKING WERE THE LOT!
No moral in the tale I see;
No plug for jolly husbandry,
A chronic history of neglect
On me no credit can reflect.
Sweet surviving geraniums,
Is THIS the secret of GREEN THUMBS???

5-23-65   GROWING OLD

IT'S A strange thing about that neighbor across the way from you - he's suddenly begun to grow old!

For the past 20 years or more, you've have been passing judgment on the weather you two, exchanging views on the political scene, dwelling in turn upon the miracles of science, the state of the Union, and the high cost of keeping the family ménage up to snuff.

Now suddenly, of a bright and beautiful spring morning, with the hot sun poking mercilessly into every nook and corner of his dear, familiar features, you are startled to discover a decided change in the dear boy.

It must have happened very gradually for you hadn't been aware of it at all!

ONE DAY, he was young and slim and bright of eye and dream; and now, quite suddenly, he's MIDDLE-AGED! And you begin to note the little things about this man of whom you've grown so completely undetected in the busy pattern of your individual lives.

No longer does he spring so swiftly from the car each night, for instance, slamming the big door behind him, and slapping his thigh with the rolled up evening paper. No, he drives serenely in, then gently moves the door about, and looks upon his world.

The step with which he navigates the walk is slow and careful; the flight of worn brick steps that once were mounted at a run, now feels the measured tread of tempered feet.

Once he played ball upon the corner lot, that tall, athletic father of a host of slim, small boys- hatless, flushed and warm beneath the harsh spring sun. Now, it's TV and the Red Sox and the Quiet porch; or maybe Little League, but from the shaded slopes of staid, initialed bleachers in the park.

Once his mower sang a raucous tune across the noonday greening of the lawn; now it's a quiet nocturne in the cool, sweet hush of evening.

A DAY or two ago, it seems he toted sons and daughters in the crooking of his arm, their eyes a carbon copy of his own. Now the trees with grandchildren, a bit more alien of mien, all vying for the warmth and wonder of his gentler years.

Once there was merry laughter on his lips, and now it's quiet joy within the settled poolings of his eyes.

Once he was quick to anger at the follies of mankind; now he has tempered rate with gentle tolerance, condemnation with a studied understanding.

Once he had every answer for the myriad ills of men; now he's quite apt to shake a puzzled head, and grope and speculate on life like all the rest...

Once long ago, his hair was dark defiance in the wind; now it's a snow capped peak that seeks no combat with the surly blasts, but moves, serenely covered, through the days. corners Laugh lines have penned their message on his mouth, and there are hieroglyphics at the corner of his chastened eyes, and lines of life upon that broad, bright forehead. Hands that cup the evening paper have a knotted look, and time has etched the fineness of his character upon the face you've watched grow soft and splendid with the tempering travail of years. Yes, it's a strange thing about that neighbor across the way from you. You've hardly noted all the passing of the years, so swift has been their pace. But now, one bright and beautiful spring morning you note the change upon his face, and find that YOU are growing old!

GUEST EDITORIAL

As the week came to an end, all indications pointed to President Nixon's imminent resignation. It may even have taken place by the time you read this. The country-and the world-waits expectantly and nervously for him to act. No matter what he does it is a dark hour for America.

For those who either look forward to or dread the fact our President will leave office in disgrace, a cynical attitude toward politics, politicians and the quality of American life seems to pervade. The feeling that politics and society have been turned over to the darkest sides of our national character is captured by something written over 4,000 years ago.

"To whom can I speak today?
The gentle man has perished
The violent man has access to everybody.

To whom can I speak today?
The iniquity that smites the land
It has no end.

To whom can I speak today?
There are no righteous men
The earth is surrendered to criminals."

The country and each individual, however, cannot afford to wallow in such despair. We cannot neglect the possibilities of renewal of what is best about America and public service. The lesson of the past difficulties must be turned into a strong resolve to call forth the best ideals of our national life. As bleak as the whole episode surrounding Watergate has been, we must not fail to look ahead.

As John Gardner, former Secretary of Health, Education and Welfare and founder of Common Cause has written, "An individual cannot achieve renewal if he does not believe in the possibility of it. Nor can a society. At all times in history there have been individuals and societies whose attitudes toward the future have been such as to thwart, or at least greatly impede, the processes of renewal…No society is likely to renew itself unless its dominant orientation is to the future."

So instead of fixating on the excesses of our politicians that have led to this dark time in American life, let every citizen resolve to call upon the best of his ideas and abilities to turn America back to the course of greatness. As Mr. Gardner writes, "Societies are renewed - if they are renewed at all - by people who believe in something, care about something and stand for something."

It is the week for all of us to show the rest of the world that American is populated by people who believe in, care about and will stand up for the best of the American spirit.

…Elizabeth N. Metayer

"I DO HOPE our Heather won't become a DROPOUT," said daughter Gael, as she and I departed for HANDLER'S SCHOOL with her prized little Cairn Terrier firmly in tow.

A mental picture of FOU FOU, the family poodle that had let us all down dreadfully by FLUNKING Obedience School, came to mind; and we both laughed.

"Lightning seldom strikes twice," I said comfortingly. "But you haven't seen Heather in ACTION," said Gael. (This was my first GO at Handler's School.) "She acts BORED with the whole proceeding.

You do have the BAIT, by the way?" I fingered the fat frankfurter or two that reposed in little "Baggies" in my purse. "I do," I said. "Good; we shall need it to BRIBE her," said Gael.

Gael plans to SHOW Heather, which is our pet name for Scot Tarre Trinket of Wofpit, a Cairn of impeccable ancestry, carefully selected by her owner with a view to her placing first in every major DOG SHOW from here to Calcutta.

"ITS FUN TO TRAIN YOUR DOG AT THE NEW ENGLAND DOG TRAINING CLUB," read the sign as we reached our destination, a rather secluded and elderly building in the vicinity of Symphony Hall, Boston. "I wish Heather thought so," said Gael wistfully...

Margot, the charming young professional in charge, was lost in a sea of dogs and owners. "This is my mother," said Gael; and even the canines seemed to smile a welcome. "Dog people are all SO friendly," she whispered. "Mother, here is MITU. Isn't that a cute name? She's an LHASPO APSO. It's a NEW breed, you've heard of them, of course?"

A wave of inadequacy enveloped me. "I'm afraid not," I said, "Oh, and this is Mitu's mother." "How do you do" said the lady in question. She lapsed immediately into an account of her darling's fine points that would have done justice to any of the doting grandmothers I know... Mitu WAS a love, however, I regarded her and remembered the toy doggies that invariably fluffed all over Gael's little crib when she was two feet high...

Margo ("Isn't she a DARLING, Mother? The dogs just LOVE her...") brought the group to order, and what a group it was...a Great

Dane, a Siberian Huskie, a Dobermann, a Dachshund, a Japanese Spaniel, and another Cairn named FANCY, with whom Heather immediately renewed acquaintance.

"Now," said the Handler pleasantly, "let us have a NICE LINEUP on four feet. Set her front feet up. Fancy, that is GOOD. Dachsie, get that ear down…When you set up the dogs, you LOOK BACK at their BACK FEET; they must be nice and parallel with the FRONT feet. Front feet should be in line with the shoulder, STRAIGHT DOWN… There now, GOOD! That is GOOD!"

The lady marched up and down the line, patting this dog and straightening that one… "Now, keep the side on which the JUDGE is standing showing BEST! Get tails up nicely. And now, SHOW ME THE BITE!" A dozen or more canine mouths were pried open in turn, revealing the perfection that Margot expected would lie within. "When the dog is on the floor, I hang the leash around my neck, which gives me two hands free," said the lady to one harassed little owner. "Nice equal distances between the dogs now. All right, let us take them around. DON'T LET HER SIDEWIND there! Talk to her` ; get her ATTENTION!"

THE DOGS and their mistresses (with one master) loped about the floor. "Go down, across and diagonally back, always keeping an eye on the judge," said their mentor. "Now ease to a stop. Set them up right, and let me have a NICE FRONT VIEW! GOOD, Heather…Now that is fine with the Dane and with the Doble! VERY GOOD…And now, LITTLE ONES up on the table one at a time!" The moment had arrived. Gael awaited her Terrier's turn like an anxious parent at a P.T.A. Conference; and I agreed instantly with her assessment of the situation when that turn finally came -HEATHER WAS PLAINLY BORED WITH THE WHOLE SILLY PROCEEDING!

As speedily as Gael maneuvered the little dear's FRONT paws into position on the "Show" table, two uncooperative BACK paws commenced to misbehave. "She's IMPOSSIBLE!" Gael's lips formed the words to me over her head; and it was at that precise moment that things began to change for the better.

Heather, we decided later must have heard! For she suddenly raised those two small shaggy ears of hers in a gesture that could have been one of indignation, and SETTLED HERSELF SERENELY ON THE

SHOW TABLE, where she stood posed and ready for the tender appraisal of Margot, or any old dyed-in-the-wool JUDGE, for that matter!

"GOOD GIRL, HEATHER!" said Margot, as one Scot Tarre Trinket of Wolfpit managed a performance that rivaled that of any dog there. The metamorphosis was, however, sadly enough a temporary one, and Heather "Larked" through the remainder of the training session like it was one big joke! 'TOOTSIES' now; put that foot down. Watch out for ARGUMENTS! (apparently the canine upper

The evening wore on; and the admonitions came thick and fast. "Don't let her go playing crust settles its differences in the civilized way.) Speak pleasantly; don't act mad, even if you are! Put the brakes on when the first dog stops. Don't get discouraged. Keep an eye on the dog and an eye on the judge. (Not an easy accomplishment with Heather…) MOVE UP - that's the spirit-1½ feet between dogs; enough room to set up your dogs, and if you have a long tailed dog ahead of you, he can't squash his tail in your face…GAEL-I SIGNALLED YOU TO FIRST PLACE! (In the Mock Show) Why did you go to SECOND? The judge would take a dim view of that; it could lead to embarrassment for him, you know. KEEP YOUR EYE ON THE JUDGE…"

HANDLERS SCHOOL- my first introduction to it. I'm not certain how much KNOW-HOW our little Cairn Terrier gained from it, but her grandmother learned a lot…

"My friend, Robert," I said comfortingly, as we journeyed back to Braintree, the session over, ("He knows a great deal about dogs, incidentally," I added.) "claims that the highly intelligent ones RESENT Handler's School and Obedience School…They dislike having to conform." Heather, hopping gaily about between us and taking in the sights and sounds of Boston, looked up as if in total agreement…Gael sighed…

"Perhaps she's a LATE BLOOMER." She said. "After all, Churchill and Edison were. I read recently that at one point in their education, they were both termed INEDUCABLE."

Scot Tarre Trinket of Wolfpit raised a bushy Cairn eyebrow. "What do you mean, a LATE Bloomer???" It seemed to say, "Didn't I come in FIRST this evening without even lifting a PAW??? Just you wait until I make up my mind to PLAY FOR KEEPS!!! Remember that impeccable BLOODLINE of mine?????? Well, we'll wait…

2-23-69   HAPPY BIRTHDAY GREG

GREGORY SCOTT COBIN had a Birthday last week and so, of course, his doting grandmother went trotting off a few days ahead of time in search of "just the right gift" for her darling.

It was a wretched day, weather-wise. The wind slipped up with murderous intent behind the unwary wayfarer on the icy streets. Winter was unleashing all of her weapons at once- snow and sleet, and wild bone-chilling rain. No one in her right mind, I decided as I met the elemental challenge head on, would have hied her off to the Arctic wastes of the Shopping Plaza on such a day...no one, that is, excepting a doting grandmother with a Birthday in the offing for a sweet small boy.

The unbusy clerk, looking with undisguised sympathy upon the pale phenomenon of alone customer in the first throes of rigor mortis, was disposed to be friendly; I responded in kind.

"Good morning," said; "I would like to see a transistor radio for my little grandson. It's his Birthday. Now - it must be a good HARDY model; and have a leather case and a strap to slip over his little hand.

You see," I added confidentially," It must be like the ones I gave his brothers for Christmas. He 'snitches' theirs constantly; and I feel he should have one of his own."

"How old is he?" asked the clerk, fingering first one and then another of the smart little models, one of which he would remove from the showcase for my perusal. "He will be TWO on Thursday," I said.

A LIKE NUMBER of eyes snapped up and regarded me as though I were the proud possessor of a like number of heads...badly mismated! "You don't think he is a little YOUNG for a transistor?" he asked. "Yes, of course," I said, "but he's a most UNUSUAL little boy!"

"NATURALLY," I could hear him say mentally as he must to all grandmothers about all small boys (and girls...)

With a slight sigh, he handed me a HARDY, complete with "leather case and strap for his little hand" transistor model, the music from which I knew on sight would find an answering song in our small Gregory's heart. Gregory, incidentally, adores music!

And so Gregory celebrated his second Birthday; and he became the proud possessor of his very own transistor radio; and he and Heather, the tiny Cairn terrier currently growing up with his young companion in the Corbin household, settle down together to what would give every evidence of becoming a steady diet of hit tunes, headlines, and what-have-you…

Gregory Scott Corbin IS a most unusual child, actually. Apart from his parents (and I hope, his grandparents) and those two big brothers who are his willing slaves, Greg's principal loves are dogs and flowers. As a matter of fact, his first word was neither "Mama" nor "Dada". It was "Doggie!"

Christmas was, for the youngest member of the Corbin family, a time of pure enchantment. His grandmother's house, with a Christmas tree in every room, was a kind of fairyland for the little boy who would open the front door of the ménage, instantly to lead a doting grandma from room to room. "Christmas tree!" "Christmas flowers!" he would say lovingly, as each bright set of window lights, and every twinkling tree had to be set alight, regardless of the time of day…

The Metayers cling desperately to Christmas long long after those we know have let the season die; nonetheless there came a day when Christmastime was tucked away. Gregory, arriving with happy expectancy at grandmother's was inconsolable.

No Kismas tree??? No Kismas fower???" Where had everything gone, two sad soulful eyes kept asking Grandma as the small boy wandered from room to room? Why was everything put away??? Why????

WHY INDEED, I asked myself, looking with anguish upon the forlorn little face…and then DASHING TO THE ATTIC…

We're probably the only family in Braintree with a small sweet Christmas tree, decked with baubles and skirted with soft tulle, upon our kitchen shelf; and another large one, fully trimmed, and standing defiantly in the corner of the playroom!

Our angel doesn't have quite as MANY rooms in which to find his Christmas, but he does have one or two…And, finding his "flowers", a little boy smiles, and makes the soft, sweet sounds we've grown to love. A most UNUSUAL child, Gregory Scott Corbin!

2-7-65   HAWAIIAN LUAU

THERE IS all of Hawaii, it seems, in a luau, and we wanted all of Hawaii, Ted and I, happily vacationing there.

Away back in the days when Hawaii was a lost jewel in the Pacific, the Master of the Feast recalled, on "sweet and special days," the grandparents of a family would call together all of its members. The little ones would gather on the white sands of the island shores while the elders of the family sang to them the stories of Hawaii - of pearl shells shining. In the sun, the trade winds blowing, the fish splashing in the blue, blue waters, the palm trees swaying. Feasting would commence, and the happy occasion would be called an "ahaaina," which is Hawaiian for "the gathering of friends to eat."

With the coming of the early missionaries and sea captains to the islands, the feast came to be called a "luau," meaning, "leaf of the taro," the plant from the root of which the Hawaiian ground his strange and starchy "poi," and from the leaf of which, sweetened with coconut juice, he derived his "spinach."

It's a ritual as ancient and colorful today as in the day of old, this gay Hawaiian luau, and Ted, attired in his aloha shirt, and I in by "muu muu," set out with a group of friends, attuned to every colorful facet of the feasting.

DARKNESS was falling upon the enchanted island that is Oahu, dropping a quiet curtain upon the rose and pink and golden gray that mark the setting of a sun that warms the wondrous Waikiki throughout its long and languorous days. The conch shell sent its mournful music to the sea as we approached.

A bronzed Hawaiian, sarong about his hips, wreath about his head, walked majestically upon the beach to where a great and ancient drum was hung. He raised the gong he carried in his outstretched hand. A booming sound caressed the night, whose advent it was heralding.

A runner, lei about his bare, brown throat, torch in hand, raced across the sand to light the lamps that were to hurl defiance at the dark, and lights the luau. The pageantry began - the sound, the racing feet, the flaring in the night…Excitement mounted.

We stood there in the dusk, to have an orchid lei placed sweetly on our necks, a kiss upon our cheeks. "Aloha," said our brown Hawaiian host, and in the liquid of his voice, we heard, "Greetings and welcome; love and farewell," and all the thousand meanings of this magic word that floats like music o'er this lonely land.

How can one call them cocktails, the soft and spicy cups of rare, exotic native juices and old "whaling ship rum." our hostess brought our way? We drank them gaily, then feasted on the crispy "pu pus" that resembled bits of pork, fired to a turn and dipped in fragrant sauce, that were our 'hors d'oeuvres."

THE LUAU was not just commencing actually. Back in the early afternoon, the conch shell's mournful voice had called the master of the Feast to where a giant pit – an underground oven or "imu" - had been prepared to hold the small, whole pigs that would provide the "puaa kalua" (baked pork), the piece de resistance of the feast, "Stuffing" the pigs with read hot "pohakus" (rocks), and placing them upon a bed of heated rocks assured the crisping of the tiny porkers, who were topped with sun dried "ti" leaves, then kindling, and then capped securely with a series of tarpaulins, which five and one half long hours, would assure the slow sweet cooking of the tiny fellows, trussed, securely in a net of strong, stiff wire, on which we'd feast.

The hour was come.

The Master of the Feast and all his "kanes" (boys) removed the canvas covers, they freed the savory porkers from their nets of wire, and with strong, dark hands, ungloved, removed the rocks from deep within, just as their ancestors did in long, long past "ahaainas."

The pigs were placed upon great trays, then borne aloft with ceremony, and brown Hawaiians danced, and soft Hawaiian voices brushed the wind.

The tables of the feast were tapa cloaked, and soft Hibiscus bloomed in nests of giant "tis". Our serving plates were wooden, and quite strangely shaped; no silverware was ours only a spoon to stir a coffee (quite, quite un-Hawaiian) that would end the feast.

There was lomi lomi salmon, kneaded and boned, and spiced with small green onions and tomatoes; and steak, with sauce, (so tender that one's fingers DID suffice); the spinach of the taro, and sweetened macaroni fashioned, we were told of fine, long rice.

There was "poi" to place upon the puaa kalua (if you were daring, and we were!) and paakai, (Hawaiian rock salt, colored rosy red, and scraped from small rock cavities along the coast), to place upon the poi; and there was sweet soft haupia (arrowroot, coconut and pineapple pudding), and short, plump, pale bananas, and spears of melting pineapple and frothy coconut cake.

We tried and found delightful every strange Hawaiian dish.

THERE WERE all the sweet Hawaiian touches. Our gentlemen were asked to place their leis about our necks, with a resunding kiss. They did.

We sat, hibiscus in our hair, we gals, (behind the left ear for all married "waihinis"; the right for single maidens), and when the feasting was quite done, the music and the dancing, the story telling of the islands, came our way.

Hula maids fashioned the tales of all the islands with their long and lovely hands, and ukuleles played. Tahitian dancers gyrated; a wild Samoan fire dancer lit the night. A sweet and languorous voice caressed the melting, magic Wedding Song of old Hawaii, and soft "alohas" floated on the wind. The luau was a memory....

Oh, the sweet and subtle magic of this enchanted land, Hawaii.

12-2-7   HOLIDAYS AHEAD

I never can wait to don my Christmas corsage. I spot the first intrepid soul to sport a Christmas boutonniere, AND I AM OFF! This year it happened the very morning after Thanksgiving...

Today I saw it smiling there,
A remnant of some yesteryear;
Its holly leaves a trifle worn,
Its berries just a mite forlorn.
THE FIRST GAY HOLIDAY CORSAGE!

(Quite premature, but no mirage!)
It's wearer smiled as if to say,
"I couldn't wait another day!"
No stylish lady, clad in furs;
No rare outstanding beauty hers;
No purity of former face;
No pretense to a special grace...
Her coat was worn; her hat not right;
But on her face, a radiance bright
Said, "Christmas is not far away.
Oh, how I LOVE that blessed day!
This holiday corsage I wear
To me is infinitely fair."
I hastened home - to attic sped;
A hundred Christmas nosegays spread,
And lovingly their forms caressed,
With memory tugging at my breast...
THIS faded treasure I acquired
From Gael, a tot in boots attired
Who tramped about on shopping spree
And sweetly brought it home to me.
The mother now of three big boys,
Her own bright Christmas she enjoys...
This one- a gift from Mother's hand;
(She dwells now in a better land.)
That one a Christmas package graced;
And this upon a sweet was placed.
That was a favor; this a boon
That rode a Santa Claus balloon!
A million precious memories cling
To keep my heart remembering...
As Christmas nosegays I caress
In sweet nostalgic happiness...
I never can quite throw away
A single holiday bouquet!
I tie them on my Christmas tree

And spend them in a lavish spree
On gay, bedeck-ed doors and walls;
With pure abandon, deck the halls
In shiny sprigs of green and gold,
And some are new...and some are old...
Their bows not now quite up to par;
A star point missing from a star;
An angel's wing that's gone awry;
A Santa Claus with but one eye!
They need not ever perfect be
To form my Christmas symphony,
But every blessed boutonniere
Brings memories so fond and fair
I cannot part with even one.
THEY ALL MUST SHARE MY CHRISTMAS FUN...
Oh, gay corsage on each lapel –
YOU RING A SPECIAL CHRISTMAS BELL!
Your cry of gladness you impart.
"Here dwells a happy kind of heart
That wishes all such Christmas cheer
And blessed joy throughout the year...
That prays, as Christmas comes again
For PEACE ON EARTH...GOOD WILL TO MEN..."

HOLIDAYS END

COMES the sad moment when our bright and beautiful Christmas is tucked away once more where it will serenely lie 'till twelve months hence - side by side with the tired skis, the unstrung tennis racket and the size one hockey skates that once belonged to our young son; the pert prom favors and the corsage remnants; the dance slippers and the frilly formals with which we cannot ever bear to part because they once made living fun for our young daughter.

Tenderly we remove - ornament by ornament - the pink and rose-gold splendor of the shining Christmas tree in our lighted window; we wind the ropes of shimmering tinsel on the waiting spools; and fold the rosy tulle that draped the trees trim base; we tuck the gifts that lay beneath its shining boughs in closets and in bureau drawers; and there is such an empty look about the once bright corner of the room…

We strip the candles from the windows of the house…We're quite convinced that - flowing there since early in December - their light must indeed have sent its message to the tiny Child for whom there was no room within the inn so long ago… "You're welcome in OUR HOME and HEARTS," they cried….

THE LAYING WASTE goes on…Off comes the lovely Christmas angel that has beautified our holiday-ing mantel this past month.

"Why not leave it there?" asked a friend. "So many people keep their golden angels on the mantel all year through."

"She's such a very special part of Christmas," I had answered. "And Christmas is a very special time. I'll tuck her up with all the rest…" the many bells whose tinkling sound had so delighted Grandson James and his two brothers all the merry Christmas season, and which would now unhappily, sound no more.

To the attic with the pinecone tree; and the sentimental memory tree - their starry twinkle lights demure and dead until another Christmas comes our way. To oblivion with the tiny tree upon my dresser top; the yule log from the master bedroom; the bright fireplace arrangements from the guest rooms all. Christmas is over!

We pile its splendor on the attic floor, and then we stop a moment to reflect, shall we be here, we wonder, as we always have, when yet another Christmas comes along? Or shall another's hand place each sweet shining bauble on a somewhat lonely future Christmas scene???

Beyond the confines of the attic windows, Nature, sensing the sadness of a Christmas gone to seed, seems to extend a soft consoling hand. We look upon her magic…No Christmas tree on earth could e'er surpass in beauty, we decide, our own tall fir, its branches white with newly fallen snow; a star that must indeed have rivalled Bethlehem's own, above it in the dark night sky!

No garlands could e'er match in breathless beauty mundane light wires in the wind, all draped with crystal ribbons, quite agleam; no Christmas village quite as lovely as our Town, all diamond-flecked and shining! We find swift comfort in the sight, and then our spirits lift...

CHRISTAMSTIME is o'er, but when the Christmastime is gone, then is not springtime surely on the way, we ask ourselves? May days are to be found in January. Rivers run in the streets, and children's coats come flapping open, and the ice floats free...and February is such a short and shining month...and merry March is almost tulip time...

And so, regretfully as always, we bid goodbye to yet another blessed beautiful Christmas, but WE LOOK AHEAD...

9-18-66 BRAINTREE SUNDAY NEWS HOW THE VOTING WENT

() withdrew before primary
- • Nominated
- * Incumbent

DEMOCRATIC
REPRESENTATIVE

	1	2	3	4	5	6	7	8	9	Braintree total	Third Norfolk total
Richard J. Adams	22	22	22	22	19	52	27	47	26	259	422
Daniel L. Capodilupo	67	46	68	41	19	50	31	23	33	378	609
Patrick F. Fitzgerald	?	166	119	122	123	98	111	248	151	1321	1955
Robert E. Frazier	288	303	163	201	185	177	217	389	229	2152	2342
Barry T. Hannon	276	223	230	251	191	209	265	241	253	2139	3035
(Richard K. LaVangle)	16	18	16	17	15	36	12	19	20	169	273
John W. LeRoy Jr.	113	119	119	154	107	162	168	165	88	1195	1456
Elizabeth N. Metayer	135	97	108	203	147	357	155	183	166	1551	1982
Blanks	134	128	119	119	126	121	118	191	108	1164	

REGISTER OF PROBRATE

9-15-66 HANNON, FRAZIER WIN DEMOCRATIC NOMINATION BRAINTREE OBSERVER

45 Percent of Voters Show

About 45 percent of Braintree's registered voters turned out Tuesday for the Primary Election.

About twice as many Democrats as Republicans voted. There are 16,399 registered voters, of whom 7,396 cast ballots this week. Of these 5,164 were Democrats and 2,232 were Republicans.

The reason for the low Republican turnout was the lack of any major contests. There are 4,625 registered Republicans and 5,602 registered Democrats. Obviously, the high Democratic turnout was due to many independents who appeared Tuesday. There were 6,172 independents when the polls opened, but there will be some changes in designation once the Town Clerk's office gets around to sorting out the names.

An independent may vote in a primary for either party, but once he does he becomes registered with the party he has voted for. On Tuesday, the Town Clerk's office was constantly phoned by people asking where to vote. This meant new voters, mostly listed as independents, changing their minds and voting for a party - in the all likelihood, the Democratic Party.

Attorney Barry T. Hannon, of West St, was the number one vote getter among seven candidates for the two Democratic nominations for State Representative for Braintree and Ward Quincy. He polled 683 more votes than Robert E. Frazier, chairman of the Board of Selectmen. Both men will however run as Democratic candidates for the two opposing seats in the General Court.

Running third was Mrs. Elizabeth N. Metayer, Town Meeting member and former head of the League of Women Voters. Patricia F. Fitzgerald ran 27 votes behind Mrs. Metayer. Teacher John I. Roy, Daniel L. Capodilupo and Richard J. Adams finished in this order, with Richard La Vangle who withdrew but remained on the ballot finishing last.

9-18-66   POLITICAL ADVERTISEMENT BRAINTREE SUNDAY NEWS

THANK YOU to
The gals who were part of my wonderful team;
Who shared all of my hopes; every wonderful dream;
Who with banners and hats, and a smile pert and bright,
Passed out flyers at those supermarkets each night
Those whose telephone arms with bursitis are burning;
And the folks who manned polls, with campaigners' hearts yearning;
And then last but not least, to the voters - they're tops!
Those who donned their chapeaux, and then pulled out the stops;
Hied them off to the polls; placed an "X" by my name....
Thanks a million, you-all! What a team! What a game!

ELIZABETH N. METAYER
DEMOCRACTIC CANDIDATE FOR STATE REPRESENTATIVE
38 Arthur Street, Braintree

8-2-70   HURRICANE SEASON

A hurricane can be a PAIN;
   That season's in the news again,
And every weatherman in sight
Is quaking in his maps-with fright.
The small craft warnings firmly fly,
   And fearful grey gulls soil the sky,
And all the beauty of the sea
   Is left unloved by you and me....
While dwellers on the fair Atlantic
   Tune in the news with faces frantic...
A hurricane is such a bore,

Each year I seem to mind them more,
Those gales with names from "A" to "Z"
That ride the skies so wantonly,
Necessitating that we tote
Upon dry land the family boat
And batten down each chair and chaise
That line the garden with such grace...
Gosh, wouldn't it really be terrific
If all "eyes" turned toward the Pacific???

G.C.H.S. "IDYLLS OF A KING" (WITH APOLOGIES TO TENNYSON) A DRAMA OF THE FUTURE AND THE PAST

Time: The dim moons of futurity.
Place: Court of Arthur, King of Knighthood.
Arthur: (rising from throne)
Blare the mighty trumpet's call, blare!
To north, to south; toward dawn, toward death.
Summon noble Knighthood from the world of past-lived glory;
Raise a court, monarch cries and calls!
Angel:
Chaste, Arthur, great King, thy holy will be done.
(blare of trumpets)
Lancelot! Ector! Placidas! Gawaine!
Ulfius! Gareth! Balin!
Out of the past cometh Knighthood,
Poised with steel upon its mount of shades,
Armed, and all accoutred.
Griflet! Uwaine! Lanceor! Kaye! Gaherin!
King of immortal glory, they be here arriven!
Arthur: (seating himself on throne)
Off from yon lofty throne, long days ago,

Chaste, Virgin Paladins. Aloft they stood
All armed and all arrayed for greatest of great Tournaments.
The ages pass,--
Their lofty combat, I, great Knights, would know.
Great Lancelot, beloved Sire, speak loud
The story of the Knights whom thou hast known
And their sweet Fate.

Lancelot:
King, Knight, and ruler of men's hearts, --
Three hath thou borne to worthy Lancelot,
Three called of Holy Mary,
God hath giv'n all a blessed more vocation.
Lo! There, in endless toil, all three
Hath labored for men's minds that they be made
To know and comprehend.
O King! Their lot is noble, highly blessed.
My weighty charge be witnessed, - God the rest.

Arthur:
Knight, thou hast been noble. Hold thy peace
Placidas, Sire of Calm,

G.C.H.S
The Virgin fair, with whom I graced thy sword, -
Pray, whither hath her lowly steps, their holy guide borne on?

Placidas:
In sacred Carmel, bowed in benediction,
King of prayer, the maid of whom thou speaketh,
Holy Margaret, lady of the Virgin, Kneels
And speaketh high to that most holy Knight,
Her pledge of lofty fealty,

Arthur:
The graces of sweet Sisterhood
Rain softly, like a falling mist,
O'er heads that God hath chosen for His own.
Are there no more whose eyes
Seek fair far battles of a higher glow
In lo! the mightiest - Crusade?

Gawaine:

> Most holiest Knight, a Rose hath I,
> Plucked from the bower of virgin souls,
> To whom the voice of God hath spoken soft;
> Sweet, move among the orphaned steps of children
> Her sweet, gracious feet.
> Great King, my Paladin
> Hath raised her arms to God!

Ector:

> King Arthur, great,
> Our Lord hath taken not my lady fair
> To be His wedded spouse in mystery.
> Thou gavest me a maid
> Whose presence in a world of weighted wisdom bright joy,
> A maid of laughter and of wit,
> A famed victor in yon Tournament of care.
> Her mailed mounts, King,
> Rideth not wild winds of sorrow sad,
> But spurreth on to jousting places,
> Gay with revelry and joy.

Arthur:

> Knight, dear beloved,
> Words weighted with high wisdom
> Fall from thy too-youthful lips.
> Yon world desireth laughter o'er its pall of hapless tears.
> Stay, Gareth, what sad reason of untimeliness
> Beareth thy steps, eager, nay, so sad,
> Beyond yon golden gate of triumph?

Gareth:

> Great Lord, I know not if to weep or glory.
> Thou hast given to my blessed hand a dreamer,
> Seer of high visions, watcher of soft stars.

G. C. H. S.

> High hath she soared.
> Yet seeketh but to call the day a day,
> The night a night, without achievement.

King of might, where leads the lofty star
My lady hath embraced?

Arthur:

That star hath lofty realm,
And time is sweet, and tides are burdened with high glory.
Ulfius, Knight,
Thy lady lies as yet in blackest dark;
I seek the light by which to know her gloried life.

Ulfius:

The body, noble King, containeth fast
The might should wherein a man is born to God,
And my great lady of the greater age
Hath followed paths that lead beyond the stars
Of corporal strength, as if to say,
"Let no Knight cry of greater deed than mine, --
I make man's body for his soul's fit shrine!"

Arthur:

Balin, grave, thy ponderous charge resteth highly
On the shoulders of a Knight.
What mighty realm doth Lady Margaret
That maketh thee so loth to tarry lightly here In sweet retreat?

Balin:

The weighty one o'er whom my sword hath hanged
Is but become a delver of deep books,
Great King,
That turneth grave and pregnant with sweet study
Her wide-seeking mind.
And so to ones that seeketh knowledge
She doth bear the shield of noble learning.
My lady Knight hath fought in might combat
Foes of ignorance. Perchance,
For greater glory than all others.

Arthur:

Yea, Knight, for he that seeketh knowledge
Findeth great content in knowing.

Kaye, high Knight of Grace,
Thy noble ladies, I, ofttimes, have seen.
The lady Alice and most fair Annette
Hath not aspired
That man may bear form worlds that gleam,
And deck the portrait of dull care
With staged peace.
Fair Lady Catherine, player of high Astolat,
G.C.H.S.
Greet gay thy gracious Lord with lofty word!"
(enter, hurriedly, the Knight Allardin)

Arthur:
Stay gentle Knight, hath thou returned at last,
And with such face as proveth joy?
What message true doth thou be come to tell
Of those sweet maids,
O'er whom I, thee, sweet Knight,
Hath placed in favor blessed?

Allardin:
That one sweet maid hath oped her silent lips
To speak of triumph, my great King,
And that, behold!
The lowly one who followeth in her soundless wake,
High Mary, hath in cloudless joy
Attained rare, lofty heights,
By holy pathway of most holy teaching.

Arthur:
Thou speakest well, with words that gladden gentle Sire.
But Lanceor, my Knight, to Irene, thine,
Hath Fate, inspired by God, seemed passing sweet?
To stars that draweth on their Knighted sisters.
For it is they
That serveth my sweet Queen, most lovely Guinevere,
And lo! Hath rested with gay ease
Upon great cloth-of-gold at her sweet feet,

To be admired.

Gaheris:

Locked fast in soft embrace of Sisterhood,
My King,
The gentle maid o'er whom thou once hath placed my sword
Doth raise her voiced words aloft to Heaven.
Terese, my lady, serveth that high King
For whom all Knights and Lords are bold With mighty boldness.

Arthur:

Knights, and Sires, and brothers, few are still
Whose word hath not been voiced that I might harken!"

Griflet:

The virgin charge whom thou hast named as mine
Hath found a world apart from lowly man,
A world of splendor, joyful light,
In city fair
Whence men all cometh for that jovial joy.

Lanceor:

More sweet, King, than all else, perchance;
Aloft on tides of men whence worlds be won

G.C.H.S.

Irene stands poises, the lady
Powered with great mind that solveth
All great things to harass hapless man."

Uwaine:

Most holy King,
As, often in the great, glad age of chivalry,
Fair Knighthood fell, keen-pierced by hated lance,
So, too, in spectral tourney, but an age ago.
I, Knight, lay fallen at the errant hand
Of black-armed Knighthood.
And my lily maid, then hath she come,
Kind Lady Mary,
Cool-sweet hand bathed in sweet tenderness,
Great, haunting eye with great-souled pain aglow
Our King, our Lord,

I know not what hath caused the mighty thing,
But there be healing in her softest touch."
Arthur:
But hark, good Knights, -
The holy bell hath made its holy music
On the thrice-calmed air of evening;
God be praised above all else.
Great Sires, thy work be nobly, greatly done.
The Virgin souls with whom I joined thy hand,
Have all high risen to high-gloried height.
Once more hath evening's music failed in arms,
At God's high sounding call to prayer.
Angel of Virtue,
Bear thou great, peerless Knighthood back to waiting Paradise.
The Pageantry is ended;
Arthur, its King, hath summoned noble Knighthood
From the world of past-lived glory,
And lo! Now doth cry farewell.
O, soundless one, bear witness to thy King,
And but depart with shades of those
That lived and fought in great-souled combat

All for God, and holy Womanhood.
Blare the mighty trumpet's call, blare!
To north, to south; toward dawn, toward death.
\And ye await your King at set of sun,
By yon dark stream twixt lowly earth, and God; -
I stay to speak high prayer with evening's Lord.
Farewell, and on!"
(Exit Knighthood, then Curtain)

ELIZABETH NENER

11-10-74 I'M A "REP"!

How do I feel??? Just GREAT! Just FINE!
Im still up there sailing on old Cloud Nine!
And I'm terribly humble; and terribly proud;
Want to climb to the rooftops and shout out loud,
"THANK YOU, GOOD PEOPLE OF BRAINTREE,
MASSACHUSETTS!
I'll try my hardest to serve you wisely and well; and with
Your good
Prayers, and the help of the Father of us all, I shall
Hopefully
Succeed in doing just that!"

7-5-70 INVOLVEMENT
SEE POLITICAL

"I love being friends with you," she said; (She'd just moved in
  to town -)
"You know, as your friend and neighbor, I meet folks of the
  true renown.
I'm politically informed; I am socially quite gay;
Oh, the day I came to your neighborhood was a very lucky day!
You know the most exciting ways of filling up one's days -
Why, life's suddenly grown delightful in a thousand different
  ways!
Now instead of doing dishes with my mind upon the suds
I rush to dry with my "weather eye" fixed gaily on the duds
Into which I'll dive for a dashing drive down to Braintree's old
  Town Hall
Or a jaunt into dusty archives that turn out to be a ball!
I attend the smartest meetings; I sip endless cups of tea;
I am exercising brain cells that were close to atrophy.

As I diaper the baby, thoughts of candidates supreme
Rise to blot from sight those pale pink pins and permeate the
    cream…
I unearth the strangest strangers, and I meet the brightest gals.
Everywhere we go folks in the know turn out to be your pals!
"Yes, I love being friends with you," she said. "Im glad I came
    your way…
Are our dishes done? Good-it's time for fun! So - where shall
    we go today???

2-28-65   INVOLVEMENT

Once, not so very long ago,
I stood, domestically aglow,
My shining kitchen sink beside,
And viewed7 my world with quiet pride.
The crisp, red curtains, framing free
The window that smiled back at me,
Dramatically, I thought, portrayed
The tenor of the world I'd made,
A snug and sweet and shining place,
Far from the earth's disturbing pace.
I raised my eyes, and then DID deign
To look beyond the window pane
To where that precious world would pass,
Serene and lovely, through the glass
I turned my eyes, approving, there
To where the clouds were white and fair;
I saw the circles dragonflies
Were etching on the summer skies
I tossed my head approvingly;
My small, sweet world looked back at me.
Germaniums. So prim and still,
Aflame upon the window-sill;

A swathe of lawn; a fringe of trees,
Correctly blowing in the breeze;
A garden gay; a playground swing;
(My little world had everything!)
The clothes reel with my wash a-sail;
The postman with my morning mail;
The garden rake; the trim, green hose;
The rakish phlox; the perfect rose.
This little world I'd carved for me
Was just as neat as it could be;
And just as narrow, I'm afraid
As it could possibly be made.
How long ago that moment seems
As I review it in my dreams…
Alas, one day not long ago,
I rose to find no special glow
Surrounding all my days routine;
No spark to make me primp and preen.
The world I watched through window small
That day, impressed me not at all.
I wondered, as I viewed it there
If other worlds were quite so fair;
I pondered; a thought came to me.
Contentment CAN bring atrophy!
And four small walls, however dear,
Do not a world encompass here.
I stirred myself; I looked about
The town, invitingly laid out;
I browsed in books; I joined the club;
I wore myself down to the nub.
Discovering cells in my poor brain
That thrilled to be employed again.
I found Town Hall; I joined "the League";
My days of fighting bored fatigue
Were suddenly suffused with light;

I burned the well-known oil at night.
I found I'd missed a thousand things;
My intellect was sprouting wings.
My soul with satisfaction shone;
I journeyed gaily on and on.
The world, I found, is wondrous wide,
And humans, walking side by side,
Can strive in countless little ways
To share the wonder of its days.
Now, as I stand the sink beside,
To wash my dishes, still with pride,
And look beyond my window free,
WHAT STIRRING VISIONS
COME TO ME!
I find a shining ship of state;
The Commonwealth beyond my gate;
I see all men of every creed
From bigotry's dark shackles freed;
I watch a hundred flags unfurled.
The avenues of all the world.
That sky that once was only mine
A canopy for all mankind.
Though my small world is still as sweet,
The universe lies at my feet!

1-9-72   JANUARY

Love the month of January...love its moods and its caprices...

Love the tiny singing rivers that run along the roadways on the days when one awakens on a January morning to find the sun flooding one's room with all the force and fervor of July. Love their cherry chuckling as they journey toward a sea that's suddenly serenely blue where yesterday 'twas gray...Love those snarling singing blizzards that blow wantonly our way by night, enveloping all the town in shiny-white embrace, keeping me snugly in my own safe, private world and all the other worlds without....

Love the sight of still proud Christmas trees upon the sidewalks of the town; or in the hands of marching boys' or on the conservationist's lawns, boughs bulging with suet, with bits of this or that or whatever it is that feeds our hungry birds...

Love the glad gay wrappings that evade the barrel tops as Braintree-ites observe their pick-up days; the bows and bits of ribbon that blow colorfully about from necks of bulging plastic baggies...Love the weathermen's predictions that Spring thaws are on the way while snowstorms rage; and snow is fast approaching Braintree while those tiny rivers that we speak about run along...merrily

Love the small boys' with enthusiastic hockey games, their sledding and their skates they drape about their necks with lacing that could strangle them at will...Love their great warm coats, their mittens and their scarves, their nice wool caps and all the other bits of warmth they seem so suddenly to affect when January comes their way and Santa's been about...

Love the way those Christmas lights that yesterday lit up the town grow gradually dim; the Love the red upon their cheeks; the snow upon their lashes; the shine about their eyes...candles fade; the music and the merriment are stilled; the partying ceases; store windows change their scenes....

Love the way one jolly Santa or one shining Christmas tree has managed to survive in some unlikely spot...

Love to find the shoppers of Christmas past, dashing about the stores as though 'twere yesterday, those gifts that were too small, too large or somehow sadly unappealing, tucked beneath their arms...

Love the first fair fadings of poinsettia plants, the curling of the holy; the fragrance of the dying pines and firs...

Love the last tired bits of turkey in the family refrigerator; (what does one do with them????); the crumbs of the once proud Christmas pudding; the flecks of fruit cake and the cashew curls; the ribbon candy's sweet remains....Love it all!

Love the thousand Christmas memories still flooding heart and soul with wonder and with family about the festive board; the ever blessed beauty of another Midnight Mass; those special Christmas handclasps and caresses; the carolers and their carols…the sheer unending beauty of it all….

Yes, it's a beautiful month, January. There are bits of Christmas left in it; and lovely, long lost days; and a hint of JUNE here and there in its complex make-up. It's a tiger and a tabby cat kind of month…a demon and a dove…and its moods and caprices never fail to delight me.

It's a time for assessments, of course…for reflection upon our lives…for resolutions on the manner in which we shall live them in another year…another brand new year…Oh, lovely, lovely thought! May it be a Happy one and a Holy one for each and every one of you, my readers. May it bring you joy, and peace, and the sweet fulfillment of those dreams and hopes that seem to be closest to your hopefully happy hearts! May God love you all in 1972!

1-28-68   JANUARY RIVERS

We all have our favorite river; Boston's dear old "Charles" is MINE!
Though I must admit a fondness for the Watchtower on the Rhine….)
Ah! The BEAUTY of our rivers; Oh! Those singing silver streams
That set poets spinning sonnets, and dreamers dreaming dreams….
Now, the fans of old "Blue Danube" (which isn't BLUE at all)
Raise their steins to sing HER praises winter, summer, spring and fall….
While the Hudson isn't pretty- tucked so tightly in a city -
Real New Yorkers THEY would tell that they loved its waters well….
Then the Thames in London Town merits all the world's reknown;
While to Holland's Zuyder Zee every Dutchman bends the knee!
There's the Liffey, Dublin's pride; and - with Florence right beside -
There's the Arno, slow and deep….(May it henceforth ever sleep!)

We admit that rushing rivers sound a symphony divine;
We're the first to hail the Hudson (or that Watchtower on the
　　Rhine!)
But if WE were asked to name the jolly river we love best,
There is one in our opinion which tops all the running rest,
Tis the January river that runs softly on our street.
When those mountainous old snow banks have begun a slow
　　retreat;
And the gutters are a-gurgle; and their music everywhere
Lends a merry old enchantment to the January air....
To be sure, it isn't pretty and its waters aren't blue;
And it seldom (if it ever) really twinkles up at you;
And its borders - NEVER grassy - for the most part are not high;
And it rarely is reflected in soft beauty in the sky....
But its voice is pure enchantment, for it carries with its song
All the snow and slush and winter-waste that makes the winter
　　long....
Gosh, the month of January is a COLD one - goodness me!
Sometimes wonder how we last until we greet dear February!
For this month that follows Christmas rushes in- devoid of guile -
Tossing snow upon our landscape like it's going out of style;
While we fuss and fume, and - fretting - carry on in high chagrin
As we shovel and we shovel and deplore the fix we're in....
Then along comes Mother Nature; she takes pity on our plight
And - within the starry confines of a January night
She blows gentle zephyr breezes that come waltzing down below
And land squarely and securely on our mountain-land of snow.
Then it is that we awaken to find gurgling softly by
Tiny JANUARY RIVERS - and we BID THAT SNOW
　　GOOD-BYE!
Yes-we guess that we're committed - love no other river more
Than that dear and welcome offshoot of the JANUARY THAW!

1-31-65   JET TRAVEL

VACATION TIME, (we love winter vacations) and Ted and I are enroute to Hawaii this year. Be not consumed with envy, you parents of tiny tykes, who entertain the firm conviction that the luster of vacations will forever more be dimmed by the dark shadows of sand pails and playpens - your day WILL come! You'll awake one morning, and out of the emptiness of large and lonely rooms and dear departed children, you will see emerging a vitalizing vision of dark and distant places, and off you'll go...

We are high above the world in a T.W.A. Boeing 707 jet, that 20th century Flying Carpet that flies with the wind, and our vacationing will begin in Los Angeles.

We are promptly introduced to the Passengers Automatic Oxygen System, (en route to Hawaii over the Pacific, our initial cheerer-upper will be a tete-a-tete with a life preserver and life rafts), and we are delighted to learn from the charming little stewardess who discusses it so gaily that these vital little gadgets will pop down adjacent to our green little faces in the event that their use is indicated. We are cautioned against the use of radio receivers while the aircraft is in flight, (they can cause interference with the navigation system) and we rise to the skies, literally.

I look back upon the familiar world so soon to lie some forty thousand feet below me, and catch my breath ever so slightly at the toy town our great City of Boston has become.

We are served our morning coffee, and have barely consumed the last crumb of sweet roll when we descend to take on passengers at Philadelphia, and to find a whopping little snowstorm making merry about the airport. Apparatus appears speedily to coat the wings of our mechanical bird with a de-icing liquid and we are off again, soaring high above the storm, where, in what seems a matter of minutes, the sun is shining with a high, hot whiteness, and snow is but a memory.

We are introduced to Strato-Cinema, Plastic earphones are ours, as from out of the ceiling there descends a large screen, and In flight Motion Pictures, Inc. presents "Topkapi", and for the next two hours we are completely unaware that we are traveling at six hundred miles per hour almost forty thousand feet above the land we love, in open defiance of the generally accepted decree of the generally accepted decree of nature that heaven is for the birds.

Time for cocktails; time for luncheon, and we are aware of the fact that the terrain below has begun to change. In the far-off distance, the Rocky Mountains are backdrops on a strange, slate stage. "Fasten your seatbelts," the pilot warns us, "there may be some turbulence at 35,000 feet." 35,000 feet....

We look about us at the little ones on board as we comply. A small boy clutches a toy dog with long, flopping ears, and we recall newsreel visions of a blackened dolly in the midst of the bubble of a downed plane, and we shiver a little.

For the most part, our fellow passengers are silent and self-contained, with one exception. A delightful lady across the aisle is graphically describing to her companion, a bus tour down Amalfi Drive in Italy. ("I was under the seat nine-tenths of the way." Italian fruit in general, (big as melons) and peaches in particular, Paris in September, the Louvre, and the "cheeky" French guide who had a "veritable tantrum" when she paused en route to the Mona Lisa, to admire a Raphael; London's fog, and Los Angeles' smog, (there's nothing there actually, but Disneyland). From her conversation, we learn that we may take a helicopter to Disneyland directly from the airport, (what an age we live in! And that Hollywood is vastly overrated.

We are renewing our acquaintance with geography now, as, the movie ended and our shades restored to normal, we look down upon the world thousands of feet below us, which has come to resemble the topography maps we made of flour and water and salt away back in school.

The Rocky Mountains lie ahead now snow-crowned, naked and black against the slate of sky, with no vegetation other than in the valleys between, where the trees lie like handfuls of black pebbles, tossed into the canyons. An Army plane crosses our path, leaving a tracer on the sky, like a smoking arrow, straight and slim.

Close to Colorado, the earth takes on a copper hue like the Indians we fancy we shall see riding out of the hills. The terrain is seamed and gullied; nature seems to have trailed great gnarled fingers across the land, as a child does across the sea sand. The Colorado River throws its muted silver at the sky, with boulder dam standing in magnificent and mighty challenge to its force. The Grand Canyon lies at our feet, a mile deep and 18 miles across - a technicolor scene in pink and rose and purple and gold, black-rimmed with trees, dark and dramatic.

The mountains of Nevada next lie beneath our wide wings, their neat little valley settlements clearly discernable in the white sunlight, their roads and railroads sleeping like slim black snakes in the wintering hills. Los Angeles, we learn, lies just ahead. We commence losing altitude; we fasten r seatbelts once more; we extinguish cigarettes. For an eternity, it seems, we are quiet in the air, with the great city rising and falling beneath our dipping wings; we ride the wide sky.

The beauty of the city hurls itself our way in a symphony of white stone, its buildings classic and pure, its boulevards broad and straight, its architectural extremes throwing spheroids and ellipsoids against our twentieth century sky. Los Angeles, City of Angels.... In later flights, we shall watch the sun rise softly in a shimmering ballet; we'll see it set in flaming, flushed abandon; we'll stretch our hands to gather stars, so close they'll seem; we'll smile upon a moon, and glory in the silver-snow of clouds beneath our feet. We'll ride in spirit close beside the pilot of our plane, and know the joy of conquering heaven's heights. We'll gaze into the soul of Mauna Loa, its cinder cones as high as the Empire State Buildings, the great and ghastly crater of Hawaii. We'll see the shores of Molokai. What an age is this, in which we have been privileged to live!

9-26-82   KENNEDY COMPOUND VISIT 1982

It was Ted Metayer's 80th Birthday, and another Ted - Senator "Ted" Kennedy to be exact, was giving the party. Ted Metayer wasn't to be the only guest, needless to say. He would share the festive occasion with about 50 members of Congress and the General Court and their spouses. Weather forecasters had predicted cloudy skies and rain for September 26, 1982 and so as we left for Hyannis Port I tucked an umbrella into my huge comprehensive bag. The weather forecasters were wrong. My grandson Jim Corbin should have been in Braintree instead of away in Vermont in School. He's usually better at predicting the weather than most of the current T.V. stars. Jim is studying Meteorology, you see; and he's been playing around with weather since the age of six or so.

At any rate, the sun was shining beautifully as we left Braintree and headed toward Hyannis Port…and it continued to shine all day long. Hallelujah!!! We followed excellent directions, and arrived at Dunfey's right on time. A bus was waiting, and we were driven to the Kennedy Compound. Coffee and a wonderful greeting from Ted and some of the Kennedy grandchildren awaited us as we left the bus. There was Pat Lawford, a beautiful youngster; and Chris Kennedy, Bob's son, along with his younger brother. Kara, Ted's lovely young daughter and his youngest boy were both on hand. His oldest son Bob is in London, Ted told us, working in connection with the current "Year of the Handicapped." Quite a young man!!!

There was considerable posing for pictures, and then a tour of the Kennedy homes. The first to be shown was "the President's home."… the home of the incomparable JFK…It's a beautiful large white structure with green shutters. It is exquisitely furnished yet not in a way to resemble a museum. It's a SUMMER HOME…We entered via a lovely wide porch to find a charming dining room and an elegant living room on the first floor. It was moving experience, this visit to the home of our assassinated and beloved president. I placed my hands upon the back of the President's chair at the dining table, and I could feel tears spring to my eyes. I pictured him and Jacquie and their little ones standing in the doorway looking out over the magnificence of the sea or toasting marshmallows by the fireplace; or sitting quietly together, reading or painting or just talking…I could see him in his sailboat racing across the harbor, this wonderfully appealing man. I could feel his presence everywhere…

Having toured the President's home, we walked merrily along a lovely road to the pier for a sail down the harbor in a large boat, the "Prudence." Here we found an Open Bar and a marvelous band which incidentally supplied music for the entire day.

Ted Kennedy had left the pier just ahead of us in his beautiful sailboat, and after sailing about and around us, his boat hove to beside ours, and he leaped aboard the larger craft with unbelievable ease. He chatted once more with us all, and my colleague Steve Karol informed him that it was Ted's birthday, and so he pumped Ted's hand in his warm way and wished him birthday happiness. The sail was delightful, and then it was back to the Kennedy Compound for chowder, an open bar, music and fun. It was announced that the "Ambassador's Home" would be open for a tour, and so Ted and I repaired to the long and lovely porch to take the tour. We were, however advised by the Tour Guide that Mrs. Rose Kennedy would be coming out to greet her guests in five minutes. "Why don't you wait until she does so," the young lady said. "You'll be in the house and you'll miss her speech." We did just that. We waited right there on the verandah, and so were right on hand to greet Mrs. Rose Kennedy when she emerged on the arm of her son, and made a speech of welcome to the crowd below.

She looked so very tiny next to her tall son. She wore a white pant suit and white sandals with medium heels. There was a dash of red at the neck of her suit, and a huge floppy red hat completed her outfit. The band struck up "My Wild Irish Rose" when she finished speaking, and she promptly reached out her arms to son Ted and waltzed with him down the length of the verandah. An elegant and remarkable lady, to be sure - in her nineties, you understand.

Ted presented her to the few who were on the verandah, ourselves included. I shook her hand, and then her son said, "Mother, it's Mr. Metayer's Birthday today,". "How nice," she said, and extended her hand and wished him happiness. It was quite a way to celebrate an 80th birthday, I thought…

The readiness of the clambake was announced next, and so we descended the gorgeous lawn to where the caterer awaited us with such delicacies as half a roast chicken, a lobster, steamed clams, corn, Italian sausage, cole slaw, rolls, and watermelon…all in a large green basket-like affair. It was all absolutely delicious, and we were seated at long tables under an awning adjacent to the "Ambassador's Home" to enjoy both the view of the sea and the clambake itself simultaneously. We next toured the "Ambassador's Home." It's a marvelous experience. The Ambassador purchased it in 1929, and promptly made a number of changes in the building. He had an old and beautiful building demolished and the wide floorboards brought to the Cape and installed in his home with hand-hewn nails. The floor is, therefore honey-colored and handsome. The house contains the most magnificent collection of photographs, memorabilia and mementos of the family one can possibly envision. There were photos of Ambassador and Mrs. Kennedy taken with all the crowned (and uncrowned) heads of the world. And what a truly beautiful young woman was this elderly lady who had wished Ted a happy birthday on this 80th!!! I particularly loved the photo of the pair with England's King and Queen, taken when all were young and gorgeous, and the elegance of that age was evidenced by the magnificence of their attire.

All the important papers of a family as unique as the Kennedy's were framed and hung on the walls the Ambassador's appointment among them, along with prestigious and historic invitations, Citations and honors and awards that had been bestowed upon family members over the decades. It was rather wonderful to view the bedroom where Jack and Robert spent their early years, and where Jack and Jacquie slept until they purchased their own summer home on the Compound. The twin beds remain untouched; and in the adjoining bathroom towels monogrammed with what looked like a "J" and an "R" "K" could be glimpsed upon the towel racks.

The band played throughout the day. The open bar had functioned as well. It was a festive occasion indeed, with everything possible done to please the guests of the Kennedy family.

Now with the Clambake over and behind us, it was off in a vehicle to visit Ted's home, a couple of miles away on Squaw Island. A truly delightful place, filled with memorabilia…scrapbooks containing photos of all aspects of his trip to the Near East and other places with his lovely ex wife Joan; photos of the Kennedy children, marvelously posed with their handsome parents, and pictured at all the various stages in their lives.

Among the memorabilia was one especially delightful item. A card from "The White House sent to Mrs. Kennedy upon the birth of son Ted, Dated February 22, 1932. The card had apparently accompanied flowers for the new mother; it termed them "perishable." The Kennedy Compound defies description. The lawns slope like huge emerald carpets down to the sea. Borders, two or three foot deep, of magnificent flowers are everywhere. Many of the varieties were quite unknown to me. In the distance the marsh grass and the famous "dunes" that are part and parcel of Cape Cod. Seagulls circling overhead, their cries floating on' the air; with the wind from the sea bearing a fragrance known only to that wonderful part of Massachusetts. "THE CAPE."

What a fringe benefit for this legislator…a wonderful day with the Kennedys in their famous Kennedy Compound…and a chance to see how the other half lives.

8-12-66   KINDERGARTEN

JAMES M. Corbin III, grandchild of our hearts is about to enter kindergarten. The home movies portraying these first, fascinating steps of his, aren't even old hat, and yet, unbelievably, here he is - a school boy.

He takes his new status extremely seriously, believe me - he's a serious little boy! "When are we going to buy my 'back to school' clothes?" he was asking the day after his kindergarten visit last And thinking back to that kindergarten visit - James demanded a lunchbox, complete with thermos, for his introduction to education. It simply wasn't the season for lunch boxes, and so, though his doting grandmother visited every drugstore in town on the Sunday evening prior to his morning at the Eldridge, not a lunchbox was to be found.

"I'll dash to one of the department stores first thing in the morning," I told him, "and I'll have it for you by eleven." The which I did.

The high moment arrived. James, accompanied by mother, brother, grandmother and great aunt, no less, set out by car for the school, twenty yards distant.

"Good morning, James," said the teacher pleasantly, holding out her hand. James Mathew Corbin took one long look at her, and bolted for the door, followed by an embarrassed entourage. He returned in the afternoon, but "with the kids, mom - not the girls' just the boys…." Mothers and grandmothers and great aunts have a lot to learn about small boys, I find.

But - to return to the "back to school" wardrobe - "I want a yellow raincoat like Michael's," he invariably stated; Michael, two years his senior, symbolizes the epitome of our James. His mother found him the yellow slicker, with a hat to match.

"I hope the whole year's rainy," James announced happily, "only the mornings, though, Byrne," he added as he noted his small brother's stricken expression at the prospect of a year of rain. His small brother, incidentally, is chartreuse with envy. "You'll go next year," James tells him patronizingly, "when you are a big boy…" "We'll be in our new house, and I'll have to cross Liberty Street by myself." Said James, "but Ellen, the Police Lady will help me; she helps all the kids." "Eleanor," corrected Byrne, "Mrs. Murch," said their mother reprovingly. "The lady across the street calls her Eleanor," said Byrne.

"How many more days, mom?" asks James daily. He's ready and impatient. His "physical" is behind him. It, too, was an experience. Mother, who is expecting a baby sister, found it necessary to visit her doctor on the day of James' scheduled examination. Grandmother proved to be an adequate pinch hitter, and we set out for the doctor's.

James literally swaggered from the car to the doctor's waiting room. "You will have to stay here," he told his brother. "you can't come into the doctor's office with me. You're not going to school. Don't worry, though," he added comfortingly, 'You'll be five next year."

The eye test was a classic. "Now, Jim," said the doctor, "tell me whether the table legs are pointing up or down. "Up." Said James, and "Down," for the first two symbols on the chart. Suddenly he changed his tactics.

Saying absolutely nothing, he pointed with an offhand finger up or down as the case might have been - a young man of few words, our James.

"No shots, I hope," he managed to say, however. The shot was endured bravely, however, and our schoolboy emerged from the doctor's office clutching the school record he insisted on carrying himself. "How many days now, mom?" he asks a least once in every twenty-four hours. "I'll be real smart when I go to school," he adds. "I'll read big fat books to you, Byrne, with stories in them like the "Three Bears," and the "Three Squirrels," and the "Three Snakes," and the "Three Little Pigs" - whole bunches of stories I'll read to you." "That will be keen, Jim," says his smaller brother. Yes, our James is ready for Kindergarten. "He looks so darling in little shorts," I said, as his mother announced she was off to shop for those "Back to school" clothes he was demanding. And then grandmother learned another lesson. Conformity begins at five. "Mother," said Gael, "they don't wear shorts to school." "I want long white pants like the other kids," said James. "Long white pants?" I repeated incredulously. "He means those light coloured chinos," said Gael. Yes, he's ready now for kindergarten - chinos, slicker, certificate and all. Our boy's babyhood is - behind him! - Shucks…

9-17-72   KINDERGARTEN

Gregory Scott Corbin, the youngest of the Metayer grandchildren has just completed his first week of kindergarten. There is something traumatic about sending the baby of the family off to school for the very first time-traumatic for his parents and grandparents, that is. There was nothing traumatic about the experience for Master Gregory Corbin. For weeks previously he had been happily anticipating the event; and planning his off-to-school wardrobe.

Greg adores clothes, and so his "outfits" (to quote him) for this all important adventure were of paramount importance. He had worn a new and particularly handsome suit for his graduation from "Library School" last June, and had requested then that his mother "put it away for Kindergarten."

"You didn't see my graduation outfit, you know," Greg had said seriously to the grandmother who was pipping about the country in the family travel trailer at the time of that momentous happening. "You will be surprised, won't you?" I agreed immediately to be TOTALLY surprised.

Greg's mother, who also adores clothes, had been busily shopping for his school "outfits" for weeks; with her small son insisting upon trying on everything she purchased - even to socks and underwear.

Mother had been assembling back to school "outfits" for Greg's two older brothers as well, but with a different reaction from these seasoned students. She had selected jackets and trousers and shirts and ties to carefully coordinated as to guarantee to produce a vision of sartorial elegance-a vision that impressed her ten and eleven year old sons not in the least. "Do we HAVE to go with you, Mom? They had wailed. "Why do we have to try things on? Can't you just buy what you like? It'll fit. You know our sizes…" etc. etc. etc.

Well, now the days of summer vacation were over, and the eventful day - Gregory Scott arrived; and though he had been assigned to the afternoon class, the young man's parents had awakened at dawn to his triumphant cry, "THIS IS THE DAY!"

Big brothers Jim and Byrne were all for accompanying him to Kindergarten. "For something as important as this you could get us excused for a half hour or so, you know," they told their mother. The pair had been on hand for Greg's graduation from Library School.

Grandmother naturally planned to be in the entourage. "Don't tell Grandma how I look in my OUTFIT." Greg had said to his mother as they headed for Arthur street; and almost before daughter Gael had applied the brakes to the family car her small son was racing up the front steps of Grandmother's ménage two at a time. "Grandma!" he was crying. "Wait till you SEE me!" He looked a perfect doll in that graduation from Library School "outfit" he had so carefully hoarded; and clutched in his hand was the little Walt Disney lunchbox "without a thermos because I don't need one" for which his grandparents had searched so madly. "I have my SNACK," said Greg. "He packed it himself," laughed his mother as our angel opened the lunchbox to reveal a nice slice of cheese, four crackers and a couple of Oreos for dessert.

Grandpa wanted to know, "Oh, gosh, no" said his mother. "He was far too excited to eat." "Well," said Grandma firmly, "You had better have a sandwich before leaving." Greg parked his little lunchbox importantly beside him and seated himself at the table while Grandmother headed for the refrigerator. "Grandma," he said suddenly, dramatically. "LEAVE THE CRUSTS ON MY BREAD; DON'T CUT THEM OFF!" His mother and grandmother looked pointedly at one another. Greg's failure to eat crusts had been a bone of contention in the family for years. Well, now we were to watch delightedly as one small boy who, now that he was entering Kindergarten, had decided to grow up all the way, TOSSED DOWN HIS CRUSTS AS THOUGH HE HAD BEEN DOING IT ALL HIS LIFE!

We were to have other evidences of Greg's sudden maturity. Having taken our young man to the front door of the school, we had expected to pick him up there. The Kindergarten class, however, was to be dismissed through the rear door and by the time we had discovered the fact, Scott Corbin was nowhere to be seen. He had gone home with his sister, said the concerned teacher; and now WE were concerned for Gregory HAS NO SISTER. "Oh, dear," said his worried mother, "And he was doing so well." He had marched into school like he'd been doing it forever. "Now this could spoil everything. We promised him we'd be here waiting for him when he came out. We were in for another pleasant surprise however. Frightened to death our gregory was not. He had simply told his 'sister' a dear little neighborhood child where he lived and he was waiting happily for us when we arrived there. "Hi, Mom!" he called merrily. "You came to the wrong door, huh?" "Hi, Grandma!" "Were you the smartest one in the class?" we asked him as Greg recounted in detail the glorious events of the day. "No." he said, "And I wasn't the BEST RESTER either. But I am BIG! Oh, and here -put away my lunchbox until next year. "We aren't allowed to bring any FOOD to school." Gregory's achievements during the past week have been many and varied. He has drawn a tree with a house and a garage and a huge big sun smiling down upon the whole with a smile that matches his own. And he has played OPEN AND SHUT "Just like in Library School!" And a game with a blindfold where you have to guess whether the other children are up or down and I was right; I guessed they were up and they were....and we played other games too; and we drawed a puddle and we might put FEET in it tomorrow!" The brand new Kindergartener babbled on happily. "And, Grandma - do you know something! If you want to TALK in school, you have to raise your hand like this! And, oh yes - we have this song like - and it says. "Together, together, together every day; Share your work and share your play..." And do you know we have a LIBRARY right next to my class. A ROOM that is a LIBRARY..."

And so the youngest of the Metayer grandchildren has become a schoolboy and even as she smiles at his delight in this fascinating fact, Grandmother finds herself brushing away a tear.

10-20-74 LADY IN THE HOUSE

I'll be a different kind of "Rep" from all the Reps you know…
To be sure, each day at dawning to the State House I shall go;
And I'll sit with all the greybeards; and I'll help to make the laws;
And when people's rights are threatened - why, I'll champion
    their cause.

I'll be dedicating monuments; and sitting down to tea
With first ladies of the Commonwealth; I'll even get to see
At close range historic visitors to this, our Sovereign State;
And - to make a spot of history myself may be my fate…

But-meanwhile - along with all the "State House" things that
    I must do
I'll be dashing home to take a slightly different point of view…
There'll be dinner to be cooked; and grocery shopping to be done.
As MALE legislators end their day, why, I'll have just begun

To catch up with matters distaff, each delightful household chore
That no female, though a "Rep," can e'er consistently ignore….
I'll be vacuuming and dusting, even though, it seems, my mind
Simultaneously is wrestling with the problems of mankind.

I'll be piling high the groceries, being painfully aware
As I do of all the burdens today's shoppers have to bear
And - as I view my checkbook with the thought of paying the bills
I'll identify completely with each poor homemaker's ills,

But, dear friends, as I regard things, this will be a PLUS, you see
'Cause the problems YOU are facing will be faced each day
    by ME!
Yes, I'll be a different kind of "Rep" from all those Reps you know;
To be sure, each day at dawning to the State House I shall go.

But, JUST BECAUSE I AM A WOMAN, I'm convinced my
   point of view
May be closer to the one that's shared by YOU and YOU and
   YOU.
My all-important CONSTITUENTS...

G.C.H.S.

Lady Moon
I am watching you
Lady moon, from my window, seeing
Your liquid silverness
Gliding thru the night,
Feeling
Your soft silence whispering
On my cheek,
You are all gleaming, like
A thousand lamps,
Lofty Lady, and
Your beam-children steal
Across my isle of dreams
To awaken me
And see!
You lie against the night, a
Tiny, glowing pool
On blackness,
And
The stars that caress you smile
At me -
They are so near to you,
Lovely Lady,
And I -
So far away.

E.A. Nener

9-28-69 LAMENT

Where, oh where has the summer went?
Spring came just yesterday, and the scent
Of New England May time was the air…
Ahead lay the summer, firm and fair.
So what happened to June? Why, it simply flew,
And the summer's face was no longer new;
And July, with its heat, left New Englander's beat!
To the sea we all flocked in a hasty retreat
From the scorchings that August invariably brings…
So what happened right then? Why, THAT month
Sprouted wings!

"Ah, well,": we opined, as the Calendar high
We consulted to learn that the autumn was nigh,
"There are wonderful days in September! We'll pip
To the neighborhood beach as in summer-to dip
our most ladylike toes in the briny and cool
what remains of the summer heat, now that in School
All our darlings are tucked, and we've leisure to roam,
For too soon 'twill be winter, and time to stay home…"
It all sounded so nice, and we say it each year
As a farewell to summer we bid with a tear
In the eyes that are set in a bronzed summer face
We've secured by just lolling all over the place…
And so, what happened next??? Though the weatherman
Said "Twould be wondrous and warm, real beach weather-
Instead the thermometer dipped, and then cold air moved in
Whistle New England's poor weatherman did a tailspin…
Now we wonder, as fall turns our world burnished gold-
Does time really fly faster, or are we growing old???

5-12-66 LEAGUE OF WOMEN VOTERS L.W.V. OF BRAINTREE ANNUAL MEETING

Your president presided at each meeting, all year through;
At each scheduled State League function, she was representing
   you.
She attended every conference, and the workshops, one and all.
While her days were very busy, she assuredly had a ball!
Now, the year that we are ending is indeed a banner one;
We've accomplished many miracles; had an awful lot of fun!
We've grown close and dear with doing; it's inevitable, I guess
That a group of people, caring, must find common happiness.
We've shared joys and confidences; we've accomplished things,
   it seems,
That we never thought we'd manage as we dreamed those wild
   old dreams…

When you're President, yours is indeed a very happy task;
In the light of all your gals unique achievements - why, you bask.
With another year now ending, and another job well done,
May I pause a while to thank my lively Leaguers, every one.

First - an ORCHID to a gal; Eleanor Callahan her name -
Who may very proudly wear it for her special claim to fame…
She's the one who first decided that a League was indicated
In our Town; she up and got us all together…The town waited
While we worked and while we labored to achieve that full
   League status.
Now our Eleanor may stand erect and catch bouquets thrown
   at us!
And a pretty PATIENT LUCY for dear Mary, League Advisor;

I can't think of any lady who is knowinger or wiser…
Now that we've achieved full status, our Consultant she's
    become;
With our Mary still beside us, we'll just naturally hum.
When she joined us, Mary set up such a program that we
    staggered;
But-my gosh - we waded through it…She'll not stand for any
    laggard.
Dear, dear Mary, we do thank you, and we owe you such a lot.
In our little old League annals, you will never be forgot…
A red rose for our own Jul, First Vice President de luxe;
As the Chairman of our Finance Drive, she sure brought in
    the bucks…
Then our Budget Chairman she became; took on another
    chore;
And now we know that thanks to Jul, next year we must ask
    more…
She's the gal who does our auditing, and counsels us on
    spending.
A Jul whose dedication to our League has been unending.
An OREINTAL POPPY to Joanne, who's next in line;
As our peppy Second Vice President, she surely has been fine.
Foreign Economic Policy our gal's handled with aplomb;
While U.N. she's tried to strengthen as a bulwark 'gainst the
    bomb.
Now a study of Red China, its relation to us all
Has been voted at Convention; she'll be leading us, come
    fall….
A daisy that won't tell for our own dear Gert LaBelle.
As a Secretary, she has surely handled things quite well
She's the gal who takes the minutes, writes the letters, spends
    the hour
Making copies of each record for the endless State League
    Powers.
She's been adept and obliging in a hundred happy ways;
So today, we would salute her, may she know more happy days…

Now a tulip to our Evie, who is guardian of our money;
Why, she'll let us spend a quarter with a mien sweet and sunny.
But, quite confidentially, ladies, though we'd hate to have this
    known,
She'd be freer by a million, were our treasury her own.
How meticulously, ladies, she records our every dime;
Gosh, we hope she'll stay our Treasure until the end of time.
A pink rose for our Rose Jordan; she's the Voters Service gal;
And for servicing our voters, she'd be hard to parallel;
She's had voter's registration; sent Town Meeting Members letters,
At each FinCom Public Hearing, that they all might function
    better.
She's made phone calls quite unnumbered; held a fine
    Candidates' Meeting;
At the big L.B.M. Seminar, her committee did the greeting.
Gosh, it seems like Voters Service carries on the whole year
    through.
Yes, indeed, dear Mrs. Jordan, it's a big pink rose for you…
Now, I think we'll pin a lily on our Press Chairman, Glad;
For the purest kind of P.R. is the kind that we have had.
If there's any Braintree resident who has yet to learn we're here
Why, it can't be blamed on Gladys; she's announced it far and
    near.

And a LILY for the apportionment portfolio she chaired;
She discussed it in such depth that every state's sick soul was bared.
When we read of Dirksen's fractured hip - we know how much
    she loved him-
Why we couldn't help but wonder- do you spose our Gladys
    shoved him???

And a HYACINTH quite gay for the gal who sailed away
Several sorry months ago; we were loath to let her go.
Human Resources is her pet; our Ann Brandt we can't forget.
She's at large in sunny Spain; may she not too long remain.
Now - what else? A WATER LILY for our own Leaguer Priscilly

Who guards our Town's water table in a manner bright and able;
Her portfolio, you know, is Water Resources, so
We've all learned, yes, one and all
Just what happens to that fall
Of delightful April rain now that spring is here again;
How we must conserve our water and our land; we really oughta.
Yes, a LILY for Priscilly - must admit this verse sounds silly…
For Peg Grabosky, a jonquil fair; she was Chairman of our
    Town Study, rare
She handled our Education Portfolio too, with efficient
    dispatch, I'm here to tell you.
She's reported on Regional Council affairs; in a manner
    suggesting she really cares.
She's handled portfolios really complex. Here's a gal who
    deserves her jonquil - NOW NEXT
A pert little pansy, smiling and sweet for our Structure of Gov't
    Chairman petite'
Our own Marge Biber; She's handled Home Rule and its study
    in a way that proclaims her a jewel.
Now she's also our Referenda Chairman, with action galore.
So-a PANSY to Marge, who sure knows the score…
ROSEMARY to ROSEMARY, our Bulletin Editor; when
    dealing with news, she's almost a predator;
She'll hound you for items; editorials write; run off the stencils
    at weird times of night.
Our Town Booklet she designed, helped to finance it, too.
Yes, ROSEMARY to Rosemary; own a lot, dear, to you.
A CARNATION to Emma, our Legislative Leaguer; few gals
    more enthusiastic; few ladies more eager;
Her 7 Offboard Chairmen she keeps well aware of activity
    brewing at the State House up there.
She eyes vital bills; public hearings attends.
Legislation's her love; and her love never ends.
A big bright bouquet full of all kinds of flowers for a gal who's
    invested billions of hours

In fostering membership… Jo Sharp's her name; and believe me, our gal has a big claim to fame;

For our membership dipped to a low 32 e'er it plummeted skyward to 65

Jo- thank you!

To the gal who handles our N.C.R.s, Peg Wallace, a fragrant carnation is yours,

For sending out bulletins all the year through, and arranging our meeting with other Leagues, too,

When for Congressman Burke she played hostess with pride; Lucky old

N.C.R.S with our Peg as their guide.

A LILAC, I think, for our Janet, the one handling all Publications, a duty well done.

Another, perhaps, for developing leaders in discussion techniques; we surely did need her.

When she came our way, this fair leaguer de luxe, she pounced on our problem and got at the crux

Of the matter, and gosh, we were soon on our way; her decision to join us was our Red Letter Day

To Penny, a BLUEBELL as bright as her eyes; when this gal came our way, we sure got a prize;

For she taught us of Units, - what pleasure! what fun! What supreme satisfaction in a Unit well done…

You know, Penny is moving from out our fair town; each time I remember, the thought gets me down.

We'll miss her, believe me; she'll be hard to replace. Yes - a bluebell for Penny, bright as her shining face.

Now, for our OFFBOARD CHAIRMEN, a penny each for their efforts in trying to dutifully teach

Our fair Leaguers the fine fundamentals of things such as State Civil Service; Carolyn Gale fairly sings

As this subject she discusses; then the System comes through at the hands of Betty McGowan, who has brought it to you.

Celia Sniffin of Constitutional Rights can proclaim; yes, these Leaguers may properly lay claim to fame.

You know, each gal who received this mythical award, has been a fair member of our fine League board.

But really, there's one who, though having no post on our Board is deserving of praise quite the most.

She is our Winnie Tarnor; she phones us each time a League happening happens - she's there on the line.

So-a TULIP, I think, of a bright shiny hue, I'll present to our Winnie, she's bright shiny, too

I think that perhaps a DAFFODIL sweet, I would like to bestow on each Leaguer I meet.

For you're all in the Club, and you're all doing fine, keeping League and its program securely in line.

Now, I wish I'd been able to really bestow all these flowers upon you, but ladies you know,

This kind of thing really is not the League way… "It just isn't done in the League," Mary'd say.

So we'll have to pretend that you each wear a flower. If you did, it would probably fade in an hour.

Now this way, just remaining a mythical bloom, though its fragrance will never quite sweeten the room,

It must stay firm and fresh in our minds' eyes, so now, wear it with pride;

You're terrific, gals…WOW…

9-22-74   LEASH LAW

In my door-to-door campaigning, when the sun shone or twas raining,

Why - I learned one thing - THE LEASH LAW REALLY WORKS!

And our Dog Officer Dawes sure does save one from the jaws of those canines and his duty never shirks…

Fort that van of his is racing as some crisis he is facing from one end of Braintree Town unto the other;

And though fines he now must levy, o'er the town he has a
    bevy of admirers who would gladly call him brother....
For what joy it is to walk now...to ring doorbells and to talk
Now....knowing daddy's nice Great Dan is a safely tied
Where his jaws they cannot reach one...Door-to Dooring
    now is GREAT
fun...almost every dog in town is tucked inside...
So-THREE CHEERS FOR THE LEASH LAW! AND
    FOUR OR FIVE FOR OUR OWN BOB DAWES! (and
    his intrepid assistant.)

3-24-68   LEGISLATOR

I am a town Meeting member. I have been given a voice in the conduct of our town's affairs by the finest people I know - my neighbors...I am their voice and their representative, I and my fellows have been termed by our town moderator the "legislators" of the town.

This is a sacred responsibility, as important as the responsibility that faces legislators on the state and national level; more so, actually, because I am more closely involved with the operation of my town, I live here. My roots are firm and fast in the soil of Braintree.

This is Town Meeting time, and as the Town Meeting progresses, I think a great deal (and dream a little) about the future of this town in which I have elected to live; and as a Town Meeting member, I make certain resolves.

I shall do my "home work" even more thoroughly next year. I shall attend every public hearing at which warrant articles are discussed - EVERY public hearing - and I shall attend with an open mind, I shall arrive at a decision on the basis of the merits of the case as presented there, and with the welfare of my constituents and of the town as a whole always in mind.

I SHALL not bow to the expediency of the moment, but shall bear in mind any and all eventualities that may arise as a result of my action, for I hope to live and die in Braintree.

I shall attend every session of the Town Meeting unless it is physically impossible for me to do so; and I shall remain on hand for the entire evening, so that my recorded presence will be an actual voting one.

I shall vote either pro or con on every issue.

I shall not use the device of abstaining from voting, because inherent in this action will be the implication that I lack the courage of my convictions - indeed that I lack convictions - or even courage!

I SHALL BOW GRACEFULLY ALWAYS TO THE WILL OF THE MAJORITY, FOR THAT IS THE DEMOCRACTIC AMERICAN WAY: right or wrong, the MAJORITY MUST PREVAIL!

And I shall refrain from mental criticism of those whose legislative philosophies differ from my own.

In short, I shall attempt to the fullest extent of my ability to perform the duties inherent in my oath of office, and to "Legislate" with wisdom and forethought and sincerity, and in the best interests of the constituents whom I represent, and of the town as a whole, for therein lies my dedicated duty...The role of a "legislator" is not an easy one to play; leadership never is easy....

4-28-74   LET IT BE SAID

I READ THIS POEM AT HER FUNERAL JUN 10TH, 1998

Let it be said of me that laughter came quite freely to my lips;
That tears quite seldom found a pathway to my eyes;
That when I faced the dying of a day;
And knelt beside my bedside for to pray;
I found with joy that with the setting sun
I counted some one kindness freely done.
Let it be said of me that ALWAYS I was kind;
And seldom cries of rancor left behind;
That for my fellow man I truly cared;
That when my courage counted, I had dared;
That those I loved were many and diverse;
That other considerations than my purse

Directed all the spending of my gold;
That to my neighbors' wants I was not cold.
Let it be said of me that I stood firm and strong
When life's grey problems came my way along;
That every single day I smiled at life
And at the gentle man with whom, as wife
I shared much more of laughter than of tears
As, side by side, we marched down all the years...
Let it be said as Mother I was fond;
That time was served to strengthen this dear bond;
That grandsons look my way with love and joy
As I have loved their coming, each sweet boy...
Then - most importantly - let it be said of me
I walked serenely toward Eternity,
For then as woman, mother and as wife
Shall I have earned the beauty of my life...

2-11-68   LET'S PLAY FAIR

WE'VE COME a long long way in our dealings with the Mass, Bay Transit Authority since the days when the teams they sent to Braintree to discuss proposed rapid transit routes professed not even to know the signals...

And the only plans that were ever open to inspection by the citizenry were those steered our way through the good offices and sheer authority of a powerful Legislator; or the journalistic detective work of the coal newspaper...

For a variety of reasons, the MBTA has decided to play fair with the people of Braintree; they are, in fact, carrying this sense of fair play to a degree of which even WE who made the demands for fairness, never dreamed...

Right now, the proposed plan for Braintree may be found in our Selectmens' office; and it is available for any town official to see and examine at his leisure - ANY town official, not just a chosen few...

The MBTA took some convincing that the best approach to their problem in Braintree was the open approach, "Only the dissenters ever show up at a public meeting," they insisted, "or the ones through whose back yards the trains will run…"

Share your problems with the people," we begged, "Drop the secrecy bit and at least identify your problems in dealing with our area. People are more understanding than you think."

So now, where do we stand? Here is the MBTA about to share its problems and their possible solutions with the people of the town. It was OUR idea; it came from the Braintree side of the table at M.A.P.C.

THEREFORE - Let's play fair!

Let's give the MBTA every opportunity to present their plan, and to defend their plan; to identify their problems; and to take YOU, the PEOPLE, in to their confidence all the way!

THEN - if you honestly feel that they haven't tried hard enough; if, after careful consideration and in all sincerity you feel that you cannot live with the solution they propose

…THEN ask, them to end the line at Capen's Bridge; or, if you decide you don't want the rapid transit extension to come to Braintree at all, ask them to stop dead in Quincy

…THEN consider taking action….

Meanwhile, the ideal is, of course, to run the entire facility underground, leaving our town untouched; that's what WE want. The economical easy way is to run the entire facility on an elevated structure through the heart of the town; this the MBTA wanted.

In the middle is a compromise sort of plan that evolved as a result of give and take on both sides of the table. This plan is what the MBTA now proposes to show and to defend before you, the people of Braintree.

THEY are playing fair! They are sending a key Authority man to spend a full week in our Town Hall, where he will be pleased to answer any and all engineering questions proposed by town officials, representatives of town organizations, and JUST PLAIN CITIZENS- YOU, the PEOPLE!

In addition to this, they propose to hold a public hearing where Braintree-ites will be permitted to speak their minds…

ONLY THEN, incidentally, will the town officials responsible for the decision making…OUR SELECTMEN….even think in terms of committing the town to the plan.

Yes, the MBTA is playing fair. Can WE be any less fair in dealing with an Authority which DOES have the power to run the line through Town Hall if it sees fit??? How about it, Braintree? LET US ALSO PLAY FAIR!

10-14-73 LIBRARY SCHOOL

Story Hour, or "Library School" as it is invariably called by the 3½ to 5 year olds who seriously and self-importantly gather each Friday morning at the Watson Park Library, got underway once again last week.

More than seventy little "eligibles" had been on hand the previous Friday morning, their hearts in their wonderful wide eyes, as they and their parents sought hopefully to secure a place among the fifty "Students" with whom we begin our Story Hour each school year. I had wondered whether some of them had spent the night there as I arrived at 8:20 for the scheduled nine o'clock registration to find a waiting queue that in sheer length would have done justice to the queuing British…

This year we had decided to assign numbers as the little ones entered the room-25 tickets in black for the nine-fifteen class and 25 in blue for ten-thirty. Many of our Story Hour mothers, you see, have smaller children, a fact which in the past has impeded their progress to the registration line so that in some instances the LAST (to arrive) turned out to be FIRST, and the first failed to make it.

Dotting the line here and there were little Story Hour alumni, those not quite old enough to Kindergarten this year, and there were hugs and kisses all around as they recognized their wonderful librarian, Mrs. Nightengale and this "teacher" of theirs. By 9:05 the tickets had all been distributed and those who had to be turned away were regarding us with disbelief. "But the paper said nine o'clock; we're only five minutes late!" The mothers chorused. "Of course we'll go on the waiting list but is there any chance of one of the children dropping out???" (There really isn't…)

But now to place the spotlight on Friday last when Story Hour was officially to begin. The little ones began to arrive, small sweet Christina Raniert, as always, among the first. The "alumni" dashed smartly to occupy their favorite chairs, the newcomers to bid a slightly more reluctant goodbye to mothers whose eyes, here and there, had a misty look. Soon every seat was filled and the three volunteer teachers, your columnist and Braintree Point Woman's Club President Mrs. Joseph Spano with Vice President Mrs. Joseph Feeney, faced a brand new Story Hour year. A fourth member of the staff, Mrs. Maurice Cristoforo had been persuaded not to sacrifice a week's trip to the Pennsylvania Dutch Country on the Library School altar. She would be back next week.

STORY HOUR opening…the record of attendance went without a hitch. Only in one or two cases would our little ones fail to respond with a nice round "Here!" when called upon. And with new little student Lisa Avery holding the flag in true parade fashion for the nine-fifteen group and alumna Elizabeth Aldorisio (we do things alphabetically in turn) for the ten-fifteen class, Old Glory was saluted in solemn style. The LIBRARY LAUGHING SONG next saw our Story Hour Alumni really coming to life as they patronized those not yet acquainted with this bit of our procedure.

Their enthusiasm as a matter of fact, had to be curbed lest the sound disrupt the speaker who was addressing Story Hour mothers in the auxiliary room not far away.

It was in the SHOW AND TELL that followed, however, that our little ones-new and old – really began to shine. This is a sequence in which the small fry who have brought toys with them may come to the front of the class and "share" them with their friends "For it is so much more fun when one SHARES a toy, is it not?" A very few of our Story Hour children had brought toys to this first meeting, however the questions, asked of each child, "And what did you do this past summer that was fun?" brought forth a variety of enchanting answers. All had, needless to say, "swimmed" or "swum" or "swam"…(They were never quite sure which…) "at the beach…in the big waves…in the pool…in my cousin's pool…in my uncle's pool…in Robbie's pool…" There had been boat rides and trips to the zoo, "Did you ever see a real live kambaroo, teacher? He jumps high as the sky…" and to the park and the lake…There were vacations in the country… "Vermont is the country," contributed small Lisa Forrest who had moved to Braintree from that lovely state barely a year ago…

What fun next to form a parade and march single file to the music of Souza, a flag or a drum in the hands of each small child, a look of delight on each small face…And then it was STORY TIME! With the preponderance of squirrels about Braintree, I had selected the tale of the good little squirrel who gathered and buried his nuts and acorns faithfully according to instructions from Mother Squirrel while his two naughty brothers played upon the high wires that crisscrossed the town.

They tossed their acorns down upon the heads of unsuspecting doggies who passed below; and they leaped from branch to branch of the big high chestnut tree instead of tucking its rich red fruit carefully away against the coming of winter. Needless to say, these naughty ones were unprepared for the storms that raged and the winds that blew and the snows that covered the landscape come wintertime…Their good brother, you will be happy to know, saved the day for them. He snatched them from starvation but only at the very last moment, and only when they promised never again to romp and play come summertime.

The small fry listened, wide-eyed, and promised to report any and all "good" squirrels they see busily at work this coming week…And now it was time to test the prowess of our diminutive students with the inevitable flash card routine, with a set at first that contained merely the letters of the alphabet, to be followed by one with a combination of the letters and pictures of articles beginning with each letter portrayed. Wow! Did these little ones shine??? Three cheers for "Sesame Street" and the Electric heater and Mr. Rogers and the rest…T.V. does have SOME advantages!

Story Hour was brought to a close with the distribution of the library books and a discussion of the care and maintenance of same. "What DON'T we do to library books?" "We don't tear them.

We don't write in them. (Small shakes of sober heads…) We don't color the pictures. We don't drop them in mud puddles. We don't let little brothers or sisters take them. (My brother TORE my sister's book. He DID, really…)." The "don'ts" went on and on as our volunteer teachers removed the pretty little autumn leaf name tags that had been so carefully made by Miss Joan Perrow, the nice new addition to our Watson Park Library staff.

And so another year of "Library School" has begun and some of the little ones who had come in almost diffidently could be seen to swagger a bit as they filed out to join their waiting mothers.

They were in SCHOOL! "Didn't I tell you?" said small Brain Hickey to a fellow classmate. "Didn't you like it? And we have a Halloween Party and Christmas Party and Santa Claus REALLY comes!"

Brian himself happens to be a newcomer to Story Hour; his sister, however, had come before him and so Brian knows the ropes…

"Next week I'm gonna bring a baseball bat and a ball!" "I'm gonna bring my doll!" "I'm bringing my fire engine!" It went on and on… Promises to be another FUN year, this Story Hour! Don't you always get returns in spades when you extend yourself for the benefit of others??? Hurrah for VOLUNTEER SERVICE!

6-7-70   LITTLE LEAGUERS

THE LITTLE League season, they tell me, is half over. It's been wonderful fun bundling up into everything wearable in the old family closet and heading for Watson Park these evenings to watch the Metayer grandchildren make like candidate for the Red Sox.

Bundling up, incidentally, is literally what we spectators do, for there are few places on earth colder than Watson Park these nice nippy spring evenings when the salt water river that hugs its shoreline and mists that rise form the marsh beyond conspire to make of it the coolest spot in town for that great American sport.

Winter coats, once carefully stored away for the season, dot the bleachers hither and yon; and even that beach blanket the family plans to utilize shortly on the sands of nearby Swift's Beach makes an occasional appearance around adult knees.

The games are delightful to watch however, and it's astonishing to note the improvement in these small boys, many of whom were AT sea as well as BY it last year. And where this columnist once headed like a homing pigeon for the editorial page of the local newspaper, now it's the sports section. "Are our boys mentioned this week???"

The Little Leaguers themselves - each and every one of them - appear to be enthralled with the national pastime. Seldom separated from those all-important jerseys and caps that identify them with their particular teams, they can be seen all over town practicing for all they are worth, hitting frequently tired and elderly baseballs as though their very lives were at stake; and needless to say following the performance of their idols, the Red Sox, like they never followed it before.

The adult segment of the Little League program appears to be equally involved. What fun it is to watch fathers managing and coaching, and mothers merrily keeping score!

Incidentally many are the tales of Little League that come the way of those "regulars" who, night after night, head for Watson Park after gulping down a ridiculously early dinner! TALES LIKE THE FOLLOWING…

JOHN SMITH, (we'll call him that because it couldn't possibly be his name) the manager of one of the thousand or so Little League teams about town, is a very charming young man. Outgoing and personable, he prides himself upon the fine relationship he enjoys not only with the small fry on his team, but also with their parents…

The Little League season lay dead ahead as Mr. Smith and his family drove into a nearby Dairy Queen for ice cream. "Hi," said a pleasant voice from a nearby car. "How are you today?"

Mr. Smith rolled down his window and looked across to where a young man sat smiling. "Aren't you the manager of the Little League team?" asked the smiling one. "Yes, I am," said Mr. Smith gaily. Now Mr. Smith had recognized his neighbor as the father of one of his team members, however in his split second encounter he was totally unable to identify him with any one of his small boys. Not so Mr. Smith's son and heir who from the back seat of dad's car was taking everything in.

We have said before that Mr. Smith is charming; he is. And so, summoning his most gracious manner, he said pleasantly, "Well, we had our last batting practice today; and we'll play our first big game tomorrow." He smiled warmly.

"As a matter of fact," he said almost confidentially, "I just got through making out the batting order. Your son is…" Mr. Smith paused while he struggled madly to line up his new found friend with one of his little ball players. He simply couldn't'. The pause lengthened until into it leaped Junior from the back seat of the car - Junior who, eating drinking and sleeping baseball as he does knows everything about everything and everybody connected with the sport.

"LAST!" he said cheerily…All of Mr. Smith's charm faded… "Well," said the father of the last" batter, trying hard to suppress a grin that threatened to engulf, "I guess he isn't too good…"

"Why in the world is dad mad at me???" wailed the small boy who being very young, has yet to learn that candor isn't for always… "I just told the truth. HE IS LAST!"

12-10-72   MADAME ZARA

"Bibs," purred the soft telephone voice of my friend Ethel a couple of weeks ago, "We're having our Christmas Bazaar at Heritage Lane on December 2. Will you come and tell fortunes for us???

Do your 'MADAME ZARA' bit????" Heritage Lane, for the uninformed, is the pretty name that has been given to Braintree's new Housing for the Elderly couples.

"I'd be delighted to come," I said gaily and immediately…which is how Madame Zara happened to make an appearance in the development's nice trim recreation hall on that first December Saturday, complete with golden earrings, scarlet head scarf and all the other accoutrements of the Gypsy fortune teller she was gotten up to represent.

The Bazaar was a colorful and merry place. Twenty or thirty of the loveliest grey-haired ladies in Braintree were manning (Whoops! With Woman's Lib about town I'm almost afeared to use that word "manning" but shall we ever be asked to use "womanning"???) a series of tables on which were displayed a collection of handmades that rivaled anything we've seen at any Christmas Bazaar to date. These gals are a clever lot, Madame Zara concluded; and versatile to boot!

"Our goal," friend Ethel had said "is to raise money for our Christmas party. Of course we've only had nine weeks to plan the Bazaar," she added almost apologetically; and the inference was plainly, "You just wait till NEXT year…"

"Hurry, Madame Zara," she said, "I've already sold seventeen tickets. There are 17 ladies all waiting to have their fortunes told." I smiled to myself at the thought of those 17 dear little elderly ladies for whom the future still held intriguing prospects.

A table for the Gypsy had been placed in the corner of what was a most attractive room; and the Bazaar's shoppers were to be kept nicely at bay by a delightful gal, on hand to assist her seventy-years-young Mother at a table close by…a table incidentally that featured handsome Christmas gifts and other delightful tidbits. "I shan't eavesdrop myself, either," she had hastened to promise, her wide blue eyes twinkling in a round and perennially smiling face. (Incidentally she would later prove to be the Fair's best customer, piling her endless purchases in shopping bags upon the window sills behind her table to the all but complete obliteration of daylight). At any rate Madame Zara went speedily into her act as my friend Ethel's voice took on a decidedly new timber with a bellowed, "Number One for Madame Zara!" Number One…She was lovely indeed, this totally feminine little Dresden china kind of lady. "Why," I said, "I see a MAN in your life. He is grey-haired and is most anxious to perform little acts of kindness for you." A decided blush suffused the sweet little face that was turned so trustingly toward my own. "Yes," she said simply; and it was obvious that some eligible "bachelor" in the Heritage Lane complex knew a charming little lady when he saw one…

"Number Two for Madame Zara," called my friend Ethel next; and the race was on! The sight of a dear soul clutching fortune telling ticket No. 26 brought a feeling of apprehension to the Gypsy F.T. "Ethel," I called, "Don't sell anymore tickets until I catch up a little. I'll be here till midnight!" "Oh," said Ethel airily, her bright and beautiful blue eyes fixed on the cashbox, "Well, don't take so long with them. Make them short and sweet." "I CAN'T!" I said helplessly; AND I COULDN'T! One look into the warm loving trusting eyes of this dear little group for Braintree's elder stateswomen and Madame Zara wanted their fortunes to be long and beautiful indeed. She wanted to predict for them more happiness than they had ever known before…

And to be sure happiness WAS in their cards… loneliness in that group of pasteboards that represented times gone by, but happiness in present and future. There was really no need to consult the cards, for this happiness was written on the faces of just about every one of the beautiful elderly people for whom a brand new door on contentment had been opened with the key to a simple little apartment on Heritage Lane. "You're not lonely any more, are you?" The Gypsy fortune teller found herself asking constantly, "You've FRIENDS here. You're happier here than you've been in a long while, aren't you?" "Oh, yes," came the answer every time. "The Housing Committee has been so good to me," said one dear lady, tears filling her eyes as she inquired about the illness of her husband. "Its WONDERFUL here," said another. "We're all such good friends; and my neighbors are just lovely." "I have a real close friend," said a third. "We've only been friends since I came here but we're so alike and we spend such a lot of our time together. It's just lovely."

The day was one of pure delight, and no one at the Bazaar had more fun than did Madame Zara … proving her contention that to extend oneself for others in the community is to guarantee rich dividends every single time.

This is Heritage Lane's first Christmas; and what Christmas spirit it has already generated! SO- RISE TALL AND PROUD, you nice Town Meeting Members who helped to bring this complex into being! And take a big fat bow, you members of Braintree's Housing Committee for the Elderly and everyone else involved in the planning and execution of the new deal for the town's Senior Citizens.…Blessings must surely descend upon you all with so many happy septuagenarians and octogenarians wishing you well; and perhaps saying a prayer or two now and then for all of you…

And oh yes, these wonderful elderly ladies raised close to nine hundred dollars that nice December afternoon. Theirs should be a humdinger of a Christmas Party!

8-5-73   MAINE VACATION

Summertime..vacationtime…and is there any place in this great wide wonderful country of ours that lends itself more beautifully to vacationing than our own picturesque unique New England??? Take Maine, for instance…

The Metayers set out for that lovely state a week or so ago…for North Shapleigh, to be exact, where on beautiful Silver Lake, those former Braintree-ites, the Timmonses have settled down to live a veritable idyll in a spot that for sheer beauty is difficult to equal…Sliver Lake, a beautiful blue expanse of water with timber covered mountains for a backdrop…a lake fed by the spring rains and the winter snows that from time immemorial have flowed from the high Maine hills into the valley below.

It's a quiet place, this Silver Lake retreat that has so speedily become home for sister Gladys and her husband, Tim…a place of peace and rest and contentment, its shores largely untenanted.

Through the shiny blue of the water, a sandy floor silvers invitingly in the sun, calling all swimmers to explore the soft July warmth of its depths.

The Timmonses have a home directly fronting on the lake. Handsome white pines crown their private beach; and beside the pier a smart motor launch rides the waves that lap against the shores with a rhythm that is quiet when dependent solely upon the summer breeze, but can be moved to action by the passing of a speedboat with a water skier behind, or a motor launch, or the occasional canoe that glides by gracefully, close to shore.

We float about on our Aqua loungers, Glad and I, having first fastened them securely to dockside so that a book may be read or a catnap taken without fear of drifting off to sea. "The peace of the Lord be with you." I find myself quoting…for peace and the handiwork of the Lord are to be found on all sides in this enchanting place. Small wonder that brother-in-law Tim now boasts a perfect blood pressure…Tim, whose soaring readings have been sending his very dear friend, our beloved Doctor Keigan, into a tailspin for lo! these many years…

The peace of the day flows gently into nighttime at Silver Lake. The breeze from off the water is gentle and cooling. Sleep folds over one like a blanket, and it lasts and lasts for even the birds appear to have joined the ranks of late risers at Silver Lake, and why not??? With a whole big forest tossing in, they have no need to congregate outside one's bedroom window come dawn the way they do at home..

The evening itself has been a beautiful one, with the setting sun dropping like a flaming copper coin into the water's rim and a hundred whippoorwills sending their roundelay over the darkening hills as the moon commences to silver the water and outline against a star splashed sky the pines that are murmuring now as they toss their nighttime fragrance to the winds…

We walk across the lawn to the water's edge. We carefully avoid the tiny holes that here and there dot the grassy slope. "Golf?" I had asked when first I spotted them. Gladys had laughed aloud.

"Chipmunks," she had said airily. "Wait a bit. You'll see them." We did. They emerged from their underground domiciles to peer curiously at us quite as though they knew we did not belong in such close proximity to their dwelling places, then did an about face and all but took from the eager little hands of our small grandsons the potato chips they delighted holding out to them. Chipmunks with their bright and shiny eyes alight and those long straight tails waving like flags above their scamperings… Adorable small creatures…

Saturday evening, and we drive to Church over the pine and birch bedecked highways with- ahead of us - the mountains lying one against the other, their shades drifting from a green that is all but black to a silver gray that blends with the paling horizon that betokens the approach of night. We keep our eyes peeled for the deer that Jeanne, our youngest sister has reported seeing a short while back…Jeanne who had canoed over the water from her own summer place further up the lake, trailing her Aqualounger behind her so that she too might join in the peaceful and beautiful interlude of the floating and reading and laughing and reminiscing and generally having a ball that was to mark our summer afternoons at Silver Lake.

Need we say with what reluctance we turned our footsteps homeward come a Sunday morning, or how very much we would have liked to stay and stay and stay in Maine's North Shapleigh, there beside the warm sweet lake with all the mountains in the background and the lavish beauty of the bounteous Mother Nature on all sides??? Or how absolutely thrilled we were when grandson Byrne, the fisherman of the family, landed a bass from off the long pier's end that would have gladdened the heart of any adult fisherman we know??? Or that our boys can't wait to go to Auntie Glad's again or that we're now already planning for a long return when February's snows have made a veritable fairyland of beautiful North Shapleigh, and its Silver Lake is ice, and we may race upon the winds in Tim's new Snowmobile and mayhap skate upon the lake or ice fish in its depths…

Ah, Maine, what a beautiful state you happen to be…and what fun to have vacationed here this happy summer!

2-23-75   MAINE WINTER

SNOWMOBILING…It's fun with a Capital "F"! I learned the delightful fact over this past weekend, a weekend which the Metayers - Grandfather and Grandmother with daughter Gael and her Jim and those three wonderful grandsons of ours - spent with sisters Gladys and Jeanne in wonderful Maine's Shapleigh. The weekend was to prove a delightful one…and an adventurous one, thanks to SNOWMOBILING…

"You should come up during the winter," the "girls" had been saying for years. Shapleigh in winter is an incredibly beautiful place." It was… As a matter of fact; Shapleigh in winter turned out to be another world, a kind of lost and lovely and snowbound and silent world. We loved it!

En route to Maine and this dear little town of eight hundred or so in habitants, we found ourselves driving along winding snow sheathed roads…roads that had indeed been plowed but to limited avail. With the scarcity of traffic using them in this little lost corner of New England, snow has, we found, a happy habit of lingering on and on…

Along the way, huge pines were tossing ice-sheathed arms; and frail birch saplings bent beneath the snow's harsh touch to form low archways on the drifts. Mountains stood like sentinels on guard against a winter sky that sent slate fingers toward the sun. And on the earth was quiet, an incredible pregnant silence that went straight into one's soul..

Maine in winter is normally a cold, cold place. The "natives" had been playing the "numbers game," temperature-wise for weeks, we were to learn. "How cold was it at your place???" The favorite daily question of those rugged dear down Mainers, had elicited responses ranging from a net 20 below, to an anything but neat 30 below…Br-r-r-r!

One-upmanship being the order of the day in them thar parts; brothers-in-law Tim and John appeared to be as addicted to the art as any down homer. "John," said Tim by way of greeting one cold day last week as Jeanne and John returned from an overnight visit to Massachusetts, "You missed the COLDEST NIGHT OF THE YEAR!" He was triumphant, reports our John. "I couldn't argue. I wasn't there," said John. "he had me and I knew it!"

Happily for the Metayers, we too missed the coldest night of the year. As a matter of fact, Shapleigh must have ordered a heat wave in our honor, for though the overnight low had been 20 below, the thermometer was hovering around 34 above at eleven a.m. when we arrived; and happily enough, that delightful temperature was to be maintained during our entire stay.

So - what exactly did we do with those two lovely leisurely days in dear old Shapleigh? Well, we visited; and we played games; we went for long lovely walks down crunchy country lanes…and I rode a SNOWMOBILE!

"I have never been on a snowmobile," I announced almost immediately upon my arrival there, "and I can't wait for my first ride!"

As it turned out, I didn't have to. Out came the family Ski Doo; and into the latest in snowmobiling attire went brother-in-law Tim; and we were off and running…up over the mountain of snow that lined the highway; down over the sloping lawns of the family menage; and onto the snow-capped solidly frozen waters of a 116-acre lake that lay like a shining jewel as the sun found it…a jewel mounted in a setting to timber-covered mountains. A lake over which we were to fly at fifty miles an hour, with the wind turning cheeks and chin and nose to stone. Pines singing and neighboring snowmobilists shouting greetings…and all the world our oyster!

Yes, it's a whole new world indeed, this dear little corner of old Maine that now is Shapleigh. Friends dropping in for coffee and a chat, fur-hatted and fur-gloved; booted and bedecked; and full of those marvelous tall tales they've come to share with this most eager columnist...

This was February vacation week, for instance, and so from dawn to dusk the children in the area were at play upon the lake and all about. "Tar bucket week, we called it," said friend Marie, snowmobiling with her grandson and dropping by to say "Hello." "Back in South Portland when I was a child, I mean" she added. Tar bucket week," I repeated. "Why on earth tar bucket week??" I was naturally hoping for a Maine tall-tale and it came. "Well," said Marie, loosening her scarf and removing mittens and hat, "each year we kids would gather up the Christmas trees just as soon after Christmas as people began to put them out; and then off we'd go to Gavett's Field where we'd pile them to the sky." Gavett's Field, it developed, was close to Gavett's Pond. It had a bog around it and so was safe for the kind of yearly bonfire the small fry of South Portland was wont to light each merry February vacation. "Gosh," said Marie, "we'd carry those trees through the woods for miles; and then the night before George Washington's Birthday, we'd light the biggest bonfire you've ever seen. We'd use a bucket-of-tar to ignite it. The town supplied the tar. That's where the name "Tar Bucket Week' came in." Marie's eyes turned misty with remembering. "Gosh, it was fun," she said, "and it was pretty and safe with the bog around it. Everybody in the town turned out for the burning. They came tramping through the woods; and they skated on the pond;' and we kids cut long sticks and toasted marshmallows and hot dogs."

"Tar bucket week," said Marie again, softly. "That's funny, I haven't thought of it in years. Oh well," she said, "I must be off. I promised my grandchildren we'd take the snowmobiles into the woods and look for rabbit tracks and deer."

"Another world," I thought as off I watched them go. Shapleigh in the winter; IS INDEED an incredibly beautiful place. I loved my weekend there.

3-12-67 MARCH

March is a kind of special month; it rushes in and warms
The frozen-fast New England scene! (unless, like now, it storms…)
It roars like mighty lions; or it bleats like tiny lamb;
Dependent on its whim, which is precisely why I am
Just the slightest bare bit skittish every year, as neighbors say,
"Ah, at last the month of March has come! Watch winter slink
    away..
"Yes, March is a kind of special month; it slips right in between
The February frosting and the gay emerging green
Of sweet April's tearful greeting; and you'll all agree, I'm sure,
That this month of old St. Patrick has its special own allure.
Just last week, dear march arrived; from the calendar we tore
That old snowy February we had struggled to endure;
And we gave three rousing cheers; scores of high hip hip hoorays,
As we settled down to revel in the ever lengthening days.
But, by gosh, we look behind us to the week that has just passed
(And believe me, there were moments when we wondered if
    we'd last…)
And we shake a puzzled forelock, as we don that cap and scarf
That were part of winter clothing we had hoped to cut in half…
How could any month whose function is to usher in the spring
Drop so many winter bombshells, we're agog with wondering…
Do those tulips that were budding back in February, still
Sleep unravished 'neath their snow-shroud on the bosom of
    the hill?
Does the robin, winging northward, have the foggiest idea
Of the arctic wastes awaiting his fair first arrival here?
Will they really run like rivers to the sea, those tons of snow
That engulf our looted landscape? Will they really sometime go?
Is this actually March-month, with dear April dead ahead;
Or has something untoward transpired to mix things up instead?
Has Dame Nature made an error for the first time in her life,
Turning back the month, not forward, hurling winter's storm
    and strife

Once again upon New England? Will she soon relent and bring
Into proper pretty sequence the nice month that houses spring?
Gosh, we hope so! We are weary…It's been winter far too long…
Please, Dame Nature, please get with it…Send our way your
   Springtime Song!

10-24-65   CABBAGES OVER
LIGHTLY MEA CULPA

THERE are sins of sad commission;
There are sins of cool commission;
But-egad! The bleak omission
Of our slick Water Commission
From the League's superb Town Study
Leaves us prostrate with constriction!
It's been said that Freud intruded;
Since we read this, we have brooded;
Unintentionally we do-ed it,
For, or course, they were included
'Till an error typographic
Caused that Board to be excluded!
All along, we've been espousing
The just cause of poor Fair Housing;
In the library's list browsing
We found club and groups quite rousing.
But no mention e'er was made there
Of promoters of Fair Housing!

YES, there are sins of omission and sins of commission, but golly,
the omission of the Commission- to be specific, the Water Commission,
from the carefully conceived pages of "Braintree – Its Government", the
Provisional League of Women Voters' prize publication, is a sin to end
all sins! It's enough to keep Mr. Matthews, our prayerful and successful
rain-maker off his knees for a month. Furthermore, it's enough to make

Mr. Whitten, that dear local banker who helped finance the deal, stop payment on his substantial check!

We do not lay claim to the close personal acquaintance with Sigmund Freud that is apparently enjoyed by the Rev. Mr. Anderson; however, if we could get to the dear fellow, our side of the story would go something like this:

Mr. Freud, sir - it was a plain, unvarnished typographical error. We were working under pressure; (ouch, no relation to the water shortage) the Water Department begins with a "WL, and that's the end of the alphabet practically... Mr. Freud, sir, it was not the subconscious; it was more like the unconscious! You see, it was to be "League of Women Voters Week" the week of September 27, and we had about ten minutes in which to edit our manuscript and get it to the printer; and everyone was on vacation.

Sig, old dear, we haven't censored out the "vawter shortage". Look- here are our water bills: the department could go broke! Sponge baths instead of showers; we take our laundry to Quincy's Laundromat: we pray for rain; and wait for the wells to come in... We make sorrowful pilgrimages to Less Than Great Pond; and we love our Water Commissioners...

Now then, Sigmund - about this Fair Housing Committee... If "in de indifidual of collectif mind zere are no seemple oversights", what "indifidual" forgot to take a tidy trip to the Public Library? Whose "collectif minds" failed to list this F.H.C. in the library's little green file of clubs and organizations our gals used for reference?

Honest, Mr. Freud, we did try. We listed everybody anyone ever had listed; we called up our friends, and our friends' friends... Maybe it's cause we haven't seen a Fair Housing pledge in a long while... So anyhow, Siggy, who repressed? Was it the party of the second part of the part or the party of the first part? Which twin, actually, has the "clear cut case of effective repression of the subconscious," dear boy?

OH YES, Mr. Freud, we're scared to death to bring this bit to your analytical attention, but-the Provisional League of Women Voters made a third mistake, you know! It's all due undoubtedly to this non partisan policy we din into each other's subconscious until we're all but unconscious, but - where do you think the lady leaguers listed themselves? You didn't notice?? Not under "political organizations", where their subconscious obviously didn't think they belonged, but under "service organizations," So now, Sig, what do you make of that? You're confoosed??? You're not half as confoosed as the Lady Leaguers…

But don't you go worrying about those guilt complexes our gals might be expected to acquire as a result of all this; they're expiating! It's writers; cramp all around the Provisional League these days for the penitent participants who are writing a thousand times under the proper headings:

"WATER COMMISSIONERS U (3)" and "FAIR HOUSING COMMITTEE" Incidentally, we've a couple of extra pens, fellas…

Now tell me, Sig, all things being equal, will this dedicated application to the ball point happily free their subconscious, or merely render them all unconscious?????

12-15-68   MEMORY LANE

I CALL IT MY MEMORY TREE! It stands there in the corner of my dining room come Christmas time, each branch awash with bit s and pieces of the very wonderful past that has been mine.

On its crest there's a glittering angel. She's a mite wrinkled as to paper wing; and her locks have a bedraggled look; and her halo is a tiny bit awry; but she's adorned one family Christmas tree or other for lo! a thousand years, or so it seems.…She was a handmade gift from Jeanne, my Garden Clubbing sister, when first she joined their ranks…

On the branches of the tree are all the Christmas corsages I have ever worn, it seems the most precious of which is the one I found upon my darling mother's coat the last sad Christmas of her life, ten years ago. Mother left us on December 27. She, too, loved Christmas…

There are all the holiday club favors I've received for years and years; and there's a string of tired glass beads and one or two quite tarnished baubles from the Christmas trees that graced MY childhood; and there's a series of the quaintest kinds of things that children find to give at Chritmastime…(I wouldn't part with one of them.) angels in every conceivable stance and condition…the large and hopeless unlovely figure of a tramp, complete with big red nose and soleless shoes, and bleary eye denoting sad inebriation, that was the Christmas gift of nephew Mike, now a United States Marine, purchased when he was six and had insisted that his mother wrap it carefully "for Auntie Bibs, and WON'T SHE LOVE IT???" And there's a red-haired skier on a stand....

There's a golden rose or two the which I had persuaded Ted, my husband, to create from endless fruit juice tins; when that fair fad was on; and there's a darling little jangling elf a friend once placed upon the dashboard of my car as off we drove to some forgotten place at Christmas time...

There are bells that now no longer ring; and cornucopias a bit forlorn in mien; and there's a tiny golden Christmas tree, bedecked with small enchanting figures, which I toted home from England just about a year ago...

There are tiny twinkle lights that shine like stars to lend enchantment to this memory tree of mine....

***

INCIDENTALLY, how the tree itself came into my possession constitutes a merry memory also, It was the hottest July day on record, and I was returning from the local beach, sloshing into my sneakers as I went-for I had had a last minute dip in the deep to fortify me against the warm walk home.

It was rubbish pickup day in our particular part of town, and all the barrels stood like sentinels along the way, ready for the big white Highway Department truck that would tote their contents off to the seagulls awaiting their arrival at the town dump.

I paused to salute a gardening friend, when suddenly her next door neighbor opened a wide front door and called a cheery greeting. She was holding in her hands a beautiful artificial Christmas tree, AND SHE HEADED STRAIGHT FOR THE BARREL THAT HELD A MOTLEY COLLECTION OF ODDS AND ENDS FROM A JULY 4 COOKOUT. I gasped. "Don't tell me you are throwing away a CHRISTMAS TREE!" I said. "That's SACRILEGE!"

"I am indeed," she replied. "I thought I'd love it...no mess...no falling needles all over the house. But I didn't. I like the fragrance of a real tree in the house. I'm, going back to nature next Christmas. All these new things we feel impelled to try…" and she shook her head disdainfully.

"But why don't you GIVE IT to someone? I wailed. "I don't know anyone who wants it," she said indifferently. I sighed. "I WANT IT," I said firmly, and I marched over and retrieved it from her unloving hands…And so there I was, on the hottest day of the year, toting a beach bag in one hand and a Christmas tree in the other. "I do hope no one I know SEES me," I said laughingly to myfriend, and headed for home.

EVERYONE SAW ME, "What are you doing with a Christmas tree?" they asked. "I know you decorate earlier than everyone else, but really IN JULY????"

The family front door has rarely looked as inviting as it did that July day. I opened it, and set the handsome tree against the foyer wall, and A CORNER OF THE FAMILY DINING ROOM HELD OUT WELCOMING ARMS…The tree has adorned it ever since…

It plays, quite naturally, a unique role in a menage that sports a Christmas tree in just about every room. This one has become a conversation piece, carrying with it as it does, its own amusing tale…

And so I created for it a unique distinction. It has also become my MEMORY Tree…And forevermore it will house the bits and pieces of the very wonderful past that has been mine…

3-17-68   MID-MARCH

Let me catch the spring wind in my pocket;
Or corral the sweet hue of a sky,
Softly finding its cloud-fluffed face mirrored
In spring rivulets whispering by.

Let me thrill to forsythia budding;
To small tulip fronds, saucily curled;
To the tassels on trees; the capricious spring breeze;
The new springier step to my world.

Let me watch, as from winter's deep slumber
The somnolent earth comes awake,
Flexing muscles that - fat fragrant furrows -
Cautious cracks in the earth's surface make.

Let me cock a bright eye for cock robin,
Who's assuredly winging his way,
Tossing haughty head high in the south's summer sky;
He'll be nodding "Hello" any day!

Sure, Election Day's snugly behind us,
And Town Meeting time's well on the way;
Our FinCom is in session; with wisest discretion
Debating the needs of the day.

Should we rezone that land? Protect flood plains? - how grand!
Heed our High School Building Committee?
Is "High Rise" really dead? Is the Town in the red?
Is it true we're becoming a city????

"Legislators" galore plan to take to the floor
As hot issues the "boys" will debate.
With the tax rate at stake, and the old give and take…
How exciting! I scarcely can wait!

What a time of pure fun when the winter is done
And the whole Town commences to stir;
When spring bonnets arrive, sure the Town comes alive
As we store away feathers and fur.

Little Leaguers start hunting up baseballs;
Tiny girl Scouts commence eyeing trails;
With their packs folded snugly, they'll soon set out smugly
With ne'er a suggestion of males…

Sweet spring merchandise lines every window;
Easter bonnets abound everywhere;
(If you know of a diet, I'd sure like to try it,
for I've ten extra pounds I can spare.)

Winter's wooing is all but behind us;
It had moments quite wondrous and fair.
Piles of snow - though they're soiled, and rather well oiled -
I view with a slightly sad air.

But three cheers, let's all sing roundelays to the spring
As the March winds escort her our way.
'Tis that time of the year when we're SO glad we're here,
And resolve in New England we'll STAY!

MIDSUMMER

MIDSUMMER and we spend the golden days with sudden thrift, for they no longer lie ahead, an endless chain. Summer is growing old.

She came to us all shining but a day ago it seems, eyes dewy moist, breast warm with life, limbs slim and virginal and sweet but she's a woman now, full blown and fading.

Yesterday gay daffodils bedecked her hair. She wept, and smiled and wept again. Today her eyes are dry; she wears a wreath of August flowers, and looks upon her fading charms and sighs.

The young new green of grass she trod with fairy steps is gone. Her lawns, tufted and gnarled like all things growing old, rise bubbling to the sun, their flawless freshness now a memory.

The yews on which she breathed with busting life, retain the close-clipped symmetry of shears, sending no fair new fronds of truant growth out to the wanton wind.

Her Christmas-red-and-green geranium beds are laced with golden leaves, bronze-tipped, and weary.

Her swaying trees, once racing with the winds, go solemnly about the business of the sustaining life, settling their root-feet firmly in a search for water, holding the stance of placid middle years.

Heavy the trail of perfume now she leaves sun-scorched the roses breath musky the mum's soft scent.

ONCE, but a day ago, I heard her voice, whispering softly downward on the wind; once, but a day ago, I watched her breath warming a withered world; once, her youth, her wanton charm, her spilling life. Now I but watch her pass and barely smile.

The robins fat that were her harbingers, no longer send my heart to soaring skies; I scarcely note their frolics on the lawn; they scarcely frolic. Starlings, 'twould seem, awaken me with voices quite mature and staid, and all their fledglings fair have learned to fly, and so the path between my dogwood tree and their sweet nesting place no longer sings with strident schooling song.

Mums are all tall and trim beside the wall, and snapdragons have lost their fairy look, and bright petunias lie in August sweeps; nasturtiums spill their gold; sweet williams stand in regimented rows.

Beetles bedevil the roses that I love, and spraying has become a must, and spring's bright, shining painted look has left the porch.

Children are running down. They spend the gold of their vacation days with less delight. Some times they think on school and friends and brooks…

The ocean's ice is melting with the days.

YES, summer is growing old. She came to us all shining but a day ago, it seems, eyes dewy moist, breasts warm, with life, limbs slim and virginal and sweet, but she's a woman now, full blown and fading, and where she walks, her footsteps mark the August dust, and they are schooled, and staid and middle-aged.

Summer's a woman now. She gathers in the harvest of her hands waiving her ripening wand to fruit and flower, and so we spend our golden days with sudden thrift for they no longer lie ahead an endless chain.

Soon we shall have Autumn.

MIXED-UP GARDEN

My garden green is all confused!
I stand within it, quite bemused
To see the mixed-up state it's in!
Will winter's changes e'er begin?

A row of pink snapdragons gay
Belies just past Thanksgiving Day.
A pansy face, as bright as all,
Winks merrily at dying Fall!

The honeysuckles swelling buds resemble
Sprouting springtime duds;
While maple trees their branches bend
With tasseled trimming, end to end.

I almost think that, passing by,
A hyacinth's green spear, I spy!
Good grief- the ants are busy there
In sweet endeavor by the stair!

Is winter really shortening?
Will each year see a sooner spring?
Has our world's madcap, merry race
Affected e'en my gardens' pace?

November's spent: 'tis past the date
When gardens fair all hibernate,
The ducks are floating on the bay;
Each robin red has flown away.

The sea is gray; the sky is grim...
Where do you get this springtime vim?
Fair flora, and fresh fauna, too.
I don't now what to make of you!

Dear little flowers, go to sleep;
Your vigil I shall fondly keep.
If you'd be bright and green and gay
When April's trumpet blows your way.

You'd best just settle down in rest
Against the earth's renewing breast.
I've tucked d you in; I've mulched you high;
Now-be good kids, and say "good bye".

1-12-75   MORE FROM THE STATE HOUSE

Life, with a capital "L" goes on on Beacon Hill; and what joy to be right there in the thick of things! Every day seems to bring to light another exciting facet of the life of a "Legislator." This week, for instance, began with a bang. I was actually appointed to the TRANSPORTATION COMMITTEE AND to the HEALTH CARE COMMITTEE! Two challenging and great appointments, both offering what I envision as unlimited opportunity for service to the people of our Town and of our Commonwealth.

The events of January 1 were the subject of my last week's "Cabbage"...and...in view of the favorable response I'm receiving to that bit of reported History, may we continue with January 2, another Red Letter day at the State House? We had assembled in the magnificent House Chamber, we Representatives. We had come to watch a brand new Governor sworn in. He had stood there, Michael S. Dukakis, young of face and form, idealistic, eager to tackle the great task that lay before him; bright of eye' confident of manner, and I had thrilled at sight of him.

His arrival in the House had been preceded by all the pomp and circumstance I have come to expect (and to enjoy) when the House "sits"…the Opening Prayer by Monsignor Kerr, the House Chaplain; the Salute to Old Glory; and the singing of our National Anthem as it was never sung before, or so it seemed. I stood there throughout the rendition; and it was as though I were hearing it for the very first time, this stirring hymn that has been woven o deeply into the fabric of our lives. The Chief Justices had been admitted; and a Committee appointed from among the members of both Houses to inform the Governor and the Lieutenant Governor Elect that we (this columnist actually included in that "we"…) awaited their arrival.

This was to be a joint session, presided over by Senate President Kevin Harrington who from his lofty 6'9" of height had warmly welcomed his fellow Senators, along with former Governors Saltonstall, Furcolo, and Peabody and a number of visiting Congressmen, including "Tip" O'Neill, the "Father of the Lt. Governor" as he was to be later introduced. And now the arrival of the Governor and Lieutenant Governor Elect and the swearing in ceremony itself…the swearing in of a Governor who "in a political sense was born, raised and nurtured in this Chamber," to quote him, "One who has served in the General Court will become the Chief Executive for the first time in two decades," he was to tell the assembled legislators; and "It will not be the last," he was to add. Governor Dukakis' speech was to be a simple straight forward one, with emphasis on the life of none other than our own Sam Adams. What a proud moment for a legislator from Braintree whose historic Town Hall houses the birth records of the two Adams Presidents! "This State is richer and more attractive than any other in the nation," he would add. "We have mountains and river valleys, and beaches along our coast without equal in any of the other 49 states." How many times Ted and I had reminded one another of these facts as we sped back and forth across this wonderful country of ours.

We have brainpower and talent unmatched anywhere in the world," he would boast; "So our standards must be high; our commitments must call for the best that is in us. And our goals must be lofty ones." "Amen, "I found myself saying softly.

This swearing in of our brand new Governor and Tom O'Neill, his Lieutenant Governor was to mark the beginning of a wonderful day, a day that would not end until the wee small hours…a day That would include our attendance, in the company of so many of those we love, at the Governors' Inaugural Gala. (Where, we might add, we had persuaded Ted to arrive in a tuxedo, only to find the Governor in a business suit… oh no, he wasn't alone; there were a great many of the formally attired gentlemen on hand, and a host of formally attired ladies.)

We were to thrill to the incomparable music of Arthur Fiedler and our own Boston Pops; to the Voices of Black Persuasion; the New England Conservatory Ragtime Ensemble (Memories of wonderful New Orleans as they played the "Blues") and the Afro American Artists Dance Company. It was to be an evening wherein we would find ourselves walking as though in a dream through a brand new world we never had hoped to inhabit.

We're still walking through that dream world incidentally; and every day the walking gets better…Take today, for instance, and that appointment to the TRANSPORTATION COMMITTEE; and to the brand new COMMITTEE ON HEALTH CARE as well. What a challenge awaits us! And what an exciting experience it all was! The appointments had been dealt with alphabetically, you see; and your columnist's name had been included with those named under the letter "H" to the Committee on HEALTH CARE. Initially disappointed, I had promptly applied my own brand of philosophy to the situation. "You really HAD set your sights too high in asking for the Transportation Committee," I had told myself firmly. "After all, you ARE a Freshman legislator…And Health Care will be very interesting. It's a brand new Committee and a mighty important issue.":

And then, in the midst of all this philosophizing, the incredible had happened. Speaker Bartley had managed to reach the letter "T" and was announcing this appointments to the prized TRANSPORATION COMMMITTEE and he was saying my name… "Metayer of Braintree." He was actually saying it; I all but cheered!

Two weeks of Orientation now and I shall come to know in more detail the workings of the Great and General Court; and to actually be apart of it. How exciting and beautiful my life has ever been! And this new turn of events is easily the most exciting time of all…Thank you, Braintree, you beautiful Town, you!

12-15-63 MORE ON CHRISTMAS

WHENCE COMES the magic of Christmas?

The CHRISTMAS CAROL, sending our warm hearts soaring to the sides…

The CHRISTMAS TREE, shining in pristine splendor on the green…

The POINSETTIA, burst of shining Christmas glory…

The CANDLE, lighting the soft, sweet Christmas darkness…

The STAR, high in the dark night sky…atop the tree…above the crèche…

The CHRISTMAS ROSE..

The CRECHE, heart of the blessed Christmas story…

And…the CHRISTMAS story…

STORY…itself….

Whence come the glories of Christmas?

The CAROL-from England.

"What sweeter musick can we bring,

Than a Carroll, for to sing,

The birth of this our Heavenly King?

…and bequeath

This Hollie and this Ivie Wreath,

To do Him honour; who's our, King,

The Lord of all this rejoicing."

The CHRISTAMS TREE - from Germany.

Bedecked with ornaments and gifts, it symbolizes the gifts of the three Kings to the little Christ Child; and of the gift to mankind of the little Christ Child Himself.

The POINSETTIA- from Mexico.

Once upon a Christmas eve, many, Many years ago, so legend says, a tiny begger girl wept because, though she had wished and wished upon the Christmas star, she had no gift for the little Infant King on Christmas morning.

She watched and waited as all the day long, the people of her village came, bearing their beautiful rich gifts, and she grew sadder and sadder.

And the hour for Holy Mass drew nigh, and finally, because she had naught else to give, the little beggar girl placed before the Christmas crèche, her one possession. It was a branch of green weeds from the forest, which she had picked because to her lonely eyes it resembled a Christmas tree.

"Dear little Christ Child,:" she prayed, "I would give you the world if I had it…"

"Remove that ugly weed," cried the scornful villagers, "lest the little Christ Child take offense and look with disfavor upon our village." And Pablo, the sexton of the Church, who had himself once been poor and orphaned, sighed, and looked from the little beggar girl to the lofty senor from the hacienda, and went reluctantly to where the great crèche told its Christmas story…

"I must do their bidding." He told the tiny child with his eyes, but as he reached out his worn, brown hand to pluck the weed, - lo! suddenly it burst into glorious crimson bloom, glowing more richly than all the priceless gifts about it. The POINSETTIA from Mexico.

The lighted CANDLE - from Ireland. Shining in all the windows of the Christian world, to light the path of the Christ Child on Christmas eve, - to bid Him welcome to the hearts and homes of Christians everywhere.

The STAR- from Holland.

The blessed symbol of the little Christ Child's birth, and of the journey of the three Wise Men from distant lands.

The CHRISTMAS ROSE - from Bethlehem.

Legend tells us that in the little town of Bethlehem, on the very first Christmas, a little shepherdess wept because she had no gift to bring to the wondrous Child in the stable on the hillside. And as her tears fell on the cold, hard ground, soft white flowers sprang therefrom, and she gathered them and brought them, and knelt there by the trough that was His crib.

The little Christ Child smiled, and held out tiny hands to her and where His fingers touched the fragrant blossom, a soft pink heart glowed in the center of each one. And so a flower that ne'er before had graced the hills of the Bethlehem, was born - the CHRISTAMS ROSE, -and lo! it blooms more abundantly at Christmastime than at any other season of the year.

The CRECHE - from Italy and France.

The very soul of the blessed Christmas story, enshrined in the hearts and the homes of the world.

And the CHRISTMAS STORY? It seems to come from everywhere…and nowhere…ever and always each Christmas - a tale of kindness rewarded, of goodness recognized, of "peace on earth, good will toward men" and lo! methinks it dwells in the hearts of all of us, the blessed beautiful, poignant CHRISMAS STORY!

3-7-71   MORE ON GRANDCHILDREN

Richard Edwards Metayer Jr., the eldest of the Metayer grandchildren spent last week in Braintree with his grandparents. In Mystic, Connecticut where Richard lives, the midwinter, school vacation is always scheduled one week after our own - a fact which appears to disturb Richard not at all. He knows full well that his Braintree cousins must be tucked away at school for much of each day and that he must consequently rely upon his elderly g.p.'s for entertainment most of the time; however, up he comes year after year. And we love to have him.

Well, with this kind of close relationship over a full week's time, many and varied are the exchanges between said elerly g.p.'s and Richard E. Metayer…some of them quite hilarious.

The young man is eleven years old and a decidedly deep child who has begun to think things through. He observed, for instance, that his grandfather, retired these past five years, failed to depart for business each day like his dad and the fathers of the boys and girls he knows.

"Grandfather," he said brightly one morning about the middle of the week. "Don't you WORK?"

"No," said his grandfather equally brightly. "Not EVER?" "No, not ever, Richard." "Not even at night while we are asleep? Or in the morning before we get up?" "No. Not even at night while you are asleep, Rich, not in the early morning either.

"Not even on weekends or anything?" persisted Richard. "No, not even on the weekends or anything. "Are you on VACATION grandfather? Are you going BACK to work?" "No, I'm not on vacation, and I'm hopefully not going back to work,…not at all, Richard."

"You mean you can sit around, grandfather, and do just what you want to do all day long every single day???" he asked, his young voice warm with wonder. "Why, yes," said grandfather in an amused tone; "I guess you may say that I can sit around and do just what I want to do all day long every single day…"

A puzzled look crossed the boy's face. He waited a moment and then suddenly the young face brightened. "Grandfather," he said, "Are you folks on the WELFARE????"

Grandfather promptly explained to his young grandson the virtues of planning for one's old age, "retirement" income, annuities, social security, etc., the whole bit. He was obviously pleased at the opportunity to deliver this kind of homily to still one more generation of Metayers. Richard absorbed every word of it. "I think that's NIZZER!" he said finally, shaking his head in out-and-out wonder, (I am not at all certain of the spelling of that modern day word that seems to mean so much to the younger generation that, however, is how it SOUNDS.)

"Grandfather," he said suddenly a while later from the depths of 'Robinson Crusoe,' You know what we talked about well, well, HOW OLD will I have to be before I can stay home from work and do everything I want to do everyday just like you do???"

"Sixty-five," said his grandfather. Richard's face fell to his knees.

"Gosh," he said dejectedly, "I'VE an awful long time to wait, haven't I?" There's no doubt about it…Grandchildren provide high moment's in the lives of their grandparents. There is young Jim Corbin, for instance who systematically-after working out a series of statistics - advances the little adjusting screw on the family scale and records his potential weight one year from now, and five years and ten years. And who immediately upon arrival plugs in every electric clock in the house, synchronizing them all at ten minutes fast because "Grandma will be late for things if the clocks aren't that much fast…" He has obviously "eavesdropped."

Young James plans to be a Meteorologist. Ask him anything about the wind velocity and the precipitation and the rest anywhere in the civilized world (or at any rate the NEWS MEDIA recorded world) and he can be depended upon to come up with the answer. The daily weather charts he fastens to the door of "James M. Corbin, IIIs Weather Observatory": which is another name of the room he shares with brother Byrne, keep the family consistently abreast of advancing storms or calms…A few years back the local T.V. stations were decrying the lack of qualified Meteorologists in the area. Young Jim, who was then about seven said to his mother solemnly, "Don't you think you should call them up and tell them I'm coming???"

Nine year old Byrne Corbin meanwhile, manages to make like a Pediatrician at the drop of a chapeau whenever anything young - human or animal - is in medical trouble. Byrne plans to be a pediatrician just like Dr. McCue!

Dr. John McCue, the family pediatrician, managed to win the heart of Gael's middle child one Christmas Day several years ago when Byrne was a very ill and very lonely little boy in a local hospital. He simply could not be persuaded to eat and the nurses were concerned. Concerned doubly was Dr. McCue - so concerned that on Christmas morning he left his lovely little Weymouth family and headed for Carney Hospital and Byrne Corbin. One very young little boy raised a tiny tear stained face to the good doctor as he entered. His Christmas dinner lay untouched before him. His family had not as yet arrived. "I can't get him to eat a thing," said the nurse worriedly. That was when the great warm heart of Dr. McCue, that wonderful man whose life is dedicated to the children in his care, took over. "What do you say you and I eat our Christmas dinner together, Byrne?" he asked quite as though such an experience would be a lark for both of them. Byrne nodded. "Bring us another tray please nurse!" he said. And one wonderful doctor and one precious small boy dined together. If Byrne Corbin becomes the splendid pediatrician we all feel certain he is destined to be, Dr. McCue may take a great deal of the credit.

Finally, there is Gregory, the four-year-old who adores Christmas. His grandmother returned from yesterday's Philergian Auction clutching a little Christmas tree which she had purchased there. Small Gregory, visiting grandfather at the time, was enchanted. "Let's put it in MY Guest Room" he said. (The Guest Room has been HIS since he first slept there.) And then the questions flowed. "Where did you get it, Grandma?" "What's an AUCTION?" "Well," I said, "I guess you would say it is a place where to take things you no longer want, and a lady or gentleman SELLS them." Gregory's big brown eyes clouded. "You mean somebody DIDN'T WANT this Christmas tree?" he asked, aghast, and then suddenly "Where are the lights?" "Oh, we'll put lights on it when Christmas comes," I said. "But for now we'll just take it to the attic and let it go to sleep with all our other Christmas trees until December. How would you like to carry it up for me?"

Gregory tenderly transported his newest holiday treasure to the "Christmas Corner" of the family attic and placed it beside the others. He stood there a moment or two, regarding it his newest holiday treasure to the "Christmas Corner" of the family attic and placed it beside the others. He stood there a moment or two, regarding it with loving eyes; then he reached down and kissed the silky green branches. "Don't worry, little tree," he added gently, almost in a whisper, "We won't EVER tell anyone that somebody didn't WANT you. GRANDCHILDREN ARE WONDERFUL!

5-12-68   MOTHERS DAY

A HAPPY Mothers Day to all the mothers of Braintree! And an ESPECIALLY happy one to those dear little mothers among us - the gals who have made us GRANDMOTHERS! May the day be sunny, so that their little ones can play outdoors; and may safety and serenity (also sanity) surround them on their own special day!

How did it all come about anyhow, this nationwide recognition of mother on her special day in May...the loveliest month, incidentally, in all the year?

Well, it had its beginning, so the story goes, in the frenzied period immediately following the Civil War.

The dark hatred that dominated the hearts of the Blues and the Greys everywhere tore at the vitals of our great nation, and left a festering sore that kept it fevered and fretful.

There were the CONQUERORS and the VANQUISHED and never, it appeared, were the twain to meet. Brother had been pitted against brother in a manner which only a great Civil War can bring about; and the bitterness that only Civil War can generate, lay upon all the South.

West Virginia was a border state, and as a consequence, the dark pall of despair covered IT like shroud, when suddenly, in the small border hamlet of Prunnytown, a gentle mother, dwelling upon her affection for ONLY LOVE, she decided, could erase the hatred that existed in the hearts of the men of America. And so Anna Reeves Jarvis - that was her name - organized what she termed a "Mother's Friendship Day". She invited all the soldiers of her area - Confederate and Union alike - together with their families, and their MOTHERS, to Prunnytown.

Her invitation was passed by word of mouth, and the soldiers of the district responded early. Across the border they streamed, enroute to Prunnytown. They came in ever increasing numbers - the Blues and the Greys!

The Great War was forgotten, and for one brief day, the soldiers of America were all just mothers' sons. And all mothers and their sons were united in friendship on this, the first organized Mothers Day in American history!

Anna Reeves Jarvis worked throughout her lifetime to promote the dream of unity through love; and, at her passing in 1905, she passed the torch to another Anna Reeves Jarvis, her daughter.

Miss Jarvis began almost from the moment of her mother's passing an intensive campaign to establish a National Mothers Day.

Had not the mothers of the ancient Greece been honored in Greek Mythology, she asked of every legislator she encountered? Were they not extolled in Biblical history, and feted at Roman festivals? Had not a "Mothering Sunday" been established in England in the early days of Christianity, with servants and apprentices alike bearing gifts to their mothers, and attending their own Churches? The dream of Anna Reeves

Jarvis began slowly but surely to catch fire. She worked feverishly to kindle the flame...And finally, in the year 1914, one Rep. Heflin of Alabama and Senator Shepard of Texas presented to Congress legislation calling for a National Mothers Day. It passed both Houses. The climate for such legislation was right in Washington, needless to say, Woodrow Wilson, a great idealist and humanitarian occupied the White House! And William Jennings Bryan was Secretary of State!

The second Sunday of May was designated as Mothers Day, and proclaimed a National Flag holiday.

A white carnation, the favorite flower of her mother, was selected as an emblem by the lady whose steadfast determination to immortalize HER the lady whose mother had established her own "Mothers' Friendship Day" - ANNA REEVES JARVIS the second, is responsible for it all. THE PURPOSE of Mothers Day, so said the immortal Bryan, (and can't you HEAR him???) was "To establish, promote and perpetuate work for the well being of the home-to give emphasis to the fountainhead of the State....

A tribute to the love of the Mother and Father", he said, resolves itself into a tribute to their law and that recognition of their law means love for country, for comrades and for God." Can we add more???

How beautiful for all the mothers...and grandmothers...we know!

2-26-67   NEW BABY

HER NAME was to have been Erin, and sure and begorrah, she was to have been born on the seventeenth of March - not, you understand, that her doctors had scheduled it that way, but Gael, my daughter, had decreed it must be so...

James Matthew III, she said, was born on March 22, and Byrne Lawrence on March 24.

"I shall have my daughter on the seventeenth and we'll celebrate all three birthdays on St. Patrick's Day! Mother, what fun!" she had added. "We'll have shillelaghs, and clay pipes and big Irish hats on the walls of the playroom, and real live shamrocks as favors for the grownups, and even the ice cream will be green!"

I half believed my child. She has a way of getting what she wants from life. Not this time, however....

Gregory Scott arrived decidedly prematurely on the twentieth of February instead. "What a pity he didn't wait two more days." her father said. "You could have called him George.!"

GREGORY is a dot of a baby. Weighing in at a trifle over four pounds, he was placed in an incubator.

"Had he waited even a week longer to arrive, you would have lost him." Said the doctor, which statement was sufficient to dispel for all time anything of disappointment his mother might have felt at Erin's about face on sex Gregory's nice dad and I raced in the night to the hospital where we pronounced out littlest angel the image of Brother Byrne, and a beautiful child indeed. Gael's was not the only overnight case that lay packed and ready for flying trip; grandmother's and grandmother (as well as grandfather) prepared to render service as a substitute mother to the two most remarkable children in Braintree -- our grandchildren...

Gael, whose Girl Scout training seems to have brushed on but good, had been ready for Gregory's arrival for months.

"Quintuplets you could accommodate," her father and I had told her as she crammed every square inch of "Erin's" smart new wardrobe with articles of apparel.

"We're going to keep her for a long time...all summer," James III had announced as he toted out and held up for inspection every baby product on the market.

"Now," said Gael, as she departed for the hospital, "in that bag are the clothes to bring Erin home. There is her little shirt and her little diaper and her little yellow rubber pants; and Sandy has crocheted me a microscopic sweater and bonnet in yellow; and her little dress and slip are on hangers; and her fluffy yellow blanket is on top..." (Greg is going to look a doll in the bonnet...)

Gael had been equally meticulous about her own accouchement apparel.

"Look, isn't everything lovely, mother? All in shades of hot to pale pink...Monochromatic colors are effective..."

With husband and father pacing the floor and sending fervent entreaties her way. Gael had prepared as carefully for her trip to the hospital as though she were dressing for the opera. Every blonde hair in place; lipstick and nail enamel and attuned…

THE HOUSE was as meticulously tidy.

"What in heavens name are you doing?" I had asked her, aghast, an hour or so before her departure time, as, with spray can and toweling, she headed for the huge thermopane doors leading to the sundeck.

"Colleen was breathing on them this morning, mother." She said. (Colleen is the family collie, as handsome a puppy as her name implies.) "She's rough on windows, but - what an angel!" The angel was shortly to be tucked safely away in the kennel. Grandmother is allergic to collie dogs as large as ponies, even collies who are angels…

James and Byrne Corbin are thrilled beyond words about their nice new baby.

"I told mommy it was going to be a boy," said James, with an air. He did. "Byrne thought it was going to be a girl; he's so often wrong about things…"

"Hi, mom," said Byrne via the telephone the following morning, "let me speak to Gregory, will you please? He's sleeping? Well, tell him to call me when he wakes up!"

"Gregory," said James, with an amused glance at his father, "will be calling all of us soon enough."

P.S. I have just returned from visiting Gregory Scott Corbin - all four pounds of him. He was kicking the front of the incubator with his feet as he pummeled the side glass with his fists. "Look at him," said the dad who had dreamed for months of having a baby daughter. "Gosh," he added proudly, his chest advanced a foot, "He's all boy, isn't he???"

10-17-65   NEW CAR

WE GOT a new car at our house this past week. Getting a new car is, for the woman of the family, a bit like getting a new baby - you have to get accustomed to the change, and it isn't easy!

"It's big," I commented.

"Its no bigger than our other car," said Ted comfortingly.

"I'll drive it tomorrow," I announced.

"You'll hop right in this minute and drive it now," said the lord of the manor.

I crawled around the block.

"We'll call this one the 'Queen Mary'", I announced. We always have named our cars. There was Gertrude, for instance - our first Oldsmobile - a nice dependable name for a solid soul of a car that went 100,000 miles without batting a piston, "Never even had the head off," Ted was fond of announcing whenever Gertrude's name was mentioned, and we must assume this fact to be undisputable evidence of her superior performance, for the news was invariably received with a degree of awe by every adult male within hearing.

There had been "Elizabeth", a pale blue Mercury which I had especially loved; and Patricia, a smart hardtop…

"NOW," SAID TED, "this is a push button car," which was the understatement of the decade. The thing has push buttons on its push buttons.

Our first trip was to Boston, and toting our darling daughter and her darling sons, we attempted to park the vehicle at Columbia Station.

"Now," I said to Gael, "Dad said that to lock it, you press one button, which locks three doors - then lock the fourth one manually." Which was all comparatively simple sounding, but – which of the 576 buttons?

There was but one way to find out.

Switches flipped; motors hummed; windows flew up and down - front and rear, rear and front; butterflies fluttered their glassy wings, windshield wipers - sang; and small jets of water washed energetically…It took ten full minutes to sort the whole works out and get the Queen Mary securely locked; and an hour or so later, as we attempted to communicate with a friend at the local gas station and to open one specific window for one small conversation, we found ourselves repeating the performance all over again.

"Who is opening and closing all the windows, Grandma? Asked Byrne, our small grandson, who is 3. "Tinkerbell??"

"Possibly…"

"NOW," said the man in my life, you really should put this car in the garage." I have a happy habit of leaving it in the driveway.

"It won't fit," I said.

"Yes, it will;" he replied, "with a little practice you'll be able to manage it."

"Ted," I protested, "I've measured it, there's no more than 4 inches on each side of the doorway."

"All you need is one inch," said my spouse, a trifle airily, I thought. I returned to the vicinity of the driveway.

"Ted," I said, one hour and 27 attempts later, "would it be possible to cut back a foot or so of the brick and widen the entrance to the garage?"

"Well, yes," he answered slowly, after the first shock of my question had worn off, "I suppose it would but I'd hate to think we'd have to do it; it shouldn't be necessary."

That was when I delivered one of my very rare ultimatums.

"Darling," I said (to soften the pronouncement a bit), "either you take a foot off the entrance, or I've a horrible feeling I shall take a foot off the car. The choice would seem to be yours!"

Ted doesn't seem to know whether the contractor who is scheduled to arrive come morning, will cut away that foot or so of brick in one fell swoop - or take it apart, brick by brick! As an engineer's daughter, I'm intrigued by the problems of stress and strain that are involved in the sundeck that tops the building. (The problem of stress and strain in our family relationship is yet to be resolved). What a pity I won't be home to watch!

WHAT A WAGON this newest of tour cars is, to quote my nephew! A switch in the glove compartment opens the trunk, the which, I have cautioned, must nevermore be slammed because the lock is - of all things - an electric one, complete with small, singing motor! With what gusto I have been slamming trunks shut for years! This behaviour change will not come easy.

There are other delightful innovations. An electric eye, which I have been informed is a photo electric cell, located strategically on the dashboard, lowers our high beams for each oncoming car; and a deep tinting of the upper windshield renders the sky, regardless of weather, ever and eternally the most heavenly shade of blue! What joys to have been born into the age of ease and aesthetics!

9-4-66   NEW HOME

IT'S A dream come true, the building of one's own first home.

Gael, my daughter, and James, her fine young husband, had selected the plans tenderly; they found just the right location; and then they settled down to the rainbow prospect of delirious days that would be bright with color schemes, and dear with decision.

The target date was to be May 15, and the children's apartment had been rented immediately. Their friends, Bill and Bebe, were expecting a baby, and were looking for the kind of large and lovely apartment the Corbin's were vacating. "The timing is perfect," Bebe had said. "We'll be in and settled before the baby arrives."

You know what happens to the "best laid plans of mice and men?" It's even worse with contractors, May 15 came and went, and the desired domicile was ten miles short of being ready for occupancy. "Oh, well," said Gael, resignedly, "June is a lovely month in which to move into a new home, and Jim can take a week of his vacation around the middle…"

And so the Corbin's cancelled their notice on Atherton Street, which set up a chain reaction that involved the couple with the baby coming; and the newlyweds who were destined to honeymoon in Bill and Bebe's Shangri-La; and the parents of one of the newlyweds, who were moving into smaller quarters…

The chain reaction didn't end there. Furniture which had been purchased for delivery May 15, had to be returned to the warehouse, and the mover's services disengaged. "Yes," said James, resignedly, "actually June is a better month in which to move."

BUT June 15 came - and June 15 went. The contractor had promised faithfully, and it wasn't his fault; the children were sure of that; but the house just wasn't ready; and this time it was bit more difficult to explain the delay to the series of landlords, and furniture dealers, and moving men....By now, Bebe's baby had arrived, and things were more than a mite crowded in their honeymoon apartment.

July 15, which also came and went, found everyone's nerves, including the contractor's at the breaking point. Gael had employed in telephoning irate furniture dealers, and mad movers, the ancient devices of a clothespin on the nostrils, and a hanky over the receiver, with "I'm calling for Mrs. Corbin; please don't deliver the furniture until August 15' or please don't have your movers come on Thursday of next week; there's been another slight delay...."

Now nobody's landlord was speaking to anybody, and it began to look like Gael's baby, due in February, could be occupying the room Bebe's baby had expected to grow up in -and Bebe's baby was growing up!

Hallelujah, however - it's all behind us now! We're moved! It was no simple accomplishment, believe me! I know. I helped. Mothers do... Incidentally, I've been employing foot muscles and throat muscles in my door-to-door campaigning, but - moving - I used muscles I never knew existed. Also, there's little or no stimulation to be found in contact with unending boxes of dishes and pans. I was tired, with a large "T".

The day itself was sunny and delightful; the movers arrived jubilantly at dawn; so did the furniture! We all but sent out for straightjackets in sizes 4 and 6 for the Corbin boys; they were beside themselves with excitement! Colleen, the four-footed little girl of the family, behaved much better; she retreated to the shade of a tall tree and lay quietly down. "Can't you tell a thoroughbred every time?" asked her mistress. The childrens' grandmother, busily defending her two angels, wondered quite what she meant, but was far too involved in moving to pursue the matter.

INCIDENTALLY, and speaking of little girls, James M. Corbin, Sr. has the handsomest den. It's wallpaper is wild; and the den set masculine and massive. The appointments were selected months ago. The room was intended by the architect as a third bedroom, but as Gael and James had said at that particular point in planning, "We'll only need one bedroom for the boys, and the master bedroom for ourselves; we can make a lovely den of that nice third room."

You know what happens to the "best laid plans of mice and men" and contractors? It happens to parents. I wonder if Jim, Senior, eyeing the comfort of that rare retreat that's all his own, really has ordered from Sir Stork the baby girl his wife desires so much? And how well will she blend with the brown and gold wallpaper and the cocoa wall to wall???

3-10-74 NEW PUPPIES

Cartier's Madame (formerly Mamselle) Tiffany is sending out birth announcements these days. It's TWINS! Twin Girls no less - and in a family where male infants have held sway for lo! These many years! Cartier's Madame is not a LADY…(though I am quite sure she would be amazed to discover the fact…) She's a white toy French Poodle who has won not only the hearts of the Corbin and Metayer families, but those of the entire neighborhood as well; and everyone in town, it seemed, was interested in her "babies" as Tiffy's offspring had been referred to from the moment her "Mother," our animal-loving daughter, had decided to breed her.

Tiffy's pre-natal care became the special concern of each and every member of the Corbin family - Father, Mother and all three sons. "Did Tiff have her vitamins, Mom?" "Shovel the stairs carefully so Tiff won't fall down them." "I shoveled a nice path around the pool so Tiff can get her exercise." It went on and on…

Tiffy's a DOT of a doggie. She weights in a mere five pounds; and we wondered what kind of mother this petted, pampered mite of a poodle might make. Well, she took to her new state like a pro, greeting the arrival of each and every visitor with a series of glad cries that led them directly to the box where her two snow white, pink-nosed, pink-eared mites of infants were on display.

All had been in readiness for the "blessed event" for days. A corner of the family room housed a handsome "whelping box." Nearby a smaller edition of the same contained a heating pad, carefully plugged in to await the arrival of Puppy No. 1. There was the family scale for weighing in the small mites, and a notebook and pen for recording such important items as birth weights, time of delivery, etc.

Gael had carefully read her instruction book. She is, however, currently struggling with an injured right hand. "What if I should DROP one of the babies???" she said in horror. "Mom, will you help?" Now Gael and I do a lot together, however, a "blessed event" is not my cup of tea. I shook my head firmly and negatively. "And don't look at ME," said her spouse. "Well," she said. "If it's during the day I know DAD will help; but I don't know what I shall do if it happens at night." "Don't worry, Mom," said twelve-year-old Byrne matter-of-factly; "I'LL help you. I'VE READ THE BOOK TOO!" Byrne, who has not as yet decided whether he'll become a Veterinarian or a Pediatrician, but who has been applying Band-aids and a sympathetic touch to anything wounded - child or animal - since he was two. (His Mother's son....)

Tiffy had had her last prenatal check-up a few days previously; and Dr. Harris, Gael's marvelous "Vet" had expressed some concern. The puppies, you see, could arrive the following weekend and he expected to be in New York at that time, attending an 80th Birthday Party for his Grandfather. Needless to say another Vet would cover for him, he assured her. "But if it should happen at a time other than the weekend", he told her seriously, "and you need me, tell my answering service that it is an obstetrical call and they will reach me immediately wherever I am, EVEN IF I SHOULD BE HAVING DINNER IN A RESTAURANT! I will call you back and give you advice over the phone if you need it. And at any rate, do call me as soon as it is over and let me know how Tiffany made out." How about that!!!!

In the final analysis everything went well indeed; and poor dear Dr. Harris was able to enjoy uninterrupted dinner engagements; though he did receive a frantic call from daughter Gael at 3:00 a.m. to which he responded as sweetly as though it were three in the afternoon....

Tiffany's first born arrived at 7:09 a.m. Gregory, who had selected the names "Peter" and "Mary" for Tiffy's babies, regarded it doubtfully. "HE doesn't look like a Peter or a Mary," he said seriously. "He's so WHITE; he looks more like a SNOWBALL," said Byrne. "We COULD call him 'Snowball, only he's so tiny he's more like a SNOWFLAKE!" He WAS tiny, six ounces, as a matter of fact. A little twin came along one hour and twenty-five minutes later. "This one is bigger," said Greg. HE was. He weighed a full eight ounces... "We can call HIM 'Snowball," said Greg joyously; "and his BROTHER 'Snowflake'!" What a shock it was later for this boy-orientated family to learn that both of Tiffy's HE'S were SHE'S!

There had been no sleep for anyone in the Corbin family that night, including, of course, the three solicitous small boys who had merely dozed on the rug beside their pet. Byrne had served as babysitter to Puppy No.1, snugly tucking the heating pad about her while awaiting the arrival of Puppy No. 2. "I don't see how these boys can go to school," said their Dad. "They've been awake all night; they'll fall asleep in class." "Oh, but Jim," said their Mother. "I don't think the Sisters would approve of our keeping them home…unless we invented some logical excuse…like a trip…with car trouble or something… "Seven-year old Gregory's head came up with a snap. "Mommy," he said in horror, "Lie??? To a SISTER????" Needless to say, they didn't and strangely enough, the Sisters appeared to understand perfectly why the arrival of "Snowball" and "Snowflake" in an animal loving family should constitute cause for disrupting its educational routine.

Tiffany and her babies are having quite a time. The little one's future families have come, bearing gifts for Mama and rendering due adulation to her little ones, who incidentally now weigh in at twelve and thirteen ounces respectively. "They've DOUBLED their birth weight," Gael is saying proudly. They've had their tails docked and their dew claws removed in the way of pedigreed poodles of the finest order; and they've been termed perfect specimens. We knew they were perfect from the beginning; and we just cannot wait to see their blue eyes open in a day or two…

2-9-69   NEW PUPPY

The Metayers have a brand new grandchild. Her name is Heather, and she's a pound and a half or so of canine dynamite. Actually her name isn't Heather at all; it's Scot Tarre Trinket of Wolfpit, the which, they opined, could constitute quite a mouthful for the three small boys who decided to make the change in names.

Heather is a Cairn terrier; and in case you are interested, you can't hardly get that breed of canine around these parts…At least, that is what daughter Gael assured us one and all as she merrily ran up the Corbin phone bill with long distance conversations until it began to resemble the national debt.

"Give your family a cold wet nose for Christmas," ran the newspaper ad of a local Puppy Emporium last December. Gael decided to take their advise. "Not just any old breed," it had continued, but "the perfect Christmas puppy for you." We had no idea what a complicated task the selection of the "perfect" Christmas puppy was going to prove.

If the puppy were perfect, our child reasoned, she would be potential SHOW material,. "I've always wanted to SHOW a dog," she said brightly. "It's primarily a matter of blood line," she added solemnly as she began a trek for the same that was to take her via the American Kennel Club and other avenues directly and indirectly to the last word in breeders of Cairns residing anywhere from Oshkosh to East Overshoe, with States to match…

"Mother," said Gael one evening, as she hung up from an hour-long phone conversation with a breeder on the New York border of Connecticut. "Can you possibly babysit little Gregory on Sunday? I have located a Cairn with a SUPERB blood line!"

And superb indeed is the bloodline of our little Heather. Her sire: Champion Bonnie Brash of Wolfpit, whose picture graces the Official Handbook of the Cairn terrier Club of America.

"Brash has set the Cairn rings on fire by finishing his championship in FOUR shows," Gael read eagerly, from the Cairn Terrier Handbook. "And Heather's dam, mother," she said, "was Lofthouse Veleta, an import from England, whose UNCLE was the English, American and Canadian Champion, Lofthouse Davey; whose MOTHER was Dorseydale Justeena, FAMOUS FOR HER HEAD AND EXPRESSION….Why, do you know, mother," Gael read proudly, "On her SIRE'S line, his GREAT GRANDFATHER on his father's side was Redletter McRuffie, an English, Canadian and American Champion, and to quote from the book, "one of the world's MOST FAMOUS Cairns????' I was duly impressed.

"There's but one drawback to Scot Tarre Trinket," said Gael. She sighed. "She has a slightly GAY tail, the breeder admits!" "What in haven's name is a gay tail?" I asked. "It's a slight curl on the end of it. Before I definitely make up my mind to go to Connecticut, I'll call Mrs. Jones, the breeder in Vermont and Mrs. Smith, the New York Breeder. I must find out what a gay tail would cost her in points….."

The breeders of Cairns were comforting. Some judges ignore it entirely, it seemed; while others consider it to be of minor importance. And so, the Corbins, James and Gael and little Byrne prepared to depart for the New York border. Baby Gregory was obliged to stay at home. It seemed also that the breeder would not "give" Scot Tarre Trinket to a family with a small child… "GIVE HER!" echoed Ted, "Why they'll have to mortgage the old homestead to PAY for the thing!"

The Corbins returned from their Sunday jaunt, bearing a small sweet bundle of bright eyes and whiskers, the which they had promptly nicknamed Heather. And, in spite of the bloodline, there wasn't a trace of the snob in her…..

"Now," said Gael, "We must face the matter of the gay tail immediately. As you can see, it's only very SLIGHTLY gay. There's a show next Saturday at the Prudential Center. Will you go with me?" I did.

"Mother," said Gael hesitantly, as we neared the place. "You know, professionals use a most unpleasant word for a female doge. It's part of their language. I hope you won't be SHOCKED….I was…

"My dear Mrs. Corbin," said a perfect and perfectly charming lady who turned out to be the breeder from whom Gael had purchased her canine angel, "How nice to see you. I hoped you'd be here. Lydia dear," she called brightly to her daughter, who would prove to be one of the judges, "This is the lovely young woman who bought Veleta's YOU-KNOW-WHAT…" I swallowed a gasp. The show was wonderful, and in the first class, a whiskered little Cairn with a decidedly gay tail copped first prize…

Gael is jubilant, and Heather is to be enrolled in Handler's school next month. I trust she will measure up to our Gael's high expectations. The only other canine member of the family to have a go at formal education - a poodle by the name of Fou Fou - FLUNKED!

Anyhoo, our Heather is shortly to be enrolled. And, though I must admit that currently obedience is anything but Heather's watchword, WHO KNOW?? She might just turn out to be an all "A" student… Wonder if HANDLER'S SCHOOL has ever had a DROPOUT???

7-29-73 NEW PUPPY

She lay there in the palm of his hand, a tiny white morsel of fluff with two bright eyes that looked trustingly up at son-in law Jim, and from him to daughter Gael and thence to the three admiring boys that make up the Corbin family. "What an angel of a puppy! Where did you get her?" Said Gael. "Is she OURS???" Not this one," said Jim. "I borrowed her. But you know what??? This toy poodle has a little sister still unsold. Would you like her?" The response was instantaneous and unanimous. The Corbins would indeed like to possess little sister; and so a call to the breeder, a trip to the kennel, and "little sister" was theirs...

"She's an absolute jewel," Gael kept saying again and again as the small puppy settled down into her little bed and made herself at home. And indeed, an absolute jewel she was...gentle, appealing, this latest little family pet was to speedily bring out the most protective instincts in each of the dog-loving Corbins.

Her name was easily decided upon. The "jewel" was to be called, appropriately enough "Cartier's Mamselle Tiffany." Her ancestry had been an impressive one...her sire, one Scooter Patrice and her dam Brat Patrice....And it showed though to be sure there was nothing of the "brat" about Mamselle Tiffany; nor seen of the "scooter." Tiffy, as she was speedily nicknamed, was to be sweet...totally and completely sweet.

Like every previous canine member of the family, Tiffy promptly attached herself to daughter Gael. There was no doubt about it, Tiffany was to be Gael's dog. Her "mother's...departure from the house for any reason saw the small white morsel settling herself at the top of the stairs she was as yet unable to descend, disconsolately awaiting her mistress's return. As the weeks passed, Tiffy developed a mad passion for riding with the lady of the house, and so preparation for Gael's daily trek to kindergarten with son Gregory invariably saw one small puppy head for the front door to plant herself firmly before it and demand to come along. It wasn't too long before the family found itself having to resort to SPELLING the word "car" if it intended to slip away without her...

Tiffany can take or leave the family swimming pool. As a matter of fact mostly she can LEAVE it. unless, of course, her "Mother" happens to be floating about on her happy little Aqualounger, in which case Tiffy can be expected to plunge in and head for the raft where she will lie cradled in Gael's arms for the afternoon. Her own little raft, Tiffany rarely ventures to use. Oh yes, each and every member of the Corbin family has his or her own little raft, not excluding Mamselle Tiffany.

Gael happens to be a gardening enthusiast of the first magnitude, with showplace rock gardens that call for constant weeding by the lady of the house. "It's a good thing for me that Tiffy only weights 5½ pounds," she keeps saying with a broad grin…for all of Gael's weeding and other gardening chores must be performed with a small white poddle tucked under one arm.

Tiffany, like every other member of the household plays her own special role she's a marvelous substitute for the alarm clock, for instance. It isn't easy for a diminutive doggie to pull the covers from three all-tucked-up-in-blankets small boys and their parents, however she manages the task, prancing from none to another of them until all and sundry have arisen and shone.

Cartier's Mamselle is not a particularly brave canine. Samantha, the toy poodle next door, reduces her to jelly by simply appearing on the family patio with her master, the Corbins' good neighbor Frank. This interesting fact is further complicated by the fact that Samantha is reduced to jelly by the sight of Tiffany's master Jim. It obviously has nothing to do with size however, for Tiffy's best friend is Ruby, the huge gangling Labrador Retriever pup on the other side of the family fence…

Tiffany is definitely a LADY. "There's no doubt about it," Gael's own grandmother was fond of saying, her nose tilted lightly upward, "Blood tells. Either one has class or one hasn't." Grandmother Nener would have approved of Tiffany. Her class shows 100 percent. For instance, who ever heard of a doggie dining in the kitchen??? When it comes to that finicky performance, each and every morsel served to the latest member of the Corbin family is destined to be toted by that little miss into the family dining room to be daintily picked at while it rests on the handsome dining room rug and why not?" asks daughter Gael with a laugh. "Where else does a LADY dine???" In addition, the decidedly tired toy bone that is her pride and joy must be considered by Tiffy to be part and parcel of the LIVIING ROOM décor. In vain does Gael attempt to change the behaviour pattern of her small pet by transferring this anything but appealing article to the downstairs family room. It reappears as if by magic in the center of the living room floor, with Tiffy standing guard over it with a "Move it again if you dare" expression on her tiny face.

Tiffany was recently transported to "Bark Inn" for her very first clipping. Gael had stubbornly held out against this essential spot of grooming, preferring the dry mop look to the Mary Had a Little Lamb motif that she knew would be forthcoming when the clipping sequence was begun. Tiffany, however, thought she found her sojourn at Back Inn a traumatic experience, refusing to even look at her mistress as she returned from Holbrook, seems to enjoy being able to see where she is going now; it must have been difficult now and then to have to rely on the radar necessitated by the mop that covered her eyes.

There is no doubt about it, however. The Corbins have at last secured a jewel of a doggie…after a Collie that nipped the neighbors now and then; a Cairn Terrier with all the symptoms of mental retardation; and a Dandie Dinmont Terrier who completely fulfilled the breeder's claim that she would "fight to the death"…, even with her Master.…

New Flash
Today I found a crocus!
He had raised his leafy head,
And was peering there in triumph
O'er my snow-rimmed flower bed.
I could swear that he was smiling;
I could almost hear him sing
As he looked in my direction
And announced impending Spring!

E.N.M

Something exciting happened last week!
We gave the old calendar one long, last tweak
And tore off a page that was aged and spent,
Then laughed right out loud in pure merriment
For behold - there lay waiting a shining new year
With twelve nice new-born months, all invitingly near…
Goodness me, what resolves shall I make for myself
As I tuck last year's failures away on the shelf?
I shall surely arise when the morning is new…
How I love curling up for an hour or two
After day's pink debut puts the night to a rout,
(And I've quietly turned the alarm clock about…)
I shall firmly resolve, when I've found a good book
Not to slip from the world into some hidden nook;
Caring not if it's daylight or whether the night
Has quite softly surrendered to morning's place light.
I shall shop quite efficiently; never run out
Of times I know I just can't do without;
To be punctual on each occasion, I'll try;
(How those last minutes manage to flutter and fly!)
I shan't interrupt; never monopolize
Conversational jousts that others might prize;
And I'll stubbornly fight the fond impulse to boast,
To produce endless snaps, and to offer a toast
To the grandest of grandchildren on this old earth;
(Nor exaggerate mightily all of their worth.)
I shall live on a budget; and pay every bill
Before it's submitted. I promise I will
Wear my boots when it rains, and an umbrella tote,
And for deluges fancy, e'en wear a raincoat!
I'll hold on to my temper, come what well may,
Counting up to fifteen as I keep her at bay…
Not prescribe for all others, on hearing their ills,
With an endless succession of powders and pills.

I'll remember my manners, and lower my voice
As in matters political I make my choice.
I shall try to bring peace where there's discord and strife,
And love where its absence has blighted a life;
To bring light where the darkness is deep and intense,
And to work for mankind, without due recompense…
I shall cease making plans for my wonderful Ted.
(From here in, I shall stop and consult him, instead!)
I'll resist all those bargains I ne'er do use;
And I promise I'll learn how to put in a fuse…
I shall ne'er overload my poor washer again
'Till it grinds to a halt, and Ted screams out in pain…
Goodness me, never dreamed all these faults I have got!
(And undoubtedly there are just tons I've forgot!)
I shan't overload circuits; or yank out the plugs;
Or wax the front hall and then line it with rugs;
Or sing in the shower (up high, and off key)
Or lose sight of the cap of the toothpaste - dear me…
Or purchase the wildest and loudest of ties
For my poor darling Ted cause "It matches his eyes…"
Or boast of my friends 'till embarrassed they grow;
Or spend long winter days madly wishing for snow…
Or forget cars use oil; or run out of gas;
Or fail to enthuse when my son lands a bass
Goodness, gracious, how near nauseatingly nice
I shall be if I bravely surrender each vice,
All these failings I've listed (and there must be more…)
How distressingly GOOD I'll become; what a bore!
Well, I'll give it a go, and it could be a ball!
Here's to me - all reformed!!! Happy Anew Year, y'all!

12-29-63   NEW YEAR'S RESOLUTIONS

HAPPY NEW YEAR resolutions to you! You're making a dozen or two, of course; I always do. The first step, naturally, is to convince yourself that you're anything less than perfect, and then it's easy!

I've been making New Year resolutions for years, with interesting results. I recall the year I solemnly resolved to be on time for all engagements with my dear husband; after two speeding tickets and half a nervous breakdown, he personally begged me to return to my desultory ways.

And the year I resolved to say on a budget. "Gosh, mom, isn't there ever going to be anything good to eat around here anymore?" wailed my son, tucking away his third chocolate éclair.

And the year I resolved to be quiet in company and let other folks do the talking. "Elizabeth," I told myself sternly, "it is high time you reformed. Be a good listener this year, instead of merrily monopolizing the conversation as you normally do." The "new me was a shock to the community. "Elizabeth just sat there disapprovingly." It was said of my debut. I received three telephone calls. "My dear," said my first caller, "You are doing too many things; you looked ill this morning." "Are you bored with our program?" asked a second. "I know you didn't enjoy yourself a bit," said the third, "and I don't blame you, that Mary Jones…" It was delightful to toss that particular New Year resolution overboard, and I've been merrily monopolizing ever since.

ONCE A FEW YEARS back, I resolved not to utter one word of gossip; what followed were, without doubt, the three loneliest days of my life; and to cease looking for "wheels within wheels", life came to a dull standstill.

And another year, I would learn to say "no". I would cease being active to the point of exhaustion in my five hundred clubs and organizations. I kept that resolution for a full year, and did not renew, believe me, when I learned that just as my dear husband had predicted, the organizations went along quite beautifully without me.

I've resolved a dozen different times in as many years not to leave things until the very last minute, however I got my most creative thoughts at 2 a.m. of every due date. You wouldn't have me settle for anything less than my best in the interest of mere punctuality, would you?

RESOLUTIONS I've made this year at the conclusion of the current holiday season:

1. Not to overload the electrical circuits in the house next Christmas with a thousand candles and stars "dear little twinkling Christmas tree lights", thereby causing father to rattle the fire insurance policy with one hand while he throws the electric switch with the other.

2. To start my Christmas shopping in July. (I shan't buy everybody bathing suits.)

Just plain 1964 resolutions:

Not to pray for snowstorms because they're beautiful. (Husband is getting along in years and applies himself with more vigah to the snow shovel than I do."

Not to boast about my grandchildren. (Even though they are the four most remarkable children in existence.)

Not to prescribe a drug at the drop of a symptom. I, personally, will gaily swallow any pill or powder tossed my way, and it always comes as a bit of a shock when someone recoils from my proffered aspirin or seventeenway cold pill.

Not to address everyone I converse with as "dear" - including the sixty year old police officer who stopped me for transgression on the highway last Sunday. (P.S. I didn't get a ticket.) Not to be a chronic do-gooder. It can backfire; it did last week. It was one of those 40-below zero Christmas Days on Tremont St. in Boston and the Salvation Army Lady was ringing her bell. She was a hundred, but come to think of it so did I after the raw winter winds had pinched my face blue. At any rate, the carols were playing on Boston Common, and the little Christ Child's figure in the snowy crèche warmed my heart, and the Christmas spirit moved me. "Would you like a cup of nice, hot coffee?" I asked the dear soul. She nodded absently; I knew later it was an absent nod, however, at the time, I was convinced that she was simply too touched by my kindness to speak.

Brighams' was several blocks away, and I dashed merrily off in its direction. "May I have a cup of coffee to go?" I asked. "To go?" the clerk behind the counter groaned as if the added burden of placing a cover on a cardboard carton was more than she could bear. "You'll have to wait." She said. I waited. The coffee "to go" finally came my way. I headed for the revolving door, through which three teen-aged boys poured simultaneously, squishing my poor dear carton, and all but squishing me.

I looked wistfully back at the forbidding face of the clerk and decided against another cup. Dripping copiously, I headed down Tremont Street, eyeing with dismay my cashmere coat, fresh from the cleaners and gradually acquiring coffee-colored stripes. In one hand I held the container; in the other the five thousand Christmas packages I had accumulated prior to my errand of mercy. My gloves were saturated; my hat awry; but I made it back finally.

"A little Christmas kindness." I told myself warmly as I fought my way among the Christmas throng. "A tiny piece of straw for the manger of the Christ Child to keep Him warm against the winter snow." as mother would say when we were children. There she was, the dear little old lady, and I handed her the inch or so of coffee that remained in the tired carton.

"I think I've spilled some it." I said apologetically, "Some boys caught it in the revolving door, and the waitress did not put the cover on tightly, and I had so many packages…but here is your coffee."

"Coffee? Coffee?." The little old lady recoiled in horror, I didn't order any coffee." She literally bristled. "I never drink the stuff."

Yes, sir, not to be a chronic do-gooder is one of my New Year resolutions for 1964.

THERE ARE OTHERS:

To be a little kinder; to invest enough of me in life to assure some measure of return, to extend the warm, wide hand of friendship; to love with ever increasing depth; to find the sterling worth of the wonderful human beings I seem to know; to live every day in this magnificent world of ours quite as though it were my last; to count our blessings, to thank the Father of us all for a wonderful, warm family in a wonderful, warm home, in a wonderful, warm town, in a wonderful, warm country, with "freedom from want and freedom from fear, and freedom to work and freedom to pray". And not to be so long-winded to my CABBAGES AND KINGS next year. Happy New Year everybody!

1-9-66 NIGHT

FOR THE most part, night falls; but there are evenings at this time of year when one gets the distinct impression it has been pushed. One moment, we are basking in the dear, deep twilight; the next, viola-darkness

How should we be able to endure life without it, however - that vital segment of our 24 hour unit of time that is devoted to "sleep that knits up the raveled sleeve of care"; to dreams; to romance, to mischief, to prayer, to crime, and I might guess, to punishment, for night would seem to be the natural cradle of remorse for any of our wrongdoing.

I drove through the soft silent nighttime of our town last evening. For the most part, Braintree, slumbered, its nice, neat houses locked up tight against the winds and wayfarers without.

HERE AND there, merrymakers splashed the shimmering shadow of the party time against a screen of light; laughing rode the wind, and muscle moved with it.

Other lights shone like buoys upon a blackened sea. The muted light, perhaps within the bedroom of an ailing child; the nite-lite of a little "Fraidy-Cat" or two; the light of Ruth, the reader, propped against her pillows, lost within the wonderful woods of words.

The light of Sam, the slim insomniac? Of Ben-big business holding closed the gates of sleep?

The light so proudly glowing on one Baby Barbie's first two o'clock feeding?

Fireboxes alight, like rich and reassuring rubies in the dark…Police boxes like sapphires bright and bold; street lights, like diamonds, fog lights like topaz…

Christmas has added a new dimension. Here a gay enchanted village holds illuminated sway; there Santa's reindeer all cavort; yonder a sleeping Child His blessed halo wears; angels keep watch!

IT'S A liquid, lovely thing, the night. Through it moves the cruiser a safe sweet island. The firehouse is dimmed, but resting lightly, attuned to e'en the smallest of alarms. "Guardians of the public welfare" guard thee well, oh sleeping town!

Yes, it's liquid and lovely - and menacing, the night. Sound slips like silk across the miles; it startles, forming frightening footfalls in your wake, and bizarre barriers before you…It is awesome and aloof; deep and detached, the night; but high above its sleeping form the sky, awakened, shines with such a bright scrubbed look; stars nod and smile. A rubied jet races the moon to the horizon-a merry moon that winks and wanes and watches. So there is magic in the night.

One raises high ones eyes, and all the menace is removed. Only majesty remains. Dear, delightful night; no wonder I'm eternally impelled to turn it into day!

8-15-68   NIGHT NOISES

When night has voiced its dark decree and banished day's authority;

When heaven's night-light calm and still will silvered silence clothes the hill;

When shadows wide and dark and deep enfold the world in starry sleep;

When those we love are dim with dreams, above the nocturne, lo! it seems

The strangest sort of sounds we hear about this menage we hold dear…

Our house a whispering begins as soft and strange as summer winds;

We hear it and our pulses race as darkness occupies the place.

Who walks upon the creaking stair? What shades are softly meeting there?

Whose echo speaks from out the walls? Whose footstep by my threshold falls?

The sigh of boards beyond the wall where there's no occupant at all…

That strange nocturnal rustling sound when there's no mortal soul around…

Do you, perhaps, oh house of mine, awake as soft sweet arms you twine

About the forms in slumber deep of those I love, all fast asleep?
Do you, oh stairs so prim and tall, gossip together by the wall?
"Gracious," you sigh, "our mistress - she is not as ladies used to be;
No longer does she work and toil; there's no such thing as midnight oil.
No woolens does she spin at all; no candle dipping spree each fall
Sets the staid pattern of her days; she has the strangest kind of ways...
No plump preservings preen themselves upon the splendor of the shelves
Of her cold cellar, dark and deep; it seems to know eternal sleep!
Instead, her day appears to be a gala button pushing spree!
One button for the family wash; a switch to flip (it's all quite posh)
And there's no need to journey out for winds to toss the clothes about;
They dry by magic! Then methinks a "pig" inhabits all her sinks!
The strangest kind of gadget spins and opens an array of tins' the which, with packets iced and sweet provide a gourmet's dining treat...
I'm tellin you, my friendly shade - today's homemaker has it made!"
Are these the kind of things they say as night-shades' murmuring holds sway???
I trust that one small spirit fair in sounding silence by the stair
Will whisperingly disagree and come to the defense of me!
"Our mistress leads a different life," she'll say, "from yesteryear's good wife...
If you will take a look around, you'll find the interests of the Town
Are hers; no lady yesterday had even HEARD of P.T.A.'
And chauffeuring the younger fry was quite unknown in days gone by...

No gardening chores did ladies know; to soil their hands was
quite de trop!

No meetings did those gals attend; tea parties were their living
end!

Our mistress presses buttons- TRUE - so she'll be free and
clear to do

The thousand things that overlay the busy moments of her
day…"

I trust one shade the time will take to these few observations
make…

\ The night is warm and shadowy and sleep's eluding weary me;

Night noises whispering about now vie with all the sounds
without…

How well my shades their vigil keep! I wish they'd let me get
to sleep!

3-24-73 NO GENTLEMEAN THIS!

There are those who look upon the merry little squirrels that pip
about Braintree in such significant numbers these days as UNDESIRABLE
neighbors. They warn of gnawing and nesting in the family attic; of trips
to the neighborhood exterminator, etc. etc. etc.

Brother-in-law Tim fell easily into that category… "They ARE
rodents," he would say disdainfully. That was, however, before he himself
found a friend among the merry ones that frequent his back yard…a
friend who came to the door, and chattering gaily, demanded a share of
his lunch each noon.

The Metayers had found friends among the little fellows right from
the start. One in particular had become a veritable member of the family.
We called him Sammy, a handsome chap with a tail that would have
easily enabled him to swing from the Empire State Building to City Hall.
With it, however, he elected merrily to sail from one to another of the
family trees, and to perform with all the professionalism of a circus star
upon the nearby telephone wires.

Sammy Squirrel was, in every sense of the word, a character. The arrival of guests at the Metayer menage, for instance, would find him scampering down to greet them, his saucy eye alight, his small mouth chattering a welcome as warm as our own. Sammy gardened along with the distaff side, and trailed the head of the house faithfully as he mowed the lawn or trimmed the hedges. He buried his winter stores openly, secure in the knowledge that we would leave his cache untouched, regardless of where he planted it. Sam's favorite spot was the broad planting area that surrounds the house itself…and thereby hangs our tale…

Unhappily this Spring Sammy was missing from the family scene. Nasturtium seeds that I had been planting for years only to have him dig up and devour each and every one of them, amazed us all by coming up beautifully in a nice neat row. "I just can't seem to get nasturtiums to grow along the fence, "I had been complaining forever, "I plant them faithfully each May, however they NEVER come up." I eventually learned the reason. I caught my friend Sammy merrily consuming each juicy seed the moment my back was turned. Well, with the arrival of said nasturtiums this Spring, our worst fears were confirmed. We faced the fact that Sammy Squirrel was with us no more. Actually he had been showing signs of advancing years for some time. His tail had taken on a rather tired, moth-eaten look; and his scampering had seemed not quite so sprightly.

We prepared to miss him, Ted and I and our grandsons' and then we made a startling discovery. Sammy, it appeared, had left a son and heir to fill his place in our hearts.…To carry on the happy relationship with the family he had grown to love…a saucy, bright-eyed fellow with a wild tail that reminded us of Sammy's at its youngest and best. The small chap descended from the maple tree and joined us at our gardening tasks quite as though his "dad's" last words had been, "Take care of the Metayers." He chattered as Sammy had chattered; and he even managed to toss down an acorn or two upon the head of a small puppy who had joined us at our labors. Shades of Sammy, Senior who for years had similarly aggravated Lady Jane, the family dog! "Janie" who was obliged to spend long summer hours droolingly parading back and forth under the high wires, ducking the chestnuts a safe and sound squirrel was tossing down upon her unprotected head! But to return to Sammy Junior, for that is what we named him. The Metayers took a lazy turn this spring. We decided on the purchase of vast quantities of pine bark chips to be spread about the family menage. There was to be little or no weeding in the first summer we've spent at home in years, we decided; and the chips were spread about the family rose garden and about the foundation planting area; and everywhere else where nice bare earth had for years been providing storage space for a small furry creature with any eye to the future. Sammy Junior was not to be seen when the chips went down. (His "father" would have been Johnny-on-the-spot; make no mistake about that!)

Came morning and we awoke to find literally hundreds of pine bark chips scattered hither and yon about the lawn and on the walk and in area after area adjacent to their original location. We tidied things up. Came the next morning however, and the situation was the same. It went on and on and on, with the Metayers painfully replacing the pine bark chips and an unknown merrily tossing them out… "Who in the world can be doing this?" we asked of one another again and again. We were eventually to find out…It was a beautiful day when, annuals in hand, I sauntered out into the garden to plant. Ted had completed the morning chore of tidying up the pine chips and I was crossing the lawn, trowel in hand, when up the long back walk came Sammy, 2nd. He was indignant and it showed. He marched right up to meet me, stopped dead and proceeded to chatteringly scold me within an inch of my life. His wonderful tail switched back and forth in what was plainly an expression of anger. Suddenly then, he stopped, marched resolutely over to the foundation planting, and, with his bright eyes still fixed on mine, proceeded to send a shower of pine bark chips in every direction. He moved a few feet away and repeated the performance, chattering the while in a tone that expressed complete, unvarnished indignation. "There," Sammy Junior was plainly saying, and as defiantly as any human ever could, "THAT'S what I think of your new anti-weed nonsense. Now, where AM I supposed to bury my acorns, will you please tell me that? If I STARVE next winter, it will be all your fault!"

Ted and I regarded the small fellow with laughing eyes. "Sammy Squirrel, 2nd," I said firmly, "YOU are not the GENTLEMAN your father was!"

12-30-73 NO LIGHTS AT CHRISTMAS?

"It doesn't FEEL like Christmas," Grandson Gregory bemoaned;
And knew just how he felt, and so all inwardly I groaned...
"The Jones-es have THEIR lights on down the street. Come
    on and see!"
I took his hand, and - sure enough - there, twinkling merrily,
Were the candles in each window, quite gloriously alight,
Shedding all their Christmas cheer upon the dark December
    night!
"Well, I'll tell you," I said; "Darling, we MUST everyone cut
    down
on the energy required to light up our little town
Though it IS the Christmas season." "What is ENGERGY?"
    he asked,
As within the glowing circle of the neighbor's light he basked...
Didn't know how to explain it to a six-year-old small lad
Especially when the myriad explanations leave me mad!
"It's an outrage," I think sometimes. "Someone's sadly off the
    beam.
Couldn't happen OVERNIGHT! Now no nice candlelight
    may gleam
From behind our Christmas windows if we take quite seriously
All those threats of cold cold days unless we use real sparingly
So I looked at grandson Gregory's wide sad eyes, and said,
    "You see,
Mom and Dad and Gram and Grandpa are a law-abiding bunch,
And though inwardly and privately, they may all have a hunch
That to raise sky high the prices on our oil and on our gas
Is the REAL and PRIVATE reason that's behind this squeeze alas!
The request for no bright candles in the windows Christmas Day.
We must keep our houses cooler, and drive less these gasless days;
In THAT way, we'll all survive this energy shortage we deplore
But, gosh! Even as I tried explaining things to one small boy

I was suddenly aware that deep inside, a surge of joy
Quite engulfed me as I stood there in the deep December night
And I must admit that inwardly I gave a happy sigh...
Thank the Lord ALL people aren't as law-abiding as am I!
HAPPY NEW YEAR, EVERYBODY!

1-25-70   NOT AGAIN!!!

IT HAS HAPPENED again! Your columnist has once more been the victim of a "typo" - as it is known to member of the Fourth Estate -- a typographical error to the general public....

This particular typo came to light last Sunday afternoon with the ringing of the family telephone.

"Hello, there," said a merry voice. "Do you know, I always HAVE wondered where you get that astonishing vitality of yours, now I know. Reading about the doing of your phenomenal mother, I understand everything. You inherited it! Eighty years old and gadding about England on her silver-spoked bicycle; and needing a CHAPERONE, to boot! What a woman!"

There was a pregnant silence on my end of the line while I tried frantically to figure what in the world she was talking about. I finally framed the question.

The lady laughed gaily, "You mean you haven't READ it yet?" she said, "Your Cabbage???" "Good heavens, no," I said. "I never READ my Cabbages. I just WRITE 'em." "Well," said my friend gaily. "You had better read THIS one!" The which I promptly did.

Last Sunday's Cabbage had concerned itself' with the adventures to be found in books; and the various family bookworms whose love of reading had been inculcated in them by our parents. The contact of those marvelous parents of ours with the English world of Dickens and Shakespeare and the rest, had been duly recounted; and interesting contact, incidentally, they were.

The paragraph in which the typo had occurred read as follows:

"Mother and Dad were born in England, and as young students had belonged to the same 'Cycle Club,' the highest ambition of whose member was, incidentally, to possess a 'wheel' with 'solid silver handlebars and wheel spokes. Mother had received this handsome badge of distinction from dad on her 80th birthday; and each weekend, CAREFULLY CHAPERONED BY 'SENIOR CYCLISTS,' the club member would set out in a group for some distant corner of their 'fabulous island.'...

MUST YOU be told that the lady received the silver-spoked bicycle on her 18th birthday, and not her 80th???

While we are on the subject of typos, here's another delightful story that came my way recently. The small town social leader was staging an extremely elaborate garden party, and the local reporter had been sent to cover the event. She was brand new at the game; this was her very first assignment; and she had been instructed by the social editor to "get all the color" she could into the story. She did just that...

Describing in detail the attire of the elegant ladies numbered among the "distinguished guests" of the social lioness, the neophyte went on to provide a glowing description of the tea table setting, the garden appointments, etc. etc.

She finished her social coverage as follows:

"Mrs. Halstead-Heath received her guests beneath a bower of golden chrysanthemums, her bronze green gown obviously having been selected to provide a striking contrast to their pale shade. The lady had plainly taken infinite pains to carry out to the minutest detail the citrus shades in the color scheme featured in her charming garden party decor. At her side were her daughters, three of whom were yellow." (The word, quite obviously, should have been "wore".)

Incidentally, what a break this "typo" was! It does not happen often; but this week, wrack my brains as I might, I failed to come up with a single subject for a Cabbage. Thanks, you nice gals who typed me one.

1-21-74   NOVEMBER

It's a tired old month, this one that has just ended. NOVEMBER! It's grey and grim, with none of the magic of snow-kissed sweet December yet about it; and all of the flaming glory of October far behind; with the year dragging its wan and wearing steps unto the dying...

Yes, it's a tired old month, yet there's a stark strange beauty in its swan song.

Against the somber smoke of the sky, the hills are hushed. They don their pilgrim cloaks of earthen brown. They draw rough homespun cowls about their greying locks; and bow their heads; and fold clawed, leafless hands upon their breasts and seek to sleep a winter sleep.

Below them a muted, brown-tone symphony is sung. Frost-kissed, the trees hang rich brown garments out to dry. Aprons of copper cast their lustrous shade; gowns of a pine-sweet green; and hose of birch-bark white; and capes of stubborn, storm-passed gold are tossed to shed their nighttime dew upon the wind-whipped reels of winter.

Trees are black lace etchings on the sun; and ancient crones, bend low to catch the last lean warmth of autumn's pale caress; and proud defenseless warriors at bay. They're ballet dancers slim and straight upon the bare earth stage; they're children, tossing their leaf balls to the wind; they're lovers, whispering softly; they're great gregarious men; and matrons, wide and warm, serene with memories...

Yes, there's a magic yet to our November...

All of the woods' fair trappings are undone, whipped wide away on winter's wanton winds, Water lies gleaming naked in the sun, catching the gold of sunset thirstily in its heart; or tossing sweet silvered coins upon its breasts; shining and shouting now - no longer among the leaf-draped glens of summer.

Bird's nests sway softly in the trees' embrace, mute merry tributes to a tender trade.

Roads are great grey puffed adders sliding about the scene, shedding leaf-patterned skins; soaking up sun; drinking in rain...

Birds-flocks write south-bound music in the sky, striking music in the sky, striking strange alien chords against the wide wire staffs they mount to rest.

Fir trees are grave black sentinels on guard as all the vastness of the woods is open to attack by winter's savage hordes.

Wild are the storm-swept moanings of the winds; eerie the haunting whisperings of errant captive zephyrs, loath to leave.

Earth wears a crazy-quilt with bits of smooth soft green; and tufts of grizzled grey; and bars of black; with sandy strips of tan; and coins of rich-brown chocolate drops upon the whole; with russet and rose; with silver and sage; and all the brilliant browns the eye can know...

Yes, it's a tired old month, November...and yet, there's a strange stark beauty in it, it has a magic all its own. Besides hasn't it just housed THANKSGIVING DAY??? And don't those happy holidays of our - the blessed Christmas season and it joys - lie dead ahead???

12-1-68   NOVEMBER GARDEN2

My garden green is all confused!
I stand within it, quite bemused.
To see the mixed-up state it's in!
Will winter's changes e'er begin??

****

A row of pink snapdragons gay
Belies just past Thanksgiving Day...
A pansy face, as bright as ALL
Winks merrily at dying Fall...

****

The honeysuckle's swelling buds
Resemble sprouting springtime duds;
While maple trees their branches bend
With tasseled trimming, end to end!

****

I almost think that passing by
A hyacinth's green spear I spy!
Good grief-the ANTS are busy there
In sweet endeavor by the stair!

****

Is winter really SHORTENING???
Will each year see sooner SPRING???
Has this world's madcap, merry race

Affected e'en my garden's pace?

****

November's spent 'tis past the date
When gardens fair should hibernate…
The ducks are floating on the bay;
Each robin red has flown away.

****

The sea is gray; the sky is grim…
Where do you GET this Springtime vim???
Fair flora and fresh fauna, too-
I DON'T KNOW WHAT TO MAKE OF YOU!!!

****

Dear little flowers, go to sleep;
Your vigil I shall fondly keep.
If you'd be bright and green and gay
When April's trumpet blows your way,
YOU BEST JUST SETTLE DOWN TO REST
Against the earth's renewing breast…
I've tucked you in I've mulched you high!
For goodness' sakes, now, SAY "GOODBYE"….

10-10-65 OCTOBER

OCTOBER is a sad old month. It houses all the fond farewells to summer.

Sunday was "say goodbye to the garden" day at our house. We folded up the awnings that spell sweet summer privacy upon the sundeck, and tucked them carefully away within the attic, to await another spring. Piles of porch furniture were toted over the green lawn to the snug shelter of the cellar. It's an easy task now that lawn furniture is feather-light, and most of it's collapsible; but what a chore it used to be not too long ago when each chaise lounge weighed fully 50 pounds, and nothing folded flat for storage; and things refused outright to pass between the cellar doors without a world of wild manipulation. It's different now.

We said a busy old goodbye. We "pipped" about the lawn with weed-killer for the old defiant ones who cling tenaciously unto the bitter end; with grass seed for the tired spots; and fertilizer for the autumn rains and early morning dews. How lush the lawn's become incidentally, now that the summer's heat has gone!

AND WHAT a busy place a garden e'er must be when it's October! Rose plants lie waiting to be served. We mound them with soft earth, and spray their sparse green leaves, and bring a gay bouquet indoors, where, 'cause it's autumn they will shed within the day those bright sweet petals that are trying - oh so hard - to hold far back the winter's swift approach within our garden green Evergreens must have one long last drink to slake the thirst that lies about their roots; and peonies must all be stripped of stalks; the bulb beds softened and prepared. Leaves must be raked, and goodness, now-how sudden is their fall!

"The leaves, I think are late," I said just yesterday, "they don't seem to be turning, and they're not falling at all." Then - down they came! I smile to see my willows tightening their joints up against the winter wind. They toss with cool contempt upon the lawn, those spindly branches at their tips that summer's drought has weakened; and we tote them off for burning...

We're not the only busy ones our garden houses on an autumn afternoon. Ants scurry by, all toting forty times their weight, or so it seems; the grasshoppers' gaiety is gone. The garden's tempo has quite suddenly all changed.

MY FRIEND the squirrel is too busy now to pause and nod a bright-eyed "hi" as she invariably does when I approach her fair preserve. She has no time these days for showing off the prowess of her young ones on the loose highwire that serves my telephone within. She's busy...so are her young ones...tucking their acorns all away against the time of snow and scarcity.

The garden snake that suns himself upon the wall is gone; the old Jap beetles have all settled down beneath the sheltering earth, to wait another year before attacking in full force my succulent blooms. No robin is in sight; nor do the starlings gather in the tree; and not one baby sparrow plays at flight, his mother's bright-eyed face upon his own.

Neighbors no longer stroll serenely by; no boys with baseball caps upon their heads pass now enroute to Little League and play. And there's a somber, sighing singing to the wind…

The fire we light within our pretty patio fireplace sheds welcome warmth; we stand within its glow, and stretch forth chilling hands, and bid a sad farewell to one more summer we have loved.

October is a sad old month.

10-13-68 OCTOBER

OCTOBER, and the golden sun of summer sets; setting a waning world aflame!

Against the gray of autumn-somber sky the hills catch fire. They don their scarlet cloaks, the golden linings shimmering in the sun. The plums they set upon their purpling caps are russet-red; their doublets dark and green; their hose a dew-kissed earthen brown…

The breeze that stirs their flame to fire is cool and kind. Streams mirror their shining beauty in soft steel. And there's a whisper in the woods that says; "Dance in the trees' great dying arms, you golden nymphs of leaves - for this has become your final hour - your gasp of glory as you pass." Off in the orchards, fruit trees spill their gold low on the vines, the nuts are brown and sweet; their fluted cheeks strain softly to be freed. Pumpkins are brash and bright; and grapes are purpling casks of wine; the cider's gold spills softly from the press.

Squirrels have ceased their rompings on the lawn; their treks - on business bent - are swift and sure; their husbandry a joy!

Birds blacken the autumn skies, fleeing the whispering winter's grim approach.

*****

PINE CONES are brown and bright beneath the feet; and beech-burrs nod their hurried heads as down they fly; and chestnuts (set for storing in all small boys pockets) SHINE and all the earth's glad glowing of a hundred days its PEAK has reached. The world is RICH and RIPE.

The garden's blaze is bright. Chrysanthemums, frost-kissed, raise blushing, full-blown faces to the soothing winds. Rose-apples vie with roses; and yews are decked with saucy scarlet rings; and each fair garden flower blooms wildly in abandon e'er it fades…

Skies sound a grave gray symphony of tone; and clouds are jarring notes upon the score.

Swiftly the DARK comes now; day hastens on, tarrying not; closing a sudden door, and night is full and deep and dire. Star-suns are sharp; and moons don icy stares…

*****

SOON the cold scythe of winter will have come, cutting its sharp, sure swathe through autumn's heart. NAKED, the hills will stand against the sky; barren the trees, and black, and bare and bowed.

7-26-70   ODDEMENTS

The delightfully turned phrases of others have a decided appeal for this concocter of "Cabbages" - like the following, which have been lifted from hither and yon, and jotted down on paper scraps during the past few book-filled vacation weeks:

"She looked like tomorrow could only be worse."

"A precious cat of a man…"

"Old house like driftwood in the rain."

"He devoured the hours."

"Mockery was flame to the quick tinder of his fury."

"He lit it with the slow care of the aged."

"And their names were thunder and their work was lightning, whose glare would light the paths of medicine forever."

"The opposite of love is not hate; it is indifference. Hate is frustrated love."

"The pictures in the art galleries are mine to stand before and reverence and be inspired by -all mine, and yet I have no fears of fire or theft; no costly premiums to pay for their insurance.

"Fog comes on little cat feet…"

And to conclude with an original reflection born also of summer leisure; We are part of everything we've seen and done-of everyone we've known. Our faces and our voices are but mirrors on which are reflected the workings of our minds, the seekings of our souls, during all the years of our lives

ON ARCHIE KEIGAN

Paul Revere's historic bit about the British that other April day nearly two hundred years ago had no more impact, I am sure, on his community than the news that spread "from village to farm" on a recent April day here in Braintree. DR. KEIGAN WAS BACK!

There are very few in Braintree who were not aware (though he strove for secrecy) that Archie G. Keigan, M.D. has been dangerously ill, for there are very few in Braintree who have not, directly or indirectly fallen within the sphere of influence of this remarkable man.

When the news of his serious illness was spread aboard on last Election Day, a pall literally descended upon East Braintree, for he is high on the list of her favorite sons. On everyone's lips, it seemed, could be heard questions, "Have you heard about Dr. Keigan?" "Is there news of Dr. Keigan?" For this is a man upon whose great heart the Hippocratic oath has been etched in steel. THIS IS A MAN!

We do not know Dr. Keigan's religious persuasion, but we would venture to guess that from the congregations of every church and synagogue of every religious denomination in Braintree a wave of prayer swept heavenward for "Archie" - as those who love him call him privately - in his hour of peril. We would venture to say further that he is no stranger to the angel who "writes in the book of gold" the fine, high deeds of mortal men.

Dr. KEIGAN was born in New Waterford, Cape Breton, Canada. He is a product of the Braintree Public School system from kindergarten through high school. He was captain of the Braintree High School track team, and also of the Tufts College track team. He served as Captain in the Army Medical Corps in Germany during World War II.

Currently serving as associate medical examiner for the 4th Norfolk Medical District, Dr. Keigan is a member of the Charitable Irish Society, the Gridiron Club of Greater Boston and the Braintree Rotary Club.

He is married to the former Dorothy Tatler, R.N. of Stow Mass.; a graduate of the Framingham Union Hospital School of Nursing. Idealistically motivated, charming and retiring, she is the perfect helpmate for her doctor husband. They have four children. Robert, 15, a student at Braintree High School. David, 11 and Margot 8, students at Watson School, and Rory 6, who is currently attending Thayerlands.

Dr. Keigan loves thoroughbred horses. A devotee of fox hunting, he makes a yearly pilgrimage to Ireland to participate in this, his favorite sport. He can be seen on an occasional free day riding his beloved "Mediation" around the little corral that adjoins his home. "Plastique" and "Royal Guide" his other two equine loves, are currently racing at Lincoln Downs.

An advocate of sports and outdoor life, Dr. Keigan has sponsored the Little League Major's Penguin Ball Club for the past seven years. He was Camp physician for the Brownies for 15 year and has contributed much to the Boy Scout movement

So much for the statistics on Dr. Keigan, now for the man himself.

THE LARGEST part of his anatomy is his great, warm beating heart. Not a spare pound of flesh cover his 6 foot frame. Spare flesh comes from regular meals and adequate sleep, and good, self-centered care, and Dr. Keigan has no time for such nonsense. There is always another father or mother, wife or husband to be reassured, another sick child to be comforted. Dr Keigan, you see, is numbered among America's unsung medical heroes. He is a general practitioner.

HIS PATIENTS are incidentally, his friends. He knows them all by name. He knows their children. He is aware of their faults and failings, their idiosyncrasies, their fears, and hopes, and dreams. Their babies, by the dozens, have been named for him. Once one of them, having been taken ill while on a visit to Ireland that coincided with his, crossed the Emerald Isle to seek his care. People, old and young, love the man.

Anyone who has ever been involved in the special town clinics to which he volunteers his services, and watched the small fry head like so many homing pigeons for Dr. Keigan's corner. John H. Crowell, Principal of East Junior High School recently termed him "the people's doctor". The people are very, very proud to claim him.

Dr Keigan is back. Thanks to an Almighty Providence he has been returned from the "valley of shadows" and the pall has been lifted from our hearts. We rejoice with him and one another. But let us now spare and protect this Lincolnesque man of medicine from the natural inclinations of his own great beating but tired heart. It is always good judgment to conserve one's assets, and Archie G. Keigan, M.D. is one of the finest assets that we in Braintree possess!

4-26-64   ON A SMILE

OH, THE monumental magic of a smile!

It is one of the few treasures in our possession which we may give away, share, or lavish with complete abandon, secure in the knowledge that its source will remain forever undiminished, inexhaustible.

Its investment will bring the richest of dividends in friends in friendship and affection. It can soften the sharp, thin edge of a rebuke, it can temper the steel of the sternest of discipline; it can be the gentle right arm of authority. It can be shared by cat and king, and each is richer for the sharing. It knows no age limit, for it is ever and always a thing of beauty. A baby's first faint smile (though frequently the pure result of colic) can lift his parents' ego to the skies. A child's warm welcoming one, can, be the most sweet reward for which the most devoted grandparents will quite openly compete and vie and stoop to any depth to win.

A smile knows no language barriers. It is the universal symbol of man's good-will toward man. Its golden application can transform the plainest face to one of beauty, for features have but little bearing on the magic of a smile. It comes from deep within. There's bit of soul in it, and a touch of the heart. It's the golden window dressing for the joy that lies inside

THERE ARE, of course, smiles and smiles. There's the quicksilver kind that flashes for a moment like the shining of a light within; and, there's the show kind of smile that gather with the crinkling of the eyes, then, wrinkles the nose slightly, then, lifts the corner of the mouth, and rounds the cheeks, and spreads the whole wide face with warmth and wonder. There are a thousand other kinds of smiles that lie between these two, all quite, quite wonder-our.

We remember smiles as we can ne'er remember tears - the soft proud smile of mother, and of father; the kind, approving smile of our beloved; the soft, starched rustling smiles that brought our first-born to our heart; the smiles of grandparents long gone; and friends fore'er remembered... We shall remember tomorrow to smile at the very young, and at the very old - and at the ones who lie between. We shall remember to share this wondrous coin we may so freely spend …to lavish it…to invest it…for such a shiny usage will most surely place the lines where they belong upon our faces, in little happy crinkles at the eyes, and upward jolly curvings at the mouth.

We shall try to be known for the gold of our smile, for this is the gold that vaults were meant to hold.

3-29-64   ON THE FIRST ROBIN

I SAW my first spring robin! He surveyed my winter lawn.
From the loftiness of hedge-top in the pale day's dusty dawn:
And the scarlet of his weskit and
The black-bright of his eyes
Made a splash of sudden glory in
the weary winter skies,
Oh, there's something 'bout the
first enchanting robin that I see
That can set my soul to soaring
on a wave of ecstasy.

I ADORE the first pale crocus
peeping sweetly by the wall!
And I love that first forsythia
apply "The Golden Ball"
I could pet each pussy willow;
and the first gay daffodil
sets my heart to silent singing as
it nods there on the hill.
I rejoice with every leaflet that
adorns the maple tree:
And andromeda in blossom makes a poet of poor me.

WHEN THE HYACINTH stands
primly with a "Come and see-
I'm here! -
Now the winter's at the waning,
and the springtime it is near.
And I thrill to find the lilac, budding gently by the door,
And the frosty hand of winter on
the rose bush is no more
I write sonnets in the garden! I'm
a poet through and through,
I'm inspired with springtime's
symphony of green and gold and blue.

BUT WHEN one shiny morning
as I rise to greet the dawn,
I find my first spring robin strutting gaily on the lawn
And he tugs the sleeping earthworm from his haven in the grass.
And winks his eye as he swaggers
by with that robin redbreast brass.
Then I send a prayer toward
heaven as I curtsy to the sun
For I know the march toward
summer has officially begun.

12-26-64 ON THE FAMILY DOG...

LADY JANE GREY Metayer is very old as the age of a dog is reckoned, and she has grown hopelessly blind. It breaks our hearts to see the frisky little puppy we once knew whimper in fright at a flight of stairs or injure her whiskery little face against the sharp end of an unseen table. She should be "put to sleep." It's the humane thing to do, I tell myself. But it's so difficult to bring myself to believe.

Janie, as we have always called her, is of no determinate origin. Her mother was a Scottie, and her father a wire-haired terrier, and Janie like many people of unimpressive background, who find themselves almost unexpectedly in a position of affluence and comfort - is a SNOB! She never leaves the confines of our property, but lies daintily on the porch, looking disdainfully down her nose at neighborhood canines. Janie does have her neighborhood favorites, of course, but they're people, not dogs. "Some day," we say, "Janie will look in a mirror and discover she's a dog, and the shock will be too much for her." I know she thinks she's a person...

"Woof" Janie will say almost to herself as certain people pass by,

"Goodness," she is announcing by her tone "there's my friend Mary Jones," and down she will trot to greet the passerby and pass the time of day.

JANIE NEVER leaves home unless, of course, she is not feeling up to par, when she will take her ailment two houses down to Auntie. Auntie is an R.N. and Janie, who knows a good nurse when she sees one, will move into her establishment, collar and leash, until she has recovered.

Janie, in spite of her questionable ancestry, once won third prize at the Braintree Pet Show. Her mistress, who was about ten, had been grooming her and training her for days. "Her name?" Asked the registration lady. "Lady Jane Grey Metayer," said Gael, quite as though she were the titled darling of King Henry's court. "What breed is she?" Gail lapsed into a recital of her ancestry. "Dog," wrote the lady with a smile. "We had to give her a prize," said the judge. "She's so darned cute... "She'd have come in first, I know mother" said her mistress, "if it hadn't been for that collie: obviously he's a show dog." Actually I don't think Janie minded losing to the collie: a male collie is the only breed of dog with which Janie ever designed to be on speaking terms.

She once had a fling at theatre. Pure "ham" like the rest of the family, she strutted with complete aplomb through scenes from "The Little Dog Laughed" in a local high school production and was a featured performer in "Mushrooms Coming Up" with a Junior Woman's Club group. (She has a press clipping, complete with picture to prove it.) She almost repeated her success in a local P.T.A. presentation. A brief fling at temperament, however, cost her the role - to a stuffed poodle. The irony of it.

This was the period in her life when Janie refused to leave our menage without her jeweled collar. She must also have read somewhere of Hollywood, and Graumnn's Chinese Theatre, for there came a day when, despite the concerted vigilance of the entire Metayer family, Janie planted her paw prints firmly in the wet cement of our new garage floor…for posterity.

JANE RESENTS any and all attention we may pay to other beasties. The fussiest of eaters she will quickly devour every stale crumb of cake or bread we toss to the birds. She has a distinct aversion to the little gray squirrel who chatters to me on the patio in summer. And she loathes cats.

Our neighbor once possessed two of them, with a large dog, who was their protector. Came the day; a summer or so ago when Paddy, the dog, departed with his family for a month at the beach, leaving his feline friends in the care of a neighbor and at Janie's mercy. Janie sauntered forth each morning "fresh as new paint" "treed" the cats and devoured their food. (She wouldn't touch dog food.) Two forlorn cats spent a full month in the apple tree with one of us feeding them at night while Janie slept. "Wait until Paddy comes home," we told her. "Wait until those kitties tell him what you've been up to." Came the day of Paddy's return, and over sauntered two large cats to where Janie had retreated on the porch. They pranced back and forth before her, their tails enormous…their heads high. "Chase us," they were saying. "We dare you…Janie lay there, cold with rage. She quivered all over; she literally drooled: she made strange, frustrated noises in her throat -- but it was "paws off". Paddy was back!

HOW CAN YOU "put to sleep" a little black and white dog who is part and parcel of a thousand family memories? It's like closing a door on the childhood of those you love. "Mother," I can still hear Gael complaining when she was very young and learning to skate. "I just can't take Janie with me any more. Every time I fall on the ice, she jumps into my lap because her paws are cold, and I can't get up..."

"That Janie..." Richard would say. "Every time I get a bead on a squirrel, she barks and chases him away. She's not going hunting with Jerry and me anymore." But she did. She tagged along with one or other of them every time, everywhere, down through the happy years...They all grew up together!

You, who have looked into the warm, trusting eyes of a dog you love, and watched the little tail that seems to have discovered perpetual motion marking your arrival, you will sympathize with me. I must put my Janie to sleep; it's the humane thing to do. Well, perhaps tomorrow.

2-2-75   ORIENTATION

We've been evolving into "Legislators," we Freshmen members of the House of Representatives...and with the most impressive set of educators the world of politics has probably ever known...The Joint Committee on Rules; assisted by the Clerk of the House of Representatives; the Program for Legislative Improvement; the Legislative Research Council and Bureau and the Legislative Service Bureau...The Institute for Government Services of the University of Massachusetts...The Institute for Politics J.F. Kennedy School of Government; Harvard University" and the Bureau of Adult Education of the Department of Education.

The Orientation program for the entering class of 1975, 169th Biennial Session of the Massachusetts Great and General Court was to be done up Brown; and it was! We were even to hold Commencement Exercises and to be awarded a Certificate issued by the Department of Education, attesting to the fact that we had completed a course in Legislative Procedures.

Our Orientation program had begun with a welcome by the Legislative Leaders and a panel discussion with Senators Anna Buckley and John F. Parker along with Representatives George Kavarian and Anthony Gallugi, all fellow legislators with their own particular philosophies and points of view. We were to attend seminars on the Massachusetts Economy (It's dismal!) to learn how the Media views the Legislator and the Legislature; to meet our Attorney General and Secretary of State, our State Treasurer and State Auditor; and to learn a bit about the functions of each of these distinguished State Officials; to become informed about the budget, revenue and taxes in a seminar that was to be conducted by key figures in each of those three areas. We were to learn much of the needs and aspirations of the Judiciary; and meanwhile, at the hands of a superb instructor, Clerk of the House of Representatives Wallace C. Mills, to become reasonably well-acquainted (we students falling far short of our teacher) with the intricacies of legislative procedure.

And at last we were to really participate in a true "sitting" of that most august body, the HOUSE OF REPRESENTATIVES! The experience was awe-inspiring. Beaneath the Speaker's rostrum a plaque bearing the words of a martyred President… "John Fitzgerald Kennedy spoke from this rostrum to the Massachusetts General Court on January 9, 1961," we read. "I carry with me from this State to that high and lonely office to which I now succeed," he had said, "the fond memories of firm friendships. The enduring qualities of Massachusetts…will not be and could not be forgotten in this nation's executive mansion. Courage-integrity-judgment-dedication- these are the historic qualities of the Bay Colony and the Bay State - the qualities which this state has consistently sent to this Chamber on Beacon Hill here in Boston and to Capitol Hill back in Washington. And these are the qualities which with God's help this son of Massachusetts hopes will characterize our government's conduct in the four stormy years that lie ahead."

Courage-integrity-judgment-dedication…" the words seeped deep into my soul; may they remain there for all the years I shall serve the people of the Town I hold dear and the State I treasure.

Other quotes were to come to my mind as I looked back over the two weeks of indoctrination just passed. "The role of the legislator is using concern to push for economic stability…Economic development must be established as a town problem, not a state problem; the State and Federal governments should play only supportive and guidance roles…(I'm a Home Ruler, so I'll agree to that.) Businessmen need an Ombudsman to guide it through the State and local governments. The

Legislature is a very human kind of institution. The business of this Chamber is to make decisions and there will be many times when you will have to vote aye or nay and will wish you might vote "MAYBE"... Now we belong to the people and the public is a hard taskmaster... You are a politician and it is an honorable and ancient profession...You can't fool anybody; your colleagues are professional...You must temper the flame of idealism with the realities of life...Your representative owes you not only industry but his intellect...Success is never final...Employ sincerity, simplicity and directness; use a ten cent word rather than a dollar one...A bill's importance is judged by the number of people it affect..." Wonderful quotes, all of them; I shall try to remember each and every one.

We have been assured by our Governor, Michael Dukakis, that because he came from the Legislature he hopes to work closely with us; and by Lieutenant-Governor Tom O'Neill that we are "the best-prepared Freshman Class the State has ever seen." We have been advised, when speaking to an issue to "be good; be brief, be gone!"

Why are we all there, I ask myself wonderingly as I look about me at the diverse group of individuals who have elected to take upon themselves the business of governing??? Essentially, I decide, our motivation is pretty much the same. We are there because each one of us in his (or her) own way is committed to improving the quality of life for the people of his town and of his State; and when it comes to improving the quality of life for our Massachusetts citizens it's here on Beacon Hill where the action is! Every day brings a new State House adventure for this happy columnist. It's beautiful on Beacon Hill! Love it! Love it! Love it!

ON EARLY SPRING

SPRING is whispering its way to Braintree these days. The great white blanket of snow that lay like a quiet mantle o'er the town is now gone. In its place we find only the occasional nondescript patch of mottled white in a shady place, like a soiled dollie tossed on the soft brown tabletop of awakening earth.

Hyacinths have sent up coy, clasped fingers, green-gloved, beside the garden wall. The maple trees wave wine rosettes upon the wanton world. Winter's golden lawn is bronzing green. The bare forsythia branch I tucked behind the playroom door is spilling gold.

Small children lose their boots in soft, dark ooze. Marbles are out, and grave boys ring my doorbell, seeking wheels for all the "buggies" that will toss them on the hill, and cause tense motorists to fret and fume, and each child's dog to sportingly give chase..

Dad is raking leaves, and sprucing up the family boat, and eyeing golf clubs, and the long sleek fishing pole he loves. Mother checks mops and pails and views the winter cobwebs with chagrin; and dad remembering last year's grim spring cleaning quietly begins.

Seed catalogs are out and winter kill's dark grasp upon the shrubs is viewed with cold dismay. Crocuses nod, and children's coats lie open to the wind, and lessons are a sudden, seasonal, bore. John dreams...and catches sunlight in a grave girl's hair....and Mary ties a bow there. (And mother with a bathing suit in mind, goes on a diet.

It will show tomorrow Capricious nature will exchange the white lace dollies for a spread. The crocuses will hide; the maples red rosettes will sliver shine. And sleds will rage once more upon the hill, and noses and mittens dare the wind.

But spring is whispering its way to Braintree. The sun is warm and soft. And so the snow will come and go, as tiny silvered rivers flow, and winds wax soft, and gently blow...For spring is whispering it way to Braintree. Can't you hear it in your hearts?

ON GRANDMOTHERHOOD

You look into two wide, wonderful child's eyes and earnestly their owner "the smartest child you have ever seen! Why, do you know he could count to ten at the age of seven weeks?" you say, quite solemnly. And furthermore, you believe it!

You respond with an air of disgusting complacency on your newest addition with the age-old observation that "they didn't make grandmothers like you when I was a boy, ha, ha…" and How many does this make? Four?"

You act like you've been awarded the croix de guerre when the local gendarme, in cautioning you against dashing madly across Main Street at risk of life and limb, accompanies his black look with a sage "Don't forget you're a grandmother." You beam, and acknowledge the, - ah - compliment, naturally-as though you engineered the whole situation yourself!

You state with an air of complete smugness that you are "so sorry you can't attend the 'Fairless Fair' of the Garden Club; you must baby-sit for your daughter." You are completely oblivious to the sniffs of those less fortunate member who, not having achieved the status of grandmother themselves, fail to comprehend the import of your statement. And you react beautifully to the knowing smiles of other grandmothers who, facing the same situation, know exactly what you mean.

YOU RESPOND delightedly to strange-sounding names like "Nama" or Nam," and would take a dim, dim view of being reminded that once, way back when grandmotherhood was new, you signed all correspondence addressed to Grandson No 1 "Grandmother Metayer." It was to be "grandmother," of course. You wouldn't have it any other way. There was dignity, a soft sweet beauty to the word…None of this "Grandma" business, or "Nana" nonsense…How many years ago was that????

You produce pictures of your darlings - all four of them - at the drop of a chapeau. "This one," you say proudly, "was taken when he was barely eight hours old." quite as though this latest of your prodigies rose and snapped the shutter. You monopolize the conversation of friends- or even of enemies with anecdotes of young achievement that occasionally gag even you.

How many do you have?" you ask obligingly of every other grandmother you meet. "All girls? How wonderful. I have all boys." You give the other grandmothers' ego a little lift. Why not? You're all members of the club. You convey to her subtly the idea that you are green with envy, but you know and she knows that you wouldn't trade a hair of your grandsons' golden heads for all the girls in the Folles Bergere, in miniature.

YOUR CATEGORY in life is changing needless to say. You are beginning quite obviously, to be known, not as Jane, the gal who loves Christmas, or Jane, Past President of the Sunday Go to Meeting on Tuesday Club, but as Jan, the Grandmother, for invariably, people, on meeting you say, "How are the grandchildren?" And how you love to tell them…

You and grandpa are having the time of your young-again lives! Just when life was getting a bit quiet, and dull, and staid, you've a brand new, grand new world to share together! You've a brand new, grand new conversational subject of which you'll never, never tire! Yes, you've joined the club. You're a grandmother!

YOU'VE joined the Club, and now your neighbors say, "Good morning! How are your grandchildren today? Time was - a thousand years ago-When this was most decidedly not so "My dear, your roses are divine," they'd say. Or maybe, "Are you still reviewing books? Do tell me how the newest fiction looks…" They might discuss the latest coup in Spain. "I see Angola's in the news again…" Or merely "It's November. Shall Fashion your Christmas magic on the hill?" The broadest range of subjects they'd pursue. In sending their "good morning" smile to you. But now they pass the time of day, and then, It's, "My dear, how are your grandchildren?" again!

PS. You love it!

3-8-64   ON HOME

TED AND I returned from a month's vacation in the south. It was a wonderful month. It included a pilgrimage to our nation's capital, where the echo of muffled drums still haunts Pennsylvania Avenue, and the spectre of a riderless horse rides the Arlington Memorial Bridge, and the tears of an unforgetting nation still fall quietly upon the gravesite of a hero

We viewed the splendor of George Washington's Mt. Vernon. We kept a rendezvous with history in restored Williamburg where, incidentally, we met quite by accident, and spent a delightful afternoon with the wife of the great, great, great, great, great, great, great, great, grandson of John Adams, Mrs. Robert Fenton Wellman. She sent regards to Braintree.

We wandered through the quaintness of St. Augustine, and viewed from a glass bottomed boat the majesty and beauty of the twelve-mile reef off Key West. We found the peace of the Bok Sanctuary. We had dinner at Antoine's in the French Quarter of New Orleans, and cafe au lait at 2 a.m. in the Cafe du-Monde after a night on the town. We shuddered at the great ice floes on Lake Erie, and watched dusk creep quietly over the Adirondacks as travelers formed impromptu torchlight parades in criss-cross beauty across the maze of highways.

IN THE little town of Canajoharie, New York, I awake at dawn with a delightful feeling of excitement. It was similar to thrill I experience each year on the morning after Thanksgiving Day when I realize that Christmas is but a month away.

"Ted," I cried. "Wake up! Today we are going home…"

Home, that blessed haven of wood and brick and dreams and memories, where the heart ever, ever is.

The home of my childhood…was it really such a large exciting place? How vividly I recall the fragrance of lilac below the window of my room, jump rope and jacks on the long driveway, the apple tree with the big dark apples that waited until fall to ripen, and so were awaiting our return from the lake each summer, and the pale spice of the big cherry tree in bloom.

And now, the home of my wondrous years.

It stands there, its shiny window-face smiling a welcome. A golden key, and we are enfolded in its wonder warm arm…

THIS IS MY HOME…I am keeper of the flame that was ignited here so many years ago. On this rug in the big living room, my little daughter played with dolls, and lay with "big fat books" before the fireplace, my son built grain elevators with his brand new Erector set and announced, "I shall be an engineer like my grandfather and build bridges."

(He is an engineer like his grandfather, but this is an age of miracles and so he builds atomic submarines.) Here Christmas toys lay heaped beneath the tree, and pajama parties left a layer of fluff I thought I'd never remove from the Oriental, and Scouts spoke solemnly of God and country. This mirror in the hall has known a Brownie headband and soft, sweet curls; it has mirrored the tilt of a mortarboard cap, and caressed a wedding veil. It has watched hair turn from brown to gray, and caught the etching of time upon a once youthful face.

This is the dining table to which Richard brought his best girl, Dolores, now his wife, and Gael brought James 'her best beau for always…' It is marked now with small, sweet scars of grandchildren…

Here at this kitchen table, we read Shakespeare together, and the wonderful Greek tragedies. "You see," I would tell my perplexed little one, "it is all a matter of reading it aloud and following your sentences through correctly; it then makes beautiful sense."

THIS SUNDECK has watched my lovely little teen-ager turn to molten gold; this patio has known the noisome hospitality of a thousand summer cook-outs.

The maple tree has housed the strutting jay. This lawn has referred many a battle between a plump red robin and the brown worm. This shrub has spilled its golden coins upon the green; that one has tossed rose petals to the summer sky. Here a fat gray squirrel danced a minuet upon the wires, and there, Janie, my friend of fond canine memory, buried her bone, or dug a tiny chasm in the shade. Here the yews have ever solemnly stood, and there the hedges guard like sentinels the wide grey walk.

This is my home, my castle, the fabric of my happy life. There is magic here, for here lies my real, my first, my lasting success. I have returned from the happiest of journeys, but oh, how wonderful today as always, to be coming HOME.

ON THANKSGIVING

On Thanksgiving…
Let us be thankful for a thousand things.
For all the glad magnificence life brings,
Let us be thankful…

Thursday is Thanksgiving Day, that bounteous bridge o'er which we pass from the golden autumn to the blessed Christmas season, pausing enroute to cast a soft soft glance heavenward, to render thanks. May we, this dear Thanksgiving Day, be truly thankful!

Let us be glad for all the sheer magnificence of life…for black lace trees against the winter sky; for snow's soft falling; for the strange sweet quietude of dawn; for sunset's flame; for rain to soothe the earth's gray, parched throat; for wind to sound the lullaby of night, let us be thankful…

Let us thank God for freedom and its pride for peace, for all the blessed bounty of our land; for glowing candles soft against the night; for savory enchantment from the hearth; for sights and sounds and smells that breath of life; let us be thankful…

Let us thank God as lo! the savage sea whispers a soft caress upon the shore; let us be thankful for the robin-song; for blossoms bright against the garden's green; for the storm-swept treetops wild against the wind: for all the sky-washed blues, and all the golds..

Let us thank God for loving, and for being loved; for all the wondrous sharing of our world; for husband, child and grandchild; for mother and father; for sister and for brother; for lullabies and laughter; for symphony and song; for all the golden magic of a smile; the bliss of a caress; the warmth of firelight glow; for the inestimable beauty of the human voice; the inestimable wonder of the human heart; the inestimable dignity of the human soul; let us be thankful…

Let us be thankful for a child's wide eyes; a puppy's soft caress; the small brown squirrel dancing on the wire; the shy gray rabbit nibbling; for bird's nests in the loft, the birds' shrill conversation on the lawns; for stardust in a midnight sky; and moondust on a quiet pool; the flash of silver bird wings in the blue; for books; and dreams; and walking in the rain; for serenity and solitude.

For love our hearts now know; and love we may yet find; for friendship's blessed balm; for birth, the peace of death; and every wondrous thing that lies between; and for the promise of a life eternal; let us be thankful…

And for the bright brown turkey that bedecks the day; the pumpkin's gold; the cranberry's red rose; the apple's shiny smile; the grapes' spilled wine; the sweetmeats and the sage; and those who share the blessings of this day, this glad Thanksgiving Day, dear Father of us all, let us be thankful…let us be truly thankful.

1-10-65   OPTIMISM...

Did you know the winter's over??? That's my pet philosophy
When we've tucked away the trimmings, and we've burned the
   Christmas tree,
And securely in the attic we've placed every Christmas bell,
Each cone wreath and quiet candle we have learned to love so
   well.
On what premise do I base, now, this strange statement that
   I make
Just the moment turkey soup has gone the way of Christmas cake,
When the new year's noisy dawning still leaves echoes on the air,
And the jolly face of Santa yet peers gaily here and there??

Well- this month of January, I am certain you'll admit,
Is beset by gay capriciousness, is moved by wanton wit.
Though she well might flex her muscles, let her baser nature show,
She has days and days when soft and spring-like zephyr sweetly
   blow.

Though she does possess the know-how to turn river into ice,
She quite frequently regards them with the gayest of caprice,
Sets them running in the gutters, sees them trickle on the lawn,
Catches sunlight in their silver as they flow across the dawn.

Though she well might be a lion, she's as gentle as a lamb
On innumerable occasions. That's precisely why I am
Saying simply, January most delightfully can fly,
Light and sweetness on its wing-tips, can quite casually pass by.

Then, of course, there's February, month of grayness and of snows,
But, with two or three days missing, it's surprising how it goes!
And besides, the pussy willows softly fur beside the wall.
You're reminded, as you find them, spring's not far away at all!

March is then around the corner, making ready her debut,
So you mutilate the calendar, and she smiles up at you.
Now the earth is warm and waking; soft, sweet crevices appear,
And you realize with laughter, springtime's rhapsody is near.
Crocuses are bravely budding, sending starshapes toward the sun,
And in small, secluded gardens, nature's magic has begun.
Tulip leaves are curling softly, jonquil fronds are stabbing free;
And a green and gentle swelling is commencing on the tree.

E'er you know it, fair Miss April dear and dancing, comes along,
And your world awakes one morning to the glory of springsong.
Robins rosy man the fence-posts; jonquils bow a greeting gay
As you trod your garden pathways, now no longer grim and gray.

You awake to buttered sunshine, walk abroad in sugared rain
Soar with wings upon your heartbeats as a world is born again.
And behold, the winter's over, and you've barely felt it pass,
But, the passing of the springtime is as swift again-ALAS!

3-21-65   ORIGIN OF BIRDS

LOVELY are the Indian legends that have come our way from those first unfettered Americans who sweetened the forest of our land with their poetic tales.

The return of two bright-breasted robins from the southland one warm day a week or so ago, brought vividly to mind the colorful Indian legend of the origin of birds.

Aeons of moons ago, the Indians related in the glow of their council fires, when the tribes were gathered to smoke the pipe of peace, and speak of solemn things, the Great Spirit walked about the world, and where his footsteps left their marks upon the earth, there rose great trees that waved their flowing locks upon the wind, and lifted strong, sweet arms in soft obeisance to their kind Creator, and stood, green and shimmering in the gold of suns, and silver in the moonwash.

The winds made music in their boughs, and the great trees danced, and tossed their heads in gay abandon in the warm and wondrous summer days; and when the nights were come, caught the silver of the stars within their outstretched hands, and hurled it back upon the dark.

Soft rains cooled their parched and pretty throats, and lo! the green leaves preened themselves upon the bright brown boughs, and there was sweet rejoicing in the forests.

BUT THEIR first soft summer season came swiftly to an end. The warm sun sped beyond the hills.

Winds carried a whispered coolness in their soft caress.

Frosts kissed the greenness of the leafy locks of all the tall tree-giants in the forests, leaving them gold and scarlet and wine-red.

The wind grew ever sharper, and the soft defenseless leaves turned up their browning toes, and raised beseeching eyes, and wept.

"Help us," they shivered in the wind, and lifted blazing hands on high to where the Great Spirit saw their saddened plight, and was distressed.

"Tiny tresses of the tree I brought to life," said the Great Spirit kindly, "how can I leave you there to die, to turn to brown and brittle ash, as down you fall upon the wintered earth, never to dance again. And the Great Kind Spirit frowned, and then He smiled a dazzling smile, and freed their gold from off the boughs. Away they flew in thousands and in tens of thousand, off upon the winds..

AND WHERE the leaves were red, there robins sang, their breasts aflame with life.

And where the leaves were golden in the sun, fair finches fluttered free..

And where the cold north winds had kissed and killed, brown chickadees and dark dear sparrows, and bold black starlings journeyed forth.

And thus were come the birds, to brighten all the forests, and to sweeten them with song.

And thus, because the Great Spirit had turned His shining countenance upon their need, and their soft pleadings heard, the tiny, feathered ones forever more would send, when dawn's first flush had stained the face of day, their paeons of sweet praise into the skies, and Him who made them.

The legend of the birds was told to me one February morning in a small Indian village on the Tamiami Trail in Florida, by a sweet young Indian maiden, with skin like sunset, and eyes like elderberries on an autumn vine, and a voice as sweet and soft as any birdsong that would ever rise to greet the legendary, kind Great Spirit, of whose distant deeds she spoke.

1-28-73   PERENNIAL DIET

It happens every year at just about this point in time…I make a fervent vow never to do it again…EAT, that is…too much turkey and too many mashed potatoes with their "rich brown gravy"…too much deep dish pumpkin pie swimming in real cream and not that low calorie substitute that does at other than the Christmas season…too many Fanny Farmer's and too many cashews, and too many of those last lingering remnants of the Cold Duck and Chateau La Salle and Chablis and other little lovelies that somehow or other inevitably manage to precede the family dinners at holiday time…

It happens every year at just about this point in time…the reason being, of course, that the lady of the house has just dredged up the strength of character to propel her larger-than-life self to the FAMILY SCALE! After which - the first said screams of dismay having died away, and the tears of disbelief having been wiped dry, all is replaced by a mad resolve. "I'll get rid of that ten extra pounds if it KILLS me!" And so it's back to the perennial diet…again…

This year's fasting fit is one that daughter Gael, herself, beginning to feel some concern about a barely discernible progression from size 7 to the vicinity of size 8 as a result of having given up smoking, dreams up for the two of us.

"You know," she says seriously, "I've been thinking Mom. There are only about 75 calories in an entire package of frozen broccoli. You and I both LOVE broccoli. And we can add Parmesan cheese, and with a slice of diet bread, sparsely buttered, it would still be less than 200 calories for our luncheon. And it's FILLING!

It WAS filling, and for the first week or ten days we managed the new deal quite well. Came the day, however, when the very thought of one more go at broccoli brought a set of tailspins to the tummies of two very disgruntled dieters. "So let's switch to French style string beans for awhile," we decide…And we do!

It was a beautiful January day, cold and bracing, and happy in the knowledge that I was shedding pounds like mad, I decided to hie me off to Boston to pick up the family's reserved number plate which we had found ourselves unable to secure in Quincy. I had carefully fortified myself with the customary string bean feast before starting out. It was a whole lot easier, I had decided, than dashing madly in and out of Boston restaurants looking for a sympathetic chef. And, arriving in Quincy, I had settled myself on the M.B.T.A. (if you'll pardon the expression) and prepared to leave town. I looked about me…and then above me…Never should have raised my eyes! For a gorgeous sign was blazing tantalizingly about. "When shopping," it read, "Won't you try a great big Bailey's SUNDAE?" To add to the putrifying picture, the ad was ILLUSTRATED! I promptly popped an "Ayds," in my watering mouth. Ayds, in case you are nauseatingly naturally slight and so blissfully uninformed on these matters, are those vitamin loaded candies that are guaranteed to satisfy the dieters craving for sweets. And really they help a lot! All of which brings me to a delightful bit about my first encounter with the little dieters' dears. I had consumed my first box and was returning ten days later to Jordan's to pick up a refill. "Have you lost any weight?" Daughter Gael wanted to know as we ascended the escalator. "No," I said, "Not a pound…And I can't understand it…" A terse explanation of the fact was to lie dead ahead. "A 30 day supply, $2.99 read the sign above my newest diet supplement…A 30 day supply, which I had merrily consumed in less than ten!

Further passage into the recesses of Boston was to bring other trials and tribulations and reminders of how a diet can change a gal's existence…The sight of a lush a lovely bunch of broccoli on Park Square Station billboard, gotten up to resemble a Christmas tree with ornaments and tinsel and the like, would normally have delighted my holiday-loving heart; today, however, it merely made me gag…

And a notification to the effect that "the most generous Italian restaurant in the world" had come to Boston; that Mamma Leone had settled herself in the vicinity of Copley Square a block or so away, caused - not a stampede in the general direction of that favorite of menages - but a succession of Ayd popping that went on for hours...

Ah me, the perennial diet...It goes on and on. We've changed to French style string beans, Gael and I...and back to broccoli...and over to beans, Italian style and to asparagus...But, boy, none of it's fun! I did succeed in losing seven of the ten pounds of excess me...at which point I could be seen happily trying on everything I own just to get the effect of a slightly tidier tummy. But that was last Saturday. Unfortunately, however, it happened to be the followed last Sunday, when Daughter Gael invited her parents to a roast beef dinner. I keep wondering if it was the wine sauce that did the damage...or the squash with brown sugar and orange juice...or the string almondine...or the chocolate cake... or the coffee with cream. At any rate, here it is Monday and would you believe it? I'VE GAINED TWO OF THOSE DARNED POUNDS BACK IN ONE FELL SWOOP! Ah me, it's lunch time! Shall it be broccoli or beans??? With or without cheese??? And could I live with me amicably if I skipped the "Ayd" at the end of it??? Decisions, Decisions... The perennial diet...

6-3-73   RAINY SPRING

I'M FED UP WITH THIS rain! Again and again,
Day in and day out, IT'S JUST ONE WATER SPOUT,
This SKY that in May should be laughing and gay...
This SKY that come June should be singing a tune!
Instead, it just WEEPS...in self-pity it steeps...
I'm bone tired of it all; SPRING SHOULD BE ONE BIG BALL!
Wanna play in my garden, a weed killer ply
That, to work, must be placed on a lawn that is DRY.
Wanna use up my Rapid-Gro on each new flower
That I managed to plant in one lone sun-kissed hour.

Wanna Spend WHOLE LONG DAYS in the garden I love;
Wanna lie in the sun, looking fondly above
On a real Springtime sky, from a lawn chair serene;
Wanna chat with my neighbors; and on my fence lean;
Wanna rake up those leaves that have slipped in between
All my hardy perennials, glorious and green
Though from this pesky rain they assuredly are....
Wanna look up at moonlight; and wish on a star!
But each day I awake to that same dripping sound
That from Monday to Sunday is always around;
And each night, so it seems, I lie down with the patter
Of rain ever drenching my roof, it doesn't matter
That cook-outs get cancelled; and ball games rained out;
And all of our Springtime plans go up the spout...
Nature tosses her head in high utter disdain
And AGAIN...and AGAIN...and AGAIN...and AGAIN...
SHE SENDS TORRENTS OF RAIN...WHAT A PAIN!

9-27-64   RAINY WEATHER...

"GOODNESS," Mother would say to us when we were children, "What is the matter with you? You are wearing a face like a wet week!"

A smile was an accepted part of a child's raiment in our home, (and of a grown-up as well), and a "wet week" to mother, as it is to all mothers of large families. (There were five of us,) was a dismal thing indeed. I can see her point quite clearly.

Somehow or other, however, I have never felt that way about a series of drippy days. I love them!

AS A CHILD it meant boots and umbrellas, (which I still enjoy) big, gorgeous puddles to splash my way through, (even now they tempt me) an occasional rainbow building a bridge to heaven for the rain-fairies' return, "days off" from school, to dream in, and read in, and spend playing in the attic with the manuscripts dad was always writing, and the wearing apparel from another era, even from another, for Grandmother

Nener stubbornly refused to part with the dozen or so pairs of shoes she had brought with her from England, a thousand years before.

"Made by Mr. Duffield, the Queen's shoemaker," she would boast, delighting in the softness of the kid, the iridescent finish to the leather, the cut steel beads and assorted paraphernalia that trimmed the long, slim pointed toes not unlike the ones that returned to style a few short years ago.

"The Queen had a pair almost like these," she would add. How we girls loved to don this strange, high-heeled footgear and pip about the attic.

Grandmother Nener would look lovingly at our feet. "They cannot make shoes in America," she would sigh, "I would never have suffered from the rheumatics if I had continued to send to England for my shoes." Dear patriotic Dad had gently set his foot down in the matter of this delightful indulgence, and inasmuch as Grandmother Nener lived with us, she had acquiesced. But, she wasn't happy about it! I wonder if the descendant of Mr. Duffield, whoever he was, are still making shoes for the Queen...

OH, THE veritable rainy-day fairyland that was our attic! Trunks and trinkets, and mother's wonderful old love letters from Dad, (and from another swain, we discovered we had found her long-light.) What fun it was until she discovered we had found her long-forgotten hiding place, and sat down there herself one day - possible one wet day in a wet week - and re-read every one, and cried a bit, and then consigned them all to the big black range that graced our kitchen. (Coal, not electricity, fired our kitchen stove.)

One rainy day is interesting, but a series of them, tied together with damp nights, becomes to affect the behaviour of a sea of normalcy for me, even now! A "wet week" eventually comes to affect the behaviour of most of us.

You acquire the conviction that no one will drop in, and so you feel quite free to prop a book against the sugar bowl and run your second cup of coffee all together - and hang the dusting.

When you telephone Mary, she's in!

Everyone you love will call, either because the day is long, or they've the weather to complain about, or they're assured you'll answer.

You wrap up leisurely in rainy day apparel and go shopping, because you are convinced the stores will be quite, quite deserted, and then you find that everyone for miles is present in the shop, and for the very same sweet reason, and it's so nice to see their shiny rain-washed smiles.

THERE'S A DARK, dear beauty to your world. The sea is gray and calm, and small fogged boats will still black shadows ride its mirroring crest, setting their leaden masts against the slate of sky. Sea gulls are sodden wraiths, as motionless as piles of white, discarded sea shells on the sand.

Trees are black old crones against the sky, slithering and slopping, and trailing dripping fingers in the wind.

Hairdo's become hair-don't, and so we lack the impetus to fuss, and thrust our face against the rain's benign caress with sudden friendship, and feel glad.

Drippy days? A wet week? After the searing drought of summer, I'm enjoying every soggy second of it; I've an attic, too, and books, and dreams…And just think, how beautiful we'll find the sun tomorrow.

8-16-70   REFLECTION

Oft as the tree its words of prayer
Whispers on the evening air
Just at twilight's softened hush….
Oft as I hear the gentle thrush
Croon its farwell to dying day
Then whirr to the long grass, then away..
Oft as all this, I think of THEE,
Lord who lets the evening be!
Oft as the sun on wings of dawn
Turns its glowing face toward morn,
Peeping above the sleepy hill…
Oft as I watch each tiny rill
Mirror the soft, sweet, pearls, and blues
Of blossoms, kissed by morning dews….

Oft as all this, I think of THEE,
Lord who lets the morning be!
For thou art hid among the flowers;
The silvered pool reflects they powers;
Thy name in whisperings is heard;
In sighing tree, and song of bird;
At eventide; at morning's fall;
They holy will behind it all…
Lord of a world! Yet just for me
Thou lettest a world's beauty be…

2-18-73   REFLECTIONS

It was a dreary winter day; the skies a sullen, somber grey;
A day when I'm inclined to look within the pages of a book
For ways to make the hours fly…the grimness of the day pass
    by…
A sudden urgent need to find, howe'er, a tome I'd tucked
    behind
Some luggage in the attic saw me ambling toward that attic
    door…
To hasten back with tome in hand was my intent, when lo! a band
Of narrow velvet caught my eye from out a box as I passed by,
Encircling - I began to think - the pretty little gown of pink
Our daughter Gael had worn with joy at her first party with
    a boy!
Thoughts raced my way of days long gone when YOUTH was
    making life a song…
I sat upon the attic stair…to realize that YOUTH was THERE!
A thousand relics of the past lay all about me…held me fast!
Gael's jodhpurs, shining smartly still; her baton on the window
    sill:
Her roller skates with their case; her dolly, slightly tired of face…
She has no little girl to use THIS treasure…nor those dancing
    shoes

That, still beribboned, seemed to say, "You little nymph once danced her way
Into so many hearts with US!" Her ice skates…How her Dad would fuss
As off to skate upon the pond would gaily march our little blonde…
"The ice is not too thick, you know," he'd always say; and watch her go
With just the whisper of a sigh; a clouding of his living eye…
A rather beat-up hockey stick…a relic of our dear son Dick…
A goalie's mask; a catcher's mitt; those shoulder pads that did not fit;
The laundry case from boarding school; the chest with every kind of tool
He'd needed for HAM RADIO…the skis on which he'd welcome snow…
A thousand memories came my way to make a suddenly shining day
Of one that just an hour before was threatening to be a bore…
ONE CAN SO EASILY WAX ECSTATIC O'ER TRIFLES
IN THE FAMILY ATTIC!

9-23-73   REFLECTIONS

A Johnny-Jump-up on the lawn, the rose pink finger of a dawn
A startlingly perfect rose; a new born baby in repose;
Birdsong against the evening air; a grey head bent in silent prayer;
A puppy in a small boy's arms; the wonder of a small girl's charm:
Sad tears upon a tiny face; two lovers in a fond embrace;
A squirrel storing winter's food; a kitten in a pensive mood;
A pine tree tall against the sky; a flock of wild geese gliding by;
A mother duck, ducklings in tow, a jet plane flying strangely low;
The moon, a silken sphere above; the cooing of a soft brown dove;
A seagull's grace against the blue of summer skies; the distant view

Of mountains rising tall and swift; the fragile fluttering first
  faint light
Of baby birds, attempting flight; the soft advancing of the night;
The wild unequalled symphony of sand and sky and sounding
  sea;
The wondrous faces fond and sweet of those I love; of friends
  I greet
What wondrous joys are mine to know as through this lovely
  life I go.

REMINISCING

His name was ALBERT. However, he was "AL" to his friends; and
from what we understand his friends included just about everyone in this
then small town of Braintree--

ALBERT F. HOLLIS, the father of Representative Herbert B. and
EARL Hollis, two of the town's most distinguished citizens; and the
FATHER, as well, of TWILIGHT LEAGUE BASEBALL!

How well I remember the TWI LEAGUE of Malden, my home
town, playing its baseball games at CRADDOCK Park on the Fellsway
where we lived. As a matter of fact, I once interrupted a TWLIGHT
League game in no uncertain way.

I had just received my first bicycle and was learning to ride. The
mechanics of mounting the bike and getting the thing going were simple
to master. However, I had not quite learned to STOP without assistance.
Furthermore, Dad had forbidden me to ride on the Fellsway under any
circumstances-a fact which, needless to say, made the Fellsway the most
glamorous spot in town to a ten-year old.

At any rate, cautioning sister Gladys to remain on hand to help in
stopping me on my return journey, I set out along the Fellsway. It was a
beautiful day and I was riding high, when suddenly I perceived Dad in
his Model "T" heading in my direction! A vision of losing my bicycle for
a week or more…the logical punishment for disobedience…rose before
my eyes, I PANICKED and, lowering my head so that hopefully Father

would fail to recognize me, I headed madly for nearby Craddock Park where a TWILIGHT Baseball game was in progress.

The spectators scattered in self-defense, allowing me room to ride smack into the middle of the diamond! I missed one baseball player after another by a hair's breadth, escaped getting hit on the head with the ball by a veritable whisker, and came to a sudden horrible halt when the front wheel of my bicycle ran smack of a park bench which had been evacuated just in time! Need I say where and how I landed!

But to return to Al Hollis, the Father of this Twilight Baseball League! He conceived the idea back in the spring of 1905 when the average man's working day was long and unrelieved. Come evening, Braintree males were want to gather in little groups here and there across the town to chat and socialize. Well, into one of these nightly gatherings stepped Al Hollis, an amateur baseball player of local distinction. Al had an idea. Why not have some of the younger boys team up and have a game of baseball, with the older citizens serving as spectators??? Braintree always had been a ball-playing town, and so the idea fell on fertile ground.

Leaders chose their teams, and the teams played one another. Competition became keen and excitement high, and the following season the "SUNSET BASEBALL LEAGUE" was formed. Very naturally Al Hollis was elected its first President. He was past the playing age but appears to have been possessed of the spirit of eternal youth for he remained a rabid baseball fan to the last of his long life.

The year of 1907 saw the beginning of organized games with a starting time set at six o'clock. President Hollis settled interest flamed anew a few years later and the Sunset League, with Al Hollis at its head, came once more into its own-to spread from town to town until a Twilight Baseball League became an accepted facet of the American Scene.

The Boston Globe, after considerable research credited Al Hollis with having been responsible for the innovation, and dubbed him the "Father of TWI-LEAGUE Ball."

Mr. Hollis, incidentally, served as a member of Braintree's first Park Commission; he was succeeded upon retirement by his son, EARL, who also served with distinction upon that very important board.

"Isn't it fun to learn about the distinguished citizens who have left their mark upon this town we love????

6-9-68   REMINISCING

WE recently learned that a group of our Braintree High School students were studying France under the German occupation. We promised to write this particular "Cabbage" primarily for them.

One of the "bonuses" of our recent European holiday was a two-hour visit with a French Resistance Fighter. The lady, who asked that her name be withheld, reminisced about life under the Germans. She is now in her early sixties. Segments of our conversation follow:

An Englishwoman, born in Yorkshire, she had married a Frenchman and gone to live in Paris. Her husband, educated in the University of Heidelburg, spoke fluent German, English, and French. The lady herself possesses dual citizenship, and proudly displayed both French and English passports. "All Americans and English who were left behind in Biarritz," said the lady, "were obliged to register with the Commissar. I went with friends, as interpreter, to have a look, because my French was perfect, and I was mentally weighing my increased effectiveness in the resistance movement if I posed as a Frenchwoman. I said, I WON'T get registered! Our French Magistrate said, 'So I BAPTIZE you French!'

The German Commissar took over. 'Would you like to go to England?' he asked my friends, with a sly smile. 'I can get you over.' 'How?' asked one. 'In a submarine!' he replied.' (which would, naturally, have been bombed by the English.)

The lady herself, who by now possessed a 17-year-old daughter, together with her husband, became resistance fighters. He was a liaison officer with the Americans.

The French, said the lady, are clever because they are unscrupulous about METHODS; it's easy to be clever if you are willing to be unscrupulous, she said. France was betrayed by the 5th Column, but resistance was everywhere.

For the last six months of the war, my friend, Madame G, whose activities had been particularly outrageous, hid in a shack in a field. The Germans would have taken her husband and daughter had her deception been discovered. She emerged from the shack only by night to secure whatever food was available - a raw turnip from the fields; a bit of bread or soup given her occasionally by a villager.

Our determination, she said was British, and therefore unshakeable. Harris of the British Army had said, "For every plane you send over here, you will get 100; and one day get 1,000 for one!" And we clung to that statement and fought on!

FALTERING courage was immediately bolstered. "I don't know," once said a peasant to the lady in question. "When you see all those tanks going through-We haven't beaten them yet…"… "Have you ever seen a CHURCHILL tank?" I asked her. "No-Have you?" "Yes. It's TWICE as big as a Tiger Tank!" (she had never beheld a Churchill tank…)

The French railway trainmen were courage personified, said the lady. Each train load of Tiger tanks that rolled across the fields was a target for RAF bombs. The underground had reported its presence. Its engineer knew it. He also knew that my friend, hiding in the shack, knew…He would wave smilingly, though discreetly, her way as the train thundered past-carrying him to destruction but CARRYING THE TIGER TANKS AS WELL! And so he smiled as he waved goodbye…

Of one "Peter, who is today private secretary to General De Gaulle," the lady said, "He was in charge of a trainful of children being evacuated. The RAF came every day to bomb Amiens. Peter saw them coming, and, as the RAF bomber approached, he rushed the children to the train windows where they would be visible to the bomber pilot, who turned and left without bombing."

Myron Herrick, she said, was American Ambassador to France prior to America's entry into the war. His French friend feared for his safety. He said, "Never mind - A DEAD Ambassador will do you more good than a live one!"

The Americans DID enter the war; and then they came to Biarritz. By now, the lady's daughter, who was 18 had like her parents joined a movement to assist the English, Americans and French. "We hadn't had MILK for four years. We had no tea. For weeks we had lived on turnip, and some sort of bread made from bran….

I opened my house to the Americans when they came, said the lady. I said "I CANNOT invite you to tea. I haven't any. And I cannot invite you to lunch, I haven't any. But you are welcome in my house!"

Later a basket was delivered to my door, the lady added. It contained ham, and powdered milk, etc. These have been PINCHED," said a smiling American

THE LADY'S health is shattered. She has slept for decades only with the assistance of a sleeping pill. Her digestive and nervous systems are in chaos.

But her bright blue English eyes smiled into mine. "You know," she said, "There's one fact the world loses sight of. You can DEFEAT a nation, but you CANNOT CONQUER it!"

P.S. My friend deplored the departure of NATO from France; and De Gaulle's foreign policy." He's been a DICTATOR too long," she said. "He won't SHARE THE REINS! And one man makes mistakes…"

3-9-75   ROSE COLORED GLASSES

I knew my life was lovely one day not long ago
When I stepped beyond a doorway that was sheathed in ice
    and snow
And then slithered down a walkway that a skating rink resembled
To a driveway, there to find a million icicles assembled
On the roof of a garage that dripped cold water on my head
As I closed my limp umbrella and turned gaily to my Ted,
And beneath a sky so stormy as to be a dappled grey
Took deep breaths and smiled serenely and said, "What a
    lovely day!"

12-28-69   SANTA CLAUS

IT HAPPENED at the Christmas party which was given by our Braintree Point Woman's Club to the 50-odd little tots enrolled in Library School at the Watson park Branch.

A festive occasion had been planned, with games and goodies; and, of course, an exchange of Christmas gifts.

Santa Claus had been invited to preside over this particular aspect of the party. He had, however, disappointed the ladies in charge by sending his regrets. Old St. Nicholas, it seemed, simply could not take time from his myriad tasks at the North Pole, where he was busily preparing gifts for millions of the world's children.

He would have to call upon one of his helpers to do the honors at Library School. Santa calls frequently upon those helpers of his at Christmastime, as we know…

Well, now, the particular helper called upon by Santa Claus to preside over the distribution of gifts at the Watson Park branch was none other than the head of the house of Metayer.

Santa arrived with a jingling of "sleigh" bells, and a "Ho! Ho! Ho!", and the fun began. The children sang for him, and recited for him, and asked a thousand questions of the red-coated fellow who brought a look of complete wonderment to half a hundred pairs of shining eyes.

"Did you come in your sleigh?" the children wanted to know, a vision of their snow-covered town fresh before them. "I did!" said Santa. "Well, where are your reindeer??" "Up on the roof," said Santa easily

The mass exodus to the roof we fondly anticipated at that point failed to come off; perhaps because Santa seated himself heavily, pillows and all, before the gaily decorated Christmas tree and prepared to do his "thing."

Gregory, the Metayer grandchild, who will be three in February, and then hopefully eligible for enrollment in the class had been invited to attend, and it was at this point in the proceedings that he arrived with his mother.

Now, Gregory is notoriously shy with most strangers, and we had anticipated some difficulty with the white-bearded gentleman seated before him. Not so, however.

Gregory, at hearing Santa call his name, went happily up for his gift, then climbed into the donor's lap for the home movies mothers everywhere were taking; and even offered his cheek to be kissed. "Yes Santa Claus," he said seriously in reply to appropriate queries from the man of the hour. "No. Santa Claus." "I think he recognized his grandfather," said Gael, my daughter. "You know how shy she is with strangers, and he went right to him. He must have recognized him."

I laughed. "Gael," I said, "had he recognized him, he would have called him 'Grandpa". You don't really think he is smart enough to go along with the game for the sake of the other children, do you? "I guess not," said Gael, "but it does seem strange." "You forget - Gregory is growing up," I said firmly

***

IT WAS LUNCH for them both at the Menage Metayer when the festivities were ended, and Santa had departed in his famous sleigh, reindeer and all.

Gregory seated himself at the table, clutching the toy truck Santa had given him, and smiling happily. "Well," I said brightly, "Did you have fun at Grandma's Library School?" "Yes," he answered promptly. "And I saw Santa Claus, and he gave me this truck."

"Yes," I continued, "and wasn't he a lovely Santa Claus? He had big black boots, didn't he?" "Yes, Grandma." "And a nice red hat with fur on it?" Gregory smiled through his peanut butter and jelly. "Yes" he said merrily. "And a pretty red suit.." "And big white hair," said Gregory. "That's right, I continued gaily. "And WHISKERS???"

The young man stopped dead, the sandwich in midair. A small frown crossed the smooth sweet forehead. "Whiskers????" he repeated under his breath, as though trying hard to remember. Suddenly he turned toward the grandfather who was seated beside him at the luncheon table. "Grandpa," he asked sweetly, "DID you have WHISKERS???"

Children react wonderfully and differently to Santa Claus. My young friend Patrick was taken by his parents to visit Santa at the South Shore Shopping Plaza one day last week. He chatted happily with the whiskered one, about the snow, and the reindeer, and things in general at the North Pole.

The line was rather long, and Santa reached the point where he realized that unless he initiated a spot of action his young friend would remain at his side until Christmas.

He gently guided our Patrick in the direction of the door, where the young man bade him goodbye and prepared to leave. "Wait a minute," said Santa, "You didn't tell me what you WANTED.." "Oh, that's all right," said Patrick easily, "I have the list all ready for you at home. You'll find it when you get there."

"And what do you want for Christmas?" Santa asked of our Gregory the other afternoon when we had wended our way to the Shopping Plaza for this annual event. The family's littlest angel, who shares his grandmother's mad enthusiasm for Christmas decorating, regarded the bearded gentlemen solemnly. He smiled. "A CHRISTMAS TREE! he announced happily

AH ME by the time this "Cabbage" will have reached its destination, the beautifully holy and happy feast of Christ's Mass will be quite behind us; and we shall have to wait another year for sweet small boys to smile angelically at Santa Claus, and the bells to ring, and lighted creches all to house the symbol of the newborn King.

Holiday Greetings, one and all. And may we add, "A Happy and Peaceful New Year" to you???

9-15-68   SEPTEMBER

I ALWAYS hate to tear the month of August off my calendar…I invariably wait until after Labor Day, kidding myself that August is still with us so long as summer remains.

It's only when the post-holiday hush has descended, and I find suddenly that all the small Cowboys and Indians are missing from the neighborhood corrals; that I live a very quiet and childless neighborhood - that I regretfully admit that August is no longer with us; and SIGH; and tear that happy summer month across the top; and greet September!

Some folks LOVE September. "There are still beach days," they say. "The Cape is beautiful in September, and the sun is still very warm." I couldn't bring myself to pack a picnic lunch and set out for the beach in September if the thermometer hit one hundred and twenty seven! It wears such a lonely look at the ending of summer, the BEACH…

"Ah," they say, "the air is so invigorating and the nights so cool." To me, the sudden chill whispers of winter; and the cool nights merely necessitate an overly warm, heated room or an electric blanket, one or 'tother.

"But the autumn foliage," they say dreamily. The foliage???? Well, maybe by October I shall have come to sigh about the reds and golds, but September is too early. The leaves winds toss my way are brown, dead ones, or nice green ones, whipped prematurely to an untimely end.

We MIGHT leave our nice comfortable lawn furniture scattered about for the now-and-then lazy days, but we never seem to be able to. Alice, or Betty, or Carol, or Gladys, or some other fat old hurricane is playing about in the Atlantic, her tail whipping my pretty lawn things like so much matchwood; and so they, too, face an untimely retirement.

**

NO, I SEE no glamour whatsoever in the brown old month of September. The lawns emerge, soft and green once again, but they'd have been more fun in July or August.

The gardens erupt in one great burst of color; but our enjoyment of their beauty is tempered by sadness; we know that it's their last lovely blooming before the frost.

It's a BROWN old month, September. There's a dark brown taste in my mouth because the season I love the best is gone, and we must wait another year for its return. There's a dark brown look to the now ever moist earth.

Over my arm there dangles a dark brown bag where just a week ago 'twas white, and on my feet, serviceable brown shoes have replaced my carefree sandals; and all the brilliance of my closet's summer hues is gone; and autumn cleaning time is come; and heating bills and balanced meals…And standard time threatens the treasured daylight of my hours. Blessed, easy summer is no more…

Another month, and I'll begin to love the fall. Thanksgiving Day will lie ahead, and Christmas blessings beckon…And snow will spread its magic on my world…But meanwhile, it's September.

**

THE YEAR begins its march toward death; cold winter sends a warning breath. To now and then the sunlight chill! The sky is gray upon the hill…

Where once we walked the beach with glee, its magic we no longer see! Thank heavens, e'er the year be dead the HOLIDAYS still lie ahead!

1-21-68   SNOWSTORM

How beautiful that mantle white
That settled on our Town by night,
Delighting us as in the dawn
We rose to face a magic morn!

We looked upon our world to find
That old Jack Frost had left behind
A sea of white, with billows high
That leaned against the morning sky.

Our trees were garlanded and fair,
Their shivery boughs - once cold and bare -
Enveloped in a robe of fir
That lent enchantment, as it were……

Our post, an ermine stole possessed;
(It lorded it o'er all the rest…..)
Our evergreens, serene and proud,
Now floated in a vast white cloud!

The rosebushes were blossoming
As though to mark the heart of spring…..
"Hooray!" I swore I heard them shout
While tossing snowy blooms about…..

How beautiful the world became
With crystal grandeur all aflame;
A pearl strand here; an opal there;
And diamond crowning everywhere.....

We LOVE the icy kiss of snow
When winter's winds about us blow;
We find a wonder in the sigh
Of snowdrifts 'neath a starry night.....

The GENTLEMAN in your menage
May wish it were a sweet mirage,
And find NO joy in shoveling;
Wish ardently indeed for spring.....

But here am I, with fingers crossed,
Appealing madly to Jack Frost!
"Just one more winter storm," I cry'
"E'er winter's wonders pass us by....."

While Ted, divining my intent,
Regards me with his eyebrows bent.
"It all depends, I'm telling you,"
He says, "upon the point of view."

"If shoveling was YOUR fine task
I doubt if in the snow you'd bask!
Believe me, dear, I'd like to know
We'd seen the last of winter's glow....."

3-9-69   SNOWSTORM

"Twas a February day, and winter donned its icy coat,
And then ties a foggy flannel 'round the rawness of its throat;
Skies were graying rather softly in a leaden sort of way
We surveyed them and decided HOME might be the place
to stay.
SNOW began a gentle brushing, and the flakes were small and
sweet,
Tossing dust upon the pathway, and a haze upon the street,
And we watched its feather falling, and were glad as we could be,
While a would-be poet's rapture made of it a SYMPHONY…
There could be no earthly reason for a panic to possess
Those who watched the winter's whitening with a mounting
happiness.
For the weatherman had hastened in his kind, consoling way
To assure us all and sundry there would be NO STORM
TODAY…
How we gloried in the starshapes silhouetted on the glass
As, entranced before the window, we watched winter's pageant
pass!
How we reveled in the music tiny snowflakes gently made
As upon the mirrored surface, quiet symphonies they played!
"February," we said gaily, "is the prettiest time of year.
When the snow falls on New England, aren't we happy to be
here???
Soon the storming will be ended; and in pristine beauty fine.
High above our frosted village, tiny stars will primly shine…
What a LOVELY month is this one; what a happy time of year…
How we'd MISS these starry snowflakes! Aren't we LUCKY to
be here???
What a SHOWPLACE is New England, when the winter's
lavish hand
Turns our February world into a feathered fairyland!"
So, we watched beside the window, and IT
SNOWED AND SNOWED AND SNOWED…

And a wind-whirl turned the corner, and IT
BLOWED AND BLOWED AND BLOWED...
"Fear thee not," we cried quite gaily, "for the weatherman has said,
'Leave your shovels in the cellar...You will not require that
 sled...'"
And the skies' soft silver mounted in a drift beside the door;
And from out our frosted window we could see the world no
 more...

***

What a lovely winter morning! See the sun demurely glow
On the crystal of the tree-shapes; on the avalanche of snow...
As we turn to face the shovels - as we strive to find the path-
WE SURVEY WITH LESS ENCHANTMENT WINTER'S
 WANTON AFTERMATH!
We bemoan the lavish driveway; we regret the lengthy walk;
At the snow plow's contribution to our problem, how we balk!
As the family car strives vainly to negotiate the hill,
And we back up, gain momentum, and are faced with failure
 still...
As we dash about with sand pails, and we pip about the chains,
HOW WE WISH WE DWELT SECURELY ON THE
 MEADOWS OR THE PLAINS!
Time to check the smoothing snow treads; time to rally to a man,
Furred and mittened, armed with shovels - time to FIRE THAT
 WEATHERMAN!
Ah, there's nothing like a snowstorm to inspire a spot of verse,
But the hitch in our New England is IT INVARIABLY GETS
 WORSE!
How we love the snow's soft falling when the flakes are small
 and sweet;
If they'd only stick to tossing winter lace upon the street!
But, there's something 'bout our weather that leaves people
 quite aghast-
When a snowstorm hits New England, it can LAST and LAST
 and LAST...

2-2-67   SPRING??

SPRING winked a warm little eye at Braintree this past week.

She turned nice frosty lawns into not so nice flats or mire; the which turned nice neat foyers into nasty little frights; the which turned nice dispositions of nice mothers everywhere, pickle-sour...

Spring's premature approach had a handsome effect on just about everybody and everything.

Sons and daughters all over town had to be subjected to the kind of dissertation on the curse on the common cold, that invariably follows the arrival of any mother's child, fresh from a winter day at school with coattails flapping widely in the wind.

Spring not only tossed her happy hat within the door this past week; (she has a way of doing that come January, we've noticed;) she entered, and stayed awhile; In fact, as I pen this little piece, she seems to have pulled up a chair and made herself to home - with most interesting results.

The family dog, for instance, has done a complete about face. He no longer lurks about the door, waiting to slide within where warmth and comfort wait, with each nice, new arrival. He runs with frisk and frolic on the hill behind the house, tossing his head in high disdain when he is called within. (dinner time excepted...)

And then, those buds upon the maple trees, which once we thought had simply bloomed quite prematurely in the autumn warmth, (way back there in the days before a Conservationist friend informed us that 'tis nature's way to form the buds in fall, for springtime growing) they are suddenly soft and swelling.

A pot of tulips which had come our way at Eastertime, and which we'd tossed within a flowerbed at some point upon the path that runs through summer-has actually begun to send up curled green leafings toward the sun! (You can't believe it? Feel free to visit me and see...)

The cracks in all the roadbeds of town are outlined now, and wet, tracking a kind of map upon the softening streets of Braintree.

Neighbors are washing cars as though the summer's come; and baseball mitts are hugging small boys' hands; and miniskirts are showing dimples, not ice crystals, on milady's knees; and bootparks are small sandboxes...

There's a nice new warmth upon the garden, and the cracking of brown earth; and one can hear, if one is still enough, quite clearly and so sweet, the fairy footsteps of a teasing spring that always has arrived in January to blow a kind of kiss in our direction, with promise pure of more, much more, so soon to come.

Tomorrow we'll have snow...

Our boots will stiffen grimly in the cold; and bootparks will be melting little fishponds in our fair front halls; and all those scarves and mittens will indeed return...

But, hidden deep beneath their soft white eiderdown, the tulips will each one, serenely smile. For fair Miss Spring made them a promise as she kissed their pert, pursed lips this wondrous week. "I shall be back," she said. "Wish I might come to stay, but winter's grasp is oh, so very strong...Wait a bit, though...The soft sweet southern winds will start to blow; they'll help. I'll talk the sun, serene and golden into joining on my side. Then we'll be back; we'll all be back. And we shall lick that icy rogue, old winter - they and I...But-not now; not today; later - but not too much later...So, until then- patience, bonny Braintree. I really am "just around that corner!"

2-20-66   SPRINGTIME AGAIN

If I but had a great gray rock about my pretty place,
    Now that spring in our direction will soon turn her fairy face,
I'd pile it up with soft brown earth, and place a crowning high
    Upon the topmost corner, within reaching of the sky;
I'd plant a wreath of daffodils about the outer rim
    So that spring's first sunny kiss would turn them smiling to Him!
I'd tuck tomboyish pansies in the crevice and cracks
    So they'd peer with fairy faces and stop robins in their tracks!

Oh, if I but had a great gray rock, I'd set it quite ablaze
    With a thousand bonny blossoms, to enrich my summer days!

If I but had a little brook about my precious place
    For the spring to set a-gurgling in a music-making pace,
Why - I'd toss a tiny bridge across the azure of its smile
    For my friend, the garden squirrel, to traverse in saucy style;
You'd find water lilies nodding; and a big old bug-eyed frog
    I'd permit to grow serenely from a tiny pollywog!
I'd drop gaily colored pebbles on the silver of the sand
    That beneath its gurgling greyness made a kind of fairyland;
I'd install a red bird feeder in a setting of green moss;
    Oh, if I'd a brook in springtime, in the air my hat I'd toss!

As soft snowy February melts serenely day by day,
    And winds whispering spread the word that spring is on the way,
I commence my time of wishing for a brook, a rock serene,
    A stand of regal birches to lend splendor to the scene
I survey from kitchen windows; yet this dreaming's but a part
    Of the surge of springtime gladness that sweeps gaily through my heart;
For my garden, if it never changed, is perfect as can be
    "Cause in every tiny corner, there's a little bit of me!
I survey it from my windows, and my heart begins to sing;
    Oh, the heaven of a garden that is waking up to spring!

4-21-74   SPRING! SPRING! SPRING!

Oh, the hyacinths are simpering; and the kitty cat is whimpering;
Now that SPRING has SPRUNG, come evening, he wants
    OUT!
While the wasps within the attic have begun to give off static;

And the birds no longer whisper…Now they SHOUT

As their morning prayers they're saying in the soft and silver
greying

Of the dawning of a day that must be fair…

There's a strange kind of abandon in the antics of each grandson

As the magic that is spring falls everywhere…

All the lush and lovely tulips raise their red and pink and blue lips,

While sweet shining Johnny-jump-ups dot the lawn;

And each schoolboy is a-wishin' he could chuck things and go
fishin'

Stead of trotting off to school each springtime morn.

All the squirrels wildly prancing and the merry chipmunks
dancing

Fill the woodland with a saucy spring delight;

And when day has gone to rest and the sun is in the west

There's a special kind of splendor to the night….

The forsythia is blooming; and spring fashion news is booming;

And the robin redbreast scampers on the grass

That each day is getting greener as that spring-returning preener

Struts about with his own special brand of brass.

All the town's begun to stir with pursuit of his or her

Special kind of recreation…THERE'S A STIRRING IN
THE NATION!

How the hearts of mankind sing when - quite suddenly - IT'S
SPRING!

7-27-69   SUBURBAN LIVING

IT HAPPENED in Connecticut, where we were visiting son
Richard and his family last week…An enormous maple tree casts a long
and lovely shadow over his long and lovely front lawn.

Centuries old, its trunk is wide and wonderful; and, like the trunk
of many an ancient tree, it happens to be ten feet or so above the ground -
quite HOLLOW; A fact which, combined with its location in the corner
rather distant from the house, would appear to make of this particular

maple tree the kind of happy habitation the wild folk seem to seek... As a matter of fact, I would wager that many a wild one has set up housekeeping therein in years gone by...

We have been lined up rather lazily on chaises, enjoying the shade this wondrous tree invariably offers of a sunny Sunday afternoon. We had no thought of anything more terrifying coming from above us, than the occasional small brown caterpillar that landed in our midst; and the afternoon passed pleasantly. With dinnertime approaching, Dolores and I retired to the house to see to the inevitable summertime COOK-OUT. It was at this point, I am happy to relate, that things began to happen...

"Dad," said small Franklin suddenly, "What is that big black thing up there in the tree? It looks like a SNAKE!" ALL EYES turned upward instantly!

IT WAS A snake, the biggest, blackest snake that any pair of them had ever beheld - five to six feet in length, and "as big around as a silver dollar", to quote my Ted...

Now Mystic, Connecticut, is NOT Braintree, Massachusetts. The decidedly wild area thereabouts can boast of copperheads and rattlers and other similarly unappealing inhabitants. There was, consequently, quite a flurry of excitement as the tree-dwelling giant came to light...a flurry which, incidentally, caused him promptly to slither away to the security of his nest right smack in the hollow of the tree - from which vantage point he proceeded to extend a curious head, followed by four to five additional curious inches through one available knothole after another in an obvious attempt to keep an eye on the eavesdropping humans below.

THERE ARE, I have since learned, very few TREE-CLILMBING snakes! The boa constrictor manages this fancy feat; but quite obviously that particular variety had not found its way to Mystic. This interloper was a brand new species of "narrow fellow" (and narrow he was NOT!) even to our outdoorsman Richard!

"I had better climb up and take a closer look at him," he said, which is the point in our story at which Dolores and I returned to the group to find the head of the house perched on a branch high above us, peering intently within the hollow trunk, an expression of deep concentration clouding his face.

"Don't tell me there are GYPSY MOTHS in your beautiful tree," I said. An epidemic of the pests had hit Connecticut this year, destroying entire sections of the area, including in nearby Ledyard, the oldest elm in the state-a 500-year old beauty, the loss of which had been mourned by the entire family.

"No," said Richard, who strangely enough volunteered no information whatsoever as he descended from the tree to head promptly for the house and one of the thousand or so encyclopedias and nature books the Metayers are wont to purchase and peruse...

Their tree-dwelling tenant turned out to be a BLACK RAT SNAKE! The growth of this charming species, Richard learned, can reach 108 inches; and it can deposit as many as 24 eggs in a cozy little nest similar to the one which had been provided for this particular specimen - a nest which, incidentally, has sheltered strange occupants before.

For a number of years, for instance, a neighborhood cat elected annually to produce her offspring there. The kittens arrived faithfully come springtime; and what FUN it was to see their little furry faces framed in those same knobby knotholes through which the current occupant was busily peering. Fun, that is, for everyone but BIM, the family Dalmatian!

Bim agonized through every springtime season. He quivered with frustration a thousand times daily as the saucy small cats, secure in the safety of their lofty perch, framed their tiny faces in the tree openings, and uttered soft seductive sounds that sent their natural enemy into a veritable frenzy!

Their mother, meanwhile, lazed away the days on the high tree branches, also quite beyond his reach; sauntering daintily down the tree come nighttime with Bim nicely tucked indoors, to go about the business of living, secure in the knowledge that her kittens were haughtily high; and would descend from their abode only when she had decided they were old enough to do so, and would personally lead them in a perky cat parade one darkened summer night, down the tree and across the lawn, then across the country road and home.

THIS ISN'T FAIR to Bim, you know," said Richard one day when he had watched the big frustrated fellow quivering with annoyance beneath the ancient tenanted tree.

"He shouldn't be subjected to this kind of torture every spring, "Kitty", he said, "I'm sorry, but you will simply have to find another cozy spot in which to have your babies!" And he filled the yawning cavity with stone and wood, thinking to make an end to the entire affair.

It did, for kitty; she never did return. She simply knew she wasn't wanted! Neither is a 106" Black Rat Snake, complete with up to 24 old reptile-producing eggs!!!! But how does one get this message across to an occupant to whom stone and wood, tucked nicely into the hollow trunk of a wonderful spreading maple tree just ten feet off the ground, presents the most inviting kind of nest there is??? Richard was wondering just that as we left his lovely Mystic, Connecticut, and headed home for Beautiful Braintree. We're waiting to learn the ending of this story…Aren't nature stores FUN, incidentally?

7-3-66   SUMMER

When the windy wilds of March and April's teardrops come
    together,
How we longingly embrace the thought of soothing summer
    weather!
Oh, to paddle in the ocean, turn to bronze upon the shore;
Prance about in summer cottons in the shades we all adore;
Wear those ice cream-luscious lipsticks; tuck our woolens all away;
Sip cool drinks beneath the willows on a sun-kissed summer
    day…

When the winter has us ragged, and our vitamins no longer
Quite suffice to keep us humans up-and coming and stronger-
How we dream of summer's magic; turn our faces toward the sun
That now lazily announces that the winter's all but done!
How we dance about the garden, and delight in every sign
Of a robin on the walkway, or a leafing on the vine…

Now, three cheers! the summer's with us; sun and sand and
   sky together
In a symphony conspiring to produce the perfect weather…
But, alas, the pretty picture that we conjured up last spring
Is about as realistic as a bell that doesn't ring…
Traffic jams beset the beaches; sunburn lurks upon the shore;
Limp and wilted are the cottons we convinced us we'd adore…

Yes, three cheers and hallelujah! It's our own New England
   summer,
And with June just barely ending, it's already quite a hummer!
Lipsticks melt upon the dresser, in limp pools we humans lie;
We're already worn and waning, shall we e'er survive July??
How I dramatize the summer when old winter's grip is fast!
But you know-I'll welcome autumn-if indeed, I ever last!

1-5-75   SWEARING IN

It was a day to remember…a day toward which all the other days
of my exciting life seem to have pointed like so many arrows….It was
climbing Mt. Everest…and crossing the Atlantic in a rowboat…and
scaling the Grand Canyon wall rolled up into one…

"I, Elizabeth Metayer, do solemnly swear…" I was actually standing
there within the half moon of the most historic Chamber, the HOUSE
OF REPRESENTATIVES…I and 239 "Legislators"…I was one of the
group; I BELONGED!

It was to be Governor Sargent's "Last Hurrah", this swearing in the
members of the General court; and I, a winner, found myself looking
toward the defeated Governor with compassionate eyes.

The words of the Oath were finding a warm response within my
soul. "Do SOLEMNLY swear….Solemn indeed, this oath and this
moment in my life; and now the Governor was echoing thoughts that
have been mine for oh so many years. "A Nation's worth," he was saying,

"is measured by the concern it has for its people… "A Nation's worth indeed, I thought; a Legislator's worth, as well…

Our arrival in the House Chamber had been preceded by a Democratic Caucus where we gathered to nominate our Candidate for Speaker of the House; and where I had the opportunity of meeting oh, so many FRIENDLY colleagues. They're a great group, I can already tell! The Hon. David M. Bartley having been selected as our Candidate; and our business having been concluded, how exciting it was now to find ourselves pushing our way through crowds of people…legislators; families and friends, we were to learn, all of whom stood patiently by the Chamber doors, hoping to be admitted finally and permitted to STAND for the 2½ hour "Sitting" of the House.

I found my heart hammering with excitement. I was now about to enter the historic Chamber for the very first time…to take my place within that august circle…to open another wonderful chapter in my life.

I entered the House Chamber, my eyes rising quickly to the Gallery above where hopefully I should find the people I love. I do! There is Ted, my wonderful husband; and my beautiful children, Gael and Jim along with their small boys, Jim and Byrne and Greg, my adored grandsons. Son Richard and his dear Dolores and their two great boys, Richard and Franklin have been prevented from coming by young Richard's sudden hospitalization, but I can feel their thoughts about me. There is Jay, my great Campaign Manager, and my "adopted" son; my terrific Precinct Seven Captain; Bernice, that much loved State House V.I.P. whose sterling worth and unmatched and brilliance as the Executive Secretary to the House Counsel will be spread upon the record a short while later by none other than Abington's own John Buckley, retiring as a "Rep" to assume a Cabinet position in the new administration…Bernice, the treasured friend who has so smoothed my pathway to the "House" that now I feel I quite belong; Rosemary and Vera, my very dear friends…I find them all. They're there; there "nods and becks and wreathed smiles" matching my own.

The day was to be easily the most exciting of my life. I was to find my seat-H-141, the seat once occupied for sixteen golden years by our Herb Hollis; and then for two by our Don Laing; and then for two by our Bob Frazier…the "Braintree Seat", it has been called; and now 'tis mine.

I was to watch, enchanted, all the protocol, the pomp and circumstance that is a facet of our government by the General Court, the oldest bicameral legislature in these great United States, incidentally; dating as it does back to 1630 when the membership meetings of the Massachusetts Bay Colony bore that selfsame name - the "General Court!"

In the early 17th century, I was to learn, it had been called the House of Deputies. Not until 1692 did it adopt the name, "House of Representatives; becoming then the world's first governing body of that name.

Yes, I was to find myself seated in H-141, looking back over the centuries…wondering who in all those years have occupied this place… what great distinguished Massachusetts men. Is there a way to find this out, I ask myself? Must check this bright detail with my Bernice…

The Speaker was to be elected by Roll Call vote - my first! And the Hon. Mr. Bartley was to win; and then the Senators and the Governor to be formally informed of the election; and by a House Committee appointed to perform the happy task…and, incidentally, to be led between the Chambers by no less a personage than the tall Sergeant-at-Arms, a gentleman resplendent in top hat and handsome staff which I am certain has a name, however I've not yet learned it…

The Clerk of the Court, the much loved Wallace Mills, was now to be appointed and to read aloud the Orders of the Day…I was to find delight in all the protocol; to thrill at sight of my own name upon the Roll Call board; if that is what 'tis called. (Must ask Bernice that one, as well; what would I do without her???) to feel somehow that I indeed BELONG within this hallowed place.

The awesomeness of the task I've undertaken stirs my soul. I'm PROUD and HUMBLE each in turn. The knowledge that what I shall do or fail to do within my term will now affect the quality of life for all the people of the Commonwealth sweeps over me like some great surging wave…

"I, Elizabeth Metayer, do solemnly swear…" My eyes rise high as now I take this oath…high above the bright gold wings that frame the great House clock; high above the handsome murals that depict those grave historic moments on the walls; high above even the Bullfinch State House dome; high above the bright blue sky that lies without this lovely day; high above all else, it seems, to where the loving Father of us all can hear the prayer within my heart. "Dear God," I ask, "Help me to measure up; help me to justify their faith in me - those wonderful people on my team; and those wonderful people who have voted for me - help me ever to remember that this legislator's worth will e'er be measured by the deep concern she has for all the people she will serve. Help me," I find myself praying; and I ask you wonderful people who have elected me to join me in that prayer that I SHALL measure up... That I SHALL justify your faith in me...

And now, a Happy and a Blessed New Year to one and all. May you have LOVE and PEACE and JOY and HEALTH and family and friends- for if you have all these, THEN YOU HAVE EVERYTHING! I do!

2-1-70   THE BUTTERFLY

IT IS STRANGE how delightful little stories come the way of a columnist... stories like the following:

Away back in the year 500 BC, so the legend goes, in a far off land that was then known as Cathay and is now called China, a handsome young Chinese boy became so entranced by the beauty of a multi-colored butterfly he was pursuing, that he lost sight of the rigid Chinese code of behavior, and raced headlong into the garden of a wealthy and powerful Mandarin.

The appearance of the man's immense and forbidding guards brought him instantly to a standstill. What had he done??? The young man, struck with the folly of his act, stood there with downcast eyes awaiting the punishment he knew full well would be his

He was led into the great hall to confront the master of the house, a man known far and wide for the harsh punishment he meted out to trespassers on his estate.

With what surprise, however, he found himself facing not the stern Mandarin at all, but his lovely daughter who, when informed of the lad's misdeed, looked his way with pity and compassion.

"I pursued a butterfly," he said, "I did not mean to come into your garden. It was such a beautiful butterfly!" "I know," said the sweet young maiden, smiling "I, too, find the butterfly beautiful."

That was the beginning of a relationship that strangely blossomed into love, a love that would culminate despite all obstacles in a marriage between the two, a marriage that was to be a symphony of sweetness for all the years to come.

To the beautiful butterfly the young lovers credited their meeting, for had not the young man been guided to his beloved as though on its delicate wings??? And so from that day forward the butterfly became for them, and with the passing of years for all Chinese, the symbol of pure love. And so on the eve of a young Chinese maiden's marriage it became the custom for her parents to place in her hands a piece of jade, fashioned in the form of a butterfly, as an assurance of wedded happiness. This custom 'tis said, is followed among the young Chinese here in America as well as in far-off China.

***

ANOTHER LEGEND of the origin of the butterfly:

Once upon a time, long, long ago, there lived a poor little crippled boy who was not able to romp or play in the fields with his brothers and sisters. Each morning his father carried the little fellow to a sheltered spot under a great oak tree where, safe from the hot summer sun, he might watch the other children of the family at play in the broad meadow beyond.

"How patient is my small sweet son," thought the father as he hoisted him high upon his shoulders each day. "Never a complaint; never a tear..."

And truly the little crippled boy WAS patient beyond belief; however, there came a day when, seated beneath the tree, he was overcome with a compelling sadness.

"If only I could run and play like the others," he thought bitterly; and suddenly hot scalding tears began to run down the sad little cheeks and settle upon the green grass. And that was when it happened.

Suddenly, so the legend goes, the tiny tears began to shimmer and shine, and then to change color, and then to take wing; and before the eyes of the wondering child to turn into a host of butterflies of every shape and color imaginable! "How beautiful!" cried the little crippled boy, and he reached out his hands as if to grasp them, but away they flew on the wind…

"Follow us," they cried to the little crippled boy. "Follow us!" "I can't," he cried in return. "I wish I might, but I can't…" "Yes, you can," they called. You CAN if you TRY. TRY!"

And the little crippled boy, so the story goes, grasped the trunk of the big oak tree and tried with all his might to lift himself to his feet. AND HE COULD!

And then he tried to race across the meadow to where the butterflies flew, to make his little crippled useless legs perform. AND HE DID!

Small boys have been chasing butterflies ever since.

***

AND JUST in case you are wondering why, with snow piled high about the eaves this cabbage treats of butterflies, a gentle reminder - January lies behind us; and February really is a short old month; and in March the tulips are up… So doesn't it really begin to feel like Spring might be just around that corner???

THE CANDIDATE

(Written in fun at a time of tension for all of us.)
I'm a Candidate for Office; I'm the undisputed choice
Of the party of ALL people, and in me they may rejoice!
In the Scouts I was an Eagle; upon cue I can be regal;
Can you vote for any other? I'm your brother! I'm your voice.

I am educated soundly; I'm a master, you can see
Of the science that is Politics. Behold my Ph.D.!
I've read all the latest books. How the ladies love my looks!
And I boast a dozen offshoots from my happy family tree.

I've a fascinating record; I've a score that can't be beat.
All the polls for my opponent predict crushing, cruel defeat.
And - if, this is any omen - why, I started as a yeoman
And, before the war was over, I was Admiral of the Fleet!

I'm a whiz at public speaking; I'm a paragon of poise;
I'm the idol and delight of all the teen-age girls and boys.
I'm for Motherhood, you bet; I'm a perfect teacher's pet.
I'm the guy whose campaign speeches every mother's son enjoys!

I've a wife who's simply charming. I've a Collie brave and sweet;
And my television image has become a household treat.
I call voters by first name; plan to make the Hall of Fame;
And in any T.V. Debate I shall happily compete.

I have promised my constituents the sun and moon and stars.
We'll be first to slip a rocket in the pocket of old Mars;
And we'll KEEP that Russian bear quite securely in his lair!
Meet the "Girls" who sing my praises as they strum their gay
    guitars!

THE CANDIDATE

I'll wage war upon corruption; I'll give juveniles the vote;
On each one of all your problems I shall personally dote;
I shall swiftly take the axe to each solitary tax
As I balance every budget (with a promissory note…)

I shall lower all the tariffs; raise the living standard high;
Top off every Sunday's chicken with a home-baked apple pie.
(With my banners all unfurled, I have pledged the blooming
    world…)
I'll send half a hundred shuttles pipping gaily through the sky!

I am certain of election, for however could I miss
With a guarantee, for all to see, of Utopia such as this!
As Election Day draws near, I slide merrily into gear!
Oh, the mothers I shall smile on, and the babies I shall kiss!

But-in private - I'm commencing (I admit it with a quiver)
To have just a few misgivings, to suppress an inward shiver…
Though old Platforms fade away, so the politicians say,
WHAT IF EVER (Heaven forbid it) I were called on to
    DELIVER!!!

G.C. H.S.

THE CECILIAN GUILD

President, Elizabeth Nener
Vice President, Rose Boland
Secretary, Louise Kennally

From the dawn of time, music has always been the voice of the soul. The soul wincing with pain, dejected with sorrow, has ever turned to music in which to pour forth its griefs in the throbbing tears of melody. Again, if the heart is happy what better means of expression can it find other than in the voice of exultation-music? And so every Sunday when we, as privileged members of the Cecilian Guild, hear the sound of the organ, we burst forth into glorious song of praise and adoration, or sorrow and hope as the feast may be.

The season of Advent finds us rehearsing in feverish excitement for the greatest event in the history of the Church, the Birth of Christ, Our Lord and Saviour, joyful, glorious and amazing. Then too, there is the season of Lent, that very sad and holy season in which we prepare for the death of Christ, sad, agnominious but triumphant, for on Easter we, exultant in Christ's triumph over death pour forth our happiness in the beautiful "Allelulias" and the most glorious of all hymns,

Truly music is always and ever "the child of prayer, the companion of religion.

"Rexurrex."

12-20-64   THE CHRISTMAS CORSAGE

IT'S HOLDIAY corsage time, and from just about every lapel in town, there sprouts a gay confection of flora and fauna and folderol that says, quite simply, "Merry Christmas!"

I never can quite wait to don my own, I spot the first intrepid holidayish soul to sport a Christmas boutonniere, and I am off! This year it happened the very morning after Thanksgiving...

Today I saw it smiling there,
A remnant of the yesteryear;
Its holly leaves a trifle worn,
Its berries just a mite forlorn, --
THE FIRST GAY HOLIDAY CORSAGE!
(Quite premature, but no mirage!)
Its wearer smiled as if to say,
"I couldn't wait another day!"
No stylish lady, clad in furs;
No rare outstanding beauty hers;
No purity of form or face;
Or pretense to a special grace.
Her coat was worn; her hat not right;
But on her face, a radiance bright
Said, "Christmas is not far away.
Oh, how I love that blessed day!
This holiday corsage I wear
To me is infinitely fair."
I hastened home, - to attic sped;
A hundred Christmas nosegays spread,
And lovingly their forms caressed,

With memory tugging at my breast
This faded treasure I acquired
From Gael, a tot in boots attired,
Who tramped about on shopping spree,
And gaily brought it home to me.
The mother now of two small boys,
Her own sweet Christmas she enjoys;
This one, a gift from Mother's hand,
(She dwells now in a better land.)
That one a Christmas package graced;
And this upon a sweet was placed,
That was a favor; this a boon
That rode a Santa Claus balloon!
A million merry memories cling
To keep my soul remembering,
As Christmas nosegays I caress
In sweet nostalgic happiness.
I never can quite throw away
A single holiday bouquet.
I tie them on my Christmas tree,
And spend them in a lavish spree
On gay, bedeck-ed doors and walls;
With sweet abandon, deck the halls
In shiny sprigs of green and gold,
And some are new, and some are old,
Their bows not now quite up to par;
A starpoint missing from a star;
An angel's wing that's all awry;
A Santa Claus without an eye!
They need not ever perfect be
To share my Christmas symphony.
But every blessed boutonniere
Brings memories so fond and fair
I cannot part with even one.
They all must share my Christmas fun.
Oh, gay corsage on each lapel, -

YOU RING A SPECIAL CHRISTMAS BELL!
Your cry of gladness you impart.
"Here dwells a happy kind of heart
That wishes all such Christmas cheer
And blessed joy throughout the year, --
That prays, as Christmas comes again,
For Peace on earth, --good will to men!"

YES, THERE'S something special about the Christmas corsage. It's a badge of distinction, - a link in the holiday chain of enchantment that binds us all together at Christmastime. I shall be wearing mine the day after next Thanksgiving Day, I'm certain if I am still upon this great, glad earth....Merry Christmas, everybody!

5-3-70   THE CLUBWOMAN

A basic black; a string of pearls;
A smart new hat on coiffured curls;
A gracious warmth; a happy smile;
An unmistakable, "Club" style..
"A-ha!" you say, "There's lucky she
Departing for another Tea,
To spend a jolly hour or two
O'er cakes and gossip!" would 'twere YOU...

Or, do you REALLY envy her,
This gal encased in flowers and fur???
Why, clubwomen lead shallow lives,
The real antithesis of wives
Whose days are dutifully spent,
You really are much more content,
You tell yourself, and toss your head...
SHE may well envy YOU instead!

"I sure do pity the poor guy,"
Your mate observes as she drives by,
"Who's married to a clubwoman.
Boy, there is a forgotten man!
Now I believe that home's the place
Wherein to house a woman's grace…"

Well, they don't know it, but our gal
Is off to Veterans' Hospital!
She'll bring the outside world with her,
A world of perfume, flowers and fur,
For those whose days are dim and drear,
She'll tote a special kind of cheer;
She'll serve them tea; their missives pen;

She'll smile upon these lonely men
With all the charm at her command.
And, furthermore, she'll think it grand!
Now then again, she may be bound
To work the well known clock around
In some outpatient clinic grey;
'Tis here she'll spend her busy day.
"Then why so chic?" you'll slyly ask
"If she's to face that sorry task?"
She'd probably just laugh and say,
"The clubwoman is built that way.
From head to toe she must look smart;
It has no bearing on her heart!"
And if you stop to think things through
You're bound to give this gal her due…
***

Who staffs the booths at Church bazaars?
Who drives the Red Cross motor cars?
Who takes those records, one and all
If things are scheduled at Town Hall?

If there's a "do" at old Town Square
Who's more than likely to be there
To sell the tickets, run the show,
And make the thing like clockwork go???
Who heads the drives for funds each time?
What gals those countless stairways climb?
Whose well known faces do you spy
When Boy or Girl Scout troops pass by?
If there's a problem in the town,
Who tracks the legislators down?

***

A perfect human dynamo
Is our clubwoman! On the go
Wherever service is required;
With selflessness and faith inspired.
She has a ball at Teas - that's true-
But, there are worse things she could do!
So, ladies, please be more benign;
This great big world of yours and mine
Is nicer for the gal I know
Who to our Woman's Club must go…
And mates of ladies - pity not
The man you feel this gal's forgot.
From him no sympathy she drains;
She has no time for aches and pains.
And fuss with neighbor??? Goodness, me -
Or fume o'er trifles??? No, not she!
The Clubwoman has other ways
In which to spend her busy days.
This gal does such a lot of good,
We wish her better understood.

WE WATCHED history being made under the great golden dome of the State House one day last week, as a bill in which we had an interest was brought before the House of Representatives. It's an impressive setting for the functioning of our government. The colorful seal of the Commonwealth graces the high, vaulted ceiling. The names of our most distinguished Massachusetts sons encircle the dome in a ribbon of history. A series of murals depicting "milestones on the road to freedom in Massachusetts" adorns the walls. The lettering beneath the murals is dimmed and faded with the years, but bright and shining is the spirit of freedom which seems to cry out from the great historic figures that are represented there. We were, incidentally, proud in the realization that the birth records of three of these distinguished Massachusetts statesmen are to be found in our Braintree Town Hall. THE MAGNIFICENT pageantry of the way we have elected to be governed, is all about us. On a dias stand the three great carved chairs, the central one of which, higher than all else, and framed by a vaulted and draped window, will shortly be occupied by the Speaker of the House, a powerful political figure indeed. His huge carved desk and the great gavel which he will wield with such resounding force as the day wears on, add to the ornate impressiveness of the platform. Four chairs, placed to the front of the desk, face the House members; in these will soon be found the young uniformed pages whose duty it is to run errands for the Legislators once the House is in session. A half moon of chairs and desks in rows, faces the platform. High above, to the left, is the press gallery, and, on the same level, across the entire rear of the House, the spectators; gallery sharply divided down the center, with ladies to the right, and gentlemen to the left. We seated ourselves in the very first row…THE GREAT CLOCK, capped by an eagle with outstretched wings, announced the opening hour of the session, and the Speaker of the House took his seat on the platform. Representatives of our great State, our own included, (we found them immediately with our eager eyes) seated themselves across the carpeted room, and a feeling of excitement, of drama, seemed to sweep across this seat of our government.

Our eyes found the Stars and Stripes, and the State Flag that flanked the great throne chair. Red, I thought, looking at Old Glory, representing honor and valor and all the blood that has been and will be spilled for this; our way of life; white for purity; blue for the high blue heavens… For more than nine score years, this flag of ours has flown, to be the symbol of a democratic land that grew from thirteen small colonies to fifty great states like this, our own.

The electric roll call is primed for action. Two rosters, one on either side; list the names of the Legislators; to the right of each has been placed a red light for a "no" vote, a green light for a "yes". The bill under present consideration (it was H 3950) is proclaimed in large, lighted numerals above the board immediately upon presentation to the House. Our legislators, we found, are vocal, articulate and informed; we were impressed.

ROLL CALL votes are exciting to watch on the electric device. A recess is called by the Speaker, with legislators dashing outside for frantic last-minute lobbying, after which, upon the reconvening of the House, a two minute period of voting is permitted, with tabulations appearing intermittently upon the roll call board. The Speaker announces, "50 seconds left in which to vote; 30 seconds left;" and finally "voting is closed."

There were moments of high drama in the House. There was, for instance, the occasion time and time again, when the Speaker brought his great gavel down with a shattering sound.

"For what purpose does the gentleman rise?" he would ask of a standing legislator. The legislator would challenge on a point of order, or a point of information, or perhaps ask a pertinent question of the legislator before the microphone.

"Does the gentleman yield?" "The gentleman yields," the legislator at the mike would reply, or, more frequently that day, "No, I do not yield."

THERE WERE wonderful utterances, impressive oratory. "I am frightened of the totalitarian powers assigned a few." "I will not have to ask why this House continues to exercise it propensity for doing the ridiculous." "We live day by day; we solve our problems day by day; and we cross our bridges day by day." We in Massachusetts have no natural resources except people, and we should give them the education they deserve.

How wonderful to know that in this great democracy of ours, wherever the laws of the land are made, provision has also been made for a spectators' gallery wherein people like you and me may sit to watch the people we have elected, enacting the laws by which we shall be governed and protected.

2-14-65   THE HAWAIIAN HULA

HAWAII is the land of legends, legends as soft and sweet as the gentle seas that whisper on its shore, legends as harsh and violent as any of the grim volcanic craters at its rim.

What, then, does legend tell us of the hula, that most graceful and inspiring of all dances? Well once upon a time long centuries ago upon a warm and languorous day Laka the younger sister of Pele, desiring to amuse this goddess of Hawaii's grim volcanos, danced for her, the very first hula. All Hawaii rang with Laka'a praise, and lo, from far and wide across the islands of this learned the movements of this lovely dance, where every motion of the eyes, the smile, the long and jeweled chain, came soft Hawaiian maidens, and big, bronzed Hawaiian kanes (boys), and they learned the movements of this lovely dance, where slender hands, would weave a tale.

Laka, herself, came to be worshipped, and the language of the hula grew, so that within this strange religious or festival dance - for that is what it soon came to be - the long and lovely brown Hawaiian hands bespoke the sun and moon, the heavens and the skies, the gentle winds, the dark and racing clouds, rainbows in the sky, and raindrops; waterfalls and lakes and pools and rivers; the mountains and high hilltops; trees, swaying in the trade winds; green grass and plains; the deep blue ocean and the rolling surf, and gentle waves and sandy beaches; and the flowers, the fragrance of the flowers, the lei, and all the thousand lovelinesses of a sweet Hawaii, land of lovely lore. Many of the dances were taboo to all but those whose lives were dedicated to the art of hula, and whose soft and chanting ritual dances were called Kapu hulas, and were performed for none save Hawaiian royalty.

All Hawaiians danced, however, as freely as they breathed, and so as many as three hundred differing hulas are thought to have been danced in ages past. When old waihinis (ladies) could no longer sway upon their feet, a "sitting down" hula was devised, for just so long as a Hawaiian lived, he danced.

The hapahaole, or as it is called, the "traditional" hula, is a soft and graceful swaying of the body. The hips move with slow and stately dignity, and there's a fluttering of hands-and therein lies the tale the hula dancer tells, for hands are palm trees, swaying in the wind, and soft seas, breaking on the coral reefs. They are rainshowers and rainbows This is the hula as it was danced when great Kamehameha I was, king, and Pele, goddess of dancing filled the languorous, carefree days.

There are almost as many hula costumes as there are hulas-brief tops and skirts of shredded "ti" the soft sarong, which young Hawaiian maids call kikepa; the long holomuu, high-necked, long- sleeved; or perhaps for formal hulas, the flowered holoku, with flowing trail, the only gown with which a hula dancer's shoes must e'er be worn.

Kanes (boys) dance a sort of hula and depict a yearning, burning love, the fire and tragedy of war, or "temple piety." Their costumes are the bright Aloha shirts, and rolled up cotton pants, or perhaps lavalavas, which are figured and sarong-like garments, reaching to the calf.

Leis adorn the neck, regardless of one's sex or age, and flowers are tucked behind the ear, and feet are bare...

Instruments are often used, accentuating all the rhythm of the dancers - kalaau, which are sticks of hardwood; pu ili, long slender rattling sticks of bamboo, ili ili, which are small, smooth stones; (these were added by the missionaries, who employed the clinking stones to teach the alphabets with chants) and ipu, hollow gourds, and uli uli, feathered gourds containing seeds, that rattle with a rhythmic, merry sound.

Other things we learned about the hula. We learned them in the grass hut of an elderly Hawaiian, known as "old Sara", on the island of Kawaii. She sat there, in a Menehune Garden, (the Menehunes were legendary little men who once roamed the land) and spoke of ancient hula drums, which sent their pahu pahu (booming sounds) out upon the islands in the days of old.

We learned from her that once there was a time when hula was considered sinful by the staid New England missionaries who had landed on Hawaii's shores, and so the hula dancing was forbidden.

We learned that hula dancers were originally men that hula was a part of their religious service, that when Great Kamehameha died in 1819, and Christian missionaries came, and fear of idols was removed, and men reacted to the outside influences of the whites, their women "took over" the hula. We're very glad they did, for there is magic in the storied swaying of a dark Hawaiian maiden; I shall nevermore hear soft Hawaiian music without visions of a gentle, brown-skinned beauty swaying on the sands, her dark eyes moist and misty, and her slim hands fashioning the tales Hawaiians love to tell of all the tender beauty of this magic land so very dear to every warm Hawaiian heart.

1-23-72   THE HYCINTHS ARE UP!

"'Twas just about ten days ago…there was no ice; there was no snow…A summery kind of sun smiled down on lovely little Braintree-town. The sound of rivers' running feet was permeating Arthur Street; And children's coats were opening…There were a hundred signs of Spring! "It's such a warm and lovely day," said Ted, my spouse. "What do you say? Let's give the family car a bath! That last storm's muddy aftermath has left the old gal looking sick; some Spic and Span should do the trick."

"Why GREAT!" I said "on such a day we really should go out to play, to seep up all this sun and such about the yard we love so much… The car, backed out from the garage, revealed the fact 'twas no mirage we faced the sand from Braintree's roads was on the family car in loads! "Let's go to work," I said "You know, the fusion of that sand and snow is more than any old "CARWASH" can quite eradicate, by gosh-The worst of spots they always MISS…" "All right," said Ted, "You handle this!" He handed me the family HOSE…then at a jog trot, off he goes to come back shortly with a pail of soapy suds that could not fail to do the job…to really clean the Metayers' own special "limousine"…Well, finally - our task well done - we turned to OTHER forms of fun, and started to perambulate about the vast??? Metayer estate…We plucked sprays of forsythia for "forcing" in a bright stone jar; Then turned attention to the wall (we hadn't looked its way since Fall) Before the which, in flower beds, our spring bulbs raise their happy heads… "Do you suppose," I said to Ted, "within their snug, leaf-covered bed Our HYACINTHS their leaves might show?" "Good heavens," said Ted, "Of course not! No! Though Spring has sprung and all that stuff, they've simply not had TIME enough…To struggle upward through the snow and ice and cold, to up and grow…" "Well, anyhow, let's look their way," I said, "It's such a lovely day…"

We strolled along the garden path now strewn with winter's aftermath, Then knelt to push away the leaves in which the gardener believes, The "mulch" that will protect his shrubs from snow and ice and grime and grubs…When, gosh - BEHOLD! SMALL CURLS OF GREEN caressed the earth… their buds serene…Already visible everywhere! Their tiny faces full and fair… "I can't believe it, Ted!" I cried. "I think that I shall BURST with pride!" "We always ARE the FIRST," he said. (He's modest too my darling Ted.) "Our pansies bloom the whole year through; those tulips that we planted, too, Full twenty years ago still spend their beauty lavishly, to lend US special magic long before the Spring has knocked at Braintree's door…

It must be our GREEN THUMBS!" he said…(Ah yes, he's modest, my dear Ted.) Quite naturally we spread the word; to neighbor shouted, "Have you heard? Our HYACINTHS are up an inch! Quite clearly, friends, it is a cinch That though it's JANUARY just, and snows MUST, and winds MUST gust, Already there's a whispering, a sign that SOON WE SHALL HAVE SPRING!" THE LIGHT OF HOPE

If after all the Christmas tinsel is no more…and all the myriad lights that grace our home are laid to rest…and countless Christmas trees that shone with such aplomb in every single room are tucked up in the attic…Braintreeites behold a single stark white candle burning in the window of the Chez Metayer, be not surprised and know it well for what it is and what it represents. "Tis the LIGHT OF HOPE, and here is how it came to glow within our window…

It is Christmas night and we are driving home from Mystic, Connecticut where son Richard and his lovely family we have just celebrated a Christmas Day that was like a poem. In Jim's big station wagon we've grown suddenly quite quiet and one by one our little boys have sunk into the kind of sleep that follows Christmas joy and holiday excitement. It is a beautiful night, warm with a hint of rain in it. Connecticut, and then Rhode Island and our own dear Massachusetts are ablaze from the windows of the humblest of those tiny homes and now and then may line our busy highways; and it bursts like a sunrise from distant estates and lush suburban dwellings. It has been a flawlessly beautiful day. Not an empty place at the long cherry table that graces Richard's charming dining room. Gael and her Jim and the boys along with Grandpas and Grandma had ridden to Connecticut in the early morning, amid fun and laughter, to find Richard's dear Dolores standing like a Christmas angel in one of those long holiday gowns our hostesses affect these pretty days, in the doorway of a lovely old Connecticut farmhouse home that was to cry "Merry Christmas" from every artistic angle.

A fire blazed in the huge fireplace beside which was a real live Christmas tree the family had selected Thanksgiving week from a Christmas tree farm nearby and cut down and toted home the first week in December. Its fragrance mingled with the scent of the "apple logs" that were to burn brightly and merrily all day long, singing and shining and warming hearts as well as footsies

The aroma of an assortment of marvelous pies blended with the fragrance of the evergreens and berries within the two huge Williamsburg globes on the long buffet. And then there was the turkey, bright and brown, and fresh from the oven, serving to remind all of us how very hungry we'd suddenly become.

Gael's three boys swooped down delightedly on Richard's two. "Our children just won't leave their toys on Christmas Day and so we have to stay home," people are forever saying. It's not so with Gael's three Christmas angels. The prospect of a day with their cousins is much more inviting than any conglomeration of Christmas toys. Even five year old Gregory had left his very first two-wheel bike without the slightest protest.

DINNERTIME with our handsome Richard asking a blessing upon all present in that deep rich voice of his, and each of the table guests smiling lovingly upon the other. There are Richard's family and Gael's and in addition to the Metayer grandparents there are Dolores' lovely Mom and Dad, Rose and George Creehan, formerly of Braintree but now settled within a stone's throw of their dear daughter and her family in Mystic...and terribly content there.

How thrilled we'd been when they'd decided to make the move, for now all of our grandchildren would know the joy of loving and indulgent grandparents, and this other set of grandparents would know the joys of having little ones about. What is it Ted and I have long called this crop of bright young men who color so our lives??? The DIVIDENDS on our original investment in life!

Only Jim's parents are missing from our Christmas gathering; and they along with the Creehans and both of our little families had shared a festive and a beautiful Thanksgiving Day with Jim and Gael. How very close we are!!! I marvel as I look about me, upon the sheer unadulterated beauty of my life. How wonderful to have brought into the world two beautiful and beloved young people and have them marry two more beautiful and beloved young people, so that love now comes our way from FOUR...as well as from their five small beautiful and beloved people, those grandchildren of ours.

The day has passed enchantingly and all too soon; and now we drive home through the warm, bright Christmas night and as we go I find my prayers rising Heavenward to the loving Father Who has made of this fine life of ours the poem it has become. And then inevitably my thoughts are turned to those whose lot so differs from my own - the poor, the oppressed, the hungry, the lonely, the ill, the boys in far off Vietnam, the prisoners of war...A vision of their families comes to mind - the promise of a holiday return of those they love snatched brutally from their hearts. Happiness and heartbreak are so much sharper when it's Christmas...

And now begins the story of that stark white candle in the window at Metayers! Jim has tuned in the car radio as he drives. It's a "talk show" and calls are coming in from distant points across our land. I'm not really listening; I am not a devotee of "talk shows". Suddenly, however, the words "Christmas lights" penetrate my consciousness. I am all ears... and the message comes through… "We delight in them," a sad and almost bitter voice is saying, "and indeed we might, but in the prison camps in far off North Vietnam there are no lights… just lonely men gazing into the darkness; longing for home and loved ones…You will all be putting away your Christmas lights in but a week or so," the caller says. "Will you consider leaving just one candle burning??? one white light within your window as a LIGHT OF HOPE - to burn there until Peace is truly ours and all those prisoners of war; those tragic missing in action, those brave young fine Americans are returned to the their land???

"If a LIGHT OF HOPE burned in the windows of millions of Americans in homes across the land, then surely Washington would realize how ardently we yearn for peace and for the consequent return of all our boys," the caller said, his voice breaking with emotion. "We hope to sweep the country with this thought," he said. "Gosh how great it would be if all within the sound of my poor voice would light their LIGHTS OF HOPE."

I've already lit our LIGHT OF HOPE, we Metayers. It shines there even now amid the tinsel and the glitter, the twinkle lights and all the rest. And there it will remain, God willing, until Peace is on the land and all our boys are home and safe and happy…Won't some of you, my readers, consider in this It IS infinitely better, you know, to "light that one small candle" than to "curse the darkness!"

11-19-72 THE MILITARY

It's a wonderful thing to be part of a family…to share its joys and its sorrows. The fact was brought home beautifully this past week as two very important events occurred in the life of John, our brother-in law. He became a full bird Colonel in the 1st Squadron, 26th Cavalry; and he retired from same, and accordingly was tendered a Retirement Dinner at the Officers' Club in Fort Devens - a place, incidentally, which this columnist was visiting for the very first time.

Few men achieve this high distinction; and so John's entire family was on hand to share his triumph, to have a ball and, incidentally to catch a glimpse of the military at play. And what a glimpse it was!

The setting was warm and rather intimate - a decidedly attractive Officers' Club where red and white bouquets graced tables and regimental and other flags formed a handsome background to the head table guest… chief among whom were, of course, brother-in-law John, resplendent in his handsome dress blues and sister Jeanne, stunning in scarlet and silver.

There was so much brass on hand for the occasion, the place resembled the Pentagon. Indeed, having recently read the latest scoop on the doing of that august body, I found myself wondering if any of the generals or colonels had arrived by helicopter.

It was a splendid affair, however, with military protocol observed to the nth degree; and we were to delight in every shiny aspect of it. The receiving line which formed about my handsome brother-in-law and his lovely wife - both looking incredibly young, we might add - included a choice assembly of the most distinguished among those present, and was so impressive it resembled a movie set. So, actually, did the head table, where the bright flowing gowns of Generals' and Colonels' ladies contrasted beautifully with the dress blues of their distinguished mates.

It was indeed a posh gathering; and what a thrill to see these men - officers all - standing at attention as the band played our National Anthem in perhaps the most hauntingly beautiful manner we've ever heard. There was a decided "Farewell" in its strains; a mixture of pride and pathos we, were quick to sense. The toast to the Colonel and the Colonel's Lady, Sister Jeanne was almost equally moving.

Across our "Family" table, the eyes of Cynthia, the couple's diminutive daughter met my own. They were filled with tears which threatened to dampen the beautiful black and white of her gown periodically throughout the evening. John, Jr. stood proudly at attention, handsome indeed in the white dress uniform of the Honor Color Guard of the Continental Army Command. As a matter of fact, people kept referring to him as the… "Student Prince" and we fully expected someone to break out with the strains of "Drink, Drink" or some other selection from that happy operetta. We found ourselves thrilling to the gracious utterances of the welcoming brass; and responding to the equally gracious utterances of brother-in-law John as we pipped about the place, photographing for posterity and having our usual ball as the ceremony progressed…a ceremony in which, incidentally, John was presented with a handsome sword, symbolic of the Cavalry and bearing his Regimental Crest and his name and rank. What an heirloom for young John's and Cynthia's children we thought lovingly…but will Cynthia's three-year old David and John's as yet unborn little men still be in uniform when future family gatherings are planned, we wondered sadly.

The evening progressed happily, and as John's distinguished military career was being reviewed and recalled, I found my thoughts going back to that tragic Sunday noontime when the news of Pearl Harbor came our way. John was dining with us; he and Jeanne were sweethearts then. As a matter of fact they had always been sweetheart, it seems. The summer homes of both our families had been built together. John and my brother John had been best friends almost from birth, with Jeanne inevitably tagging along on any and all of their adventures, and the "Colonel" seeing to it that she did.

But to return to the Sunday of Pearl Harbor. John, who was in college at the time, had come to an immediate decision. "I'll enlist tomorrow," he had stated firmly. We had persuaded him to wait until after the holidays, but depart he did on January 3 to begin an army career that was to include service in World War II and in Korea, and to ultimately end in a retirement dinner at the Officer's Club in Devens with the rank of full bird Colonel.

And now my thoughts went to his son, seated across the table from the Metayers, another generation in uniform. John, Jr. had also enlisted during the most horrendous war, perhaps, in American history. He had been fortunate, however. A particularly handsome young man, John had been speedily selected to join the Honor Color Guard of CONARC, the Continental Army Command, whose dress white he was so adoring this evening. John is stationed at Fort Munroe, Virginia. Known originally as "Fortress" Munroe, this army post has had a fascinating history which he was to share with us as the evening progressed, to our delight and enlightenment. No less colorful character than Robert E. Lee had designed its fortifications, we were to learn, which is why it never was attacked by the Confederates. As a matter of fact, Lee's first child was born there in perfectly preserved quarters that are currently being occupied by a Lieutenant Colonel and his family.

It was there that President Lincoln planned the attacks on Norfolk and Richmond' and President Jefferson Davis was confined in what is called its Casemate for two years following war's end. The Battle between the Monitor and the Merrimac was fought off the fort in Hampton Roads.

John's interest in things historical was obviously as great as our own. "And do you know," he added happily, "Fort Munroe hasn't changed a bit. As a matter of fact, CONARC's Commander, General Ralph Haines is occupying the same big handsome southern mansion his predecessors have occupied for a hundred years."

As our young soldier presented these historic facts with all the charm and articulateness of both his parents, my heart gave a sudden wrench. John might well have been sent to Vietnam instead of to Virginia. I thought with a kind of horror. Instead of those handsome dress whites of CONARC's ceremonial guard, he might be wearing a robe in some Veterans' Hospital. His father could be wearing one as well. That chair placed next to his lovely little sister Cynthia might well have been an empty one. His father might never have lived to know the homage of this night. For the business of the Military is War…and behind the splendor and the ceremony such as we were witnessing this day, there lies the terror and the death…the nightmare and the never-ending…

A wonderful evening, but it ended with a prayer…Dear Father of us all…PEACE - PEACE - PEACE- will it ever ever come to stay?"

3-25-73   THE MONTH OF MARCH

When young I was, the month of March was not my cup of tea;
Four weeks of fighting ice-tipped winds that flailed at schoolgirl me…
Though January's snow was often difficult to bear,
And Valentine's Day storms were sure and certain to be there,
One was still aglow from Christmas…or enchanted with the song
Of the merry little freshets new-year thawing sent along…
But then MARCH came leoninely! (or crept, lamb-like
   through the door…)

And the wildest winds of winter seemed to roar and roar and roar!
How they whistled through my pigtails as I walked the mile to school;
(With a total cold abandon of that nice old golden rule.)
How they hammered at my heartbeats; how they nibbled at my ears;
How they whipped about my leggings, filling wide young eyes
  with tears!
Oh, how endless was the Fellsway as we journeyed, young
  head down
On those merciless March mornings, in our own fair
  Malden-town.
Oh, how far away that schoolroom-e'er we reached it, we were
  blue!
Such a joy to tear the page off when THAT calendar month
  was through!
How the ancient order changeth; how the years one's
  viewpoints dim!
Why, I NOW approach the scoundrel that is March with
  verve and vim...
And each footstep I am taking is replete with SPRING's allure.
Here the earth is soft and squishy 'neath my rubber-coated toes,
And the seasonal enchantment day by day more wondrous grows.
Crocuses their arms are waving in the wind that rushes free;
And my matronly green hyacinth nods on even terms with me.
Jonquil fronds are huddled closely, seeking warmth beside the
  wall,
Make ready to turn gold in no blessed time at all.
Maple trees are moist and beaded in exciting kinds of ways;
And above we find a blue-ing in the sky's assorted greys.
There's a friskiness about the way the willows toss their arms;
And a row of low Sweet Williams has begun to show its charms.
Look! A pair of chilly robins huff and puff with rosy pride-
Two gay premature young heralds from the Southland, warm
  and wide,
Who-like me - could wait no longer to announce approaching
  SPRING
So had set their sight on Braintree, and quite gaily taken wing.

As I dash from house to auto, I can scarce recall the day
When I faced the monster month with such childish, dark dismay,
For NOW March is but a gateway, though its winds may rush
    and roar,
To the happy Springtime season that has come our way once more…

5-17-70 THE MONTH OF MAY

LITTLE MIS MAY danced gaily up my garden path last week. She wore a sky blue ribbon in her hair. Her gown, of greenest velvet, brushed soft lawns, and gave them glow.

A rainbow scarfed behind her in the wind. She wept a bit, then smiled a golden smile from out her tears as maidens have a way of doing in the spring.

Little Miss May then stirred the birds beneath our eaves to lovely morningsong. She nodded gaily to the robin and the moist brown earthworm, locked in deadly tug-of-war upon the grass.

Squirrels, tightroping on the wires, waved merry tails her way; shyly they watched her pass through great white brides' bouquets of apple tree and pear tree, rich with bloom.

Little Miss May waved tiny, sun-tipped wands o'er all the silent corners of our place. Tulips opened wide red hearts to her; they splashed rich jeweled chalices of gold and white and pink upon the nut-brown warmth of earth.

Pansies tossed welcoming heads, their pansy faces smiling 'neath a thousand slender stems. Music came with crimson-shod Miss May… sighing of gentle windsong in the dawns. Music came…All of my garden wind-chimes silver sang, while bold brash poppies waved long Oriental arms and tossed green heads in gay exotic dancing by the wall.

Haughty rich azaleas heard her step, springing in magic flamings as she came, or tossing their snowy heaps beneath her feet, or blushing with coral glow, or laying their luscious lavender about…

Great yews sedately bowed their handsome heads, sweeping at softly scented springtime air with all the tiny new-green whiskbrooms in their hands.

LITTLE MISS MAY caressed the pale magnolia with her touch, leaving magenta moonglow in her wake.

She tiptoed past the tiny garden snake, sunning himself upon the granite wall-black eyes bright-beaded with the joy of May.

The gentle white andromeda's soft bells sounded a silent greeting as she passed. The hedges fluffed rosettes were waved her way; and brown and shining rose stalks raised plumed heads in sweet salute.

Slowly she tossed great handfuls of low phlox - here in a scarlet heap and there in a mound of white; rich pot-of-gold she burnished with bright hands; iris she tipped with blue, or kissed with flame.

Little Miss May fashioned a Maypole fair, using the slim straight dogwood as her staff. Gaily she pinned pink blossoms in its crown. Softly she summoned birdsong to its side.

Spiders saw fit to weave their silvered strands; spinning the sunlit streamers for dance. Starlings flew by and caught the magic spell, bearing the streamers sweetly to the skies.

Little Miss May's gay laughter moved about. It whispered on the scented springtime wind. It sounded in the willows' lullabies.

Where has the winter gone that yesterday withered the earth's brown cheeks with ancient hand? How can it be that but a week ago, this paradise Miss May has wrought was bleak and bare? How can one Maytime week transform a world?

May's the month of magic. May's the precious prologue to the great compelling drama we shall know.

Little Miss May danced gaily up my garden path last week. She wore a sky blue ribbon in her hair. She wept a bit, then smiled pure gold from out her tears. AND WHERE SHE WALKED WENT WONDER!

7-4-71   THE NEIGHBORHOOD CAT

Fluffy is our neighborhood cat. She is big and black and wears a bright red collar and a bell like any self-respecting feline.

Fluffy is middle-aged...no flighty adolescent this lady...and she is as poised and purr-fect a female as ever graced the pert front porch of a trim white house in a tidy suburban town.

Fluffy is an early riser; consequently, so is her mistress! Promptly at seven, the front door opens and she emerges to appraise the day. Her middle name must be Thomas-ina, for she places no credence whatever in the sight or sound of falling rain. Fluffy invariably extends a haughty feline head and a tentative paw over the door sill as a prelude to turning tail and stalking back to the comfort of a soft wicker basket and a dry world.

Let the day be sunny, however, and Fluffy saunters forth. There is feline decorum in the quiet measured pace with which she executes the walk. Her tail is high; her back arched. Her paws rise and fall daintily and deliberately; and every dog in the neighborhood - large and small - takes to the hills!

Her daily schedule is quite static. Winter naps are taken on the warm hood of whatever car happens to have been at large in the neighborhood that day. Summer naps see Fluffy curled up in the cool confines of our brick garage or stretched beneath the low-hanging willow tree.

Fluffy is supremely egotistical. The house in which she dwells is HER home, with its human occupants living there on sufferance.

The neighborhood is replete with tales of Fluffy and her machinations. We had our own personal experience.

A workman had left an aluminum ladder propped against the wrought iron railing of the porch that adjoins my room. It was a warm summer evening and the porch door was open. I awakened suddenly to hear stealthy footsteps ascending the ladder, which moved gently with every step, metal sounding softly against metal. I quietly awakened my spouse and knowing the screen door to be securely locked, we staged an elaborate plot to catch the culprit. Ted stole silently down the front stairs and across the lawn, clutching a weapon of sorts while I frantically dialed the police department on the upstairs extension. Fortunately I heard his laughter e'er the call was completed and sped to join him on the lawn. The burglar was stepping daintily off the last rung of the ladder onto my tempting porch. It was Fluffy. She meowed a silent greeting appropriate to the early morning quiet, she is Of several things you can be quite sure. Fluffy will never be petted by your grandchild, or devour your table scraps, or sit upon your lap, or turn on her tiny motor just to make you happy! And yet she definitely prefers PEOPLE to other CATS. I am certain that on her next little trip around this earth, Fluffy will be a dowager, complete with pearls! Fluffy is one kind of cat; there are others. A friend has three delightful little felines. Charlie, named for a "dear brother who didn't amount to much", is a hail-fellow-well-met sort of cat. One ear is off at a rakish angle, and there's a bend in his tail where his devil-may-care attitude obviously bought Him, on one occasion, to grief. Arthur, "named for the milkman" is a Scairdie Cat. He takes a furtive look at anything human and dives headlong into the nearest thicket. George, on the other hand "named for my husband" (sometimes it's a little confusing to them both) is a gentleman. He does everything but bow from the waist when encountered. (So does his master!) George has never in all the years of his life caused his mistress a moment of anxiety. Charlie, on the other hand, has been missing for days at a time; and Arthur, popping unexpectedly from the weirdest places, has reduced the dear lady to borderline heart failure on more than one occasion.

The mistress of these three feline darlings had a private entrance installed for them in the cellar wall. You've seen this delightful new addition to the comfort of the feline world, I'm sure. It failed, however to work out!

"Charlie insisted on bringing in his friends," said his mistress. "I would awaken in the morning to find the house filled with the wretched creatures. I couldn't take it."

How did you know it was Charlie?" I asked. "My dear," she said. "One could tell at a glance. They were always, invariable, Charlie's type!"

A cat is a strange, complex, inscrutable creature. She will respond with complete loyalty so long as you bring her a saucer of milk; AND UNTIL SOMEONE ELSE COMES ALONG WHO WILL BRING HER A SAUCER OF CREAM! Fascinating, though, aren't the little dears???

1-26-69   THE OPTIMIST

DID YOU KNOW THE WINTER'S OVER??? That's my
   pet philosophy
When we've tucked away the trimmings, and we've burned the
   Christmas tree;
And securely in the attic we've placed every Christmas bell,
Each cone wreath and quiet candle we have learned to love so well…
***

On what premise do I base now, this strange statement that I make
Barely as the turkey soup has gone the way of Christmas cake;
When the new year's noisy dawning still leaves echoes on the air
And the jolly face of Santa yet peers gaily here and there???

***

Well, this month of January, I am certain you'll admit
Is beset by gay capriciousness; is moved by wanton wit…
Though she well might flex her muscles; let her baser nature show-
She has days and days when soft and spring-like zephyrs sweetly blow!

***

Though she does posses the know-how to turn rivers into ice,
She quite frequently regards them with the gayest of caprice;
Sets them running in the gutters; sees them trickle on the lawn;
Catches sunlight in their silver as they flow across the dawn.

***

Though she well might be a lion, she's as gentle as a lamb
On innumerable occasions…That's precisely why I am
Saying simply, January most delightfully can fly;
Light and sweetness on its wing-tips, can quite casually pass by.

***

Then, of course, there's February, month of grayness and of snows,
But with two or three days missing, it's surprising how it goes!
And besides, the pussy willows softly fur beside the wall…
You're reminded, as you find them; SPRING'S not far away at all!

***

March is then around the corner, making ready her debut,
So you mutilate the calendar, and she smiles up at you…
Now the earth is warm and waking; soft, sweet crevices appear
And you realize with laughter, SPRINGTIME'S RHAPSODY
     is near…

***

Crocuses are bravely budding, sending starshapes toward the sun;
And in small secluded gardens, nature's magic has begun.
Tulip leaves are curling softly; jonquil fronds are stabbing free;
And a green and gentle swelling is commencing on the tree!

***

E'er you know it, fair Miss April, dear and dancing, comes along
And your world awakes one morning to the glory of spring-song
Robins rosy man the fence-posts; jonquils bow a greeting gay
As you trod your garden pathways, now no longer grim and gray...

***

You awake to buttered sunshine; walk abroad in sugared rain;
Soar with wings upon your heartbeats as a world is born again..
And BEHOLD, THE WINTER'S OVER, and you've barely
  felt it pass;
BUT, THE PASSING OF THE SPRINGTIME IS AS
  SWIFT AGAIN - Alas!

2-21-71 THE PHILERGIANS TAKE A TOUR BY E. IONE LOCKWOOD

Those who "stirred their stumps: and got down to the Philergians' meeting Tuesday at Emmanuel parish hall were rewarded by a marvelous travelogue by "Bibs" Metayer. This took them to Yellowstone National Park, the Grand Tetons, Banff and Lake Louise in Alberta, Canada, and into Jasper National Park and the Columbia ice Fields. Mrs. Metayer was introduced by Mrs. John G. Hedman.

Mrs. Metayer was a spellbinder with her easy delivery and spontaneity, and Philergians and their Senior Citizen guests just didn't notice time passing as Mrs. Metayer wove her fascinating story. Her inquiring mind led her to explore many spots much more extensively than other tourists, and she plied the Rangers and others with pertinent questions, finding out little-know facts about these natural phenomena.

She and her husband, Ted, now devotees of trailer living, bought one which they named "Fanny" because it "was always behind." The model home on wheels was "self-contained," having all facilities for cooking, sanitation, electric living, and all the comforts of home while traveling cross-country. She told of the cooperative and genial atmosphere of the trailer camps where they stopped, and said they were both itching for Spring, 1971, to take off again.

Highlights of the trip included her pictures of Yellowstone, including those of "Old Faithful" and other geysers, the Continental Divide, a real live black bear, mountains, et al, which were something to see. Her commentary was priceless as she described some of the predicaments Ted and she got into, such as entering Yellowstone by the East Gate!

"Yellowstone she said, "is a fairy-land for photography." and she proceeded to prove it. A good part of the "Lecture" was taken up with pictures of an informative discussion about geysers, their causes and effects. "Bibs" found out when one was to erupt and was on hand to witness the Castle Geyser erupt 100 feet into the air. She talked of rocket geysers, daisy geysers, and small geysers called fumerols. The temperature of the geysers is 190 degrees, making them very dangerous to approach...

Her parting advice on leaving the fabulous Park was to advise against going there in July or August, as it is a nightmare for tourists. (She starts with Ted on their next "safari" on May 21, just before school lets out!)

"This country is incredibly beautiful," she enthused in reference to journeying to Banff and Lake Louise. She projected slides of the snow-covered mountain peaks of the lofty Canadian Rockies. She showed a herd of bison. She managed to shoot a mother elk and her baby, caribou and some evidences of beavers' industry. Lake Louise is a "gem of a lake," "a Turquoise" in the Canadian Rockies, and Victoria Glacier is something to write home about. Ted and Bibs left their trailer for the luxurious atmosphere of "The Chateau" at Lake Louise where they had lunch, dinner, and stayed the night. While at Lake Louise, they went up a mountain in a cable car (but of course!)

Then they toured Jasper National Park where they saw the Snowbird Glacier which they perpetuated with a lovely picture. The Columbia Ice Fields are the largest glacial field in the North American continent-100 square miles, which have been there since the Ice Age. (Here Bibs said she almost froze despite all her warm winter gear which she had stowed into the trailer.)

Before coming home, they stayed 18 days in San Jose at the Mobil Country Club where they "pamper the camper." That was the end of their travels, and of Mrs. Metayer's travel talk for the afternoon. In appreciation, she was presented with the gorgeous centerpiece of red and white carnations from the coffee table. She looked scrumptious holding them against her snappy red and white pants suit. Everybody loves to hear "Bibs," and it's certainly understandable because she takes you traveling so inexpensively and excitingly. One just sits in a chair and thinks she's there, which, after all, is the purpose of any good travelogue.

Mrs. Daniel F. Cameron presided at the business meeting which opened with patriotic exercises with Mrs. Roy W. Lawson, pianist. Mrs. Bryce M. Lockwood, historian, read memorials for Mrs. G. Vinton Jones and Mrs. Albert P. Nelson, long-term members of the Philergians, and Mrs. Cameron placed white carnations in a vase for them Service house must be turned in before March 1, club members were advised.

Mrs. W. Donald Crispin

7-5-64   THE SEA

ON SUNDAY we went down to the sea in a ship Ted and I. The "ship" was the "Sea Gate" of Connecticut home port of Richard, our eldest, and his family.

We arrived in Groton at dawn, slipped the "Sea Gate" from her berth, between two trim little finger piers at the marina, and headed for another world.

Wide metal buoys, black with the wash of winter toiled a throaty greeting.

Sunday was a symphony of blues and silvers on Pine Island Sound. The sea tossed about us, pale blue against the soft white of our wake cold steel against the horizon. With great throws of smoky grey, or tawny green or stark stiff white scattered about its surface. Oh, the sight and the sound and the smell of it!

Richard and his father alternating at the wheel, were mentally rounding the Horn, or skirting the twelve mile reef. They were small boys playing at being men. I thought watching them, or perhaps men, playing at being small boys.

It was a day of pure enchantment! Out of the indescribably sea rose Race Rock Light, on the west end of Fisher's Island. New York. The "Race" is a challenge. Here all the waters of Long Island Sound funnel through a tiny opening causing a powerful rip-as high at time as six knots - every six hours, as the tide changes direction.

Sea-sweet appellations flowed from Richard's knowing lips - Wilderness Point, and Silver Eel Pond, and Watch Hill Reefs, and Seaflower Reef, and the Dumpling Islands, North and South looking for all the world like two soft green dumplings arising from a churning stew. All the fishermen in the world, or so it seemed, lay at anchor. There were the hardy Blue Fishermen (this huge inhabitant of the deep gives quite a battle) and the old fisherman, and distant etched figures seeking "the highest stripe bass in the world." THE "SEA GATE" is a handsome craft, sleek and shining and speedy. She sleeps two, and after an hour of wind and wave she was sleeping our two small grandsons.

Oh, the wonders of a day on the savage sea, with the great, gulls crying, and the rocky reef writhing with full, fat cormorants at play, and slender, silvered terns hunting the bait fish in graceful packs, high above the churning water. Deep in the menacing sea the great "blue" clamps his wide wild jaws about his prey, sealing his doom with one great bite, then leaving the half-mooned victim to but drift above. Oh, the blessed beauty of the tiny flame-billed tern against the summer sky - a slim, slender pencil of a bird writing his poetry on the slate of sky, swooping sharply downward to the floating feast, claiming the mangled prey.

West Harbor, Fisher's Island and the sleek yachts and yawls of the wealthy lie at rest. To the right is, "Blue Hen", half a million dollars of sea-going luxury; a white jacketed steward shakes a snowy cloth above the sea, and for a moment or two the delight we take in our own little "Sea Gate" is shaken; but not for long. The world we see from the deck of our dear little craft is the same, wide, wonderful world as theirs!

THE SEA seems to be staging a special show for us as we cruise the waters of the Sound. A submarine surfaces, far off to starboard, headed for New London. There are great, gorgeous yawls and ketches on all sides, the difference between which, I learn, has something to do with the mizzenmast, which is forward of the helm on the ketch, and aft of the helm on the yawl (or vice versa). The wonderful, wide sails are colored, strangely enough, bright shocking pink, and blue, and candy striped, and lavender and lime. A magnificently carved Chinese junk towers across our bow, complete with pale orange sails, ribbed across like great bats' wings.

"This is something new," Ted tells us. He has read it somewhere. "They are importing Chinese junks; Americans may purchase them for as low as $3,000 but not that baby," he adds, with a laugh.

The sun slips into the sea, splashing the sky as it goes, with a great wide sweep of rose and red and gold, and our ocean grows softly, strangely calm. We journey home.

Richard has been fishing for stripers at Watch Hill Reefs, and so we grill fresh fat fillets over a charcoal fire, and pick up Littlenecks at Noank, and daub at wind-burned faces with sun-tan oil, and rest under the landlocked trees, and speak of the sea and its magic.

How wonderful is the world our God has given us!

6-7-64   THE WEEPING WILLOW

EDWARD and Elizabeth are gorgeous, graceful willow trees on our place. We adore them. There are those who see no great beauty in the softly draping folding of a weeping willow. "They are like weepy people," my dear mother used to say, "I cannot see what you find to like in them. Give me a tree with a fine, stiff black backbone against the sky, and leaves of size and substance." I don't like weepy people. But I love my weeping willow trees. They are not very old. Their parent tree waves lofty arms above the lawn of a very dear friend in South Braintree.

"What a beautiful tree," I said to her admiringly one hot summer afternoon as we sat together sipping tall lemonades and talking family in its shade. "I'd love to put one in the lower area below my stone wall."

"I'll root one for you," she said. "I'll root two in case one doesn't take. They root with no difficulty in a cool, dark place," And she did root not one but two little willow saplings for me. Naturally we planted them both in the lower area below the stone wall.

I never can discard anything that grows. I have passed on my dear friend's kindness, and ours have become the parent trees for slim, straight saplings securely taking root in Melrose, and in Weymouth, and in several other little corners of our own town, which, of course, makes of my dear friend's willow a stately grandparent.

One of the willows was robust and cocky. Its arms were flexed as though to show its muscle; the other was tall and slender and willowy. We named them Edward and Elizabeth after us, and Ted planted them with much ceremony. Each summer evening he gave them long, luscious drinks of cool water, (they require whole lakes of it) while I stood by laughingly, demanding an equal share for Elizabeth who remained slender and undernourished, while Edward sent out strong, straight arms toward the sky. The neighbors watched with amusement; we've wonderfully tolerant neighbors. A HURRICANE that fall and Ted and I watched with horror as our latest garden inhabitants writhed in agony in the cruel wind.

"They cannot survive," we thought, but they did.

"How about Edward and Elizabeth?" the neighbors asked as we walked together over the littered streets, when the calm had come.

"They're safe, thank heavens," we replied quite as thought they were members of the family, that which by now they had become.

Elizabeth, like the lady for whom she was named, has grown plump and matronly with the years. Edward's chest expansion is enormous. In fact, the lower area below my stone wall is absolutely chock full of weeping willow. We might adore the shade our giants contrive to offer, if we had but room to tuck a chaise lounge or two between them, or if we could bring ourselves to seek shelter from the summer heat in the great caves that lie beneath the long, slim fingers by the thousands that caress the lawn. Our grandchildren, when they are older, will have no need to pitch tent or build tree huts.

We sigh just a mite as we recall friends with willows, like the one who placed a "dear little sapling" on the front lawn of her ranch house ten years ago, and now has to volunteer directions for first time guests, like "turn in driveway by weeping willow; follow (willow) for three miles around until you come to sandalwood front door." Or the folks in an exclusive Washington D.C. suburban development who planted them as a happy community project and have been obliged to remove them one by one, replacing water pipes, gas mains and the rest enroute, and sacrificing lawns, and shrubbery, and everything else, until the willows weep no more.

THERE'S NO DOUBT about it. Willow are fast-growing trees. And they do get about. They are beautiful. The soft winds of June provide the music for a thousand garden ballets. The symphony of summer storms inspires an effect of choreography never quite achieved by mortal man.

But they are BIG. You turn your back upon them and they've grown a mile or two around. Ted no longer favors Edward with the hose every summer evening. They're on their own. Someday one of each of us willow or willow-worshippers may have to go! Meanwhile, life is so much richer for their large, lush presence.

We're currently enjoying a sudden Maytime shower, and the lower area of my garden is featuring a water ballet. Soon the sun will scatter handful of emeralds upon the grooved leaves and robins will frolic underneath; and toss the showered drops Edward and Elizabeth send their way back and forth with gay feather arms up the green.

"Great oaks from tiny acorns grow," the poet says…A word of warning-willows grow great as well.

7-24-66   THE VANISHING TRAIN

IT happened the other morning. I heard the close, frantic blowing of a train whistle as I drove through South Boston, enroute to South Station. I followed the impatient sounds, and laughed aloud at what I saw.

A trailer truck was slung carelessly across the railroad tracks, its owner undoubtedly serenely sipping coffee in one of the little neighborhood bistros that dot the area.

The great long freight train which should have been proceeding majestically down East First Street had come to an abrupt halt while its engineer tried lustily to rouse the missing truck driver from his little old coffee break.

"Clear my tracks this instant," the train whistle seemed to be saying… "Lo, have the mighty fallen!" I said to the small grandson who rode beside me. The quote is probably inaccurate, and it passed over his head anyhow, but the idea isn't!

"I wish I could be on that big train," said young James wistfully, and his great brown eyes followed it hungrily until it was quite out of sight.

Of course he does, I thought fondly, and patted his small blonde head, and remembered the countless journeys I had taken on a "big train" when I was small James age or less-to Fitchburg with mother, who never did learn to drive and to our summer place on days when we had driven to Boston with dad in the early morning, but didn't wish to return quite as late as he did; to New York or further on exciting family holidays…

OH, the special kind of excitement to be found in the high vaulted railroad stations we remember - the rush for a seat by the train window; the prickly feel of the upholstery against the backs of the legs our socks failed quite to cover; the song of the rails; telephone poles whizzing by too fast for us to count them, though we always tried, we children; cows dozing in fields of milky daisies and bright brown-eyed-Susans; the little "depots" with their waiting trainmen, green eyeshields and all catching the inevitable mail bags on those long looped hooks…

Ah, the innumerable trips we managed to make to the water cooler behind the train door, with those fascinating paper cups that came out flat, but formed small satisfying cones as they were filled with water.

The fun of the dining car, and the staggery journey through the length of the train to get there; the joy of being met by brothers and sisters at the lake; by innumerable cousins and a smiling, wonderful uncle or two at the more distant places! Long station platforms and uniformed conductors to help with that last high step and redcaps with smiling white teeth…Baggage racks, and brakemen's lanterns, and train whistles by night and reunions and farewells…

"I wish I could be on that big train," young James had said so wistfully. "I wish you could," I thought, and remember a summer day in Quincy not too long ago. The children and I were awaiting the return of their mother from a small shopping spree. We were parked in the vicinity of the old railroad station in the square.

"Don't go near the tracks," I cried in alarm as young Byrne headed automatically in their direction. "It's all right, ma'am," said a small boy close by. "The train won't be back for an hour or so. I'm waiting for it.

It passes here and goes way down there beyond the signals and then it takes on freight; finally it comes back. There's only one train the whole afternoon.

"I come down every day to watch it. The engineer waves to me. I love trains," he added, his eyes wistful. "My friends and I-we come down every day. We wish there were a lot of them, with a lot of people on them, getting on and getting off; but there's only one..."

I hadn't really realized what a rarity trains have come to be. Once they tell me, freight trains sixty cars long, slithered across Braintree any afternoon at all, they "crawled" along in the vicinity of Elm Street, I've been told...The tracks met in a sort of "V" up ahead. The train would stop, then with a sound like thunder change its tracks, and finally come slowly back. A full half hour it took in all. I've heard...YOU know, I cannot help but think, today's children have a fantastic world to live in---outer space and all; but they're missing things to know that you and I remember well from our past-things like the "big trains," with their waving engineers, that bring such a wan wistful look to any small boy's eyes, and even cause a grandmother to pause occasionally herself, and look fondly back...

2-8-70   THE WIG

If, fashion-wise, you would make it big
This sweet spring season - why, wear a wig!
A close cropped cap, or a set of curls
Can perform a miracle for us girls.
It has really become no longer rare
For one gal to wear another's hair;
And a dynel wig on milady's crown
Will send nary an eyebrow up or down...
Time was when your own best friend might ask
"Does she or doesn't she??? and the task
Of knowing for sure must remain with her,
Your friendly; tight-lipped hairdresser...
Not so today; why, if you abhor

Your dull hair shade or its texture, pshaw!
Tis a simple task to quickly change,
To glorify and to rearrange
That crowning glory beneath your hat...
(Believe me, gals - you may lay to that!)
You're blonde, and perhaps you have secretly
Yearned for a dark brunette beauty???
Well, take a chance; don a striking wig;
Transform yourself; you may make it big!
You're a brunette now? Or a brownette drab?
Don't bemoan your fate; instead, hail a cab
And dash on down with a daring smile
To where shimmering golden wigs beguile...
Have you perhaps longed for that happy day
When friend nature will turn to a lovely grey
Those locks of yours that now misbehave?
Have you felt you might journey to the grave
With that wretched old salt and pepper look?
There now, don't despair; and don't get shook.
A grey as gorgeous as it can be
Can be yours for the asking, instantly...
And it really is fun, incidentally.
Take it from one who has tried it - me!
Why, you find you're set at a moment's note
To leave by plane or by train or boat;
To join any party anywhere
With smoothly coiffured and handsome hair...
There are, of course, the asides to face:
Remove it, and wow! Your fall from grace
Can be devastating. That plastered head
Is difficult, ladies, to take to bed...
And shall we be, as we've oft been told
Bald when the years have made us old,
Mayhap we shall live to rue the day
When we tossed our own drab curls away...
But meanwhile, gals, how serene is life

For each gentleman's busy, besieged wife!
No curlers to tuck in one's locks each night;
(And curlers can be such a sorry sight…)
No hours 'neath the dryer; appointments to keep
On cold winter mornings…Just curl up and sleep!
Not forgetting to bless the dear scientist, girls,
Who developed the concept of push-button curls!
Ah, me, what an age…Well, to shower now; and then
My own pearl-grey dynel to rinse out once again,
And than hang way up high on the old shower head
For to dry while I slumber serenely in bed…

THIS AND THAT

All sorts of bit and pieces come my way, like the tale of a recent experience of a family of my acquaintance.

They became aware awhile back of a strange singing sound that intruded itself upon the serenity??? of the family of their lovely large Colonial home. It was a significant noise. It had to be significant to be heard above the din customarily being made by the three spirited young boys of the family whose decidedly handsome habitat the noise was invading.

"What do you suppose it is?" the boys had asked of one another, and failing to come up with an answer, they had brought the matter to the attention of their nice young parents. Now those nice young parents, like most of the nice young parents I know who possess a family room, customarily leave this part of the establishment pretty much to the small fry, generally retreating-come evening to the peace and privacy of the family living room; which undoubtedly accounts for the fact that the strange sing noise had up to that point gone undetected by them…

Said nice young parents, whom I shall call John and Mary simply because two parents are seldom called John and Mary, faced finally with the problem, found themselves equally at a loss to identify the racket.

The puzzle went on until one sunny afternoon when the arrival of Grandmother solved the riddle.

"It's a CRICKET!" she announced excitedly. "How wonderfully lucky! You know - the Cricket on the Hearth, etc. etc. Good fortune... Good luck...Don't KILL it whatever you do!"

And so the cricket was permitted to go on cricking and gradually the little family grew so accustomed to the sound they barely noticed it - like the adjustment they assure us our Braintree citizens will speedily make to the joyous experience of living beside the M.B.T.A. tracks...

Now, what the little family...and the cricket-treasuring grandmother...did not know, however, was the fact that the cricket had a friend...a LADY cricket!

She had to have been a lady cricket to produce those darling little baby crickets that began suddenly to leap about the family room...on and off the furniture, the walls, and the window sills, and the heads of the small fry.

At any rate while one small cricket, performing his intermittent calisthenics, is not too difficult to take the formation of a succession of chorus lines with each of their member vying with his fellow to hit the highest points in the "theater", can become a bit much! A bit much, that is, for adults; the kids loved it. "You can't KILL them," they assured one another gleefully. "They're LUCKY! Grandmother says so..."

Mary and John were beginning, however, to have reservations about Grandmother's merry predictions of family good fortune. How lucky is it really, Mary wondered, to be hit on the head by a flying object each time one entered the family room. The cricket quite obviously had FRIENDS... "We're going to have to DO something about this," she told her husband. But actually John and Mary seldom entered the lush large family room while the advent of evening was bringing out the "ham" in the saltatorial insect intruders; and the three small boys of the family were having the time of their lives with their merry companions. So the crickets cricked on...

Came the climax, however, one middle of a dark winter night recently when the lady of the house attempted to enter the family bathroom UPSTAIRS - a goodly number of large and lovely steps from the confines of the family room. AN ENORMOUS BLACK CRICKET

LAY DIRECTLY IN HER PATH. "He stood there," she said, "glaring at me out of those crazy black eyes they have, and rubbing his big antennae hands in glee…I was terrified!"

"John," she screamed. "There's one in the bathroom - a cricket! The most enormous thing I've ever seen. To heck with luck! KILL it!"

Needless to say the gentleman of the house performed in true gentlemanly fashion, sending the intruder to the hinterlands with firm dispatch. Mary, meanwhile, was reaching a decision "THOSE CRICKETS" she announced firmly to her small sons, "HAVE GOT TO GO! Luck or no luck…I'll pay a bounty of 25 cents per corpus delicti for every cricket you catch!"

The boys were off like so many arrows the following morning. Only they were aware of the number of corpus delicti they would unearth. When, however, the safari turned up thirty-five defunct you-know-whats within a two hour period, Mary reneged. "The bounty," she said "will have to be reduced. Ten cents per cricket is my absolute limit!"

The safari went one, and on, and on…mother's budget underwent a severe strain as the week flew by…but the singing sound came to a screeching halt. The family may be in for less good fortune, but the family room of my friends John and Mary is a much more comfortable though far less amusing, so the small fry tell me, place in which to relax these cricketless days…Another delightful tale…the story of a friend of mine who while on a family visit was tucked nicely into bed in a decidedly handsome convertible divan which had been opened into the world's most comfortable you-know-what. She lay there contemplating happily the eight hours of blissful slumber that lay ahead. Now the fact that with the opening of the divan a full eight inches of space was suddenly visible between the bed and the floor impressed my friend not at all; it did however impress the family pets-a pair of very frisky felines…mother and son…and one outsized Labrador Retriever dog…

"Aha," cried the two cats quite obviously in sheer delight. "A nice new PLAY AREA!" And they promptly proceededto chase one another in and about and back and forth beneath the bed. Their canine companion, meanwhile, who was much too large to fit within the new playpen, wept and wailed as with leaps and lunges he vainly attempted to enter the gorgeous game of tag that was going on so merrily BENEATH THE

PRONE FIGURE OF MY DEAR FRIEND, who rose and fell with the regularity of a Yo-Yo all night long until the dawn's early light saw the frisky felines fall exhaustedly by the wayside themselves...Needless to say the family pet were tucked neatly away on following nights...

3-5-72   THIS AND THAT

At long last those vacationing schoolchildren of ours had a beautiful week, weatherwise. ("Tis seldom so...) There was all the snow in the world for the skiers...and for the proud possessors of those Christmas sleds that once were part of the New England winter landscape, but in recent years have scarcely left the confines of the family storage areas.

Hockey players and would-be hockey players alike found ready-made blades upon arising one vacation morning after a night of rain, and snow and rain again.

The small fry...Hallelujah!...for once in their lives did not have to wait until the Park Department saw fit to flood those skating rinks at Watson Park and elsewhere...(and the larger fry, too, for that matter...) They were to be seen darting merrily by the hundreds in every direction over what appeared to be the entire expanse of park land on a skating rink to end all skating rinks...an area that could easily have accommodated the Bruins in one of their home games...and they had come by it freely, from nature's bounty.

The Metayer grandchildren were absolutely in their element. They entered the family abode only to eat and sleep. The abode itself was as quiet as though the small fry were in school, but WOW! the family backyard!!! Every boy in the neighborhood appeared to have converged upon it with shovels and brooms the moment the snow had ceased on one particular day, to create from the ice that had formed beneath it a private skating rink of beautiful proportions, upon which the young Jim and Byrne Corbin and their friends enjoyed for hours on end their favorite winter sport...HOCKEY...our boys playing it with a gusto that found them drooping over the dinner table come evening, and readily yielding to Mother's suggestion that they view another group of players, their idols, the Bruins, from the comfort of their nice warm bed via a portable TV.

We watched the merry scene, delighting in the happiness of a thousand kids we know and love…and then we began to look back and to remember, Ted and I…

Skating was always my favorite winter sport. Living as our family did on Malden's Fellsway, we had access to wonderful Craddock Park (now bearing an entirely different name, we learned upon passing it recently; however, all old Malden residents will recall the place…) Well, there is no doubt about it, we must have had the world's most cooperative and concerned Park Department in those days for the dropping of the thermometer invariably signaled the call to action of the dozen or so jets that brought about the flooding of this winter playground for the young. And as the jets sprang into action with their streams of wonderfully welcome water, so did the family telephone. "They are flooding the park! The park is flooding!" the Neners whose living room window afforded a clear view of the action, announced far and wide to every skating enthusiast in town.

Skating was definitely the "in" thing in the vicinity of the Fellsway and so the freezing of the flooded area saw all hands heading for Craddock.

WE who lived close by invariably donned our skates in the nice warm privacy of the family front hall, as did our friends. We then pranced over the roadway and across the dark brown stubble of what come summertime was nice green park land, to the "rink" beyond. I cannot recall our ever being the least bit concerned about what the trip might do to our skates; their sharpness or lack of it never seemed to affect the races across the ice or those wonderful "whips" we joined hands to form when evening came and the small fry were home in bed.

Incidentally, thinking in terms of evening and skating, as has been said previously the family living room window faced the slightly distant but nonetheless clearly visible ice of Craddock; so did the window of the family den, a floor above, and thereby hangs a tale. Mother was extremely strict with her growing girls. Though others in the neighborhood might be permitted out when darkness fell, not so the Neners. Living with us, however, was our paternal grandmother, a sweet, gentle, loving soul who resembled nothing so much as a Dresden figurine and was possessed of as much discipline as one. She never could refuse us anything. Now Mother and Dad were gadabouts. Dad belonged to the Lions' Club and the Rotary, the Knights and all the rest, and Mother to the local women's clubs, and so socializing was the order of the day or perhaps we should say the order of the night. And so, "Gaga," I would say sweetly to our darling grandmother when said night had fallen and our parents were safely on their way, "my homework is all finished. May I go skating in the park for just a little while? You watch the clock and at 8:30 put the light on in the den and I'll come right in. You know," I'd add, "I just lose track of time when I'm skating."

Gaga invariably consented and so on went the skates and off across the way went your columnist. Now, needless to say it was not long before my "signal" became know to everyone on the ice. "Bibs, your light is on!" they would cry, and I would turn reluctant skate-steps homeward. There were times, however, when Fate manage to toss a monkey-wrench into the you-know-what. Mother would produce a headache and Dad be persuaded to return home earlier than expected. Emergency! On and off would go the leaping light. On and off! On and off! "Come quickly; mother is home!" Thank heaven for a nice long driveway and a cooperative Dad who managed to drive ever so slowly into the yard, tuck the family car even more slowly into the family barn, and with even slower deliberation escort his wife to the rear door before which he fumbled madly as he produced the key that opened it…by which time I would have succeeded in entering grandmother's unlocked front door to speed - skates, knickers, scarf, sweater, mittens and all up the two flights of stairs to the safety of my room…and into the turned-down bed that Gaga's thoughtfulness had waiting…where, with my hat tucked under the pillow and the covers over my head I was out like the proverbial light that had summoned me when Mother came to check.

"Good heavens, Mother," said Gael, my daughter when I shared with her this tale, "If Richard or I had done that sort of thing, you would have been horrified!" And, you know she's right; I WOULD have…

Well, anyhoo, how grand for all the small fry in our town that last week THEY succeeded in storing up some ice-oriented memories of their own for the sometime way ahead when THEY are sixty and remembering…

'Tis a Cape Cod garden where the quaint things are,
An old-fashioned garden with a blown glass jar
And old-fashioned flowers, and a tiny wooden dog,
A whirling, happy wind-mill perched high atop a log;
With soft, swishing breezes blowing downward from the blue
On a little, laughing cloud-ship sailing softly down to you,
And a butterfly a 'flitting' round the green glass jar
In the Cape Cod garden where the quaint things are.
But it's quaintest of all seasons when the night bird cries
As the little, laughing cloud-ship sails away on darkened skies,
For 'tis then staid bachelor button hums a faintly coaxing tune
To coquettish lady larkspur as they dance beneath the moon,
While the pink and blue of blossoms turns to tiny fair folk
Who look upon the dog and say, "tis time that he awoke,"
Then tease him until barking, he goes dancing down the green
To knock upon the wind-mill door and rouse the fairy queen,
While the fairy men and maidens cry challenge to the star
And then scamper nimbly down within the blown glass jar.
Ah, you'll never find a garden though you travel very far,
Though you search the wide world over for a green glass jar,
And you bid life's choicest flowers cry a challenge to the star
Like my little Cape Cod garden where the quaint things are.

12-8-68   'TIS CHRISTMASTIME!

It's Christmastime again!
It's Christmastime again!
Realization of the fact came beautifully to me this past week as Braintree's own Philergian Bell Ringers rang out the familiar strains of "We Wish You a Merry Christmas" - bringing to a delightful conclusion a concert which had included all the old and precious Christmas Carols, presented amid the beauty and solemnity of First Congregational Church Sanctuary.

AND the Madrigal Singers from Eastern Nazarene College brought our way such wondrous Christmas music as "Lay Down You Staffs, O Shepherd" and "Jesu Parvule."

Oh, the inestimable dignity and beauty of the human voice, than which no finer instrument will ever by devised by mortal man!

As the music filled the sanctuary, I could sense the Christmas angel winging his way to Braintree. "Behold," I almost heard upon the wind as home I went, the concert o'er. "I bring you tidings of great joy!"

The Christmas season, I decided, with all its gold and glory, had for me suddenly begun. The realization sent my glad heart skyward in a pure cascade of Christmas dreams..

The very next morning, I found myself high in the family attic, in sweet search of my Christmas treasure trove - the stuff of which my Christmas dreams are made

The tinsel tree in the corner quite obviously note my approach, for it caught the sunlight that streamed from out the window in a glowing, gleeful way

****

"Here I am," it seemed to be saying, "ready for another go at Christmas! And what a long and lonely year it's been for me - imprisoned here…Deck me with Christmas garlands; scatter your gleaming glory o'er my lovely branches; MAKE ME TO LIVE AGAIN!"

The big bronze pine cone wreath upon the attic wall shed one small cone, as though endeavoring to draw my passing eye without disturbing symmetry or grace.

"Place me upon your find front door where I belong," it said sedately, I could swear!

The pine cone TREE, with all its twinkling lights that soon would glow like stars upon the Christmas scene, tilted in awkward stance, as though by bringing me in rescue to its side, 'twould rouse awareness of its charm.

Garlands of holly stirred slightly by the breath of nearby louvres raised tiny, berried heads. Christmas," they seemed to-SWAYING say. "Christmas at last!"

The very windows of our dear menage cried out for lights - or so it seemed. "Let there by light," I could feel them saying, "that our cold glass hearts may pulse with warmth once more; and that the little Christmas Child be thus assured of loving welcome…"

Christmas cards in nice neat boxes cried aloud each time I glanced their way, "SEND US!" They said. "Let us away with greetings, soft and sweet. Tis Christmastime!"

Tiny elves on last year's Christmas corsage winked wide winsome eyes; and all the village greens for miles around commenced to don a bright expectant look, as though they had already seen the Christmas trees soon destined to bedeck the holidays within their fair confines.

****

"'Tis Christmastime!" called the crammed store windows in a burst of sudden pride. "'Tis Christmastime!" cried the fir trees in the high, heaped vans..

"'Tis Christmastime!" said the grandmother of the Metayer family, scooping up the tinsel tree, the pine cone wreath, the holly and the berries - AND THE TINY CHRISTMAS CRECHE THAT HOLDS THE LITTLE INFANT KING - and all the meaning of this blessed time of year…

"Surely now, December 8 is not too soon a date. The neighbors know that I've a wild wide YEN for Christmas…Bid the candles twinkle! Bid the trees shine! Bid the pine cone wreath adorn the doorway AND BID THE CRECHE ITS SMALL SWEET CHILD EMBRACE! 'Tis Christmastime!""

12-14-69 'TIS CHRISTMASTIME!

AND SO at last 'tis Christmastime, season of "Peace On Earth; Good Will Toward Men!"…Time of holiness and happiness.

Whence comes the magic of the Christmastide? The Christmas Carol, sending our warm hearts soaring to the skies…The Christmas Tree, shining in pristine splendor on the green…The Poinsettia bursting with Christmas glory…The Candle, lighting the soft sweet Christmas darkness…The Star, high in the dark night sky…atop the tree…above the creche…The Christmas Rose…The CRECHE…heart of the blessed Christmas story, And the CHRISTMAS STORY itself….Whence come the glories of Christmas?

***

The Carol - from England.

"What sweeter music can we bring
Than a Carol, for to sing,
The birth of this our Heavenly King?
…and bequeath
This Holly and this Ivy Wreath,
To do Him honour; who's our King,
The Lord of all this rejoicing."
The Christmas Tree - from Germany.

Bedecked with ornaments and gifts, it symbolizes the gifts of the three Kings to the little Christ Child; and of the gift to all mankind of the little Christ Child himself

***

The Poinsettia - from Mexico.

Once upon a Christmas eve many many years ago, so the legend says, a tiny beggar girl wept because though she had wished and wished upon the Christmas star - she had no gift for the little Infant King on Christmas morning.

She watched and waited as all the day long the people of her village came, bearing their beautiful rich gifts; and she grew sadder and sadder.

And the hour for Holy Mass drew nigh and finally, because she had naught else to give, the little beggar girl placed before the Christmas creche her ONE possession. It was a branch of green weeds from the forest which she had picked because to her lonely eyes it had resembled the Christmas tree that other children everywhere danced about and loved.

"Dear little Christ Child," she prayed, "I would give you the world if I might…"

"Remove that ugly weed," cried the scornful villagers, "lest the little Christ Child take offense, and look with disfavor upon our village."

And Pablo, the sexton of the Church who had himself once been poor and orphaned sighed, and looked from the little beggar girl to the lofty senor from the hacienda; and went reluctantly to where the Quiet Creche told its Christmas story..

"I must do their bidding," he told the tiny child with his eyes; but as he reached out his worn brown hand to pluck the weed-lo! suddenly it burst into glorious crimson bloom, glowing more richly than all the priceless gifts about it…The Poinsettia from Mexico…

***

The Lighted Candle - from Ireland

Shining in all the windows of the Christian world, to light the path of the Christ Child on Christmas eve; to bid Him welcome to the hearts and homes of Christians everywhere.

***

The Star- from Holland.

The Blessed symbol of the little Christ Child's birth; and of the journcy of thc three Wise Men from distant lands.

***

Legend tells us that in the little town of Bethlehem, on the very first Christmas, a little shepherdess wept because she had no gift to bring to the wondrous Child in the stable on the hillside. And as her tears fell on the cold hard ground, soft white flowers sprang therefrom, and she gathered them and brought them quickly to Him, and knelt there by the trough that was His crib.

The little Christ Child smiled, and held out tiny hands to her; and where His fingers touched the fragrant blooms, a soft pink heart glowed in the center of each one. And so a flower that ne'er efore had graced the hills of Bethlehem was born - the Christmas Rose - and lo! it blooms more abundantly at Christmastime than at any other season of the year.

***

The CRECHE - from Italy and France.

The very soul of the blessed Christmas story, enshrined in the hearts and the homes of the world!

***

And the Christmas STORY???

It seems to come from everywhere…and from nowhere…ever and always at Christmastime – a tale of kindness rewarded and goodness recognized; of "peace on earth, good will toward men". Doesn't it actually spring to life within the hearts of all good men and women, this recreation of the blessed Christmas story, once the beautiful season of Advent comes our way, and we stand on the threshold of another celebration of the Little Christ Child's birth? We think it does!

4-20-69   'TIS SPRING

An event occurred this morning; I had donned my walking flats,
And had filled the gay bird feeders; plied with milk the pussy cats,
Then saluted each young puppy playing games upon the lawn,
Quite enchanted with the sweetness of an April Sunday morn.
*

I bethought me, "I shall garden; 'tis a perfect day for this,
With the world awake and turning toward an April sun's first kiss…"
Sought the rake, and found the shovel; wheeled the trash cart to the fore,
Thrilling softly to the knowledge that the spring had sprung once more!
*

Oh, it's fun to ply the lawn rake when the winter's spell is through,
And the soft, sweet scent of springtime floats benignly back at you.
What a joy to now uncover, quite secure and quite serene
Tiny star-shapes of pale ivory; gentle growing things of green!

*

By the door, a row of CROCI, (how I love that plural noun!)
Smiling golden and pale violet, on the springtime's bosom brown.
Then, the plump, matronly hyacinths standing stiffly by the wall;
The Weigela bush, quite shamelessly a-courting spring's soft call.

*

Robins, watching for the earthworms I have wrenched from slumber
    sweet
With the rake's disturbing earthquake, and the tread of giant feet.
How they toss their rosy weskits, and regard me, eyes alight!
How they liven up the fir tree; what a welcome springtime sight!

*

Tarnished gold on old forsythia, waiting there its coins to spill
From their cask of golden glory, on the bosom of the hill...
How I search each barren rosebush for the magic swelling small
That will make of twigs and tatters, quite the fairest sight of all!

*

Lilac trees, with tossing tassels; haughty honeysuckle red,
Simply bursting with impatience to beguile the flower bed;
Look! A jonquil stands there, budding; see its broad and buttered spear,
Raised with hauteur o'er the tulips curled in henna-ed leaf-nests near!

*

Perfect peace within the garden; ah, there's naught can match the worth
Of an April Sunday morning in a garden, close to earth.
But, what gay event this Sunday served to make my spirits soar,
To convince me quite, quite firmly that the winter is no more?

*

Well, 'twas not the sight of squirrels, dancing ballet on the wire,
Nor the scent of burning leaves upon their springtime funeral pyre;
And it wasn't greeting neighbors, toting garden rakes like mine,
Though on any Sunday morning, greeting neighbors can be fine.

*

No, IT HAPPENED OF A SUDDEN! I had dropped upon my knees
'Neath the staid and solemn sighing of the winsome willow trees,
And, with soft, exploring fingers, matted leaf mounds I had spread
From the sweet and subtle confines of my favorite flower bed.

*

I could scarce believe my vision! I cried out in utter glee,
For whatever do you think was looking gaily back at me?
Just the brightest bed of pansies, growing there in splendid style,
Every tiny pansy face just simply wreathed in springtime's smile!

*

Now, I know you won't believe it; April's barely here, you'll state,
Why Miss Springtime's hardly set her foot inside the garden gate.
Jonquils, yes, and even hyacinths you quite willingly would buy,
But, A BED OF BLOOMING PANSIES??? have to look it in the eye!

*

Well, they're blooming by the fence posts, and they're blooming by
    the wall;
There's a sweet bouquet of blossoms on the table in the hall,
And I touch their velvet softness, fondle free each fairy face,
Touched anew by nature's magic, and transformed by nature's grace.

*

They're the deepest shade of purple, and the brightest shade of blue,
And their tiny pansy faces smile serenely up at you;
And you see them nodding gaily, and your heart is moved to sing,
For though lately you have doubted, NOW YOU KNOW FOR
SURE, 'TIS SPRING!

10-26-69 TODAY'S TEENAGER

LIFE ALWAYS has been a bit rough on the teenager. Half way
between childhood and maturity, he flounders about, seeking to find
himself; and to fit himself into the kind of niche his family and society
dictates he shall occupy. It's a difficult time of life - for him, and for those

about him; and only the most patient and tactful of parents manage successfully to contend with it.

This fact was never more apparent than it is today. Confused; buffeted by conflicting forces from the Left and the Right; exposed via "instant communication" to the tragic kind of history that is being made in so many corners of a tortured globe, the teenager must frequently experience the feeling of being alone and lost in an adult world, the which, with childhood falling behind him, he is struggling to enter.

At a recent meeting, I had the privilege of hearing Miss Basilla E. Neilan, a youth consultant discuss this very situation. "Buzz", as she is called by teenagers everywhere, talks their language, and understands the complexity of their problems.

She read the following original poem, written for "Hancock Day," a seminar for high school students which was sponsored by the John Hancock Mutual Life Insurance Company last November.

It is called "Prayer for Today's Teenager."

"When I speak and no one listens,
Lord, let me understand…
When I listen but wish I'd not hear it,
Lord, let me understand
When I try so hard but fail so easy,
Lord, let me understand…
Let me understand this world I live in,
Let me try to take my place,
Let me do for the sake of others
And be part of the great human race.
Lord, help me to jump life's hurdles,
To meet and to pass the test.
Let me take my place with the others.
I'm not asking to be the best.
I want to meet others squarely,
To extend those in need my hand…
Oh Lord, this big world's a hard one…
Please help me to understand."

Oh Lord, this big world's a hard one for parents and grandparents as well; please help all of us to understand one another, for the problems we all face today appear insurmountable. And it is only by understanding one another, and helping one another, that we shall ever, in any way, solve them.

3-3-74   TO TOMORROW'S LOSERS

There's just ONE winner in every race…still a smile of pride should adorn the face

Of EACH CANDIDATE who has fought the fight that precedes the din of Election Night!

You have sought to serve with a willing heart; to become a vibrant pulsing part

Of the Town in which you elect to dwell; you have vowed to serve her and serve her well.

It's a THANKLESS task, you hear people say…Goodness, why should you seek it? There's no pay!

And the hours are long; and the HEADACHES…Wow!

(Life is so delightfully simple now…)

Well, you've run the race, and alas! You've LOST…And you're at the stage where you count the cost

And assess the value of what you tried to do for the Town you regard with pride.

There's little doubt you've invested much of your time and effort and self and such;

But hasn't it all be quite worthwhile? You've GROWN, you know; you've acquired STYLE!

You're stronger for walking those million miles; (and wrinkled from smiling those million smiles…)

You've learned fortitude and self control as you traveled the pathways toward your goal…

As you stood your ground on that platform bare, with worth opponents everywhere,

And answered questions until quite blue. (Why are they all directed to YOU???)

You've made hosts of brand new friends, it seems; and for one brief span you've indulged your dreams...

You've been for a time the shining star in a drama that's playing wherever you are...

So you HIT SOME SNAGS as you trailed along; sure and nothing is ever just one sweet song!

You've grown weary of meetings; and leery of greetings and tired of handshakes and questions like earthquakes...

But, say - do you know - though you LOST the game, life for you will never be quite the same???

You'll be "JOHN - he ran for Selectman once. Almost made it. This guy is indeed no dunce..."

Or "FRANK" - he tried for the Park Commission; not electing him was a big omission."

Or "PAM - (she's a lamb!) What a doggoned pity she didn't make it for School Committee!"

Yes, you may have LOST! WE CAN'T ALL WIN...But hold up your head! And lift up your chin!

And throw out your chest! YOU'VE DONE ALL RIGHT! YOU LIT THAT ONE SMALL CANDLE TONIGHT!!!

3-28-75   TOWN MEETING

'Tis the month of pussy willows; 'tis the month of daffodils,
When the first faint flush of summer seems to tint the waking hills.
(And we sing about the springtime as we fight those winter chills.)
'Tis the season of spring cleaning; time of diet, geared to crash;
Of accounting to dear Uncle for the spending of our cash;
And, of Annual Town Meeting. Has our course been wise or rash??

Oh, the problems that beset a "legislator's" busy days!
Why, from dawn to dark, we wandered in a melancholy maze,
Unrelieved by e'en the prospect of a mink in autumn haze.

Should we really make so free with our dwindling E. & D."
Was the Highlands School addition truly a necessity?
Should we not, perhaps, have voted for East Braintree's library?

And, that yen for Conservation that's engulfed the blooming
    nation,
Can we guard our quaking bog? Treasure every fallen log?
Safeguard vital Cranb'ry Pond for the years that lie beyond???

'Tis the time of Annual Meeting, when with conscientious heart
Each Finance Committee member tears the warrant wide apart,
Just to watch the "legislators" overturn the apple cart...

How we dwell, and how we ponder, as we journey over yonder
To Town Hall, to reconvene in solemn session; how we wonder
If last evening's rash decisions will our tax rate rend asunder.

What of that industrial sewer? Should the firemen's ranks be
    fewer?
Will the Fire Chief now replace his radios with something newer?
If the Town Hall were remodelled, would its tenants skies be
    bluer?

Each and every meeting member'll have occasion to remember
As the month of January leads the way too old December
How his voting, the accounts of Mr. Parker did dismember.

What post mortems we indulge in at the meeting's final ending,
Cheery cries of jubilation with a mournful sadness blending;
And those prudent Finance members quite aghast at all the
    spending...

Right and left, each legislator, with his brain an emptied crater,
Facts and figures in a maze having left him in a daze,
Looks regretfully, alas, at some moment he let pass...

Ah, IF ONLY HE HAD LEAPED WITH ANIMATION TO
HIS FEET,
And poured forth with charming rhetoric, a plea, quite short,
but neat,
Why, I'll bet his special article would not have known defeat!

Oh, if only she'd arisen, and with gay, masterful stroke,
In a speech articulate and fine, astounded all the folk,
Why, all salaries could be doubled, (though the Town might
well go broke.)

Gosh, if only we'd succeeded e'er Town Meeting was quite
through,
In impressing legislators with our special point of view,
There's no end to what we might have done for you and you
and you.

'Tis the month of legislation; 'tis our fair Town Meeting time,
When upon the experts' judgment, merry legislators climb.
Well, ahead lies rude awakening. Brother can you spare a dime???

9-7-69   TYPO

...which is the Fourth Estate's term for a typographical error!

Just about every newspaper-man (or woman) worth his salt has at
least ONE to boast about whenever newspaper people gather, and the
subject comes up...Well, I'm delighted to report that I HAVE BECOME
ONE OF THE GANG! I, too, have had a TYPO; and what a blooper it
is! I discovered it yesterday...

I've been carefully tucking away in a special lily-white Scrapbook each "splendid" installment of the "Seventy Years of Splendor" that is the Philergian Story…Well, of late, what with the delightful demands of summer…the beaching and the rest, the project seems to have gotten ahead of me. What I mean to say is, the last filed installment was dated about the first of July; and so of free time on my hands, I decided to bring the thing up to date…I had reached installment number XVIII, dated August 17. "I was getting there," I told myself happily! I smear the inevitable Elmer's on the back of the clipping, and lay it gently in place, when - VOILA - the word SUSPICIOUS leaped right up and hit me - hard! "Suspicious, just didn't seem to BELONG to the Philergian Story…

I raced back to the beginning of the paragraph, reading madly; and then I LAUGHED RIGHT OUT LOUD! "Mrs. Lawrence W. Guild," it read, "the charming Philergian president who would go on to become president of the New Hampshire State Federation of Women's Clubs - and, incidentally, publicly attribute the success of her club career to its SUSPICIOUS Philergian beginning…" "Ted," I screamed, choking with laughter, "Read this!"

The word should have been AUSPICIOUS, of course - and that will "learn" me to read the thing I submit to the Forum, or any other newspaper, for that matter…I never do…I shall.

Now, I keep asking myself, did the "typo" go unnoticed??? I have been deluged with queries as to the final disposition of the big black snake in son Richard's maple tree; and at least 20 Braintree-ites have called to ask, "What in the world are GEORGE BOOTS??? Why, I wonder, has not someone mentioned this SUSPICIOUS bit???

At any rate, what a "fun" story this will make; and what a series of similar "typos" it will unearth from other journalistic sources.

Like the tale of a fellow fourth estater who covered a local Battle of the Bands not long ago. "Now," she told herself firmly as she departed for the bit of Bedlam close by, "I shall review this carefully. I'll show these young people that there is no generation gap here; that even an over-30 adult can understand and review this kind of entertainment."

My friend worked hard over that particular review. She employed the language of youth; and analyzed every facet of the program from the teenage point of view. She tried Heaven knows how hard she tried. She sighed with satisfaction as she handed the thing to her Editor. "A job superbly done," she told herself proudly.

And then the article reached the press room; and some enterprising soul REAR-RANGED THE PAGES so that the colorful critique that had been developed so carefully by my friend, reached its readers WITH THE FIRST FIVE PARAGRAPHS DELETED FROM THE BEGINNING AND ADDED TO THE END of the tall tale. It made of the lady's endeavor a tribute to the greatest Generation Gap in the history of mad music...

I keep recalling other tales of colorful types...There was the occasion, for instance, when "Mrs....", we read in the Social News, "entertained the ladies with a musical program; she was attired in a pale green sheath, with the inevitable RED NOSE that is the trade mark of this delightful performer, firmly in place..." The word should have been ROSE, of course!

And then, there was the report of the lodge meeting as it appeared in the local tabloid, where "the Speaker, who came, as always, one hundred miles to share in the group's birthday celebration, was "Deadly Dull"! The gentleman's name was "Dudley Dill"

Ah, me, so much for TYPOS! P. S. I like my own quite as well as any I've heard to date...

4-25-65   UMBRELLAS

"I WOULD rather," said my dear husband, one delightfully rainy morning last week as we pipped about a shopping plaza, "face an army with fixed bayonets, than a group of women with umbrellas." He may have a point there.

Actually, during the rainbow-beribboned month of April, the old family umbrella becomes standard equipment, and I, for one, wouldn't be without it. It gives one the most refreshing feeling of anonymity to keep one's eyes affixed to the small, multi-colored puddles on the oil-splashed pavements while permitting the rose-colored mushroom (all ladies umbrella should be red you know; it's so flattering) to cast its soft glow over the top of one's head, as one splashes along through every little fat sidewalk brooklet that can exercise the same strong allure for little Mary's mother as for little Mary, especially if she is secure in the knowledge that no one will recognize her as an errant child.

UMBRELLAS, like everything else in this age of variety, come in many styles. There's the tall, pagoda-like affair with the long tassels and the Chinese look, beneath which one couldn't possibly stoop to such childish sports as puddle exploring; and there's the parasol-type of rain repeller, which must send every young spring zephyr into a perfect frenzy of temptation to playfully whisk it inside out.

There's the big, black masculine umbrella, teddibly British, designed for the weaker members of the stronger sex, and associated indelibly in our minds with such delightful personalities as Mr. Neville Chamberlain or the late George Apley.

The umbrella is an article that is lost more often than anything else on earth. Ask any "Lost and Found" department if they have come upon a blue umbrella with purple stripes and a pink tassel, and you'll invariably be invited to "come in and have a look" among the three hundred and twenty five umbrellas which precisely fit that description. I know. I've been coming and having looks all my life…

Some people wouldn't carry an umbrella if they floated downstream without one; and others will tote one at the drop of a molecule of precipitation. (like ME.)

THERE'S something akin to being marooned on an island, or snowed under in a blizzard, or tucked away on a railroad siding, about journeying forth under an umbrella, especially in April. Walking along, snug under a rosy roof, one dwells in a private world of tantalizing extremities, all quite readily recognizable.

There are the large, firm feet of the local banker (he's carrying an umbrella himself, but in probability, utterly unaware of the fact that YOU possess extremities), on his way to tote up his tidy sums, and rattle the financial world; and here are the feet of the little housewife, shod in her second-best, hurrying to early bird at the local market; the high-heeled feet of the secretary, fresh from business training, and brisk with new-broom efficiency; the not quite so high-heeling, but smart extremities of the first year teacher at the nearby elementary school, and the sensible oxford of her old educator-sister; the reluctant small feet of the boy next door, (somewhat in need of a shine), en-hesitant-route to school and the purposeful and maternal little steps of his younger sister, seeking to speed the small, would-be truant on his unhappy way.

There are the slow peds of grandmother, on her way to baby-sitting duty, laden with packages unlimited for a set of small darlings, and the slightly aimless feet of John L. Jones; retired, with no place actually to be going in the early morn; and the gray topped extremities of the postman, the navy topped brogans of the corner policeman.

There are the well shod feet of the clubwoman, on her way to a stint at the Historical Society or the organization bazaar; there are the shopping bag-accompanied feet, and those suitcase-accompanied; the schoolbag-laden feet and those accompanied by smart attache case; and they are all bound somewhere, even as you yourself, enfolded in your own small world, and sauntering along quite as though you, and you alone, were guardian over the sweet and scented sidewalks that lie wash with April rain these merry mornings..

"Oops…I beg your pardon, Mr. Smith, I wouldn't have deliberately removed your right eye for anything in the world." My, my, perhaps my Ted does have a point there, "an army with fixed bayonets." We inoffensive women, with our rosy-red perfectly harmless umbrellas.

2-11-73   VALETINE'S DAY

Wednesday is Valentine's Day - time for expressions of sentiment and sweetness…day for LOVERS…and for LOVE!

The feast had its beginning away back when Rome was Mistress of the World, and on February 15, "Lupercalia" or the "Lovers' Festival was celebrated there. Young people were paired off by chance for the year that lay ahead, with the gods presumably directing the choices from on high. In the year 496, Pope Gelasius injected a note of Christianity into the festival of lovers, calling it St. Valentine's Day and changing the date to February 14, where it has remained to this day. But why St. VALENTINE???

Well, legend has it that once upon an age long ago, a mighty tyrant ruled the citizens of ancient Rome. Claudius the Cruel was his name, and all feared him. At the same time, there dwelt in the temple close by, a high priest whose name was Valentine. As kind a man as he was learned, Valentine was loved as fervently by the Romans as Claudius was hated.

War was the prime interest of Claudiùs, the tyrant. He sent his unfortunate subjects unceasingly into battle until at long last the married men of Rome demurred at having to constantly leave their families; and those in love and as yet unmarried rebelled at being torn from the arms of their dear ones; and suddenly the tyrannical ruler found that all of Rome was refusing to do his bidding. Accordingly, Claudius the Cruel issued a devastating decree. There should be no more marriage in Rome; NOR EVEN ENGAGEMENTS!

Months passed, and all of Rome appeared to be dying for want of love; and Valentine, the high priest, came to a decision. He would marry those in love secretly before the sacred altar in defiance of his emperor.

Eventually, Claudius the Cruel learned of the defiance of the kindly old high priest. "Cast him into the dungeon," he cried. "This foolish priest will live to rue the day he dared to defy the might of Rome!"

Valentine was indeed to languish and eventually to die in the dungeons of Rome; but those he had befriended were never to forget his kindness…And each year on the anniversary of his birth, Romans in love were to gather and to pay him homage.

Needless to say, Valentine, who later became known as St. Valentine, is the patron saint of everyone in love, and is said to possess the divine gift of healing lovers' quarrels…

Valentines have changed over the years, but the hint of lavender and lace seems not to have succumbed entirely to the ravages of time. From the coarse brown paper missives of our great grandmother's age, with their tender and touching sonnets, to today's elaborate confections, they are geared to an amorous declaration of ardent love.

"The Young Man's Valentine Writer" guided the swains of the 18th century in penning their Valentine messages! In the early 19th century, "Cupid's Repository of Choice Valentines" yielded Valentines that were geared to the profession of the sender, viz; From A Shoemaker to his Lady: "A piece of charming kid you are - As e'er mine eyes did see. No calf-skin that e'er I saw - Can be compared to thee. You are my all, do no refuse - To let us tack together; But let us join, my Valentine, Like sole and upper leather." How about that??

Fiction is filled with fascinating references to Valentine's Day. There is, for instance, the classic effort of the "lovesick Pickwick."

"Lovely creetur...afore I see you I thought all women was alike, but now I find what a regular soft-headed, inkred'lous turnip I must ha' been, for there ain't nobody like you though I like you better than nothin' at all...Except of me, Mary my dear, as your valentine..." Ho Him... Well, there ARE Valentines and Valentines!

At any rate, Wednesday is, once again, Valentine's Day. There's so little time for sentiment these busy days. We've so few opportunities really to tell those who share our lives how bleak 'twould be without them. Let's all get downright sentimental! Let's find the silliest, frilliest valentine upon the card shop shelf and drop it into Cupid's mailbox... Let's (but not MINE - I'm still wrestling with that string bean DIET...or perhaps waft the loving fragrance of a small bouquet of soft Spring violets through someone's happy day...Just remember dear old St. Valentine, who DIED because of love! Happy Valentine's Day everybody!

P.S. Guess what??? My ROSE BUSHES are budding and my HYACINTHS are up! And I note the curious curling of a scarlet TULIP cup!

And...LAST SUNDAY, bright and early, I was GARDENING...

So There!

With the scent and feel and touch and sound of Springtime in the air Didn't I TELL YOU???

11-17-74 VETERANS DAY

Veterans Day was observed in Braintree last Sunday morning. It was a beautiful day-cold, crisp and sunny. Representatives from our various veterans' organizations were on hand. There were uniforms and the flags; the speeches and the solemnity; and on the morning air the echo of the inevitable volley that accompanies such sad events and serves invariably to chill the blood within my veins. Only the townspeople were missing. To be sure the day was cold, but our town officials had braved the weather perhaps because they, too, or most of them at least are veterans and so are well aware of what the word implies.

I sat there upon our Braintree Mall, listening to the speeches; looking into the faces of the veterans themselves and recalling in my sadness a day not long ago when we were there dedicating a brand new monument to those deceased heroes of the Vietnam "Conflict". I had on that occasion looked into the faces of the loved ones of those fallen heroes. I had felt my woman's heart constrict with grief as I beheld their strained expressions. There were friends among the group; and I was sharing thoughts with wonderful fond parents who had lost sons; and a beautiful young woman who had lost a husband she adored. I had looked about me at a similar monument to the fallen heroes of the Spanish-American War; and of World War I; and of World War II; and of the Korean conflict and now, the Vietnam Conflict...

Will it never end, I thought this senselesss killing of our nation's young??? Of all the young of the world??? Words came unbidden to my lips; and, as I sat there, feeling the depths of each one's sorrow, the following bit of verse came into being:

They have not died though every heart was stilled
And each young hero's dreaming unfulfilled;
Though on that foreign land they looked no more,
Their sleep untouched by all the cannons' roar;
That land in which no friendly face they found,
Its mountains and its vales a battleground...
They have not died; their tortured spirits live,
To cry aloud, "Father, can we forgive?
Was it in vain, the death we found afar?
Did we close fast, or leave the door ajar
That leads to further bloodshed on some plain,
Some distant battleground? Shall WAR again
Lay siege to YOUTH as leaders lust for power
To term BLACK HELL their country's 'FINEST HOUR???'
Our shades cry out an anguished 'NEVERMORE'

SEND THOU THY FLOWERING MANHOOD OFF TO
WAR!""

7-18-73   WE CELEBRATE
THE FOURTH!

There never has been a more rollicking Fourth of July! In the town where independence was born, so our history books tell us - and our Town Records, as well…(and if they ever commence to denigrate good old John Adams as they have poor Daniel Webster and so many others among our national heroes, this sixty-one year old grandmother will take up PROTESTING, and on a GRAND scale!!!), the celebration of this historic date was absolutely unparalleled!

Your columnist had elected to MARCH in the Braintree Point Woman's Club parade entry. Well, she really hadn't ELECTED to march; she was sort of pushed into it. "we really should have two of our members march, carrying the club banner," someone suggested. "It would set the stage for the remainder of our entry…" "A good idea!" we agreed; and we proceeded to seek candidates for the happy task. "MARCH two miles in the hot July sun?? I couldn't!" "Good heavens - MARCH?? I wouldn't dream of it!" "I'd never last!" "My feet just wouldn't stand it" "I'd never make it." etc., etc., etc. It went on and on. Well, you know what happens when you serve as Chairman of an event; you wind up doing all the most difficult things yourself. "I'LL just have to carry the banner," I told my family finally, a family still smarting over the jolly news that I was not to share their holiday fun at all; that I would indeed be occupied with the Club's Field Day involvement the entire afternoon. They reacted with a series of audible snorts…

"You'll have a heart attack for sure," daughter Gael moaned. "You'll NEVER do it. I wouldn't do it, at MY age." Her all-knowing father intervened as usual. "Mother will do it," he said. "She will by so busy waving to friends all along the line she'll forget she HAS feet, or a heart, or anything else." Which is precisely what happened. The companion I had selected to represent our many YOUNG members, lovely Carolyn

Fitzsimmons, delighted me by accepting happily. Our banner would indicate the club's 52 years of community service; it would serve merely as a prelude to the highlight of our entry - young scholarship winner Patricia Stokes and her friend Cheryl Brems riding a tandem bicycle, and attired in the kind of bathing suits the younger set affected in 1921, the year we began. One of the bathing suits, incidentally, was actually worn by the mother of past president Pearl Goldsworthy, a lady named Fanny Hawthorne, and a direct descendant of good old Nathaniel.

A brand new 1973 car, driven by past president Helen Peterson and housing past president Pearl and present president Ethel Spano was to conclude the entry. It read, "1973… WE CONTINUE TO SERVE!"

Our group was first to arrive at the parking lot of the First Congregational Church where Division Two was to assemble; and what fun to watch the various contingents arrive…the Drum and Bugle Corps; the Championship Bands; the floats, the Shriners in their colorful hats; the baton twirling babies, the clowns and the rest. The Braintree League of Women Voters had a darling entry. Faith Smith, attired as a very charming Suffragette, was to ride in an elderly buggy with a sign, "We hate to NAG, but wish you'd register to vote!" (or words to that effect). The buggy was to be drawn by a nice white horse, Count Nicolai by name, whose pretty young owner, Patty tried vainly to keep him in line as the bands blared and the cymbals crashed. Quite obviously the "Count's" aristocratic blood was offended by the din. He finally had to be unharnessed and the entry scrapped; and we grieved for Faith who had arranged it all with such pride.

The parade was magnificently planned and executed. Not a single "Parade Rest" marred its passage over the streets where once the early colonists marched to the tune of a crotchety old farmer with a thin reedy voice and a consuming desire for freedom - old Sam Adams, who was to beget a President who would in turn beget another president, both of whom were to play such a prominent part in shaping the history of this lovely land whose birthday we were celebrating and, incidentally, how appropriate it was to have the parade begin by the historic spot where the "Braintree Resolutions" or the "Braintree Resolves" as they are also called, are memorialized for all time!

Needless to say, your columnist did indeed "last" to the end of the parade. Ted was right as always. I wasn't even particularly tired. I was indeed so busy acknowledging friends along the way that I completely forgot that I had feet or heart or anything else but a warm, wide, wonderful feeling of patriotism and pride in being part of our Town's sensational Fourth of July observance. Hope we have a similar one next year; we're already planning our entry, using our beautiful little Story Hour Children…

The Braintree July 4th Celebration Committee deserves accolades unlimited for the most delightful Independence Day celebration I can ever recall…in spite of the weather…those clouds that refused to allow our Sky Divers to leap into Sunset Lake…and those cloudbursts that saw us madly tucking our Field Day wares beneath tables and chairs and umbrellas and the rest…It was SOME affair! And as for our own Olive Laing and her P.R. performance - we've never seen anything like it! Congratulations, all of you wonderful Braintreeites! WHAT A DAY!

7-7-68   WE PAPERHANGERS

It HAD seemed like such a splendid idea… "I think I'll change the wallpaper in the hall," we had said gaily on one of a series of long rainy days when boredom threatened…

NOW, however, with the thermometer bursting at its hot seams, we wonder why we ever dreamed the project up. We shall, however, love it when its done, we tell ourselves, as we labor over a hot papering board in a hotter atmosphere…

There are, we've decided, few accomplishments which challenge the humility we strive for quite as completely as the sight of a room, freshly papered by our own two grubby little hands!

Papering is, you see, a comparatively new accomplishment for us. It had never occurred to us that JUST PLAIN PEOPLE papered their own walls, until we encountered our good neighbor, Helen, some years ago.

We had been taught over the years to show proper respect for the veritable ARTIST who, each year in June, upon our departure for our summer home, was handed the key to the Nener establishment, with instructions to paper and paint one room or other. As a mater of fact, come to think of it, people had not come to the point where they changed their wallpaper as frequently as they changed their hair styles. Paper stayed on the walls until it was SOILED or SPOILED!

Anyhow, the advent of the paperhanger was preceded by hours of consultation with the sample books he dutifully brought for mother's perusal. I wish I might be able to say that we young Neners were consulted about our preferences. It simply wasn't so. A "pale buttery yellow" of "soft sky blue" constituted the limits of mother's thinking for her daughters…

ONCE SISTER Gladys and I "struck", so to speak, against the maternal authority. It was the era of "old rose", a kind of muted version of today's hot pink. We were MAD about it, but mother had declaimed against the color long and loudly. She was, however, to take a winter vacation with dad. We decided on a bold course of action…and a SURPRISE for mother…

Wall paint which could be affixed over paper, had just appeared on the market. We purchased a gallon in the glorious old rose shade with a carefully hoarded allowance. Over the pale yellow I went the lovely new pink. Down came the crisp white curtains and up went new old rose ones.

the lampshade - an old rose one being unavailable - was spruced up with a crepe paper overskirt, complete with fluting and ruffles.

We were CARRIED AWAY on an old rose tide…Even the traditional statue of the Virgin wore an old rose mantle and robe, when Mother returned from TRIPPING…and TURNED RIPPING…The paperhanger made his winter debut at our establishment that year; and we and the pale yellow lived happily afterwards…

But-to return to our introduction to the fine art of paperhanging. Helen, our good neighbor, had invited us to her home for tea. We arrived to find a sort of staging set up in her dining room. "What are you doing?" we had asked idly.

"Papering", she had said. "But I'm giving up for the day, I'm tired." "Oh", we said, and then "YOU are papering???" "Why, yes," she replied. "I have just finished the bedroom and the kitchen." We were speechless with admiration. "This is a brilliant girl," we told one another, Gladys and I. and time went on. "Do you know," we said suddenly, one fine day several years later. "Helen is no more brilliant that WE are actually. If SHE can paper a room, I'll bet we could. Let's TRY IT." The which we promptly did - - repairing to a nearby shop to purchase a splashy and beautiful design in coral and white. We opened the first roll, measured the length of the wall, cut and applied the piece…so far, so good…But then-CONFUSION.

For the next piece DID NOT FIT where it should follow the pattern at all! we tried another roll, and then another. "Well," we decided finally, "they have given us the wrong paper. WE shall have to call them and tell them so. One roll does not fit into the other…"

At which point we were rescued happily from our dilemma by the timely arrival of HELEN herself! she heard our story with amusement. We simply did not know that one CUT THE SECTION OFF until the pattern matched….

THAT was a number of years ago. We are, of course, expert at cutting off the pattern by now; also expert at tangling with a strip of gooey wallpaper; and creating lumpy paste; and cutting the strip with that horrible one-eight inch short because of irregularities in the wall etc. etc.

A friend of ours, a very prominent club woman, had a favorite wallpaper tale. The wife of a doctor and the mother of several athletic sons, she always donned one of their sweatshirts and a pair of their jeans while doing the family papering, a task which she enjoyed as much as we do.

A lady of considerable size, she presented quite a picture to begin with in this fancy garb. Add to this, then the inevitable "HAIR DON'T", and the sticky face and fingers; and Isabel was not at her best when the doorbell rang one autumn afternoon. "Come in!" she called cheerily.

A young man entered and peered upward to the top of the rather decrepit ladder on which the lady perched. "Mrs. C?" he asked. "Yes," she said cheerfully. "What can I do for you?" He cleared his throat.

"Mrs. C." he said, "Your name has been suggested…We are looking for a community leader for Town Chairman of the Cancer Crusade. Now I know that YOU are a lady of considerable social standing; president of several clubs; that you possess a great deal of charm and the ability to inspire OTHERS to work under YOUR direction…that you have the kind of executive ability which leaves YOU free for leadership with OTHERS doing the ACTUAL WORK FOR YOU…" His voice trailed off, she sent the young man to us, incidentally; we led the Crusade…

Once we papered a room with the most engaging array of huge green trees across a white background. "It's so DIFFERENT!" everyone said. "Yes, isn't it?" we agreed happily. "What kind of tree is it?" they would ask. "We really don't know," we would reply, "some kind of exotic foliage.."

It had been up for a number of years when a friend, dropping something on the floor of the room, bent to retrieve it. Her eyes strayed upward as she rose.

She suddenly straightened. "They're PALM TREES!" she exclaimed. "UPSIDE DOWN! The Wallpaper is UPSIDE DOWN. They're palm trees - that's what they are!" We all proceeded to stand on our heads. The merriest and most maddeningly ordinary group of PALM TREES imaginable wallpaper is greeted our eyes, the lady was RIGHT.

Oh well- back to the papering board. It IS a FUN kind of endeavor, really HITLER should have STAYED at it!

2-17-74 WHAT A WINTER!

"Tis a crazy kind of Winter, so they tell us…so they say…
All those cheerful weathermen who bring us forecasts every day.
Why, thermometers hit sixty as old January thaws
Then along comes February and a northeast blizzard roars…
All our closets must be stuffed with clothes of every different kind;
How to DRESS??? Poor Mother's frantic, for she can't make up her mind!
Shall small Suzie wear her raincoat??? Will the boys their boots require???
If they don that extra sweater will the little ones perspire???
With the energy crunch pinching, are the thermostats too low???
Through those underheated classrooms do the bonny breezes blow???

Will those snowflakes that are falling, drifting so serenely down
In a twinkling change their tactics and engulf our little town???
Shall the traffic snag and falter, and those "No School" whistles
    blow???
Will a coat of silver icing be affixed now to the snow???
This HAS been a crazy winter, quite unlike the normal kind;
Gosh, it sure has all the flowers in our gardens in a bind!
SAUCY SNAPDRAGONS were blooming as Thanksgiving
    Day drew near;
Why, I plucked a great bouquet of them to add Thanksgiving
    cheer...
Then came Christmas! They still bloomed there in the garden
    by the wall
So behold - a vase of snapdragons upon the table in the hall,
Interspersed with blooming PANSIES! they had not yet gone
    to sleep.
We began to wonder if a YEAR LONG vigil they might keep...
Then, one January morning, 'twas the 24th, I spied
Two delightful curling green things coming up the wall beside...
Gosh, my HYACINTHS were budding! They were up an inch
    or more,
And I cried out in excitement as I bolted for the door
To announce to all and sundry, "Spring, my friends, is on the way!
Just guess what I've discovered in my flower bed today!"
Well then, darn it, February shortly after came along,
In her arms a dozen snowstorms to cut short my nice Springsong...
Oh well, soon it will be March, and then we've not too long to go
E'er we see the last of winter and we see the end of snow...
Meanwhile IS this winter CRAZY??? Seems to me, it's quite
    routine,
All this "Wait a minute" weather on our New England scene...

2-4-73   WHATEVER HAPPENED TO JANUARY?

Whatever happened to January??? "Twas just one glorious THAW!

New Englanders were firmly convinced that their winter was no more...

The streets were rivers; soft zephyrs murmured; and ladybugs by the score

Came climbing up on the window sills, and peeping in at the door...

A fly or two I chanced to view; and squirrels seemed to me

To be calling down, "hey, SPRING has sprung!" as they scampered from tree to tree,

Or tossed their tails on the high light wires; or chortled with squirrel glee

As they spied - at work on my garden paths - that premature gardener...ME!

Shouldn't be surprised if one morning I wakened to the sight

Of another "Preemy" - a ROBIN - who'd arrived under cover of night;

Who had tuned in to Weatherman Norman, and decided 'twas quite all right

To pack his things and spread his wings for his annual Northern flight...

We realize 'tis February, and we're certain to have SNOW...

But the sun is high in our softening sky, so it speedily must go.

And then March, though it's wild and windy IS the precursor of SPRING...

We may get out our scarves and sweaters once more, but gosh! April's on the wing...

Why do folks ever leave New England for those "sunny???" Florida shores

When the month is January, and ahead lie our lovely THAWS???

Why do folks ever leave New England anyhow, when winter's here???

Some New Englanders feel that our wintertime is the happiest
    time of year...
MYSELF INCLUDED...

6-8-69   WILD LIFE

WHAT A HAPPY response there was to last week's "Cabbage"
on my friend Fay's Orioles, and my friend Rosemary's Robins! It would
appear that people enjoy reading about something other than OTHER
people; and so, flush with success, I decided to trot out another story
concerning a houseguest of my own!

Well, actually, he isn't a HOUSEGUEST as such; he dwells in the
hollow trunk of a big old apple tree in a neighbor's yard, a fact of which
the head of the household thoroughly approves. Ted has heard too many
tales of the ravages that can be attributed to a houseguest such as the one of
which I write. You see, my little wild life pet is a SQUIRREL!

SAMMY is his name. As a matter of fact, Sammy always has been
the name of any pet squirrel that moseyed - either in actuality or by the
fictional route I have traveled for years with small children - into the lives
of the Metayers. And, incidentally, Sammy has been moseying into the
lives of the Metayers for a goodly number of those years...

"But how do you know he IS Sammy?" ask my friends; after all,
you've seen ONE squirrel, and you've seen them all. They look alike, I am
informed. Well, I say, WE really DON'T HAVE TO KNOW SAMMY;
HE KNOWS US!

We've watched the years leave their mark on the little fellow we call
our own, even as the years have left their mark on us! His tail, for instance,
is decidedly "ratty". When he waves it in greeting, it no longer represents
the handsome gesture it once was; it's a bit like waving a torn flag! But we
pretend not to notice, just in case he's sensitive about his age...

Sammy is totally tame; and totally concerned with the comings
and goings of a family that seems to come and go more than most. The
arrival of daughter Gael's convertible, for instance, top down and spilling
over with small boys, is a signal for Sammy to come swinging along the

telephone wires to the tall maple tree that stands beside the drive, from the lower branch of which he is able to cast a bright eye on their antics.

When Gael brought her brand new Cairn terrier puppy our way for the very first time, Sammy not only eyed the little fellow, but chattered a noisy greeting.

"Ahah," I could hear him saying mentally, "I shall have a ball with this one!" Sammy had indeed had a ball with Lady Jane, the Metayer DOG of fond memory, who was my constant gardening companion. Lady Jane was incredibly jealous by nature.

She took a dim view of my noticing anyone other than herself. She abhorred the neighborhood birds whom I faithfully, as I stated in last week's "Cabbage", fed. As a matter of fact, our canine companion carried this jealousy to such an extent that, although she was the fussiest eater on earth, she would immediately devour every crumb of the stale bread or cake I tossed upon the lawn for our poor starving birdies.

And I am certain that, kindly though she was, starving out the little dears was precisely what she had in mind.

Lady Jane particularly disliked Sammy who, perched high on a branch of a nearby tree, delighted in chattering away to me while I worked at the incessant summer weeding which, ridiculously enough, I enjoy.

It was plain to see that Sammy and I were FRIENDS; and Lady Jane saw, and reacted. Her barking would have aroused the deceased. Sammy evened up the score. He ran merrily back and forth on the telephone wires safely out of reach; while Lady Jane ran anything but merrily back and forth below him, quivering with annoyance at his inaccessibility, and howling dismally in frustration. Occasionally, just for kicks, Sammy would pause, retrieve a nut or an acorn from someplace deep within his small jowls, and aim it playfully at our poor dog's harassed head...

Sammy and Ted have their happy relationship as well. Secure in the knowledge of this friendship, the little grey fellow buries his nuts and acorns in our pretty green lawn from morning to night. How amusing it is to see Ted mowing the family lawn, with Sammy three or four jumps ahead, burying his tiny tidbits like nothing was afoot.

"Watch out there, Sammy," Ted will say playfully, "or I'll mow that tail of yours along with the grass!" Occasionally I hear a rumble or two as my spouse finds himself pulling up the resultant oak trees that sprout by the dozens in the lawn he loves, however, Ted for the most part, is as tolerant and fond of Sammy as are the rest of us.

MONDAY was a beautiful day for gardening. I decided to plant the several packets of nasturtium seeds I had been meaning to sow for weeks. Sammy came to watch, his eyes bright with interest as he trailed me about the place. "I hope they grow this year, "I told a friend.

"Last year I had about three plants out of the lot; I must have planted them too early." My friend laughed. "Didn't you just tell me that SAMMY watched your every move?" she said; "So what's different about digging up acorns and nasturtium seeds"?

"I wish WE had a pet like Sammy," young Jim said one day last week. "How did you TRAIN him, Grandma?"

"Well," I said, "I really don't think WE trained him; I think HE trained US!"

1-27-74 WINTER WONDERLAND

The snow came first. It draped a mantle of white ermine 'round the shoulders of our world. Then came the ice storm to set a diadem upon its brow and make of it a place of breathless beauty, a WINTER WONDERLAND!

It was forecast as a possible inch or two, the snow that had been threatening - or so it had appeared by all the leaden skies that seemed to meet our gaze day in and dark day out for several days before. An inch or two would have barely covered the bleak brown earth, we thought, and e'er long would have turned to tattered shreds beneath a January sun. Instead our snow had deigned to fall in great gay gorgeous quantities that were to drape the hills in pristine splendor and the valleys covered with a quilt of softest down.

Our Winter Wonderland had begun…It was to stay that way but briefly for a cold front soon would march our way from Canada to bring us great grey sheets of freezing rain that were to silver all the earth and lay a shimmering gorgeous crust upon the snows that lay below.

A Bishop's Mitre soon would crown the sculpture in my garden; the yews were all to wear soft fleecy robes, their graceful arms encased in wide sweet white kimono sleeves that would all fall demurely from the long and slender hands that were to turn to rich green gold as sunlight sought them out…While all the skeletons of oaks and maples and the rest, divested of the Fall's fair leafings would be garlanded once more with crystal drapes that were to shine like myriad diamonds in the sun and turn to rosy red when day was o'er and catch the magic of the moon in silver softness on the black of boughs when night had come…

Our world was now a veritable treasure chest, spilling over wildly with the fire of diamond gleam, the multi-faceted glow of opal, the shimmering shining softness of pure pearl…

It was to last for days and days, this WINTER WONDERLAND… The beautifully garlanded lush Christmas trees we had so lately set aside were all to pale beside the beauty of the Christmas trees that still stood tall and straight in Nature's gardens, trimmed as they were with all the lushness and the lavishness of nature's own fair hand…and now in such a way that our own puny efforts at creating beauty were to pale by sad comparison.

It was all to end quite suddenly, this WINTER WONDERLAND that was our own-one January night when lo! the pale caress of moonlight would give way to sweeping winds that soon would send their strident voices through our world, despoiling black lace trees whose swan songs were to echo on the winds as crystal garlands fell and silver bangles slithered from the arms of great grey bearded giants and of striplings all alike…The WINTER WONDERLAND was to be, alas! partly at an end. To be sure snow would drape the harsh high contours of our world with its own special beauty for awhile; but January's tired traditional time of thawing would arrive and send the ice in racing rivers to the sea; and turn to ragged refuse-strewn and puny piles the sun-kissed snows that we had known.

Our WINTER WONDERLAND would be no more…But wasn't it all unbelievably beautiful the while it lasted??? And isn't our own wild New England weather with its changing moods and patterns; its wantonness and caprices - the living end??? LOVE it!!!

7-19-64   YOUR VOTE DOES COUNT

IN THE HARSH, hard spotlight of publicity, via the most far-reaching and comprehensive communications system of any age, the national political conventions will carve their chaotic pages upon the history of the world. The great voices of the party of our political persuasion will be counted on the side of justice or injustice; and Americans will either weep with shame, or shine withpride at what they witness.

The delegates who mould their party's platform, and choose their party's candidates, have come from all the corners of our land. They include the very young and idealistic, the middle aged, the elderly, the novice, the seasoned politician. They represent a divergency of ethnic backgrounds, walks of life, patterns of thinking and rightly so.

They have one thing in common. In an age torn by the struggle for individual freedom, by international upheaval, by foreign and domestic issues of almost unparalleled proportions, they were entrusted with the fate of the greatest nation on earth - our own by YOU and ME, and the people of our town; and thousands of small towns similar to ours; for it is at the grass roots level that the men and women whose voices will sound above the chaos of our times commence the portentous trek toward the national convention of our political persuasion.

When we hear the authoritative voice of a Saltonstall or a Kennedy intoning the vital vote of our State's delegation, on candidates or issues that can well change the shape of our world, we may pause for a moment and reflect solemnly, "I placed him there. I gave him voice in the shaping of my destiny, either by voting for, or failing to vote for, the delegates at grass roots level, who would ultimately lead this man to the floor of this convention. How very vital is my vote!"

The women of America, who might have been expected to exercise to the utmost degree the franchise for which they fought so bitterly and so long, fail dismally in their voting record. The Gallup polls indicate that 33,600,000 were cast by women in the last Presidential election, as against 34,700,000 votes cast by men - this in a land where women constitute an overwhelmingly larger segment of the adult population than men. (We live longer because we take better care of ourselves, we are told...)

The importance of our vote emphasized by President Johnson in proclaiming September 13-19 "Women Voters Week". This proclamation was announced at the national convention of the League of Women Voters in Pittsburgh on April 24. Ours is a solemn obligation to vote, for, to quote Mrs. Katie Louchelm, of the United States Department, where, perhaps more than anywhere else, the vital impact of a vote is apparent, "For today's American women, the community is not only her town, her city or even her nation. Her community is the world."

Our community, however, can be the place where we begin to exercise the blessed privilege of participating in the selections of the politicians who will write the future of our world. For it is here in our town that their march down the political trail will begin. It is here that men and women of integrity and worth must be encouraged to seek public service.

How many of us had even made the acquaintance of the Town Committee of the party of our choice for whom we voted in the recent presidential primary election? How many of us even bothered to vote in the recent presidential primary election? How many of us stated smugly, "Nothing of consequence is decided here; I never bother with primaries."

"Nothing of consequence????" The Town Committee names the delegates to our State Convention; the State Convention moulds the political figure our State will cut before the Nation (and the world, thanks to the scope of our communications system), and starts the delegates on their way to the national convention. It is as simple as that. Once a delegate is entrusted with the awesome responsibility of choosing a candidate and a party platform in a world in peril, the die is cast.

We women should be the first at the polls in any election; our vote does make a difference. We are the "hearts" of our families; we can be the "hearts" of the families of nations. Let us lend our hearts and our voices, our time and our talent to the support of the kind of man we want to run our town, to bear the standard of our state, to sit at our national convention, and have a part in the shaping of our world. OUR VOTE DOES MAKE A DIFFERENCE!

A TRIBUTE
PUBLISHED IN THE PAGES OF THE QUINCY PATRIOT

LEDGER, QUINCY, MASS.
JUN 10 1998

MEMORIAL OBITUARY
Entered into Eternal Rest
Sunday, June 7, 1998
Funeral Mass Saturday for Elizabeth Metayer

BRAINTREE - A funeral Mass for former state Rep Elizabeth "Bibs" (Nener) Metayer will be celebrated at 10 a..m. Saturday at Sacred Heart Church in Weymouth. Burial will be in Blue Hill Cemetery. Mrs. Metayer, a resident of Braintree for many years, died Sunday in Fort Lauderdale, Fla., after a long battle with cancer, she was 86. She had lived in Pompano Beach, Fla. since 1985.

Mrs. Metayer served in the House from 1974 to 1984. She was assistant majority leader.

She served as a town meeting member for 20 years, but had no other political experience when she ran for state representative at age 63. She visited almost every home in the district, and defeated two-term Rep. William Dignan in the Democratic primary. The campaign that cost her just $900. Mrs. Metayer served as president of the Quincy Deanery, the Archdiocese Council of Catholic Women, the Sacred Heart Church Guild and the Archbishop Williams' Women's Guild.

She also served as president of the Braintree Point Woman's Club, the Second District Past Presidents' Club and Past Chairman Club of the Massachusetts Federation of Women's Clubs. She was founding president of the Braintree League of Women Voters and a member of the Northeast Braintree Civic Association, the advisory committee of Braintree Hospital and the Braintree Historical society.

She was a corporator of the Braintree Savings Bank.

Mrs. Metayer was also chairwoman of the local fund-raising campaigns of the American Cancer Society and American Heart Association.

She wrote columns for the Braintree Observer, Braintree Star and Braintree Forum for 21 years. she changed the name of her column from "Cabbages and Kings" to "Lady of the House" after she was elected to the Legislature; Mrs. Metayer was named to more than a dozen "Who' Who" volumes.

Born in Boston, she graduated from Girls Catholic High School in Malden, Hickox Secretarial College and Harvard University.

Wife of the late Edward A. Metayer, she is survived by a son, Richard E. Metayer of Mystic, Conn.; a daughter, Gael M. Corbin of Pompano Beach, Fla.; and four grandchildren and three great-grandchildren. She was also the grandmother of the late Richard E. Metayer Jr.

Visiting hours will be 2 to 4 and 7 to 9 p.m. Friday at the Cartwright-Venuti Funeral Home, 845 Washington St.

Donations may be made to the Braintree Historical Society, 786 Washington St.

Trailer Traveling

Contents

1-19-75 CALIFORNIA!

Beauty lies in wait as we drive through Oregon's Cascade Range of Rockies, with the green of the timber line continuing its sharp contrast to the burnt gold of the hills.

This is timber country and the sawmills lie adjacent to the highway. The broad S. Umpqua River that winds peacefully through the valley is filled with logs. Thousands of the great felled trees lie stacked on barges; while immense streams of water play upon others piled high on the river banks - so as to slow the process of their drying out, Ted tells me. Immense kilns are sending smoke signals (and pollution) skyward. Leaving the valley behind, the engineering marvel that is our highway slices its way through the immense mountains of this excitingly beautiful range, leaving HERE a wall whose copper heart glows in the sunlight… THERE a sheer rise of gray slate and coral clay…the whole vying for beauty with the deep dark green of the towering mountain's crest…

We drive through Stage Road Pass, where a vivid imagination takes over. Was this the road taken by the old stagecoaches that fought their way through the Wild West, we wonder??? (with hostile Indians roaring down the mountainsides, Hollywood style???) And then it is Wolf Creek…(where, perhaps, the wolves lay in wait for the traveler AND the Indian…)

Occasionally a mountain will have been cut back in tiers, uniform in size and beautifully rounded, with a hundred variations in the coppery shades that light the Oregon hills…The logging trucks that labor along the highway, their tremendous logs jutting out behind them, all but rock our car and trailer as they pass.

We journey through Sexton Pass and suddenly the whole of magnificent Oregon appears to lie below us…the timber covered range of mountains lying one upon the other, ending in a hazy fringe of hills against a dusky horizon. "For purple mountain majesties…" The words of the song "America" rise unbidden to our lips…

The thought of reaching California this very day excites us, however, we decide to stop awhile at Kerbyville, an old western "Ghost Town", and at Kerby, a log scaling center. Scaling, we learn, is removing the bark from the great trees.

We pass the Siskiyou Smokejumper Base where men are trained, Ted tells me, to leap from planes to fight forest fires. Then through the tiny town of O'Brien, whose curving old country road reminds us wonderfully of New England; and we are leaving Oregon. "We hope you enjoyed your visit. Come again," reads the roadside sign. and now it is "Welcome to California". San Francisco, here we come!

Through the long "Collier Tunnel" that cuts through a towering mountain peak and we enter Six Rivers National Forest.

We wind our way down the Redwood Highway, up and down and around the Rockies, encountering one blind curve after another - on a two way highway that will barely accommodate two cars, traveling in either direction. We have no way of knowing who or what (including an occasional cyclist with his backpack strapped upon his back) lies just around these curves that are so unbelievably blind. "This," says Ted finally, "is fully as bad as Italy's Amalfi Drive!" "I think it is worse," I wail, "because here we are toting a TRAILER!"

The redwoods rise 100' in the air, on all sides. Speed in some areas is restricted to twenty miles per hour. We had been warned of this Redwood Highway back at Grant's Pass. "It will take you 3½ hours to get to Crescent City." the gas station attendant had said, "The road is one snaking mass of curves!" He was not exaggerating…

Across Hardscrabble Creek and the trees grow taller and more enormous. These are California's famous redwoods and they constitute a thrilling sight for an Easterner.

Redwood State Park, and now the trees are 20' in diameter and 200' high and we begin to leave the tortuous drive behind us. For we are but 380 miles from San Francisco…We encounter "Highway Patrol" cars; and we remember the T.V. program that features them.

Crescent City…the wonderful Pacific Ocean lies dead ahead. A wild impatience seizes me for I realize suddenly how desperately I have missed the sight of the sounding ocean I love so very much. Mountains, to be sure, are beautiful; my first love, however, is the sea. And suddenly it lies before us - the blue Pacific, its shore littered to a depth of two hundred feet or more with driftwood from the wild northwest…great felled tree trunks, and burned bits of ships; and the flotsam and jetsam of a hundred storms…Foghorns sound across the water from Crescent

City; and the fragrance of the redwoods and the sea mingle to delight the senses; and we must park the trailer so that I might scramble across the driftwood and walk along the sand and feed my soul, starved, as Ted well knows, for the sight of the sounding sea…I pick up bits of driftwood while Ted shakes a doleful head. "If you keep accumulating things," he informs me, "we'll not be able to perambulate…" I am persuaded finally to return to the car. "The sea is visible intermittently all along the coast," Ted tells me by way of consolation; and it is!

We are driving now through Del Norte Coast Redwood State Park. The vegetation is thick and luxuriant; it fringes the highways and the redwood groves; each of which bears the name of one of California's distinguished citizens or civic groups. We note Earl Warren Grove and Rotary Grove. Every so often we glimpse the sea, with the surf thundering against the rocky cliffs that line the shore. we are reminded, Ted and I, of Greece - the ride from Patras toward Athens along the wild and winding coast with the mountains rising on one side and the sea thundering on the other… "Ah, my love, the sea, how I have missed thee!"

The beautiful coastal ranges lie to our left, but I've eyes only for the bright blue of the Pacific…the wild breakers and the driftwood strewn coves and beaches…How our nephews Kevin and Michael would love to surf in these wild waters!

"Wouldn't you just love to park our car and trailer beside one of those wonderful beaches and sleep to the sound of the sea?" I ask Ted wistfully. Ted, who insists on the security of a well-supervised trailer park, leaves the question unanswered; and later when we have settled ourselves in San Jose for what turns out to be an eighteen day stay, and turned on the family T.V. for a news broadcast, I decide he is right, for we learn of three young men who succumbed to this urge to park their camper beside the sea - down San Bernardino way I believe - and curl up in sleeping bags beneath the stars with the ocean sounding its lullaby. Two of the three were found murdered in the morning, with the third clinging faintly to life. It is difficult for peace loving middle-aged people to grasp the implications of this new wave of violence that has swept our truly magnificent country.

CALIFORNIA AGAIN!

The Indians "captured" Alcatraz in a twentieth century uprising which undoubtedly had its roots in the current wave of minority group upheavals. They propose to make of the island an Indian Cultural Center, and they refuse to leave, despite the lack of water and medical care, and a thousand other privations they must be enduring in the middle of the windswept waters of San Francisco Bay. The first Indian child was born there a few months back; while in San Jose we read of the impending birth and marveled at the courage of the young Indian parents.

Alcatraz was purchased by the U.S. Government in 1849 for the sum of five thousand dollars, we were told. The island, used for so many years as an escape-proof prison, now sports the traditional Indian Thunderbird, that supernatural eagle which was conceived as the god of thunder. Signs posted conspicuously across the island declare it to be Indian property. We exchange friendly waves with a group of the first Americans of ours who are gathered on the rocky island ledges; possible to watch the Harbor Princess go by. We sail under the San Rafael-Richmond bridge, another magnificent span. The traffic moves like an army of ants across the towering two-tier highways above us. The bay has become rough and white-capped as we pass the Treasure Island Naval Base and proceed under the San Francisco-Oakland Bay Bridge, the world's largest...4½ miles long, towering 519' in the air...its cost, we are told, a staggering 77 zillion dollars! (Don't believe I ever heard of a zillion dollars before...) A crew of sixty painters must be maintained year-round for servicing this enormous structure, we learn. Two years are required to cover the bridge with 200,000 gallons of most expensive paint, the workmen commencing their task on the Oakland side and finishing in San Francisco - just in time to begin all over again on the opposite side.

We pass the Ferry Tower with its sixty five year old clock that has withstood the 1906 earthquake as well as fire and flood and other calamities. for one year after the earthquake, we are told, the hands of the clock remained at 5:12, the hour of the tragedy, as a reminder of the disaster that was to change the face of fabulous San Francisco for all time...(and bring my own civil engineer father from London to America, though having landed on the East coast and come first to my mother's Boston relatives he decided to remain here…)

Past the Coit Tower now, with its delightful bit of history. Lillian Hitchcock Coit, a wealthy eccentric, was the official mascot of the Knickerbocker Fire Brigade back in the Gay Nineties, we learned. She followed all fires, smoked cigars, and cussed, and generally shocked the more staid San Franciscans all to bits. Upon her death it was found she had willed one third of her estate to the City, to be used in a beautification project. Coit Tower was promptly erected by the imaginative city fathers as a memorial to the colorful lady; it is shaped precisely like the nozzle of a fire hose…Now, having seen San Francisco from the Bay, we proceed on successive trips to explore the great city itself, sauntering through Chinatown, that colorful part that houses the greatest concentration of Chinese-outside of China - of any place in the world. Ah, the magic and mystery of San Francisco's Chinatown with its tiny doll-like Oriental ladies, delicate as flowers; its dear little children with their dark slanting eyes and small somber faces; its Oriental families taking their leisure in the shade of doorways or on sidewalks adjacent to their humble homes, the engaging language that is theirs flowing about like the music of wind chimes back at home…Chinese vegetables in the markets…vegetables I've never before encountered; and Chinese numerals on the street signs…

Enchanting…

San Francisco is a joyous city to visit and to find stretched out before one from the Top of the Mark. We explore it all from end to end before turning our attention - most reluctantly, we might add - elsewhere in this beautiful State that is California…to Carmel and Monterey, for instance, which we reach via the storied "Seventeen Mile Drive" through the Del Monte Forest, a toll road that is worth every penny of the charge of several dollars that permits the entry of a car and its driver into this enchanted place.

We stop again and again along the way…at shepherd's Knoll with its breathtaking view of Monterey Bay, the Santa Cruz mountains dim and distant on the northern horizon; at Huckleberry Hill; and Carberry Knoll with its spectacular view of Carmel Bay and Point Lobos and the Santa Lucia Mountains. Pebble Beach lies directly below - delighting as does all of this ocean oriented area - our momentarily mountain-surfeited souls.

We delight in the sights and sounds of Seal and Bird Rocks, wildlife sanctuaries where gulls and cormorants by the thousands sun themselves upon the rocks, and sea lions disport themselves about the place below. Seal Rock, we learn, is a haven for Leopard and Harbor seals which are a great deal smaller than the sea lions. We watch, via a mounted telescope, as the fascinating creatures play about the rocks, or doze lazily in the golden California sun.

We inspect the Spyglass Hill Golf Course and the Fanshell Beach which is crescent-shaped and frequently covered with vividly colored sea shells and stones, we are informed, though none are visible that day. Cypress Point next, with Point Sur visible in the distance; and Crocker Grove where we view the oldest and largest Monterey Cypress existent - moss draped and beautiful. Then suddenly there is the Lone Cypress lying against a gorgeous California sky with the sea beneath...a familiar California landmark. We've seen it pictured a thousand times and now what a thrill to be actually looking upon it. The Monterey Cypress assumes the weirdest of forms. There is the Ghost Tree and the Witch Tree, both aptly named, trailing their mossy drapings like ghostly garments in the moving summer air.

Pescadero Point next, the northwestern extremity of Carmel Bay. And now we stop to lunch and shop and pip about the fabulous Del Monte Lodge where we manage to tuck in a visit to Mr. Crosby's famous Pebble Beach Golf Links...Our Seventeen Mile Drive is over...and seventeen miles of opulence it has indeed been...of magnificent estates, and breathtaking scenery, of coastal California at its most superb. Carmel by the Sea. We park the car and walk for miles along the beach, with the surf pounding against the shore and surfers disporting themselves despite the "No Swimming" signs that line much of the shore. The seaweed lies heavy on the sand and we gather shells and revel in the fresh wild fragrance of the sea air about us...The quaint little Carmel shops delight us, as does the Carmel Mission of San Carlos Borromeo...and enduring monument to Padre Junipero Serra, the "Great Conquistador of the Cross," who with other Jesuit priests was able to establish an enduring chain of Missions along the California coast.

Carmel's first buildings, both the Church and the dwellings, were made of wood; they were enclosed by a palisade fashioned of poles, we learn. These were to be soon replaced with adobe and then finally with a structure of the native sandstone as it stands today, quarried from nearby Santa Lucia Mountains. Its architecture is lovely. The interior walls of the church curve upward as they rise, with the ceiling following the wall sweep to form an eye-pleasing Catenary Arch.

The Church walls are finished with a lime plaster made of burnt sea shells. The edifice, which was four years in the making, was dedicated in 1797; and the side chapel, which served as a mortuary for the Indians, was added in 1821; more than 3,000 Indians, incidentally, are buried in the adjoining cemetery where we viewed with interest one particular cemetery marker reading "To Memory of Old Gabriel who died March 14, 1890. Aged 151 years." How about that???

Padre Serra is buried within the sanctuary of the beautiful old Mission Church whose deep yellow exterior blends so beautifully with the gold of the California sunshine. His sarcophagus is made of stone, with a bronze figure of the Missionary lying full length, a young bear at his feet. The bear, we are told, is symbolic of the young State of California to which he came.

The Chapel contains the original altar furnishings, many of which were brought by Father Serra from Baja, California in 1769, expressly for the founding of the Mission.

In the museum section of Carmel Mission we come upon a delightful bit of history - a flintlock rifle which was once the property of Captain William Goodman Dana, the brother of Richard Henry Dana Jr, an illustrious Braintree boy who grew up to write social conscience-stirring novel, "Two Years Before the Mast." Captain Dana came to California in 1821, we learn. He married one Maria Josefa Carrillo and received a grant of 38,000 acres of land in Southern San Luis Obispo Country in 1835, which he promptly named NIPOMO, the Indian word for "Foot of the Hills." Ah me, have we said recently that we LOVED beautiful California???

11-15-70 CANADA

CANADA...We crossed the border at Carway - I with fear and trembling, I might add - for I had forgotten my birth certificate of all things! Ted assured me I wouldn't need it, however, my days had been haunted by the spectre of an irate immigration officer shaking a stern hand and shouting, "Thou shalt not pass!"

Ted was right, as usual; the gentleman did not even ask for my birth certificate. He did, however, show a profound interest in the contents of our trailer. "Are you carrying firearms?" he wanted to know. "Yes," said Ted, who had tucked son Richard's trusty old "Betsy" into a corner of the trailer closet just in case we encountered any of those Western black hats en route. "A shotgun," said Ted. "No pistols or automatics?" "No." "Are you carrying meats, plants or flowers?" It was my turn to answer; and all the gay and exciting unusual plants I had picked in Yellowstone and Montana and pressed between the pages of my Woodall's Travel Dictionary and elsewhere, took a mental nosedive right down the drain as I confessed in a very small voice to having done that very thing. "May I see the flowers?" asked the officer, rather sternly, I thought. I waited while he laboriously turned the pages and examined one by one my bits of pressed blue and pink and purple and green. "I picked them in Yellowstone," I said in a rather pleading tone. "and in Glacier National Park...I LOVE pressed flowers," I added. and I waited and waited and waited while he examined and examined and examined...

The uniformed Canadian finally, however, closed the book and then suddenly smiled, and his rather long nose seemed to wrinkle in amusement. "You may keep them," he said, and patted my hand; I all but kissed him...

The fluff from the cottonwood trees that had been pursuing us for weeks followed along into Alberta, a rich green rolling province of ranches and farms, with the Canadian flag flying on all sides. We are still in Indian country, the "Land of the Bloods," and I who always thrilled to the exploits of those early settlers of our North American continent, delight in the lore that surrounds us.

At lunch we are entertained with the story of Red Crow, a great warrior and apparently and equally great statesman of this Blood tribe of

Indians whose descendants still inhabit the area. Red Crow was the leader of the "Fish Eaters" band, or Mamyoyi, we are told, and in 33 daring raids against his enemies he was never once wounded. His fame among the Bloods increased as the years passed, and he became their principal Chief in the year of 1870. It was he who signed "Treaty Number Seven," our informant said proudly. (I was tempted to ask about the other SIX, however, I did not want to embarrass the young Indian boy, or perhaps, as a white woman, to be embarrassed myself by his reply.)

Red Crow selected the "Land of the Belly Buttes" as a reserve for the Blood Indians in the year 1883. He became the tribe's first rancher and was the first to abandon his Indian dwelling and build a log house for his family. His last resting place, we learned, is beside the bright blue Belly River that rolls gently through the countryside about this Indian "Reserve." Another Indian tale at Standoff, a tiny settlement with a bit of local history behind it. The year was 1870 and a group of obviously unscrupulous Americans left the Missouri River and came north to trade whiskey to the Blood tribe. Hot in pursuit of the outlaws was one Sheriff Charles D. Herd who caught up with them at a point about forty miles south. Herd ordered them to surrender, however, they cunningly informed him that they were in Canada, and therefore, beyond his reach legally. They threatened him with death if he attempted to arrest them.

The International Boundary had not as yet been surveyed, and so the Sheriff - uncertain of his ground-withdrew. The rogues, rejoicing in the success of their deviousness, went on their merry way to this area - where they built their trading post, calling it "Standoff" to commemorate the "standing off" of the law. Standoff Post was short lived, however, we were happy to note; the arrival of the Northwest Mounted Police to the area in 1874 speedily brought about its abandonment. The name remains, however, as well as the tale which is told to passing travelers by the descendants of those original Blood Indians who were involved.

And now we must visit the headquarters of the gallant Mounties who brought law and order to the Canadian West - restored Fort MacLeod and the Mounties museum!

The original fort was built by a band of 150 scarlet clad Mounties, who arrived here after a hazardous trek of 1,000 miles across the Canadian prairies, and the restored fort is a delightful place, filled with mementos of early Canadian pioneer days-memorials to the first Mounted Policemen to die in this then remote wilderness area - Henry Parker and Thomas Wilson and Frank Baxter, who were caught in a blizzard between Fort MacLeod and Fort Kipp; and a spade which was used by one Mrs. Helen Mills, the third white girl child to be born in the area - when the sod was turned in 1957, marking the beginning of the old fort's restoration.

The restored Fort MacLeod is an exact replica of the original one, blockhouses and all; and it is fun to visit, especially when one has the good fortune to meet as we did Chief Crowfoot, the grandson of the old Indian Chief who negotiated the peace treaty with Colonel MacLeod a century ago. "How did it all begin, the restoration of this wonderful old wilderness fort?" we naturally wanted to know. An historical association, formed for the purpose, secured a federal grant and a provincial grant totaling $45,000, we were told. This figure was swelled by private donations and contributions from businesses - much in the manner of our own local Thayer Birthplace Restoration, we noted. The upkeep of the place is beautifully handled by the current admission fees to the Fort, which last year amounted to $63,000.

Have we said how handsome are these Northwest Mounted Police Officers in their scarlet trappings??? They seem to represent the very soul of Canada.

The Canadian Rockies are dimly visible far off in the distance, however, not even a hill breaks the monotony of the plains over which we are driving now, en route to Calgary and thence to Banff. We stop for the night at Nanton, and what fun it is to see a police car patrolling the streets of this little town, bearing the Maple Leaf and the letters R.C.M.P. on its sides???

It is 10:30 p.m. when we tuck ourselves in, and it is still broad daylight here in Alberta - sunlight, in fact! The sun which must have set finally is to arise again on the morrow at 4:30a.m. I am not on deck to note its arrival; I rely for the information on Ted who, unlike his spouse, does not always sleep like the proverbial tree trunk...Ted duly reports this premature reappearance of Old Sol, reminding me at the same time that here in Alberta we are indeed rather close to the top of the World...

8-15-71   CANADA SAFARI

It will be happening - God willing-each Spring from here in! The Metayers will go about freeing "Fanny", the fabulous family trailer, from her warm winter wraps to set forth on the summer safari they have been merrily planning the long winter through. This past June they were to explore the Maritime Provinces and a few other corners of that fabulous land to the north-CANADA! It was Ted's task to see to it that every inch of Fanny was functioning beautifully- to check the electrical system; fill the bottled gas tanks; test the heating unit for performance, for we were heading- so all the former natives told us for COLD country; and the family refrigerator-freezer, carried with her all the comforts and conveniences of home…

To the distaff side of the family was left the provisioning of our home-on-wheels for the six weeks to two months trip that lay ahead; and for providing it with all the necessary household gadgets. "Why don't you keep a list of everything you use at home in the course of a week or so of housekeeping," suggested practical daughter Gael. "In that way you won't forget anything." I did It read like the inventory of Jordan Marsh.

And so it was tuck and push and shove item after item into the various and sundry cupboards and drawers of our gal Fan until she literally groaned.

Ted's "Do you HAVE to take four pocketbooks and seven pairs of shoes?" was promptly put a stop to by dispatching him early to the nightly Little League games at Watson Park where grandsons Jim and Byrne performed - while, on the pretense of setting the kitchen to rights after our afternoon Little League season dinner - the distaff side could function unobserved before joining him. Came the day of departure. "I hope I'll be able to get the thing off the ground," said Ted - his customary classic remark as the Metayers trail off…

He did; and we left beautiful Braintree behind us. It was a lovely June day and we were merry as a pair of crickets on the family hearth as we headed towards the Mass. Pike. Our smiles seemed to come straight up from our toes at the prospect of one more vacation in that home away from home we had learned to love.

"You know," said Ted suddenly, "this trailer is acting strangely. It's rocking and swaying to the right as though there is too much weight on that side." Now running along the neat right side of Fanny are the family refrigerator-freezer, the family stove, sundry other appurtenances and a decidedly ample food cabinet, complete with three large shelves spaced beautifully apart. "How much food did you bring?" he asked as we headed for the nearest Turnpike rest stop to check the whys and wherefores of Fanny's untoward behavior. "Well," I said, "I didn't want to spend my good time food shopping. I guess I brought a LOT."

Ted's expression as he opened the family food cupboard should have been photographed for posterity. "Good heavens," he screamed (Well, anyhow, that's a reasonable facsimile of what the dear boy DID say...) For the gal in charge of provisioning had piled every inch of each shelf in the food closet THREE CANS HIGH. There were cans of chicken and cans of crabmeat and cans of shrimp and cans of corn and cans of pears and jars of coffee and jars of pickles and tins of soup... "Where did you think we were going?" he asked, "To the Arctic? They DO have grocery stores in Canada, you know. Oh brother, why didn't I check this area as well "Ted," I said hastily as he commenced tossing cans and bottles and jars in all directions, "You wouldn't throw it out...all this food...Think of the starving children of Europe!" He didn't throw it out, I mean; he did however, stop at the nearest grocery store where we managed to secure a raft of nice sturdy cartons into which the family food supply was tucked to be deposited on the floor of the car and the floor of the trailer, from which inconvenient areas we "shopped" from then on. "A veritable grocery store," he kept muttering as we continued on our no-longer-rocking way...

Now - where shall we begin our tale of this latest idyll - a 6,000 mile trip that found us exploring just about every inch of New Brunswick, Nova Scotia, Cape Breton, P.E.I., and Quebec, with bits and pieces of Ontario thrown in for good measure...to end our journey into history and the past with a memorable visit to Fort Ticonderoga, pet preserve of that valiant Ethan Allen and his Green Mountain boys??? A journey, incidentally, in which we kept the sea almost eternally within sight.

Perhaps we should begin at St. Andrews-by-the-sea, a charming little resort town on the Passamaquoddy Bay. Once a bustling port for the great sailing ships of the world, this delightful settlement of 2,000 people (founded by United Empire Loyalists from Penobscott, Maine in the year 1784 - is now a fishing center. 65,000 lbs of lobster are shipped daily to the United States, Canada and Europe from the Conley Lobster Company, the largest live lobster distributing plant in all the world. 200 of the homes here were built more than a century ago; and we wandered about, admiring their sturdy lines…

Much of history here; and a tale or two….like the story that lies behind the beautiful Greenock Presbyterian Church, completed in 1824-a must for tourists.

Captain Christopher Scott was noted for his Scottish thrift and when in the autumn of 1822 the congregation of his church gathered at a public dinner to discuss building a new edifice, "a few uncomplimentary remarks" were made in regard to the gentleman's reluctance to open his purse. Needless to say the Captain took exception to the remarks so much so that in a burst of anger he took upon himself the entire project of building and financing the most beautiful church for miles around - a Church of absolutely perfect proportions and superior architectural design, completed without the use of a single nail or metal fastener. And having completed his gift to the Presbyterians of St. Andrews, he made certain that his generosity would not be forgotten by placing upon the front of the edifice the coat of arms of Greenock, Scotland, his place of birth.

The loyal son of Scotland went one step further. He instructed the architect to have placed in each of the four corners of the ceilings, a beautiful scotch thistle, its purple and green lying gracefully against the ceiling's stark white and instantly catching the eye of every visitor.

Our eyes kept straying upward toward these lovely symbols of Scotland as we sat in the hand-carved pews enjoying a splendid organ concert we had arrived just in time to hear.

A beautiful town, St. Andrews-by-the-sea. We settled ourselves in a lovely trailer park there, with the wild full sweep of the St. Croix River lying before us. And at low tide we drove across the ocean floor to nearby Minister's Island, hurrying back e'er the tide roared in - for at high tide the roadway to this delightful place is inundated by ten or more feet of green sea water. A unique phenomenon, and one of so many we were to witness during our stay in beautiful Canada, a land the which I wish everyone I love might visit…

9-7-70   DEPARTURE

As June made her yearly appearance in Braintree the Metayers departed from it on a golden kind of day that happily matched the gold of our thoughts as we headed toward our great adventure in the self-contained and self-assured little travel trailer that was to prove such a joy to both of us.

***

Family friends and neighbors were on hand to see us off. We left them with mingled feelings of excitement and apprehension. What kind of experiences, I wondered secretly, lay ahead for a couple of anything but young persons who had never before set foot in a trailer and were embarked on a journey that could lead absolutely anywhere.

***

Traffic was heavy as always on the Southeast Expressway, it lightened, however, as we entered the Mass. Turnpike in the vicinity of Boston. Ahead of us almost immediately lay the first of a great many toll stations through which we would be passing during the weeks ahead. the sign read: "CARS - 30c", and so Ted merrily handed his three dimes to the attendant and drove off. A yell from the gentleman in question - who had incidentally vacated his station with the speed of sound - brought us to a screeching halt. "Hey, wait a minute, fella," said an irate voice, "You have a TRAILER! It's 70c!" "sorry, Ted said apologetically, "I didn't know, I'm new at the game. This is my first trailer trip, etc., etc". the expression on the tollee's face clearly indicated that he considered the entire explanation a tissue of lies-none of them very white. Nonetheless, we proceeded on our merry way, laughing over the incident until we reached Ludlow, where we stopped for gas.

The day proceeded happily nonetheless. "Everyone dreams of doing the things you do," a neighbor had said as we bid her goodbye, "but no-one but you DOES them." "How fortunate we are!" I said to Ted as the merry miles began to fall behind us...miles that would lead us from east to west and then some...from the magnificence of the Geyser Basin at Yellowstone National Park to the rare beauty of Lake Louise and the wonder of the Columbia Ice Fields...and across the barren Mojave Desert, in the middle of which unlikely place we would meet a family from home - from Braintree, Mass - Betty and Victor Franceschini of Whittier Road, vacationing like ourselves, together with their fine young son, Bob...Bob, a dedicated history buff who happened to have been a third grade student at Penniman School last January when that historic publication "Braintree - Our Town" was presented to the town's third graders; and who had been so enamored of the third grade teaching aid with the publishing of which I had been involved, that he had badgered his parents into driving him immediately to Town Hall to purchase his very own copy from our fine Town Clerk, Bob Bruynell, who was, as always, doing his civic bit by handling the sale of our book.

"What did you like best about "Braintree - Our Town?" I asked him when identifications had been exchanged and we had settled down to a wonderful three hours of exchanged experiences in the cool of the desert evening. "I liked the stories in the back of the book about John Adams and John Quincy Adams," he said instantly, a reply which delighted me no end because there were those who thought the biographies we had included in our book would have little or no appeal for third graders!

I walked back to the trailer to deposit the sweater I had thought I would need and found I didn't. I opened the trailer door and GASPED. Everything we had been misguided enough to leave decoratively on the counter and elsewhere lay in a heap on the trailer floor. A canister of sugar lay on its side. gently spilling its sticky contents into the heating plant.

"Ted," I wailed. "everything is upside down and the gas heater is full of sugar. Will it be ruined?" "Oh no," said Ted. "It will probably smell a bit oddly when we light it- like the cakes you're always burning - but it won't be ruined. It was that sudden stop at the toll booth," he added. "Wow, I wonder what else is spilled..."

We headed fearfully toward our refrigerator door, the which I gingerly opened TO CATCH AN EGG SQUARELY IN MY HAND... The door of the food cabinet was target #2. I opened IT gently. A SHAFT OF ARROWS ASSAILED ME FROM AN UPPER SHELF! "What on earth?" I gasped as supplementary shafts cascaded in all directions. We hadn't even APPROACHED Indian Country. The arrows turned out to be strands of spaghetti - from a box I had been foolish enough to open before storing.

WE hasten to add that Bob Franceschini is anything but an ordinary third grader. His contribution to the evening's entertainment was to produce a marvelous collection of Polaroid pictures which he himself had taken and which he proceeded to discuss animatedly. shots of Disneyland and of the fabulous Hearst Castle, where he solemnly informed us, whole closets of clothing of every description and in all sizes were kept always on hand so that in the event a guest neglected to bring tennis clothes or bathing attire or anything else that might be called for in a weekend visit, the garments would be provided by William Randolph Hearst, a truly remarkable host who permitted the guest in question to keep the borrowed treasure as a memento of the occasion. (Fur coats only excepted, these had to be returned, he told us.)

What a happy coincidence, this meeting with our Braintree neighbors...one of many happy coincidences, incidentally, and experiences that were to make our first "go" at trailer travel and absolutely flawless adventure, about which you will be reading in the weeks that lie ahead.

DINOSAURLAND UTAH - an incredibly beautiful state-much of it having an Alpine flavor...Lush soaring mountain peaks; Swiss-type chalets; farming areas, their out buildings fashioned of split logs, with here and there an actual sod roof...

Cliffs of red Navajo sandstone as we approach VERNAL, a fascinating small city which because of our acquaintance with the Watsons back in Salt Lake City and their acquaintance with the wonders of their great state, is our next Port of Call

Vernal, Utah and DINOSAURLAND. "A Free Dinosaur Hunting License" is being offered at the Vernal Drug Store as we approach this colorful little city that is the gateway to Dinosaurland. Plateaus and canyons, desolate and untenanted, have followed us there for absolute miles across a country almost as arid as the Mojave Desert. Hill on hill, and hill against hill - with their Navajo sandstone and clay lying hot and bright against a leaden summer sky. One easily visualizes those great awkward Dinosaurs lumbering about this remote area that is Northeast Utah.

VERNAL, and we settle ourselves in a lovely private trailer park with a splendid shade tree and a patio, and then head promptly for the Dinosaur National Monument that houses the exciting Dinosaur Quarry where scientists and archaeologists may be seen busily at work excavating the great bones of the prehistoric monsters from the mountain's sides.

ABOUT SAID DINOSAURS…I must certainly have known they once existed but I fear I could not quite bring myself to believe it until we journeyed westward to find their giant tracks at Zion Park and elsewhere.

The realization that we were about to see their remains in wonderfully great numbers brought me back mentally with a chuckle or two to an evening several years back when a merry little Christmas gathering was in progress at my home for the children of my friend Rosemary. As a prelude to the Christmas stories I proposed to tell by way of entertainment, I looked into their lovely young smiling faces and said sweetly, "Now tell me, children, what kind of stories do you like?" I fully expected the little ones to reply equally sweetly, "I like Fairy Tales" at which point I would have been in my element…Or at the very worst, "I like Adventure Stories!" at which turn of events I would have had to think real fast…I was, however, in for a bit of a shock. It came when Warren Jr. who was all of ten at the time, looked me squarely in the eye. "I like books on Paleontology," he said firmly…Warren Jr. would have had a ball in Dinosaurland…

Reproductions of the huge beasties graced the storefronts and motel entrances and every restaurant in Vernal quite as though Dinosaurs steaks were being offered on the Bill-of-Fare every day in the week. the dinosaur Museum beckoned, however, we first proceeded along a twenty mile stretch of granite mountains to the place itself!

The series of small rounded sand hills that ring the entrance to this National Monument suggest an Arab encampment as we approach, and truly such a facility would have blended beautifully with the desert land we found ourselves now entering. We drove to the Visitor's Center where we transferred to a delightful little open shuttle bus in which for 10c one is whisked comfortably to the mountain top…up a steep mountain road between two peaks to the Quarry itself which is located directly beneath a huge sheltering building which the National Park service has had erected over the mountain's summit.

Dinosaur bones by the hundreds lay exposed on the sides of the mountain and from a movable platform archaeologists drilled carefully into the rock with pneumatic drills. Enormous bones were emerging everywhere under their touch.

We listened eagerly to the Ranger whose lecture on the Geology of the Area answered most of the questions that were racing through our minds. The literally thousands of feet of those folded rock layers that made up the split mountain we were viewing have - over the ages-been eroded away, exposing Dinosaur bones that have lain buried for millions of years, he told us. These bones lie in a "sandstone lens" whose thickness varies from 8 to 12'

How did this vast storehouse of dinosaur bones come to light, we wanted to know; and the Ranger had the answer to that one also. Earl Douglas was a young Paleontologist who made the original discovery in 1909 and for several years afterwards the Carnegie Museum removed the mountaintop and the Dinosaur bones. Their archaeologists marked the great cliff off in 4' squares for more accurate location of the bones. In 1953, however, the National Park Service happily took over the area and the quarry. Their goal is, of course, to preserve this rich archaeological find for all time.

From evidence gathered by studying the fossil bones, scientists have been enabled to reconstruct the appearance of these giant plant-devouring animals that in the opinion of those who know such things undoubtedly walked on dry land and subsisted on sub-tropical vegetation.

The process of exposing the fossils is a delicate one indeed, our Ranger said. The archaeologists use ice picks and tiny dentists' drills and proceed with infinite care and precision in the delicate task of preserving as they expose their invaluable finds.

Why aren't you finding skeletons intact, we wanted to know? "Why a collection of miscellaneous bones from different species???" And once more our Ranger came up with the answer…

About 140 million years ago, he said, the low land in the area was very close to sea level and the rock on the mountainside is believed by paleontologists to have been a sandbar in the river. Dinosaurs, they believe-like many other animals - invariably came to the river to die, and at high flood times their bodies were carried down the river to be picked clean by vultures in due time or as the shifting river sands covered their carcasses - to DECAY, leaving only the bones to be covered by mud and sand. Millions of years passed and rivers and lakes and oceans dropped their sediments so that layers of mud and sand and lime accumulated and hardened…Meanwhile the underground water was seeping into the bones, filling their cavities with minerals which combined with the deposits above them to bring about a change from bone to stone.

During the last 60 million years a mountain system developed in the area, with earth forces forcing mountains to rise and then tearing them down again through rain and ice and wind and erosion so that rock more than half a billion years in age has been uncovered in this exciting area. Incidentally, the disarray of bones that remains had been moved and tossed about during recurring floods and earth action.

Over 350 tons of bones have been recovered, we learned, from this remote area - bones of those dinosaurs who became extinct 70 million years ago. why had they become extinct, we wanted to know, as the realization of the fact that MAN has been around for a mere 1 million years at the very most swept over us. "No one really knows," said our Ranger. "it was probably a matter of environment." And then he reminded us of the present threat to our own environment that is so existent today…

"How do you break the rocks to uncover the bones?" we asked next. "Well," said the Ranger, "Obviously dynamit would be far too dangerous to the specimens and to our visitors and so we employ a method of removing stone that has been in use with very little modification since the days of the Egyptians. The archaeologist drills a series of holes in the rock, then places two wrought iron half-rounds in each of the drilled holes and proceeds to drive an iron wedge between them. Eventually the rock breaks along the line of holes.

As the rock is stripped away with the pneumatic drills and heavier tools, a petrified bone appears. It is very carefully cleaned and measured and then coated with a plastic spray which hardens the shattered bone. A plaster and burlap casing is used to protect the specimen, with wet tissue separating the bone from the plaster.

The block is then loosened from the face of the quarry and sent to the laboratory for cleaning where skilled scientists scrape away the surrounding rock, using extremely fine tools, dental picks among them. After many hours of painstaking labor a well-preserved bone appears.

What kind of story lies behind this fabulous story, we ask ourselves wonderingly? How much of the earth's history is contained in this long step from living breathing Dinosaurs to fossil bones buried deep in a series of tilted sandstone cliffs??? Oh, to be a geologist and understand it all! "Drive Through the Ages", we read as returned daily from fabulous trip after fabulous trip through this land of long ago. "Nearly One Billion Years in 30 Miles!" says a huge sign in Vernal, What an intoxicating feeling to know we have done just that…DRIVEN THROUGH THE AGES! AND SEEN EVIDENCE OF IT ALL!

From Vernal we are to journey to Denver, Colorado, a fabulous city lying at the foot of a vast chain of mountains…a city approached via a series of long lovely tunnels out through the heart of those towering mountain peaks…And at Denver we decide suddenly after our weekly telephone call home, to race back east for a rendezvous with vacationing Gael and Jim and their little ones at Bennington, Vermont where we shall bring our summer idyll to the happiest kind of conclusion with a grand reunion with the dear ones we have missed so desperately and love so dearly. And so our 1,000 mile journey is over, and we have indeed DISCOVERED AMERICA as Columbus never did!

END OF SAFARI

Off next for a two hour cruise about the Thousand Islands on the "Ida M" out of Rockport, Ontario (flying the American flag, by the way…)

The Thousand Islands…Actually there are about 1800 of them, varying in size from large shoals to islands several miles in length. To be legally an island, a shoal must have grass, and at least two trees; and the smallest island of them all, "Tom Thumb" just about qualifies.

This area was once the home of the legendary hero, Hiawatha; and it was known in his day as "Manitonna" or the "Garden of the Great Spirit."

Most of the islands are privately owned and decidedly costly. a 20' × 20' waterfront lot, for instance, costs $2,000; and handsome Senator Island sold recently for $275,000. Two thirds of the islands are located on the Canadian side, however, 70 percent of them are owned by Americans; so we might say facetiously that the Canadians have the islands but the Americans have the money.

By the way, there is a "Boatel" and restaurant located on Sunset Island. Splendid for boaters, however, non-boaters are not excluded. They may phone from the coastal village of Ivy Lea and have a craft pick them up at no charge, returning them neatly to the village when the dinner hour is over.

We pass Woolrich Island which is really two islands joined together by the world's shortest international bridge - 32' in length. The owner's home, we learn, is situated on a Canadian island, while his flagpole and flag are located on the American one.

What fun to visit for awhile the famous Boldt Castle on Heart Island, monument of a great love, a "historically romantic ruin" in a magnificent setting. Its story delights us. George C. Boldt was born in Prussia of rather poor parents, and as a small boy while sailing up the Rhine River he dreamed of one day owning a great towering castle like those that line its banks. Boldt came to America quite young and found work in a Gentlemen's Club in New York. A brilliant young man, he rose over the years to the position of manager and then, backed by a number of New York businessmen, he purchased a hotel of his own. Boldt called it the Waldorf-Astoria - Waldorf after his German place of birth and Astor for his wife's name. the phenomenal success of the Waldorf-Astoria is history; and our hero who subsequently purchased Philadelphia's Bellevue-Stratford as well, became a multi-millionaire.

It was then that he turned his attention to the dream of his youth. Boldt came to the Thousand Islands where he found a perfect setting for the 'Castle on the Rhine" he proposed to build. the island was owned by one G.K.Hart, and Boldt's first undertaking, after purchasing it, was to transform it via a series of stone walls into the precise form of ancient mantelpieces of shining white marble for the great rooms, and from the four corners of the world came the mosaics and sculptures, the carvings and tapestries, that were to adorn the lovely place. The castle itself was to be large enough to accommodate one hundred guests, and the central point of a proposed eleven building complex. It would include a ballroom, a reception room, a library, and billiard room and innumerable handsome apartments. Tapestries arrived to adorn the walls above the regal stairways and immense chandeliers of gleaming crystal awaited installation.

At the water's edge the Alster Tower rose skyward, approached on all four sides by great stone steps bordered by handsome balustrades. Its ballroom and bowling alley, its billiard room and café were designed to contribute to the entertainment of the castle guests. It resembled a Rhine chateau and it was connected by an underground passage to the great castle itself.

Boats would enter a flower-decked 500' lagoon through an Arch of Triumph, and proceed through the heart of the island to their happy destination, the Castle.

It was to have been the dream-come-true of one very remarkable man and one very unusual woman, for whom it was intended to be a tribute, a monument to her love. Two million dollars had already been expended as the nineteenth century waned, with additional millions earmarked and waiting when the world of George Boldt came to a crashing end! His beloved wife, the lady who was to have graced Boldt Castle, died suddenly, tragically....The millionaire's dream died with her, and a telegram from the anguished man brought the building of his "Castle on the Rhine" to a dramatic tragic halt...

Workmen tucked away their tools, and birds and bats built their nests among the silent halls. spiders spun their silver about the marble fireplaces and the gleaming chandeliers. Small boys picnicked on the spacious grounds and played among the waters of the lonely lagoon… and the years passed…As for George Boldt, never again did he visit what was to have been the dream of his lifetime, the monument to his one great love - his wife…

The romantic ruins are the wonder of the Thousand Islands. The place was purchased not too many years ago by one E.J. Noble, the inventor of Beechnut Gum and Life Savers, so we learn; and it is open to the public-with the admission fee one pays to walk about the tragic ruins, visualizing the dream that might have been used to support a number of hospitals located on the American side…

Our American boat trip, taken from lovely little Alexandria Bay, New York yielded little by way of additional history but was fun nonetheless. "Come Again Where the Thousand Islands Are", we read; and we head for Massena, New York where we shall visit the famous St. Lawrence River known as the "River without End", and the Great Lakes that lay beyond. The size of the ships however, had to be severely limited. Now, however, the Great Lakes are open to deep-draft shipping.

the Eisenhower Locks, which will permit the passage of ships 730' long and 75' wide…ocean going vessels from all the world's seas…are fascinating to behold. and each year, we are told, new vessels apply for passage through this engineering marvel; and new languages are heard at the lake piers. The St. Lawrence Seaway includes some 9,500 square miles of waterway, we learn. The water at Montreal is 20' above sea level while at the "Soo" Locks, 383 miles away it has risen to 602' above sea level. Passage along it is accomplished by a series of locks like the Eisenhower. We watch the Martin Schroder out of Bremen, Germany as it passes through. It is four in the afternoon and we are told that the liner hit the wall in the early morning and has been held up while its owner posted a bond for the damage.

The Martin Schroder is not quite the size of an ocean liner; the "Texaco Mississippi" which follows her through the lock IS, however, and we thrill to her exciting passage. The captain first sounds the ship's whistle, then brings her stern around in line with the lock entrance, the bow is then lined up correctly. There is a scant two or three foot clearance on either side of the lock, however, the pilot maneuvers his ship through beautifully. The Texaco Mississippi is now snugly placed in the lock at a level with the platform from which we are viewing her. Winches are brought into play and she is fastened to the sides of the great lock. All St. Lawrence Seaway locks are filled or emptied by gravity; and so the valves are opened and the water begins to leave the dock…20 million gallons of it in 10 minutes!

we watch, fascinated as the great liner sinks lower and lower until at a certain point the huge gates swing open to hasten the process and bring the water level of the lock in line with the water level of the St. Lawrence, forty feet below. We are tempted to cheer as the sea-farers release the cables and the great ship moves serenely out of the lock and into the broad sweep of the waiting St. Lawrence.

Almost equally fascinating is our visit to the Moses-Saunders Power Plant, where, in addition to the story of the conquest of Niagara and the St. Lawrence, we come upon another bit of history, the museum houses two handsome red leather chairs, beside which we read: "These chairs occupied by then Vice-President Richard M. Nixon and Prince Phillip on the occasion of the dedication of the St. Lawrence Power Project, June 27, 1959." Nearby we find, as well, a most impressive booklet; it reads: "This book records the historical occasion when Her Majesty Queen Elizabeth II and the Hon. Richard M. Nixon. Vice-President of the United States which symbolizes the peaceful cooperation of these two nations to advance the prosperity and well-being of their people. (signed) Elizabeth, R. June 27, 1959.

It seems fitting that we should end our Canadian safari on this most happy note…

8-27-72   GETTYSBURG

And now reluctantly we leave the heart of the Pennsylvania Dutch Country, the Conestoga Valley area, birthplace of the Conestoga wagon, we are told and so in a sense the gateway to the Old West. We are comforted only by the knowledge that ahead lies Gettysburg, a battlefield which two history buffs like the Metayers have long desired to visit. Gettysburg…scene of Lincoln's magnificent address and we are there! We pass the Sleepy Hollow Lodgings proudly announcing the existence of "bullet holes in the house" and head for the National Museum which reputedly houses the world's largest collection of Civil War relics and that famous Electric Map on which one may follow with the commentator the dramatic story of this battle in the war between the States, this "High Water Mark of the Confederacy"", this "turning point of the entire Civil War."

The battle began, we learn, on July 1, 1863 as General Robert E. Lee and his famous Confederate Army of Northern Virginia made an attempt to defeat Gen. George G. Meade's Union Army of the Potomac. Lee's confidence had been bolstered by previous victories over the Union Army at Fredericksburg and Chancellorsville. He had attempted a second invasion of the north but was repulsed at Antietam. Now he and his advisors felt that only a real victory on northern soil would serve to bring about a negotiated peace "on the basis of Southern independence." And so in June of 1863, the Confederate Army of North Virginia marched northward from Fredericksburg into Maryland and Pennsylvania. It had been reorganized into three infantry corps and totaled 75,000 men.

Meanwhile President Lincoln had ordered the 100,000 strong Union Army of the Potomac to maintain a strategic position between the Confederacy and Washington, thus safeguarding the Nation's capital. The two armies were to clash at Gettysburg and the resultant battle, termed "the greatest in American history" would end on July 3 with the retreat of Lee, Longstreet and Stuart and victory for the North. The back of the Confederacy would have been broken, and 4½ months later, on November 19, President Abraham Lincoln would return by train to this historic place to deliver his famous address. The lights in every farmhouse along the railroad right-of-way were to burn, we learn, in a dramatic greeting to this man who had preserved the Union and whose address was for all time to "crystallize the ideals for which free men, then and since, have lived and died." The Museum which we visited does indeed house the world's largest collection of Civil War relics. We thrilled to the sight of such fascinating memorabilia as the saddle cover, for instance, which was used by Mr. Lincoln when he rode horseback to the dedication ceremony at Gettysburg National Cemetery where his address was to be delivered; and to the tattered blood-stained litter on which Stonewall Jackson was carried from the battlefield at Chancellorsville after having been shot by his own men in one of the Civil War's most tragic episodes; and the blood-stained table on which his arm had to be amputated in the pre-dawn of the May morning that followed the accident. (This great general died of pneumonia three days later.)

A cloak which once belonged to John Wilkes Booth, Lincoln's assassin stirred tragic memories; as did the personal correspondence of one William McPeck, an ordinary soldier whose unhappy privilege it was to assist in carrying the fallen President from Ford's theater. We were interested to read of the inscription on this all-but-unknown soldier's gravestone: "His spirit gone to the unknown land where he helped usher that of the martyred hero, Abraham Lincoln," it reads. There was General Grant's cigar case, and a framed-under-glass little basket of dried flowers, which were picked on the Gettysburg field on the battle days; by whom, we wondered…and General Custer's Civil War epaulets; and a Confederate drum, its edges badly worn and for an astonishing reason. The drummer, while on night marches would beat the wooden band around the drum head rather than the drum head itself, we learned, because the sound of wood striking wood fails to carry very far and so the danger of disclosing troop movements to the enemy would have been considerably lessened.

Incidentally, we were to see 106 different kinds of bullets, all of which had been picked up on the Gettysburg Battlefield; and to learn that at the battle's ending 37,574 muskets were picked up and forwarded to Washington. Of these 24,000 were loaded; approximately 6,000 had one load each; 12.000 two loads each and one musket had 23 loads. Many of the musket barrels contained untorn cartridges or cartridges that had been placed upside down, rendering the muskets useless. It was at that point, we learned, that our Government began to encourage inventors to develop and submit breech-loading systems.

We were to gaze with awe upon the very chains which were used on the Speaker's Platform on the dedication day. Which one was honored by the presence of that great gaunt figure whose memory dwells so lovingly within the hearts of most Americans, we found ourselves wondering.

And now a bit about the Gettysburg National Cemetery itself. It was one of the first national cemeteries to be established here in the United States. The war-time governor of Pennsylvania, the Hon. Andrew G. Curtin, visiting the Gettysburg Battlefield not long after the tragic battle, was appalled at the temporary graves of the battlefield dead. He initiated a drive to secure funds from the other 17 northern and western states whose fallen troops were buried there, and a more fitting resting place for the Union dead was established. State monuments tower over the graves; and excerpts from Theodore O'Hara's "The Bivouac of the Dead" are etched upon bronze tablets under century-old trees.

"No vision of the morrow's strife
The Warrior dream alarms
No braying horn nor screaming fife
At dawn shall call to arms…
The neighing troop, the flashing blade,
The charge, the dreadful cannonade,
The din and shout, are past…
Your own proud land's heroic soil
Must be your fitter grave;
She claims from war his richest spoil."
Gettysburg-a memorable and moving experience!

9-10-72   KENTUCKY AND LINCOLN

The great state of Pennsylvania falls behind us as we head for Kentucky through a Maryland ablaze with laurel in full and beautiful bloom. The timbered Cococtin Mountains provide a continuing dramatic backdrop for the red-earthed area farmlands through which we are driving…farmlands alive with dainty little foals and their magnificent Maryland sires and dams…

"Welcome to wide wonderful West Virginia," we read; and now it is past Saddle Mountain where Nancy Hanks, the mother of Abraham Lincoln, was born; and through and over and around the Appalachian

Mountains and the Allegheny Mountains and what seems to be an unending series of mountains…and not particularly high ones as peaks go…3,000' or so…but incredibly challenging with their hard hairpin turns and ridiculously sharp angles. It is a hair raising experience, and there is a pregnant silence in the family car as Ted negotiates on nasty bit of roadway after another. "Ted," I say finally in a voice made small by the absence of the breath I am holding in near terror as we drive along. "Do we have to COME HOME this way?" My husband utters his first profanity of the day. "Good God, NO!" he says; after which I breathe easier.

Even Fanny the ever trusty travel trailer that climbed over Wyoming's Big Horn without turning a hair, is having a spot of trouble. The electric brakes with which she is equipped are emitting a burning odor. This is most unusual…and decidedly disturbing. I worry. I worry a lot! "Ted," I say finally, "It really smells badly, our BRAKE, I mean…Is it BAD?"

"Oh, no," says Ted who manages to take everything in his stride in this great old life of ours - or we wouldn't be traveling by trailer over all the winding world - "It isn't SMOKING yet. When it smokes, we'll be in trouble!" Well, it never did smoke, and we never were in trouble, but WOW! It was descent, ascent, descent, ascent…over miles and miles of horrendously curving roadways…a hair-raising journey that found us taking eight hours to negotiate a mere 242 miles…Clarksburg and we visit the Jackson Park Historical Cemetery to view the graves of the Jackson family, including the famous "Stonewall's" father and son…and now we have still more mountains, but not such wild ones. There are misty scarves draped about the timber-covered heads of this far softer chain, with an exposed mountainside revealing an extraordinary sight - layer upon layer of golden sand and amethyst and rose and garnet rock, with here and there a layer of grave gray granite. A fascinating sight geologically and otherwise…Night falls over Virginia. We settle ourselves in a beautiful trailer park close by Huntington; to dine and then to visit one of the many shops that feature the handsome hand-blown glass for which this state is famous; and then to return to find our world ALIVE WITH FIREFLIES…millions and millions of fireflies! They cover the ground with silver, and set the trees and shrubs aglow, and lie like myriad stars against the dark night sky. We drift to sleep amid a veritable fairyland, tying our curtains back that we may revel in the sight. We drift to sleep - to waken on a shiny bright June morning to resume our journey…shortly to be welcomed to Kentucky.

We leave the parkway to head over the Lincoln Heritage Trail toward Abraham Lincoln's birthplace not too far away, and thrill to find the park in which the memorial to this magnificent American is located ENCLOSED WITH SPLIT RAIL FENCES; and to behold-etched in glass upon the window of the visitor's center - the figure of this man among men. His words speak to us from the huge memorial window.

"I was born, and have ever remained in the most humble walks of life," we read. "Every man is said to have his peculiar ambition…I have no other so great as that of being truly esteemed of my fellow men by rendering myself worthy of their esteem." The words of the American president are followed by William Taft's assessment of the man. "His mind was luminous with truth, his conscience was governed by devotion to right, and the tenderness of his heart was only restrained by his intellect and his conscience."

"The story of the Lincoln family interest us. Abraham Lincoln, the President's grandfather crossed the mountains into Kentucky in the early 1780's we learn, where he was ambushed and killed by an Indian. His son, Thomas, left fatherless at the age of ten, grew to be a man of simple tastes and rustic nature. a carpenter, he settled in Elizabethtown where he met and married Nancy Hanks in 1806. A child, Sarah, was born to the couple in 1807 and in 1808 with another child due shortly, Thomas Lincoln purchased for the sum of $200 the 300 acre Sinking Spring Farm in the vicinity of Hodgen's Mill.

The Lincoln family moved into a tiny one-room cabin on the place, located near the huge limestone spring which had given the farm its name, and which still remains…and here, on Feb. 12, 1809 Abraham Lincoln was born.

And now a bit about that one-room cabin in which the man who was to preserve the Union first beheld his corner of America. It is preserved for all time within a handsome memorial building that towers at the top of 56 stone steps…one for each year of the Great Emancipator's tragically short life.

It's a handsome Memorial...a fitting setting for the birthplace of Lincoln. Erected from funds obtained by popular subscription from 100,000 Americans - mostly school children - its 16 ceiling rosettes symbolize Lincoln as having been our 16th President. It was designed by John Russell Pope; and the edifice is constructed of Connecticut pink granite and Tennessee marble; and it reads, "Destined to preserve the Union and free the slave."

The log house itself is simple and crude and small and happily perfectly preserved. So is the limestone spring for which the farm was named; and a huge impressive boundary white oak that in the era of the Lincolns represented a landmark and is listed on the original 180-5 survey of the farm area that was to be purchased by the Lincoln family. "The only LIVING thing from the time of Lincoln," our guide informs us. It's a towering 90' tree with a trunk 6' in diameter and a spread of 150' or more; and it is reputed to be at least 300 years old, we're told. We view it and photograph it...It and the spring and - with awe - the cabin itself.

Incidentally at the Visitor's Center we are privileged to examine the family bible of Thomas Lincoln, the President's father...and to learn that he lost the Sinking Spring Farm after a mere 2½ years of ownership... because of a defective land title. AMERICANA!

MONTANA

Leaving Yellowstone National Park we find ourselves almost immediately in the "Big Sky Country" of Montana, and we view for the first time our American Rockies. They lie beyond the wild Yellowstone River that races beside us, fed by their melting snows. We pass forlorn little abandoned log cabins, their sod roofs rotting and an occasional herd of cattle.

We have learned that the road to Yellowstone is closed from November 1 to May 1, and as we view the high snow-capped Rockies and the desolate land that leads there, we understand the restriction. Lilac, purple and white, now in ridiculous bloom everywhere is the one colorful note in a stark and almost forbidding landscape that leads fortunately after not too many miles to the lush and lovely Shields River Valley. The river, we are told, was named by Captain William Clark of the Lewis and Clark Expedition in tribute to the bravery of John Shields, a member of his heroic band. This is the river at the mouth of which the Captain and his gallant men camped in 1806 when, guided by Sacajawea, the Shoshone squaw, they explored Yellowstone on their return trip from the west coast.

****

It's an historic land through which we are driving, lying as it does along the old Bonanza Trail over which, during the sixties, the scout Jim Bridger guided those early emigrants in their wagon trains from Ft. Laramie in Wyoming to Virginia City - through what was then decidedly hostile Indian country. Bridger, we are told, led his settlers up this valley from Yellowstone; he followed Brackett Creek crossing the Continental Divide to the west, and reaching Bridger Creek along which he proceeded to the Gallatin Valley - through an unknown untamed wilderness. The courage of the pioneers!

****

The realization that we are on the historic Lewis & Clark Trail is an exciting one. Its fun to be an easterner living the western history of which we have read so much. Through the Smith River Valley and we are in the Lewis & Clark National Forest, the which we appear to have all to ourselves. Through Cascade County with its huge affluent ranches, and Great Falls, a trim city of 10,000. The farmlands now lie against the sky in perfect symmetry, a brown field, a green field, a field of stubble, a crop fully ripened moving like flowing silk under a summer breeze - a vast natural patchwork quilt of pastoral land that pleases the eye as it sweeps toward the horizon.

****

We continue to drive along the Lewis & Clark Trail and the Old West Trail, with history rising to meet us all along the way. Just beyond Dupuyer we come upon an area colored by the memory of Captain Meriwether Lewis who explored this region along with three of his companions. The date was July 26, 1806, and they were camped with a group of Gros Ventres Indians, we are told, on Two Medicine Creek. The Indians attempted in the dead of night to steal the explorers' horses and weapons, and in the fighting that followed two of the Indians were slain.

****

This is the kind of tale we hear in this Indian country through which we are now passing, a land rich with the lore of tribes previously unknown to us, like the Pikuni, and the Piegans and the Bloods and others. We are in the Blackfeet Indian Reservation, a 2380 square mile area housing an Indian population of 6,400 and encompassing 180 miles of trout streams and famous lakes like Duck and St. Mary's and Two Medicine Lake. This is an open range and motorists are warned to watch for stock on the roadways, and we do, and it is there.

****

We pass a group of berry-brown Indian children busily engaged in catching butterflies in a net amid the flower-flocked fields that are black with grazing cattle.

The Rockies that now lie ahead of us are barren and bleak and quite awesome to contemplate as they thrust their snow-capped crowns almost defiantly, it seems, through the blue of a summer sky. Our destination is Montana's Glacier National Park and we reach the town of St. Mary where we find we must drive an extra two miles of gravel road to reach the K.O.A. Kampgrounds. The K.O.A. Kampgrounds that lie along the way are our holiday Inns. The do indeed "pamper the camper" as their commercials suggest; and the setting of this particular one is quite wonderful. It lies in a lush valley with pine-covered hills and snow-capped mountains on all sides. We walk about the place to find a wonderful mountain stream that will sing us a lullaby by night, and ice-cold natural springs from which we may drink. Tiny prairie dogs raise their inquiring faces from their tunnel entrances as we pass, and wildflowers lie in a maze of color against the incredible green of the fields that are fed with the melting snows of the glaciers that lie forever about them.

***

Sunday morning and Church services of all faiths are held in the recreation hall of a nearby motel at St. Mary Lake where, incidentally, we dine; after which having left our trailer back with its pamperers, we set out to tour the area.

****

Grinnell Glacier is our initial destination and we look forward to it eagerly as we have to date only viewed these phenomena from afar - from the roadways or the moraines that lie before them. Grinnell's present day glaciers, we are told, unlike those we shall see as we reach the Canadian Rockies, are a mere 4,000 to 8,000 years old and are not remnants of the Ice Age at all. Strangely enough they reached their peak around 1900 have actually decreased since that time both in volume and surface.

****

During the Ice Age from about 100,000 years ago to 10,000 years ago, we learn, this valley was filled with ice when by grinding and scouring and moving carved the Glacier Park Valleys into their present exciting forms. One may visit Grinnell Glacier, we are told, only by taking an all-day naturalist conducted trip along a thirteen mile trail. It leaves the hotel each morning, and so we postpone our exciting adventure until the following day, taking a scenic ride around the Park instead, with a stop at the glacier-fed Swiftcurrent River and Lake, the slate-gray waters of which keep reminding us of the Alpine rivers we encountered a few years back in Switzerland.

****

We return to camp for a "fun" evening. We had met a delightful couple from Tinley Park, Illinois earlier in the day - Charles and Mildred

Austendorf - and had swapped travel yarns with them and their lovely daughter Barbara, a sophomore at the University of Illinois and a journalism major; and as we were about to join them for coffee in their handsome holiday trailer, a huge Airstream hove into view and parked merrily fifty yards away. "It's Carter and Liz Ayres!" Ted said excitedly. "It CAN'T be!" I said. We had left these two delightful people from Maryland away back on the Ohio Turnpike where we had met them a few days after leaving Braintree. What a lark we had had with the two seasoned trailer travelers who had howled with delight upon learning that we had not as yet even stepped foot into a trailer park and scarcely knew one end of our brand new trailer from another; and had, nonetheless, set out on a three month's jaunt into the unknown, without turning a hair... And what fast friends we had become from the very beginning.

****

"It HAS to be Carter," said Ted. "That HAT!" and to be sure, Carter Ayres sported the weirdest fisherman's hat we ever hope to behold...It WAS Carter's hat and we had indeed found our friends and what a grand reunion followed - a reunion that extended far into the early hours and, with an exchange of now firmly fixed routes, was to be repeated at Banff and at other places along our fabulous way.

****

This was to be one of the big "pluses" of trailer traveling, this meeting and forming friendships with people from all parts of this big and beautiful country of ours - the kind of thing that had not happened in the motels and hotels we had frequented in previous journeys across our lovely land. Unless one elected to haunt the cocktail lounge, evenings could be rather dull with entertainment a must. Not so in a trailer park. Here, everyone who arrives is everyone else's immediate neighbor. Friendships ripen fast, and the people we were to encounter would color our journeying and enrich our lives by sharing their adventures to which they seemed as responsive and beautifully attuned as we ourselves. Ah yes, this traveling by trailer is the only way to go - or have we ventured that opinion before?

MORE ON CALIFORNIA

The Humboldt Redwoods State Park...Within this 43,000 acre wonderland that is located in the Eel River Basin of exciting northern California we witnessed with a feeling of utter awe the magnificent forests of Sequoia Sempervirens, primeval coast redwoods two thousand years in age.

For 160 million years, we learned, immense redwood forests have existed in this planet of ours. Geologic and climatic changes have destroyed a variety of species; nonetheless, since the age of the dinosaur the redwoods have somehow managed to survive.

The coast redwoods of California are generally conceded to be the tallest of all living things; many of the magnificent specimens reach a height of 350'. Statistics, however, tell little or nothing of the grandeur of these dense groves of trees that lie upon the alluvial flats beside the streams of the California north country. The immense soaring trunks covered with rough bark in a rust red hue; the soft green of an amazingly delicate and lacy foliage; the lush moss green of the forest floor with its carpet of growing things; and the silence...the majestic grandeur and serenity of a silence that speaks eloquently and loudly of all the wonder that is Creation...the flawless beauty of the whole lifted our hearts in soaring gratitude to Him who has given us the untamed unequalled beauty of this land that is our own. the redwoods have survived the forest fires that raged throughout the ages. They can survive, we were told, extensive damage by fire; and they will work at healing the scars of fire for a century if need be, or even longer. The floods that have swept over this savage land throughout long ages past may well have left a deep deposit of silt about the trunks of these forest giants; they merely commence to establish NEW root systems as the waters recede-root systems that have soon replaced the former new buried roots. Countless small redwood seedlings, meanwhile, take root in the new silt that now covers the earth and is so essential for their germination...Hardy sprouts will appear about a stump or from the roots of a felled tree. Not for nothing has this giant of the forest been named "sempervirens," meaning "the everliving Ravens and huge golden eagles fly against the sun as we leave our comfortable trailer park in "Myers Flats" (doesn't that sound exciting???) and head toward San Francisco once again. The mountains hereabouts are anything but high by previous standards, they are, however, incessant; and we continue to curl around them over a highway that curves…and curves…and curves…

We drive through the city of Asti where we are besieged with billboard invitations to visit and taste the wondrous wares of the famous Italian Swiss Colony Wine preserve; Ted, however, feels that he will need all his faculties operating at peak performance to take our Trailer over the final 100 miles to san Francisco where we plan to stay and do the fabulous city in depth. and so we pass it by…

It is extremely warm. The thermometer reads 94 degrees and it will reach 100 by noon, we are told by the service station attendant. Vineyards lie against the warm sides of the hills. WE pass the Wells Fargo Bank - another bit of the Old West! A weathered poster offers "$100 reward. Deposit $827 for 2 years at Wells Fargo Bank." Ingenious!

Through Marin County and we pass the Civic Center and the Hall of Justice, two magnificent structures in modern architecture, their pale blue dome-like roofs lying against the deeper blue of the sky in a dazzling color contrast.

Past the Mission of San Rafael Arcangel; then over the bridge at Richardson Bay as the sign emerges - "Golden State Bridge - San Francisco!" And San Francisco Bay lies there beneath us, the bridge towering above, looking precisely as it has looked in a thousand tantalizing T.V. sequences. "Lafayette, we are here!" I say triumphantly; "Lafayette" is tensely absorbed in the horrendous task of keeping our property afloat in a sea of the most enormous trucks and buses I have ever encountered, each one racing toward the big city at what appears to be a hundred miles or more.!"

The bridge crossed we proceed down 19th Avenue, drive through a mountain tunnel and pass the Park Presidio. We have encountered a superfluity of "hippies" in our travels -particularly in Banff, Alberta, where Ted had almost to be restrained from tackling a rugged young American defector with Old Glory sewn to the seat of his trousers. The Hippie colony that greets our eyes at the Presidio, however, is unbelievable in size and content.

The architecture that lies about us is, understandably, Spanish in style. we drive past PARKMERCED, a gorgeous "Residential Community owned and operated by the Metropolitan Life Insurance Company." How about that???

Trailer parks in and around San Francisco, we speedily learn, are negligible and so we continue on fifty miles or so to San Jose where we settle down in the Mobil Country Club, a fantastic private park, complete with Olympic size swimming pool, restaurant, beauty shop, bus service, a recreation center, whose décor might well rival a Hollywood set, and with a garden and shade trees adjoining each beautifully laid out, large trailer space. We settle down to swim in the big pool and lie on our chaises under the flowering trees and to so fall in love with our surroundings as to stay a full eighteen days.

San Francisco is a bare hour's drive away. We shall visit there several times-boarding the famed Cable Car at the corner of Eddy and Powell Streets as we head inevitably for Fisherman's Wharf with all its sights and sounds and enchantment. The car comes clanging down the hill to a turntable located in the center of the intersection, where stalwart employees of the line turn it manually for a return trip up the hill. There is ever and always an enormous crowd waiting. WE and they board the car. The more adventurous of the tourists cling to the sides of the Cable Car, laughing gaily as it rides straight up and down the sides of one hill after another. We are inside the car, however, the merriment here is equally as great as passengers hop on and off the car while in transit. We stop to visit Lombard Street, "the crookedest street in the world." It is red brick walled and delightful to behold, winding as it does through the sculptured landscaping that adjoins the road. FISHERMAN'S WHARF. We stroll through the colorful area, stopping to admire the fishing boats that lie at anchor and to nibble at fresh shrimp and crab and sweet hard crusted Italian bread. Dinner time finds us heading optimistically for Joe DiMaggio's, we invariably tire, however, of waiting for hours in a long queue of people and settle instead for Alihoto's or Fisherman's Grotto where the seafood is quite as wonderful though we fail to catch a glimpse of the fabulous "Joe." Oh, those oysters and prawns and scallops and the rest...

A ride around the Bay aboard the "Harbor Princess," a harbor cruiser. Above it a blue and white pennant flies, reading "Save the Bay," and I remember our S.O.S Campaign back home to "Save Our Shores." the boat whistles sound their warning; strains of the inevitable "Anchors Aweigh" float upon the golden breeze; and then it is "All aboard. all hands make ready to cast off lines." We look back upon the receding shoreline. Telegraph Hill…the Mark Hopkins Hotel where on a subsequent visit we shall like all good tourists repair to the "Top of the Mark" for cocktails and a view of the skyline…

The streets of San Francisco run like shiny sun-bright ribbons in perfectly straight lines upon the myriad hills upon which the city is built. we had been warned on this particular day to wear heavy clothing; San Francisco people were saying and so was the weather, man, it was bitterly cold. We donned everything we owned for this special trip which would include a sail around the Bay; you may well imagine how happy we were when we found Fisherman's Wharf basking in the high seventies…

The sight of the Golden Gate Bridge from the Bay brought our hearts to our throats. "I hope it will be fog-draped," I had said to Ted. it was. The ghostly gray stuff lay draped like a giant scarf about the towers that rise 746' in the San Francisco air. And now we are abreast of Alcatraz, the "Rock," about which there will be more next week…MORE ON GASPE

That clever little "Time Machine" we use locally when the Town's fifth graders visit historical center - Thayer House - to bring the small fry back in time to days long gone, would not be needed in this peace-filled, colorful, centuries-behind-the-rest-of-the-world corner of Canada. One is there already!

We leave Perce and curl around Mont Blanc via a dizzying series of sharp descents and hairpin curves that remind us unpleasantly of Wyoming's "Big Horn" Mountain. The situation is further complicated by road construction that manages to toss the family car and its occupants to such a degree that we fear for the safety of Fanny, that faithful little gal that trails behind us. she survives the journey, however, you will be happy to know; and so do we!

The scenery sends us both into a stunned admiring silence, however, as we finally descend. There is the ocean, matching the deep blue of the sky with a blue all its own; the mountains, a hundred shades of green relieved here and there by the broad ice gray of a host of waterfalls.

The "Rock" of Perce is clearly visible-arch and all- twenty miles away across the shining waters of "Mal Baie" (Bad Bay). we wonder what is bad about it; it looks gorgeous. Later we are to learn that a naval engagement, disastrous for the French, took place there.

White church spires everywhere send their messages of faith skyward. Caves line the shores where the hungry sea seeks eternally to devour the towering cliffs above. This is the Gulf of St. Lawrence and at this point on the Gaspe soft silver beaches and coves line the shore for miles. Great sweeps of daisies and buttercups in full summer bloom cover the fields like a fall of snow flecked with rich butter-pats.

Gaspe itself - a bustling town. Jacques Cartier planted a wooden cross here on the hilltop on a July day in 1534, claiming Canada for France as he did so. Today there is a huge stone cross to mark the site, and as for the French influence so dearly desired by the explorer - it is not quite as discernable here as elsewhere on the Peninsula. As a matter of fact, we learn, a large part of the population is descended directly from those United Empire Loyalists who fled our own young struggling country after the Revolution. We leave the little town, where in one of Canada's oldest fish hatcheries, two million salmon and trout fry are produced annually for deposit in the lakes and streams that dot the area.

And now the land really begins to come into its own as we drive along Gaspe Bay. The sea is steel like here--so dark is the deep cold blue of it - and the timber covered mountains rise starkly out of its exciting depths; with the highway running between. The headwinds are wild; and Ted must keep a firm grip upon the wheel; and for once we are rather happy that Fanny is loaded to the gunwhales with those gorgeous rock specimens I have been beachcombing daily to acquire.

Thousands of golden cod are drying on racks as we drive leisurely through Riviere -au-Renard, a dear little fishing port near the northeast tip of the Gaspe. the population of this tiny settlement is a blend of French and Irish and for a fascinating reason, we learn as we stop here for lunch. A ship carrying Irish immigrants fleeing the Famine was wrecked near the Cap-des-Rosiers and the survivors of the tragedy elected to settle there.

We settle ourselves in a beautiful trailer park near Gros Morne (Big Bluff) where a towering sea wall struggles vainly to hold back a tide that is sending great geysers of spray upon the curving roadway. The mountains on our left are now black in color with the shale clearly visible upon them. We are told by our trailer park manager that they are formed of limestones conglomerate and shale and date back to the mid-Ordovician period.

The shore which is visible beneath the wild breakers that are pounding in from the sea is utterly devoid of sand. Instead, great jagged layers of this strange black rock - with here and there a layer of white-fold in toward the mountainside. The road will run for perfect miles like this, the sea wall on our right holding back the wild devouring surf that roared against it at high tide…the mountains rising on our left, now stark and black; now timber-covered and lovely.

We walk by the sea, Ted and I, when the night is all but come, and the tide is going out. It is actually the St. Lawrence River, however, at this point the sea has asserted its dominance over the mighty salt water stream that will traverse the very heart of Canada. At low tide the ocean floor is strange indeed…layers of uplifted rock with channels running between them. What sand there is, is dark gray and volcanic - all but black-and the magnificent cold steel blue of the sea lies against it like a poem. Sunset adds its high dramatic note of scarlet and of gold; and when the moon appears the world is silver.

Ted and I lie on our chaises as the surf whispers or roars, thrilling to the beauty of this most remote of lands where children wave a greeting as we pass, and bread is baked for us in open ovens out-of-doors…great golden loaves that invite one to gorgeous gluttony; and fishing families live precisely as their forbears did - earning their living from the bounteous sea and seeking no more from life than the privilege of dwelling here in this enchanting place.

Ste-Anne-Des-Monts next as we reluctantly leave Gros Morne to journey further along the Gaspe. Here, high above the mountain is a huge cross that, honoring the patron saint of sailors, may be seen for miles up the broad St. Lawrence. And now we reach the delightful resort areas of the Gaspe with their soft sand beaches and infinitely softer seas.

We stop to visit Le Moulin Historique de Sainte-Luce. (The Old Mill). Here an immense water wheel, twenty feet in diameter, still turns a shaft which turns three grinding stones. The wheat to be ground falls into the grinding stones, we are told, and then proceeds down a shaft and into a sifter. The construction of the mil which was begun in 1803, is almost entirely of wood. The gear is of metal, however its teeth are wooden; and an axle of wood turns on a stone bearing.

The mill has what we considered a fascinating history. It dates back to the era when the cultivation of wheat was decidedly profitable and when it was produced locally in such large quantities that the wheat was exported to larger areas.

One Joseph Drapeau who was at that time proprietor of the Lessard Seigniory (the domain or landed estate of a French seigneur under feudal tenure - this ceased in 1854) built the mill which was to be used as a communal one during the period of seigniorial regime. Water was supplied by the Ruisseau a la Loutre which also furnished power for the settlement's other mills. By 1848 the mill had fallen into such disrepair that the miller feared to use it and the farmers of the region were obliged to carry their wheat to Rimouski to be ground - a rather long journey which angered them each time they had to undertake it. One day in July of 1848 they decided to put an end to the situation. They met and before a notary issued an ultimatum to the miller. "Either you rebuild the mill," they told him, "or we will do it ourselves." The record of that historic meeting delighted us.

"Today, 25th day of month of July, 1948…at request of Messrs. Andre-Elzear Gavreau, simeon Joseph Chalifoux, etc…(a long list of names), the notaries public J.B. Pelletier and colleague Pierre Gavreau traveled expressly to residence of Melchoir Rehen, in parish of Saint-Germain, where we have found Mrs. Luce Drapeau, proprietor and co-seignioress of the fiefs and seigniories of Lessard Lepage, Thivierge and other places…and we have notified and pointed out to her that the communal wheat mill presently located on La Loutre stream…is in a state of near ruin, that the structure of building is tilted over and the plumbing system is not working because of decay, that the interior of said mill, both mechanics and movable parts wise, are also insufficient and worn out…(that the farmers) now are actually obliged to travel to Rimouski to have their grain milled, at a distance, for most of them, of from 5 to 6 leagues from their homes…that the said mill needs to be rebuilt in the new and that it should be larger than the one now threatened with ruin, and that this should be done during the present year…in default of which…the above-mentioned petitioners and tenants will build it at their own cost and expense."

Joseph Drapeau's heirs bowed to this formal complaint and a magnificent stone mill replaced the wooden shack, so beautifully equipped that Sainte-Luce became a most important flour-milling center. After the abolition of the seigniorial tenure in the year 1856, the stone mill ceased to operate as a communal affair though milling continued until the streams that operated it became - with road construction and area development - mere trickles that could do nothing more useful than finding their way to the sea.

The flour mill is silent now, however it has become a "must" for tourists with its government-restored buildings housing a treasured small bit of a past that is forever gone.

9-3-72   MORE ON GETTYSBURG

It's a beautiful spot, the last resting place of those fallen heroes of Gettysburg, the National Cemetery…Native wisteria vines have formed a canopy above the handsome brick rostrum from which, for 103 Memorial Days, speakers have sent the immortal words of Abraham Lincoln, the greatest fallen hero of them all, over the sweet Spring air.

The Soldiers National Monument marks the exact spot where on a simple platform THE MAN delivered his dedication address. The corners of this towering granite column are ornamented with four gleaming Carrara Italian figures. Allegorical in concept, they represent PLENTY, PEACE, WAR and HISTORY, with high above them the soaring GENIUS OF LIBERTY. The northern and mid-Western states, whose honored dead lie sleeping in this silent place, are represented by a band of 18 stars. The figures are the work of Randolph Rogers, celebrated American sculptor of the Civil War period, and one J.G. Batterson designed the monument.

Abraham Lincoln…we pause upon the spot to re-read for the thousand th time his immortal words…words that were to ride the winds of history and reach all corners of the world forevermore.

Fifty years later Lord Curzon, then Chancellor of England's Oxford University, was to visit Cambridge University and addressing the student body on "Modern Parliamentary Eloquence" cite as three "supreme masterpieces of eloquence in the English language" THE TOAS OF WILLIAM PITT BEFORE AND AFTER ADMIRAL NELOSN'S VICTORY AT TRAFALGAR, ABRAHAM LINCOLN'S GETTYSBURG ADDRESS and ABRAHAM LINCOLN'S SECOND INAUGURAL ADDRESS.

We wander about the cemetery grounds. The massive stillness is broken only by the singing of a spring wind in the century old trees... trees that include the European purple beech, its brilliant foliage exciting us to admiration, and the rare gingko tree, reputedly the world's oldest known species. Our guide's strange stories move us - stories like that of Sergeant Amos Humiston whose grave we visited.

The body of an unidentified Union soldier, he said, had been found in the streets of Gettysburg, a daguerreotype of three small children clutched firmly in his hand. Word of the incident went out, and a Philadelphia lawyer conceived the idea of having copies of the photograph struck and forwarded to leading Northern newspapers in the hope of identifying the fallen soldier.

His ruse worked and a Portsville, New York mother learned tragically of her widowhood. she hastened to the Pennsylvania town and national attention was focused on the incident. It was then that a movement to establish a SOLDIERS' ORPHANAGE at Gettysburg sprang into being. It instantly gained momentum. Funds poured in from Sunday School children throughout the North and the State of Pennsylvania contributed funds and granted the new organization a charter, and so the SOLDIERS' ORPHANAGE WAS BORN.

Each year the orphans were permitted to lead the Memorial Day Parade and to strew flowers on the graves of the fallen heroes in the National Cemetery. The SOLDIERS' ORPHANAGE was regrettably, short-lived. It lasted a mere ten years, however, its memory lingers on as each year on Memorial Day Gettysburg school children decorate the graves in the National Cemetery and Civil War students look back upon the Soldiers' Orphanage and remember...

We visited another interesting grave, that of Private George Nixon, great-grandfather of our President. a member of Company B, 73rd Ohio Infantry Regiment, he lies buried in the Ohio plot, a place which Mr. Nixon has visited both as President and as Vice President, to place a memorial wreath upon his ancestor's grave.

We were to have a glimpse of the Battle of Gettysburg from another point of view as, upon an overlook at the famed Battle of Gettysburg Cyclorama, a park ranger, attired as a Confederate soldier, was to share with us the thoughts that would have raced through his mind on that tragic July day when the battle ended.

"Two years ago, Saturday morning," he said, "I was goin' to town to buy grain. ridin' into Leesburg (Virginia) I heard people yellin'. We bombarded Fort Sumpter! we're goin' to make a new Confederate States of America!"

"They were offerin' a new gray uniform and $13 a month and a new gun and maybe the cavalry. I joined with Stonewall Jackson. They called him 'Old Bluelight' cause he had pretty blue eyes. Jackson's Foot Cavalry, they called us. I followed him to Chancellorsville, where we licked the Yankees; but Jackson was wounded, the surgeon removed his arm and he died of pneumonia. Then I fought with A.P. Hill, 'Baldy Hill...'"

"I ain't fightin' for slavery. I don't own no slaves. and I ain't fightin' for States' rights. I don't even know what it means. I'm just a farmer. Only had two years education. Can read and write got it though! I'm fightin' for my land - 45 acres south of Leesburg - rollin' hills and a stream and cowsfrom HIS daddy. and chickens and pigs. I got it from my daddy and he got it from his daddy and his daddy "My Ma wrote me last week. she said Yankee soldiers was tearin' down my fences - fences I built with the sweat of my brow-tearin' 'em down for firewood, and eatin' my cows and chickens and pigs. well, no Yankees' goin' to take that land from me. that's one reason I'm fightin'; and I'm fightin' for a man named Robert E. Lee. He's my best friend and he don't even know my name. "Them Yankees are setters. They just set on them big hills yonder but we did all the fightin'. Started off with 75,000. Lots of boys I set with, and marched with and ate with ain't goin' to be goin' home; but we ain't goin' to quit. I ain't goin' to quit...only if I get killed or if Lee tells me I don't have to fight anymore the soldier described his uniform...an ancient felt hat with a brim. "Saw an old farmer standing on the side of the road and I just naturally reached out my hand. He don't need it much as I do. Keeps the sun out of my eyes and the rain out of my face; makes a good pillow at night…" and a shirt, "Ma made this shirt - homespun." and pants… "Yankee pants off'n a dead Yankee. Figured where he was goin' he wouldn't need those warm wool pants." and shoes… "Summer time I go barefoot. Come winter I'll borrow some from some Yankee who don't need them anymore." and a haversack… "Keep my valuables init; a cup, hard tack, a knife for whittlin' a harmonica, a sewing kit, letter from home, spare underwear." and a bayonet… "Put a rabbit on the end and turn it over the fire; stick it in the ground and stick a candle in it at night for writin' letters." and an 1861 Mississippi Rifle.

The soldier fired the rifle. The smell of powder assailed our nostrils and floated in mid-air. "You wanna know something?" he said. "You wanna know what this here battle was like? Well now, you just multiply the smell of that powder by 97,000 Union and 75,000 Confederate soldiers and string it out for 72 hours. That was the Battle of Gettysburg!"

11-12-72 MORE ON NEW MEXICO

Most of us have been stirred and saddened by the many alarming stories that have come to light of late - via a series of best-selling writings - of the tragic fate of those first fascinating Americans who roamed our forest lanes - the Indians!

Now in New Mexico we were to come face to face with their culture - to explore the ruins of their ancient pueblos and to look back upon their earliest civilizations…it was to be one of the highlights of this year's summer safari; and a revelation indeed; for as early as 13,000 B.C., we were amazed to learn, ELEPHANT HUNTING nomads had roamed the plains of what is now New Mexico and Arizona, following the herds of elephants and bison that were to be found there.

By 5,000 B.C. the land's first FARMERS were building shelters of brush, and hunting smaller animals. Their food included the corn and squash they had learned to plant each spring and the berries and nuts and seeds they had found in the forest come fall. We delighted in the museum relics of that era…the yucca sandals, and the fire-making sticks…

Incidentally we had no idea of the importance of those huge unwieldy yucca plants we had summarily discarded years ago after having been given them as a gift by a gardener neighbor. We had planted the things happily, never realizing the proportions to which they would grow…Our earliest Americans, we now learned, used them not only for the sandals they wore during the more severe weather, but for food and medicine as well.

By A.D. 1, our early American farmers had learned to build more substantial dwellings, built partly underground; and excavated ruins dating around A.D. 700 were to reveal multi-storied adobe buildings - apartment dwellings, so to speak. Pottery making techniques of this era would prove to have been decidedly well-advanced. We were, as a matter of fact, to marvel at the colorful exhibits of this Pueblo pottery as it had developed by A.D. 1100, as well as at the prehistoric bone and turquoise jewelry and the necklaces of shells, delicately wrought, that we were coming upon in the countless little Indian museums that dot the American West. It was all fascinating, fascinating, FASCINATING…

And now, having explored a number of ancient Indian pueblo ruins to marvel at the ingenuity of our first Americans and to delight in their culture, we decide to visit a MODERN pueblo; and so we head toward Santa Fe and the Santa Domingo Pueblo, over miles and miles of roadway with the desert sand on all sides. The Santa Domingo Pueblo…one of the least changed Indian villages in all of New Mexico, we have been told; and the largest of the Rio Grande Keres Pueblos. We found ourselves happily reloading cameras and planning wild sprees of picture-taking as we drove along, only to have our hopes blasted by a sign at the entrance to the Pueblo "$50 fine," we were warned, "for taking pictures in the Pueblo or bringing a tape recorder" into it…per order of the Governor. Perhaps he feels that the squalor and shabbiness of the village are best left unrecorded, for squalor and shabbiness were indeed to be found there. Interesting sights as well, however, like the little adobe Mission Church, the original bell of which was cast in Spain in 1700, we were to learn, and salvaged when the then mighty Rio Grande flooded the first Mission to be built there. We noted the four small crude stoves, placed against the walls, that provide the only heat for the Indian congregation; and we delighted in the church interior which was bright with colorful Indian figures and fascinating Indian symbols.

We are interested to come across a statement of one Dr. John Polich, Curator of the History Division, museum of New Mexico as it relates to these wonderful old Mission chapels we are finding in the Indian Southeast: "New Mexico is a hostile land which has traditionally sustained only those who would successfully struggle for survival against both the elements and competing men. Indians struggled along centuries before the Spanish arrived. In their turn the Spanish created in New Mexico a remote European enclave.

Their struggle commenced before the first settlement in 1598 and unlike later English settlers on the Atlantic seaboard they had no ocean avenue for support. Their only link with the outside world was a tortuous trail over more than a thousand miles of desert. The coming of the Anglo-American only added another competitor...

The Churches reflect their builders' struggles. Rains, heavy snows, floods and fires constantly threaten their existence. Without constant attention the buildings return to the earth of which they are composed. Yet as long as each exists it projects dignity and provides its faithful a secure retreat in which to implore the blessing of a severe but just God."

And now it is off to visit Acoma, the Sky City, the oldest community in the United States...built between 1629 and 1641, a fascinating sight with its "Enchanted Mesa" and another famous Mission Church, the San Estevan Mission, towering 357' above the plains that surround it. Once this Church housed 3,000 souls, we were told. To build it, materials had to be carried up the mountainside on the backs of the people, over unbelievably precipitous trails. Much of the original building is encompassed within the present Chapel which we view with awe and delight.

The Indian dwellings of today are for the most part constructed of the same adobe clay as those found in the pueblos ruins, we note as we drive across the desert expanse of New Mexico and Arizona. In many of them the family oven still remains outside the building itself and only the addition of doors and windows really distinguishes the Pueblo Dwellings from those to be found among the excavations going on on all sides.

We are incidentally to wander from one of these "digs" to another; and to learn from the Indian Postmaster at NAVAJO that each of the area ranches is dotted with ruins and that we may explore those on his own huge ranch at will.

He is delighted with our interest in things Indian, and assists us in planning an itinerary that will include a drive about the Painted desert and a walk through the Petrified Forest, and the exploration of a dozen additional wonders in between.

MORE ON NOVA SCOTIA

Farewell now to Cape Breton as we head for Annapolis Valley, land of Evangeline; and vivid indeed is the memory of those little girl's tears your columnist shed over the plight of the tragic young Acadian and her lost lover in our favorite Longfellow poem.

Grande Pre- meaning Great Meadow - Evangeline's village. Today it is housed in Grand pre National Park and we find first of all a replica of the original old Church of St. Charles from which on a tragic September day in 1755 the Acadians were expelled from their Canadian homeland. The church is a museum nowadays, housing wonderful collections of Acadian and New England artifacts, and we delighted in such antique treasures as wooden shoes (worn because of the area's wet land), butter molds, a host iron, spinning wheel, oxen yoke, a bench for tapering house shingles, butter churn, etc. Framed conspicuously is the order from Britain's Col. Charles Lawrence to Col. John Winslow ordering him to hold all ships (English) that came into port to be used for deporting the Acadians… to "clear the country of such bad subjects."…And, incidentally, although a list of all men and children deported from Acadia was scrupulously kept and is on exhibit, there is no mention at all of the women who accompanied them.

What were the events that led to the expulsion of the Acadians from Canada, we wondered anew? Well, it was around 1675 when the French made their first populous settlement on the shores of the Basin of Minas at Grand Pre, we were told. They were prosperous and happy there and their contentment irked the occupying English who smarted under the refusal of these Acadians to take the oath of allegiance to the British King, a refusal that stemmed in part from loyalty to their mother country France and partly from their friendship with the Indians who feared and disliked the British.

The English tolerated the situation and matters may have continued at a standstill indefinitely had not one Col. Charles Lawrence been named governor of Canada. He had suffered a military defeat at the hands of the French and so entertained a marked dislike of them; and having decided to "have Nova Scotia British and British to the core", he proceeded to post a series of proclamations designed to harass the mild-mannered French in every way. Their freedom of movement was curtailed; their arms were taken away; they were accused of neglecting their fisheries and their funds. And finally came the order to Col. Winslow that brought about their expulsion to Boston, to Louisiana, to the West Indies and to other corners of the globe...the order commanding "all male inhabitants from ten years up to attend at Church on Fri. 5th at 3:00 p.m. (1755) to hear instructions from the governor."... "Your lands and tenements, cattle of all kinds and livestock of all sorts, are to be forfeited to the Crown, with all other effects, saving your money and household goods and you yourselves to be removed from this his province."

Among those tragic refugees was, of course, Evangeline, the Longfellow heroine who was to seek her lost love Gabriel during all the days of her life.

"the long sad years glided on and in the seasons and places...

Divers and distant far was seen the wandering maiden - Now in the tents of the meek MOVIAN Missions - Now in the noisy camps and battlefields of the army-Now in secluded hamlets, in towns and populas cities - Like a phantom she came and passed away unremembered - Fair was she and young when in hope she began her long journey, - Faded was she and old when in disappointment it ended."

In the historic park are to be found a handsome Cairn, erected to John Frederick Herbin, historian and Acadian descendant who made a gift of the land on which the memorial is located. There's a bust of Longfellow who immortalized the Acadians' story; and "Evangeline's Well", a well dug by Colonel Winslow himself, which with the three huge willows behind it remain today as they were two centuries ago. Incidentally we were delighted to learn that the Acadians kept a large trout in this well to eat whatever insects ventured there. and…most exciting of all…there's an immense bronze sculpture of Evangeline herself…She looks back wistfully on her beloved country and on the rich rocky bluffs of the Basin's sentinel, the majestic Blomidon. It's an unusual sculpture because it was brought into being by two artists, father and son, Acadians "by birth and blood", each of whom saw the tragic heroine in a different light. Phillippe Herbert died with his masterpiece but half finished; his son Henri completed it and if one looks closely upon their creation one can readily see where the work of the two artists begins and ends. FOR FROM ONE ANGLE EVANGELINE AS PORTRAYED BY HENRI IS A BEAUTIFUL YOUNG GIRL! AND FROM THE OTHER, AS SEEN BY THE SENIOR HERBERT, SHE IS A TIRED AND CAREWORN WOMAN, HER EYES DIMMED WITH TEARS… Off next to Fort Anne in which historic park museum we found tucked among the historic memorabilia the following delightful sampler created by one Elizabeth Burket, aged 7 years, in "the year of Our Lord A.D. 1783":

"Thus have I done to let you see What care my parents took of me - Whilst I was yet in infancy -When I am dead and laid in my grave and all my bones are rotten - When this you see remember me that I am not forgotten."

Annapolis Royal next. We visited the "Habitation" recently restored by the "Associates of Port Royal", a group of distinguished citizens of MASSACHUSSETS and Virginia, headed by one Mrs. Harriet Taber Richardson. the lady had summered in Annapolis Royal for many years and having fallen in love with the area's history, had decided the old fort ought to be restored. A fun aspect of the Habitation is the "Order of Good Cheer", America's first social club which was organized by Samuel de Champlain to while away the winter of 1606-07. It drew it's members from the settlements fifteen principal male colonists who gathered each day at noon at the table of the Baron de Poutrincourt. Each of the fifteen served in turn as Grand Master of the feast that followed, a feast to which the area's most influential Indian chiefs might be invited. Incidentally records indicate that one Membertou, a venerable old warrior friend of the French, was always on hand. It was the duty of the Grand Master to prepare and serve a sumptuous repast from the rich rare bounty of the forests and seas about him; and on the last stroke of noon to enter the dining hall, wearing the Collar of the Order of Good Cheer and carrying his staff of office, followed in turn by the remaining fourteen order members, each bearing aloft a steaming or succulent dish. Presumably the feasting went on all day for we learned that just prior to the Grace as the EVENING meal the Grand Master relinquished the badge of office to his successor, toasting the morrow's host in a cup of wine as he placed the Collar about his neck. Incidentally today a la Champlain's Order of Good Cheer Nova Scotia offers those visitors who will spend at least three days within her exciting confines full membership in the "Order of the Good Time." An application for same may be secured from the Tourists' Center upon arrival in this lovely province and the certificates will be mailed from Halifax. The Metayers are still awaiting theirs…so much for Tourism…

Now with beautiful Annapolis Valley tucked behind us it is "Welcome to Yarmouth. World famous seaport", and we are about to explore Nova Scotia's scenic South Shore, returning to Halifax along the beautiful southern coast. A fascinating place Yarmouth! Its historic museum, for instance, houses among its treasures the famous "Runic Stone" which indicates that the Vikings landed on these shores centuries before Columbus. This 400 lb. stone was found in a small cove at the head of the Yarmouth Harbour on the property of one Dr. Fletcher in the early nineteenth century; and it carries a strange Runic inscription.

The well-tooled cuts must have been executed with a highly tempered instrument and a number of translations of this inscription have been offered by archaeologists and runeologists all of whom are in agreement as to its Norwegian authenticity. We liked that of one Olaf Strandwold of Benton Cy, Washington, a man who has translated from a great many original sources, a number of which concur with the early voyages of the Vikings to North American locations. He feels that Leif himself was responsible for the Runic inscription which he claims reads "LEIF TO ERIC RAISES", and indicates that Ericson raised the memorial to honor his father, Eric the Red who then ruled Greenland, the place from which the expedition had sailed.

Incidentally, as if to support this theory a number of ancient cellars recently unearthed in an archaeological dig at Tusket Falls, a scant five miles away, are believed by Norse experts to have been those of the "Great House" of Leif Ericson who in their opinion about the year A.D. 100 established the capital of an American Norse colony there - a colony that was to last for several centuries. And they ask, if the Norsemen were able to navigate the waters from Norway to Greenland, why not from Greenland to Nova Scotia???

There were other delightful treasures in Yarmouth's historical museum...like the old sea chest with a fascinating history. In 1844, we learned, one Capt. Alexander MacKenzie sailed from Valparaiso for London aboard the "Saladin", carrying a rich cargo of silver, money etc. On board were Capt. George Fielding and his son who were being given a free passage home by MacKenzie. Fielding fomented a mutiny killing his benefactor with his own hands even as other mutineers killed all loyal officers and crew members. Later, suspecting the Fieldings of treachery, the mutineers threw both father and son overboard. The Saladin was wrecked near Country Harbour and the criminals arrested and transported to Halifax on a cruiser commanded by one Capt. J.W.E. Darby. Four of their number were hanged; and at a salvage auction the sea chest of both Fieldings, father and evil son, were purchased by Darby, whose grandson, Guy C. Pelton, presented one of them to the Museum.

MORE ON P.EI

From Province House it was but a few steps to the magnificent Memorial Building which was officially opened by queen Elizabeth in 1964. It is a complex of five beautiful edifices- a museum, a theatre, an art gallery, a library, and a memorial hall; and, like Province House, it is built of sandstone from Wallace, Nova Scotia.

The theatre's summer festival was featuring a series of musicals, and suitably enough, we thought, it included "Mary, Queen of Scots", "Jane Eyre", and "Anne of Green Gables." the buildings were a delight to visit, their architecture modern, their appointments colorful and luxurious.

On to Victoria Park next where we stopped to view the historic old Government House, the official residence of the Island's Lieutenant Governors. "Be sure not to miss Fort Edward", we had been cautioned by several of the islanders. We did, admiring the nice neat row of ancient cannons that stood sentinel above the beautiful broad harbor.

We visited Rustico, a typically French settlement, where we were told a remarkable tale. One Father George Belcourt, a forward-thinking Catholic priest was stationed there from 1859 to 1869. It was he who established the farmers' bank, our informant said proudly; however that was not the fact that intrigued us. In 1966, before a number of witnesses who promptly recorded the fact, Father Belcourt appeared in the Town of Rustico, driving an ordinary driving carriage; it was however, being powered by a small steam engine! "It was the world's first automobile!" said our Rustico-an proudly.

This area is, of course, adjacent to the Gulf of St. Lawrence; and tiny fishing villages slumbered in the sun that turns the sea coast ruby red and silvers the incoming tides by way of contrast. At Prince Edward Island National Park we found a "Change House" which turned out to be a cabin where one might change one's clothing for bathing; and we decided to do just that. Cavendish at last - that "gorgeous beach with the silver sand dunes" we had been urged by so many to visit. The Micmac Indians called it "Sandy Beach" and it is just that. The winds however, are wild at Cavendish this day, for P.E.I. is bracing itself for oncoming hurricanes; and the sand is being swirled about along with the people who are attempting to set up their chaises there; and so we decide to forego swimming even though the water IS reputed to be 70 degrees or warmer. we thrill anew however to the dramatic beauty of the dark green pines and firs, the lighter green of rich ripening fields and that gravestones (fascinating) that twenty one American sailors are buried there- the crew of the "Yankee Star" which sank off Cavendish many years ago. there was a twenty second drowning victim and therein lies another tale. The father of the young man had come to P.E.I. to claim his son's remains and was returning with them to the United States for burial when the ship on which he was sailing also went down enroute to America, entombing both father and son in the cold Atlantic.

A visit next to "Green Gables", that fascinating mansion where the memory of the wonderful adventures of "Anne" returned to delight me; and then a visit to the birthplace of Lucy Maud Montgomery, the gifted author of those exciting children's stories. Lucy's own favorite tale, we learned, was "The Story Girl", a story of Rachel Ward and a mysterious blue chest in the corner of the room that was eternally kept tight locked. Such a chest does exist, our informat said, it may be found in the home of Lucy's cousins, the Campbells, in Park Corner, P.E.I., and a replica of the mysterious piece may be seen here in the birthplace. there was other memorabilia to delight us - Mrs. Montgomery's personal scrapbooks, albums of her early prose and poetry, and her wedding dress along with the accessories that completed her wedding costume. I have re-read and enjoyed the Anne of Green Gables since our return.

And now a delightful tidbit from one of our PE.I. news broadcasts. The moose hunting season had opened officially that day and inasmuch as only 1,000 licenses are issued annually there, and there are infinitely more would be moose hunters than available licenses, Canadians had been invited to make application, the applications are then placed in a huge bowl, and one of the game and fisheries officials appointed to draw the first thousand names from the lot. 16,500 applications had been received this year and an unexpected examination of them revealed an interesting fact - some of the would-be moose hunters, it seemed, were applying more than once. One gentleman, in fact, had filed twenty-three separate applications!

"Remedial steps will be taken", said the announcer tersely.

Ours is a beautiful trailer park here at Cornwall; it is located high on a cliff with the bright blue sea before it. There is an entrance to the beach a few hundred yards away, however, Ted and I elected to scramble down the cliff side each evening for our promenade along the shore. We were pipping along the beach one summer evening, gathering our sea shells and our stones, when two elderly ladies hailed us from the top of the dune. they quite easily weighed 250 bs. - each one of them. As a matter of fact even as they the enormity of his merry suggestions struck my Teddy! it is here at Cornwall and from our delightful trailer neighbors Judy and Mel Alexander that we learn another interesting tale regarding Charlottetown, which was named for Queen Charlotte, by the way - the wife of George III of England. The site was selected for a Capital by Capt. Samuel Holland, Canada's first surveyor. And in 1775 the settlement was invaded by a couple of American privateers whose crews literally looted the town; carrying off with them as they left the Attorney General of the Province. He had been functioning as Acting Governor during the latter's absence.

This gentleman was carried off along with a few lesser officials, to the United States where all were quickly released by our General George Washington who "severely reprimanded" the two privateer captains. Incidentally the Great Seal of the Province was carried away as well during this raid, and it has never been returned to the people of P.E.I.

The air is like wine as having moved the family trailer to a Chelton Beach trailer camp - we set out to tour the eastern end of the Island. A sign "Dangerous Crosswind" as we approach Summerside causes us to congratulate ourselves on the fact that we must concern ourselves only with the family car, for dangerous indeed they are; and wild! Summerside is a beautiful seaside town with large lovely shops like Holman's where we pipped about for a bit; and a handsome high tide tinged with pink; and a lighthouse clearly visible across the bay. We drive about over "Lady Slipper Drive" delighting in the great white farmhouses that lie against the sky; the tall church spires that pierce it; and the sea, that purpling above the brick red sandbars, follows us along the way. Flowers are everywhere - wide fields of clover and of daisies, lupins in endless mounds, and those wonderful orange-red lilies that grow on clusters in each family garden. How dearly I wished for the courage to knock upon the door of just one home and seek to purchase a bulb or two of this delightful garden lily!

"Welcome to Port Hill", and to Bideford, to Tignish and to Cape Wolfe where 'tis said General Wolfe stopped off on his way to Quebec in 1759. And now it is home along the shoreline where the setting sun is staining the world a deep dark red and we shall have to wait until morning to walk upon the sands of Chelton Beach where seaweed and sea moss and a lovely pale flower-like sea growth that looks for all the world like orchids, screams to be tucked into the family trailer. "They'll SMELL! says Ted wisely as I make the silly suggestion…We scramble over the rocks which are deep wine in color and stratified and incredibly beautiful. we are hundreds of miles out in the Atlantic her and so, needless to say, strange objects are to be found along these seldom-traveled sands. Prince Edward Island is beautiful; how loath we shall be to leave it!

8-6-72 MORE ON THE AMISH COUNTRY

A Spring dawn in the Pennsylvania Dutch country. A cock crows from afar, awakening the occupants of the scrubbed-clean farmhouses that lie mistily against the morning sky; nighttime dew has fashioned a robe of seed pearls for the fields, and the stars are no more; and there is a stirring in the great barns as the sun rises with a swiftness that is almost startling; to gild the farmhouse roofs and send banners of gold and rose, red-tinged, across the gray-blue ocean of the sky.

An early morning wind carries the sound of birdsong through great trees that move with the slow deliberate steps of ancient crones within our sight.

A Spring dawn that invites even lazy me to rise an don wings and fly.

We are to visit an Amish homestead, the 200 year old farmhouse that once upon a century or two knew the longings and yearnings of the grandsons of the William Penn family. It is an "old order" Amish farm, and the sun is glorious and golden as we reach it. A Water wheel from a nearby creek works as a "cucumber pump" before the weathered farmhouse. The water is pumped to the pump itself, and to a second floor tank from which by gravity flow it reaches all parts of the house, we learn. Fifty years ago running water in the barns was made mandatory by the State of Pennsylvania, we are told. "Well," said our guide, "the Amish women decided that if the COWS were to have inside water so would they!" Daisy, the family donkey, greets us with her own distinctive bray. This particular farm is RENTED by the farm family, the farmer being one of TWELVE children whose parents simply could not afford to purchase for him the traditional wedding gift of a farm of his own. The farmhouse kitchen is primitive but neat. A black iron wood-burning stove with built-in waffle iron stands in the corner…no ELECTRICITY anywhere on the farm-that would constitute a permanent connection with the outside world…a situation shunned by the Amish people. There are no curtains on the windows, "Too FANCY," says our guide. "Besides, window shades provide sufficient privacy." The walls are painted. Amish walls may never be papered, and only painted blue or green - "nature's colors." The early American clock on the kitchen wall shows STANDARD TIME-"God's Time; this daylight saving is simply for YOUR convenience…" The pantry bulges with preserves, and the kitchen furniture, hand-made by the Amish, is decorated with fruits and flowers - "God's decorations" - nothing else! Potted plants line the window sills; no CUT flowers will ever be brought within the Amish home, we are told.

The living room is plain…a decorated bench (not upholstered - "too frivolous!") with six chairs and built-in china cabinet on one side and benches for "House Worship" on the other…a large stove in the center of the room. We seat ourselves upon the bench to learn of the "House Worship" service of the Amish people, and more of the people themselves…There are five types of Amish, we are told. Some are allowed to drive to cars, some only BLACK cars; some whose chrome must be painted black; some colored cars; and some even tractors. An Amish individual may leave the "old order Amish" and try other forms and still return to his original sect. He may try the outside world and return within a year if he finds he is unhappy there.

Each family hosts a House Worship service once or twice a year, and the hostess is obliged to serve everyone (sometimes 150 or 200 people) a simple meal. The service lasts from 8:00am to 12N, and children from two years old up sit through it, "If they act up, they are taken to the woodshed and when they return, they behave," said our guide matter-of factly. A Bishop; two preachers and two deacons may preach, and each for as long as an hour. They hymn-book or "Ausbund" houses the laments of those martyrs to the Amish faith who, imprisoned during the 1500s composed moving hymns to while away the years of their tragic prison terms. These hymns are sung slowly in the manner of Gregorian Chants.

The Amish people practice adult baptism, and the average age for this rite is 16, however, "the girls like to be like their mothers, so they are generally baptized at 12, the boys however, like to get away with as much as they can, and so their average age is 18." Prior to baptism the clothing of small girls may be colored with the exception of red, yellow or orange, however, after baptism, it is BLACK. The Amish prayer cap of white organdy is worn at all times as a sign of the prayerful lives the ladies of the Pennsylvania Dutch country elect to lead. It covers the uncut hair of the Amish woman, which is parted in the center and twisted and arranged in a tight bun.

The Amish man wears a hat at all times, with creased hats worn by laymen and smooth-crowned hats worn by small, un-baptized boys and by clergymen. His suit has no collar, lapels, or buttons; these were all removed by 17th century Amish as a protest against the European soldiers who persecuted them and whose uniforms featured all three. His coat is fastened with hooks; his wife's dresses and the dresses of his daughters with straight pins.

His trousers resemble those of our sailors, but with one fascinating difference. The sailor's trousers originally sported thirteen buttons; and the Amish people being conscientious objectors and this being part of a service uniform - their pants will be made with either 12 or 14 buttons – never 13! Incidentally, small boys wear BARN DOOR britches, adjustable for size. Our Amish farmer uses suspenders; and should his wife PURCHASE his shirts, Heaven forbid - she will remove the pockets to alter them. His shirt buttons will be concealed by a black bow tie, incidentally, until the traditional BEARD of the married Amish man grows long enough to cover them.

An Amish farm is run for the most part by the family, however, outside hands, if needed, need not be Amish. Milking machines with Diesel engines and gasoline-powered farm equipment and home appliances may be used, but never electrically operated affairs. Each farm has a family garden - organic of course-ploughed by the husband and planted, weeded and tended by the wife. Broad-leaf cigar tobacco is an important farm crop, and so the Amish man is permitted to smoke cigars or pipes, though cigarettes are forbidden. Tobacco seed, which is as fine as face powder, must be sowed in a watering can; and, when planted, is covered with hog bristles and moth balls to repel insects, and finally with a protective white cloth covering. It is harvested when waist high, and stored in the barns until it is picked up and purchased in December. This crop, the "Green Gold" of the Pennsylvania Dutch country, is responsible for much of its affluence.

And now a bit about the farm horses of the Amish country. Their carriage horses are already broken to the harness, LOSERS of countless area sulky races, which are sold there at periodic auctions. Both work horses and mules are used for farming, with a preponderance of mules which, though not as smart as horses, EAT LESS! Corn fodder for the cattle is ground up and stored in huge silos, up the outside ladders of which the farmer must climb to shovel the corn down a long chute to receptacles below. The corn at the bottom of the silo FERMENTS, you see…and the Amish farmer feels that his animals are frisky enough! It is decidedly De Trop to be frisky in the Pennsylvania Dutch country… however, WHAT A LAND OF PEACE AND SERENITY IT IS!

8-13-72   MORE ON THE DUTCH

The forefathers of the Pennsylvania Dutch came for the most part from the German Rhineland and many of today's Dutch still speak their "Deitsch" language; however the German word order and the German idioms when carried over into the language of the English speaking Dutch make for some conversational gems indeed!

Around dinner time for instance, one could easily hear "Jacob, come from the woodpile; Mom's on the table, and Pop's et himself done already…" or "Smear me all over with jam a bit of bread…Amos eat your mouth empty before you say…Don't eat yourself full there's cake back yet…the cake is all but the pie is yet…"

And should one ask directions in the Pennsylvania Dutch country, one might well be told: "there's two roads to Smoketown. They are both the same as far, but one is more the hill up…" or "Go the bridge over and the street a little up…Jacob and Jane live the hill over, out where the road gets all…"

And should the matter of the weather come up, one might hear, "The paper wants ome kind of fallin' weather…" or "I sink it's going to make down heavy…It's going to give a thunder gust, it looks like…It's hands-in-the-pocket weather and it's slippy yet…"

And then there are other miscellanea that might bring forth pearls like, "The bus seats are so near (narrow) for me - I sit BROAD…I belled the door but it didn't make…aunt Becky's wonderful sick…She don't feel so pretty good, and they've got her laid down still…Don't horn the machine so, you'll blow the baby awake…Throw Papa down from the haymow, his hat…Outen the dog and make the door shut…Rachel's wearing new shoes on the baby…"

Pennsylvania Dutch proverbs are something else again. We delighted in such words of wisdom as, "Better it is to single live than to the wife the britches give…A plump wife and a big barn, never did any man harm… Kissin' wears out, cookin' don't…"

And now a bit about those HEX signs we were seeing everywhere on the big soaring barns with their inevitable forebays that dot the area - not, to be sure, on the barns of the Amish or Mennonites, but only on those of the Lutherans, Reformed or other church people. "the Gay or Fancy Dutch!" This folk art is, of course, a feature of the homogenous culture that emerged from the melting pot of those original religious refugees from the countries about the German Rhineland…the Amish and the Mennonites, the French Huguenots and the Dutch, Quakers and the Lutherans, Reformed…all of whom contributed to this culture their varying religious customs and their great faith in the God who had brought them to our shores.

We delighted in the stars and rosettes, the teardrops and the whorling "swastikas" and the hearts and flowers of the Hex signs, but why, we kept wondering, were they placed there originally? Were they used to distinguish friend for friend, for instance, here in a strange land. Or to prevent witches from entering the great barns that housed their slowly accumulating possessions? We heard a variety of explanations. At Lancasteris Landis Valley Farm Museum for instance, we were assured of the religious origins of the Hex and shown such interesting memorabilia as an early door latch with crosses carved into the handle bar. All seemed to agree, however, that for the most part the Hex marks were Talismans designed to prevent the entry of evil spirits and to bring good fortune to the struggling farmers of the valleys and foothills and towering mountains that lie between the Susquehanna and Delaware Rivers.

At any rate, we beheld them, fascinated…signs that featured the Double Rosette, apparently the oldest of the Hex symbols. This particular sign, we were told, may be found beside the entrance of an ancient Greek Church in Athens, a church dating back to 1453. And then there was the Single Rosette, which assured good fortune…and the Sixteen Pointed Rosette, which also dates back to that Byzantine Church in Athens on whose walls it may be found.

We LOVED the story of the Irish Hex we viewed - a delightful one that feature a SHAMROCK of all things! There were both Irish and Pennsylvania Dutch troops among the armies of General Washington during the long tragic winter at Valley forge, and to while away the terrible monotony of their days they indulged now and then in a private little battle of their own. On such occasions, we were told, the Irish employed a special chant on their friendly foes. "Hooray for the Irish! They're not very much, but they're a darn sight better than the Pennsylvania Dutch…"

Well, history records that during one of these "battles", an Irishman drew a shamrock on a Dutchman's Hex sign just for luck! The Irish won the fight and the shamrock has been there ever since.

The particular Irish Hex we viewed included the shamrock, of course, "for the luck of the Irish", a couple of "distlefinks" or good luck birds, a heart which symbolized love for one's fellow man, and the Trinity Tulips for faith, hope and charity. It was bordered by scallops indicative of ocean waves, and guaranteeing smooth sailing for life.

We delighted in the special Hex signs for Rain, sun, and Fertility; and those that featured the Double Headed Eagle for strength and courage…and the Mighty Oak for character; the Rosettes and Hearts for love and romance; the Eight Pointed Star for goodwill and abundance; and the Haus-Segen, or House Blessing whose flowers contain a prayer for protection of home and family. And, oh yes, a special bit about the Distlefink we seemed to find everywhere on the Hex signs of the Dutch country. He was the good luck bird of the early settlers, we were told…a goldfinch whose diet included thistle seed and who used thistle down to build his nest and so the early Dutch called him Thistlefinch, a name which, in the Pennsylvania Dutch fashion, degenerated over the years into "Distlefink". LOVED the Pennsylvania Dutch country with its clean shining order and its folklore and its Legends.

10-25-70   MORE ON YELLOWSTONE

The snow-capped mountains are etched sharply against a cloudless sky as we head toward our first glimpse of "Old Faithful"…over the Continental Divide, elev. 8391 to the Old Faithful Basin area, elev. 7367.

A bulletin at the Visitors' Center announces that the geyser "MAY erupt between 10:05 and 10:15," and we seat ourselves expectantly before the giant cone to await the magic moment. A strong odor of sulphur pervades the immense basin area where we note the Little Plume Geyser beautifully erupting and a certain amount of steam pouring skyward from them all. The water temperature, we have been told by a guide, ranges from 190 degrees up.

A thermal basin such as this one is a barren place. There is no soil over the Geyserite and so there is little or no vegetation. Dead trees usually dot the area. What IS a geyser really, we wonder as we await Old Faithful's scheduled performance, and we seek the answer. It's a particular type of hot spring that erupts periodically. The ground water that has seeped to a depth of thousands of feet below the earth's surface is heated by the magma or molten rock buried below and moves by the process of convection following channels that led upward towards the earth's surface. It becomes progressively hotter as it ascends, with bubbles of steam forming until they become too large and too numerous to rise to the surface in the narrow channels that house the water. Eventually they lift the water in the geyser tube and the geyser overflows decreasing the pressure and setting up a chain reaction that results in the water at depth flashing into steam and forcing an eruption of water and steam alike through the vent in the earth's crust. It is rather like what happens in our kitchen pressure cooker, we opine, where we obtain high temperature by heating liquid under pressure in a tightly confined area. Or is it? At any rate, Old Faithful erupts right on schedule at 10:07, first hesitantly, then with a hissing sound and slightly more force to rise suddenly skyward to a height of more than 100 feet with a wild burst of water and steam, that roaring savagely, rolls away toward a now cloud flecked sky; and then to subside gradually over a period of two or more minutes leaving a wondering wave of visitors breathless and awed in its wake.

Fascinated, we walk along the boardwalk that covers the desolate geyser basin, past Surging Spring and the Paint Pot Geysers. The colors that surround these beautiful boiling water pools delight us - the shores of pink and white and yellow and coral are formed, we learn, by bacteria; and the orange and dark green and brown are formed from algae.

"Thin crust area," we read, "for your own safety and the protection of fragile features, STAY ON BOARDWALK." We do. We cross a beautiful river that runs through the heart of this barren bit of the earth's surface that keeps reminding us of the moon shots we witnessed on T.V. not too long ago.

The odor of sulphur is very strong as we walk past one gorgeous geyser after another - past the fountain-type Giantess Geyser, the area around which, we are told, shakes from explosions deep within the earth's heart while it is erupting and the Pump Geyser, with water shooting forth as though literally being pumped from below.

The earth beneath the boardwalk is flooded with steaming water and orange and green with algae as we pass Depression Geyser and the dozens and dozens of other geysers - some large, some small, that dot this fascinating place. We delight in Beehive Geyser which takes the precise form of a beehive and which varies from one eruption in the course of a month to two or three in a single week. these eruptions frequently reach a height of 150 to 200 feet, we are told.

The Metayers spend hours wandering about the boardwalk - sulphurous fumes and all - before returning to the family car for a drive along a wonderful highway with geysers and hot springs rising on all sides. We reach Castle Geyser which has the largest cone of all and is thought to be the oldest of all Yellowstone Park geysers. Here we run into a sudden rain squall, which daunts this photographer not at all as she dashes from the family car, umbrella and all, to catch this marvelous castle-shaped cone prior to and then during an eruption. Goodness, I have just realized that I had termed the snowstorm through which we struggled toward Yellowstone our last bout with precipitation. It wasn't! THIS was…or was it?

Past wildly erupting Rocket Geyser and Riverside Geyser, which rest on the bank of the colorful Firehole River and sends its picturesquely arching column of water gracefully over the river's shining surface. The Firehole is a beautiful river. It runs along the highway dotted by rapids. It tumbles over the huge boulders that block its path - boulders in the crevasses of which pine trees grow.

We visit Morning Glory Pool, an immense boiling water pool of rich morning-glory blue, surrounded by a shore of pure and palest pink - breathtakingly beautiful in the sunlight that has returned to Yellowstone.

We come upon a mother elk and her baby as we drive along and are happy because we are able to catch the sight in film as we pass by.

The little patches and ribbons of green in the thermal basin of Yellowstone provide, we learn, a wonderful sanctuary for many of the higher forms of wildlife. Swans and ducks and geese winter on the waters that never freeze, finding an abundance of food there; and elk and bison escape the deep snows by moving into the thermal areas where plant life grows year round.

The natural aspects of Yellowstone are interesting. Fallen trees are permitted to remain where they lie across the streams and upon the mountainsides and in the fields. There are many of them for the storms are frequent and wild in Yellowstone; and fallen, they provide food and breeding places for insects and assist in maintaining the balance of nature.

We drive past Gibbons Falls (height 84') with the Gibbon River swollen with rain and snow of recent days, roaring beside us; and cross Gibbon Meadows, a rich green area beautifully flat and pine studded, to arrive at the wonderful Virginia Cascades.

On then to the Grand Canyon of Yellowstone, a tremendous gorge whose width varies from 1500' to 4000', and depth from 750' to 1200'. Eroded by decomposed rhyolite layer rock, it is a magnificent sight, its sand and rock and earth blending in a riot of color-gold and yellow and pink and purple - with splashes of black earth, and great green pines clinging to its sides, the roaring river racing through its heart, with the falls wild and white against the whole.

We head toward Tower Falls and Tower Junction climbing the while with the snow growing deeper with every mile. Trough Dunraven Pass, elev. 8859, with its spectacular view of the mountains that rise on either side, pine-studded and majestic; and the valleys that lie beyond with their myriad shades of green blending, form a scene of incomparable beauty.

We pass a huge black bear dining anything but daintily on some poor dear lesser animal, and a huge cow moose at the sight of which I grab my camera and dash madly from the car to be pulled back summarily by an irate husband with the wild and wooly notion that she just might have a mean old bull moose by somewhere ready to pounce on puny photographers. We cross Hayden Valley, "Grizzly Bear Country"where we are cautioned to view wildlife from the safety of our car and I get my darling's point. And we do just that…Over Trout Creek where I have a mental picture of said grizzlies catching a leisurely breakfast on its banks.

We visit Mud Volcano, wildly boiling mud spring; and Dragon's Mouth Spring, whose spectacular belching action results from the escape of steam and sulphurous gases from deep beneath its banks; and whose roaring noise is occasioned by the splashing of water against the sides of the caverns. And we visit Roaring Mountain, with its myriad fumeroles bursting from all angles, tiny vents that carry minor quantities of carbon dioxide and chlorine and other gases as well as steam. Roaring Mountain which once was extremely active but has subsided in recent years and is formed of a gray ash-like substance which, when reflected in the turgid pool that lies before it - a pool dotted with blackened ghost-like tree forms - at an elev. of 8130', presents a decidedly weird picture indeed. Have I given the impression that we saw all this in one day's drive - we Metayers??? I haven't meant to. We spent a week at Yellowstone and could easily have spent a month there. But what a wonderful week it was!

MOUNT RUSHMORE

And on our third day of journeying, we discovered Woodall and Rand McNally and traveled happily ever afterwards - for here, we found, were listed every approved trailer park in these dear United States, together with directions for reaching them, facilities offered - the whole bit! Why, or why had we not investigated these nice little directories in the first place??? At any rate, from here in, like the discriminating trailer travelers we intended to be, our "musts" included pretty surroundings, a swimming pool *heated if possible) or a lush little lake - comfort with a capital "C"…

And so, having journeyed over the "Old West Trail", and through the Badlands of South Dakota, we reached Mt. Rushmore, the second scenic high spot on our cross-country journey. Our trailer park lay in the midst of the mountains, 21/h miles from the sculptured Presidents, that "Shrine of Democracy" we had come to see - a lovely facility, incidentally surrounded by lilac in full bloom. MORNING - and we set out for the Mt. Rushmore Memorial, driving along a curving roadway through immense forests of pine, their fragrance all about us. A bend in the road, and suddenly there he was - 6000' above us on the face of the mountain - The Great Emancipator, his thoughtful brooding profile etched against a summer sky of cobalt blue. Great white cotton clouds were draped about his head, with here and there a rain-swollen cloud mass of gaunt gray, slate-edged…

"Oh, Ted," I breathed, then, "How he must have loved him - Borglum, I mean- the Sculptor…How he must have loved Lincoln…" Teddy Roosevelt emerged as we moved along the highway; then Jefferson; then Washington; each of the majestic heads 60' in height; their wide immortal eyes looking out upon our nothingness with all the wisdom of the ages…Lincoln, we were soon to learn, was the Sculptor's favorite among those four illustrious Presidents whose "lives symbolized and gave birth to the American dream." Washington, who represents the American struggle for independence and the Republic's birth; Jefferson, whose political philosophy of self-government assured a "government of the people, by the people, for the people"; Lincoln, who typifies the nation's permanency, and the struggle for equality among its citizens; and Roosevelt, the Conservationist, whose years in office saw the emergence of America as a determining influence in the affairs of the world.

How did it all begin, this hurling of the Presidential heads against a dark blue Dakota sky??? Well, back in the twenties, we were told, at the invitation of State Historian Doane Robinson, Gutzon Borglum arrived in the Black Hills to consider carving on those granite formations known as the "Needles" the figures of a number of romantic Western heroes. The patriotic and nationalistic artist saw instead an opportunity to create on the smooth-grained granite surface of Mt. Rushmore, a National Memorial which would serve as an inspiration for centuries to come

On August 10, 1927, President Calvin Coolidge handed Borglum the drill bits and he was lowered over the cliff to begin work on the Washington face; and by 1941 - his death having put an end to the immortality the Sculptor was carving into stone - his son completed the head of Roosevelt and put the finishing touches upon his father's dream…now beautifully realized.

And how was it accomplished, the actual carving of these four heads into the mountainside? Well, drillers were suspended in "swing seats" over the face of the mountain, we learned. The seats were controlled by winches - hand operated - and the drillers employed jackhammers to drill holes for dynamiting. Excess rock to within 3 to 4 inches of the surface was removed by blasting; and holes drilled at intervals of 3 inches or so vertically across the surface. A small drill or a hammer and wedging tool were used to wedge off the remaining rock, with the Sculpture brought to its smooth finish by "bumping" with a small air hammer. Incidentally, over 400,000 tons of rock had to be removed before the sculpture was completed…

If the sight of the Lincoln profile had moved us by day, the effect was as nothing compared with the vision of the brooding President when we returned to the scene at eight that evening…a sweep of storm clouds behind it-suggestive, I thought, of the storms that enveloped the land as this beloved President sought to win equality for all men - the immensity of the sky with the incomparable majesty of the pine-forested Black Hills movingly behind it…

A concert orchestra played "America" as the Forest Ranger in charge, raised the Stars and Stripes as a prelude to the drama that was about to unfold, the program that each evening precedes the ceremonial lighting of this National Monument. We sat there in the half-dark within the Amphitheatre that is cut in the heart of the mountain. "Hail to the Chief" echoed and re-echoed among the hills. The majestic faces of the four Presidents looked out across the valley, their great eyes somber and reflective - behind them the sky; before them this magnificent portion of the land they had loved and served. Darkness came gradually over the Black Hills, and with its advent Old Glory, spotlighted from below, began to dominate the scene. The moon appeared suddenly from beneath the clouds. The huge pine trees were black and ragged against a sky that was suddenly, despite the clouds, filled with stars!

Pines have begun to fill in the area beneath the giant carving, thrusting Cathedral-like heads through the mounds of granite chips that lie piled there; landscaping lovingly this scene of incomparable beauty.

The music America loves floated on the summer air; and a profound stillness settled on the Amphitheatre. How, I wondered, did the workmen climb those impregnable heights day after day? What gigantic obstacles did they face??? Well, their story and the story of the Monument itself was soon to unfold upon the summernight, while the Heads would stand there against the clouds – like gods; they were MEN. the fashioners of our beloved Democracy. The Star Spangled Banner added a last magnificent note to the symphony as the program ended and suddenly the four figures were bathed in a beautiful soft white light. The audience rose as one. We had been invited to sing, but I could not sing. Tears kept running down my face and choking my voice in my throat; tears that I saw reflected in the eyes of men and women all about me; tears that blurred the slate blue of the star-studded sky that framed the "gods" above.

"It made me SAD," said a small boy to his mother as we emerged from the Amphitheatre. It made me sad as well, but oh, so hopeful for the future of an America that could produce these giants among men - now immortalized so magnificently against the granite face of glorious Mt. Rushmore…

9-20-70   NIAGARA FALLS

NIAGARA FALLS! The sheer unadulterated wonder of it…the American and Canadian Falls, with pretty little Goat Island in their seething center…

There once lived, we were told, on this - the largest fresh water island in the world - an old fellow who raised goats and cattle for a living.

An exceptionally severe winter had held the area in its grip some years ago, and with the advent of spring area residents found but one lone survivor on the bare bleak place - a goat, half-starved and wretched... The island, which incidentally belongs to the United States, was known as Goat Island from that day forward...There are, in addition, three sister islands in the Niagara River which body of water runs from Lake Erie and is three quarters of a mile in width. The air on the American side of Niagara is fouled with industry. Immense chemical and other plants rear their ugly air-polluting heads, the majority of them having been placed there to utilize the tremendous water power available - all this in the days before the problem of air pollution had begun to trouble humanity.

We drove past wonderful old homes, and across Rainbow Bridge to the Falls. Rainbow Bridge has replaced Honeymoon Bridge, that romantic structure that collapsed on a January day in 1938 when, with the ice 100' thick in the gorge, the January thaw arrived unheralded to break the ice and bring down the immense bridge along with it. The U.S.-Canadian boundary line lies half-way across the river, incidentally.

***

NIAGARA FALLS at last! we looked back upon the spectacle from the Canadian side - Rainbow Falls first, and then Lunar Island, then Bridal Veil Falls, 1000' across, six million gallons of thundering water falling each minute in a 167' drop to reach a depth of 160' at their base; the Falls; mist-shrouded and awe-inspiring, their waters tumbling over the immense boulders that block their path.

It was easy to see why the Indians believed that the Thunder God dwelt at the foot of Niagara Falls - a fearful deity to whom each year at harvest time they offered sacrifice - a beautifully fashioned canoe, loaded with the fruits of the nearby forest, and containing the loveliest maiden in all the tribe, to be hurled upon the rapids and sent over the Falls to the Thunder God below.

On then to Canada's magnificent Horseshoe Falls-2000' feet across with a drop of 162'; the water - 114 million thundering gallons of which pour over each minute - falling to a depth of 180' at the base. FIVE MILLION HORSEPOWER, we were told! We listened and viewed with awe.

Tourism is the order of the day on the Canadian side, the industrial development of which happily failed to keep pace with our own; we rejoice that the new concepts of ecology will now prevent forever the despoiling of this magnificent spectacle of nature.

***

And now on to the estates and gardens of Sir Harry Oakes, the colorful Canadian who presented these magnificent possessions to the Canadian people within his own lifetime. Picture frames and other articles of pure gold may be found within his imposing mansion, we were told.

Harry had not been born a gentleman. Once he was a HOBO, and while riding the rails had been ignominiously hurled from a moving train, to land - along with a Chinese traveling companion -at a spot where the two arose and dusted themselves off to discover GOLD at their tattered feet. Harry soon bought out his good friend's interest - for a song, no doubt - in the gold mine which was to make of him one of the world's richest men. Incidentally Harry's gift to the Canadian people included provision for the upkeep of his estate for a full century to come. A drive next along the 3000 acre Queen Victoria.

1,000 employees are required to maintain the perfection of this vast showplace whose greenhouses represent still one more facet of Sir Harry's munificence.

***

On to the Rapids, where we find an immense weather-beaten scow held fast in their thundering depths. Half a century ago, we learned, this imprisoned vessel broke loose from the tug that was towing it and was swept swiftly downstream toward the brink of the Falls. Two men were aboard the imperiled scow, one of whom happened to be a wise old sea captain who promptly opened the seacocks of the vessel, filling it with water to hold it fast upon the rocks. The two aboard prayed frantically through the longest night of their lives for the rescue that came at dawn when a cannon was brought from nearby Fort Niagara, to shoot a cable across the rapids, over which the two men were able to crawl to safety.

The mists over the Horseshoe Falls were incredibly beautiful. In winter, we were told, they freeze in midair, creating a vision of unsurpassed splendor. This, however, was a summer evening, and so a RAINBOW was our lot instead. The rain that had plagued the waning day had stopped, and there it hung in the immense summer sky - an immense half-moon of iridescent color - delighting the eyes and soothing the souls of the hundreds of tourists who beheld it.

Night fell as, having viewed the frightening eye of the whirlpool nearby, we returned to the wonder of the Falls once more, to find them bathed in light! It swept across their thundering faces in a splendid sweep of pink and yellow and blue and green. It filtered through the magic of the mists to light the Falls beyond. And to add another noble and compelling note to the symphony that is Niagara - a symphony that will forever leave it soundings in your hearts…

NEW BRUNSWICK

FUNDY NATIONAL PARK - the next point of interest in our fabulous Canadian trip…a beautiful New Brunswick feature, this eighty square mile recreational area, skirting as it does the incomparable Bay of Fundy for almost eight colorful miles…

We thrill to the dramatic beauty of the steep red sandstone cliffs that rise from the park's sea coast with their innumerable coves and caves, formed by the lashing of some of the world's highest tides…tides that have been known to reach heights of up to 53' in certain areas of New Brunswick and in the park itself to range from 20 to 40; in height.

Behind those sea-lashed cliffs that tower as high as 100; skyward, the fertile land rises in a rolling plateau that is cut by deep delicious valleys into which waterfalls tumble from the steep rock walls above,

How did it get this strange name "Fundy", we wanted to know. It is believed to have been derived from the words "Fondo Rio", the Portuguese for "deep river", we were told. Portuguese and French fishermen found their way to this fascinating corner of New Brunswick as early as the 16th century, we learned.

"Take only pictures - leave only footsteps" we were cautioned as we followed the trails through the evergreen forests of the Fundy Coast, delighting in every aspect of this beautiful park.

A visit to Herring Cove where we learn that Fundy's strange funnel shape serves to force the incoming tide higher and higher as it advances up the Bay, surging back and forth simultaneously with a rocking motion that doubles the height of the giant tides, tearing out as it comes such ragged coves as Herring where the tide at full height fills the area to a depth of twenty to thirty feet. We visit Hopewell Rocks, those weird wild sculptures that extend for almost a mile along the shores of Shepody… great giants of conglomerate carved by wind and frost and the erosion of the world's highest tides as, surging up the Bay, they race and swirl among the 100' cliffs…conglomerate rock, brick red in color, formed in eons past of sand and pebbles and gravel and oceanic debris. We thrill to the rocky profile of "The Old Man", towering as he does high above us, keeping his eternal watch upon the Bay; and the "Sentinel", also on guard. We make our way through "Keyhold Rock" from one cove to another; and we explore "The Devil's Cave" and "Twin Caves"; and find a special kind of delight in the storied "Indian's Head."

There is, an old Indian legend about Hopewell Rocks. Glooscap, the guardian spirit of the Micmac Indians, kept a watchful eye as well on the animals of the forests in which his people dwelt. One day while looking out upon the seas of Fundy, he heard a furious barking and noticed stag being pursued through the woods by a pack of enormous hounds. As the frantic animal reached the Bay he raced across the thin ice that capped the water's edge that winter's day, with the hounds in close pursuit. The handsome animal would have been slain had not Glooscap, who was capable of all manner of magic, taken a hand, changing the pursuing hounds into the giant rocks that to this day line the shore of Shepody…A delightful bit of lore…

The most exciting feature of Hopewell is easily the "World's Largest Flower Pots", to quote Robert Ripley who wrote of them some years ago, a group of high rounded rock formations set upon the beach and shaped precisely as the name suggests, complete with trees and shrubs and flowers all growing gracefully skyward. At low tide, the World's Largest Flower Pots lie serenely on dry land. When the giant tides of Fundy sweep the area however they are all but covered by the boiling sea. A huge clock, carefully placed at the point where visitors might descend the rambling staircase from the cliffs above and set at twelve-hour intervals, serves to warn the beachcombers of the time at which their lives are endangered by remaining on the beach.

It was not the advancing tide that spelled danger for the Metayers however, though it was at Hopewell Rocks that we experienced our one and only mishap. we had just emerged from the exploration of a particularly fascinating cave and were happily rounding the cliff when we came face to face with the most enormous German Shepherd dog on earth, a beast who, growling fiercely, SPRANG DIRECTLY AT MY THROAT. Ted, lion that he is, came promptly to my rescue by hurling himself in front of me and lashing out with the only weapon at hand - his camera - only to be severely bitten on the hand for his bravery. And so it was off to the nearest hospital for shots and treatment and an end to the Metayers adventure at Hopewell Rocks.

Incidentally, you may depend upon it Ted carried a club each time we beach-promenaded from then on though he never had to use it.

Off next to New Brunswick's famous Magnetic Hill. "To appreciate this phenomena", we read, "proceed to spot indicated by the White Post. Turn off motor. Release brakes." Your car, we were told, will promptly back merrily up the hill all by itself. We followed instructions and the car did just that. It was fun!

Off to Moncton next and the fabulous Tidal Bore which though its size has been diminished by the building of the Causeway, is nonetheless still an exciting phenomenon. We traveled there through one after another of enchanting covered bridges that even now are to be found in beautiful New Brunswick. "See Moncton's Unique Tidal Bore at Moncton's Bore Park, we read, and we were there! The Bore was due to arrive at 9:10, we learned; and we were on hand early to secure a front-row spot in the little park from which one views the Bore's arrival. The tide was completely out and the red mud flats of the Petitcodiac River lay beneath us, gouged and furrowed strangely by the angry action of an eternity of mighty tides. a narrow tidal river ran swiftly toward the left. Seagulls screamed above the flats or floated lazily on the shallow pools that here and there filled the furrowed inlets. It was cold in the little park high above the river;

and the crowd was strangely quiet. We were soon to learn why. They were awaiting the sound that swept suddenly up the river from the left, a strange exciting sound that began as a sort of whisper and became a roar.

"Here it comes!" someone cried. And it did come, changing the direction of the river's flow…a great roaring wave that rushed up from the Bay of Fundy and swept into the Petitcodiac River, filling the river bed in a matter of minutes with a creeping crimson sea that licked hungrily against the river's sides as it rose higher and higher toward the low cliff on which the Boreview Park is built…

Ah, the drama of scenic New Brunswick with its red sandstone cliffs, and those red sand beaches over which a copper colored ocean rolls, its waves white-capped and high. Beyond it the steel blue beauty of the Atlantic; above it a sky that is forever laced with cotton-candy clouds; and over all -above and about the cliffs - the emerald green of growing things fed constantly by rushing rivers and those rains that seemed eternally to fall as night enveloped beautiful New Brunswick…A land enchantment. We loved it…every exciting inch of it.

NOVA SCOTIA

And now it is "WELCOME TO NOVA SCOTIA" and we are piped over the border by a Scotsman, the music of whose bagpipes is almost as appealing as those handsome MacKenzie kilts he swirls about. We cross at a point where once lay the little Acadian Village of Beaubassin. Founded in 1672, we were interested to learn that it was raided in 1696 and again 1703 by an invading force from BOSTON under the command of one Captain Ben Church. having absorbed this interesting bit of history we proceed to look about us upon the beautiful valleys of Nova Scotia. The scene is one of incredible beauty and prosperity - shining distant towns and well-kept farms lying upon an emerald green landscape that rises to meet an incredible expanse of sky.

Our immediate destination is to be Cape Breton where we plan to explore the storied Cabot Trail. We settle ourselves in a beautiful trailer park at Baddeck, a few short miles from the trail's beginning. Baddeck, a delightful town, was settled in 1790- for the most part by Scotsmen from the Highlands - and it resembles Scotland in many respects. Alexander Graham Bell built his summer home here. He called it "Beinn Bhreagh" which is Gaelic for the "Beautiful Mountain" overlooking the Bras d'Or Lakes where he elected to build it and where we find the final resting place of the great inventor and his beloved wife.

A visit to the Alexander Graham Bell Museum reveals the unbelievable extent of this man's genius "The Inventor", he once wrote, "is a man who looks around upon the world and is not contented with things as they are. He wants to improve whatever he sees. He wants to benefit the world; he is haunted by an idea, the spirit of invention possesses him, seeking materialization." We boast to the Museum's Curator that our home is built upon what was once the Braintree estate of Bell's co-worker, Thomas A. Watson; and immediately we are IN! We spend hours in this fabulous place, learning much about a most unique individual. Did you know, for instance, that Dr. Bell devised and used an iron lung several decades before it was used elsewhere? And that in 1871, Bell, whose interest in the problems of the hard of hearing, stemmed from the deafness of both his mother and his wife, began lecturing to teachers of the deaf here in Boston; and that with the $10,000 Volta Prize which he received from France for the invention of the telephone, he established the Volta Laboratories for research and development in teaching speech to the deaf? And that it was his research in this field that led to the development of the telephone and the photophone and the graphophone and the multiple harmonic telegraph? And that Helen Keller, who termed deafness "that inhuman silence which severs and estranges" was educated under the guiding hand of Dr. Bell?

Dr. Bell himself taught the deaf at Northampton, Mass. He established a small school in Boston in 1872 for the instruction of teachers of the deaf; and he taught at the University of Boston where he received an appointment as Professor of Vocal Physiology.

The inventor made speech visible to the deaf by devising an alphabet-like system that employed printed symbols to represent the various positions taken by vocal organs in uttering consonants and vowels. His countless other achievements are, of course, history.

And now it is off to tiny St. Peter's Anglican Church where we find a Saxon christening font 1200 years old, an ancient stone masterpiece… The Cabot Trail itself is indeed beautiful. It curves about the mountains with the steel blue sea lying eternally below. It races beside great rivers with farms lying against their banks, their crops a hundred shades of lush and lovely green, reminiscent, we thought, of Ireland. The tall white spires of churches in the villages along the riverbanks tremble in the moving waters below even as they pierce a soft blue sky above simultaneously and beautifully. Here, we are told, is the "most nearly Scottish scenery in America" and we believe that as well, for the mists lie about the mountains and the mountains descend to the "lochs" in a manner that does indeed suggest Scotland's Trossachs. We visit the "Margaree Monster" in picturesque Magaree Harbor, a weird rock formation spawned of the hungry sea and possessing a scaly body with a foreleg and three distinct toes, a head with eyes and eyebrows, nostrils and a mouth. A grassy growth at the top suggests its hair, completing the weird monster-like effect. The 184 mile Trail was named for the great explorer and navigator, John Cabot, who first sighted Cape Breton Island on a balmy June day in 1497.

We park the car frequently to walk upon the beaches that dot the Cabot Trail, beaches of incomparable beauty like the gem at Neil Harbor where a coral mountain sweeps down into the sea and there's the whisper of a fog about the rocks where white caps thunder against a gold sand beach.

Cape Breton has other delights to offer. We visit the Miners' Museum and the Ocean Deeps Colliery at Glace Bay. Here the first regular coal mining in America was undertaken to supply fuel for the magnificent 18th century Fortress of Louisbourg nearby; and hear we don rubber coats and hats and boots and enter the coal mine itself - a mine which incidentally, extends for several miles beneath the ocean as far as the Continental Shelf. Our guide is a retired miner who began working in the mines at the age of eleven years and three months; and lurid indeed was the picture he would paint for us of those early mining days when men worked for twelve hours a day upon their stomachs or backs in a mine 2½' high and were paid 8c per ton and only for the coal they personally dug and nothing for the time required for dynamiting the coal and shoring up the mine. With this fascinating miner who had, incidentally, lost two brothers in mine explosions, we walked through a simulated carboniferous swamp where millions of years ago trees would have sunk into the swampy earth with the hardwood trees turning to stone and the softwood to coal; and we followed the actual process of coal mining from beginning to end.

It was equally exciting to view a model of the "Mary Celeste" here - that mystery ship which in 1872 was found floating aimlessly between the Azores and Portugal, its Captain, his wife and daughter and the seven man crew all missing. The ship's log was on board but without entries for the preceding eleven days. The remains of a meal, partially eaten, lay upon the table' with only the chronometer and the ship's papers missing. This salvaged mystery ship which had been built locally, was said to be cursed. It brought a series of misfortunes to one owner after another, and was finally wrecked upon a reef off Haiti, only to have its Captain indicted for barratry when his cargo which had been insured for $30,000 was found to be worthless. Our local historian Edward Rowe Snowe wrote of the "Mary Celeste" in his delightful column.

On next to the magnificent 18th century Fortress of Louisbourg which is currently in the process of restoration. Louisbourg has a fascinating history. Completed by the French about 1845, this 74 acre fortress with its immense bastions overlooking the mighty Atlantic, once housed a veritable Town. Its citizens lived beyond the walls, coming into the Citadel only in time of attack. Attack was expected only from the sea, for behind the fortress lay three miles of bog and hilly terrain over which so the military experts opined - heavy cannon could never be hauled. They were, however, to be proved incorrect in their judgement for in 1745 4,000 New England volunteers under Massachusetts Governor William Shirley (supported by the British fleet) hauled their cannon over the forbidding area on sledges to attack the fortress from the rear; and the French, their food and ammunition supply exhausted had no alternative but to finally surrender.

Louisbourg was returned to the French by Treaty some years later; however in 1758 hostilities having been resumed between the two countries, it was attacked once more by the British and this time completely destroyed. Currently it is being restored on the foundations and with the materials unearthed in an archaeological dig; and a portion of it is fully restored. Consequently we visited the Place Royale or Parade Square; and the Chateau St. Louis where we viewed the Guard House and a typical Officer's Room with its beamed ceiling and fireplace, the French hand-rolled glass of its windows bubbly and imperfect and beautiful. Here we found a canopied bed and a gaming table and a black bear rug thrown gracefully upon the floor. A contrast indeed to this comparative luxury was the Troops' Room with its common bed running the length of the wall. Here the soldiers slept head to top and feet to bottom, wrapped only in their cloaks for blankets were issued only to officers. We visited the Chapel with its original 18th century confessional and holy water font and portrait of St. Louis. The skeletons of five people were found here amid the ruins, all identified as military governors and dignitaries with the exception of one mysterious one - that of a small child whose remains had been wrapped in cloth and buried in a shallow grave…

We delighted in the Governor's Dining Room with its immense "U" shaped table; his kitchens and their original bread ovens; and his bedroom with its gold Louis XV mercury barometer and thermometer, as well as the adjoining bath which sported a wooden tub. We were interested in the High Court of the Colony where, we were told, criminal cases required five councillors and civil three.

The Fortress Louisbourg which was designed by the French military engineers Verville and Verrier, was begun in 1719 and when completed had cost 10M dollars. Its Caen stone and much of its brick was brought from France. The town when complete boasted a coalyard, a fishmarket, bakery, icehouse, a woman's shop, a prison, and a "bill ard" or tavern where the game of billiards was played..

Above the Chateau one finds the royal crest, the pieces of which were found within the dig; and the blue faced clock with its original 18th century works. Incidentally the drawbridge of the old fortress still functions over what was once a moat. What a fascinating place this was to visit..

NOVA SCOTIA CONTINUED

The museum of the historic town of Yarmouth yielded yet another treasure to delight the Metayers...the magnificent old Yarmouth Light that for more than a century guarded Cape Forchu at the west side of the entrance to Yarmouth Harbor. A fascinating light this. Its smoky gray lens was designed by the French physicist Augustin Jean Fresnel who was responsible for developing a method of producing circularly polarized light, and because of whom mirrors were replaced by compound lenses in lighthouses across the world. The handsome lens was built in Paris at a cost of $38,000 in 1840. Its 170 prisms catch and reflect the light shining through the high museum windows. Its beam could be seen twenty miles out at sea, shining for 1 4 minute intervals and being invisible for 2 minute; and we loved it!

Canada was celebrating her 104th birthday as we left Yarmouth; it was Dominion Day, July 1; and we were to lope along behind parades that sported entire families on horseback costumed in 19th century fashion. Our route took us along Nova Scotia's "Scenic South Shore" and scenic indeed it was to be. Hundreds of lobster traps pyramided in just about everyone's back yard; piles of sea moss spread out to dry beside the roadways; and cordwood piled to the roofs of the picturesque fishermens' dwellings that for the most part lined the way.

Loved the little towns...Shag Harbor with its beautiful view of Sable Island, the extreme southwestern point of Nova Scotia, from which delightful place we were able to view by night the lights of FIVE area lighthouses...

Liverpool, a lovely place founded in 1759 by a group of settlers from Cape Cod, no less – most of them descendants of the early pilgrims. Liverpool was celebrating Dominion Day in style and we found ourselves following horsemen by the dozen, all enroute to the town square for parade formation. Floats floated about; and a ball game was in progress; we felt real Fourth of July-ish as we tucked ourselves into the local scene.

We were wonderfully amused by the Nova Scotia bridges we are encountering as we follow the sea to Halifax. With few exceptions they are one-lane affairs and so one must wait until they are clear of all on-coming traffic before entering their narrow confines.

Lunenburg next - the home of the famous "Bluenose", that undefeated champion of the North Atlantic fishing fleet and the winner of no less than four International schooner races. And now we are at Ovens National Park. It's a rather short sea-side stretch of great caves from which, when the customary high winds and waves sweep the area, immense clouds of snow-white foam arise. It was the early Micmac Indians who gave it the Micmac name for "ovens." Naturally we shared an old Indian legend. The Great Spirit chose this beautiful part of the province for the feasting he enjoyed while celebrating the many marriages of his Indian people, their bountiful harvests and peaceful loving way of life, preparing his delicacies in the immense "ovens" or caves that line the area. And the Micmacs were a peaceful loving people, we learned. They befriended the French and indeed it was largely because of that friendship that the French refused to swear allegiance to the British King, so an old Micmac Indian told us. Incidentally, grains of gold may still be panned at the "Ovens" where in 1861 an actual Gold Rush occurred.

Mahone Bay, our next port of call. It's an exciting place where for almost two centuries men have actually been digging for buried treasure. "Welcome to Mahone Bay", we read, "We love the beauty around us and welcome you to share it." The saga of the buried treasure began away back in 1797 when a group of hunters came upon an old ship's block hanging from the limb of an oak tree. Under it, a depression thirty feet in circumference stirred the imagination of the hunters who spent the remainder of their lives seeking in vain the treasure they felt certain had been buried there. Mahone Bay has other delightful bits and pieces of history. There was once a privateer called "The Young Teazer", we were told, which was cornered there by warships during the war of 1812. Facing capture her captain ordered the pirate ship blown to bits, and so it was. "The Ghost Ship of Mahone Bay" as it is now called, The Young Teazer, afire and burning helplessly, is seen in the harbor from time to time even to this day. Its appearance usually precedes a hurricane and the ghostly fire can be seen far out to sea, so the fanciful fisherfolk say…In this area we find the weird Nova Scotian "Drumlins" as well-200 or more of them-enormous drift mounds formed of boulders and clay and sand and shells, all deposited by glacial ice in eons long past.

Chester next, a handsome summer resort which was founded in 1759 by settlers from MASSACHUSETTS; then Queensland with its white sand, rock-strewn beaches. Very few pleasure craft are to be seen upon the waves of the great coves that lie along this Nova Scotia coast; and we are surprised at the fact. At home such an ocean area would teem with sailing craft. Halifax finally, a magnificent harbor extending 16 miles in from the sea, and spanned by two enormous bridges. It was founded in 1749 by Lord Cornwallis as a base to defend the North American territory of the English and to counteract the French Fortress Louisbourg. Its "Citadel" is a brilliantly designed star-shaped fortress that straddles the 270' high Citadel Hill and dominates the peninsula. Citadel museums depict the fort's history and are exciting to visit. Fun also are the moon gun for which for 150 years has been fired there; and the colorful Junior Bengal Lancers that mount guard during the summer months.

From Halifax to Pictou now for the annual Lobster Carnival or "Carnival of the Fisherfolk, Mardi Gras of the Sea." Pictou is the shire town of the County. Its population is 4500 and 2000 men work the area's fishing grounds. It was settled in 1767 by a group of immigrants from Philadelphia who were joined six years later by Scottish settlers. The Carnival was originated in 1934 to entertain the lobster fishermen of the Northumberland Strait at the conclusion of their dangerous two months lobster fishing (May and June).

Quaint old stone houses line its principal street, the old English chimney pots topping their roofs dating back to the time when the ships of the world dropped anchor in what was then a bustling port… It's a typical Carnival this a bit less sophisticated than our own in many respects but with all the trimmings. There's the inevitable Carnival Queen, and what a beauty she was with her long dark hair and great shining eyes…and a group of princesses all equally lovely. Last year's Queen crowned her successor amid the customary tears and smiles; and the charming young lady promptly cut the ribbon, officially opening the festivities. There was the usual Guest Speaker; he was the Hon. Benoit Comeau, Minister of Fisheries of the Provincial Government, and from him we were to learn a lot about the incomparable lobster we would be consuming in great quantities for the next two days… indeed throughout our Canadian tour. The Heatherbell Girls Pipe Band of Pictou presented a Concert, their pipes sounding and their kilts swirling; and from one of the spectators we learned that "those girls, not one of whom is over 17, took first prize at that great big Brockton Fair up there in the States."

America had sent a Coast Guard Ship, the "Owasco" and all Carnivalers were invited to inspect her; and Lobster Boats raced across the Bay to the fishing grounds to stake out their prize claims on the sea for the coming year; and we were on hand to photograph the finish of a sailboat race which had commenced in Charlottetown, P.E.I. that morning at six and ended in mid-afternoon. Its escort, incidentally, was the R.C.M.P. boat "Nicholson", named according to custom for a former commissioner; and we enjoyed a chat with two handsome young officers, Donald B. MacMillan (like the explorer) and Brian Wryde, both of whom were attired in the brand new uniform of the Mounties. "We used to wear long blues," said Donald, "but the new commissioner prefers boots and breeks." (breeches.)

A Country Western Band pipped about the Midway area constantly, by the way, pausing before each restaurant, gas station, etc. to advertise the wares of the establishment and to entertain the audience that followed it from place to place. This area, incidentally, is called the "Highlands of Nova Scotia" and is predominantly Scotch which explains why the hardy Carnivalers patronized the Festival en masse sans umbrella or other head covering even though the rain poured continually on their 117 year old heads. The only umbrella on the Midway was usually my own. And looking back upon that Midway with its games of chance - they were so unsophisticated that the management might just as well have had its hawkers empty the victims' pockets…without pretense…and yet those games of chance were patronized to the nines…

One more bit about Pictou. Our stay there included a visit to a fascinating Micmac Indian Museum at nearby Bayview. It contains the contents of a series of burial mounds unearthed by one of its citizens, Kenneth Hopps, who was digging a new drain on his property when the find was uncovered. Archaeologists were promptly called in and the dig explored. And among hundreds of Indian artifacts of untold value there were found twenty two huge copper kettles that had been traded by Champlain in 1605-06. The burial mounds were in fine condition only because the copper oxide from the kettles had over the centuries acted as a poisonous preventative to the insects that ordinarily would have destroyed them.

One huge kettle had housed a skull for 300 years and the explanation we were offered was intriguing. The Micmacs buried their dead but once a year, and until the ceremonial burial the bodies of their deceased would be wrapped in bark and furs and placed on platforms or hung from the trees. Archaeologists are of the opinion that the brave whose skull was found beneath the kettle had only just died and so his face was protected. There were other fascinating artifacts…A fortune in furs; several scalps, including that of a white man; articles woven of reeds and grasses; double-edged and single-edged swords of French manufacture; arrow and spear hooks, and fish hooks which the Indians fashioned from ribs of field mice. A fascinating story.

ONTARIO

"ONTARIO WELCOMES YOU - PROVINCE OF OPPORTUNITY!"…and we have left Quebec behind us. We drive along the King's Highway through the scenic Ottawa Valley. The Ottawa River - historic Trans-Canada canoe route of days long past-flows swiftly beside us and leads us directly to our destination, the Provincial Capital of Ottawa!

Were this Springtime, tulips would literally cover the beautiful city, we learn - the gift of Queen Juliana of the Netherlands who, with her little family found refuge here during World War II. The tulips are not in bloom this July day, but the city itself is!

The Rideau River winds its way through it to flow by way of a curtain-like waterfall into the swirling depths of the Ottawa River. The Rideau Canal, log-jammed because of the local paper mills, bisects the city to lead as well - via a series of small locks - to its mighty partner, that same Ottawa River. Towering above the whole are the magnificent Gothic Parliament Buildings, high atop Parliament Hill; and we hasten to explore them.

"The wholesome sea is at her gates," we read above their main entrance. "Her gates both east and west." Ottawa…We look about us. How very true! We stop to examine the building's cornerstone. "This stone was laid by Edward, Prince of Wales, Sep 1, in this year of victory," we read. "Finis Coronat Opus 1919." Once upon a time and not too long ago young (or old) ladies attired in shorts were given "wraparounds" to don before entering this special place, we are told by an Ottawan.

We enter the Rotunda or Confederation Hall as it is called, columned and beautiful; and then proceed to the House of Commons or Lower House. There are 264 members elected every five years, we are told. The traditional Mace is placed on the foremost table when the House is in session; and a translation booth here as in the Senate Chamber converts English to French and vice versa, immediately as House members speak.

Magnificent carvings of Canadian Red Oak line the walls; and the ceiling is covered with Irish linen which was painted after its installation, we learn. A "Miss Miln" together with five assistants works on the carving each evening upon the close of Parliament, we are told; and the completion of the work will take an additional thirty years.

The Library is incredibly beautiful. Hand-carved throughout with the exception of the parquet floors, it features a sculpture of Queen Victoria, shown, for a change, as a YOUNG woman. The foyer to the Senate Chamber houses the portraits of former British monarchs including George III (the British American King, they call him) and a portrait of Queen Victoria that strangely enough has survived two devastating fires. "Wasn't the old Queen indestructible, though?" asks our guide fondly. The portrait is most unusual as it portrays the Queen in a standing position and having suffered from severe back difficulties the Queen seldom permitted an artist to paint her in a standing position, so we are told.

The Senate Chamber next - the Upper House of Parliament where meet the 102 members from the ten provinces who are, interestingly enough, not elected at all but have been summoned by the Governor-General on recommendation of the Prime Minister…this chamber too, is panelled in Canadian oak. Paintings of the Canadian forces in action during World War I - gifts of Lord Beaverbrook-line the walls.

The center throne upon the dais is used by the Queen or her Canadian representative, the Governor-General on such ceremonial occasions as the opening of Parliament. A small throne on her left will seat her consort or the Governor-General. At the opening of Parliament, a strict ritual is observed, we are told. The Throne Speech is to be read; it will present the Government's plans for the coming year and it is therefore fitting that both the Upper and Lower Houses both hear it. Accordingly, when all is in readiness, the "Gentleman Usher of the Black Rod" as he is called proceeds to the House of Commons where he knocks three times upon the door. The door opens and House members emerge to follow the G.U. of the B.R. to the Senate Chamber. These lesser mortals however are not admitted to this Sanctum Sanctorum but must wait just outside the enclosure while the Throne Speech is read.

It's a magnificent room, this Senate Chamber. Its massive chandeliers of Russian bronze weight two tons each, we are told; and Britain's patron saints, David, Andrew, George and Patrick are all dutifully featured in the décor.

We follow our guide to the Memorial Chapel next where the names of Canada's war dead are entombed and where on the walls one may read "The Story of Canada in the Great War." "Read how free men throughout the land kept faith in the hour of trial", we read; "and in the day of Battle, remembering the traditions they had been taught, counting life nothing without liberty." 20,000 volunteers had been sought by Britain in her hour of need, we learn; and 40,000 volunteers answered in a month...

We visit the Peace Tower next, at the top of the Parliament building...the Peace Tower with its carillon of 53 bells. The weight of the Bourdon Bell 11 tons; its note "E"; the weight of the smallest bell 10 lbs.; its note "A". There's a huge clock here, the diameter of whose face is 15'9"; and an immense flag 15' x 7 and one half feet that floats from a flagpole 35' high. all of Ottawa lies beneath us it seems as we stand on the parapet of the Peace Tower and look below us; with all of Quebec facing us across the river.

We naturally visit the Museum to see such fascinating memorabilia as the inkstand used by the Delegates of Canada and Newfoundland to sign the terms of their union and the original signed oath of allegiance of Members of the House of Commons of the Dominion's FIRST Parliament. "I do swear" it reads "that I will be faithful and bear true allegiance to her Majesty Queen Victoria." Queen Victoria again…that extraordinary monarch who in 1857 shocked Canadians everywhere when she selected the then rough and ready settlement of Ottawa as the Capital of the United Provinces.

And now it is off to Sparks Mall with its wonderful shops and that exciting Rock Garden that contains immense slabs of rock from each of the Canadian Provinces, among which we find - from the Province of Ontario - part of the Precambrian Shield estimated to be a billion years old…We visit the Centennial Flame which was lighted on the eve of January 1, 1967 to mark the Centennial of Canada's Confederation; and we view the Changing of the Guard, a 45 minute ceremony on the lawns of Parliament Hill. Colorful and exciting!

And now we spend our days pipping about the city, parking the family car in the immense underground garage of the National Arts Center with its three great theaters and restaurants and delightful shops.

The city's Museums house a multitude of treasures, we find, including - interestingly enough-the staff car of Field Marshal Alexander, in which he was driven from Egypt to Tunis and elsewhere during the Italian Campaign - to the tune of 180,000 miles.

And now it is off to Upper Canada Village as we head homeward toward the American border. "When you pass through the 1850 toll gate into it," we read, "you step back 100 years and more into Ontario's past." Here one may wander through and about the forty or more old buildings-homes, Churches, shops, taverns and mills.

We visit the pioneer shanty of 1790; the first log cabin of 1795; a log home of 1820 and a fine stone farm house of 1860. They represent indeed "the evolution of Canadian life." We are amused to read that the park itself commemorates, among others, the "Loyal British Regiments of America." We delight in the old Willard's Hotel with the cattle grazing before it; and the log schoolhouse of "Glengarry School Days fame"; and Cook's Tavern with the mail coach standing nearby: the oxen ploughing in the fields; and the blacksmith's shop with its smithy hard at work.

And now it is off to the Thousand Islands with our own beautiful America lying excitingly across the broad St. Lawrence before us. We plan a boat trip here on the Canadian side with one to follow from the American side when we have crossed one of the many beautiful bridges that keep the countries apart or bring them together, whichever you prefer. But these adventures will be covered in next week's column, which should bring our Canadian Safari to an end...

11-22-70

Our Indian friend kept reminding me somehow of those bright hanging cones we find in our New England woods-in that his skin was shiny and seamed and on the horny side. His name, we learned, was Johnny Longfellow. Charlie, the "wag" of the group was to call him "Johnny Wrongfellow" as the day progressed, but that is another story.

At any rate we sat with him in the trailer park on Tunnel Mountain, and I who delight in the company of a new friend, plied him with questions. "Tell me," I said, "What's with those wonderful signposts we see all around Banff and Jasper and the rest?" And wonderful indeed they were.

Straight smooth posts with immense knobs, rounded and symmetrical, where branches once had grown on the stately trunks.

"Oh," said our friend, "the BEAVERS make them. We've wonderful beaver colonies hereabouts. For instance, there's a lake - Beaver Lake it's called - where you may see a typical example of the kind of Beaver Colony one finds everywhere around here."

"We must see it," I said immediately, and later on we did. "But tell me where we are likely to find the other animals we are told are to be seen in this vicinity?" "Well," said Johnny with a knowing air, "If it's moose you're interested in; there's a beautiful six-point fellow that comes regularly every evening at seven thirty right up at the top of the hill there behind the trailer park. He comes to drink in the little stream!" "How wonderful!" I said instantly "Let's all go up tonight to see him. We can leave around seven and get there early- just in case his watch is fast!"

"You know, hon," said Ted later on as our Indian friend having departed, "I find it difficult to swallow that bit about the beavers. To begin with every street sign is held up by one of those gnarled knobby posts, and every inn and restaurant for miles around has one outside it; and homes have summerhouses made of the things. The beavers hereabouts must be pretty industrious to furnish all that. Besides, I admit I've always known beavers to be ENGINEERS, but artists??? Those knobs are absolutely perfect - round and symmetrical…" "Ted," I said, "The Indian should know, it's his country." And Ted shrugged. "Well," he said, "he may be right…"

The fact that a sudden thunder shower struck the area - just as we planned to leave to keep our rendezvous with nature on that high hill behind the park-deterred the intrepid band of adventurers we had become not in the least. Clutching cameras to our collective bosoms as we drove merrily to the area - that is, to a point as close to the area as it was possible to drive. We tramped the wet woods and then hid behind a tree to await the arrival of the six point one. We waited and waited and waited, while the rain dripped forlornly on our heads and umbrellas, and facial expressions grew increasingly more grim. The males in the party were all for quitting almost from the beginning. They eyed us females with an increasingly baleful air - while we pretended not to notice their diminishing enthusiasm. "Something tells me," said one of them finally, "that Johnny's timetable is off - Johnny's or nature's, let's squish home and allow a nice case of pneumonia to settle in gradually…" the which we did, reluctantly, I might add for this adventurer.

Our disenchantment with Johnny Wrongfellow was complete the following day when Ted and I, on visiting beautiful Cascade Gardens, an eleven acre wonderland leading to Banff, that exquisite little alpine-type village that lies in the heart of the Canadian Rockies-learned from the naturalist in charge that those lovely gnarled and knobby posts we had been admiring so enthusiastically were not fashioned by beavers at all, but came about as a result of a disease called "gall", in which insects enter the tree trunk at the point of branching, to disease the tree and cause the picturesque swelling of the joints that makes of it such a marvelously decorative creation. "He seemed so GENUINE, our Indian," I wailed when Ted's "I told you so" look had put me properly in my place. "And you, my dear," said Ted, "Are so GULLIBLE." A trait to which I confess I have admitted for more years than I remember…

A bit about Cascade Gardens, for here lies the headquarters of the Canadian National Park Service, and how those Canadians love their garden spots! The area is enveloped in a wrap of shining emerald green for grass, with beds of annuals in full bloom in every conceivable form and color - all lying like rainbows against the green; waterfalls trail gently over rocks that are strewn with growing things and bronze with moss; tiny pools mirror the sweep of trees that lie about them.

Rustic summerhouses sleep within the glades of the delightful place- havens for tourists wearied from the sun. Serenity and peace pervade this place of beauty that sweeps along a curbing drive to find the bridge that - crossing the slate gray glacial streams - leads one to Banff, a jewel of a town that kept reminding us of Innsbruck all the while we spent there.

Needless to say, we were impatient to find Lake Louise. I headed there with Ted, experiencing a quickening of the heartbeat and a tightening of the throat with every passing mile…Lake Louise, that precious bit of Paradise I've always wanted to know.

We stopped to photograph a herd of bison on the way. Mt. Eisenhower towered above us at altitude 9076'. Slate gray glacial streams raced murkily beside the roadway as we passed. The wind grew strong and wild as we passed through the high Bow Pass and over the rushing Bow River. We stopped, however, for coffee at a point beyond, in a tiny inn where silence was now suddenly immense; and small wild strawberries grew beside the path; and there was such a haunting heady fragrance to the pines that lay in heavy stillness all about us as to delight the soul.

We climbed a curving mountain road and parked the car and walked a scented path through the woods. Lake Louise! It lay there in the heart of Paradise Valley, a shining sparkling flawless turquoise, its setting the splendor of the Rockies all around it…behind it towering Victoria Glacier silvering in the sun, its snowy crown ablaze with diamonds from the morning mists and growing light…

We had expected it to be large somehow - a Titan of a lake, it wasn't! It was small, exquisitely small like most of the flawless jewels that light the world. the unbelievable blue of it stood out in sharp contrast to the deep dark green of timbered mountains to the right and left.

The Chateau Lake Louise towered nearby, a magnificent edifice which we approached across a small stone bridge, there to lunch and watch the splendor of a scene whose equal we shall seldom find again. Lake Louise! It exceeded all my fondest dearest dreams…

And now it was over Canada's spectacular Ice Field Highway as we headed toward the Columbia Ice Fields and Jasper National Park. We have not previously SEEN a glacier, we concluded, as now we sweep along - not the kind of glittering gorgeous glacier that we find with every passing mile! But that's another story which we shall unfold next week.

A wee bit more on Banff, however. Its main street runs straight as an arrow through this tiny town beside which mountains tower. The streets are each named for animals which once apparently roamed about this storied land in great glad numbers. There is a Caribou Street and Buffalo Street and Wolf Street and Otter Street. It is fun to wend one's way through all these pretty little somehow sad reminders of a time that is no more in North America…an era long since lost to this, the civilization that has brought us and others…tourists by the millions, to marvel at the beauty of the land.

OUR TRAVELS CONTINUED

To continue with the saga of the traveling Metayers, we cross the desolate Mojave Desert from California to Nevada, traveling only from six to nine each morning before the sun is high. At nine we settle down to pass the humid desert day in the cool comfort of a trailer park swimming pool - first at Tehechapi and then at Barstow, where- wonder of wonders - we meet a family of fellow Braintree-ites, the Franeschinis, Betty and Victo, and their bright little nine-year-old, Bob! What a reunion!

We drive past the exits to such fascinatingly named towns as Zzyzx (How would you pronounce that one?) in the vicinity of Death Valley. And we see a MIRAGE! It appears for all the world like a broad and beautiful river flowing across the valley floor. "It must be part of Lake Mead," Ted opines. And then we reach it - a RIVER OF FLOWING SAND! I had always assumed that the movie hero who staggered across the Sahara toward this non-existent river was maddened by heat and thirst; he wasn't!

And shortly after our arrival in Las Vegas, we encounter a desert thunderstorm. The sky for some time had been dark and threatening against the surrounding mountain peaks. We watched it with increasing excitement. First came the wind, a savage wind that sent the desert sand flying in all directions. It sifted through the all-but-closed windows of our trailer, literally choking us. Through the pale brown sand-filled air we watched the park trees tossing frenzied arms about in the rain that came in great round sandy coins that hammered on the trailer roof and coated the car and trailer with golden mud...

Las Vegas by night...We thrill to the unforgettable sight quite as though we are seeing it for the very first time-this immense sprawling city lighted an immense sweep of multi-colored lights lying on the valley floor and sweeping up into the foothills...To the right a maze of glittering white lights lie like an enormous diamond necklace against the jet black throat of night - the diamonds relieved here and there by swathes of rubies or emeralds or sapphires or topaz. Magnificent!

The Casinos are in full swing. Don Rickles is performing at the Sahara; and Liza Minnelli at the Riviera; and Vic Damone at the Frontier; and Petula Clark at Caesar's Palace; and Julie London at the Tropicana.

"Free aspirin and tender sympathy" are being offered at one of the "Strip" service stations...The thermometer keeps registering 115 degrees or worse even by night; and so, having flown to Vegas previously while en route to Hawaii and done the town from end to end on that occasion, we limit our night life pretty much to the recently added Caesar's Palace and Circus. Circus where, incidentally, the small fry have their own minute gambling games as well as circus acts to entertain them while their parents indulge in more serious play on another level...So much for Vegas...

Zion Canyon is to be our next port of call, and we are soon settled in a lovely tree-shaded trailer space on the national campground, where tiny lizards slither about and our next door neighbor, a retired Texan engineer once affiliated with Boston's Stone and Webster, invites us to share a family reunion where we cool off with tall frosted glasses of iced tea and wedges of a huge watermelon which had been chilled previously in a shining mountain stream and kept on ice for the occasion. They were precious people, especially the small grandchildren…Aren't people wonderful???

"Zion" where great deep canyons have, with the passing of centuries, gouged immense stair-stepped plateaus into an exciting scenic chaos of strange stark form and line.

Navajo sandstone, the "cliff maker," has formed the immense arches of red or white that dot the mountainsides, their coloring dependant upon the rust or iron oxide content of the land itself…

Zion, we learn, was a place of refuge for the Latter Day saints, a fact which accounts for the biblical names that grace its mountain peaks. Towering above are the "Three Patriarchs," named for Abraham, Isaac and Jacob; and the 7800' Towers of the Virgin; and the tall spires of Cathedral Mountain; and the Great White Throne; and Lady Mountain; and, most exciting of all, the 5785' soaring peak that, because of the several pairs of perfectly angel wings that encircle the stark white mountain top, is known as "Angel's Landing". Zion Canyon is a place of breathtaking color contrasts. There is the incredibly beautiful rose and red and copper that lie side by side with the pure stark white of the peaks and plateaus themselves, the deep dark green of the pines and firs that dot the area; the soft pale blue of the Virgin River that races below; and above all the bright brash blue of a brilliant summer sky.

The walls of Zion Canyon, which is cut into the Kolob Terrace, tower 2400' above the Virgin River. Here are the ancient rocks of the Mesozoic Era formed some 150 million years ago when dinosaurs roamed the land.

Bryce Canyon, which is cut into the rim of Paunsqugunt Plateau, is the widest; it is ten miles across-and the deepest - one mile in depth… And in its walls the geologist reads the very earliest chapters of our earth's history, those Precambrian and Paleozoic eras that spanned a billion years and ended 180 million years ago. Oh, to be a geologist!

All three canyons incidentally, were carved by the waters of the mighty Colorado River and its tributaries, this MAKER of the national parks that dot the West…

So much to see and marvel at in Zion. The Temple of the Sinewava, for instance. Legend has it that Sinewava was a beautiful Indian Princess whose BRAVE was drowned in the raging waters below the giant cliff that now bears her name. Overcome with grief, the Princess climbed to the top of the soaring mountain peak and leaped to join her beloved in death upon the rocks below.

Other legends and tales, ranger-told, delight us. Wild grapevines dot the park. They grew there in abundance during the nineteenth century when the Latter Day Saints found refuge in this wonderland. When Brigham Young arrived in the 1870's, he found his people making merry with the wine these grapes afforded; and, angered, he changed the name of the bible-oriented settlement to "NOT ZION;" and "Not Zion" it remained for many years.

Grapevines still form part of the hanging gardens that dot the mountainsides, gardens above which the Golden Eagle sweeps in daring dignity. Western Yellow Pine soars from the hanging valleys high above.

Ted and I trail the ranger for miles along the trails - many of them cut by C.C.C. boys during the thirties - that curl about the mountains. We send our voice through Echo Valley to hear them race along for miles. We stop to examine the "Ant Lion," a weird little insect that digs a hole in the sand into which unwary ants fall, to be caught in his powerful claws and crunched in his powerful jaws.

Lizards scamper about the trail; and a plane, passing overhead, brings a threat of landslide. There was such a landslide two years ago, we learn, when tons of rock barely missed a group of hikers on this very trail. A helicopter was brought in from the South Rim of the Grand Canyon to dislodge the loosened rock that remained above. It dynamited the area, but the situation merely worsened. And so the MARINES landed. They climbed to the mountain top and fired rockets which brought down the loose rock and restored the area to comparative safety.

Once the range of the grizzly, the wolf, and the cougar, the kings of Carnivores, only the cougar has managed to survive man's dominance in this part of the great Southwest.

Zion's boulder-covered slopes bear silent witness to its toppled cliffs. The ground water of the region washes away the natural cement and undermines the cliff walls. With the coming of winter it freezes, widening the cracks, and the suddenly - a Rock Fall!

Many centuries ago an immense rock slide moved down the west wall of Zion Canyon damming the Virgin River by the Court of

Patriarchs, an immense basin lying between the three biblical mountain peaks. The boulders it carried with it were part of the soaring cliffs that lay one-third of a mile behind. Landslides constantly alter the magnificent scenery of Zion and Bryce Canyons, we were told - those smaller and - in the opinion of many - even more beautiful prototypes of the incredible Grand Canyon itself.

PRINCE EDWARD ISLAND

Prince Edward Island next, and we head there aboard a magnificent ferry, the "Prince Nova." A slight waiting period at the dock affords Ted an opportunity to engage the fishermen there in conversation. Their lobster boats for the most part are tied up along the wharf. There's "The Blue Strait," "Pictou," "Jacob's Pride No. 1," "Veraz," etc. Did we say engage the gentlemen in conversation??? A taciturn bunch, these men of the sea.

Ted speaks of the difficulties our Cape Cod lobstermen are having with the Russian trawlers; they have not heard of it. He questions them about their catch; they are non-committal. He remarks on the beauties of the province, and they regard him as though he was sporting two heads – badly mismated. "Give up!" I whisper laughingly.

One young fisherman is painting the stern of an enormous craft with a 4" brush, the which he dips to a depth of about ½" in shiny white paint. He doesn't spill a drop…and it will be three months before he finishes painting the thing, a 4" strip at a time! These Canadians, we have been assured, are never in a hurry…The craft is a scalloper and boasts a huge platform built in two sections which can be lowered by separate sets of block and tackle. The dragger is hauled upon the platform and scallops removed from it, leaving the mud to be washed off. Needless to say, it is Ted who explains the workings of the thing to me, and not the fisherman!

"Wait till you see the ISLAND!" said one of our shipmates, a Mrs. Angie Power, R..N. who had trained at Everett's Whidden Hospital, "The farms are gorgeous! Don't miss Stanhope and Cavendish Beaches with their beautiful sand dunes. And when you reach Summerside, call me," she said warmly. "I always have the kettle on for tea!" So typical of the hospitality we were to encounter all along the line in the friendly Maritimes.

And so we reached there - Prince Edward Island - and it was over the King's By-Way to Murray River. It still maintains the sweet charm of a century ago, this pastoral province with its 1100 miles of seacoast, we soon decided. It is completely surrounded by water, by the Northumberland Strait and the Gulf of St. Lawrence; and it claims the warmest ocean swimming north of Florida. Its soil is rich and red; the sand dunes silver; and the landscape the rich rare green we found in Ireland.

We settled ourselves in a beautiful trailer park in Cornwall, a place of enormous proportions where we walked the red sand beach for perfect miles each lovely evening, with the tide sounding in our ears and the gulls crying. What was it Jacques Cartier wrote of P.E.I. after his return from that 1534 exploration of his? "A wave-washed, wind-swept, sun-kissed, air-cooled province." Amen to that!

It's the proverbial fisherman's paradise of course, with the world's record for giant tuna broken consistently year after year. Last year, we were told, the first bluefin to weigh more than 1000 lbs. was caught off North Lake and by a young law student from the U.S. no less!

It was at P.E.I. that your columnist was stricken with rock fever. "Ted," I remarked one evening, eyeing the profusion of colorful rocks and shells that literally covered the beach, "You know among five grandsons we are bound to turn up at least one ROCKHOUND, especially," I added, "Since this grandmother of theirs adores rocks so. Don't you think we might take a few home from these beautiful Canadian beaches?"

Ted looked doubtful. We were by now about one month into our journey and he was merrily rejoicing in the knowledge that we were consuming by leaps and bounds the gigantic stock of food I had managed to tuck surreptitiously into the family trailer. "You wouldn't believe what a difference it makes," he kept assuring me as he vowed never again to leave to my lavish hand the family larder. "The trailer literally FLIES!" "We won't take too many," I hastily added, "I know you don't want too much weight, dear; but it really would be criminal not to take a few of these rocks from the wild Atlantic!"

Ted's enthusiasm for the idea was slightly less than large, however, he agreed that we might "take a few - not too many - just a few!" It was surprising how quickly pockets were filled that summer evening; and tote bags produced; and purses pushed out at the seams…that evening and the next and the next and the next…in P.E.I. and Nova Scotia and New Brunswick and Quebec and Ontario… "Don't let's put them in the trailer," I had said magnanimously, "because of the weight. Let's put them in the back of the car" - which sank lower and lower and lower and had to have more and more air pumped into the air shocks with each succeeding spree of beachcombing. By now, Ted was helping the cause along; picking up the treasures and tucking them nobly into the receptacles and then carrying them to the waiting cartons, though he DID opine now and then that he now hoped he'd be able to get the CAR off the ground. I was congratulating myself like mad. Ted was being a perfect darling, as usual, I told me. And then-quite by accident-I DISCOVERED THAT FOR EVERYONE OF MY TREASURES HE TUCKED INTO THE FAMILY CAR, TEDDIE WAS TOSSING SIX OR SEVEN OVERBOARD!

Charlottetown, the Capital of this lovely province and we naturally visited historic Province House. Here we learned that the island was successively named Abegweit, Saint-Jean and Prince Edward to denote the Micmac, French and English regimes. It was at Charlottetown that the First Confederation Conference was held in 1864, however, it was not until 1873 that P.E.I. joined the Dominion of Canada. "Why??" we wanted to know; and one Howard Hobbs, host in the Chamber, came up with an interesting reason. The island was owned almost entirely by absentee landlords in those days, he said - landholders who had rendered some service to the Crown and had been given the land in return. These landholders would have to be paid off; and at that time the Province had not the wherewith to accomplish this. It was not until 1873 that arrangements were worked out with the Dominion Government which loaned P.E.I. the money to pay off the absent ones, along with building the railroad they were struggling with, and the wharves and piers they needed so badly, said our informant.

"In this historic chamber around this table," we read from a handsome plaque, "on Sept. 1st, 1864, were gathered those statesmen whose deliberations led to the formation of the Dominion of Canada." It's a beautiful Chamber, with stark white walls and an Italian marble fireplace, rugs and window hangings in royal red…handsome chandeliers. Its ceiling design features in true British Style the thistle, shamrock and rose. A magnificent bronze mural graces one wall, with the crest of the uniting provinces in each of its corners and the names of the delegates inscribed in the margins. At the center top the Arms of England; in the center bottom the Canadian Arms…

Meaningful inscriptions inform us that "Providence being their Guide" (from Milton's Paradise Lost") "They builded better than they knew" (from Emerson)…And that "Thy Dominion shall extend from sea to sea and unto the river's end." Truly the Dominion of Canada does extend from the Atlantic to the Pacific, we reflected, and from the St. Lawrence River to the MacKenzie…and all of it so incredibly beautiful.

QUEBEC CITY

It is called the "Cradle of Canadian History", this story-book kind of place we have come to visit Quebec City, capital of the Province; it was founded in 1608 by Samuel de Champlain upon the very site where Jacques Cartier wintered in 1535; and it is really two cities in one.

There is the Upper Town, spread magnificently upon the crown of Cape Diamond; and the Lower Town, lying along the shore of the St. Lawrence River. The Upper City needs no restoration; here to be found are the incomparable Chateau Frontenac, rising from the cliffs like a medieval castle, and the great fortress, La Citadelle; the Parliament buildings and the storied Plains of Abraham. Throughout the entire Lower City, however, restoration work is in progress as a special team of historical architects, backed by the interest and finances of a history-minded government, turn back the centuries and restore this historic bit of Canada to its former grandeur. Interestingly enough, however, the wonderful old cut stone houses are to be lived in, and not to be mere shrines for visiting tourists - at extremely high rental costs, we might add.

We pause just long enough to visit one of these already reconstructed buildings that IS a museum - the Hotel Chevalier which was built in

1752 for one Jean Baptiste chevalier. Then it is up the towering cliffside to Dufferin Terrace in the "Ascenseur", the entrance to which has a story all of its own. It lies within a dear little stone house built by the architect Baillif in the year 1683 for Jolliet, the discoverer of the Mississippi, no less. He occupied it until his death in 1700; and one wonders what went on in the subterranean passage leading to Cul-de-Sac Cove, the existence of which we learn.

Dufferin Terrace, and we now tower 200' above the mighty St. Lawrence and find ourselves in another world. Here Champlain's first fort was built in 1620 here is where he died on a snowy Christmas Day in 1635. We stand wonderingly in the Place d'Armes or parade ground and look skyward toward the towering towers of the Frontenac. Once it was called the Chateau Haldimand, we learn, in honor of the British governor of that name. Roosevelt and Churchill and MacKenzie King hammered out much of the Allied policy here during World War II. WE shall return there for lunch, we decide, after which we shall investigate those interesting little horse-drawn carriages that are pipping about. First, however, we shall walk about the historic streets, stopping at will to poke into their quaint little corners…streets like Rue du Tresor with its artists and their exhibits…

The area is scuppers awash with monuments; they are to be seen in every park and bit of green we pass. We proceed along the Promenade des Gouverneurs to the Jardins des Gouverneurs where we find the most exciting monument of them all the famous Wolfe-Montcalm monument which is perhaps unique in history because it was erected in honor of two opposing generals, both of whom died in the Battle of the Plains of Abraham. Its Latin inscription moves us. "mortem Virtus Communem, Famam Historia, Monumentum Posterias Dedit." (Valour gave them a common death, history a common fame, posterity a common monument.) wonderful! Incidentally, that tragic battle lasted a mere twenty minutes, we learn to our horror.

We walk along the Promenade thrilling to the sight of the lovely St. Lawrence below; and now we proceed to climb the 500 or more steps to the Citadel above - where we arrive spent and bent only to learn that we might have DRIVEN there effortlessly in the family car, for which we are paying parking fees in the Lower City, by the way! Ah, well…

We decide to forgo a visit to the Citadel that day and instead to meander back over the wonderful streets that lie - jammed with traffic, but beautiful nonetheless - invitingly before us. And so it is down the Grande-Allee and past the Parliament buildings whose immense sprawling Gothic loveliness rises from a park of typical Canadian beauty.

Handsome cut stone house after handsome cut stone house carried its historic plaque. At No.25, for instance, we find the 1648 Kent House. From 1792 to 1794 the Duke of Kent, Queen Victoria's father, made this his town residence. A short distance beyond we delight in finding the dwelling of Jonathon Sewell, the son of John Adams' law partner, born in Cambridge, Mass. We approach the handsome 19th century Saint-Louis Gate which has replaced the original one through which the body of Montcalm was carried after the Plains Battle and through which the Regiment de Carignan marched in 1690 to relieve Frontenac during the siege by Phipps. History!

The 1639 Ursuline Convent is next - in the lovely chapel of which Montcalm was buried; here was conducted the first girls' school in America, we learn. And now it is back to the Frontenac for lunch; and then a tour of the Lower City, the center of which is the Place Royale. In time, this area, completely restored, will handsomely recreate the past.

Notre Dame-des-Victoires Church has a remarkable history, we find. Suspended from its ceiling is what is thought to be the original ship model of the "Breze". the sailing ship on which the Marquis de Tracy sailed to Canada from France, in 1664 with four companies of the historic Regiment de Carignan. The Marquis placed the model in "ex voto" in the vault of the Cathedral where it remained until 1759 when, in the course of the siege, it crumbled with the burning church. Preserved as an Historic treasure by the authorities of Laval University, it was restored by the Quebec Historical Society in 1954 and placed once again in the church.

The history of each of the wonderful old cut stone houses in the Place Royale is a matter of public record, we are happy to note, No.13, for instance, built in 1722, housed Jolliett's son-in-law and his family; No.11 was the home of the Formel family, members of the 18th century Sovereign Council; and No.29 was built in 1683 for Francois Hazeur, a very wealthy merchant.

We return on the morrow to visit the Citadel. MacKenzie King, F.D.R., and Churchill met here as well while planning strategy for W.W.II; and we view the historic room in which they met. Adjoining Commanding Officer's residence and the officers' quarters are next, followed by the domicile of the regimental mascot, a handsome goat named "Batisse III". The oldest building in the citadel, the "Redoubt" was built by the French in 1693, we learn; and there's a bombproof hospital dating back to 1849 whose 7' thick walls face us as we pip about within the Citadel. The walls on the river side, incidentally, are 9' in thickness and the roof of the building is 10'.

We visit the Citadel Museum which was built by the French as a powder magazine in 1750; and here we view a handsome diorama depicting the history of this wonderful city; its many sieges; its victories and its defeats including the final tragic one that saw it prostrate on the Plains of Abraham. Incidentally, the walls of the citadel facing those fateful Plains is 14' thick, and one may walk through it and examine the gun slots through which the French hoped to hold the enemy at bay with their fire.

We love the historic documents we find in the Museum, a building with huge buttresses which were built, we are told, "to store 2388 barrel of powder." There is, for instance, the "Order by Brig. Gen. James Murray, Governor of Quebec; ordering the officers of the Militia of the parish of Ste. Foy to send to Quebec within two days 30 carts of hay, warning them that failing to obey this order, their parish will be burnt. (Dated at Quebec on 3rd Nov 1759) And a little book: "General Wolfe's Instructions to Young Officers: Also his Orders for a battalion and an Army together with the orders and signals used in Embarking and Debarking an Army by Flat-bottomed boats etc. and A Placart to the Canadians to which is prefixed the resolution of the House of Commons for his Monument; and his character and the dates of all his commissions…also the duty of an Adjutant and Quarter Master…"

We read it and remember that wonderful monument he shares with Montcalm…

It's a marvelous fort, La Citadelle, we decide. It crowns Cap Diamont and was built by the British upon the advice of the Duke of Wellington, no less. British troops were garrisoned there until 1871 when they were relived by Canadian units. We enjoyed every minute of our visit there; and by the way, what fun it is now, with all our pipping behind us, to sit easily in one of those handsome little horse-drawn carriages and effortlessly retrace our steps over the same historic places.

And now with the dawning of another day it is off to the Shrine of St. Anne de Beaupre along the mist-shrouded St. Lawrence, past handsome Montmorency Falls, eastern Canada's highest, to the magnificent Basilica. We attend Mass here and then, having absorbed the beauty of the edifice we visit the site of the original old shrine dating back to 1658, and the second shrine that was built on that site in 1878, using the original materials and the original altar. From this Memorial Chapel it is on to the Scala Santa (the sacred stairway), a reproduction of the 28 steps ascended by Christ before undergoing His Judgement in Pilate's Praetorium. Pilgrims by the hundreds are ascending the stairway on their knees, praying the while for world peace.

A visit next to the Cyclorama of Jerusalem, a panoramic painting 360' long and 45' high on which, from an observation point, one may view the City of Jerusalem and its environs as it was 2000 years ago on the day of the Crucifixion. Mountains rise against a sinister threatening sky and the countryside is bathed in a strange mysterious light. WE identify the tomb of Jeroboam the First, Israel's first ruler; and the roads leading to Jaffa and to Damascus; we see the Xystus, the gymnasium of the Roman soldiers; and the Tower of Antonia, Pilate's residence; and the Palace of the High Priests along with the Tomb of Absalom, son of King David. Most moving of all is, of course, Calvary, the Place of Crucifixion, where the figure of the Christus hangs suspended between the two thieves. Moving and memorable.

QUEBEC CONTINUED

Trois Rivieres is next on our travels and we journey merrily there with the wide Saint Laurent running swiftly beside us...stopping hither and yon en route to visit wonderful little churches where we continue to find the masterpieces of the Canadian artist, Antoine Plamondon and the altars and carved wooden figures and bas-reliefs of the incomparable Francois Baillairge. Beautiful!

Through Donnacona which was once an old French military post and was named for the Huron Indian Chief whom Cartier carted off to France where he died in 1536, never having returned to his native land…

At Cap-Sante we hear an interesting tale. Fort Jacques-Cartier once stood nearby, and it was to this fort that the remnants of Montcalm's army withdrew after the fateful Battle of the Plains of Abraham. It was the last bit of French to surrender to the English after the capture of Montreal, and its defenders held out so long and fought so bravely "they earned the right to retire with the honors of war." How about that!

And then through Batiscan where we are astounded to learn that archaeologists have unearthed the ruins of a permanent Indian settlement dating back some thousand years before the Christian era! Cap-de-la-Madeleine, and yet another Basilica towering majestically beside the original little 1714 chapel - the oldest church in Canada and perfectly preserved in its original form. And now we are at Trois Rivieres which represents the gateway to the storied Saint-Maurice Valley. Here the famous Rabaskas were built during the last century - those 35-40' birchbark freight canoes in which voyageurs and fur traders journeyed to the Athabasca River in the far Canadian west. "Rabaskas", as a matter of fact, is a corruption of the word "Athabasca."

It's a wonderful town, Trois Rivieres, filled with ancient historic houses and fascinating places to visit including the famous Ursuline Convent where we hear one more delightful bit of history. Here is where the sick and wounded American soldiers were hospitalized and cared for during the Occupation of the town after the battle of June 8, 1776. The nuns, we are told, submitted their bill for dressings and medications to the American government. It was duly endorsed by the American Commander, William Gosforth; and it amounted to $130.00 AND IT WAS NEVER PAID! And in 1968 one Raymond Douville, a local historian, came up with the delightful fact that, disregarding the statute of limitations and figuring the amount at the rate of 6 percent compound interest, Washington would by that time have owed the Ursuline ladies of Trois Rivieres the handsome sum of $8,519,630.00.

And now we reach Pointe-aux-Trembles, just eight miles from the city of Montreal. We tuck ourselves merrily into the most enormous trailer park on earth and promptly discover to our delight that we are entrenched directly behind an enormous recreation hall beyond which a vast and beautiful swimming pool beckons. "How great!" we say as we settle down upon our chaises to watch the world go by, which it does…on Thursday evening and Friday evening…to play cards and pip about and toss its collective coins into a juke box which is pitched remarkably low. Came Saturday evening and the teenagers began arriving especially early. "There must be something special doing tonight." we remark. There was. A ROCK AND ROLL BAND that sharply at seven traipsed across the lawns before us and set up shop in the recreation hall that might as well have been outdoors…to play screamingly until midnight in an unending torrent of sound that bounced off our trailer walls and aching heads like a fall of hail. Oh well, you can't win them all!

and now it is off to Montreal, an immense city located on an island thirty miles long and built about the mountain that gave it its name - Mont Royal. When Jacques Cartier first arrived there in 1535 it was called Hochelaga by the 3500 Indians whose sophisticated settlement included fifty huge wooden houses fashioned of logs and covered with sheets of bark. Seventy-five years later, thanks undoubtedly to the Indian Wars that were constantly in progress, Champlain found nothing there but the broad meadow, fertile and inviting.

There are two beach levels in this immense sprawling city. There is the lower or "cradle" section which includes Le Vieux Montreal and Notre-Dame Church, the court houses, the city government and the financial district; and the upper level, a short but steep grade above.

We find the Place Royale and d'Youville Square and proceed on a walking tour along St. Paul Street, the oldest street in the city. We visit Notre Dame Church which holds 5,000 people and is utterly magnificent. Its architect, one James O'Donnell, an Irish Protestant, is the only man entombed there, we learn.

The edifice has two towers - Perseverance Tower on the west which contains "Le gros bourdon", one of the world's most famous bells weighing 24,780 lbs.…and Temperance Tower on the east, with its Carillon of ten bell chimes. We arrive in time to hear the unbelievably beautiful combination of the two… "le gros" and the Carillon…the most unusual sound imaginable, a blending of rare and unique beauty.

The rose windows of the great Cathedral church…the mother church of Montreal…and the 40' stained glass windows that line its walls catch the noon sun as we arrive, creating a vision of almost unearthly loveliness. On each of the Church pews we find a carved head. These are the founders…the first parishioners of the Church.

We are delighted to find Montreal's oldest house, which was built in 1698 on foundations of an earlier building that was designed to receive the King's Wards, young French girls of fine families who were sent to this new strange land to become wives of colonists.

Montreal is a magnificent city, almost 10 percent of it devoted to beautiful parklands. The Mt. Royal Park especially is a must…with its tiny artificial Beaver Lake and the incomparable view from the Chalet Lookout.

We naturally visit St. Joseph's Oratory and look back upon the life of the storied Brother Andre whom we remember from childhood and whose warm compassionate heart is encased there "as a symbol of his great love for fellow humans"…Brother Andre at whose death in 1937 a terrifying storm with the most savage of seas swept against the island for a full frantic week, so the story goes.

We are off to Ontario next, the last Canadian province we shall visit e'er we return via the Thousand Islands to our own dear U.S.A. and so our journeying goes.

8-23-70   RENDEZVOUS

Life for the Metayers has taken on a new hitch - A TRAILER HITCH! "If we plan to see OUR OWN wonderful country next," I had said to Ted a couple of years back when we returned after six adventure-filled months in Europe, "we should buy a TRAILER!"

Ted had regarded me as though I was wearing two heads - badly mis-matched… "In that way," I added, "we would have our own little home on wheels and could wander about the country for several months, stopping where we wished, with no regard for 'No Vacancy' signs etc. etc."

Ted's response had been considerably less than enthusiastic. He enjoys the comfort of a good motel room and bath. As a matter of fact, it had taken me two full years to reach the point where the head of the house of Metayer handed over the check that made a beautiful trim little seventeen foot FAN trailer ours! (And then it had taken me nine months to clear my calendar sufficiently for us to trip away with it…)

At any rate, the Metayers left Braintree the first of June for a three months' trip around the glorious U.S.A. and parts of western Canada, a trip from which they have just returned…- rendezvousing as we came, with Gael and Jim and their precious boys last Sunday afternoon in Burlington, Vermont, in a reunion that brought one magnificent trip to a magnificent climax…

The plan to rendezvous in the Green Mountain State had emerged full-blown a couple of weeks back as we engaged in our weekly Sunday evening telephone conversation with Gael and her loved ones. "Jim and the boys and I are going to upper New York State and Vermont on vacation," she had said. "Oh, how lovely," I had replied. "Dad and I are returning home via Vermont and New Hampshire." And then a sudden thought had struck. "When do you expect to be leaving?" I had asked. "Wouldn't it be marvelous if we could MEET somewhere?" Gael's immediate enthusiastic response had brought Jim to the downstairs extension and Ted to the phone booth; and a rendezvous was promptly planned - for Burlington, Vermont, on Sunday, August 16…

We'll be staying," said Jim, "at Holiday Inn or Howard Johnsons' Motor Lodge." "And we," said Ted, "will be saying at a trailer park at a lake or with a pool. There won't be many in Burlington," he added. "New England is not the West Coast." (where, we might add, three out of five vehicles on the main highways are either campers or cars hauling trailers…)

"Going home," sang the car wheels as Monday morning found us bidding farewell to Iowa and heading East. Ted piloted our little house on wheels toward the Green Mountain State as though he had ten minutes to make it; and we arrived at North Beach, on beautiful Lake Champlain, on Friday afternoon.

A call to three motels…The Corbins had not as yet arrived…And so we settled ourselves down to do the Town, with a visit to the beautiful Shelburne Museum about which you will read more later on; and to the Ethan Allen Monument, etc. etc.

On Sunday afternoon, right on schedule, came the telephone call that brought the trailer park manager dashing over to our campsite. "They are at Holiday Inn," she announced triumphantly, "They'll be right over. Your daughter asked me not to tell you; she wants to surprise you, but I just HAD TO!" And then we were all racing across the lawn and into one another's arms for the most marvelous reunion on earth. We all talked at once, the children-who looked to our starved eyes like Botticelli angels of Frontier Town and the North Pole, and the ferry ride across Lake Champlain and Ausable Chasm and the boat ride down the rapids! And we of our incredible adventures…Our boys had grown a foot. They excitedly presented us with a beautiful Christmas Music Box to hang in my foyer come Christmastime, following which ceremony an elaborate silence had to be maintained for the playing of "Jingle Bells" again and again and again…

"How do you fasten that car on your trailer?" asked Gregory, who has had a big boy's haircut and looks like a little boy doll. "Will you buy ME a car and a trailer?" he asks; and then, "When my CAR grows up, I'm going to Calipornia," he announces determinedly. Three year old Greg's "F's" always did come out as "P's." "That's my Pather," he adds solemnly, nodding toward Jim.

And now it is off to the beach and the playground, our boys handsome and dashing in the real Western cowboy hats we brought them from Steamboat Springs, Colorado, and then out to dinner where our wonderful son-in-law who is really a son to us, played host, wining and dining us elaborately in celebration of our return…Then back to the Corbin's beautiful room at Holiday Inn and a long lovely swim in the hotel pool…And how those boys can swim and dive…

We watched "Bonanza" on the colored T.V. until our boys fell sound asleep on the big roomy beds, and Jim returned us to our trailer park about midnight.

Our rendezvous at Burlington had become the wonderful climax to a completely wonderful trip…Gael and her family were to leave for home in the morning, and Ted and I would pip around the mountains of our beautiful Vermont and fair New Hampshire e'er once more we'd be together back in Braintree…But what a day was Sunday, August 16th! A time to treasure and remember.

SAFARI CONTINUED

And now, with the beautiful Christmas season behind us, we return to the State of Washington and a continuance of our American Safari.

Waterfalls had become a familiar sight as we journeyed through the mountainous West. They cascaded down the gleaming mountainsides, or meandered along the recesses between the lowering peaks. We had even ceased to photograph them…

But "Dry Falls" the "spectacular" feature of Dry Falls State Park - that was something else again! What on earth, I wondered, was a "Dry Falls" and what made it so spectacular???

We found it located at the head of the Lower Grande Coulee, a "ghost falls," it was called; and it represents, we learned, one of the world's geological wonders. It was 400 feet high and 34 miles across the crest. Once the thunder of its waters must have raced across what was then a savage land; now, of course, its thunder is stilled; its waters no longer flow…

Eons ago, we were told, a wind and savage river flowed from the immense glaciers of the Ice Age, to carve this mighty canyon and thence to retire as the glaciers receded. the "ghost falls" it left behind that "spectacular" sight which we viewed with a kind of awe, bears evidence of a prehistoric cataract that is reputed to have been "40 times mightier than Niagara…" Oh, to be a geologist on the wonderful trip to really comprehend the marvels we are viewing.

And now with Dry Falls just one more photographed memory, we find ourselves driving for miles and miles along the canyon floor, with black towering mountain walls rising on all sides. Erosion and glacial action have carved them into weird and wild forms. They crouch like prehistoric monsters ready to spring upon us as we drive beneath them.

Their sides are black. with ridges of copper and green; and dark caverns yawn grimly beneath stark overhanging crags.

We stop for lunch by the Ginkgo Petrified Forest en route to Yakima. Here geologists have uncovered the petrified remains of more than 200 species of trees - among them the Ginkgo, a sacred tree that is currently found only in the Orient…

Millions of years ago, we learned, this section of our wonderful country was a tree-covered swampland. It was bordered on the north by mountains, and the towering trees that covered both the mountains and the lowlands lived out their life spans and then settled as logs on the swampy earth. With the passing of time, lava flows covered the area and buried the vegetation completely. The elements in this wild and desolate area have eroded the lava strata and exposed the petrified remains of the trees that we now view from the edge of an immense cliff overlooking the wide Colorado River below.

We enter the Snoqualmie National forest, and now, says Ted, we must look for a trailer park. He is growing tired; mountain driving is especially taxing when one is toting one's home on wheels up and over one precipitous peak after another. WE pass several likely-looking national campsites, however, we are seeking a private trailer park and so we carry on- and on- and on- and finally we give up!

"Goodness knows how far we shall have to travel before we reach a private park," Ted announces finally. "We'll have to settle for a national campsite." The which we do!

it is located adjacent to the highway, and unlike those we passed back, it is merely a broad clearing with camping instructions and facilities for the payment of the camping fee, but no sign of a Ranger or camp attendant. To complete matters, there is not another soul parked in the campsite. Recalling little warnings we have received from trailer toters along the way against ever being the first to settle in ANY trailer park - let alone a national campsite in the deep forest - I find myself sending appeals Heavenward for even one additional trailer family to join us. Heaven, for once, fails to respond…

Darkness falls as only darkness CAN fall in the wild and remote Snoqualmie; and we remain alone in a campsite that is clearly visible from the nearby mountain highway.

I begin to feel a kinship with little old Red Riding Hood and wonder what course of action I shall pursue when the wolf comes…

"Ted," I say, as with dinner behind us and bedtime looming, he settles down with a good book. "Aren't you scared?" "Of course not," the head of the house says blithely. "Don't forget we have 'Betsy'." And out of the trailer closet comes the family shotgun, to be loaded and placed neatly beside his bed.

We settle ourselves for the blackest night I ever remember, with the towering mountains and the dense forest shutting even the night sky. I lie there…Little news items I have read rise to haunt me-like the one about the bears who descended from the mountains to shake and upset a trailer, sending its occupants into panic; and the criminals who robbed and murdered a nice elderly couple just like the Metayers beside a remote highway just like this one…

"A criminal could easily cover Ted with his gun from the window beside me," I tell myself in fright. "He wouldn't be able to REACH Betsy in time." Oh, well, I decide finally, we've had more fun than most in our nice lives; and our children are both grown up and happily married and situated. And so, reassured by the deep regular breathing of a spouse who never permits ANYTHING to interfere with his nice night's sleep, I drifted finally into mine.

DAWN in the Snoqualmie was an adventure. the sun rose over the soaring mountain peaks in a play of light and shadow that kept us spellbound. Ted and I,- both of whom were awake in time to see the rose and gold and black and mauve and purple of a spectacular to end all spectaculars. Oregon…The section of the State through which we must drive en route to California lies close to the sky for it is a wide open area lit with rolling hills and tidy farmland and scattered small settlements - the whole ringed with timbered mountains.

The grass covered mountain slopes have dried to a golden brown under the hot summer sun; and against this bronzed hue the deep green of pine and fir provide dramatic contrast.

We stop for the night in a tiny town called Curtin, settling ourselves in a dear little trailer park with a man-made lake stocked beautifully with fish, the which we might catch had we been fishermen. The park is handsomely landscaped, and each trailer space has been precisely laid out on a raised platform of cement with a ramp before it. There may have been an extra foot of space allowed on either side of the concrete area - for vagaries in parking - there was certainly, however, no more than that.

"This is not going to be easy for an amateur," said Ted, "You'll have to guide me in." I hopped from the car and Ted commenced to back the trailer toward its base, when, A FULL SCALE RECEPTION COMMITTEE ARRIVED TO GREET US! It consisted of one proud mother duck and the half dozen members of her brand new brood. The lady trotted her babies over for our inspection in a manner faintly suggestive of all the doting grandmothers I know - myself included! "Wait!" I screamed as Ted continued to maneuver "Fanny" toward the decidedly narrow ramp. "You will run over the ducks!" which merry little beasties happened at that moment to be running over and under and around the trailer in a mad pattern of behavior, with no two going in the same direction.

Ted, however, deep as he was in concentration upon the difficult task before him, failed utterly to hear my screams. He continued to back the thing up while I tried vainly to hold back our house on wheels with one frantic hand and shoo the little committee members out of harm's way with the other.

The ducks were saved, however, I wound up with A badly bruised arm and Ted with a case of the horrors as the message finally got through to him that his spouse was endeavoring to protect six silly little ducklings at the risk of her own silly little neck. And the ducklings and their proud parent??? They simply turned tail and trotted off to the pond for a nice cool swim the moment the fracas was over. One more bit on dear little Curtin, Oregon. "Let's take a walk to town," I said to Ted when, our dinner over, we had settled down to a sweet summer evening. Ted, as always, agreed to do just that.

"Would you please tell us," he asked the very charming couple who ran the trailer park, "in which direction we shall walk to find the town?" The two laughed merrily. "You are LOOKING at the town," they said. "The gas station and the snack bar and the post office and the trailer park that's it!" "But gosh," I said, It's on the MAP. How can it be on the map if it's that small?" "It has a POST OFFICE," said the lady gaily. "The minute they built the Post Office, we found ourselves on the map…"

So much for Curtin, Oregon, and our adventured there. The ducks, by the way, became our constant companions. We fed them and had fun with them, however, when the time came for Ted to descend from the concrete you-know-what and proceed on our way I shooed the little dears off personally and headed them all in the direction of the pond, from which point they solemnly regarded us as we bade them "Adieu" and headed once more for the open road…

STILL MORE ON GASPE

We could dwell forever, it seems, upon the loveliness of the Gaspe Peninsula…especially the land that lies between the Sacre Coeur and Riviere-du-Loup…for it is one of unending beauty. Riviere-du-Loup named for the great loups-marins or seals that once abounded there.

We approach BIC for instance, to marvel at its scenic charm. There's a legend about this enchanting place. Away back when the world was at its beginnings, so the story goes, a special angel was charged with the dispensing of the mountains and of the islands and of the seas and all the other lovely elements of this, our wondrous world. The celestial spirit arrived at Bic at the very end of a deeply tiring day. He was weary and he longed for respite from the task he had been assigned; however - trailing behind him like a glorious scarf - were multitudes of mountains and of islands, of valleys, and of silver seas, each one of which was yet to be assigned. The angel paused, thinking to rest a little while before proceeding on his way. He sank upon the cold brown earth and then - almost as an afterthought- this being-from-another-world draped the trailing scarf…the mountains and the islands, the valleys and the seas… across the land that lay about him.

Awakening after a little while, he found himself spellbound at the beauty of the scene he had created. "I cannot bear to it," he said softly, "I shall leave it as it is, that man may know forever the boundlessness of God's great love!" and thus was it created, so the legend goes, this lush and lovely corner of the world where more of mountains and of islands may be found than one might ever dream to find in any corner of the world…BIC, a deformation of the word "Pic", of course, which means "Peak;" but there is no other hint of deformation about this lovely place!

Incidentally, it's the setting for much of the very first novel ever to be written on Canadian soil "The History of Emily Montagu" by Mrs. Francis Brooke, wife of a chaplain of the Imperial troops stationed there, which was published in London in 1767.

We leave this lovely spot to journey further along the Peninsula. The handsome stone walls that have for miles separated the pasture lands have now given way to countless log fences, silvered and weathered by the suns of many years; they crisscross the rich green fields in careless abandon, it seems, adding to the charm of the pastoral scenes that move in all directions.

Each little village or settlement has a spot of history, it seems. "Trois Pistoles", for instance, is so called, 'tis said, because once-away back in the year 1621-a silver cup fell overboard from a small fishing craft as it moved up the churning river. "There go three pistoles," said the oarsman, a pistole being an ancient French coin, and the cup being worth about three of them. The village is called Trois Pistoles to this very day! Le aux Basques is named for those fearless Basque whale fishermen who long before Cartier ever sighted the area were busily building their ovens there and extracting the oil from the great ocean-dwelling mammals captured along the North Shore. The remains of those ancient ovens may still be seen, incidentally-huge affairs with an outside diameter as large as nine feet.

We are delighted at sight of "Pelerins", which is French for "pilgrims." That is precisely what this little group of four islands resemble as they emerge mistily from the fog-like atmosphere which is created in summer by a meeting of hot and cold air currents- four hooded pilgrims advancing wearily across a churning sea.

And now we are made suddenly aware of the fact that the lovely little churches we are observing and visiting as we journey along the Gaspe - each one an architectural gem - have been designed and adorned, even as are the wonderful European churches, by the same architects and sculptors, the same artists and artisans. Generations of Berlinguets and Leprohons, of Baillairges and Levasseurs and Plamondons have left the stamp of their genius upon the temples and tabernacles of the

Gaspe. Many of them are now designated by the Canadian government as "National Monuments" – one of them at Saint-Jean-Port-Joli dates back to the year 1776 and remains virtually unchanged from that time.

The Kamouraska Archipelago is clearly visible now - Kamouraska, which is Indian for "where there are rushes on the edge of the water." And there are!

The Gaspe was once a land of seigniories, of fiefdoms, and wonderful old manor houses remain to be duly visited and admired. Governors of New France, we learned, granted seigniories or fiefs to former officers or other individuals especially friendly to the Crown. At La Pocaterie we were interested to learn that the fief was granted in 1672 to the widow of a gentleman for whom it is named, and whose daughter became the wife of Pierre Le Moyne d'Iberville, the founder of Louisiana. Tie after tie after tie with our own beautiful country is to be found here in this lovely land across our northern borders.

And now we are nearing the end of the Gaspe, and we settle ourselves in a beautiful trailer park in Beaumont from which point we shall explore Quebec City and the Shrine of St. Anne de Beaupre and the Ile d'Orleans and the rest. The trailer is tucked neatly away and we head for Levis in the family car, pausing as we go to examine an ancient church, on the door of which Wolfe posted his Proclamation of 1759, demanding the surrender of the French. The villagers promptly destroyed it, we were told, and the soldiers retaliated by setting fire to the little church. "But only the door burned," said the sexton proudly as he showed us about this dear historic place.

Have we thought to mention the tiny procession chapels that line the roadways and towns of the Gaspe? They are precious small miniatures of the handsome old churches that abound in such unbelievable numbers in this deeply devout little corner of the land that is our neighbor. And they are lovely to behold!

LEVIS- it lies across the strait from the historic City of Quebec… "Quebec" which means "narrowing" in the Indian language of the Micmacs. Its streets, like the streets of Quebec City, are sloping and lined with wonderful old houses. We reach there and we drive about the place and then we board the ferry that will carry us across the broad St. Lawrence River to the splendid city itself - AND THERE IT IS! It towers upon the cliffs above, a sprawling beautiful walled city - the ONE walled city on the continent north of Mexico.

Quebec City! The splendid towers of the Chateau Frontenac are buried against a sky that is now bright with sun, now dark with unshed rain. We look above to where a giant fortress crowns Cap Diamont with a proud commanding air. Quebec City! The old city here below the wall where we propose to dock; the upper city soaring brilliantly above.

The ferry touches land. We drive across the ancient cobbled streets of yet one more of those enchanting places we are managing to know on this our first real introduction to the splendors of the Maritimes and their neighbor; fair Quebec.

Quebec City! We propose to explore it from end to shining end, and we do; and ours are a hundred merry adventures about which - hopefully - you will be reading in this column next week.

10-8-72   TEXAS

Texas next! The State's name was derived from an Indian word, "Tejas," meaning "friends", we are to learn. Six flags have flown over its mile high mountains and semi-tropical valleys...the Spanish flag; the French and then the Mexican flag; the flag of the Republic of Texas; the Confederate flag, and the Stars and Stripes...

It's a land of oil wells and ghost towns; of citrus groves and cotton fields; of dude ranches and swank resorts; of springfed lakes and desert sands.

Cattle roams the range land as we head for the City of Dallas... "Big D"...where we shall view the site of the John F. Kennedy assassination and see the Memorial Texans have raised to his memory. We settle ourselves in Arlington, a city nearby, because the trailer park we have elected to patronize boasts a swimming pool 150' long and 80' wide, and it is HOT-95 degrees.

The Metayers arrange for MORNING sight-seeing when the thermometer is THAT high...preferably very early in the morning so as to leave the afternoon free for swimming and lazing; accordingly the sun is barely up as we head for the JFK Memorial and the additional sights that Dallas has to offer...past such fascinating phenomena, we might add, as a "Drive-Through Pawn Shop" and a dining spot that offers a "Foot-Long Hot Dog"; and a "Yellow Belly Drag Strip" and countless "Washaterias."

The John F. Kennedy Plaza slumbers in the sunlight. It's a beautiful area, its lawns so perfectly maintained as to find us doubting the authenticity of the grass. Nearby is the cabin of John Neely Bryan, founder of Dallas. He it was who organized Dallas County, we learn. He was responsible for establishing the one and only Post Office in the City of Dallas under the Republic of Texas; and he built the first County Courthouse. As a matter of fact, he donated to the County the area where the Courthouse stands today, as well as the spot where his primitive log cabin now rests. Perhaps the land on which the JFK Memorial is erected was part of that original gift; at any rate it is located a stone's throw away...a magnificent monument - huge, imposing, a shining white granite poem in modern architecture rising skyward to a height of 60 feet or so...

The plaque before it...affixed to a broad concrete apron...reads: "The joy and excitement of John Fitzgerald Kennedy's life belonged to all men. So did the pain and sorrow of his death.

When he died on Nov 22, 1963 shock and agony touched human conscience throughout the world.

In Dallas there was a special sorrow.

The young President died in Dallas. The death bullets were fired 200 yards west of this site. This memorial designed by Philip Johnson was erected by the people of Dallas. Thousands of people contributed support, money and effort.

It is not a memorial to the pain and sorrow of death, but stands as a permanent tribute to the joy and excitement of one man's life. John Fitzgerald Kennedy's life."

Within the outer monument, a shining edifice of blue-black marble, ten feet square, to bear his name forever more, John Fitzgerald Kennedy... We stand there, looking back upon the Book Depository Building where the killer stalked his prey; marking the route by which the Cavalcade had borne our own dear Massachusetts martyr to his death...remembering the horror and the pain...We stand there, and somehow we are impelled to LEAVE the State of Texas...

WE had planned to store the family car and trailer there in Houston and fly from Texas into Mexico for what would doubtless prove to be another gay adventure, we decide however, to call the whole thing off and fly from Boston later, which we now propose to do.

So it is now off across the Texas Lakes Trail and then the Texas Forts Trail. Armadillos – victims of too speedy motorists - line the highways; we've not seen these curious creatures other than in zoos. The road is visible for miles ahead, threading its off-white way through timber-covered mountains and wide wild arroyos. A lone hawk circles perpetually above us as we drive along, it seems.

Texas is wearing a hundred different faces. There are cacti everywhere; and oil wells and storage tanks; and farmlands with their crops serenely waving, and barren sagebrush-covered mountains… something for everyone…

We leave Abilene behind and then, stopping for gas, read the following notice upon the station wall: "Exact cash or credit cards after dark. To prevent robberies purchases may be made only with exact cash or approved credit cards. After each sale card is placed in locked safe. Salesman does not have key". "Is that really necessary???" we ask. The station attendant shakes a sorry head, "It sure is, ma'am," he drawls.

An endless procession of trucks rumbles along the highway. They are transporting cattle to the State's innumerable stockyards…stockyards that house countless thousands of head of cattle that are waiting to be shipped…waiting beneath the nightmare of a broiling Texas sun. In one of the trucks we spot a little calf, its eyes closed with weariness, leaning against his mother's side…leaning because there is no room for him to fall, so crowded is the vehicle.

Through Roscoe, Texas, now, where the land is completely flat that one can see for miles and miles on every side. Windmills soar above the farmlands with their rich red soil. And then it is over a desert-like wasteland. Occasional flat-topped mountains now square off bleakly against a sky devoid of color, a sky that - drained of fleecy clouds and cooling winds - gives off a pale parched

Look…

Oil wells are everywhere.

Over the Double Mountain Fork of the Brasos River next, and here we stop to view one more historic landmark, "Garza County's First Oil Well", we read; and then we learn that the first oil producing wells in this oil producing area were established at Justiceburg in 1926; and that the 1500 oil wells of Garza County have produced more than 85 million barrels of oil in the past half century.

The scene, though rugged and wild, is spectacular. Distant hillsides of royal purple sand lie soothingly against the drab sky. The mountains are layered; and great colorful dunes rise from the canyon floors. They run from pink to rose to mauve and then to plush, pure purple. Sagebrush dots the scene. Yes indeed, 'tis a spectacular State, this Texas…And is it ever BIG!

10-4-70   SOUTH DAKOTA

The Badlands of south Dakota…For as long as there have been Western movies, outlaws have been losing sheriffs in their desolate depths. I had thought about them, and read about them, and now, suddenly there they were, grimy and gray. A ragged swathe of pinnacles and peaks of saw-toothed hills and barren gorges, flush against a slate blue sky that seemed as strange in aspect as the land itself.

The French Canadian trappers who are generally conceded to have been the first white men to stumble upon these barren bits of our America called them "les mauvaise terres a traverser," which translated means "bad lands to travel across." The Indians who had roamed their wastes for centuries before had named the region "Mako sica," which means just about the same thing…

The 170 square mile area is today known as the "Badlands Monument," legislation for the authorization of which National Park having been approved by Congress in 1929. The Monument itself was officially established ten years later with the cooperation, it might be noted, of the State of South Dakota.

Oh, to be a geologist! To really comprehend the evolvement of this wild and desolate area, the Badlands, as it was unfolded to the visitors who oh-ed! and ah-ed! while roaming through its fastnesses.

Once, millions of years ago, we were told, this "land of the White river" was a wide and marshy plain where huge, now extinct, animals lived and died to leave their remains buried in the sediments of the wide, swift river. Mountain streams, sweeping quantities of silt before them as they came, buried them still deeper in the mud.

Eons passed; and then volcanic activity far to the west hurled enormous quantities of material eastward - the prevailing west wind depositing it as a blanket of ash upon the barren land.

The many climatic changes in the millions of years that have elapsed since the beginning of the Badlands produced lush grasslands, we are told, where once were marshes; and prairies where once swamplands cloaked the earth…

The water from the highlands above began to form tributaries of the wide White River- tributaries that to this very day erode the soft layers of rock within the mountain areas, to cut a swathe of soaring spires and pinnacles and buttes where golden eagles come to nest; and swifts and cliff swallows to rear their noisy young; and rock wrens too, to nest within the crevasses that dot the mountain heights.

There is scant vegetation in the Badlands of South Dakota. Only an occasional patch of juniper lying against the sickly gray of canyon or of pass; or Yuccas, sending their sparse spires reaching toward the sky.

The Monument's wet areas, to be sure, have yielded trim little cottonwood islands; and an occasional patch of wild rose - all welcome sights within this area of desolation where prairie rattler lie in wait; and bullsnakes and blue racers slip about; and summer's heat is harsh; and winter's kiss a cruel caress of ice.

Sunset on the Badlands…the jagged saw-tooth ridges are aflame, their gaunt grim grayness swathed in pink and rose and gold, their lines softened and made sweet by the glittering gleaming robe that Mother Nature drapes our world at sunset.…

Reluctantly we leave this fascinating section of the fascinating place that is Dakota, her barren Badlands.

It is Dakota's great gaunt granite "Needles" that we visit next, the most exciting topographical feature, we have been told, of those beautiful Black Hills whose origin must also be volcanic, we opine. Tall, slim towering pinnacles and crags rise one upon the other, rearing proud heads from out the lush and lovely setting that is Custer Park State.

We drive about the mountains along unbelievably curving roadways toward the top. We journey even higher to what seems to be the summit of the world, through narrow little tunnels cut into the mountain's heart across rustic bridge upon rustic bridge…bluebells and wild iris lining the hairpin turns.

The game refuge emerges, and we are warned that "Buffalo are dangerous. Stay on the highway near your car!" we are cautioned; and we do. What fun, however, to find the forms of Bison rising from the brush that lines our way!

Small wild begging burros stop our car to find the sweets that we and other travelers pass their way.

We come at last to the "Needle's Eye," one towering crag that could be threaded with a giant string; and here we pause to look upon the jagged panorama of the Needles all strung out now like mammoth teeth against the sky.

Day's end…we seem to have covered all 72,000 awe-inspiring acres of our fair, fair South Dakota's Custer State Park.

Have we thought to mention the "Pigtails?" South Dakota's name for a series of fascinating mountain arches and tiny mountain tunnels - cach one placed in such a way as to superbly frame the beauty of Mt. Rushmore's wondrous Sculpture, far behind.

The lofty granite faces look our way. They seem to send a silent stern farewell to us and all those other proud Americans who have come to look upon the heights of what was once Mt. Rushmore, just another mountain peak within our land; but what has now become a "Shrine of Democracy" indeed, a lasting memorial to the memory of four "movers and shakers" who had a hand in fashioning the American dream.

THE AMISH COUNTRY

The Metayers have returned from one more "Summer Safari" in the delightful company of "Fanny," the self-contained little travel trailer that now, in its third season of operation, seems to fit the family like a second skin. To quote a colorful and appropriate expression borrowed from those fascinating inhabitants of the Pennsylvania Dutch Country, this year's first port of call; "Our OFF is

ALL," meaning "Our vacation is over."

And what a vacation it has been…a 7,000 mile trek over what surely be the loveliest land on this grand old earth of ours - incredibly beautiful America. Take Lancaster, for instance, the heart of the Pennsylvania Dutch Country, with its huge rolling superbly cultivated farmlands, lying beneath a limitless expanse of sky; its trim little farmhouses and immense old barns; its shining silos and its sounding windmills; its rolling hills and verdant valleys, and in its fields those lean bearded farmers with their broad-brimmed hats and battered braces; and the weathered farm women with their long black skirts and the small white prayer caps that seem to hug grimly the plaited plastered hair that is the trademark of the Amish women, old or young.

Yes, these are the Amish people, the "Plain Dutch," as opposed to the "Fancy Dutch," those modern ones who place Hex signs upon their barns and drive motorcars and run their great farms electrically… the quaint independent descendants of German émigrés who landed on our shores in the early 1700's. Today they number 8,000 stalwart souls, dedicated to humility and hard work; and by rejecting all outside influences they have erected a symbolic wall about themselves…A farming people who, scorning the use of electricity as a means of connecting them permanently to the outside world, know not the entertainment of T.V. or radio, the convenience of a car or of a tractor or of any of the all-encompassing items of farm machinery that makes life easier for today's tiller of the soil. An absolutely fascinating people these - dedicated to the one-room school house concept where their children are permitted to attend only eight grades of schooling and must graduate at fifteen to a life of hard work. As a consequence of this philosophy there are no Amish professionals and we were relieved to learn upon inquiry that the

Amish people are at least allowed to consult outside professionals when the need arises.

An Amish family, we learn, is EXPECTED to include eight or more children. This represents an insurance against "defectors," we were told. Should two of the children defect, there will still be six or more to produce eight future Amishers each, our informant said quite simply.

The children learn early to farm; and each one has his chores. How we marveled at the sight of a ten year old lad attired exactly like his father even to the broad-brimmed hat, diligently following the horse-drawn plough across the family farmlands!

Incidentally, the unmarried Amish girl starts early to collect the glassware and china that will be part of her trousseau; and to save any and all rags that come her way - for these will be dyed by her mother and carefully set aside; and when plaited into a rug by the official Amish weaver, will constitute the lady's wedding gift to her adult daughter... And by the way, we were intrigued to note that the rug will be woven in strips so that a worn section may be replaced if necessary. The rug, you see, is expected to last a lifetime!

And now a bit about Amish weddings...They are always celebrated during the month of November when the harvest is over; and on a Tuesday or a Thursday, these being the least busy days for Amish housewives.

The bride's wedding attire is a simple affair - a white cape and apron which are worn over her Sunday dress; and the cape has a special significance, for at the conclusion of the ceremony it will be given for safekeeping to the bride's best friend where it will remain until the death of the bride who will be buried in it! It is adjustable for expansion, we were assured solemnly! And another delightful bit-a cow is purchased with what would have constituted the cost of a "fancy" wedding dress. The groom, incidentally, is married in white as a symbol of the Resurrection. And the couple is joined for life, there being no divorce in the Amish Church.

Newlyweds enjoy a decidedly DIFFERENT honeymoon, departing on their travels in a "Courting Buggy," an open affair - the parents gift to each boy grown old enough to date. They will not leave the community, they will, however, travel from the home of one friend or relative to that of another, visiting for a while and picking up the wedding gifts which are never brought to the ceremony itself. As the buggy overflows with gifts it is turned homeward where the couple tucks away the loot, resuming the honeymoon with a now empty vehicle…a honeymoon that will end only when the month of March arrives to bring with it the planting season that will introduce the newlyweds to the duties and responsibilities that will be theirs for all of their lives.

As the Amish family increases in size, the Courting Buggy will be replaced by a "Family Wagon," a covered affair; which will eventually be replaced by a "Market Wagon," a covered vehicle capable of tucking in the ten anticipated family members and good for thirty to forty years of solid service. Thrift must, of necessity, be the watchword of the Amish farmer who is expected to provide a farm of at least 51 acres for each of his married sons, and at a cost of approximately $2,000 per acre. The last son to marry will inherit his father's own property, building an addition that will be known as "Granddaddy's House," where his parents will retire to live in peaceful serenity for the remainder of their days.

More next week about the fascinating way of life of the Amish people…including a report of a visit to an authentic Amish farmhouse, a 200 year old affair that was owned originally by Richard and Thomas Penn, grandsons of the fabulous William…

How delightful it is to be writing a weekly "Cabbage" once again; I've missed it!

THE GASPE PENINSULA

The Gaspe Peninsula! The very words set my heart racing as we looked back upon the rapidly receding shoreline of beautiful Prince Edward Island from the deck of the Borden Ferry that would carry us and our trailer across the blue of the Gulf to Cape Tormentine, New Brunswick – from which point we were to head for this scenic wonderland in historic Quebec, The Gaspe Peninsula! It seemed I had always wanted to visit it…

The day was wonderful, however, as we pipped about the trailer park making ready our departure. Ted and I had found ourselves having to don great high boots against the slither and mud of the terrain. "it must have rained heavily last night," I had remarked to our next door trailer neighbor, Mel, as he arrived to offer his services in casting off. "Oh, no," said this hardy Prince Edward Islander firmly. "That's just the HEAVY DEW!" I had laughed merrily. "So heavy it PUDDLES???" I had asked.

"CN Ferry Traversier" we read as we approached the sea and found ourselves lining up for a wait at the ferry crossing. "Don't forget!" I cautioned Ted. "If it's the Abby (Abegweit) we have to back off and wait for the next one." WE had been warned against the Abby; it was dynamite for trailer disembarking, we had been told. It was not the Abby, however, that arrived right on schedule; it was the M.V. Holiday Island, brand spanking new this season and every inch a beauty.

WE read the Emergency instructions absently and were reminded of an interesting story we had heard in Cape Breton involving the North Sydney ferry there. It had just landed from Newfoundland and one stormy winter evening last year when a distress signal was from a fishing boat nearby. The ferry quickly disembarked its passengers and headed back out into the storm to aid the distressed fishermen - who, happily for them, had already been rescued by the crew of another fishing vessel - WHILE THE FERRY ITSELF SANK IN THE WILD ATLANTIC WITH ALL HER CREW ABOARD.

The Gaspe is several hundred miles away across New Brunswick and we travel through Shediac, "The Lobster Capital of the World" where the annual Lobster Festival - four fun-filled days long – is in progress. Shediac where the streets and shops carry their names in both French and English…a quaint and charming little town that seemed to bulge at the seams with carnival-ers (whom we promptly joined…)

The one-lane bridge over the Shediac River delights us. It's a novel experience indeed to wait until a bridge is free of on-coming traffic before one ventures to cross it…And to drive through one covered bridge after another.

"Welcome to Chatham-75th Anniversary - Old Home Week August 16-21-next! And guess who happened to have founded in the year 1800 this limbering and commercial fishing center on the murky Miramichi River - one Frances Peabody of MAUGERVILLE, MASSACHUSETT! (Wherever THAT is…) The enterprising little town was named for

William Pitt, the Earl of Chatham, by the way; and its landmark is beautiful old St. Michael's Church, the lighted cross above the spire of which serves as a beacon for the aircraft from the Canadian Forces base nearby.

We leave the shoreline briefly to drive through the deep dark forests of the Greystone National Park area; then through the Village of Beresford, the "Resort Center of the North Shore." We are following the Acadian Trail with Quebec visible across a shining silver harbor that is strung with dozens of long wide fishermen's nets…

We are to cross to the Gaspe Peninsula on a ferry called the "Inch Arran," and we arrive at our destination at last - The Gaspe Peninsula - to find that we must ascend, from a dead stop on the ferry, a hill that rises almost perpendicularly for what appears to be miles; and then a second "hill"; and then a third…Fanny takes it all neatly in her stride, however. What a great gal she is, this home on wheels that is our own! And now ahead of us lies a valley of indescribable beauty with a hundred shades of green rising to caress our wide admiring eyes as on the scene we gaze from what appears to us to be the top of the world…the dear little town of Miguasha!

It has grown warm now and the sea is diamond-studded beneath the silvering sun. Small flower-bedecked shrines dot the roadside. Nets…the long kind we have seen across the seas below…dry in the sun. There is driftwood along the shore and the tide crawls lazily up the miles and miles of golden beaches that line the edges of this utterly enchanting land.

We arrive at Perce, mecca for artists and photographers from all corners of the world – Perce with the immense rock that rises from the sea a few hundred yards from shore, 1420' long and 288' high. It is pierced by a central arch 60' in height through which, at low tide, one may walk merrily, having traversed the wide sandbars that emerge to lead one to the Rock itself. Millions of fossils are to be found there, we are told, and we hunt them up on a sunny Sunday morning…we and our trailer neighbors, the Grays, a darling young couple with a sweet small son who keeps reminding us of treasured boys we've left behind in far-off Braintree. We scramble over the rocks like a herd of mountain goats, rolling up pant legs and removing socks and sneakers as we hit the tiny inundated areas that emerge here and there on the sandbars; gathering the fossils and the quartz crystals and the starfish and the rest, stopping to photograph the immense porpoise that has drifted up upon the beach by night.

The "Rock" itself is a beautiful shade of coral veined here and there with shiny black or stark white; and what adventuring we enjoy there!

We had stumbled upon a gorgeous rainbow here at Perce the evening before. It had rained while we were at Mass in St. Michael's Church, a handsome old stone edifice high upon a hill overlooking the colorful seaside town. Church bells had called the congregation to prayer in true European style; and then a Carillon of unbelievable tone had sent its glorious music out upon the night. A concert on the great and ancient organ had preceded and then followed the celebration of the Mass; and we emerged from the lovely evening of prayer hushed and humbled - and suddenly there it was shining high above the Rock far out to sea; and sweeping inward toward the shore in one wide colorful embrace - A RAINBOW!

"Ted," I said. "Look! Doesn't it just seem to be part of that beautiful Divine Service??? A RAINBOW???" Ted matched my rapt smile with one of his own. "Who knows?" he said as he guided me, unseeing, for my eyes were fixed on the scene above, down the long steep flight of steps that led from the Church. "Perhaps now we shall find our pot of gold!" He said. I felt the sting of tears as an awareness of God's goodness to the Metayers filled my heart. "Ted," I said, "If ever two people have found their pot of gold, it is you and I."

THE GRAND TETONS

The Grand Tetons of Wyoming lie one hundred miles or so south of Yellowstone Park and we set out to visit them on a rather chilly June morning with the sun barely up and at it - we being the early birds we had by now become.

The immense mountains, snow-capped and cloud-draped, form an imposing backdrop for the early morning drama of Yellowstone Lake, with its gull-inhabited island resting like a trailing green scarf upon the blue-gray water.

The pines that fill the forests of Yellowstone are enormously high and grow close together so that -the sun failing to penetrate the forest depths - only their crowns bear needles. The cones are small and the preponderance of fallen pines that lie upon the forest floor add to an early morning illusion of the forest primeval as we journey through it.

Traffic is stopped dead as a huge brown bear ambles across the roadway. The bears we have earlier encountered have all been black; this fellow reminds us of the big brown teddy bear at home on Grandson Gregory's bed.

The area fishermen are out in force and the geysers are greeting the new day with enthusiasm erupting all over the place; and we cross the Continental Divide and head toward the South Endurance through which we must pass en route to the Grand Tetons. The Teton National Forest, and we are in Grand Teton National Park. The scenery is breathtaking - immense glacier-crowned mountains piercing the skies, great scarfs of mist thrown wildly about their icy throats.

We stop for a moment to render thanks for the beauty of our lives in a rustic little chapel fashioned of logs and situated beside a jewel of a lake in the heart of the wilderness.

The Tetons at last! The Grand Teton, elev. 13,766' and the Middle Teton, elev. 12.788'; with Mt. Owen, 12,822' and the Teewinot Mountain, 12,317', along with a line of lesser mountain peaks…Clouds obscure their summits. Ted is not too happy as I plead with him to pull up non-existent chairs and await the right photographic moment - hour after hour after hour…

Others are sitting it out with us, cameras at the ready' among whom is a charming couple from Florida. They are the proud possessors of a huge Winnebago Motor Home and they plan to leave in September for a Winnebago variety of SAFARI in Africa. They are to fly there, pick up a Winnebago and driver, and head-along with hundreds of others - for the African bush!

We swap travel tales. Their journeys over the past year have included a Caravan trip to Mexico and a toot over the Alcan Highway to Alaska. "Oh, tell us about that one," I say enthusiastically. I would adore a trip to Alaska, that dynamic and wonderful 49th State of ours. Where the forces that were responsible for sculpturing this earth as we know it, are still at work…the tremendous glaciers that slowly, inexorably advance or recede over the mountain peaks, the savage earthquakes and the violent volcanoes…

Ted, however, remains cool to the idea of negotiating the several thousand mile stretch of gravel highway that will take us there - with or without a trailer…and I have been laboriously working on him. "The Alcan Highway really isn't all that bad, is it?" I ask hopefully. Our friends laugh gaily. "Oh, no," they say lightly. "It isn't bad at all-unless, or course, you mind such trivia as a couple of windshields smashed to atoms by flying rocks, and a few dozen wheels loosening and shearing the studs that hold them-to break off and leave you stranded in the wilderness…" I change the subject. "About that African safari…" I say quickly.

As we wait for the clouds to leave these enormous mountain peaks that are eternal ABOVE the clouds, we gaze about us at the incredible beauty of the terrain that is their setting. Before them lies the forested Piedmont Moraine - a moraine being a sizable deposit of glacial debris; and beyond this beautifully green moraine area, a shallow valley called Glacier Gulch carved by glacial action, dropping down the mountain front from the immense Teton Glaciers high above.

Evidences of glacial carving is all about us in the Teton valleys and Canyons. The sun shines brightly by mid-afternoon, picks up the gleam of the rock "benches" which were polished and smoothed, we are told, by the flowing glacial ice of ages past.

The beautiful Snake River flows between us and the Grand Tetons as we circle the area in a loop drive of seventy five miles or so next morning. Magnificent Mt. Moran lies reflected in its blue and beautiful depths; and from every angle the Grant Tetons rise above the scene like reigning monarchs remote and majestic.

We walk across a wonderful little prairie town to visit the Cunningham Cabin. It seems incredible that the first homesteaders settled in this valley less than a century ago in 1885. it had been abandoned half a century earlier by fur traders who had undoubtedly robbed the area of its wild life and gone on to richer pastures. Pierce Cunningham was among those first homesteaders and built the little cabin we now survey, with its sod roof and wooden pegs and axe marks so typical of early Western wilderness construction. We are interested to read that in 1893 a group of horse thieves were shot by a posse in Mr. Cunningham's shed. We are out WEST. The prairie dog town, which is such a fascinating feature of western America, delights us. We watch eagerly as the little fellows jump up from the dozens of tiny holes that dot the area – holes which are connected by a series of underground tunnels they have laboriously dug. We dash about with our cameras and the little dears don't seem to mind at all, as a matter of fact, we decide they've a bit of the "ham" in them, these delightful little Western animals that may by seen along the highways, standing up with front paws in mid-air, their small head swiveling with undisguised interest as they survey the motorists passing by.

Things have changed, needless to say, in this handsome valley which is now dotted with huge and beautiful ranches, their cattle black against the fields and the crossed rail fences that separate them silver in the sunlight.

The day ends in a burst of splendor as the flame of a setting sun pauses just long enough above the Tetons to set their snow-capped tops aflame e'er it departs to leave the grayness and the grandeur of a summer Teton evening in its wake.

"You know, hon," says Ted that night as we tuck ourselves into our little downy amid the magnificence of the Tetons. "We probably shall take that trip to Alaska you want so much, but let me clue you - we'll drive "Fanny" onto a big beautiful boat in Seattle and SAIL her up the coast to Juneau or wherever it is the thing docks. I'm not lacking in courage but that Alcan Highway is a bit much even for me."

This method of travel, I tell him, will suit me fine, just so long as some day I see the splendor of Alaska. When shall we tuck in THAT journey, I wonder. However, next Spring it will be off to the Maritime provinces and southern Canada; and then there's that trip across our country's southern states with Mexico at the end - that will be a winter trip. Oh well, so long as the years continue to be kind to Ted and me, and Fanny remains trim and enticing.

THE SEQUOIAS

SEQUOIA NATIONAL FOREST, California. We enter it at elevation 3000' However, we are to climb higher and higher into the wild desolate Sierra Nevada Mountains until at close to 7000' we reach Sequoia National Park.

We are about to embark on yet one more adventure. We have hitherto - being the amateurs at trailering that we are-stayed at privately owned trailer parks. You don't know what you are passing up on the National Park Campgrounds, we have been told repeatedly; and so we decide finally to investigate them - not while toting the family trailer but in the family car. The trailer spaces we discover are wide and wonderful the ways in and out beautifully marked; and so at Sequoia we decide to have a go at staying in a National Campground.

We select a beautiful spot among the pines high on a mountainside with the Kaweah River, a rushing mountain stream, fifty yard or so below us. Swim suited campers are cooling off in the tingling icy waters, and we, too don our bathing suits and scramble down the mountainside and hoist ourselves on rocky ledges midstream and dangle our feet deliciously while we watch the big black bears lumber along the opposite bank and the anglers angle.

Early evening finds us investigating another aspect of National Park life. We follow the crowd to an amphitheater for an open campfire and a sing-a-long night among the Sequoias. a million stars shine against a sky that seems quite close enough to touch and is pollution free. The wind sings in the giant trees and the mountain stream adds its beautiful bass note to the symphony of this the Giant Forest area. the lights from hundreds of campers shine like huge fireflies within the deep dark woods. Campfires flicker and glow and send their crackling sounds against the night; and then from every side there is the sound of singing....SO, THIS IS A NATIONAL PARK CAMPSITE. why, oh why have we not investigated it sooner???

And now for the Sequoias…In 1858, we learn, one Hale D. Tharp discovered the giant trees which had only been known to the Yokuts Indians of the area. He was the first white man to know of their existence and he decided to establish a ranch on one of the mountain meadows.

For a dwelling he used a fallen log which we visited, to find that he had built for himself within its huge confines a fireplace, a bed, a bench and table and an entry hall, all fashioned of beautifully weathered redwood and all perfectly preserved more than a century later. How, we wondered, did this rancher manage to move his cattle over the mountain trails of the Sierras to the adjoining meadow on which from 1861 until 1890, when the Sequoia National Park was established, the animals summered while their rancher owner steeped himself in the peace of the surrounding forests.

Dawn in the Sequoia National park and we are both awake to see it. By 7:30 a.m. we have unhitched and left behind the family trailer and are en route to visit this land of the giants. The sequoias shut out the sun, rising as they do side by side hundreds of feet in the air. The road curves through the forest, its direction fully determined by the placement of the ancient trees, the mountains rise above us on all sides.

WE visit the General Sherman Tree, "the largest living thing on earth," its estimated age 3000-3500; the estimated weight of its trunk, 1319 tons; its height above the base 272.4'; its circumference at the base 101.6'. this tree, we reflect, was alive and growing in the era of the Trojan Horse. It towered above the land when the Holy Roman Empire ruled the world and when the Vikings preyed upon it, and when Columbus discovered America and the Declaration of Independence took form.

Stephen Endlicher, an Austrian botanist named this forest giant we are finding on all sides for one Sequoyah, a Cherokee Indian Chief, who gave to his people an alphabet system of writing.

We decided not to wait for the ranger guided tour of the famous Congress Trail scheduled for nine thirty and we pip off through the forest by ourselves. It's a wonderful place, this "Giant Forest" of the Sequoias. WE exclaim over the "Chief Sequoyah Tree", a gnarled and twisted "venerable giant" of a sequoia, reflecting, we thought, the storms and stresses of ages past. We delight in the beauty of the "Resident Tree," a magnificent specimen which was dedicated, we learn, in honor of Warren G. Harding, the 29th President of the U.S. at the hour of his funeral on august 10th, 1923. It stands apart, just above the "Senate" and the "House" groupings of those wonderful sequoias. We explore the interior of the "Room Tree," burned by fire, but still beautifully alive, its deep interior large enough to contain 35 to 40 adults; and the "McKinley Tree"; and the "Bear Den Log," a fallen sequoia with a large cave-like opening in which bears are said to hibernate.

Another striking example of an immense living sequoia with a large part of its heartwood burned out is the "Telescope Tree." We view it with delight. We look skyward through the blackened towering chimney that remains inside the tree to where the blue sky is clearly visible. The rusty red of the bark of these magnificent trees that defy fire and flood to survive throughout the ages provides a striking contrast to the greens and browns of the pine and fir of beautiful Sequoia.

Off to Moro Rock whose towering 800' summit is reached via hundreds of steps cut into the granite of the mountainside. Legend has it that Moro was a beautiful roan mustang. He roamed the wild Sierras glimpsed now and then against the skylines by the Indians who hunted him unsuccessfully, so fleet were the hooves of this wild and wonderful creature. He was finally trapped by his pursuers here on the high mountaintop. Rather than surrender, however, Moro hurled himself to death within the gorge below. His spirit survives, so the legend goes, to haunt all those who dare to walk the mountain trails of the Sierras. And so it is up the hundreds of steps to the top of Moro Rock where we are rewarded with a breath-taking view of the Great Western Divide - its glacier-crowned peaks rising as high as 12,600' against the immense blue sky.

How exciting to visit nearby King's Canyon, the magnificent "General Grant Tree," declared by President Roosevelt to be the "Nation's Christmas Tree" and a living memorial to its war dead; and to see the pen with which he signed the proclamation. Candlelight services are held here each year on Christmas Eve, we learn, for the peace of the nation and of the world. a beautiful thought. Time was when the sequoias were threatened with possible extinction, we were told. In 1868 Israel and Thomas Gamlin, two enterprising Vermonters, filed a timber claim on 160 acres in Grant Grove. Their headquarters in the "Fallen Monarch" served as an employee camp in 1890 when the grove was set aside as the General Grant National Park, and at one time, we learn, this fallen giant we are viewing stabled the 60 horses of a cavalry troop quartered nearby. A public outcry saved the sequoias. Heaven be praised! "As well sell the rain clouds"'" wrote the famous botanist and explorer, John Muir, "and the snow and the rivers to be cut up and carried away, if that were possible." How deep and dark and mysterious is this Land of the Sequoias, I reflect as I lie abed in our snug little trailer on our last night in the Giant Forest. Our trailer windows are open and the curtains wide. The wind fans my face and the stream sings. I look skyward. The pines twisted limbs form strange patters of black lace against the night. The stars are silver on the sky; the campfires of my neighbors send their flickering shadows high; the fragrance of the burning embers assail my senses. Laughter rides the wind and snatches of song; and there is peace within this land of the Sequoias, a kind of precious peace we have not previously found upon our journey o'er this land that we traverse.

HOW BEAUTIFUL! BEAUTIFUL! BEAUTIFUL! is this country AMERICA

8-30-70 THE TRAILER

The Metayers had never been inside a TRAILER; they were yet to see the inside of a TRAILER PARK! It is surprising, therefore, that the trailer they selected for purchase turned out to be precisely what they would have chosen had they seen a million of them...

"Fanny" - so called because she's a FAN trailer, and for 11,000 miles she trailed along at the rear of our anatomy is totally self-contained and very handsome. Her interior paneling is warmly honey-colored; her décor gold and white; with touches of aqua. Her refrigerator runs on gas while traveling and electricity while at a trailer park; her light fixtures function with gas, electricity or marine-battery. Her stove and lavatory are adequate and pretty; her closet space phenomenal. Cross ventilation keeps her cool for sleeping on the warmest nights. She's a LOVE!

The purchase of "Fanny" completed, Ted lost no time in surrounding himself with every known Publication on trailer travel. "Oh, oh," he said almost immediately, "We'll shall have to buy NEW CAR!" "Why?"

I asked. "Well," he said, "the book says you can expect half your car's normal mileage while hauling a trailer. The Cadillac gives us 10 miles to the gallon; half of that is five. We wouldn't make it between gas stations."

"Why don't you buy a Blazer?" asked son Richard. "It's a good sturdy car with a station wagon body and a truck motor…a Chevrolet…"

"Somehow, dear," said Ted as we surveyed the thing at the local Chevrolet dealers, "I can't see you pipping off to Club meetings in that thing. Up mountains, yes; but not around the Federation. "Besides," he added, "it's built like a truck. It would rattle; I can't live with a car that rattles."

It was easy to gravitate from the Blazer to the Impala. "How big is your trailer?" asked the salesman whom Ted had questioned on the car's ability to haul it. "Well," said Ted, "It is 17' long and weighs 2700 pounds empty. You can double that weight, however," he added, "My wife's planning to take everything we own with us."

The salesman shook an envious head. "Boy," he said, "a three months trip across the country, that's every American's dream. The Impala can handle the trailer beautifully, but of course, you'll need an oversized radiator - you'll be going up over the Rockies, no doubt; and a heavy duty battery; and you really should have a heavy duty transmission with an extra gear for mountain driving; and a positraction differential - it's wonderful for getting you out of sand if you should get stuck in the desert; and for SNOW too. And power steering, naturally; and disc brakes; and - to withstand the heat you should have tinted windows throughout the car…and super air lifts - they're a positive necessity; and what you really could use is a special 265 horse 400 cubic engine…and then there are fender mirrors, etc. etc. It is called, we learned from the sales manager who - together with every salesman in the place regarded us enviously as he made myriad suggestions, a TRAILER PACKAGE. Needless to say we wound up with the whole works. "It's safer than taking a chance on getting stuck somewhere," said Ted, who ALWAYS winds up with the whole works whenever we go to make a purchase. He's a salesman's best friend…

In due time, the new car arrived, and a Reese trailer hitch was installed. "Now," said Ted, "Let's take the car and trailer on a trial run to Mystic, Conn. Richard and his family haven't seen it.

It made a handsome combination. The blue of the trailer and the blue of the new car were identical. "First," said Ted after hooking things up, "we'll stop at the gas station and put air in the super air lifts." Now, the function of the super airs is to raise the back of the car to compensate for the weight of the trailer; and without turning a hair, Ted shot 50 lbs. of air into their waiting depths.

"It's like having a baby buggy," said Ted merrily to Richard on our arrival. "I wouldn't have known I had the thing behind me if I couldn't see it in the mirrors."

"Well," said Richard after our caravan had been safely stowed away. "Let's disconnect the car." Came the first of several crises that would affect the lives of the trailer-toting Metayers. Disconnecting the car was far easier said than done. Every time the gentlemen of the family raised the tongue of the trailer, the car came right up with it. Friends and neighbors arrived with advice and tools and strong right arms to no avail. "Obviously," said one volunteer, "your trailer hitch has been installed wrong." "I took the car to the best place in town," wailed Ted, "all they do is install trailer hitches. They should know what they're doing. I'll take it back to them on Monday," he added dismally.

The weekend passed with car and trailer locked in fond embrace. And it was not until we were in sight of Braintree on our return trip that light dawned upon the head of the household of Metayer. 50 lbs. was just about 40 lbs. too much. The car simply COULDN'T let go. The amount of ozone was reduced to 10, and we've lived happily ever afterwards with the super air lifts that do indeed compensate for the weight of the trailer so loaded with NECESSARY items that my darling's spirits sank lower and lower with each passing trip to the trailer. "I'll be lucky if I get the darned thing out of the driveway," he said finally. He DID, you'll be happy to know get the darned thing out of the driveway and haul it 11,000 exciting miles for the most fabulous vacation we shall ever enjoy; to return to Braintree madly in love with "Fanny" and firmly convinced that trailer travel is the only way to go.

TRAVELS CONTINUED

Back to the discovery of America and what fun it is to be at it again…mentally journeying toward Arizona and the North Rim of the Grand Canyon! Tourists generally visit the Canyon's South Rim primarily because the normal route West passes through Phoenix and Phoenix happens to be a scant fifty miles or so from the south Rim, while a visit to the North Rim involves an additional 200 or so miles. Nonetheless, it was toward the North Rim we were heading on a beautiful day in late July. Our reason? The temperature at the South Rim was reportedly 110 degrees or higher, while at the North rim the weather can generally be relied upon to be considerably cooler.

Through the magnificent and impenetrable Kaibab National Forest and we find ourselves in Grand Canyon National Park. Wild flowers riot beside the highways and delightful birds we identify as roadrunners sweep across the meadows that line our path.

Ours is a beautiful campsite at Bright Angel Point. We've a fireplace and a picnic table and space to spread out our chaises under a wonderful stand of quaking aspens (which I promptly identify as birches…) The elevation ranges from 7800' to 8800' hereabouts and so it is cool and beautiful.

We set out immediately for Point Imperial. Having thrilled to the purple magnificence of the Grand Canyon from the air, I am impatient to have it spread before me; and suddenly there it is! Great jagged peaks rise from the canyon floor, one upon the other, their cliffs brick red in the fore front, then pinking and purpling as they reach toward the horizon. For sheer magnificence the Grand Canyon has exceeded our most extravagant dreams, we decide, Ted and I….

Over the Walhalla Plateau next as we head for Cape Royal and the famous Angel's Window. The area is sagebrush covered. Sagebrush appears to be the most abundant shrub in the far west. Its extensive root system resists drought, we are told. The Indians have for centuries used this hardy plant for luck and as medicine to treat their colds and fevers.

The Angel's Window is just that - an enormous window cut in the side of a towering cliff which juts out into the canyon for a hundred feet or more. It was formed, we learn, during the uplift of the Kaibab Plateau

(Kaibab being a Paiute Indian word meaning "mountain lying down") when stress and strain brought about fracture of the rock to form vertical joints intersecting horizontal bedding planes. The extremes of wind and weather have eroded the Kaibab limestone to form this hole or window in the cliff's side, through which, incidentally, the mighty Colorado River can be glimpsed a mile below. the wind whistling through the great trees and echoing in the Canyon sounds for all the world like a roaring rushing stream as we stand atop the great cliff that houses Angel's Window and look upon the chasm below. We are enchanted by everything we see and hear…This is the first of several days we shall spend in the Grand Canyon e'er we head our trailer elsewhere- days when hour after exciting hour, we watch the shades of this wonderland turn from pink to plum to purple to gold to rose to gray to blue and to black…The many side canyons and buttes of the North Rim conspire to send deep dark shadows over this place of beauty, shadows that add one more exciting note to the symphony that is the Grand Canyon of the Colorado…We hike with the Rangers over the canyon trails; and attend evening "Campfires" with their wonderfully informative programs; and are careful not to miss a single one of the fascinating Naturalist's lectures that are scheduled daily for interested tourists…

And seldom have they encountered more interested tourists than the Metayers…

Once upon a time this area was below sea level, we learn. Water moved in bringing mud and sand and gravel with it, all of which settled and pushed down. Eventually Nature tired of pushing down and began to push up, and the mountain peaks evolved. The rock at the bottom of the canyon is two billion years old, we are told; it is extremely dark in color. The second layer, which is one billion years old, is tilted at an angle and is pink or white with here and there a layer of a darker shade. The 3rd Chapter rock is a mere 600 million years old. This area, we are told, was once the beach of an inland sea; clams have been found embedded in the stone. The 4th Chapter rock from 25M to 62M years in age is to be found in the Painted Desert. The 5th Chapter rock of the Grand Canyon area represents the period from 900 A.D. to 1125 A.D.

In the grandeur of the awesome spectacle that is the Grand Canyon of the Colorado River are recorded the very earliest chapters of the world's history, their significance unequalled elsewhere in this great exciting earth that is our own. The wearing away of the land by erosion…the immense cliffs and varied colored slopes of the tremendous chasm that is the Grand Canyon delight the eye as it descends to the deep dark cleft a mile below where the mighty Colorado River continues to carve ever deeper into the earth's crust.

We view across the Canyon the wonderful Painted Desert with its landscapes of strange form and color. Dinosaurs once roamed the lowlands of this area; their footprints are preserved in stone. shifting desert sands were formed by wind and weather into great dunes which were hardened into the colorful Navajo sandstone that is 150M years old. the Indians of this area, incidentally, continue today to use the low grade coal that is available from deposits 75M years in age.

As each day wanes Ted and I walk along the canyon rim to see again and again the long shadows of evening send their exploring fingers into the chasms and ridges of the canyon gorge. It is a vast ocean of color, this aptly named "grand" Canyon of the Colorado, rising from the misty depths of which are great islands of crimson Navajo sandstone, their undulating strata softening in color and form as they approach the horizon. Vermilion cliffs rise like towering Cathedral spires or castle domes from the canyon floor- their outlines bold and beautiful against the deep blue of the Arizona sky; in the distance the mighty Colorado River wends its twisting tortuous way across the colorful Painted Desert in its eternal race toward the sea.

A bit about the history of the area as recounted by our Naturalists. Four thousand years ago Indians dwelt in the great caves that line the mountainsides; they fashioned figurines which were used in religious ceremonies performed to assure success in tribal hunting.

1 A.D. and the Basketmakers arrived.

1050 A.D. - The Indians had managed to survive by hunting and trapping and farming the area.

1540- The Spaniards, seeking gold, saw the sun shining on the dwellings of the Pueblo Indians, on investigating, however, they were disappointed to find only the Indians.

1857 - An Army Officer entered the Colorado River where his craft encountered the Rapids and sank.

1869 - John Wesley Powell led the first expedition down the Colorado; he was given up for dead as the months passed without word of the adventurer, however Powell returned eventually – to read of his death in the newspapers. Later other settlers attempted to mine copper, gold etc.

1883 - John Hans, one of the first residents of the South Rim, a miner turned guide, entertained visitors with his tall tales - whoppers - typical of which is the tale of the Indians who pursued him so relentlessly he was obliged to jump astride his horse from Canyon rim to butte to escape them.+

1950s-Uranium was mined in the canyon area.

1960s-Owen Fletcher, and Englishman, visited the Canyon. He was en route to California with a party of friends, however, he was enchanted by what he saw. "I shall return and walk the inner gorge," he said; and did just that, writing an exciting book about his adventures, the title of which was to be "The Man Who Walked Through Time."

The Grand Canyon of the Colorado is ever-changing. How old is this mighty river anyhow, we wanted to know. the river, we learn, is between 60M and 100M years of age. Its waters flow 1450 miles to the sea. 200 inches of snow melt annually to run into the canyon and bring about constant erosion. The river carries away each day one million tons of sand and gravel from the sides of the canyon and the canyon walls. When we return, God willing, we shall find changes in the magnificent Grand Canyon for it is ever changing.

How reluctantly we leave this wonder spot where even one species of rattlesnake that is found upon the canyon floor is PINK! Nowhere in the world, we are certain, is there to be seen such a breathtaking display of natural form and color! And at last WE have beheld it!

10-29-72   TRAVELS CONTINUED

"THE New Mexico State Line" and we drive toward Albuquerque through the Llado Estacado or Staked Plains, and enormous flat grassy cattle-raising area. We reach Clovis, a cattle market city; and then the Pecos River silvers in the sunlight as we journey through the Pecos

Valley…the river that provides water for the farms that line this wide agricultural belt. The terrain is much like that of Texas - flat, red sand, rangeland - with occasional cactus and sagebrush.

We pause to inspect the "site of the original Military Village of Ft. Sumner, established in 1862 to control the activities of the Plains Indians. The Pecos Valley around the fort then became Bosque Redondo Indian Reservation from 1863-68," we read, "where over 400 Mescalero Apaches and 8000 Navajos resettled after being rounded up by Col. Kit Carson." The saga of the American Indian and his tragic undoing comes crowding in upon our consciousness as we drive through the historic state where so much of our early history is recorded…but how wonderful to be actually in the PECOS! We've been reading about it forever…

Strong winds buffet the family car and rock our indomitable ":Fanny," travel trailer extraordinaire, as we haul her up one mountain after another en route to our initial port-of-call…Albuquerque-we are to love it, this enormous city of a third of a million people lying along the Rio Grande in the twin shadows of the Sandia Mountains on one side and the Manzanos on the other!

What a fascinating history this city has! Founded in 1706 by Spanish Colonists, a section of the original settlement is still perfectly preserved in what is known as the "Old Town." The first descendants of Europeans to settle here were actually the Trujillos and the Caravajals, two illustrious families from the epic of Spanish Conquest in the New World. In the early 17th century they built great haciendas in an area that included an existent Indian pueblo…haciendas that were to be burned to the ground later during the Indian Rebellion with their inhabitants forced to flee for their very lives.

For 18 years the hacienda ruins scarred the desert land; and then Gen. Diego de Vargas reconquered the colony and the Trujillos returned - alone this time to rebuild and resettle, the less adventurous Caravajals preferring to remain elsewhere. Rich crops flourished in the area's river-bottom farmlands; and sheep grazed on the grassy mesas; and then in the year 1706, thirty additional families from the villa of Bernalillo, a few miles to the North, received permission from governor Valdez to also establish a hacienda close by that of the Trujillos. The Trujillos had incidentally named their settlement for the duke of Alburquerque. The

"R" was to be later dropped, but the name was destined to remain and the settlement to take firm root. Soldiers were ordered to protect the settlers from the "wild" Indians - the Navajos and Apaches and Plains Indians, so unlike the peaceful Pueblo Indians of the Rio Grande valley.

A tiny adobe chapel was the first structure to be built in this new hacienda, it was to be named for San Felipe de Neri, the Patron Saint of the Spanish. The original walls of this little chapel may still be seen within those of the present Church which we visited. Albuquerque soon became a vital way-station on the storied Chihuahua Trail from Santa Fe to Mexico City. By the year 1800 American mountain men and trappers began to find their way to New Mexico; then in 1821 "New Spain," which is now Mexico, declared its independence from Spain and New Mexico became a "Department of Mexico," 1846 and Albuquerque became an army post and a supply center for southwestern forts. The City was captured by the confederates in the early days of the Civil War and the confederate Flag flew briefly over the Plaza through the streets of which we delight in roaming. The Plaza, which is gas lit and charming, is lined with inviting white wrought iron benches.

The wonderful old San Felipe Church seems to smile benevolently upon the galleries and shops where the many cultures that have combined to produce the rich heritage that is Albuquerque's have brought forth arts and crafts that are seldom matched for originality and beauty. We are to pop about the shops and pick up Mexican sombreros and Indian bead belts for our five little grandsons and silver jewelry from the skilled hands of Navajo silversmiths.

The days are beautiful and warm. Our mornings are spent in sightseeing and our afternoons in the trailer park pool which is fed by mountain streams and infinitely icy and wonderfully bracing. We drive to the top of Sandia Peak for an 11,000 square mile panoramic view that is unparalleled.

Now, having explored Albuquerque from end to end, we head for Coronado State Monument where we are to view our first real ancient Pueblo Indian ruins. Here are to be found the remains of the Pueblo of Kuaua, Indians were living here when Coronado explored New Mexico. The excavation and restoration is still going on; and the adobe is being made today just as it was in early times-of the area clay mixed with water.

Here, too, we find the famous "Painted Kiva" or ceremonial chamber painted with no less than 85 layers of adobe plaster, 17 of which contain colorful murals, religious symbols and figures of Masked Kachina gods with their sacred paraphernalia - the whole in shades of black and white and green and yellow and red. So, what is a Kiva, we wanted to know. 500 years ago in the Pueblo of Kuaua, the chief social and religious organization was a clan which maintained a Kiva where the men conducted religious ceremonies honoring the "Sun Father." In his many sons' persons - the elements, the birds and the animals. It's a miracle of primitive engineering, this Kiva. It is entered, like all Pueblo dwellings, via a ladder through the roof, and it contains a ventilator shaft, an altar and a fire pit. The ventilating shaft is placed low on the wall; and the fire pit built directly under the entrance which serves as an escape opening for the smoke. As the heat rises from the fire through the ladder hole, fresh air is drawn down the ventilating shaft and a deflector slab, placed between the fire pit and the ventilator, serves to protect the fresh air from blowing directly into the fire. How about that for ingenuity???

We marvel at the murals on the walls of this ceremonial chamber and then climb the ladder to the surface and roam about the excavated area to wave gaily to the Indian "archaeologists" – mostly young- not too hard at work on the historic dig.

It is our first encounter with the Indian ruins that dot New Mexico and Arizona. Others will perhaps be even more fascinating, but this is the first and we explore them with an excitement we have seldom before experienced. What a country to be let loose in is our wonderful America!

10-01-72   WE JOURNEY ON

We leave Kentucky to enter "the Great State of Tennessee." The name is Cherokee Indian origin, we learn; and no one is quite certain of its meaning…Tennessee…a state that boasts of three American Presidents - Andrew Jackson, James K. Polk and Andrew Johnson.

We visit "The Hermitage," Jackson's magnificent home. The beautiful 625 acre "farm" on which it is located was purchased by Jackson in 1804, we are told. Two small log cabins located a couple of yards north of the mansion were part of the original purchase; and Jackson was living there with his family when he defeated the Creek Indians, and later when he emerged as the hero of the Battle New Orleans.

The original mansion was erected in 1819 and remodeled extensively in 1831 while Jackson was President, only to be heavily damaged by fire three years later. The present mansion with its handsome white pillars and the wide verandas that front it…with its huge spiral staircase rising gracefully from the broad front hall…is a splendid example of southern colonial architecture of the Pre-Civil War era. The walls and foundations of the original building have been retained, we are told, and the farm and mansion remain today as they were in Jackson's time. We delight in the sight of the paintings and mirrors, the crystal and china that were actually used by the Jackson family; and the huge banqueting table at which this historic figure presided; and the bed in which he slept; his military insignia and his swords and rifles…and the carriage in which he rode about the rolling Middle Tennessee hills.

Amateur gardeners that we are, we thrill to the Hermitage Garden which was designed, of course, for Rachel, the General's beloved wife. Fifty varieties of plants are to be found there; and hickory and magnolia trees abound. It is early America landscape art at its very best.

Those hickory trees that surround the tomb of the General and his wife have a particularly appealing history, we learn. They were planted from a package of hickory nuts given as a gift to the President in 1830. "Old Hickory" as he was affectionately called gained national recognition for his successful expedition against the Creek Indians in 1813…and expeditions which ended forever the power of those warring tribes in the Gulf States…That recognition was increased by his tremendous military victory, a scant two years later - over British forces in the Battle of New Orleans.

Jackson's administration (he was America's 7th President) was known as "The Age of Jackson," we learn. Under his skillful administration America's stature was raised to that of world power. He inspired in the American people a new sense of pride and purpose. He was a superb leader for a rapidly advancing nation.

Jackson served two terms a President - terms that were marked, we are told, by tremendous patriotism and devotion to the Constitution as well as a true awareness of fiscal responsibility. The great military hero turned President is credited historically with having "paid the National debt, returned a Federal surplus to the States and Collected our debts from France" as well as with "giving our emerging Western Territory a dominant voice in national affairs." We pondered upon his motto as we reluctantly bid his "hermitage" farewell - "Our Federal Union - it must be preserved!"

And now it is over the Ozark Frontier Trail as he head for Hot Springs, Arkansas, a place about which we know absolutely nothing excepting that it manages to appear prominently upon every MAP we view. The Ozarks lie all about us - timber covered and lovely against a pale blue cloud-flecked sky. We pass the "I.Q. Zoo," where "educated animals" are to be found; and were we not looking forward madly to a swim in the nice cool pool that awaits us in our K.O.A. campground, we should certainly have stopped to investigate that phenomenon.

The pool is a beauty, and we swim happily about, postponing our exploration of Hot Springs National park until the morrow.

A beautiful June sun is shining as we head for the nearby Visitors Center next day. "Good morning," I say pleasantly to the sweet young thing at the Information desk. "We would like to know just what to see in the area." I am in hopes that she will reply swiftly and briefly because Ted, who has been forced to drive around town for a full half hour before finding this carefully hidden spot, is now outside parked apprehensively in a ten-minute parking zone. "Well," says the young thing sweetly, "The BATH HOUSES are all located on Bath House Row, here on the map; and there are DRINKING FOUNTAINS along Reserve Avenue her; and along the Promenade..." "Drinking Fountains?" I repeat. "Bath Houses???" "yes," says the charmer happily, "The Springs are SPLENDID for ARTHRITIS and RHEUMATISM." "B-but," I stutter, "W-w-we DON'T HAVE arthritis and rheumatism! What else is there to see???"

The sweet one shrugs a pretty shoulder; she stifles a yawn....Quite obviously in her opinion one who fails to qualify in those important areas is beyond her concern; and then she tries again. "Kidney Malfunctions?" she asks hopefully. I shake an apologetic head. "No." "well," she says finally "There are TRAILS...and FISHING..."

And now a bit about this Spa whose delights we do not plan to explore. It was hallowed ground long before the white Europeans arrived on our shores, we are told. Here Indian warriors with arthritis and rheumatism??? laid aside their arms and bathed together in peace and friendship. The underground pathway of the thermal water has its beginnings in rainwater which finds its way through fractured rocks to drain deeply into the earth's crust and be heated by the molten rock encountered there. It returns through a "fault" or ancient break in the earth's crust, to be dispensed through 47 springs to the bathhouses and fountains in the National Park area. No, we are not to test the therapeutic value of the thermal springs we encounter there. We are, however, to saunter happily over the lovely wooded trails of the Hot Springs National Park area…trails with oak and hickory forests, rising above them…trails bordered by white and purple passion flowers in full bloom, and giant cacti, rich with fruit; trails that have a beauty all their own and make us glad we came; and glad as well that, having naught of rheumatism or arthritis, we are free to find that special beauty and relish it.

We spent our first trailer-traveling night in a roadside rest area in Fultonville, N.Y. It had been recommended to us by a friend whose hearing loss must be total… "How wonderful," I said to Ted as we dined, tuned in our transistor, and settled down to read, "to be parked here, watching the world go by!" It was a lovely spot. The Mohawk River wended its way beside us through a wooded area that delighted the eye, and managed to cloak beautifully several nasty little area details that were to come to light later on-like two sets of railroad tracks, one on either side of a dual highway etc. etc.

"We'll turn in early," we decided, "and get a good night's sleep, then start for Buffalo at dawn." Sleep??? The night was rent from beginning to end with the wildest assortment of noises modern man can manage-like 1,000 car freight trains roaring by in both directions every ten minutes; barges chugging and tooting their way along the Mohawk to the Eerie Canal; and TRUCKS-millions of tractor-trailer monsters, each one striving to break speed records and eardrums at the same time… Did the sign say REST AREA??? at about 2:00 a.m., with everything roaring simultaneously, I began to giggle. Ted, who had been gently snoring in spite of it all, awoke. "It's a freight train going by, dear," he said gently, quite as though it had been the first sound to break a night of silvered silence. I howled. "AND a thousand trucks," I said, "AND barges and motorcycles, and everything else that hoots and moves. "Ted," I added, "anyone who doubts that the world moves on wheels should try SLEEPING here!"

Night number two was even funnier. Arrived at Buffalo where we planned to view Niagara, we set out in search of a private trailer park. Rand McNally and the Woodhall Directories were as yet alien territory. "You need not worry about finding a trailer park at Niagara," our dear deaf friend had said, "There will be dozens of them there…"

And there's a wonderful Indian Spring etc etc., and all for the very low price of $9.75 each. It would cost you more than that for GAS!" "But," I said, "we're looking for a trailer park. With all this literature (the place was scuppers awash with pamphlets covering every attraction in the area) surely you must know the location on ONE trailer park." "sorry," said the gentleman pleasantly, "I'm afraid I don't." "Well," said Ted after a kind of stricken silence, "I'll tell you what. You find us a trailer park and get us a reservation and we'll take your tickets." "Well," said the you-know-what instantly interested, "I'll see what I can do." "But Ted," I wailed, "It's raining! We'll get double pneumonia prancing about Niagara Falls in a deluge, Cadillac or no," I turned to the entrepreneur "Couldn't you get us a trailer park and let us buy our tickets tomorrow?" I asked. "What does the weatherman say about tomorrow?" The gentleman picked up the local paper and gave it a quick glance. "Heavy rain," he said flatly. "Well, he may be wrong, we can take a chance on tomorrow." The gentleman shook his head. "There may not be a tour tomorrow," he said. "The rain may be TOO bad." "Well," said Ted, who was not about to seek out another rest area if he could help it, "perhaps it will stop. We'll take the tickets if you get the reservation."

We were amazed at how quickly he secured us the necessary reservation at the Beacon Trailer Park. "Their charge is $4.00 a night," he said his voice dripping honey. "and now - here are your tickets, that will be $19.50 plus tax, and - oh yes - 10c for the telephone call. The limousine will pick you up at the Beacon Trailer Park at 6:30. "Now," said Ted, after travelers' check and tickets had been exchanged (and our boy had mistakenly handed us change for a twenty instead of the fifty dollar check Ted had handed him, talking pleasantly all the while...) "Where is the Beacon Trailer Park, and how do we get there???" the salesman of the year smiled sweetly. TT'S JUST A FEW BLOCKS STRAIGHT DOWN THE ROAD-ON THE RIGHT," he said, without the slightest qualm of conscience.

UTAH

"Welcome to Utah!" with its swirling layered copper colored cliffs laced with their lush green vegetation, the great clumps of Yucca rising stiffly from copper-colored sand; the sagebrush gray-green.

Our destination is Salt Lake City and eventually we are to reach it, but not until we have climbed up and down and around and across MOUNTAINS...

We settle ourselves happily in the V.I.P. Campground, a lovely place with the Wasatch Range rising in the east of us and the Oquirrh Range to the west. Our next door trailer neighbors, Dave and Colleen Watson happen to be Salt Lake City teachers who have checked into the trailer park for the weekend that they might ready their trailer for a trip east and we avail ourselves of their friendly assistance as we plan a program of sightseeing that will include everything of consequence in Utah...Our usual luck!

Salt Lake City, the "Center of Scenic America," is just that! On the 10 acre site that is Temple Square stand the sacred buildings of the Church of Jesus Christ of the Latter-Day Saints - the Mormons! We must view the magnificent granite which was hauled by ox teams from one of the many canyons that surround the city, the temple was 40 years under construction. (From 1853 to 1893). It is now used for special ceremonies only.

The Tabernacle, however, is open to the public and we visit it to hear a concert of sacred music by the famed Tabernacle Choir. It's a wonderful structure with a seating capacity of over 8,000. completed in 1867, the buildings beams and joints are held together totally by rawhide thongs and wooden pegs. Its huge soaring dome shaped roof is completely without interior pillars and so its acoustical system is all but perfect. "A pin," we are told, "dropped at the front of the Auditorium can be heard distinctly at the extreme rear of the building…a distance of 200"."

11-17-74 YELLOWSTONE NATIONAL PARK

(With apologies to any geologist who might read this column.)

AND SO WE CAME TO YELLOWSTONE…over "the most scenic fifty miles in the West," having crossed that grim forbidding mountain range we had viewed with such dismay back there in Cody by way of a series of beautiful mountain TUNNELS, (What an age we live in!); and dropped by to oh! and ah! over the impressive Buffalo Bill Dam and Shosone Power Plant that brings water to the arid desert regions that lie about it. We laugh as we gaze from our mountain-top roadway upon the immense gorge through which the Shoshone River flows, to find a merry sign reading "Danger. Do not throw rocks, men and equipment below."

The Absaroka Range is next, and then the Absaroka Volcanic Field. We are driving through a land of strange wild rock formations, formed by millions of years of wind and weather and erosion and volcanic action. Their descriptive names delight us: Laughing Pig, Camel Rock, Elephant Head Rock, Chimney Rock…And thence along the valley floor, with the world green and graceful about us and the mountains rising on either side like a great regiment of sentinels on guard.

Once the American Indian roamed across this wild majestic valley we now view. He camped beside the shining streams that lace its heart; and fished within their depths; and hunted all the wild wild game that even now abounds within this forest we traverse. He loved and laughed and lived and died in this primaeval paradise that was all his alone…We fancy we can see him there, still gaunt and grim and brave and bronze against a soft Wyoming sky…

We are to enter Yellowstone National Park by the East Gate which turns out to be the two mile high mountainous one- naturally! There are others far less difficult to negotiate, however, we have no way of knowing this as we delight in the sign that announces our arrival, "ENTERING YELLOWSTONE PARK," we read; and we thrill to the sight of Old Glory singing in the stiff breeze one invariably finds about a mountain's summit, "Watch for falling rock," we are warned; and then "thank you," the sign reads. For not getting HIT, we wonder???

Onward and upward once again and now we find it all around us - that SIX INCH SNOWFALL we had heard about a few days back in fair Mt. Rushmore. It lies in soiled heaps against the mountain's sides, and lines the roadway like a tarnished crust. It creeps about the giant pines that roar above us toward the sky; and rests like a pristine blanket over the frozen lakes and rivers we are meeting on all sides.

AND SUDDENLY IT BEGINS TO FALL AGAIN! We are driving through a blinding snowstorm over the highest point in Yellowstone… The snow comes mixed with sleet and hail. It screams against the windshield of our car and hurls itself upon the trailer we are toting, with a savage force that makes us wish, just momentarily, THAT WE WERE BACK IN BRAINTREE SAFE AND SOUND…

The windshield wipers are of little use against its fury; and so we must open wide the windows of the car and drive along, shivering and shaking in the wild wild wind that pierces easily the lightweight clothing that we wear, everything warmer having been tucked away neatly in our trailer closet…This is to be the last "precipitation" we shall encounter on our three-months journey through America; however, we have no way of knowing that as we struggle along a rutted mountain road toward Fishing Bridge, the site of our next selected trailer park. The season is early for Yellowstone, and the way there via the high East Gate is strewn with the potholes and road ruts that winter brings. We bounce along; our trailer bounces along; we pray a little; and then we begin our descent. The snow ceases; the rainclouds swallow their pride and their contents; and the sun peeps timidly through. Is this, we ask ourselves, to be typical of Yellowstone weather???

Yellowstone Lake - at last. altitude 7731'. A magnificent gray-blue jewel lying against the rich green of the mountains' sides. Nature has dotted its shores with tiny campfires - a series of gay little geysers that send their smoke skyward. We tuck ourselves within the comfortable confines of a trailer park called Fishing Bridge, beautifully situated in a sylvan setting, with the pines murmuring all about us and the prospect of finding a bear or two beyond our windows at any given moment, a most exciting one. We have already been welcomed to Yellowstone, incidentally, by a gorgeous black mother bear and her cub who stood beside the roadway long enough for us to photograph them through the windshield of the car as we drove by.

YELLOWSTONE NATIONAL PARK. What had we really known about this miracle of nature before we found our way to its magnificent confines? Nothing, really. We had expected Old Faithful to be on hand and were prepared for her dramatic eruption; but never did we dream that she would be just one of absolutely hundreds if gigantic geysers and boiling water pools, of springs and fumaroles that all erupted from a mammoth geyser basin that made us think as we traversed its crusted surface, of walking on the moon…

How had it all come about, we wondered? How had this strange wild land evolved, in Nature's savage plan? Well, fifty million years ago, we learned, what were then the semitropical forests of Yellowstone were killed by gigantic volcanic eruptions. The periodic floods of water and silt that descending formed a heavy mud, along with the vast avalanches of volcanic material, cascaded down the slopes of the surrounding mountains to cover the forests and fill the valleys and change the entire face of this remote land.

No less than three different times during the past million years, according to geologists, "mountain born glaciers" encased Yellowstone in a vast mantle of ice. The lakes and riverless valleys cloaked with volcanic debris bear silent witness, geologists say, to the frozen world that once was Yellowstone.

The mountains that rim the northern and eastern sections are formed of "volcanic breccia," which is composed primarily of cooled fragments of dust and rock - NOT lava. And so the forests that once were there were preserved and not destroyed by the volcanic action. These volcanic eruptions came to the area periodically, with sufficient time separating them to allow new forests to grow above the ones that lay buried beneath them. to date twenty seven different forest layers have been uncovered in Yellowstone, we were told.

And what of these mountain ranges that lie forever about us? Oh, to be a geologist and really comprehend the savage story that unfolds as we traverse these mighty fortresses that guard the forests of Yellowstone! The ranges that once crowned the land from Mt. Washburn to Mt. Sheridan have vanished completely. we learned-blown to pieces by volcanic action or lost to sight in a sea of lava.

A million years or so ago, we were told, the mountainous Yellowstone area roofed a tremendous chamber that was filled with molten rock-a burst of which combined with dissolved gas-shattered the chamber roof. Immense quantities of volcanic ash poured forth through the mountaintop aperture and were swept across Yellowstone by a savage wind, destroying all life within the area.

The removal of such vast quantities of molten rock from the bowels of the earth caused the chamber roof to collapse, and much of the mountainous area sank to form a barren basin.

As the mountains tipped downward and then sank to the basin floor. The lava spread eastward toward the Absaroka Range over which we had driven en route to Yellowstone. It never quite reached the mountain chain, however, and with the cooling of the lava flow the basin filled with water to form gigantic Yellowstone Lake. A lake which has changed its face with the passing of time to become now larger, now smaller, and to drain through different valleys as glaciers and periodic movements of the mountain blocks brought about such changes. Oh, to be a geologist and really comprehend it all the miracle that is Yellowstone a miracle about which there will be so much more next week:

European Holiday

Contents

WE ARE shortly departing, my husband and I, for a six months tour of Europe. We plan to visit eighteen countries, and a few miscellaneous - and bewitchingly beautiful, we've been told – islands off the coast of Greece.

Greece itself is, needless to say, one of the eighteen, one for the enjoyment of which, we might add, we've made especially elaborate plans. The which is why we read with dismay a week or so ago that a neat little revolution has been scheduled there for sometime in May.

"So that," commented Ted, "settles that. Unless it's all over by September or October," which are the months we've assigned to that particular section of the continent, "Greece is out. With you, we could wind up in the middle of the War…"

Ted has similar views in regard to the Iron Curtain countries, I'd dive behind that mythical barrier in ten seconds flat, but not Ted.

"With your mad zest for a camera." He announces, "we'd be arrested as spies ten minutes after we crossed the border…"

Ted holds similar views regarding East Berlin; I have assured him, however, that I can not return from Europe without having seen for myself, and journeyed behind, the Berlin Wall. I think perhaps he'll humor me on this one for we can travel there safely in the company of a tour guide, our travel agent tells us.

***

WE'VE BEEN planning this little jaunt since a thousand or so B.C.-B.C. standing, in private family parlance, for "Before Children Left the Nest." The which is that frustrating period of time just prior to the final family split, and totally disconnected in any way to A.D., which, standing for "After Departure," follows B.C. as the night the day, though you're absolutely sure it never will.

It is at B.C., we've observed, that most parents plan jaunts like ours- usually, however, to remote corners of the world, like Alaska, or Siberia… And why not??

You've invested twenty or so of the most productive years of your life in raising what you earnestly hope will be a family of fine young Americans, superior in every sense of the word. You find yourselves now holding your conjugal breaths and awaiting the outcome of your labors. You've done your level best; however, you haven't the foggiest notion whether your techniques for developing fine young Americans are right or wrong…And the sad part is that by the time you find out, it's going to be too late to use the knowledge…

You might have found it difficult to believe at that particular moment in your lives, but B.C. if followed finally by A.D., and here the picture changes. You find quite suddenly that those plans for spending your waning years in California or other distant climes are somehow totally lacking in appeal. How can one leave the children? You ask of one another, dismally…

***

TED AND I are flying-to Paris initially, for fifteen days, thence to Rome for fifteen; and thence to London, after which it's two months in the British Isles, followed by three more on the continent. All sorts of fun things are happening as we proceed along the route that leads to Paris.

There was, for instance, the lady who phoned our travel agent within our hearing, to learn how she might bring her cello from the Burlington Music Festival, without placing the beloved thing in the baggage room.

"Put a hat on it and buy it a ticket," I said airily to the highly congenial group who were planning tours. It turned out to be a hat with streamers - half fare - but that was the airline's solution…Passports were secured at the magnificent John F Kennedy Building in government Center; and here we learned how very little we knew about ourselves…and each other…

Now, what, we asked ourselves, does one do with a home for six summer months while one meanders across the face of Europe? Visions of unkempt lawns and unloved privets kept recurring…We decided to sublet, the which we have done, to two charming young businessmen who will arrive, complete with hi-fi and ping-pong table, easy chair and dry sink, and who have fallen in love with our home already.

***

IT'S AN ADVENTURE just to plan an adventure like ours. We're devouring guide books madly; discovering history in lands where age is measured in centuries...

"Have you seen all of America, you two," a friend asked this week, "that you're trotting' off to Europe for all that time?"

"No," we replied, "but America will be next..." next year, hopefully...if we survive the eighteen countries...and the islands...and the revolutions...and the Berlin Wall...and the whole bit...

4-16-67   THE LUGGAGE PROBLEM

NOW THAT Ted and I have announced publicly our forthcoming trip to Europe, we're having a ball!

All sorts of friends are offering all sorts of advice, with delightful results.

There was, for instance, the call from my good friend, Ann.

"Bibs," she said, "do you, by any chance, have arthritis?"

Well, I had to admit to a twinge or two now and then, as would become one of my age and parts.

"Well," she said, "now the climate of much of Europe is murder on arthritis." (or words to that effect...) On one of our trips abroad' (Ann is the well-know seasoned traveler) "I all but died from the dampness. But last time I was smarter. I brought along my wheat germ. You know," she said, "wheat germ is a miraculous cure for arthritis. both Phil and I take it regularly."

"Why, nice to know," I said warmly.

"How much wheat germ do you take?"

"well," said Ann thoughtfully, "I would say about one quarter cup per day."

I thanked her profusely, communicating the information to my mate, who must also own to an occasional twinge or two of arthritis, and for the same reason as my own...

"WELL," said the practical head of the family, "there are two of us. At one quarter cup each per day - that will be one-half cup of wheat germ - multiplied by the 180 days of the trip, with one or two days extra thrown in to allow for the calendar…I'd say that would add up to just about a suitcase full of wheat germ. Now, by air, we are allowed 66 pounds of luggage, I believer, or is it 77?

But still…"

***

THE SECOND CALL came from my good friend, Rosemary.

"Bibs," she said, "you are not traveling with a doctor, are you?"

I had to admit that I was not.

"In that case," she said, "you had better bring a plentiful supply of drugs. You know the drug safeguards aren't as high in European countries as they are in our own. Be sure to take plenty of aspirin and cold pills and something for sea sickness and something for air sickness; and vitamins in case your diet is inadequate in spots, and bisodol mints, and any prescriptions you regularly need, and something for upset stomach, etc., etc., etc.

"so now," said Ted, to whom I recounted the latest advice, "we take one suitcase of wheat germ and one of drugs…"

***

ADRIENNE'S call came next. "You are planning to take Dr. Denton's Sleeping Garments if you're going to England, I hope," she added.

"Adrienne," I said, "they don't make Dr. Denton's garments for grown-ups, do they?"

"They sure do," she said, "I took them."

"But, dear," I said laughing, "we're going to England in July!"

"Dear," she said, "I went to England in July and, believe me, I needed my Dr. Denton's Sleeping Garments!"

MY EYE strayed, as he spoke, to the six foot pile of books and pamphlets I'd purchased and purloined from every friend I own, dealing with every aspect of life in all the eighteen countries we plan to visit. A fourth suitcase rapidly took form…

Oh well, we really don't have to take those seventeen dresses and thirteen pairs of shoes, and the lightweight wool topper to go over the black dress…and the white faille topper to go over the melon…

On the other hand, we could add a bulky knit sweater and bedsocks to our sleepwear in Great Britain; and substitute Vitamin C tablets for the wheat germ…

Just think - in two short weeks, we'll have to solve the whole darn problem!

Columnist Metayer is touring Europe. Unfortunately, through a mix-up in the mails, her second two columns from Europe arrived and were printed before the first one, describing the hectic getaway of travelers leaving home. It has arrived in the meantime and is printed this week.- Ed.

"AU REVOIR"

5-28-67

There's no doubt about it - the Metayers are not the efficient couple they fondly intended to be when they planned their European holiday!

When Ted and I ought to have been packing things madly into boxes and toting them to cold storage in the attic, we were lost to the world in the pages of the great gorgeous tomes we were devouring - viewing the bridges across the Seine, strolling about the palace at Versailles, living the magnificence of the Louvre, tasting the perfume of the chestnut trees…

We were IN Paris and we should have been in Braintree - especially since the tenants who have sublet our home during our absence were fondly anticipating a vast??? collection of empty closets and drawers and wide-open spaces - the tenants who have sublet our apartment, ah, therein lies another tale!

"WE HOPE you don't mind.," they had said sweetly. "We've a few things we would like to bring with us…a hifi and a dry sink a pingpong table and an easy chair…"

"Of course we don't mind," we agreed readily. "Just find little appropriate places and tuck them in!"

Saturday was a lovely day for moving in, especially so for two young executives who would have two days free and who obviously wished to dash to Braintree at the end of their business day on Monday.

It was close to eleven when the first little old orange U-Haul turned into our driveway. Its arrival had been preceded by a phone call. "You're sure you don't mind if we bring some things today?"

"Not in the least; come right ahead!" they took us at our words.

Ted's eyes were dancing as he turned from the front door to confront little old madly packing me.

"They have Hollywood beds and a dining room set and a refrigerator and heaven knows what else in the trailer," he said. By now to was too late for us to anything but laugh. We had tucked away their check and they were clutching our receipt. Besides, they are such darling young men... They had an explanation, or course. "the girls" were taking an apartment on June 1. They'd use the furniture. They didn't want to "throw it away" which was the only alternative for disposing of such priceless objects as black walnut captain's chairs and a round dining table of exquisite beauty and a wolfskin rug, more than a century in age, with a head so magnificent that each time we entered our living room and met the thing face to face, we all but reached for a gun. Ah well, thank heaven for a nice huge basement. The FOUR U-Haul trailer loads managed to find a home below decks. The story of Saturday morning wasn't a one-sided tale, however.

ALMOST simultaneously with the Hollywood beds and the great armchair; the pingpong table; at 33 Arthur Street a motley collection of children of all ages and descriptions. They converged upon and the basketball net; the weights, the cribbage board and the tennis racquets, there began arriving our corner-noisily! They swung from the "Stop" sign and climbed the fire alarm pole and cavorted about the hedges and lawns. They leaped from tree to tree - raucously! Mothers (who had also been arriving in droves) screamed at offspring and offspring out-shouted one another until the air in the "quiet residential neighborhood" we had promised our young men was a veritable azure! It was the Little League Parade, of course, and it won't happen again, but I wonder if the boys thought the troops had been called out to witness the arrival of the furniture they had to wade through crowds to deliver...

And so now we have come to the hour when we bid adieu to Braintree, town of our hearts, and to those we love. Our next "Cabbage" will come, god willing, from Paris, city of dreams.

Au Revoir, everyone!

FROM PARIS

Ed Note
On a six month visit to Europe with her husband, Mrs. Metayer is continuing her weekly column, sharing impressions of her first tip abroad with her friends and readers at home.

PARIS

HOW can one find words to describe the magnificence and enchantment of Paris? Indescribable, Ted says of it all, and I agree...

The chestnut trees with their round fat brown fruits swaying against the sparse foliage of May; the cobbled streets with their interlocking half moons of stone; the bouquets of lilac or muguet du bois each morning, as small jets of water rise from the sidewalks to lave the gutters of the city; the rain that graced every other market basket; the street sweepers with their twigged brooms, hard at work showers that leave Paris either smiling or in tears a dozen times each day; the gendarmes with their rubber coats; the geraniums high upon the window sills; lighted windows in the rooftops of the great high buildings all around (writers or artists starving there???), French cooking and wine with every meal; croissants light as air; and small sweet metal chairs in every open space; and wrought iron balconies and great, grand doors with shining brass, and short slime chimneys with a dozen stacks...and church bells!

The Church of the Madeleine, standing like a Greek Temple with its 52 Corinthian pillars...Here was Chopin's funeral march performed for the very first time, at the funeral of the composer. WE attended mass at one of the eight side altars and shrines, and gazed with awe upon the domed main altar, and the statute of Jeanne d'Arc.

La Voie Triomphale (Way of Triumph) stretching from the incomparably magnificent Louvre to the Arc de Triomphe, with the Tuileries Gardens fountains playing, sculptures in marble and bronze and great, gaunt urns rising from the green of formal gardens; tulips ablaze; paradise in the heart of Paris.

The Place de la Concorde with the Obelisk of Luxor, a monument of stone, rising 76 feet into the Paris sky. This gift of Mahommed ali Pasha Khedive of Egypt to Louis Philippe in 1836 occupies the exact site where the guillotine took the lives of 2800 victims of the French Revolution, Louis XVI, Marie Antoinette, Mme. du Barry and Robespierre included.

The horses of Marly, the two groups of statuary that form the entrance to the champs Elysees which flows magnificently to the Arc de Triomphe.

The Pont de la Concorde nearby - a bridge across the Seine, the stonework of which was furnished from building material of the old Bastille.

THE COMEDIE-FRANCAISE where we witnessed an unforgettable performance of "Le Bourgeois Gentilhomme" by Moliere, a "comedie-ballet en cinq actes, en prose, with one Mr. Louis Seigner as M. Jourdain.

How can I convey to you the magic of the Comedie-Francaise? Built by the architect Louis in 1786-90, it was last renovated in 1935. Sculptured bas-reliefs of Victor Hugo, Racine, Moliere, and Corneille faced us as we entered the theater. The crimson carpetings and hangings in brocade; the chair coverings of scarlet velvet and the furnishings in gold…the massive crystal chandeliers…the enchanting combination, I thought, of splendor and the genteel shabbiness of a grande dame who has known better centuries!

I looked about me. Was that, perhaps, the royal box, long years ago - that box beside the stage, where all the chairs have quite a different gilded look? Did Louis and Marie, perhaps. once occupy the place, to witness Moliere himself?

My eyes strayed all about. Seats rose in tiers up to the very roof itself and not one seat was vacant - students, from their appearance, primarily!

Small boys were present, in groups accompanied by their teachers; they occupied the loges and galeries, and watched with rapt attention. There were a dozen curtain calls and "bravos" rang out from above and never shall I ever see Moliere performed with so much style. A night to be remembered…As are all the nights and days that we are spending, Ted and I, in this enchanting place.

Cabbages & Kings

5-21-67   CITE MAGNIFIQUE

AGAIN and again and again - blessings on the German General who refused to destroy Paris! We continue, Ted and I, to revel in the delights of this incredibly beautiful city. We arise each morning, wearing the smug look of two cats who are about to devour the most luscious of canaries!

Out travels take us to all the exciting places like the Palais Royal and the formal gardens of Cardinal Richlieu, with their monument to the study of Latin - and to the Petit Palais (paris is alive with palaces) where we saw a magnificent exhibition of objects from the tomb of King Tutankhamen including his death mask of gold - and to Notre Dame Cathedral, that masterpiece of Gothic architecture and French art. In the Roman period the Temple of Jupiter stood on the site of this great cathedral. The Rue de la Cite before it was the site of an ancient Roman highway. The massive figure of Charlemagne stands at the entrance. Napoleon was crowned Emperor here. The celebration of high mass was beginning as we entered, beneath the organ loft. Two immense pillars rose on each side, supporting the towers. Galleries rose above the side aisles and chapels lined the walls between the buttresses and the two magnificent Rose windows in the transept caught the sun. THE MASS began and the organ sounded from above, sending its melodious thunder through the great cathedral. My heart tore its way into my throat and lay there hammering. Never before have I heard such music! The choir chanted softly and the organ thundered in reply; Ted had given a coin to a blind beggar as he entered and I had paused to thank le bon Dieu for the sight with which to see this great cathedral. I thanked Him, now, again, fors ears with which to hear its glorious voice. On to Saint Chapelle-that exquisite Gothic chapel, with its 31 magnificent stained glass windows rising from to floor to ceiling. It was built, we learn, by Saint Louis, to house the Crown of Thorns which he obtained from Baudoin, Emperor of Constantinople. And then a brief pause at the Sunday morning Bird Market, where the tiniest and most colorful of birds, as well as such delightful creatures as bantam roosters and all the appointments required for bird fanciers, are offered for sale.

TODAY, however, was the highlight of our stay in Paris, for we paid our first visit to the Louvre! This immense palace, the largest in the world, defies description. It is magnificent! How shall I begin to share its treasures with you? The breathtaking spectacle of the Victory of Samothrace (Winged Victory) at the top of an immense marble stairway; the Venus de Milo which I touched; Egyptian antiquities like the immense bronze figure of Isis, the tomb of Ramses III, papyrus scrolls from the book of death of some Egyptian ruler, centuries ago.

French treasures like the sword of Louis XV and the shield of Charles IX; the scepter of Charles V and the sword of Charlemagne; the diamond-studded sword of Charles X; the cover of the reliquary of the ancient treasurer of Sainte Chapelle and "Le Regent," a diamond of 136 carats…

And then, at last the Mona Lisa. It was seven years in the painting, we learned. Leonardo da Vinci failed to sell it to the husband who had commissioned it, for it looked not at all like his wife. It remained unsold and was given to Francis I, benefactor of the artist, who in his 80th year made a gift of all his remaining works to the King - which is why so many of da Vinci's works adorn the Louvre in France, instead of in Italy.

All of da Vinci's paintings, we learned, have the same model. The face of his St. John the Baptist is a more masculine version of the face of Mona Lisa.

ALMOST as exciting as the Mona Lisa were the 21 immense paintings by Rubens, depicting scenes in the life of Marie de Medici. Breathtaking! and we have only begun to know the Louvre. Back again tomorrow!

Today is a holiday in France and ceremonies were scheduled for 6:30 this evening at the Arc de Triomphe. Our hotel is situated on Avenue Marceau, close to the Champs Elysees, and from 5 o'clock on, the parade began gathering there. They rode past our window, first the Cavalry, with the Cavalry band mounted and playing, their silver helmets shining in the sun, horses' manes braided neatly, ranks close and precise and beautiful. Then the Infantry, arms swinging, heads high…

The French tri-colors were everywhere. We joined the crowd on the Champs Elysees and hadn't long to wait. In the lead, standing erect and stately in an open car, saluting the populace like a monarch came Charles De Gaulle! I cheered him with the rest!

Gendarmes were silhouetted against the sky from every rooftop around. General de Gaulle had been shot at on numerous occasions. Still, he rode alone, an immense, proud target. We marveled at his courage, and then we came to a conclusion - he'd probably love to die a martyr's death, this enigmatic ruler whom we saw today!

Incidentally, isn't it wonderful - I wanted to see de Gaulle we timed it well - a holiday in France and we were here to share it with him!

Ed. Note: By coincidence another Braintree resident was in Paris the same day and witnessed the ceremony - in honor of French Resistance heroes - which Mrs. Metayer described. Library Trustee Ernest D. Frawley of 80 Monatiquot Avenue, in Europe to visit publishing houses, and the Metayers did not know they were there together.

6-11-67   GLIMPSES OF PARIS

THIS IS the WEEK that was...for SPRING with its gaiety and laughter - the warmth of its caress and the song of its myriad frolicking fountains - burst upon Paris!

It had been raining since our arrival, which did not seem to slow us up a great deal, but DID add to the eternal burden of camera, guide books and maps, etc., the inevitable umbrella, which went up and down with monotonous regularity, as Paris - like the wide-eyed visitors who were enchanted by her - was torn between laughter and tears, day after day after day!

Ted DID apply the brakes a little this week, to our mad spree of sight-seeing. "My dear wife," he said in his very best French, "if you continue this pace-seven days a week for six months - they will bury us (with full military honors naturally) on one of the little Greek islands..."

Nonetheless, we are still "pipping" about Paris reveling in a magnificence that leaves us breathless.

There was, for instance, our visit to Sacre Coeur, the immense white 19th century basilica that crowns Montmartre, and the little church of

St. Pierre beside it. Once the proud Abbey of Montmartre, St. Pierre's is the third oldest church in Paris.

We ascend the steep hill via a funiculaire (cable car) from the quaint little Place Suzanne Valadon, named for a resistance fighter, we were told by a delightful French Army officer, who died bravely during the German occupation.

Sacre Coeur, he added, and Notre Dame both received direct hits from the German Big Berthas during world War I. And, he added, during the last week of the more recent occupation, the FFI (French forces of the Interior) knowing that the Americans were but a week or so away, fought the Germans in the square before Notre Dame Cathedral and in the very Cathedral itself! We had noted the bullet holes there and at ECOLE MILITAIRE…

How does one describe Sacre Coeur…the massive mosaics under the great dome, the Army Chapel with its simple statue of Joan of Arc, the great bronze doors, decorated with bas-reliefs based on the scriptures, the massive bell, the Vox Dei, one of the world's largest…and all of Paris below it!

A boat trip up the Seine, and the magnificent series of bridges-no two of them alike-sweep before our eyes as well as the Conciergerie where Marie Antoinette was imprisoned, and the gargoyles of Notre Dame.

**

AND ON to Versailles - the Palace and the gardens! "A toutes les gloires de la France," we read as we enter the massive golden gate and salute the equestrian statue of Louis XIV. And here again, the magnificence we witness defies description.

The chapel, with its exquisite paintings and marble columns and the galerie above…the king we were told by our guide, would accept petitions as he mounted the marble staircase to the chapel each day. The handsome parquet floors, the walls and ceilings of the great state apartments, with their noble materials - marble, bronze, chased or gilded brass and copper; and their immense tapestries and paintings. The Salon of Hercules, with its Lemoyne painting of Hercules and the gods; the Royal Suites; the magnificent chandeliers and fireplaces; the Hall of Mirrors and the painting of Marie Antoinette; the Chambre of

Louis XIV…the Gallery of Battles, with its massive paintings of the great battles in the history of France; the Napoleonic paintings…

Tapis Vert (Green Carpet) and the Grand canal dividing them in the center; fountains and sculpture And then on to the breathtaking beauty of the formal palace gardens…250 acres of them…The adding to the symmetrical walks and tree groupings…The Luxembourg Gardens we found to be far less formal, with their tiny octagonal pool housing the small boats of a hundred happy boys and the daisies enveloping the lawns.

***

ON NOW to the Pantheon, modeled beautifully after the temples of Greece, and housing the tombs of Voltaire and Rousseau, Victor Hugo and others… "aux grands hommes," we read, "la Patrie reconnaisante." (to great men, their grateful country.)

Thence to the Sorbonne, where with permission of the gracious concierge, we viewed the great staircase and the grand amphitheater. The chapel where lie the remains and the hat of Cardinal Richlieu was unable to be seen today…we'll be back!

Art Carney would definitely approve of the weirdly exciting boat ride we took through the sewers beneath Paris. The water, purified in a plant beyond the city, is returned for re-use; and we floated along in a rather large craft propelled by boatmen who walked on walkways beside the canal, huge ropes about their waists pulling us with all the style of the Volga boatmen.

During the German occupation, we were told, the resistance fighters continually harassed and sabotaged the Germans from the sewers beneath the city.

Have I mentioned the fact that we've discovered the Metro, Ted and I, that's the Paris version of our MBTA, but how different!

For eleven cents one can cross the entire city in a facility that is entirely automatic and includes lifts (for exit from subway stations beneath the Seine) and a "Trottoir" or moving sidewalks, if you please, for one particularly long connecting link.

Ah ME - take it from two enchanted Americans - Paris has everything!

6-18-67   AU REVOIR, PARIS

We are already planning to return, Ted and I, to this cities of cities… the year after next, perhaps. Meanwhile we continue to enrich our lives with treasured memories…of the treasure of Notre Dame which we saw today, for instance.

The magnificence of the sacred vestments from ages past - among them the golden vestments which were a gift of Napoleon III to be used at the baptism of his Imperial Prince-chalices, the gifts of Popes over the centuries, including that of good Pope John' gold and silver vessels, exquisitely wrought, dating from the nineteenth century, when this magnificent art seems to have reached its zenith; the crozier used at the coronation of Napoleon I; exquisite cameos of the popes and saints of the Church.

We smiled to see the last Cardinal's red hat above the main altar, where it will hang until it turns to dust.

Memories of the flower Market and the Theatre Sarah Bernhardt and the Concergerie, where we viewed the cell in which Marie Antoinette was imprisoned, as well as her possessions' a crucifix, an armchair, and a facsimile of a letter which she scratched with a pen in an appeal for help.

We saw the wretched hovel in which prisoners were prepared for execution and the door through which they passed to take their places in the "tumbrel for 12" which would bear them to the guillotine knife.

We viewed ancient relics of the first century, which are being unearthed in the Square Vivanti, before Notre Dame Cathedral-relics which include part of the first wall built around the city which was called, in ancient Roman times, Lutece..

We viewed the charm and serenity of the lle St. Louis and the magnificence of the great church. AND WE WITNESSED a superb performance of Wagner's opera "Tristan and Isolde" in the the immense marble staircase beyond?

Opera House. How to describe this magnificence building? Shall we begin with the great foyer and The elegance of the décor of this nineteenth century masterpiece with its double balustrade of the left, which made it possible for the carriage of Napoleon III to be driven right up to the Imperial box? The immense ceiling by Marc Chagall?

The sets and costumes, we learned from a charming Frenchwoman with whom we shared our evening, were designed by the great grandson of the composer, Wagner himself - M. Wieland Wagner. The performance, which commenced at 6:30, ended at midnight. Magnificent! On to the markets of Paris, Les Halles; and to the Colonne de Juliet (July column), an immense memorial crowned by the Godess of Liberty which marks the site of the old Bastille! And to the great Church of St. Eustache close by the markets, modeled after Notre Dame, Masterpieces of Liszt were heard here for the first time, we learned. And Moliere's funeral was held in this magnificent edifice.

HOW TO DESCRIBE the quaint and beautiful Place des Vosges, the oldest square in paris? Victor Hugo himself lived here from 1832 to 1848, and we visited his home and its museum. What treasures!

We viewed with awe the drawings of this versatile genius Exquisite carbed furniture.

Made by him; his death mask by Dalou; theater memorabilia including a crown worn by Sarah Bernhardt herself, original manuscripts and drawings; busts by Rodin; his chamber with its great carved bed and writing desk and quills; the magnificent dining room, the walls of which were decorated by the poet himself.

High mass in the beautiful ancient church of St. Germain des Pres, which included a concert on the magnificent organ. The incense floated upward to the lofty nave of the great church and lay there. The sun brought to dazzling life the figures on the exquisitely stained glass windows. Unforgettable!

***

AND A CHANGE OF PACE - we're not spending all of our time in churches - and evening at the incomparable Folies-Bergere! Oo-la-la - we are still in a daze. The grand foyer with its immense bar and galerie of original paintings delighted us immediately, but - the performance!

The dazzling scenes - several with American influence - the magnificent costumes; the elaborate staging; and the incomparable beauty and talent of the handsome young men and women of France. Never have we witnessed so appealing a spectacle!

Have I mentioned the "flood-lit" Paris, which is a two hour tour of all the great monuments of Paris lighted against the darkened Paris sky? We proceeded down the rue de Rivoli, to Place Vendome, the Louvre, Pont Neuf, the French Academy, St. Germain, the Latin Quarter, the Pantheon, Notre Dame, City Hall, the Concergerie, Champs Elysees, Arc de Triomphe, Eiffel Tower, Invalides, Rue Royale, Boulevarde Montmartre, Place Pigalle, Place Blanche and the Opera. Magnifique!

We shall soon be leaving Paris, Ted and I. Only a few days left which we shall spend in the Rodin Museum and the Louvre. How can we bear to say even "au revoir?" This has been a city of magic. Now-on we go-to Rome!

6-25-67   FROM ROMA - WITH LOVE

SPRING has come to Rome after two long weeks of rain, which, happily pipping about Paris, we missed. In fact, spring and the Metayers managed to arrive together!

The impact appears electric (of spring - not of the Metayers…)

The streets, day and night, are thronged with happy people. There are, of course, the religious - thousands of them; and the tourists…

"Now," said my friend, the student who had "done" Europe last year and who considered herself an authority, "don't make the mistake of wandering about, guidebook in hand…"

Heavens, without the guidebook in Rome, we'd be unable to find our way to the hotel restaurant!

The Italian people, who most of all, are pipping about the handsome "vias" are wonderfully helpful, however.

Today, while enquiring our way to the Colosseum, we were offered assistance by a tall, suave, handsome, bearded gentleman who spoke flawless English, and would, I am confident, have turned out to be the traditional impoverished nobleman, had I been my daughter- and unescorted!

SPRING is something one feels, rather than sees, in Rome, for there are few tree-lined vias. Potted plantings line the stone sidewalks but, unlike Paris, there are no flowers as yet abloom within the City parks here and there, tufts of wild yellow flowers cling precariously, and deep within the Roman Forum, small white flowerlets are sprinkled on the green. Students are demonstrating - noisily but quite good-naturedly and it's not against America; the traffic is mad, and crossing the streets a task; and there's of course siesta!

Everything closes down beautifully from noon to four. Workers return to homes, to eat their heavy meal and take a nap, from which they all return at four.

When in Rome - we also took a nap today; there's really nothing else to do with Rome asleep. We rose at four and started on our way once more. We dined and then returned. Our beds had been remade and fresh white towels spread upon the floor beside them. I never shall be able to return to mundane keeping house, I am afeared...

***

OUR FLIGHT to Rome was flawless. The day was bright and blue; the ride like silk; we watched the snow-capped Alps below; passed over tiny Elba Island, which I strained to see but couldn't- the strong Napoleonic influence still upon us!

Landing near Rome, we drove to the Eternal City. It smiled under the warm spring sun. the grass was lush and green. Hay, stacked in handsome high arrangements like small, sweet-roofed houses, dotted all the fields.

Motor scooters raced along the highway with entire families aboard, and European small cars were everywhere. The way led through tiny villages, past houses with their red-tiled roofs...children smiled and waved.

The Colosseum brought our hearts within our throats...the Roman Forum...ruins upon ruins upon ruins...great Roman stones marking, here and there, the ways where once the Roman soldiers marched.

The Colosseum by night…floodlit and beautiful…and a German religious service in progress. Pilgrims carrying shielded lighted candles; and prayer and music floating to the sky. High in our hotel room we listen to the voices of the city…muffled in this handsome place, by two sets of glass windows, two sets of shutters, with great lined drapes! (It's air-conditioned) Tomorrow we shall find St. Peter's…

WE MEET people from home - Newton, a couple with whom we have Braintree friends in common; Americans from Weymouth and Quincy…More importantly, we are meeting Europeans. The French, with their exquisite courtesy; the warm gracious Italians…

As we wander about, here on this side of the world where our own beautiful part of the world had its beginnings. How wonderful it is!

7-9-67   SPRING IN ROME

ROME..

Today we visited the Roman National Museum with its immense collection of Greek, and Roman and Christian Art monuments found in Rome. We sat upon an ancient Roman bench within the cloister, which was designed - like so much of the magnificence of Rome - by Michelangelo. Great golden roses bloomed upon the vines. Tiny lizards, creatures that seemed so thoroughly at home among the ruins of Ancient Rome, lazed in the sun.

Tonight we walked above the din of all the city, high upon the Capitoline Hill - the Campidoglio, as it is called in Rome. Below us lay the Roman Forum. A great white moon smiled above the palm trees and sent soft glances toward the Temple of Vespasian and Concordia; the Curia; where the Roman Senate met; (was it before these walls that Caesar met his end?), the tomb of Romulus, co-founder of Rome; the great grave arches of Septimius Severus and of Titus; the remains of the Templum Divi Julii, which was erected by Octavian in 29 B.C., on the place where Caesar was cremated! The Palatine Hills tore a jagged rent in the soft night sky. Off to the left, the Colosseum glowed, floodlit as are the mighty monuments of Rome when darkness falls. Have I said there were no signs of Spring in the Eternal City?

***

The night was a soft warm scarf about our throats…spring has surely come to Rome these past few days. Lovers abound: and laughter lights the way; the Carabinieri stroll about quite handsome in their uniforms of blue.

They smile and tuck incessant tickets in the windshield wipers of the gay Italians who park their motor cars in all the strangest places. Hawkers sell wares; and every sidewalk café is filled; and families stroll within city parks. Bambini looking for all the world like Botticelli angels (with Madonnas for mothers) romp everywhere.

Could it be anytime but spring when great gay crowns of scarlet poppies perch atop the walls that line the ancient Appian Way; and calla lilies bloom within the gardens high above the Catacombs of St. Callista?

How to describe the sheer magnificence of St. Peter's and the Vatican Museum? Michelangelo's "Pieta"…all the genius of Michelangelo, who designed the massive structure; Bernini's immense bronze canopy over the center altar; his holy water fount; his monuments and masterpieces; the Sistine Chapel with Michelangelo's immortal frescoes, on one of which gigantic mystic inspirations, the "Final Judgement," the incomparable artist worked for seven years.

How to convey the awe-inspiring experience of a Papal audience, where thanks to the good offices of Cardinal Cushing, Ted and I sat on soft plush seats directly in front of the Pontiff, the most preferred location in the immense basilica where less than a thousand people were seated, and forty-nine thousand pilgrims stood, according to a Vatican attendant we met. This number, incidentally, was in addition, he said, to the hundred thousand people in the courtyard just outside.

How to express the feeling that suffused our hearts as a magnificent choral group from Maine, rendered the beautiful hymn, "Let There Be Peace On Earth, and Let It Begin With Thee!" It thundered in the great basilica and rose like a mighty prayer which found echo in the hearts, I am certain, of everyone of us. A memorable experience for the Metayers.

***

EVERYTHING about the Eternal City is memorable- and wonderful. WE spend our days walking with history, learning...

Of the Etruscans, for instance, one of the three original tribes living on the hills of Rome (Latins, Sabines and Etruscans) whose "cerveteri," immense circular dwelling places erected beneath the ground yielded sculpture, jewelry, pottery and household goods that reveal an astonishingly advanced civilization.

Their museum houses "safety pins" almost identical to our own, and exquisite filigree golden jewelry, and vases, one of which could pass for a Picasso!

We are meeting in the museums of Rome all the ancient Romans we have ever found in history books, putting faces to them, "getting to know" them...we gaze upon "The Dying Gaul," and the "Capitoline Venus" and the "Thorn Extractor" and the rest...

We revel in it, and we are humble before it, and how very, very reluctantly we shall leave it...

7-2-67   SUNDAY IN ROME

THE IMMENSE dome of St. Peter's ever and eternally casts its shadow over the face of Rome; but never more completely than on a warm Italian Sunday with the sun high in the cobalt blue sky...High Mass at ten in the Basilica, with the great bronze figures above the altar springing to life in the candle flame; and the organ thundering; and the full rich voices of the choir rising to the dome. St. Peter's square is thronged with thousands of people even as we arrive, for on each Sunday at noon, Pope Paul will appear at the window of his workroom in the Apostolic Palace to bless the "pilgrims" gathered below.

By the ending of Mass, the square is a mass of humanity of every race and shade. We regard them with delight - the turbanned and sari-clad Hindus; the Moslems; the Orientals; service men from all the countries of Europe, it seems. Our English is a small island in a sea of languages that swirls about us.

***

Who, we ask, are the little girls in beautiful floor-length bridal attire, who stand so solemnly about, proud parents in their wake - holding their small white missals in their sweet gloved hands? It is customary among French and Italian families of means, we learn, to bring their First Communicants to Rome on the Sunday following their reception of the sacrament to receive the Papal blessing.

We are seized with the excitement of the impending event.

High in the Vatican tower the hands of the great gold clock move on the window high up inch silently towards noon. Tens of thousands of cameras are focused on the window high up in the Apostolic Palace, at which Pope Paul will make his appearance. And now the window opens; and the Papal banner is hung from the sill. A murmur passes over the hitherto strangely silent crows. A band commences a solemn hymn which lasts until the great clock of St. Peter's - "Vox Dei," as it is called within church circles - begins to strike the hour of noon. The band ceases instantly. The great bell tolls the hour, slowly, sonorously…

As the last stroke sounds, he appears at the palace window, Pope Paul VI, a slight figure clad in simple white. He raises his hand in greeting.

The crows thunders it s applause. Thousands of white silk kerchiefs flutter in the summer aid. "Viva Papa" rises from the throats of Italians everywhere. The rest are content to wave their arms, or to applaud.

The clicking of thousands of cameras is lost in the din…

The Pontiff salutes the crowd affectionately. The warmth of his smile carries into the rich, full voice which comes beautifully over the sound system as he addresses the crowd.

He pauses briefly, and then a hundred thousand people fall on their knees or bow their heads, as the spiritual of one faith leads people of all faiths, and of all lands, in a prayer for world peace – a prayer which sweeps over the great courtyard and rises to the blue Italian sky…Pope Paul raises his hand in blessing, and the thunder starts anew!

He is gone; and now the great bell sounds as never before, it seems - joyously, unceasingly! The pilgrims move in a mighty wave toward the Basilica.

Baptism is in progress as we enter St. Peter's, and within the Baptismal Chapel, the sun streams from above, playing on the faces of the figures that adorn the great bronze fount. The center of this impressive vessel is an ancient porphiry bowl from the sarcophagus of Otto II, we learn. Everywhere, or so it seems, tiny Botticelli angels in gorgeous christening robes, are being held Proudly in the arms of handsomely groomed godmothers. Godfathers in formal attire stand by. A delightful sight! We walk again within the Basilica, where the red robes of Cardinals mingle with the drab brown of humble monks. We gaze, enraptured once again, upon the sheer magnificence that is St. Peter's. Michelangelo's genius is everywhere; and the hand of Bernini speaks to us from all the wondrous corners of this hallowed place.

All the beauty of Italy is exemplified here, we decide. Her artists and her sculptors; her artisans and craftsmen - the combined genius of centuries of Italian art is in full bloom in the great church that is the heart of Rome…And we are seeing it, studying it, thrilling to it! Incredible…

UP WITH PEOPLE!

There's no doubt about it…we're for people all the way; and those we are meeting in Europe we find are almost as wonderful as those we left behind us in Braintree!

Some of them, of course, leave us laughing-like the very wealthy elderly lady from New Orleans whom we met in our hotel in Paris. She and her portly spouse were spending six weeks on the Continent.

Their travel agent had arranged to have a limousine with chauffeur placed at their disposal at each of the major cities they visited. "My dear, have you seen Montmartre?" she asked me.

"We drove to Montmartre yesterday," she confided, "up to the very top, where the artists were at work at their easels and with all of Paris lying beneath us."

"Wouldn't you like to get out and walk around?' asked the chauffeur. 'Oh, I don't know,' I said," she told us seriously. "Are the natives friendly?"

Incidentally, we did of course, see Montmartre - by day and night with the artists at work, and the Bohemians at play. Montmartre, we were told by our guide, is a law unto itself. Its inhabitants pay very little taxes; they elect their own Mayor; and their "night spots" are wide open twenty-four hours a day.

(We fear Columnist Metayer's guide may have exaggerated slightly, although within the bounds of poetic license. The Independent Republic of Montmartre also issues its own passports, but they have as little official validity as the Mayor.-Ed.)

***

But to return to "people." While we were in Rome, the "pensioners" of Italy staged a demonstration at the Colosseum. They were seeking reform in the pension system, and an increase in pension amounts.

They arrived by bus from every corner of Italy. The Via dei Fori Imperiali was choked with the great parked vehicles. And the elderly of Italy - men and women -- marched to the music that blared from a sound system high above the Roman Forum.

They marched by the tens of thousands! Some were on crutches; tiny, fragile old ladies were escorted by stronger ones; the more aggressive carried crude home-made banners; and the elderly men -- hundreds of them -- sported a faded boutonniere.

We never did learn whether or not they won their point; but it was a colorful sight to see them trying.

***

Actually, we managed to meet interesting and delightful people on all sides -- like the young Italian who, seated at an adjacent table in the sidewalk café, heard us commenting about a particularly fetching hat (huge with feathers) which was part of a young Italian soldier's uniform.

He knew not a word of English, however, he managed to convey to us the information that the soldier was a member of the Alpine Corps. We thanked him profusely for the information - - so profusely, in fact, that he responded by summoning every soldier who passed by wearing a different insignia to our table, where with gestures, he identified his branch of service (rank and serial number).

In no time at all, we were surrounded by a group of precious young boys who looked and acted exactly like our own; and with whom we found ourselves shaking hands and exchanging photographs (they of their brothers and sisters and of themselves in uniform and we of our grandchildren).

***

Most delightful of all, I think, was the lady whom we met at the top of the magnificent Spanish Steps in the Plaza di Spagna. We were enroute to the Villa Medici and we inquired the way of the handsomely attired woman with whom I seemed to establish instant rapport.

In no time at all, we were exchanging confidences - which was not so easy as one might think! The lady, who was French (a widow, whose husband was an Italian diplomat) could understand, but not speak, English.

My French leaves vast amounts to be desired. Ted, however, speaks French fluently! And so, there ensued the most fascinating three-way conversation in history - with Ted interpreting for both of us, and all three of us having a ball.

But therein lies the tale - the French Academy and the Villa Medici were having on that very day, a special exhibition of Rodin's works. Admission was by invitation only, and the lady had an invitation.

A VIP, she exerted her influence and had us admitted to this all-important affair, which was being sponsored by the Ministers of Cultural Affairs of half a dozen nations, our own included. We were her guests, she informed them.

The aristocracy of Rome were present, as well as the influential French for miles around. All the great couturiers of Paris had dressed the ladies; never have I beheld such style!

And there we were, Ted and I, taken in tow by our charming new friend - two American tourists among the elite of the Eternal City -- hand-kissing going on all about us…reveling in the genius of the sculptor whose works included "The Thinker" and "The Kiss!"

***

Afterwards, our new friend insistently invited us to what I assumed to be a two hour Roman luncheon, the idea of which was not appealing as we had had an enormous breakfast. Ted kept graciously refusing; the lady kept insisting.

We parted sadly, with kissing on both cheeks in the pretty French manner, and it was several minutes before I learned the nature of the lady's invitation - it was to tea at her home!

I all but divorced my darling husband on the spot. How wonderful to have visited an Italian home in Rome! Ought to have brushed up on my French before leaving home.

Ah, Roma, how shall we ever bear to leave thee!

6-20-67   THE ENGLISH COUNTRYSIDE

Fate continues to smile our way. Today, by the merest chance, we attended in Westminster Abbey the Committal Service of John Masefield, England's poet laureate!

It was a beautiful day. The sun streamed through the magnificent rose window and framed the face of one C. Day Lewis, Esq. whose glorious voice carried the beauty of the poet's "West Wind," and "Dauber" and "The Everlasting Mercy" straight to the souls of those who mourned the great man's passing.

The eulogy was appropriately moving, and the committal wherein the poet's ashes were placed prayerfully beneath the gray stone floor of the Abbey, solemn and beautiful.

We watched afterwards as, the mourners having departed the great cathedral, masons cemented the tiny wooden cask that held the mortal remains of England's poet laureate in a soft, sweet place by the Poet's Corner, close to the tombs of the Brownings, Robert and Elizabeth, and Alfred Lord Tennyson.

How strange that we should be in England for the passing of a man whose poetry we've always loved!

"Illuminate and inspire, we beseech Thee," the rich deep voice of the Archdeacon intoned solemnly, "all poets, writers, artists and craftsmen; that, in whatsoever is true and pure and lovely, Thy name may be hallowed and Thy kingdom come on earth."

***

Earlier in the week our fancy took us to Shakespeare's Warwickshire. We left the lovely town houses of London -- with their wrought iron railings and deeply blooming rose gardens - far behind us and were off to the English countryside, the which, we might add, is remarkably like our own. In the County of Buckingham, we learned the delightful story of "The Chilton Hundreds," a division of the county so called because it comprised one hundred "hides" of land.

A "hide" we were told, was in early years, as much land as a man could cultivate in one year with one plough.

In medieval times, the king hired a "steward" to farm his "hides" of Chilton land. To this day, a member of Parliament cannot resign his seat once elected unless he takes another government position and so an M.P. who wishes to resign seeks the mythical post of "Steward" of Chilton Hundreds.

There is no longer a steward; there is not even a Chilton Hundreds. It is a device. However, it works! He is free of the duties of Parliament!

**

On we went past the little towns of Chalfont St. Peter and Chalfont St. Giles. From here we were told, came many of the Pilgrim fathers who sought religious freedom in our own dear land. Close by Jordan, we were shown an ancient barn that was built from the timbers of the Mayflower itself!

The fresh scent of the earth, newly turned, was all about us. We entered Amersham, the tiny market town where one "Miss Springett," wife of William Penn, was born.

Poppies lay, blood-red, on the lush greed fields and buttercups tossed golden heads our way. We thought of home…

The villages of Banbury and Wroxton, with lovely little thatched-roofed cottages lining the narrow road that wound about it and the ironstone being mined from the fields with "open cast mining." And then - sweeping before us from the crest of Hedge Hill - Shakespeare's Warwickshire. With the view across the Warwick Plain sending us dashing madly for cameras and films!

How to describe the delights of a visit to Anne Hathaway's tiny daub and wattle cottage in Shottery, with the thatched roof and the settle upon which the bard of Avon courted his lady love…And Stratford-Upon-Avon itself, with the great white swans on the river Isis; and the handsome Memorial Theatre; Holy Trinity Church and the tomb of the "Swan of Avon" himself; the grammar school he attended; and the house where he was born.

And then - how wonderful to behold - the American flag riding the breeze above "Harvard House," the home of Catherine Rogers, mother of John Harvard, and now the property of Harvard University!

Over the colorful Cotswold Country now to Oxford University, which we were surprised to learn, is not one university at all, but is comprised of twenty-five men's colleges and five women's accumulated over nine centuries.

We visited "New College," with its great beamed hall and ancient chapel. The oldest of the Oxford Colleges, we learned, had their beginnings as monasteries and the monastic style of building has survived to this day.

Have we neglected to mention our visit to Blenheim Palace where Sir Winston Churchill was born… "impetuous as always," to quote our guide, in a cloakroom, on an old fashioned bedstead which had been "made up" for a servant, his mother having been surprised by his arrival while she was walking about the grounds. It is, today, a museum…

And have we mentioned lovely little Eton College, the original building of which is supported by timbers from the Spanish Armada.

Incidentally, the schoolboys in their white collars and cutaway coats are "smashing," to quote the English schoolgirls…

7-23-67   FROM LONDON TOWN

"When a man is tired of London, he is tired of life; for there is in London all that life can afford." I believe it was Samuel Johnson who said it, but I'm not really sure. In fact, I'm not even certain of the accuracy of the quotation. But, after a week in this city of color and splendor, are we ever in agreement with the sentiment!!!

Our hotel overlooks the lush green wall-to-wall of Hyde Park…and were we Conservationists delighted to learn that a London ordinance will forever insure the setting aside of one-fourth square mile of park land just like Hyde Park within the city for every square mile of development.

Before us lies the Marble Arch and the famous "Speakers' Corner" where before the tolerant eye of the park "bobbie" the Englishman exercises his freedom of speech before his fellows. We brought the spring with us from Rome. After the coldest, wettest weeks in London's memory the sun is rising merrily each morn at four or thereabouts and setting at nine or ten. (The English call it "twilight!")

People are coming out from behind their MacIntoshes and umbrellas. Flowers are bursting everywhere (in a restrained British way, of course)…We've yet to encounter that fog we've heard about; and we've had no call to date, to break out the Dr. Denton's sleeping garments…

**

We're beautifully at home. It hasn't taken us long to plunge into the bloody world of British history via the great Tower of London, with the dungeon apartments of sir Walter Raleigh and Sir Thomas More; (We saw "A Man for All Seasons" right here in London); the burial places of Ann Boleyn and Catherine Howard and Lady Jane Grey and the rest; the private execution site of mad Henry VIII where "the grass failed ever to grow, for all the blood that flowed upon the post" to quote our "Yeoman Warder," (the term "Beefeater" is out, he said) "and so good Queen Victoria caused the wretched site to be cobbled…"

We've cast wondering eyes over the magnificent armor of Henry VIII, with its initialed border "W" and "H" entwined with lover's knots. (For Henry and Catherine Howard his beloved wife- before the execution.) We've viewed the sabre of the Duke of Wellington, once Constable of the Tower; and the cloak of General Wolfe, who died on the Plains of Abraham.

**

We've heard the delightful tale of Colonel Blood, who made off with the crown jewels in 1671 and, when apprehended, was rewarded by merry King Charles II with five hundred pounds a year for life.

("Any man who could make off with the crown jewels," etc., etc.) And -- we've seen the crown jewels themselves, which defy description.

We've made the acquaintance of the "Maundy coins." Each year, we learned, on Maundy Thursday, which is the Thursday before Easter, Britain's ruling sovereign distributes to as many "senior citizens of each sex as there are in her age," "Maundy Coins" (golden penny, two pence, three and four pence.)

The coins are distributed from a great golden "Maundy Dish," and the ceremony is held in a different Cathedral each year. An ancient custom!

We've heard the tale of the six ravens, whose clipped wings assure their never leaving the Tower of London, for it was been prophesied that should the ravens (who have been present since the time of William the Conqueror) ever leave the Tower, then should the British Empire cease to be! We've visited magnificent Westminster Abbey and found our ancestress there -- "The Countess Clanricard, wife of the Earl of Clanricard, of the Noble Family of Burke of the Kingdom of Ireland" to quote the handsome crested inscription above the lady's tomb.

We had been advised by our British Aunt precisely where to look -- to the left of the Tomb of the Unknown Warrior. And we've found all the magnificent landmarks we witnessed via television at Queen Elizabeth's coronation...

***

We were enchanted to find in Victoria Tower Park, a handsome bronze of Emmeline Pankhurst, who, with her daughter, Dame Christabel Pankhurst, were so honored for their "courageous leadership of the movement for the enfranchisement of women"...and who "led the militant suffrage campaign" in Britain.

Emmeline, we were told, chained herself to the Parliament railings at one point in her obviously colorful career. Delighted our Leaguer's soul, naturally!

We're compiling a set of marvelous English expressions. "The toaster has packed up on us this evening; will you take a roll?" from the waitress in the corner restaurant after the theater.

"St. James Palace? It's at the top of the street," "What's the matter, love? You're wearing a face like a wet week;" "Shrewsbury straight on;" etc., etc.

We're staying in London an extra week - we know that already; in fact, we just may never leave it! What a city!

7-30-67   ONE DAY IN LONDON

The fates, we have decided, are conspiring to tuck every possible bit of drama and delight into our European holiday!

On a recent Monday Ted and I were attending a session of Parliament's House of Lords when George Brown, Britain's Foreign Secretary, came to report to "Milords" on the Israeli-Arab conflict, and it was high drama indeed!

The day had begun in London, as I am certain it began in Braintree, with a screaming newspaper headline. "It's war," we read, with horror. The Israeli-Arab situation had exploded!

We had planned a visit to the National Gallery for the morning, and so we went to be enchanted by an entire room of Rembrandts, scores of Titians and Rubens, Gainsboroughs and the rest. Around the corner then to the National Portrait Gallery, where we found every Englishman (and Englishwoman) of consequence we'd ever known. Delightful.

Lunch and then we proposed to visit Parliament. "Big Ben" was sounding the hour as we proceeded along Whitehall, past Downing Street…

Number 10 Downing, the unpretentious residence of Britain's Prime Minister, was alive with activity. Two English "Bobbies" stood on either side of the doorway, while England's policy-makers arrived in their chauffeur-driven cars to be ushered quickly within.

A crisis was bringing the heads of State together.

Across the narrow street, people stood quietly, somberly. We joined the crowd. I looked about me at these Londoners to whom war represents a very personal experience - at the veteran with an empty sleeve; at the vacationing lady from Malta who confided to me in low tones that her one child had been born without medical attention in a cave eighty feet underground during the bombing of that tragic island in the last great war. She could never have another.

Our hearts were heavy as we made our way to the magnificent Westminster Palace of Parliament. Beside it flowed the Thames quietly, sedately.

Exquisite mosaics representing St. Stephen, King Stephen and Edward the Confessor graced the inner portal. Sculptures of England's monarchs lined the outer wall.

***

England's House of Lords - with its royal trappings and great throne and chair; the bewigged, berobed Lord Chancellor and the great golden mace correctly in place…the Baroness Gaitskell was discussing a National Health Service Bill as we entered and took our seats.

And then the arrival of George Brown from 10 Downing Street! Unexpected drama!

"The situation," he stated, "is still unclear. Jerusalem is engulfed in war. I have been in touch," he said, "with representatives from the United States, the Soviet Union, Italy, France and the United Nations.

"Our immediate aim is a cease fire. Our interests are the same as the rest of the world. We seek a peaceful solution. Instructions have gone out to our forces to avoid conflict.

"All merchant shipping due to pass through the canal will be advised to lay to for 24 hours." "What happened in Washington and New York?" asked one old gentleman seriously. "No statement has been made," he was told.

The matter must be debated, the Lords agreed. A personal appeal from the Secretary General of the United Nations might be effective, it was decided.

And then, a most distinguished looking peer of the realm took the floor. He wanted assurances that "we are working closely with the United Nations in this."

He received them. "In this matter," he was told, "right from the outset the government is working closely with the United States government." I wanted to cheer.

On next to a session of the House of Commons where I could feel good old Sir Winston Churchill all about me. Social legislation was being debated with intermittent references to the "Government" report on the grave international situation "that had been made earlier that day." Tea in the handsome Parliament Restaurant before our departure - with "M.P.'s" and their constituents dining and conferring about us. What fun!

Back now through the soft summer evening along Whitehall to the Horse Guards Parade, and another unexpected treat for here we found the famous massed bands of the Royal Marines - many hundreds in number and superb in performance.

They were rehearsing for "Beating Retreat," a ceremony to be held on Thursday evening when H.R.H. the Duke of Edinburgh accompanied by the Queen, would take a salute as their captain General. (We dashed off and purchased tickets for the event!)

***

And so a rather typical day in this extraordinary city came to an end…Oh yes…P.S. with further reference to Mr. Brown's appearance before the House of Lords…Compulsive note-taker and "Cabbage"-minded individual that I am, I was merrily scribbling away while the gentleman's speech was in progress when a voice whispered into my ear.

"We no longer chop off their heads," said one of the gentlemen who, in white tie and tails, and, wearing great seals about their necks, protect the dignity and decorum of Parliament, "but we've been known to send to the Tower ladies who take notes in Parliament!"

PS. On Wednesday morning, Ted and I visited the British Museum which lies close to London University. Students everywhere were displaying professionally printed stickers on either side of their briefcases "Stop Nasser Now" read on one side and "Support Israel" on the other. Extraordinary people, these Britishers!

8-6-67   BRITTAIN-IA

Bits and pieces gathered from guides, Londoners and Yeoman of the Guards - unauthenticated: The magnificent American Embassy is an architectural triumph; it is surmounted, however, by a gigantic and gorgeous gold eagle, the which, for some unaccountable reason, is facing the wrong direction…

A handsome statue of the Duke of York, second son of King George III, stands facing the mall with its back to Regent St. The gentleman financed the monument by appropriating a days' pay from each of his officers and men.

He owed the sum of 10,500 pounds which he never paid to the creditors of Regent Street. 'Tis said in London that to the very end, he always turned his back on the creditors…

The famous Admiralty Arch was dedicated to Queen Victoria and its gates are kept locked. They can be opened only for a coronation or state business.

All distances in London are measured from the statue of Charles I in Trafalgar Square.

***

Captain John Smith is buried in the Holy Sepulchre near St. Paul's Cathedral. The base of the monument to Queen Anne before the Cathedral steps contains the figure of Pocahontas. The firm of Berry Brothers and Rudd distillers of Cutty Sark whiskey, has for 200 years been located at 2 St. James Street. From 1842 to 1845, while Texas was a Republic, this building housed the Texas legation.

George Frederick Handel played the organ in the Royal Chapel at St. James Palace; and at the Queen's Chapel, Mendelssohn played the organ.

Lord Cobbold, the Lord Chamberlain of England, occupies in St. James Palace the apartments which housed Queen Anne (wife of George III) the "last Queen of America."

The tiered steeple of St. Bride's Church, which was designed by Sir Christopher Wren, is said to be the model of all wedding cakes.

***

Metal from cannon captured during the Crimean War is melted down to fashion Britain's highest award, the Victoria Cross.

The Lord Mayor of London, who serves only a one-year term is paid a salary of 10,000 pounds annually; it costs him, however, 100,000 annually to maintain the office. It is, nonetheless, the most sought-after post in London.

The Queen cannot enter London without his official permission; she is met by him always at the Temple Bar and escorted into the city.

Sir Christopher Wren is buried beneath the floor of St. Paul's Cathedral. His memorial reads: "If you wish to see my monument, look around you." (He designed the cathedral).

Friezes on the base of the Albert Memorial Monument are said to contain the faces of all the great men in history…

The "American Chapel" at St. Paul's, which was erected to repair a bomb-damaged section of the cathedral, contains a monument to American airmen who lost their lives in the Battle of Britain. It reads: "To the American Dead of the Second World War from the People of Britain."

The statue of George III in Haymarket has its back turned on the statue of George Washington, directly behind in Trafalgar Square.

Prince Charles will enter Cambridge College in the fall. The royal children have formerly been privately taught. Credit to Prince Phillip!

So precisely was the "Trooping the Colour" celebration of the Queen's birthday (which we witnessed) that a non-com, armed with three foot long dividers, measured the distance between the Coldstream guards who lined the mall six paces apart, and between them and the mall curbing. The uniform of the Coldstream guards is the same throughout; only the arrangement of the brass buttons on the tunic distinguishes the Grenadier, Irish, Scotch, and Welsh guards.

Sir Francis Chichester, who recently sailed alone in a small sailing vessel from Australia to England around the Horn, was knighted by Queen Elizabeth with the sword with which Sir Francis Drake was knighted.

An "astronomical clock" in "Clock Court" at Hampton Court Palace, which was made by Nicholas Oursian in 1540 and is still running, shows the hour, the day, the month, the number of days since New Year, the phases of the moon and the times of High Water at London Bridge…

Dulwich Village celebrated its 1000th anniversary, and we were there…It's a small English village, a very few miles from the bustling heart of London, over the Tower Bridge…

The day was warm and sweet as we arrived upon the pennant-bedecked scene. (London has, believe it or not, staged a drought in our honor, so we've yet to see rain.) Dulwich, we decided, was like a 19th century painting.

Neat red brick houses stood in rows, their slate roofs shining in the sun; the lawns before them trimmed with T.L.C. Every flower in Dulwich's handsome gardens seemed to have bloomed just for the occasion.

English roses in a myriad of colors spent their summer perfume lavishly. Rhododendrons hurled great masses of purple and pink against the wine of walls.

Holly was everywhere - rich and green…Tiny pansies smiled and red geraniums glowed! Townspeople in 5th and 12th and 16th century attire (you name it…) smiled from all the doorways of the shops, or walked the village green as Dulwichites (and others) converged upon the park from which the fair Millennium "Procession" would proceed to Dulwich village and the Gallery Road, and thenceforth to Belair, the handsome mansion where a pageant would commemorate the thousand years of Dulwich history.

***

A concert, "Music at Belair," would mark the proud event; and then -- as darkness fell -- a fireworks display would bring the merrymaking to a close.

Dulwich, Anglo-Saxon for "Village in the Valley," we learned, traces its history back to the year 967 A.D. when Edgar the Peaceful, whose reign was marked by no Crusades, no foreign conquests, no invasions, nor assassinations - granted Dilwihs to one of his Thanes.

For 900 years, we were told, the little village whose name was changed to Dulwich in 1530, was independent of the outside world.

It was brushed occasionally by history. Cromwell quartered a contingent at the college; and Charles II hunted in its woods.

The village has known three owners - the Crown; the Priory, or Abbey of Bermondsey – a Benedictine Order which was endowed by Henry I in 1127 with the "Manor of Dulwich"; and "Alleyn's College of God's Gift"…Edward Alleyn was of the Age of Shakespeare. An actor and star of the Lord Admiral's Company, Christopher Marlowe's Barrabas was created especially for him.

He was, also, a man with a dream. And so, we learned, in 1619, James I bequeathed to the actor, now retired, the "Manor" or village, on order that he might build there "a chappell, a schoole house and twelve almshouses," the which he did.

***

Alleyn's College of God's Gift remains today, to dominate the little town and color its history. Its "Picture Gallery" houses the finest private collection of paintings in the world.

And how did this magnificent art collection - Rubens, Rembrandts, Gainesboroughs, etc. find its way to Dulwich College? Well, that's another story.

One Noel Desenfans, an art connoisseur of note, had been commissioned by King Stanislaus to collect paintings for a Polish National Gallery. Stanislaus died, however; and Poland was invaded by the Armies of Russia and Prussia; and Desenfans was left with the collection on his hands. It was bequeathed eventually to Alleyn's College of God's Gift. God's Gift, of course, was the magnificent talent of Edward Alleyn, actor.

In December of 1966, the theft of eight of the paintings, including the Rubens and the Rembrandt, was duly reported in our newspapers. Do you remember?

They were, happily, recovered, however - in the "Rookery" we were told, and are back at the Picture Gallery where we viewed them.

***

But to return to the Millennium festivities. The "procession" was decidedly amateurish by American standards - crude "floats" on truck bodies; crepe paper trappings, etc.

There was, however, nothing amateurish about the three-hour pageant which was presented on the green English grass of Belair, with a great sweep of ancient trees as a backdrop; and a gray sky overhead; and the faintest roll of thunder in the air; and the river flowing softly by, white swans upon its silver surface.

And "Cameo" following "Cameo" with the clashing of swords; the sounds of knightly combat; the mantles and crowns of monarchs and the soft silks of their ladies; the mitres of bishops and the holgbows of yeomen; the color, the costumes.

The pageantry of England - with each performer's voice resounding on the fields like dear James Mason at his darling best, or Deborah Kerr in person. It was a triumph!

"Music at Belair" was lively also, and the fireworks!

It was a delightful day with lunch at "The Crown and Greyhound," a charming inn where Dickens was a frequent patron and where a special Dickensian menu was served by costumed waitresses and barmen. Sam Pickwick lived in Dulwich actually!

A precious little village, Dulwich. John Harvard, founder of Harvard University, we learned, was born here. It is possible, said the dear vicar who communicated the fact to us, that the recollection of what his father's friend, Edward Alleyn, had done in Dulwich prompted his action!

Yes, a delightful day indeed. And when, the concert ended, "God Save the Queen" floated above the starlit English night, we closed our eyes contentedly and in our hearts we sang "America" as always.

8-27-67   FROM DUBLIN

Sure and the top of the mornin' to you all from Dublin!

We left London on the crack train, "Irish Mail" - so called because it meets the Irish Mail Boat - and a delight to the Metayers, who realized with a sense of shock 'tis close to twenty years since their last journey by train!

The sun was warm on the deep green fields of the English countryside. Storms were to rip through England that very day, claiming several lives; but there was no indication of their coming in the bright, brash blueness of the summer morning we took with us from London.

Cattle and sheep lazed in the fields of the English country through which we rode. Blooded horses raised inquiring heads as the long train thundered past.

There were miles of green fields, criss-crossed with hedgerows, an occasional stand of ancient trees flat against the sky.

Tiny thatched cottages rested lightly in clusters on the landscape; little stone churches sent their ancient spires aloft; graveyards slumbered… Here and there a castle hurled itself against the blue- and great fortresses they were indeed - Conway Castle and the rest…Occasional hills with the mist about them marked the distant skyline…

There were charming people with whom to share the journey, and tales of delightful places like the little village of Cemaesboy in northern Wales, where no one ever locks a door.

"I don't believe there's a key in the village," the wife of a young engineer told us. She spoke of other things also - of the Wylle Nuclear Power Plant on which her husband is engaged -- a gigantic project which will supply electric power for most of Wales and for which the tip will be left standing in order to bury the entire installation in twenty years.

"It's obsolete already," she told us, "and it's not yet finished - so rapidly is the nuclear development picture changing. And 20 years is the life span of such a plant…"

The train roared on, and now the Snowdonian Mountains were proud and high on the horizon and a softsweet mist lay on Anglesey Island and Cymru Mam, which is called the "Mother of Wales".

***

The Cambria lay at anchor as our train arrived at Holyhead at the northern tip of Wales -- a huge, handsome craft, with accommodations for more than 2300 passengers; and we boarded her for the three and one half hour trip across the Irish Sea - the which we might add, was on its very best behavior, and so our little ocean voyage is a delightful one indeed!

And now we came to Dublin, capital of Eire, and there was O'Connell Street - at its head the splendid monument to a prized ancestor of ours, Daniel O'Connell, the great Irish liberator…

And the mist was on the River Liffey as it flowed under O'Connell Bridge and on its way to the sea…and the grass was greener than any grass we've ever ever known…

And the soft Dublin Mountains peered gently over our shoulders… and the trim gay flower beds everywhere were ablaze with snapdragons and sweet Williams and primroses and salvia…

And we remembered our own sweet gardens at home…and the mist upon the River Liffey deepened and then turned to quiet rain, but no one seemed to note the change.

Dubliners sauntered on the wide and handsome street, their clothing light and gay, their laughter free. For this is Ireland's summer… and it's the warm season…

We and the other summer visitors may wrap ourselves in woolens if we must: not the Irish! We wander, shivering now and then in the "summer" wind, through all of Dublin's wondrous places…

Trinity College, with its ancient buildings and the magnificent illuminated Book of Kells - the four gospels, written in Irish majuscule script about the year 800…

Dublin Castle, erected as the residence of the Danish Kings of Dublin in 820 A.D. - a great fortress of stone which has known the Normans and the English…

***

We entered its Royal Chapel, where, thanks to a charming warden, we climbed the "broken spiral stairway" (built totally without supports) and entered the Royal Box in the gallery above. Seated in the royal throne chairs, we listened with delight to a wonderful Irish storyteller and his wonderful Irish tales…

Of the chapel around the gallery of which in 1921 there was "no room for the coat-of-arms of one English ruler." "We'd have made room for more," said the English, "But we said 'thank you, no' and took our country back…"

And of one Michael Collins, an Irish rebel who, "during the trouble," with a price of 2,000 pounds on his head, bribed the "coal man" to carry him, his face smeared with the black stuff, into Dublin Castle itself, where he seated himself in the chair of the Chief Secretary, and with the reward poster clearly visible behind his head, had the "coal man" snap his picture, the which appeared, "big as life" in the local papers...

And the story of the ancient wood carver who gained immortality by placing his own little face in the carving about the window frame...

And of Jonathon Swift, whose likeness, "if you please" may be found above the head of St. Peter with the keys, at the entrance of the chapel...

And of the mischievous Irish sculptor who placed the one angel without wings directly over the name "Cromwell" in the records of English rulers...

Shure and 'begorrah we've scarcely scratched the surface of this wonderful Irish city, and we're head over heels in love with it already!

9-3-67 EMERALD ISLE

Ask any Irishman and he'll tell you that his is the most beautiful country in the world; and, if we hadn't the memory of our own lovely New England fresh in our hearts, we might be inclined to agree with him.

For Ireland, we have decided, is a lot like New England, a great deal like Hawaii -- of all places --and a land of utter scenic enchantment.

It lies-this beautiful Emerald Isle - on the bosom of the Atlantic, like a great shining saucer with a fluted edge - the fluting being, of course, the soft rolling mountains that ring it.

Journey anywhere, and the landscape will stretch ever and always for miles before one, like a giant patchwork quilt, the bits and pieces of irregular sizes and shapes, fastened together with hedgerows and stands of trees and shrubs.

The fields carry a hundred different exquisite shades of green, one upon the other, with their encasing foliage dark and beautiful beside them.

Bales of hay lie like golden nuggets on the bronzing stubble; here and there one sees a patch of brown or copper earth, symmetrical and lovely; the olive green of a rich turf bog and the black of piled turf beside it...

Mountains lie in groups against the skyline, their heads crowned with the Irish mist…a cloak of green draped gracefully over their gray rock shoulders…

Above all, ever and always, there's the sky, immense and awe-inspiring, with great sweeps of clouds-wide mushroom clouds of gray and mauve and slate and white, swollen with the waters of the Atlantic, and ever ready to weep their tears on Ireland…

Streamers of sun descending radiantly to turn ponds to silver and mountain tops to gold…here a turquoise banner, soft and sweet; there a swathe of shining cobalt blue…a sky unparalleled in beauty!

Roads, threaded like ribbon through the green of fields…and ruins of great stone castles gray against the blue…sheep and cattle on the hillsides; sheepdogs herding…

***

What shall we say about this lovely land? Shall we write of Southern Ireland - of Glengariffe, ablaze with tropical plants and flowers and the breezes warm from the sea?

Or Killarney, with its lakes flowing one upon another to the sea amid a vegetation totally unparalleled - a thousand house-high rhododendrons, all in bloom, setting the lovely scene…Killarney, home of the Irish jaunting car, in which, we might add, we rode happily about the lakes - our very first experience behind a horse…

Shall we follow the River Shannon to its lakes - Lough Allen and Lough Arrow and the rest, with the small, sweet islands lying like water lilies on their silver surface?

Shall we head west to Galway Bay? Stone walls have replaced the hedgerows now as we cross the emerald heart of central Ireland. The farmers are cutting turf as we pass by.

They labor in the rich black bogs, and lay the "bricks" of peat in waist-high stacks for drying in the summer sun. The smoke from winter-warm turf fires will perfume Erin's air, the country folk all say…

***

Shall we not write of Galway Bay, with the limestone hills of County Clare serene beyond it? It lies at the rim of the sea, with the rich dark blue of the sky above reflected in its heart…

Islands like emeralds, shining softly on its surface; trees on its shores gnarled by the sweeping winds, each one facing out to sea…

"A hundred thousand welcomes" is traditional for Galway. Galway City, once a great walled place that housed the fourteen Anglo-Saxon tribes. Only the Spanish Arch remains of the long ago. Galway, with the Connemara Mountains all around -- black faced, black footed mountain sheep clinging to their crags; soft white "bog cotton" blowing…

What shall I write of Ireland? Shall my "Cabbage" treat of her castles, grey and grim? The ruins of her abbeys, hard against the sky, the laughter of her people, and the soft sweet voices of them, and the wit that is their own?

The little people one fancies one can see racing with the small slim colt, the gentle calf, about the velvet fields?

Shall I write of the journey north of Belfast, with the Irish Sea at our elbow, sweeping free? Now and then a village marks its shores; mostly however, it rolls upon the silver sand, untouched by any century it has known in perfect pristine beauty…

Shall I write of the curragh, the Irish Derby which, for a day, shakes Dublin to its core? Or shall my "Cabbage" deal with Irishmen of note - "Shay" O'Hanlon, for example -- fourth time winner of the International seven-day bicycle race about the Emerald Isle…

Sure and my difficulty is - I could write a Cabbage a day! Especially in Ireland…

9-10-67   HOOT MON!

Swinging kilts and swirling bagpipes; snow upon the mountain and mist upon the moor; we're in Scotland!

What to write home of this lovely land of "Brigadoon" -- of "heather on the hill"…

We could produce a full blown "Cabbage" on the Trossachs alone -- that beautiful Scottish sweep of mountains, lochs and glens - the setting for Sir Walter Scott's immortal "Lady of the Lake!" We sailed in the handsome steamer, S.S. Sir Walter Scott, about Loch Katrine, the loveliest of all the Trossach lochs! Ah, yes indeed - The Trossachs, with its heather a royal purple mantle about the shoulders of the monarch- mountains that embrace it; an ermine collar of snow caressing their firm dark throats; swirling mists forming the lofty silver crowns they ALWAYS wear, our courier said…Rosy foxglove tossing its jesters bright-belled caps at them… rhododendrons blooming in a blazing-bold attempt to seek their favor…

We might easily produce a sprout or two on Stirling Castle, that sweeping stone retreat of Mary, Queen of Scots, with the two ancient cannons before it trained, even to this day, upon the home of poor, ill-fated Darnley, Mary's spouse…

Mary, who was crowned Queen of all Scotland, so we've learned, at the age of but nine months…We could write of Robert the Bruce, and the Battle of Bannockburn in 1314 -- Robert, who whilst in hiding from the British, lodged himself within a cove so the story goes and watched a spider spin his web against apparently insuperable odds; the which encouraged Robert, King -- defeated many times in battle -- to make one more sustained attempt at victory and so to WIN!

We could write of Ayr and the Burns country, with the tiny white thatched cottage in which Burns, the poet, was born…of Brig-O-Doon, an arched stone bridge across the River Doon, with its "Banks and Braes," (Tam-O-Shanter raced across the "Brig" to escape the witches…) And we could quote from Burns' letter of his friend, Alexander Cunningham, writer, of Edinburgh, the original of which we found in the Burns museum.

"Q. What is Politics? A. Politics is a science wherewith, by means of nefarious conniving and hypocritical pretense, we govern civic politics for the emolument of ourselves and our adherents."…OUCH…?

We could write of the bleak and desolate moors, with their mists by day, and the dark night fog that waits to claim them…with the heather that alone bedecks their barrenness. "Heathcliffe," we found ourselves crying silently, "Heathcliffe…" as we gazed upon their desolation. We could write of the beautiful Firth (Estuary) of Clyde, and of the Scottish seaside towns that line its banks; of Dunoon, and of nearby Holy Loch, where we found our own American Submarine Depot, with its great gray supply ship, and huge dry dock, and the blessed Stars and Stripes sublimely flying over all - a wondrous, welcome sight to two expatriates!

We could write of palm trees and pampas grasses and roses red as fire and large as dinner-plates about the sunny seaside rim of Rothesay and of Wemyss Bay; of sail boats in the wind, and wild, dark mountains on the shores beyond; and of those handsome river steamers on which we sailed the Clyde…and of the Hilly Brae above the lovely Scottish town of Largs, with all the sweeping silver of the Firth spread out below…

We could write of the lovely Loch Lomond, which defies description; the blue of lazy loch mirroring the blue of summer sky amid the scowls of menacing mountains…

***

And we could well devote a "Cabbage" fair to Edinburgh, "Athens of the North," with the stony fortress castle rising menacingly above it; and the "Royal Mile" -- long centuries ago, the heart of Edinburgh -- racing before it to Holyrood, the present royal residence. Holyrood Palace with the ruins of the ancient abbey of Holyrood stark and silent there beside it…We might speak indeed of the majesty of Scotland's War Memorial - a massive bronze casket similar in size and form to the ancient Ark of the Covenant containing the names of Scotland's World War I heroes and resting within the castle upon the highest rocky peak in lofty Edinburgh.

We might speak of the great carved statue of Michael, patron saint of warriors, which rests high above the hallowed place - an immense achievement carved from a great OAK tree…We MUST speak of bagpipes by the seaside and of tartan kilts within the glens. And of the somber Scottish mists. Beautiful, beautiful Scotland.

9-17-67   "SCANDANAVIA"

Not for nothing are the colors blue and gold traditionally those of Scandanavia. Her seas move alternately from cobalt to slate, we found, and everything about her is golden- from the soft tow-heads and fresh tanned faces of her people to the muted sun-silver gilt that splashes her ancient yellow buildings and paves her streets with gold.

Scandanavia wears a scrubbed clean look. We were aware of it almost from the moment we crossed the border into Denmark. Well ordered farmlands stretched on either side. There was nothing haphazard about the farm buildings that served them. They were architecturally aligned. Modern farm machinery lay close by and electricity flowed from pole to farmhouse on all sides. The occasional thatched roof dwellings were trim and neat. Chaste white daisies had replaced the poppies and the effect was right.

Copenhagen was, we found, an elegant city, reminding us considerably of Boston. We delighted in the Barometer Girls whose function it is to foretell the weather from atop the tallest building in the square one slim young thing beside her bicycle; the other toting an umbrella.

We were amused equally by scores of "hippies" about Town Hall -- youths whose long blonde locks looked absurdly like sister Susie's "fall' - and by the grande dames who delicately puffed on slim havanas as they pranced about they City Hall Square.

We played Cupid, Ted and I, to a charming young man from Bierut, Lebanon, and his lady love - a precious young teacher from New Mexico. Don had been educated in the American Institute, and is currently studying at the American University. He insisted upon introducing Kathy to his "American Friends" (We shared hotel acquaintance).

Norway was enchanting. Its fjords and its mountains and glaciers crowned with snow; the wonderful Viking ship Osebert, more than 1000 years old. Queen Aase, grandmother of King Harold the Fair-Haired was buried on this emmense "Skibet.'

It was buried in the ground, according to ancient custom, in the year 960 and covered with a special clay to preserve it. The remains of the ancient queen were no more. Her household effects, and elaborately carved sleds were intact.

What fun to see the raft Kon Tiki after having enjoyed the bestseller so enormously! And to read from the original log the details of its fabulous journey from Peru to Polynesia! And to settle ourselves into a 'hospits' at the top of an Oslo mountain with Dennis, a thoroughly charming young American from Chicago (apparently lonely for his parents, for he adopted Ted and me) and a group of his young friends-for what turned out to be the most delightful three days on record. - from Sioux City, Iowa and Yonkers, New York, from Pasedena Calif., and Casper, Wyoming -- from Europe, we found out upon our return to the Continent, is literally overrun by young Americans.

everywhere, in fact, but Boston, Mass.

We've yet to meet our first young Bostonian. "Ingang" and "Outgang" read the busses of Amsterdam, where we first noted the invasion, and "gang" indeed it was!

We just naturally annexed them-in parks and in palaces, in museums and in city halls – wherever our budget lent itself to a guidebook and theirs did not.

"Would you mind if we tagged along' they would ask (or words to that effect). We were delighted to have them do just that; and to chat with them occasionally afterwards over a cup of coffee or a glass of coke. They live, we learned, primarily in youth hotels which are provided for students by European governments for a minimal amount.

Two dollars per day, we were told, is sufficient to provide food and lodging for a student traveling abroad. They bemoaned our government's failure to provide such opportunities for travel in our own wonderful country and promised a move in that direction inspired by the International Student Union- and so on.

Sweden was an adventure! We visited the Wasavaret, a museum housing an ancient Swedish warship, the Wasa, which was sunk in 1628 on her maiden voyage in Stockholm Harbor.

Three centuries passed before one Anders Franzen of Stockholm, an archaeologist, learning that the low salt content of the harbor would not permit the existence of destructive sea worms, opined that the ship would be intact at the bottom of the sea. Crisscrossing the area in a motor launch over a period of several summers, sending down lines to dredge up objects from the deep, he came upon a small plug of ancient wood which led to the discovery and subsequent raising of the Wasa, a veritable treasure trove and the largest waterlogged object in history under preservation.

The Wasa would crumble if permitted to dry out, and so in its specially constructed museum, the humidity is kept at 95 per cent. Jets of water stream intermittently upon her, filling the museum with a vapor-like fog which is eerie and exciting.

On an island park called Skansen, also in a typical Lapp Station Camp, similar to those in use by the Lapps who range with their reindeer herds across the Laplands of Sweden and Norway, I visited with a charming Lapp girl whose English was flawless, and whose beauty was arresting. Had my picture taken with her also!

YES - Scandinavia was delightful. And now we're off for what could truly be the most exciting trip of all- to Berlin!

We shall travel via Hanover, Germany, from which capital of the State of Lower Saxony, we can board a plane for West Berlin. The words of President Kennedy ring within my ears as I contemplate viewing the infamous Berlin Wall. Ich bin ein Berliner.'

What an adventure this European Holiday has become!

9-24-67 "GERMANY"

Germany's Hanover is a handsome city. Its shiny newness delights the eye. Immense stone structures - architectural dreams come true, obviously -- stand in trim geometric patterns against the sky.

Super-highways and fly-overs (overpasses) tie everything nicely together. It wasn't, however, until we took a city tour - a tour that led us to Town Hall and a series of "models" of Hanover- past, present and to come -- that we understood the newness of it all.

For Hanover, like Coventry, was a casualty of World War II, with 100 per cent of all buildings in the inner town, and 65 per cent of all buildings in the town and its suburbs destroyed -- the other side of the hideous coin!

It had seemed strange arriving in a country with which, within our not too distant memory, we had been at war. I noted a group of German sailors in the railway station, and an involuntary shudder passed through me.

Visions of late late movies and prowling U-boats crossed my mind, and I remembered Ted, in uniform, on my dresser at home.

The German flag flying above Army Headquarters all but stopped my heartbeat...I had viewed with curiosity the Customs Inspector who had asked to see my passport on the train. An S.S. man, I had wondered???

Now here I was, face to face in a Town Hall foyer with the model of an almost totally bombed city, naked in its destruction. Our guide had reverted to German, and so I was unable to understand his comments about it.

It was easy, however, to read in the faces of his audience (we were the sole Americans) the horror of the devastation he was discussing. I looked at their haunted eyes, and then at the shattered buildings, and my woman's heart translated the whole into human misery and death.

Have they learned, I wondered sadly, and then a feeling of remorse swept me, for it is not "they" who must learn - not the people who pay the price of war...Who, then???

****

Rolf Straten, our guide, was a charming German gentleman. A member of the city's Administrative staff, concerned with the building program, we visited with him at the conclusion of the tour, and found ourselves driving with him in his car to view the Marktkerchel.

"There's something there," he told us, "which I particularly wish you to see." It was the great bronze door - a gift to the bombed cathedral from the artisans of Hanover; and it depicted in a series of sculptures the consequences of following the Nazi philosophy -- the murder and the violence in the name of the State; bombing and burning; the death of children and the disruption of family life; the rape of German women.

It portrayed the rebuilding of the land, the farmer ploughing; the church, its functions restored; the family, reunited.

Do not let, however - the sculptures warn the German people - prosperity bring excesses; and do not forget the "late returning soldiers," those battered and beaten men whom the Russians failed to release for as long as ten years after the war...An incredible masterpiece, this great bronze door. Our new friend drove us to view the ruin of the great church of St. Aegidien, a ruin which will be permitted to stand forever un-restored as a mute reminder of war....

Have the Germans learned, we wondered again, as we rode with our host to view the incredibly beautiful pre-fabricated suburb of Auf der Horst, and heard him say jokingly as he pointed with pride to the renaissance about us, "There is a saying in Germany - the Allies won the war, but the Germans won the peace!" Does anyone ever learn?????

We had come to Hanover with the avowed intention of boarding a plane and heading for West Berlin. We had learned, however, from our new-found German friend of the ramifications of the partitioning of Germany; of the deep and dire meaning of the double line of chain-link and barbed wire fencing, stretching from the Baltic to Czechoslovakia, which serves as the border between the Deutsche Demokratische Republic and the German Federal Republic.

We had been told of the monument in Lietzensee Park, Berlin - dedicated to "Liberty, Justice and Peace," with the flame which "shall never be extinguished until Germany is again united..."

***

"Ted," I said, "would you be willing to take a train across East Germany to Berlin? I want to see the barbed wire border -- to see East Germany, not just fly over it..."

Lucky me! Tomorrow is my birthday and Ted never has refused me anything on my birthday.

We leave this morning for Berlin by train...

10-1-67   "BERLIN"

It was a lovely morning as the Berlin train moved slowly out of the Hannover Railway Station, Ted and I were seated in a second-class compartment with a steely-eyed young man and two very elderly ladies.

We had attempted to secure first-class reservations and had been told they were unavailable. We might take our chances on finding a seat, etc., etc. We purchased first-class tickets and headed for the second-class section with the intention of seeking a seat elsewhere after the train left the station. We were to be strangely successful, finding the entire first-class section occupied by but one other couple!

Oh, well…At this point, however, the elderly lady on our left was bidding a tearful goodbye to a daughter and a grandson on the platform below. Her hands clasped theirs through the open window until the movement of the train separated them. She seated herself quietly, then gave us a tearful smile. "Do you speak German?" she asked. We replied that we were Americans and could not speak her language. "Do you go to Berlin?" she asked. "Yes," I said. "West Berlin, and you?"

The little lady sighed. "East Berlin," she said. "I too," said our other female companion. "The Soviet Zone," she added.

"Oh," I said, and there was a world of sympathy in my voice. The ladies responded with knowing eyes. "Yes," they said. "Oh!" The steely-eyed youth missed none of it. He looked pointedly from one to another of us. Ted pressed my arm in warning. The journey across East Germany was beginning…

***

We might purchase a ticket at Helmstedt, we had been told - where the East German authorities assumed control of the train -- for the journey from this last West German town to Berlin. Visas could be secured at this point also and we were warned to purchase two-way visas from the train conductor.

East German customs officials arrived immediately. Passports were checked and a statement of all currency of any kind in our possession demanded. We were on our way across the eastern half of divided Germany.

The chain-link barbed wire fence came into view as we crossed the border. Miles of forest lay on either side of the rails. We glimpsed Russian soldiers in the villages through which we sped, and here and there uniformed members of the East German Volks-Polizei.

On the whole, however, there was little to suggest the tyranny about which we'd heard so very much in Hannover. East Germany appeared old and shabby, we decided -- not charming old, but tired old.

Goldenrod in bloom was giving it a dose of hay fever, but above the sky was a fleece-flecked blue and church spires lay against a quiet horizon…

Pottsdam- and the picture began to change. High chain-like barbed wire fence encompassed the railway area, and armed Russian soldiers were very much in evidence.

Griebnitzsee - we were coming closer to Berlin…Great wire mesh barriers now lay across the banks, floodlights in readiness; the Russian guards had taken up positions at vantage points along the platforms -- their rifles ready. Vopos were in evidence on all sides. The delays at the railway station were interminable. I stared through the window at the steely faces of the guards, the heavy guns.

Why could I not have been satisfied with a nice safe plane trip, I wondered miserably. I sent Ted a sickly smile; he patted my hand.

The train moved finally to speed through Berlin, Gruenwald and Berlin Charlottenburg and Savigny Place nonstop…Then, at last -- Berlin!

Checkpoint Charlie - and a tour into the Eastern Zone of Berlin! Our passports and financial statements have been duly checked and recorded. East German marks may not be brought into Berlin at all, we learned.

We had attempted to secure them at the Hannover Bank for use in purchasing our railway tickets and had been told that although the actual value of the West German mark is three times greater than the East German mark, the East Germans demand one for one, which fact undoubtedly explains their preoccupation with our currency.

We enter the first of about ten barriers, and the Berlin Wall is before us.

Its double walls of concrete are topped by thousands of yards of rolled barbed wire, which stretches as far as the eye can see. My heart pounds and I fancy I can hear it in the pregnant silence that has suddenly gripped the occupants of the bus.

We proceed from barrier to barrier. They lie across the street, these immense walls of concrete with barely enough room for a car to pass through on one side. The openings alternate - on the right side of barrier one; the left side of barrier two, etc., etc. The bus lumbers through, making the turns in several stages, and is diverted into a side inspection area. The grey-uniformed vopos stand in readiness.

We are ordered out of the bus and the bus is searched. Mirrors on wheels are passed under the vehicle. (We note that in a bus nearby U.S. Military personnel remain seated). We are checked against our passports and currency declarations and returned, one by one, to the bus.

Our charming little West German guide has been detained on the American side, to be replaced by a grim-faced Communist lady -- by the name of Mrs. Schmidt. We are taken on a tour of a dreary, battle-scarred region of despair.

Scarcely a car on the lonely streets (one taxi in two hours); scarcely a smile on the sullen faces…We are shown the bunker "in which Hitler committed suicide;" the ruins of building after building "which we plan to restore soon;" the facade on Unter den Linden; Frankfurter Allee, the first "Socialist Street," with its state-owned apartments, shops and restaurants…(It is lovely!).

We are shown the magnificent Russian War Memorial with its ancient Russian burial mound and the monument to the six Russian Order of Victory recipients.

The fact that Eisenhower and Bradley are among the six interests us. We are handed the party line…And we are returned to Checkpoint Charlie for more passport checking; more searching the bus; more mirrors and more red tape…

***

Finally we are turned to bright, beautiful ultra-modern West Berlin.

We have not been permitted to photograph the wall, or the guards. We have, however, photographed the agonizing people who stand behind the barrier on the Eastern side and watch from the corners of the streets that intersect there, and from the doorways and vantage points that line the way, the blessed, fortunate people - ourselves included - who ride across to freedom…

10-8-67 "BAVARIA"

Our return across East Germany from Berlin was - we are happy to relate -- without incident. The Russian soldiers, having added police dogs to their machine guns, guarded the East German border town of Marienborn even more fiercely; the Red flag with the star above it was perceived at several small villages; there were two breaks in the barbed wire fence - one was being guarded and one was not; and a rifle-toting female guarded a female work detail...

We were on the apprehensive side, for we had visited the Schoeneberg town hall, scene of the famous John F. Kennedy "Ich Bin ein Berliner" speech the previous afternoon.

We had been taken on a grand tour of this handsome building, located now in "John F. Kennedy Platz;" and had climbed the 128 steps to view the "Freedom Bell," purchased with the contributions of 17 million "Crusade for Freedom" Americans.

Incidentally, this immense bronze bell, which is rung daily at noon, can be heard by the East Germans, we were told, as far as the Brandenberg Gate. We had had our picture snapped occupying the President's seat in Parliament, no less -- and had been given colorful mementos of the JFK visit, and a map of the city outlining the indescribably tragic "wall".

We had been advised to mail our treasures home, for if we were searched by the East Germans they would be confiscated. Instead, however, of dashing to the nearest post office we rode off with Hermine Sommerer to the Templehow Acrodrome with its monument to the brave American flyers who lost their lives in the Berlin Airlift!

The East German officials were not friendly. However, they left our "loot" quite undisturbed, thank heaven!

***

West Germany again, and the old Scandinavian order returned - trim villages, red-roofed, nestling against the Harz and other mountains; fertile fields; crops ready for harvesting; tractors and baling apparatus and a Volkswagen in every farmer's "castle," instead of the lone East

German horse; and townspeople waving at, not woefully watching, passing trains…

Munich, where promptly at eleven a.m. the Clockenspiel sent its carillon over the Marienplatz and set its charming figures to dancing-soldiers marching, banners erect; knights tilting; Bavarian peasants performing…our cameras clicked away! A perfectly beautiful city -- Munich! Dachau, and a visit to the indescribably horror of the almost untouched concentration camp. A museum now occupies the site of the former "kitchen, laundry, storage rooms for prisoners' clothing and personal belongings, and the notorious shower baths where the SS would torture prisoners (forminor infractions) by flogging and hanging them at the stake."

The museum documents the development of the Nazi "reign of terror." We viewed with horror heartbreaking photographs of small children on their way to the gas chambers; of medical experiments and their results; and of the stacked bodies of the starved dead that greeted our American soldiers upon their arrival at Dachau; the electrified barbed wire fence and barricade; the water-filled ditch and the electrically charged barbed wire and concrete wall that prevented escape of the unfortunate prisoners; the daisy-strewn grass plots before the wire - an area forbidden to the prisoners under threat of immediate death. Did the daisies grow there then and butterflies abound we wondered…

***

Frau Meier, a Munich friend who has reason to remember the Hitler era, resided with her Jewish grandfather in a small Bavarian village. She was an art teacher in the local school and her grandfather a dearly loved doctor. And then Hitler came to power!

Frau Meier, one quarter Jewish, could not be allowed to teach the German children. There was no food or tobacco for the aging doctor, who for years was a virtual prisoner in his home.

The villagers, however, who remembered his years of service to them, fed and protected him. Somehow he and she survived.

She told us her story sadly…

A more cheerful note - directly behind the Dachau Museum is a building currently occupied by the U.S. Army. Just because we view with delight everything American over here, Ted and I peered through a barbed wire fence (not electrified) at the back of the long low structure.

"Hi," said a masculine voice, and a long bare arm waved in our direction through a small barred window! Another waving arm joined it.

"Are you Americans?" I called. "Yep," said a cheerful voice.

"That we are! Are you in prison?" I asked, aghast.

"No, ma-am," said the voice. "Just in jail!" (There is, apparently, a difference…)

"Oh, I said lamely. "Well, I hope you get out soon…"

"Oh, we will," said the voice. The arms waved a cheery goodbye (We snapped a picture of that scene also.)

***

Berchtesgarden next, and a visit to Obersalzburg, 1800 feet above the village, and once the residence of Hitler and Goering and the 200 SS men who guarded them; and a climbto the "Nid D'Aigle," (Eagle's nest), the former hitler hideaway now Kehlstein Haus, an inn run by the German Alpine Club.

How to describe the frightening ride over the famous Hochalpenstrasse, up the more than a mile high mountain peak - the gorges falling into nothingness behind us - the hairpin turns and the steep rock faces sending our hearts hammering.

The terminus finally, and then a walk through a 395-foot tunnel to the electric "lift" for an additional 400 feet ascent through the heart of the mountain to the Eagle's Nest!

Oh, the breathtaking beauty of the scene from the tip, with the alps rising on all sides, and the Koenigssee, a soft lump of silver in the misty distance!

We had dinner, Ted and I, before the huge Italian marble fireplace in what once used to be the Hitler grande salon and is now a handsome dining room. hitler and Eva Braun, the actress, frequently dined in that precise place, our waitress told us. (It did not spoil our appetites!)

***

Oberammergau next, and a visit to the Passionsspielhaus, where once in each decade the Passion play is presented. It originated, we learned, during the 30 Years War.

The Black Plague had descended upon the little village, and many had died. The villagers of Oberammergau vowed to perform the Passion play every ten years if the plague were lifted. There were no more deaths, and so the first performance was given in the parish churchyard in 1634. It has been presented every ten years since that date. The play lasts seven and a half hours and its actors must have been born in Oberammergau. No makeup or artificial lighting is used for the daytime performance on the mammoth outdoor stage which is 28 meters deep and has the majestic Alps for a background.

Have we said that Bavaria is beautiful??? It is!

"PEOPLE ARE WONDERFUL"

We met them in Berlin - Friedrich and Hermine Sommerer of Munich, and their 12-year-old son, Peter.

They were delighted to learn that we came from President Kennedy's home state and acting as interpreters (Friedrich spoke English beautifully) they accompanied us on what turned out to be a royal tour of Schoeneberg Town Hall, the scene of JFK's memorable "Ich Bin Ein Berliner" speech. We spent the evening together and parted regretfully. We were to return to West Berlin the following morning, while their Berlin vacation was not to end for several days.

"You must visit us in Munich," they said. "Come for the Octobrefest and we'll spend the day together." Munich's Octobrefest is famous throughout Europe. Munich beer flows; Bavarian music and revelry abounds; good food; good fellowship; good fun… "Call us the minute you reach Munich," they said.

We did not do so. However, fate was not to allow our newfound friendship with the Sommerers to die!

We were walking, Ted and I, guide book in hand, toward the Theatiner Church in this enchanting city, Munich. Someone clutched my arm.

"Mrs. Metayer," said a delighted voice. It was Friedrich. "Why didn't you call us?" he demanded and promptly made plans for us to spend the next day together.

Friedrich arrived at our hotel at nine the following morning. (Friedrich is a salesman and had simply taken the day off!) A wonderful whirl about town in his little "Volks," with a visit to the bustling scene of the Octobrefest - immense prefabricated buildings capable of holding 5,000 being assembled on all sides, many with the inevitable fir tree tucked snugly on top, the significance of which our host gaily explained.

In Bavaria, he said, when the roof "goes on" a new building, the workers are given a holiday feast, and red and white ribbons are hung from the little tree. Woe betide the skinflint, however, who fails to provide such a reward, for a long-handle broom is hung instead, from the sad little evergreen, for all of Bavaria to see!

Octobrefest, we were told, had its beginning with the marriage of the son of a Bavarian king, long centuries ago. The townspeople were invited to the wedding, and a horse race was provided for their entertainment. Octobrefest has come a long way since then!

Luncheon next at Friedrich's veritable showplace of a little home. And what a luncheon it was! Soup made with cream and beaten egg, Bavarian style; pork with knodels (mashed potato mixed with meat, stuffed with seasoned toast bits and boiled - delicious!); a beverage that was half lemonade and half Munich beer…

Off then to the estate of Friedrich's mother (his father had been Munich's postmaster) for coffee and whipped cream cakes and cognac with that thoroughly charming woman, whose home was on the outskirts of the city.

Bordering it was the Nymphenburg Palace. Friedrich had played in its magnificent park a and so a tour of this wonderful castle was included in the afternoon's itinerary, as well as a visit to the grave of his father.

"He's not very far away," Friedrich's mother had said. "Just over there," she had added, pointing in the direction of the ancient cemetery which also adjoined her grounds.

Strangely enough, this house into which we Americans were received with such warmth was taken over for a time after World War II by our American Armed Forces. We learned an injured Army captain and his secretary were installed there, forcing the Sommerer Family to vacate – Mrs Sommerer to the home of a neighbor, and Friedrich and his father to the cemetery chapel...

***

Dinner time, and we were off to the famous Hofbrau Haus, in the second-floor restaurant of which we dined wonderfully. A concert of Bavarian music in the concert hall upstairs rounded out the evening beautifully. Friedrich's fine baritone and Hermine's contralto handled the German handsomely; Ted and I, surprised at how many of the tunes we knew, added gaily to the general din of happy Bavaria at its merry making.

"Good friends, you simply must return to Munich for the Octobrefest," Friedrich and Hermine urged. "You will be our guests. No hotel room! Come right to our home for the whole two weeks..."

Now why, really, is this such an unusual story as to warrant our sending it back to Braintree for publication in our favorite newspaper?

Apart from the fact that our four people of differing age groups and of differing nationalities, having come to maturity half a world apart, could find such pleasure in each other's company-there is another facet to the story, for Friedrich Sommerer, aged 37, was a Hitler Youth.

And we could picture this tall, incredibly handsome young man in his boyhood years...a typical example of the so-called "Master Race"...

"It was wonderful," he said. "We learned to sail and to fly a plane and to ride a motorbike. We were too young, of course, to realize that we were being groomed for war."

Friedrich was just 15 when in the last terrible months of the war he found himself, along with other young boys and very old men, manning anti-aircraft batteries around Munich. "We were scared to death," he confided. "We were only boys," Friedrich was one of the casualties of a bomb that fell on East Munich. A Jagged Scar marks his right eyebrow, and Friedrich wears a glass eye to replace the one he lost on that terrifying night.

"Your poor mother," I said involuntarily when he told us the tale. "Yes," he said. "You say "This is my son' and the German mother says, 'This is my son' and why in the name of God do nation's war?"

***

Friedrich's son, Peter, is currently studying English and in the course of conversation we discussed the use of "proud and proudly." "I can't seem to see the difference," said Peter. "Well now let me see," I said.

"You salute your flag proudly."

"Yes," added Ted, "because you are proud to be a German." Friedrich looked at us almost pleadingly. "Can we be proud to be German?" he asked. "The German people haven't lost the war," he said at another point. "We have our homes and our cars and our freedom. It is the East Germans. They have nothing. They have lost the war." We would love to have time to return to Munich and we pray that someday, somehow our path will cross the Sommerers' again.

Meanwhile- does it sound ridiculous to say that Ted and I felt as utterly at home with these two delightful young Germans as though they had been our own?

If only the "just plain people" of all nations could get to know one another, there'd never be a war, I warrant. For we've decided, looking back over the folks we've met in all the countries we have visited to date - people everywhere really are rather wonderful!" "Up with people!"

"WE'VE SEEN THE ALPS!"

From the lusty music of Bavaria to the slender elegance of Strauss… from Munich to Vienna and the incredible grandeur of the Hofburg complex that once housed the seat of the Holy Roman Empire…

What fun to roam the castle wherein Marie Antoinette dwelt as a little girl; to relive the glories of the age of Maria Theresa and the rest. Mozart himself played the piano at the age of six in the gold and white drawing room of the Schoenbrunn Palace. "When I grow up," he told Marie Antoinette as a teen-ager, "I am going to marry you!"

The Spanish Riding School, another Hofburg legacy, and the incredible performance of the magnificent horses which are born black, but turn to dappled grey as young stallions, and white when full-grown. The stars of the show -- a group of handsome animals -- not only dance on their hind legs, but leap from them into the air like frisky dogs.

No opera - disappointingly - for the Metayers…The Vienna City Opera Company opened its season in Montreal at Expo '67 and not in Vienna; the ballet "Swan Lake," scheduled in its place, a sell-out, thanks to the ever-present doctors' convention. A wonderful tour of the Opera House, nonetheless, with a trip backstage!

The stage, incidentally, is 150 feet long, 90 feet wide and 90 feet high, and is actually composed of three stages and a revolving one.

From a visit to the stage setting of Swan Lake, we wandered back to the Prima Donna's dressing room -- a simple affair in white, rose and green-

How we would have reveled in any one of the three magnificent new Promenades, the walls of one of which are lined with immense tapestries, their motifs from Mozart's works- the Magic Flute, etc. These represent for 20 women five years of needlework, we learned; the cost 1 million Austrian shillings.

What a magnificent building - this opera house is! We drooled over the wide white marble staircase with its moss green carpeting; the sheer magic of the seven Grecian marble statues of the arts above the balustrades; the immense fireplace in the foyer, and the utterly at-home busts of Mozart and Beethoven and Strauss and the rest - all of whose spirits walk by day and sing by night in the soft sweet silence of Vienna…

***

A Journey by train through just about every Austrian Alp that rears even an infant head! Alas we were so occupied in oh-ing and ah-ing and photographing the scenery that we failed utterly to note the diversion of our section to another line.

What a shock to learn that our "Innsbruck" express was about to saunter merrily about the Alpine villages, picking up University students here and depositing them there, for an additional seven hour journey that was to end in Innsbruck in the wee small hours of a morning which housed the first real rainstorm (this was a cloudburst) the Metayers have encountered since May 1. Oh well, we've seen the Alps!

Innsbruck and the golden dome of Maximilian I with its 3400 gold plated titles. It was created in 1500, we learned, as a royal box for the entertainments which were presented in the little square below -- a Gothic bay-window kind of appendage on a handsome and ancient building. Oh those Hapsburgs! Their imperial palaces dot Innsbruck as well as Vienna!

To Zurich next via a five hour train journey which lasted about five minutes, thanks to the Harrisons, a charming English couple with whom we shared a compartment. He is an architect who has visited Boston and knows it well, and she is a jewel.

We are invited to call them upon our return to London and to come "for a meal" in the "rather wonderful old Victorian house" they "picked up and had remodeled in Wimbledon, London." They will "show us the Wimbledon Courts (tennis) and some things in the vicinity of London which we, perhaps, missed.

***

How do we find these wonderful Europeans, we asked ourselves, Ted and I as we were discussing The Harrisons.

First off, where???? Well in trains and hotels; in restaurants and museums and palaces – anywhere at all, where a smile manages to break through a language barrier quite as though it never existed - and frequently, in this age of multilingual individuals, it doesn't exist anyhow.

It hasn't taken us very long to conclude that people everywhere have several things in common, incidentally.

They laugh and they cry; their eyes are "the windows of their souls" and their children are beautiful! Furthermore they are as interested in knowing Americans as we are in meeting Europeans!

***

Zurich, where we are within touring distance of Lucerne and so we found ourselves on a three hour sail about the lake which is as beautiful as we were led to believe with the Alps sloping right to the water's edge and the snow-caps shining beyond them in the sun.

And a trip to Interlaken, named by the ancient Romans for it lies between the Turquoise waters of Lake Brienz and the slate grey of Lake Thune Glacial waters, we learned, flowing from the Alps above, are responsible for the variation in the color of the sister lakes.

Glacier water, incidentally, is not at all transparent. The Swiss say it must run over seven rocks before it runs clear. Sailing over Lake Thune, we concluded that the water had done just that, for we could watch the fish darting about in its dark slate depths.

The Alps, snow-clad, add a note of gorgeous grandeur to all of tiny Interlaken.

The Jungfrau is a short two hours away; we are, however, persuaded not to take a cable car to the top of this nearly three mile high mountain marvel. Only the strongest hearts can take the altitude, etc. etc. We weep…

***

And so we pass from Switzerland across a picture postcard land, and we return to Italy. and where in Italy? Venice to be precise -- and where in this wonderful world of ours is there a more delightful city to explore???

The Grand Canal, the "most beautiful street in the world," with its ancient Venetian palazzos standing as silent symbol of the genius of the 13th, 14th and 15th centuries and onward.

St. Mark's Square, with the immense basilica which is the heart of this ancient place that has known all the history of Venice from its beginning.

St. Mark's, with its 14th century mosaics, within and without, shining golden in the sun, and its astonishing and enchanting fusion of oriental, Gothic, Moresque and Renaissance elements of architecture - its towers and turrets, its niches and statuary…And in its splendid baptistery, a block of granite brought from Tiro in 1126 from which Christ is supposed to have spoken to the multitudes!

"WE'RE HOMESICK!"

With what reluctance we shall leave sunny Italy! From Brindisi, the coastal town from which the Crusaders left for the Holy Land (we saw the Tancredit Fountain where they watered their horses sailing away) we traveled across the country to Naples - a colorful journey! Farmland plastered to the steep mountainsides…strings of scarlet peppers and pearly white onions festooning the ancient farmhouses…lumbering white oxen in pairs, attached to primitive plows…

Napoli finally and a visit to the Palazzo del Corallo, where we learned how cameos are made. Only Sardonic or Cornelian shells may be used, we were told, and only the small top section of the shells, which are found in Madagascar or Zanzibar.

The shell section, which has three layers, is glued to the top of a stick for handling. The top layer is removed; a design is drawn on the second layer; after which the artist goes to work. The dark third layer of the shell provides the color contrast to be found in a cameo. Interesting??? We thought so We naturally visited Pompeii, which is especially fascinating because here are to be found the ruins of an entire town, complete with shops, homes, etc. Pompeii - population 20 to 25 thousand, was destroyed by an eruption of Mt. Vesuvius in 79 A.D., along with Herculaneum.

We visited the Basilica which housed the Palace of Justice and the Stock Exchange; and did you know (we didn't) that churches and cathedrals follow to this day the architectural design of the ancient Roman basilica, having generally three naves, a central and two side naves, with supporting pillars; the altar being placed where the ancient tribunal stood.

Ashes - not lava - buried Pompeii to a depth of 40 feet. Incidentally, excavations, begun in 1748, are still going on.

We visited the public baths, where we made some startling discoveries. The cold water in the frigidarium ran from a metal "tap" in the wall! In 79 A.D! And the Calidarium (hope we spelled that one correctly) featured central heating! Hot steam passed through the double walls beneath the floor, and the ceiling - if you please - was grooved so that the water caused by condensation slid gently to the side walls, rather than falling upon the ancient heads!

Saw the famous canine mosaic "Cave Canem" that invariably graced the entrance of an ancient Roman home…Pompeii was wonderful!!!

***

We drove along the incomparable Amalfi Drive, with the steep Lattari Mountains high above us, and the cobalt blue Mediterranean far below. Towns - Amalfi, Positano, Sorrento - terraced into the mountain sides; their lemon trees nestling under their slatted bamboo coverings, against the slightest mountain chill…(lemons as large as oranges).

Mt. Vesuvius, to the top of which we traveled by cab, praying that the driver's brakes would hold. (We hadn't time to take the official tour). A strange wild world of lava mountains and hills, with the morning mists swirling about them, and the winds are fiercely free…like the face of the moon, we thought. Long tough grasses and hardy pines growing out of the slate grey masses; lava caves and strange weird formations.

We had the driver stop by the antique crater so that we might bring back lava samples to Kevin and John, our rock-collecting nephews. We must also have samples of the Grande Crater, immediately announced. It buried San Sebastiano in 1944. My arm was seized in a powerful grip and we went leaping like two merry mountain goats from crag to crag - lizards scurrying before us - half way across Vesuvius, it seemed; at the end of which hazardous enterprise I found myself the proud possessor of another 10 pounds or so of interesting substance absolutely indistinguishable from its elder brother Antiqua…Oh, well!

***

To the French Riviera next, via the west coast of Italy with the sea alternately lashing angrily at the mountains that dared to intrude upon its depths and raining oft, salt tears upon a stretch of silver shore. We watched the setting sun draw a purple veil across the face of the Mediterranean, and we arrived in the south of France…

Nice is nice! And Cannes just can't be topped! And in Monaco we gambled a bit in Monte Carlo and saw the noontime fairy tale changing of the guard at Princess Grace's palace.

We sat in deck chairs beneath gay umbrellas on the Promenade des Anglais and the Boulevard de la Croisette, and now we know why the International Set settles down upon the French Riviera! We surveyed the yachts and the Silver Spoon crowd in the great gay basins of Monaco and Cannes; and we watched the bejeweled ladies and the bored gentlemen swell the treasury of Prince Rainer at his famous Casino (It is his, isn't it?)

***

And we began to think lovingly in terms of home and Braintree... Only Spain and Portugal lie ahead and then the return journey to London for a homeward flight to Heaven, which is in U.S.A! (Ed. Note: The Metayers - Bibs and Ted - return to their home in Braintree this coming Wednesday, six months to the day of their departure last spring).

"JOURNEY'S END"

Sunny Spain...Barcelona with its colorful Ramblas, and then Madrid!

We arrived there on Election Day, the first the country has known in 31 years - a result of the 1966 Constitutional law which, we understand, was instituted primarily to provide the mechanics for the naming of Franco's successor. We had expected a little excitement; there wasn't any.

In Barcelona posters everywhere were urging Spainards to vote in their "democracy." In the more sophisticated capital city of Madrid, we noted the posters were conspicuous by their absence, nevertheless, we opined, an election is an election!

"What is there to be excited about?" asked a Spanish gentleman at our hotel, with whom we discussed the matter. "In a one party system, who can win but Fanco and his National Movement?" So what about this election, we wondered, and proceeded to ask questions...

The Spanish people went to the polls, we learned, to elect 19 per cent of the deputies to their "Cortes" or Parliament- all candidates running on the slate of Franco's National Movement. Of Spain's 564 deputies, the remaining 81 per cent will reach the Cortes from official appointments and from selections by the National Movement; labor unions (controlled by the regime); and from municipal and provincial government and professional and cultural groups. The anti-Francos had urged an election boycott. The turnout was light. Incidentally, the Cortes has not the power to initiate legislation, we were told. It merely votes on government bills. It will, however, have a voice in the naming of the aging Franco's successor. That's about it!

We don't stop often enough to count our blessings -- we free people - do we???

***

Ah, Yes, Madrid, where they jolly well celebrated October 12, even as we do.

"Day of the Spanish Peoples," it was called. "Which means what?" I asked a Spaniard I met. "Why," he said, obviously surprised at my question, "it's the day on which Columbus discovered America, of course."

Incidentally, a tidbit on our discoverer, from the local edition of the International Herald Tribune… "75 years ago-Oct. 11, 1892. President Henneaux of San Domingo…offered to dispose of the remains of Columbus for $100,000…authorities at Washington have respectfully declined to purchase."

Yes indeed-Madrid and a tour to the 16th century Escorial Monastery, with its magnificent Basilica, and the marble Pantheon below the main altar, containing the tombs of all the Spanish Kings and Queens and mothers of Kings from Charles V-- also the white marble tomb of Don Juan of Austria, natural son of Charles!

And to the Valle de Los Caidos, a monument and Basilica 300 meters in length, built into the mountain rock by Franco to honor the fallen of the Spanish Civil War. Eighty thousand soldiers are buried here.

And to Toledo, an ancient walled medieval city with a natural moat (the Tagus River) 100 feet deep about it and buildings of vary-styles from Moors to Gothics to Renaissance - including the casa el Greco, 14th century home of the artist, which contains entire rooms of his masterpieces. And speaking of El Greco…did you know that he was a Greek born in Crete; and that he studied in Italy with Titian, Tintoreto and Bassano; (it shows in his work, doesn't it?) and then he lived his life in Toledo, where the many churches in the little town encouraged him in the mysticism which dominates his paintings?

That the whereabouts of his burial place is unknown for "we know El Greco, the artist," whose genius was recognized only during the last two centuries; "we do not know El Greco, the man?" Incidentally in his gallery of saints and apostles -- many of the paintings unfinished - the only one to bear his signature (his actual name) is the portrait of St. Paul, who preached in Greece - in Crete, El Greco's birthplace. Interesting???

***

Madrid, where we naturally attended a bull fight. "Colorful and revolting" was our private opinion of this highly touted form of entertainment!

Colorful, we must admit, it was! A blare of trumpets promptly at 4:30 of a Sunday afternoon, and two medieval horsemen called Alguaciles galloped across the bull ring to request of the President (who, with his party, was seated in the flag-draped official box just above us) the key of the Toril in which the bulls were locked. The keys, thrown by the President, were caught in a hat. The horse gate was opened and the Cuadrillas paraded into the ring.

The toreros, (there were three bullfighters, each of whom would kill two bulls), handsomely attired, and wearing the wonderful gold embroidered capes which they would later offer to their admirers in the boxes or at the barriers, replacing them with working capes - were followed by their Peones and subordinates, all of whom were in glittering attire.

A signal, and the first bull entered the ring, to be received first by the Peones and then by the Matador, who employed most spectacular turns, known as faroles, with his cape.

Following which, and at a signal from the clarion, two Picadores, riding heavily protected (thank Heaven!) blindfolded, and beautifully trained horses awaited the bull's attack, the which they repulsed with pikes, severely wounding the animal.

After three such attacks and the intervening play of capes by the subordinates, the trumpet's blare announced the introduction of Las Banderillas, the decorated sharp darts, six of which must be placed by the Peones or the Matador himself, in movements called "quiebro" or "de poder a poder," in the sides of the bull.

At this point, the clarion call indicated that it was time for the kill.

The Torero accepted the franelo (sword) and the montera (cape) and, removing his hat, requested of the President permission to kill the bull. With permission granted, he raised his hat in a toast to the animal, and then advanced to the center of the ring, where his daring skill was flaunted with a variety of passes and theatrical gestures which delighted his audience no end.

***

The torero is allowed 15 minutes for the kill, and his sword must pierce a very small vital area at the base of the animal's neck.

The public reaction to the killing determines the torero's reward. An especially heavy flutter of handkerchiefs and applause may bring him the bull's ear, or perhaps both ears; a spectacular kill the tail and the foot.

Our first Torero received an ear, which he triumphantly paraded about the bull ring. Handkerchiefs, tossed to the ring, were returned by him or his peones; a flask of wine, hurled down, was raised dramatically to his lips! The audience went wild!

Incidentally, the Spanish take their bullfighting very seriously. "Ole" is yelled only when a American particularly brilliant play is made, and we were informed confidentially that our young people who roam about Spain during the summer months yell "Ole" at all the wrong moments, deeply disturbing the Spaniards!

I laughed right out loud when I heard it. Wouldn't you know??

The audience reaction to an inept torero is a series of three claps which convey a message to the hapless matador. Clap Clap Clap they urge insistently, meaning Kill That Bull!

Our first bullfight was quite an experience. We saw two toreros gored, and I was all but under the concrete bleachers (one purchases a small leather cushion, thank goodness) most of the time, quaking now for the bullfighter and now for the bull!

***

From Madrid to Lisbon, Portugal, and thence to Fatima, the little mountain town where 50 years ago, three little shepherds--a boy and two girls--saw a series of apparitions of the Virgin Mary, who urged world prayer for world peace.

And from Fatima to Lourdes, where close to a century ago, Bernadette Soubirous, a little shepherd girl, had a similar experience...

And so we ended our Grand Tour of Europe on a note of inspiration, and thanksgiving for six flawless months in 19 fascinating countries, from which we would return to the loveliest land of them all!

For we'll let you in on a little secret, an observation shared by hundreds of traveling Americans we've met these summer months - there's nothing like a look at the rest of the world to make better Americans of us.

What a wonderful land to be coming home to -- the United States of America! How very fortunate we are, the Metayers!

11-12-67 HOME FROM EUROPE

Our luggage wears a battered look
From planes and trains; our travel book-
Its cover tired, its edges curled,
Proclaims acquaintance with the world.
Our purse - from filling it with stuff
For which we'd never room enough-
Won't close its catch; its handle stout
Persists in turning inside out…
Our nice new shoes show signs of use;
Our hush puppies of real abuse;
Our lingerie is tattle grey
From hotel lavings day by day.
Our gloves are everything but frayed;
(With Dior they'd never make the grade!)
The umbrella we squired about
Is everything but inside out…
Our pearls adorn a theatre floor;
Our golden bracelet is no more;
Our earrings - pair by pair - have gone
Until there's just the pair we've on…
Our haute coiffure is haute no more.
In every town but Singapore
Our hair in differing styles they'd place
Until we scarcely knew our face!
Our lace peignoir is shabby,
And gosh-even Ted is gabby;
And 'twill take a year or two or three

E'er all our candid shots we see…
But, goodness me, our six months trip-
In all respects - it was a pip!
And for the balance of our years,
Whenever boredom's shadow nears,
We'll simply smile, and Ted will say,
"Do you recall that rainy day
In Istanbul…the mosque of blue,
Wherein you lost your beat-up shoe???
Do you remember dear, the trip
We took aboard that Russian ship???
The way you searched our cabin for
The hidden microphone you swore
Was securely somewhere fine???
(You are a character, wifey mine…)"
And then we'll laugh and reminisce;
And I'll say, "Ted what utter bliss-
Those days in Nice and Cannes…the sea
And sky a cobalt symphony…"
Or, "Ted, dear, will you e'er forget
(I close my eyes and see it yet)
The Parthenon, all bathed in light;
The beauty of the marble white
That forms each starlit edifice
Of Athen's own Acropolis???
The poetry of ancient Rome?
The grandeur of St. Peter's dome?
The charm of Paris when it's spring?
And London's magic? Everything
We found to see, and dared to do
In what was just a dream come true…
What fun it was the world to roam!
But gosh, it's heaven to be home…

11-19-67 "AMATEUR PHOTOGRAPHY"

A couple of thousand Kodak slides, the Metayers are rapidly discovering, represents a powerful lot of celluloid. And identifying the contents of those small packs of travel treasure Uncle Sam is delivering daily to the Metayer ménage is no mean accomplishment.

"Look, Ted" I said fondly, gazing upon a handsome edifice in one of the eleven packets of slides our dear letter carrier had placed in my waiting hands yesterday morning...("How many are you expecting today?" he had asked gaily in his nice friendly fashion; he's practically a member of the family... "Eleven," I had answered. "They're here," he had said happily. I was happy too.)

"Look, Ted," I repeated, "Here's Paris - the Versailles Palace, with the statue of Louis XIV!" "No, dear," he replied. "It's the Castle Nymphenburg in Munich. See the garden where we walked with Friedrich and Hermine that afternoon..."

It turned out to be the Hopsburg Complex in Vienna, and we were both wrong...for the hundredth time...

Thank heaven, we say constantly, for the careful record we kept of each film as it was shot; For at this point, the five hundred palaces, six hundred cathedrals, and seven hundred Roman ruins we visited during our wonderful six months stay in Europe seem to be blending in a kaleidoscope of opulence and splendor that is utterly bewildering. That total recall we've often been accused of having, seems to have been totally recalled from our little old brain.

Photography, however, is fun. Every traveling American, of course, came complete with camera, and most of us were toting "his" and "hers". Slides were produced at the drop of a shutter in hotel rooms and railway carriages; on beaches and travel tours. "I don't want to bore you," said a new-found friend one day in Stockholm "but I just happen to have a viewer and the six hundred fabulous slides I took of my trip to the top of the Matterhorn and back. I know you'd love them." We did. He, in fact, loved the seven hundred and fifty slides we handed him for his perusal of our meanderings.

***

Naturally, in the matter of "his" and "her" photographic equipment, there were differences of opinion over what constitutes a likely subject.

Our friends, the Lumsdens, from New Zealand - we met them aboard a cruise ship in the Adriatic-Disagreed constantly.

Cloe, a Garden Clubber, had apparently photographed every bush, grass blade and wild flower from Auckland to the Aegean. There appeared to have been exposure shots at twilight, and eerie little expeditions at dawn; and flowers and flowers and more flowers…

"Now really," Lum, her husband, had asked us plaintively, "Isn't she wasting time and money? Who will ever spend an evening viewing bluebells in the rain and daffodils at dawning, and a bud with a bee on it???"

I will," said Cloe firmly. "But it's silly, Cloe," he had said. "Is it sensible to take mini skirts to London and mud flats on the Mediterranean and moors in Malta?" she had replied. "You stick to your oddities, Lum, and I'll stick to mine." Which they did.

Ted is the quick snap type photographer - raise the black box and click. I, on the other hand, am the careful type. Center the picture just so, set the lighting and labor over the subject matter, and hold postmortems over each and every shot. We've some wonderful shots incidentally -- both of us!

As far as the Metayers are concerned, by the way when it comes to slides, you may choose your country! Carousels bearing such fascinating titles as "Istanbul" "Pompeii, its Ruins," "Athens and the Islands" and the rest, grace every corner of our living room these days. And the travelogues go on…More films; more slides to be incorporated; more cataloguing, and more fun!

Slides of small boys performing such remarkable feats as chewing on a Pyrex nurser, tossing an indifferent snowball, or standing, ankle deep, in the briny blue, have given way these days before such super sights as Hitler's Hideaway, Michelangelo's David, and the wonderful British Islanders at work and play. And are we having fun, and reliving experiences, and storing up permanent memories…Photography is a wonderful hobby. And hats off, especially, to the man who invented that delightful adjunct to travel - the slide! WE seem to have accumulated thousands of them!

11-26-67 "STILL REMINISCING

We're taking a little more interest in the news that comes our way from the Soviet Union these days because, you see, the Metayers sailed from Athens to Istanbul on the Bashkiria, a Russian liner out of the port of Odessa! Not intentionally, you may be sure…It was quite accidental, but what a lovely accident for a newspaper columnist seeking foreign adventure!

We had every intention of flying to Turkey, however the cruise from Brindisi to Patras on the Egnatia had been such fun…

"Ted," I said suddenly of a lovely Saturday evening as we headed back to our Athens hotel after having witnessed a memorable performance of the fabled "Sound and Light" drama at the Acropolis, "how about taking a ship to Istanbul instead of a plane???" Ted was, as usual, in agreement and so on Sunday morning early, we set out in search of a shipping agency and cruise reservations.

At Peraeus, the ancient port of Athens, we found but one travel agent doing business, and the reservations for departure at 2 the following afternoon, were speedily made -- a one-way reservation only incidentally, for, as he informed us, Istanbul was a stopover on the route to more distant eastern seaports, and return ticket would involve awaiting the return of the liner, etc., etc. A different shipping line handled the cruise each day, he said brightly. It did not occur to us to inquire WHICH line would be handling our journey on the morrow…

***

Our usual weather was with us as we headed happily for the harbor. Our first destination was the Police Department, for passport check; our second Customs; and our third the gangplank of the Bashkiria.

We tripped gaily along the pier toward the lovely liner which lay at anchor on the delft blue sea. My eyes swept it lovingly, then bugged! The RED FLAG, complete with hammer and sickle, floated serenely from its mast!

"Ted," I gasped, "She's a Russian ship!"

We were aware suddenly of the interested stares of a group of passengers at the foot of the gangplank, and of the crew members who waited above. I all but took to my heels and bolted! "Ted," I said, "I'm scared."

"There's nothing to fear," said Ted. "But I criticized the Russians in my Cabbage about East Berlin," I said. "Believe me, dear," he said, "you'll be perfectly safe. I doubt very much if they read the Forum; besides you won't be in a Communist country.

They're flying the Greek flag as well..."

I lagged behind --not before as was customary -- the head of the household every inch of the way up that very long and somehow lonely gangplank...

We were greeted graciously by the ship's officers, who incidentally came complete with Oxford accents, and the voyage began. I must admit I looked for hidden microphones in the cabin, which was decidedly a beautiful one; and convinced myself I'd found one.

We were, needless to say, the only Americans aboard. Our cabin radio furnished us with the latest Russian news. (We heard the word "American" used frequently.)

We attended a full-length Russian feature in the lounge, and though we couldn't understand a word of it, did observe that the British C.O. and the kilted scotch Highlanders were made to appear pretty silly...It was amusing to hear the audience "boo-ing" the good guys, figuratively speaking, and applauding the bad ones...

We dined luxuriously every ten minutes or so, it seemed. (The Russian cuisine was marvelous!) We visited with a young Syrian who was enroute to Moscow for advanced engineering training at the invitation of the Soviet Government. "Why don't you come to Moscow?" he inquired to us, slyly.

Incidentally, he called our attention to a nondescript little ship passing us on the Aegean Sea in mid-morning. "There's an American ship," he said, "a warship..." he added. I'm ashamed to admit that I reacted instantly. "I can assure you," I said - proudly yet - "that our warships are a great deal larger than that..." We received, Ted and I, to misquote a favorite L.W.V. term, "most favored passenger treatment" the purser himself presented each of us with an enameled gold pin portraying the Bashkiria in all her glory, as well as a picture post card in his pride and joy. And she was a beauty - built in East Germany in

1964, he told us. "We are very happy to have had Americans on board," he added cordially.

***

We had a few hilarious moments, needless to say. There was, for instance, my wild determination to possess a slide of the Red Flag flying so formidably from our masthead. Every time I aimed the camera in its direction, a member of the ship's crew peered about a corner or through a window, or looked down or up in our direction. Talk about your proverbial shadow…we were "tailed" to quote our friend Ian Fleming, every step of the way we took about the ship.

I was convinced we were being spied upon; and it was only after we docked and considered the matter objectively from all angles that we realized that we, as Americans, were of as much interest to the Russians aboard, as they were to us!

Yes, of course we got the slide -- slides, to be precise - of the Red Flag, and the ship's lifeboat, and Ted, ensconced in a deck chair, coincidentally placed directly in front of a life preserver, labeled in Russian!

12-3-67   "MORE REMINISCING"

S'WONDERFUL! Each time we fling open a magazine - Ted and I - we are face to face with some marvel, architecturally or otherwise, which we encountered on our recent prowl about Europe! On Monday evening, for instance, when Ted, immersed in the depths of the Patriot Ledger, let out a whoop… "Hon," he called excitedly, "here's the 'Regina Maris!'"…and sure enough, there in the ever-fascinating column of Edward Rowe Snow, "Sea and Shore Gleanings," was the story of the Norwegian Clipper Ship, Regina Maris, our encounter with which last summer in Oslo Harbor had been one of the high points of our Norway visit.

From the columnist we learned that this handsome craft "displaces 480 tons…had a length of 150 feet over all…" that her "highest mast is 110 feet" and that "she has 32 sails in all, including the 'Jamie Green' below the bowsprit." We know that the Regina Maris (Queen of the

Seas) had, in addition, grace and charm and beauty unparalleled, for we witnessed her triumphant return on August 11, from a westward sail around Cape Horn!

***

It was a beautiful day.

We had crossed Oslo Harbor that morning, headed for Bygdoy and the museums that house the thousand-year-old Viking Ship Oseberg, and the raft Kon Tiki, and Capt. Roald Amundsen's polar ship, Fram; and, as we awaited the ferry's departure, had observed a wonderful windjammer, the Christian Radich, lying at anchor at Pier C. We promptly photographed her, and then by persistent questioning, learned that she had been used in the film, "Windjammer" and was on hand to house the grand reception to be given by the Norway Cape Horn Club - an organization made up of Norwegians who had sailed around the Horn - for the crew of the clipper ship Regina Maris, the latest sailing vessel to have achieved this danger-fraught accomplishment.

The Regina Maria, we were told, had sailed from Oslo Harbor on or about May 1, the date of our own departure from Braintree-a fact which delighted us. We had read references to her in our Oslo Bulletin of Events. However, knowing nothing about her, they had meant little to us.

Bygdoy was enchanting, and, as we strolled along the pier, awaiting our return ferry to Oslo, we noticed a fireboat in operation out upon the beautiful clear waters of the bay.

"Ted," I said, "there must be a fire at sea. See all the boats clustered together, and the fireboat is spraying water!" And then, even at that distance, the air of excitement that surrounded the group, was obvious, and we leaped to a happy conclusion. "It's the Regina Maris!" we cried excitely, and our little old cameras came out singing. having raced it to the pier, we secured a wonderful shot of her Regina Maris - as she swept We snapped the flotilla as it sailed triumphantly across the harbor's mouth, and then, our ferry majestically into her home port.

The reception accorded her was pure enchantment! Her crew was piped off the ship by the crew of the Christian Radich, which, we neglected to say, is a training ship for young Norwegian sailors. The voices of these fine young boys were raised in the most rollicking set of Norwegian sea chanties we ever expect to hear. They flew from the sound system and raced on the bright Norwegian wind across the waters of the harbor, and the waiting crowd tapped its collective feet, and roared its excitement… And the sun was golden on the clipper ship Regina Maris, with the bright Norwegian flag upon her mast…And the bronzed Norwegian crew who stepped upon the pier might well have been at home upon the Viking ship Oseberg, which we'd seen that very day in the marvelous museum of Bygdoy. What a day it was, this August 11- and once more we were there…How kind the fates…

***

Oh, yes - Mr. Snow tells us that the master of the fair Regina Maris is one Captain John Wilson of Norway, who will now, we were told by the "Texaco Tourist Pilots", two lovely young Norwegian girls on motor scooters, whose function is to be of service to tourists (how about that???) and whom we pelted with questions, naturally who will now, we repeat, be permitted to join a fascinating organization composed solely of Norwegians who have sailed around the Horn in a schooner, and who were responsible for the welcome and civic reception, which we were happily to witness - another lucky accident!

We must add one more note…(Why is it that my Cabbages keep growing larger!)

Mr. Snow quotes one Giles Tod who "would question the opinion expressed by some that the 'Regina Maris' is the little sister of the famous tea clipper, 'Cutty Sark'" She's not. We know that also, for we visited the Cutty Sark and roamed about her fascinating old decks…She's in drydock at Greenwich, England, and we sailed upon the Thames to find her. But that's another tale…

We must write Mr. Snow, whose article indicated heartbreak at his failure to arrive in Connecticut waters e'er the clipper ship Regina Maris left them for New York last summer on her way around the Horn, or maybe on her journey home.

Bet he'd love to see our slides of her arrival back in Oslo! And of the fireboat in the harbor, and the Cristian Radich at the pier, and of the two great sailing vessels lying side by side…They're marvelous!

IRISH CULTURE

"O Ireland let be it thy high duty
To Teach the World the might of moral beauty
And stamp God's image truly on the struggling soul."

The history of Ireland' is a story of dawns and declines, of outstanding figures, of frantic struggles, of pitiful tragedies, and of a final dawn, mighty, almost miraculous. The history of Ireland's civilization is the history of Ireland.

As the first sun of time rose on Ireland, there dawned an age, primitive and uncultured. Lands echoed the footsteps of barbarism. The flight of centuries produced Rome, "Mistress of the World" in power and culture. Europe received her, accepted her pagan influence. But alone in the West, Erin a beautiful gold-green isle, bent not her maiden head. This little land of indomitable love of freedom scorning the culture of the "Empire of the World" carved for herself a culture unparalleled.

Simultaneous with this era of primitive civilization, came the bards, kings in the realm of legendary literature, strolling subjects along "The Road Round Ireland" singing "tales of magic, love, or arms from days when princes met." Fostering culture in a race, which at the close of the seventh century "was synonymous with learning and literally blazed like the stars of the firmament with the glory of her scholars, these wandering minstrels laid for Ireland the corner-stone of her Temple of Culture. The Age of the Bards has left literary-relics, it has bequeathed masterpieces in the world of Art. Ireland's treasured bronzed, the primitive beauty of her tumuli, contemporary with the courtly verse makers who roamed thru mountainy places.

"Ever in view of the sea and the fields,
With the rough wind
Blowing over the leagues behind "

All these proclaim the culture that was pre-Christian Ireland's. With the fifth century, a new day dawned for the Celt of Ireland.

The traditions of centuries were to be forgotten. The flower of pagan culture was to be uprooted and in its place there were to germinate the seeds of Christian truths and principles. This new day was ushered in with the advent of the sainted Patrick, eminent for his scholarship, more eminent in his exalted vocation of a nation's Patron Saint. Then Ireland's paganism yielded to Christianity; her primitive civilization, to hallowed culture. Out of the depths of an uninformed nation, arose in all directions stately schools-at Armagh, Noendrum, Louth, and Kildare. The sixth and seventh centuries saw further establishments of monastic schools at Clonfert, Clonard, Arran, Bangor, Glendalough, and Lismore. And from the fifth to the ninth century, Ireland led the nations of Europe in learning, thus deserving the undisputed title of the Island of Saints and Scholars."

Irish monks proved to be not only apostles of souls, but also masters of intellectual life. St. Virgilius, an Irish missionary, taught in the eighth century the sphericity of the earth and the existence of the Antipodes. It was this same teaching that Copernicus and later astronomers formulated into the system now in vogue and Newly-Christian Ireland gave to Literature the " Book of Armagh," the Life of St. Columba" the "Book of Kells," and the "Annals of the Four Masters," besides hymns, poems, commentaries on the Psalms, and classical transcriptions; to Sculpture, the "High Crosses" treasured, embossed figures in metal, milestones of antiquity, ornamented with a blazonry of colors, and to Architecture, the gray, sombre Round Towers, cone-capped fingers of mystery pointing between the green valleys and the heaven of the saints over them."

But scarcely had of the Light of Christian Culture reflected the beauty of the "Emerald of Europe" than powers of oppression, of devastation, bending nations to their ruthless will, sought to tarnish her lustre. But soon the sea was "white with hurrying oars "of the men of Erin as they sped to the call of their kinsmen, threatened with imperial servitude."

In this land "constantly wet with the blood and tears of its children", culture might with facility have perished. But to each warring dawn of Ireland by the tyranny of foes, there was offered eternal resistance—the keynote to each subsequent attack thru Danish, Norman, Tudor, Stuart and Cromwellian invasion. Ireland lived and loved the beautiful for

"She was not made for shame or ruth,
For trampled right, triumphant wrong.
Her hope was high, her heart was true,
The fire of freedom, lit her eye,
Her homes were pure as morning dew;
Reverence was hers and charity."

Although her blue-green streams and sounding seas send forth their sigh of sympathy for persecuted Erin; although her very hills and dales her towering mountains bespeack with sad noises a story of noble sacrifices of glorious patriotism, of priceless Faith, there are heard in all the greivings and laments tones of the culture which, like a loyal mother, the little Isle of the West preserved for her offspring.

And she preserved it even in the ten dim centureies between the Fall of Rome and the Renaissance. Who kept alive in Northern Europe, during the Middle Ages the culture of Greece and Rome? Scholars from Ireland's forty universities. England, France, Belgium, Switzerland, Germany, and even Italy turned expectant gaze toward Ireland, the little free-souled Isle, torn by ignominious oppression, but innately culture loving. And so from Ireland came forth her Saints and Scholars, bearing aloft the torch of learning, founding schools, universities, notable centers erected on Faith and reverence for culture. Shedding her beams of native refinement into the shades of farthest Europe, this little "knight-errant nation" whose cities and ports of culture remained so steadfastly perpetual, clinging with such dominant tenacity to the potent spiritual ideals which marked their foundations," civilized the world.

Like the history of Mediaeval Ireland, her Mediaeval Culture comprised a succession of dawns and declines. As the soundings of barbarism echoed in the Land of Erin, she absorbed their vibrant tones, embraced their pagan sagas and song, and, guided by the beacon of highly spiritual ideals, despite the effects of rabid assaults, gave to Literature offerings beautiful in their fringe of suffering, musical in their strains of Nature love:

"Ebbing, the wave of the sea,
Leaves where it wantoned before,

Wan and naked the shore,
Heavy the clothed weed.
And in my heart, woe is me
Ebbing a wave of the sea!
Ebbing the wave of the sea
Leaves where it wantoned before
Changed past knowing the shore
Lean and lonely and gray.
And far and farther from me
Ebbs the wave of the sea."

As the Middle Ages crashed into obscurity against the ruthless onslaught of Time, as Modernism succeeded Mediaevalism, the culture of Ireland upon whom "The Lord God will ever smile with guardian grace," progressed gradually rising with intermittent strides to the apex of its development. From the years of the mid-nineteenth century when Callanan, Banim, Griffin, Mahoney, Mangan, and Sir Samuel Ferguson raise their frizzied cries for Revival to the present position of Ireland in Literature, her history has glowed, has burned with soul-stirring appeals to the cultured mind of a cultured race thru the effective medium of literary expression.

Arthur O'Shaughnessy sang of the children of Erin,

"We are the music makers,
And we are the dreamers of dreams,
Wandering by lone sea-breakers,
And sitting by desolate streams.
World-losers and world forsakers,
On whom the pale moon gleams;
Yet we are the movers and shakers
Of the world forever, it seems.

And so from William Butler Yeats with his exquisite, lyric moods; Lady Gregory, God's gracious gift to Ireland's womanhood; and George Russell the mystic lover of a mystic land came the strains of a Celtic

Revival. For the sun of an Irish Renaissance had risen. The beauty of the Literature, the Drama, Art, and even the liquid tongue of the Gael again thru the opalescent hues of a new morn.

Ireland's poets, high-priests of beauty, chanted their melodies across her green-tinged bog-lands—Douglas Hyde with John Millington Synge, his literary protege, peasant-mad Alfred Graves; and God-given Katherine Tynan. And as the great "singing fire" of youth blazed the new Ireland, "poets of the soil", like Padraic Colum sighed.

> "Oh, to have a little house!
> To own the hearth and stool and all!"

and Joseph Campbell, of whom A.E. unwittingly sang

> The child of earth in his heart grows burning
> Mad for the night and the deep unknown.

As this mystic voice of mystic Ireland wails to a world thru the pen of her mystic writer, the keynote of a tortured nation's undying culture, her prophets of beauty raise aloft thru the sky of the Revival proud hands for literary deliverance.

Her priestesses of Art plead equally- Moira O'Neill, sweetest of Erin's sweethearts; Alice Miligan; ideallic Eva Gore-Booth; Dora Sigerson Shorter; and Susan Mitchell, lady of the clouds.

On the towering walls of Ireland's Temple of Culture, men will read thru the dawns and declines of future ages the valiant story of Ireland's response to the peremptory call of the Drama sounded thru her realms with the passing of the nineteenth century.

And men will see inscribed on the shrines of age: Edward Martyn, George Moore; and on the panels of youth, Lennox Robinson, Rutherford Mayne; and the tragic Murray.

We have seen that the Irish Culture has stood, despite the onslaughts of cruelty, invasion and war, undaunted, towering and triumphant for

"Not let lost is their power to quicken, to exalt, to purify.
Still they live, and reign and shall reign."

Christian Culture is a mighty monarch: His kingdom extends to all climes. All nations are his loyal subjects. Oppressed but cultured Ireland is one of the many who pay him tribute. With the passing of ages this little Isle of the West has quietly mounted the steps ascending to his throne. And tonight as we the Class of 1929, leave the hallowed portals of our loved Girls' Catholic High School and look in retrospect and prospect, we find ourselves within the courtly halls aspiring to pay homage to the same monarch.

Those who have directed our childhood and maiden steps along the path to Culture, are with us as we bid our "Vale." From these devoted handmaidens of the queen of Heavenly Culture we have learned by word and by example that "Culture, like all of life's blessings, can not be hoarded- it is for service." And of its service we have most generously received.

"In all things showing himself as example in good works, in doctrine, in integrity, in gravity," our own good Father and Pastor, Rt. Rev. Richard Neagle, has spent himself that we may be reared in the atmosphere of truly Christian Culture— "a culture that he, as "Ambassador of Christ" would know." His vigilance, his labors, in all things, his work as an evangelist, the fulfilment of his ministry, will merit the promise of the inspired words:

"As to the rest there is laid up for me a crown of justice which
the Lord, the just judge, will render to me in that day."

As we stand this eve at the gate of an unknown world, as we witness the dawn of a new day glowing in the dim east of our lives, the fervid gaze of each one of us seeks for those "dearer to us than life is dear", the ones who rocked us in the Cradle of Culture, a pure, Christian home—our mothers, tender model Christian mothers—our kind, virtuous Christian fathers, representative of the One who reigns in Heaven. They have ruled our hearts, our minds. In childhood strifes have they been our refuge;

in maiden joys, sharers. May God bless them and grant them length of day and "the peace which surpasseth all understanding." May they be privileged to say "I have no greater grace than this, to hear that my children walk in truth."

Fellow students of 1929, let us then for their dear sakes never discard the armour of Truth and Culture with which we, as virgin Paladins of our loved Patroness, Mary Immaculate, have been accoutred.

May we preserve with glowing ardor our shining breastplate of the principles of justice with its insignia of hope and trust, "Deus Lux Mea," God my Light.

And before we journey further in the Crusade of Life, let us renew our pledge of loyalty and fealty to the King of the Heavenly Court under whose glorious standard we are enrolled.

> Under our colors, celestial Blue and White Mary's own
> We shall fight the good fight "against the foes of
> Christian Faith and Culture, jousting for the favor of
> Our Lady—her starry smile."

> May it e'er bless us from above
> Keep pure our souls from passion's guile
> Our hearts from earthly love
> Still save each soul from guilt apart
> As stainless as each sword
> And guard undimmed in every heart
> The image of our Lord

Valedictory Speech

"Quo Vadis?"

"Parting and forgetting? What faithful heart can do these? Our great thoughts, our great affections, the truths of our own life, never leave us. Surely they cannot separate from our consciousness; they shall follow it wheresoever it shall go; and are of their nature divine and immortal."

William Thackeray.

We have reached a climax in the drama of life, a cross-road in life's journey. Our past has been but a stepping stone to the present and the future is ours to make or mar. This evening we stand on the brink of the precipice of time peering into the profound abyss of mystery before us. Heretofore, we have trodden a sylvan path along which sorrow was an intruder; care, an outcast, for, as youthful wayfarers, the beneficent care of loving parents or guardians has guided and directed our tottering steps. Yes, from babyhood they have with the most tender vigilance and unfailing generosity nurtured us, conscientiously tilling the fertile soil of our young hearts and faithfully sowing the seeds of Faith and goodness that they "might bring forth fruit in abundance"; and plucking meanwhile, the weeds which from time to time, threatened to taint the beauty of our budding souls. Truly our good mothers and fathers are loyal laborers in the garden of life.

"The child is father of the man." With this dominant thought, our teachers, those chosen-elect of God, have sacrificed their lives to the service of Religion. Under their benign influence, the benefits derived both morally and educationally are inconceivable. Every broad-minded man or woman is compelled to acknowledge even reluctantly that the results of such religious training are evident and far reaching. Not only do these noble women impart to the student mind the principles of education, but they instil into it a clear knowledge of right and wrong, thus erecting stone by stone from the very foundation the mighty edifice of a strong and upright character, a staunch bulwark amid the winds of adversity. By force of their own exemplary lives, these Sisters impress upon their charges a love of the good which must needs prompt them in later life to follow the path of duty, the only path of right which "reaches down the ages in its effects and into eternity; and when one goes about it resolutely, it seems to me now as though his footsteps were echoing beyond the stars, though heard only faintly in the atmosphere of the World."

In 1909, the "Girls' Catholic High School" was established under the supervision of our most revered Pastor, ever solicitous of both the spiritual and temporal welfare of the children of his parish. Each year saw the field of its influence widened until it became impossible to accomodate the number whose parents were eager to have their daughters trained in truly Catholic environment, But difficulties ceased in 1922 with the completion of the imposing edifice which now graces our School grounds - a fitting memorial and manifestation of that real, fatherly love and priestly devotion which - prompted his plan of construction. That our Eternal Father bless him with the plenitude of grace is the prayer of every girl in the class of 1925.

Each year during the vernal season, when all Nature is awakening, when frail boughs are bearing their precious buds and blossoms to light, and birds are gladdening the world with song, a class of girls has bidden its farewell to the Girls' Catholic High School, its "Alma Mater" beneath the folds of its celestial blue and virginal white, with many a qualm of sadness at the parting, for

"To meet, to know, and then to part
Is the saddest thing to a school-girl's heart."

So we, another group, stand ready to launch forth upon the open sea of life to battle for Eternity. 'Tis scarcely a month ago since one of our number was taken to her heavenly reward, a frail bud nipped from the garden of youth. "Life is before us - not only earthly life, but life - a thread running interminably through the warp of eternity." The mainland is vast and endless, yet we know not the day nor the hour when we too, shall answer the angel's summons to the Great Beyond, armed only with the meritorious works we have accomplished. Now, our thoughts are of joy tinged with sadness, joy at the recollection of the happy, care-free existence through which we have passed; sadness at the consideration that our childhood has passed forever. Now, we are bordering on womanhood; henceforth, we must tread our· own path guided by the beacon of our Faith - Faith, "that subtle chain which binds us to the Infinite."

Life is a coursing rivulet that flows with ever increasing speed, babbling its messages of joy and mirth to the world. Its path is straight and fresh, its banks are dewy and verdant. Abruptly, its mileage is impeded, the source is severed dividing it into narrow channels, each pursuing a course independent of the other. We, travelers on the journey have reached this severed source, this parting of the ways, and there looms up for meditation "Quo Vadis? – "Whither goes thou?" Short, it is true, and still so momentous a question that we must ponder before deciding the issue upon which our future happiness and welfare shall depend.

"Every individual has a place to fill in the world and is important in some respect whether he chooses to be so or not." Nature has endowed each of us with certain distinctive qualities, which acting like magnetic forces, seem to imbue us with diverse attractions to the many avocations in life. And thus we are led by varied paths to that particular goal in view of which we wend our way with earnest care for the fulfilment of our life's mission. In the labyrinth before us is the broad highway on which so many choose· to travel, that avenue to the world of commerce, that daily scene of struggle and confusion agitated by the click of the typewriter and the constant turmoil of the passing crowd. Yet, this center of activity and livelihood offers attractions and allurements. To some, it spells success; to· others, dreary monotony and keen disappointment. Ah, deep and mysterious future, if we could but discover the key to your locked treasures!

In contradistinction to this approach to the world of trade, is that regular and disciplined path of the nurse - a path cleared of the thorns of selfishness only. The career of a nurse is a role of continuous self-denial and steadfastness to duty. In her daily round of duties, well does she understand the worth of patience, that unrivaled virtue which "ornaments the woman and proves the man". But her sacrifice is not unrecorded, for from the lips of the sufferer whose fevered brow her hands have cooled, comes a whispered prayer for the benediction of her Divine Physician.

Tending toward contact with the youth of humanity is the course of the teacher. Hers is a route of responsibilities of a nature not educational alone but ethical as well. It is her charge to endeavor to analyze each character, to inspire confidence and, finally, to imprint indelibly by her own example, the essentials of true manhood and womanhood. The teacher conquers not by strength but by perseverance. Thus will she "instruct others unto justice that she may shine as a star through all Eternity."

In view of these aspects, what weighty consideration is due to that salient question, "Quo Vadis?", that we may not err in the pursuit of that path directed to that sphere in which Divine Providence has destined us to exert our influence that we may do great deeds not for our own renown but for the greater glory of God and the good of our fellowmen. Ruskin says: -

"The voice of parents is the voice of gods,
for to their children, they are heaven's lieutenants."

After our parents, our thoughts must needs revert to our beloved Pastor through whose magnanimity of soul, like to a good shepherd, being ever mindful of that first mandate of the Divine Shepherd - "Feed my lambs; feed my sheep" - we have been the joyful recipients of benefits whereby we are induced to habits of "plain living and high thinking". Besides these temporal advantages, however, we have enjoyed as fruit of his priestly. zeal, spiritual opportunities for "laying up treasures in Heaven which neither the moth nor rust doth consume" that at the final reckoning we "may not be found wanting." In all his endeavors, our· Right Reverend Pastor Monsignor Neagle, has been aided by the earnest cooperation of the good Sisters, ever zealous for the salvation of souls. They are indeed true friends and a faithful friend is better than gold.

Tonight as we set out upon our· earthly pilgrimage, may our thoughts with one accord center around that parting advice of Polonius to his son Laertes:

"This above all;
To thine own self be true,
And it must follow, as the night the day,
Thou canst not then be false to any man."

And as we bid "Adieu" to our loved Alma Mater, in this her own month of May, beneath the pure folds of the banner of Heaven's Bright Queen, Mary Immaculate, and our Virgin Patroness, may we see

"With clearer faith her majesty,
And learn her sweet humility",

that we may be commended through life as faithful children of Mary, and at the end of life's pilgrimage that we may be found kneeling at

"The throne of the Queen of Heaven",
enjoying there with her the Beatific Vision of "God, our Light!"

"Bright Queen of Heaven, Virgin most fair,
Mary most gentle, list to our pray'r,
Mother protect us, aid to us bring,
Sweetly enfold us 'neath sheltering wing.

Star of the Ocean, shedding soft light,
Solace in sorrow, and rest 'mid the night;
Send in our slumbers, peace from above,
Shine on us ever, Bright Star of Love."

Words for Elizabeth from her last doctor...

Over 25 years I've seen it all…the gracious and the rude, the selfish and the generous. A lot of nice folks and lots of not so nice people as well. Those who face illness and death with great courage and those who are cowed and tremulous at the least infraction of their bodies. And maybe once or twice in those 25 years a person comes who has such grace and courage, such selflessness, even gallantry that they fall well outside the norms of humankind.

Elizabeth was such a person. Her goodness, wisdom and grace almost fall outside the human compass. The only word that does her justice is saintly. Saintly in the sense of great love and great faith and great deeds.

If America is famous for its farmer-soldiers then Elizabeth was our mother- legislator, our moral leader…an example of what a human being could and ought to be. Thank God she lived long enough to receive yet another honor from her community. It was an honor to have known her and to have been her doctor. She confronted every obstacle with a quiet determination that bordered on fanatic. I always had the feeling that if a problem had a solution she would find it.

In our cynical age of commercials and commercialism, spin-doctors and dissemblers, of the superficial compounding the gaudy, she did honor to our humanity and to our country. This is my homage to the work of art that was her life.

May she rest in peace.

Howard B. Perer MD
6/98

PALADIN

Look forth the summit and the pinnacles of a gray steeple-
thence at intervals a low bell pealing.
Endurance is the crowning quality and patience all the passion
of great hearts.
Pure with all faithful passion,
With tender smiles that come and go;
And comforting as April air after the snow.
I love everything that's old.
Old friends, old times, old manners, old books.
Life has its dreamer, its seer of lofty visions.
Its watchers of the stars. We have our dreamer,
our idealist–she is Beatrice.
Far greater the joy to this daughter of evening, of walking
through the world of booklore wandering by the silvery
poesy streams than anywhere else.
But would you have a dreamer without a strain of humor in
her dreams?
Out "Beats" is a gay little dreamer her merry laugh sounds
always where there is the tiniest trace of trickery amongst
"we classmates"
The destiny of Beatrice is quite unfathomed; apparently quite
unfathomable; for who can understand the thinkings of a
dreamer?
Elizabeth when you are weary after a day's work look at this
book and remember the happy days of GCHS
Welcome as the swift cool fall of the white pure snow on our
uplifted faces is Rose with her eyes dancing, radiant with
happiness and friendliness. Often Rose has led us a great
pace through basketball games and again and again in a
swift excellent race over the ice lips singing in merry song
and pulses tingling with joyous life. In Rose truly the joy of
youth and health her eyes displayed and ease of her heart
every look conveyed.

Elizabeth when you reach your biggest dream remember me as the girl who sat beside you in dear old GCHS Love & success.

The bright countenance of truth in the quiet and still air of delightful studies.

She is as good as she is fair

None–none on earth above her

As pure in thought as angels are

To know her is to love her

Never have we seen Elizabeth other than content, true, idealistic and our leader. Constantly our "Beth" as we know her, striving to do her utmost both in literature and art.

Fine manners are the mantles of fair minds.

Laugh, the world laughs with you

Weep and you weep alone!

There's in you all that we believe of heaven–amazing brightness purity and truth.

In the dimness of futurity may her lofty head rise ever toward the noble clouds whereupon Catherine delights to gaze.

Who mixed reason with pleasure, and wisdom with mirth

If she has any faults, she has left us in doubt

Grace was in all her steps

In every gesture dignity

As sunshine broken in the rill

Though turned astray is sunshine still

The business of art is not to represent things as nature makes them, but as she ought to make them.

Looking back on the girls of the Senior Class there is one that stands out, a gem of personality, efficiency, and friendship that sparkles on the forefinger of time.

Geneva so unaffected so composed a mind so firm yet soft so strong yet refined is our president who shows us by her perfect example the road to success.

It has been said that in business three things are necessary: knowledge, patience, and time. As Geneva believes that; they build too low who build beneath the skies.

They are never alone that are accompanied by noble thoughts

Often I have watched a sunbeam flitter and light in a shadowy place. Often I have heard a robin sing with joyous abandon at the first little sign of Spring. Still more often I have heard children laugh with delight at some childish prank.

Beth, I am not wishing you success because there is no need since you have always been successful. But here's hoping you'll remember me when you become famous. Margaret Mary Chisholm "Peggy"

Be thine own self and thou art lovable.

Humility, that low sweet root from which all heavenly virtues shoot.

From the crown of her head to the sole of her foot she is all mirth.

Never Never change Elizabeth Sister Mary James

Wednesday is a day of great moment in the High

White bloused figures can be seen running hither and thither before the great period arrives–athletic period.

With the sound of the gong we form in line and eagerly march to our gymnasium, where with cheeks glowing and eyes sparkling we are put through a series of grilling exercises by our very popular coach Miss Louise Welsh

The sports club also has been striving in games of basket volley and dodge ball. If we are defeated after a hard and desperate fight we have always striven to accept loss in a sportsmanlike way, with a smile and a cheer for the others.

Clean sports signify clean living. Hence we shall strive always to keep our bodies in perfect condition so that the mind and heart may ever follow that beautiful path of our Blessed Lady.

May we feel her smiling down on us in her lovely way from the blue and the white of the skies above.

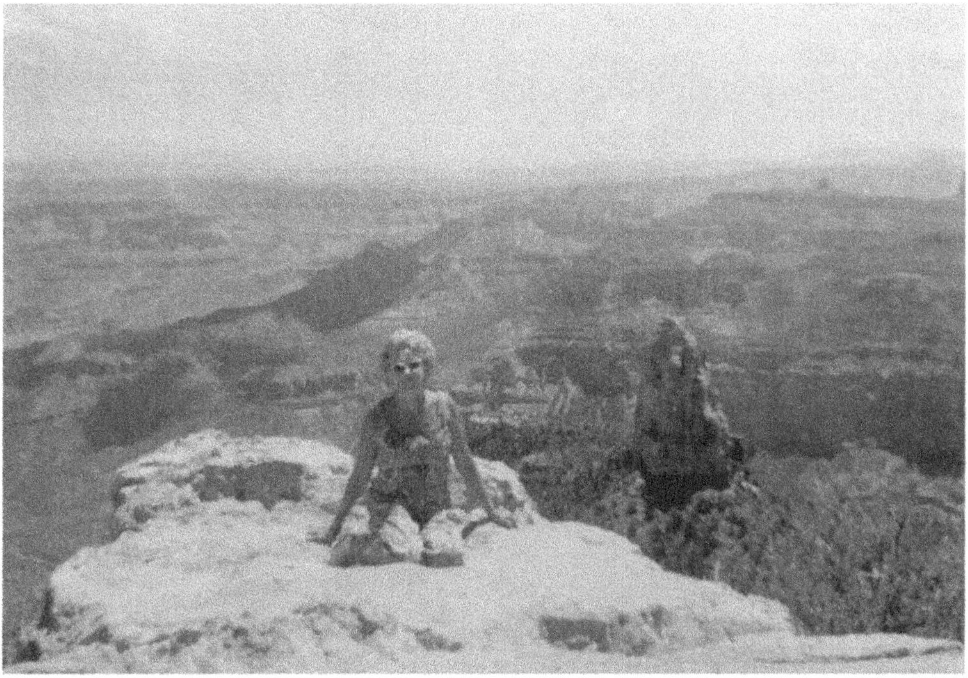

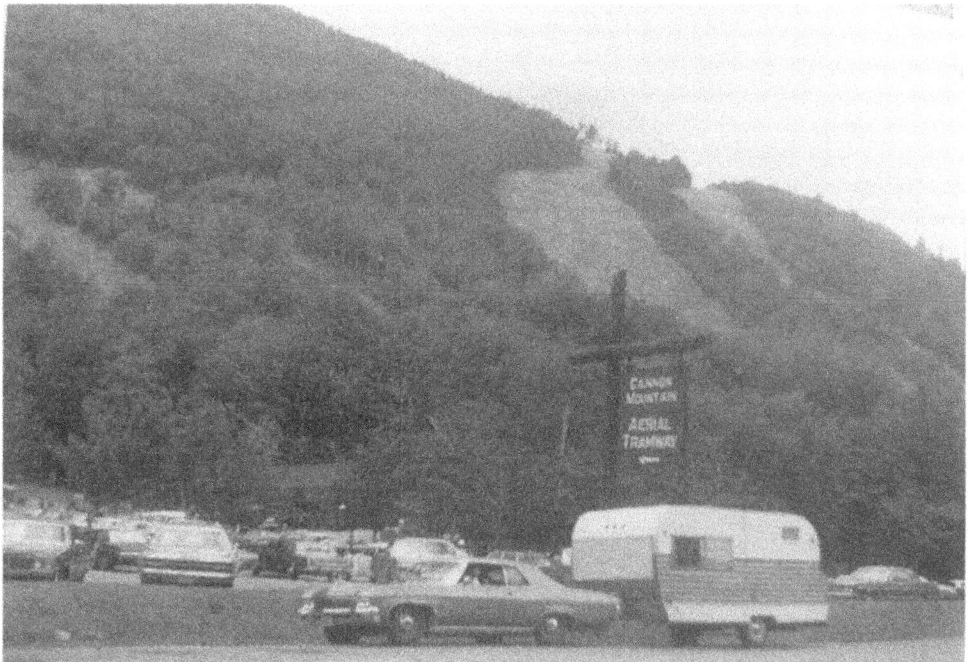
CANNON MOUNTAIN
AERIAL TRAMWAY

To Elizabeth
With best wishes
Ted Kennedy

GRAND MARSHAL
ELIZABETH
METAYER

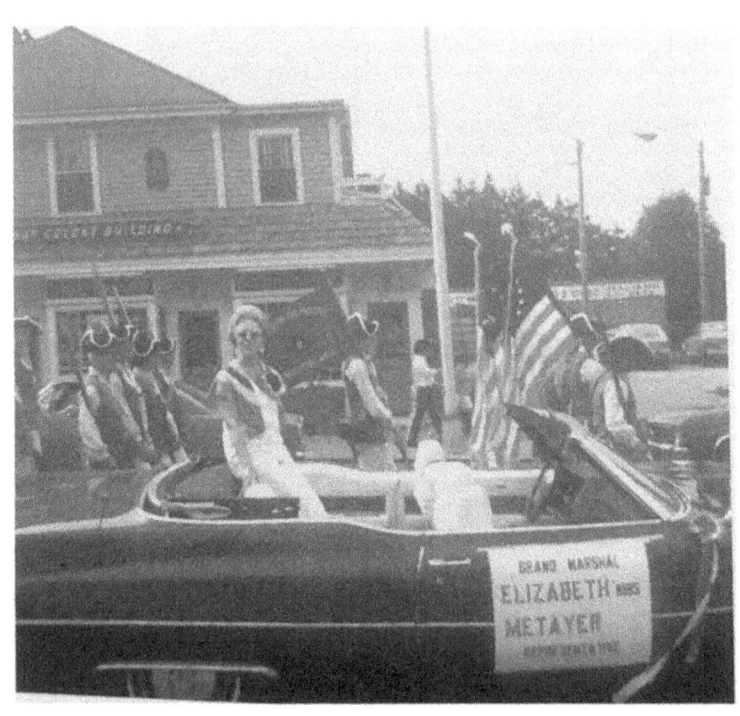

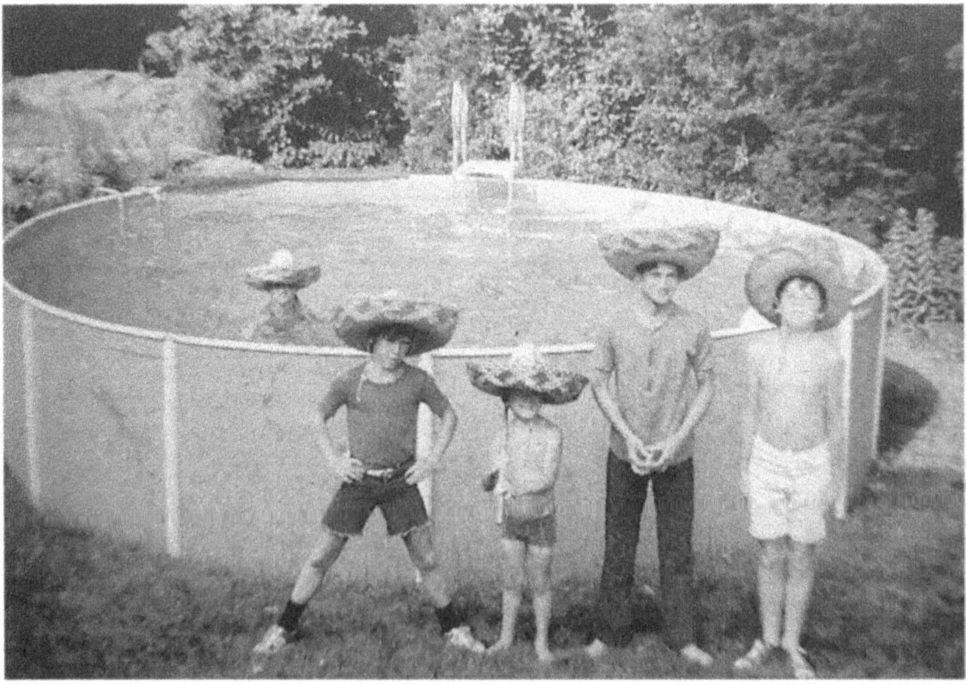

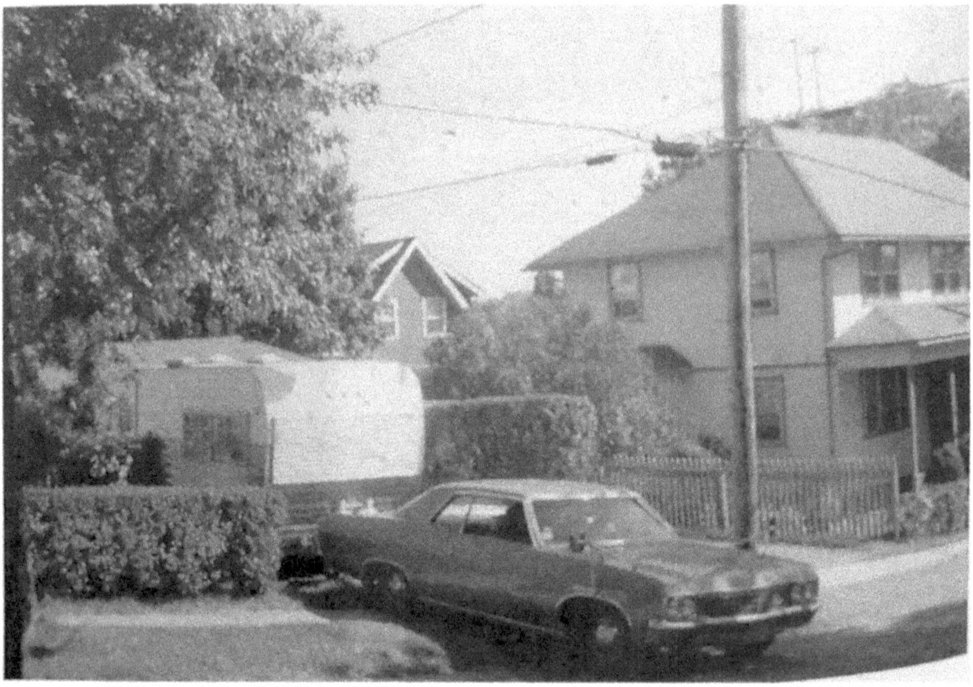

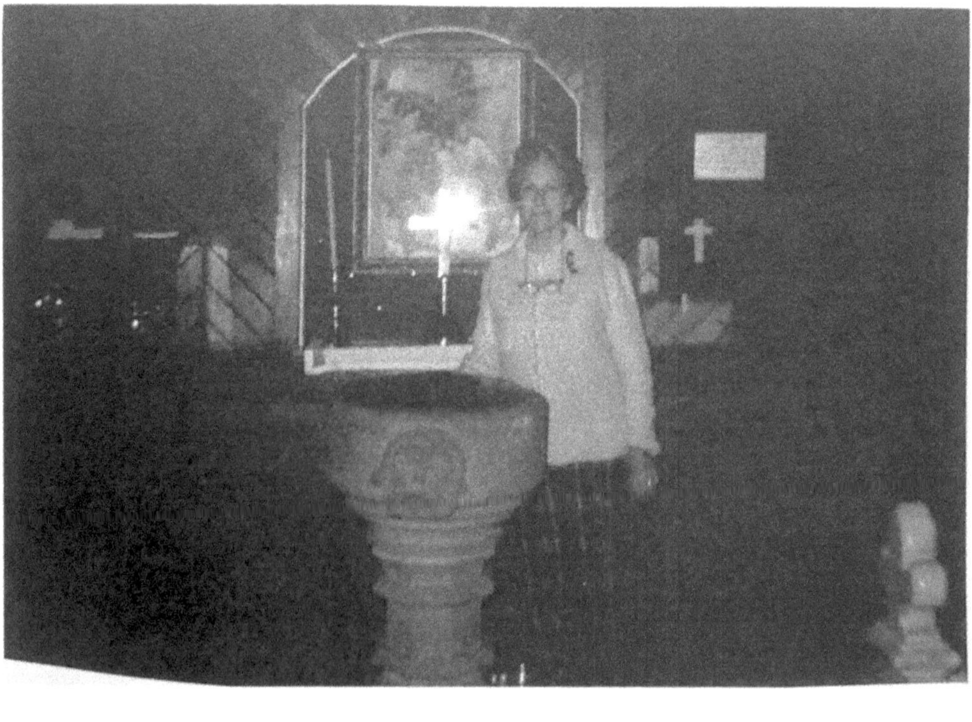

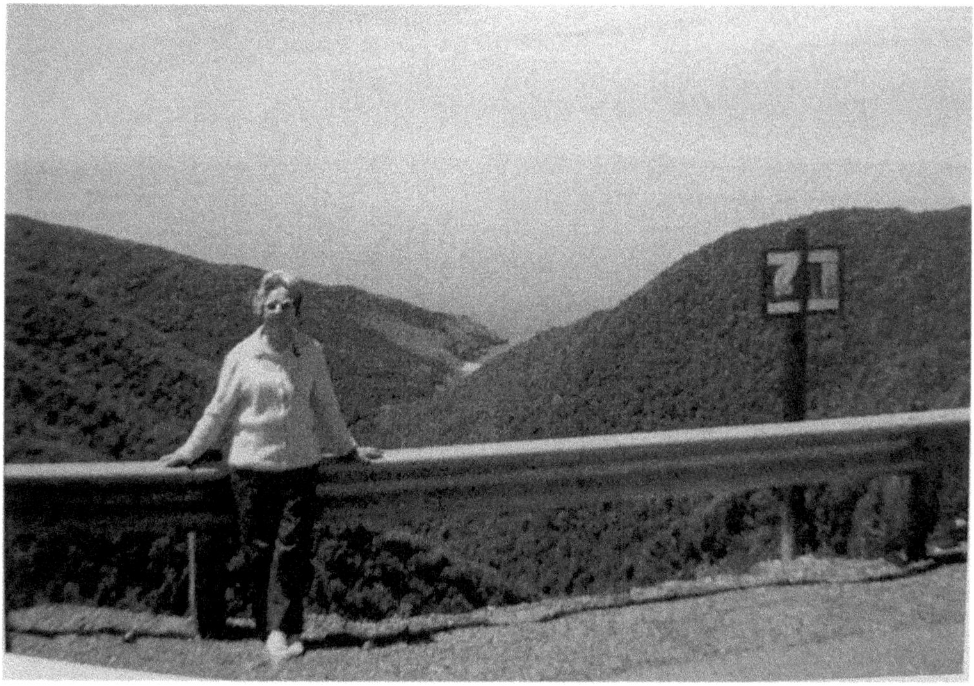
71

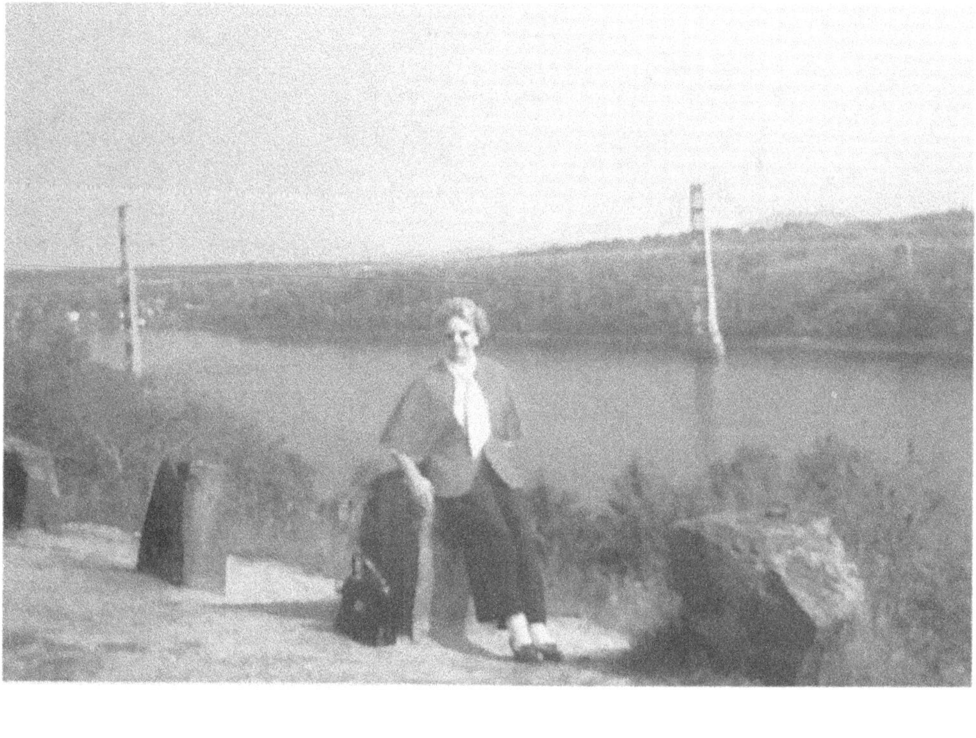

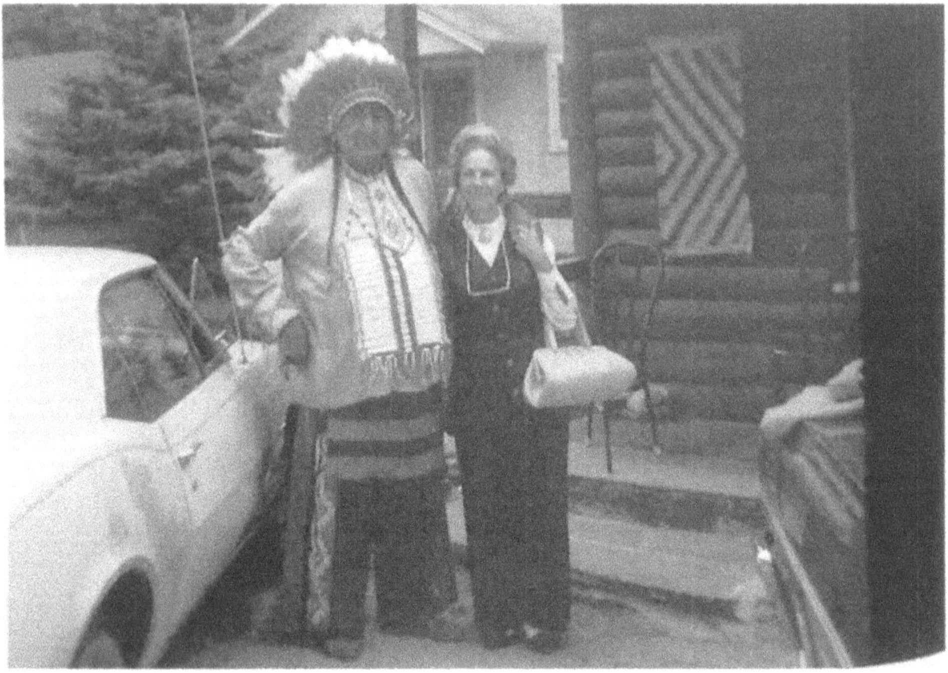

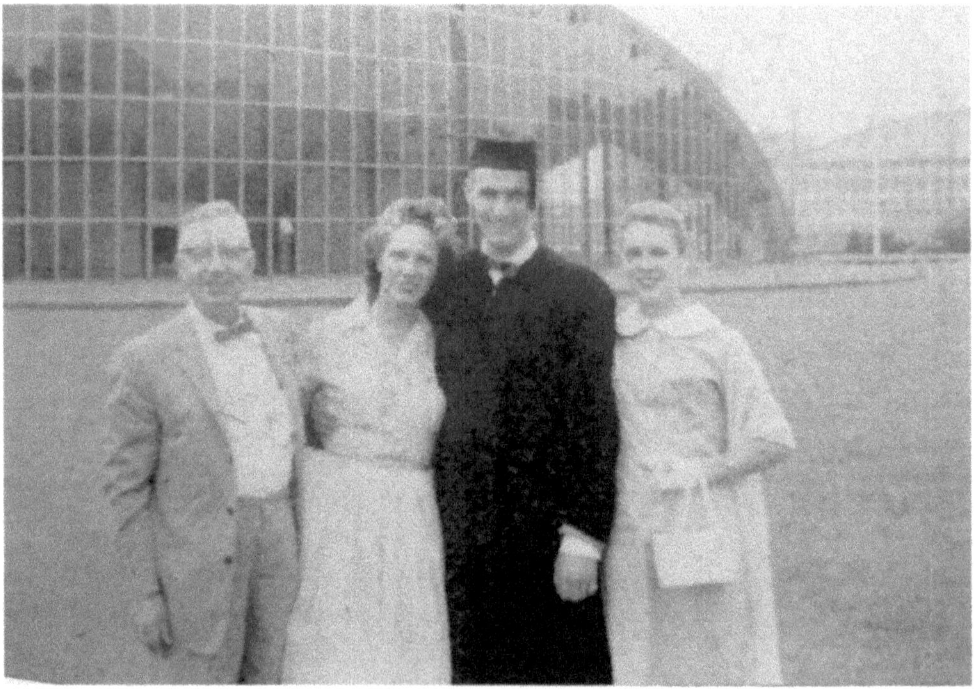

South Dakota
POINTS OF INTEREST
1. MT. RUSHMORE NAT'L. MON. 131 M. W
2. W. KNEE BATTLEFIELD, 120 M. S W
3. SIOUX FALLS ZOO, 219 M. E

4. SLIM BUTTES, 202 M. N W.
5. CORN PALACE, 194 M. E

FRIENDLY LAND
OF INFINITE VARIETY

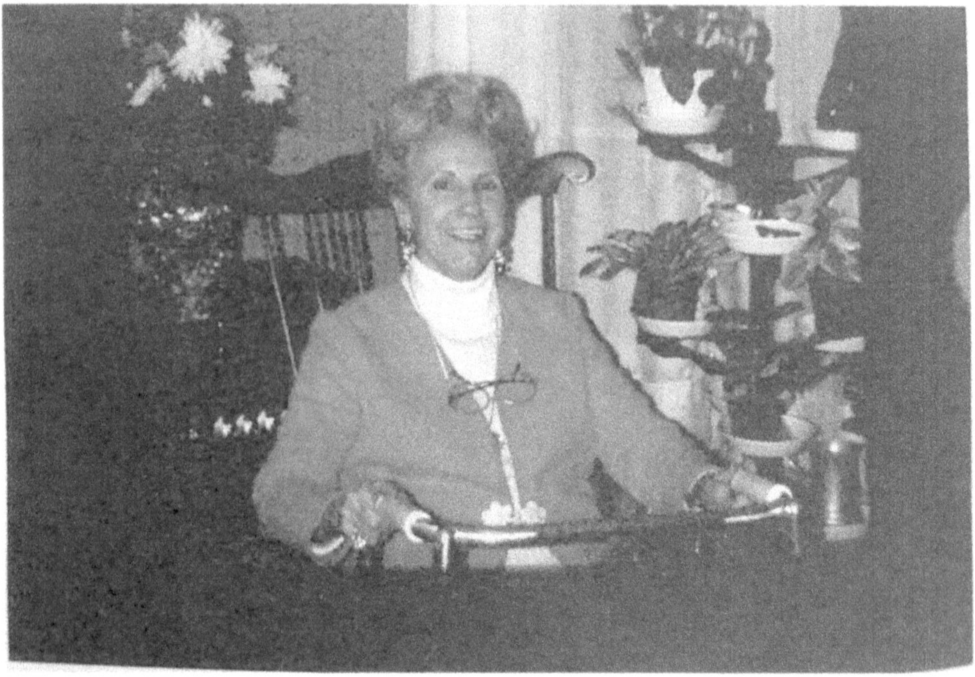

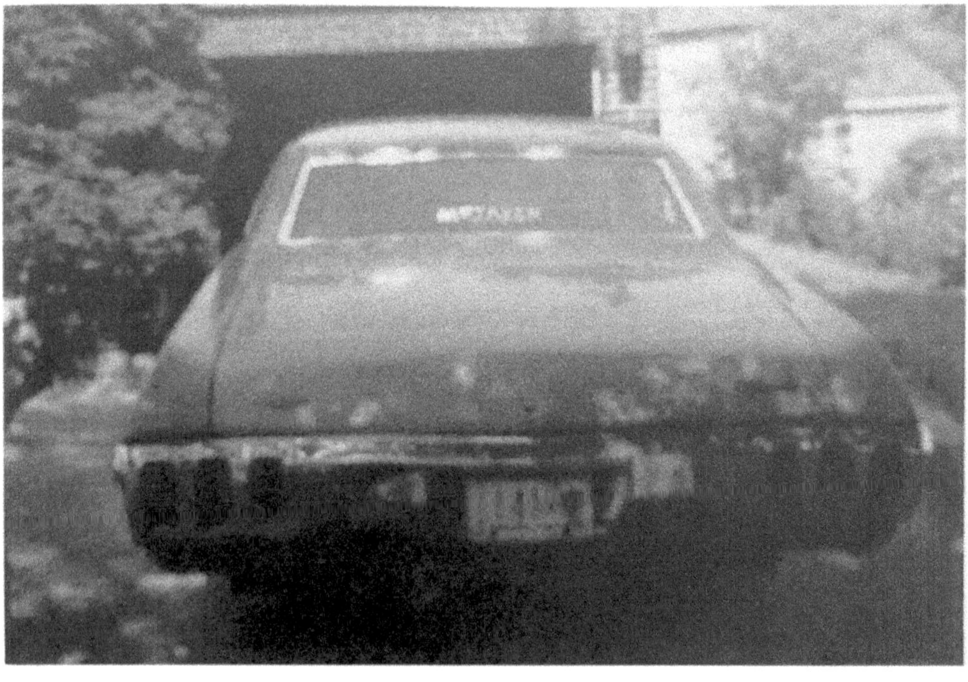

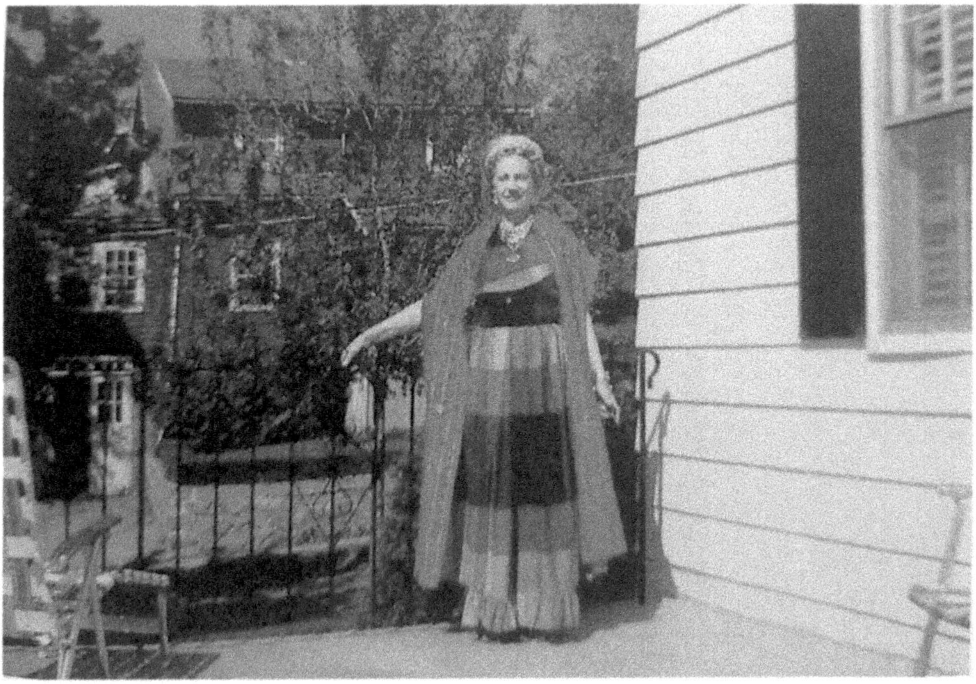

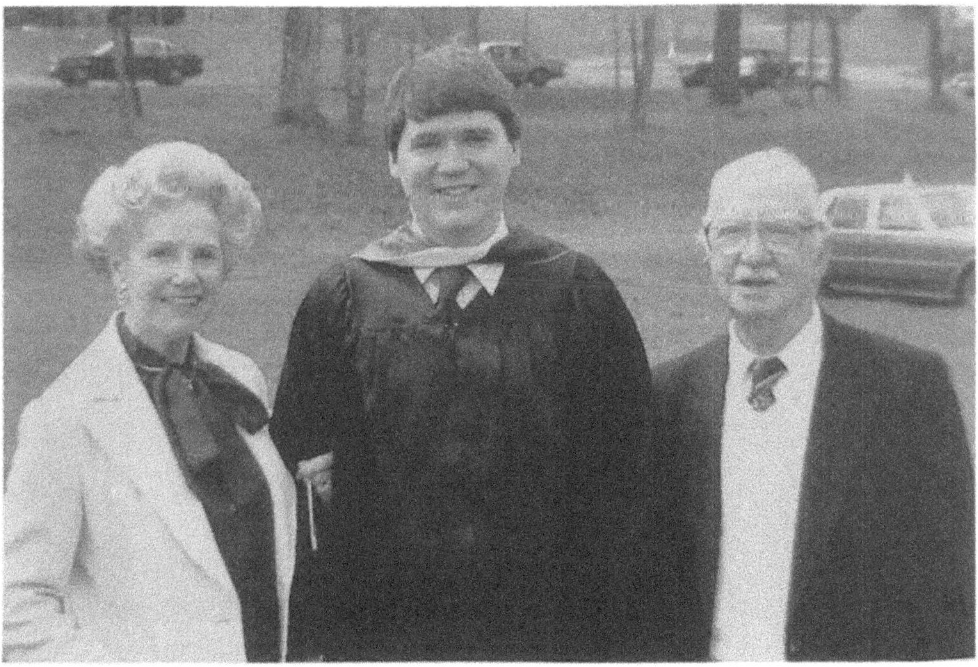

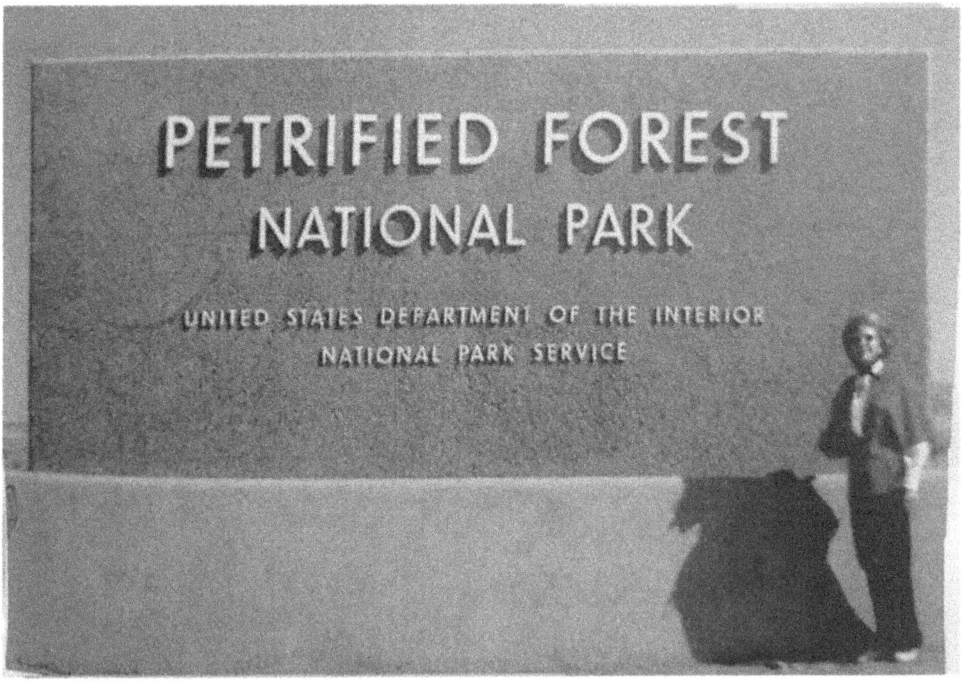
PETRIFIED FOREST
NATIONAL PARK
UNITED STATES DEPARTMENT OF THE INTERIOR
NATIONAL PARK SERVICE

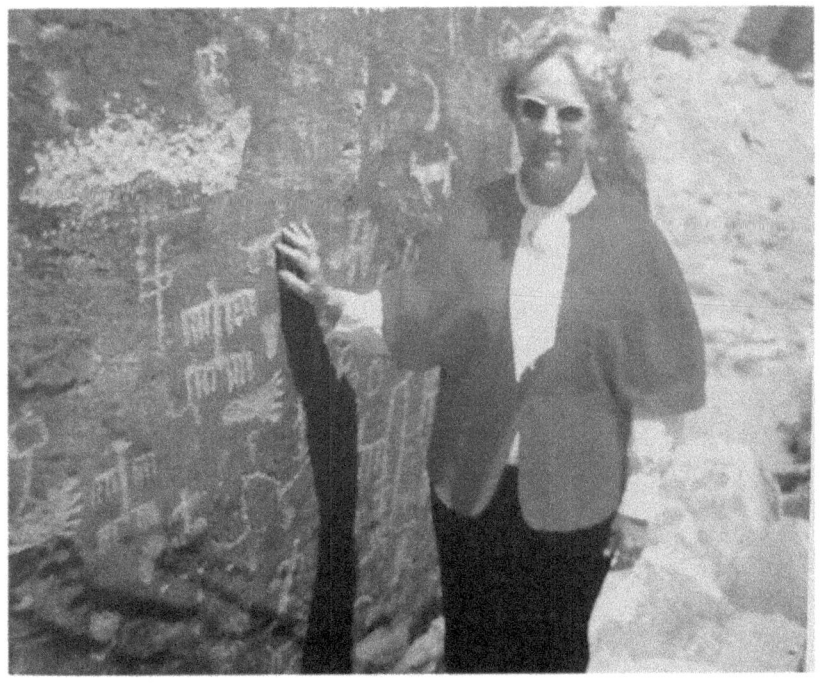

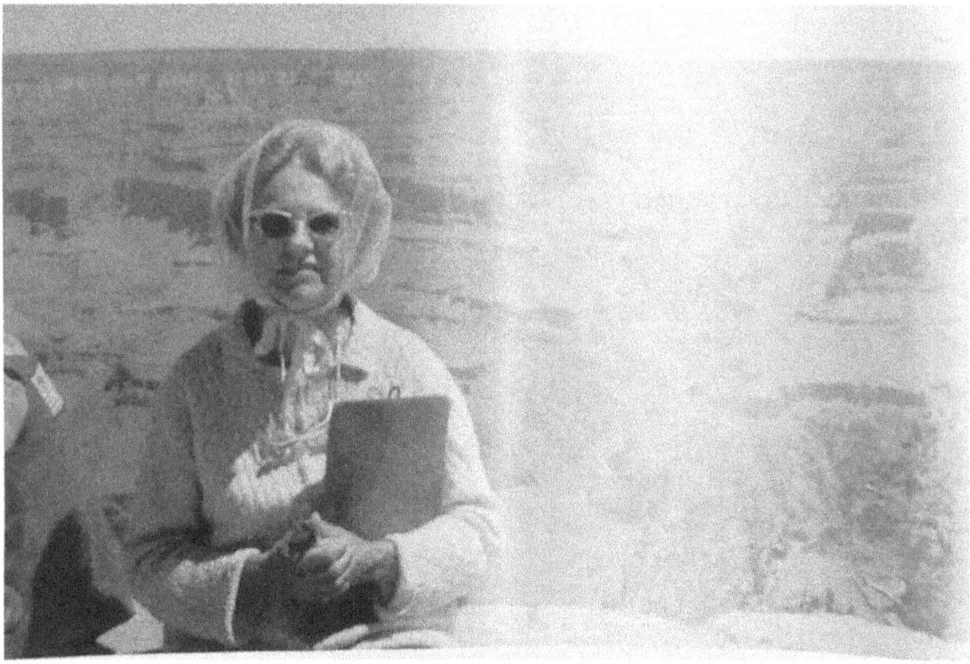

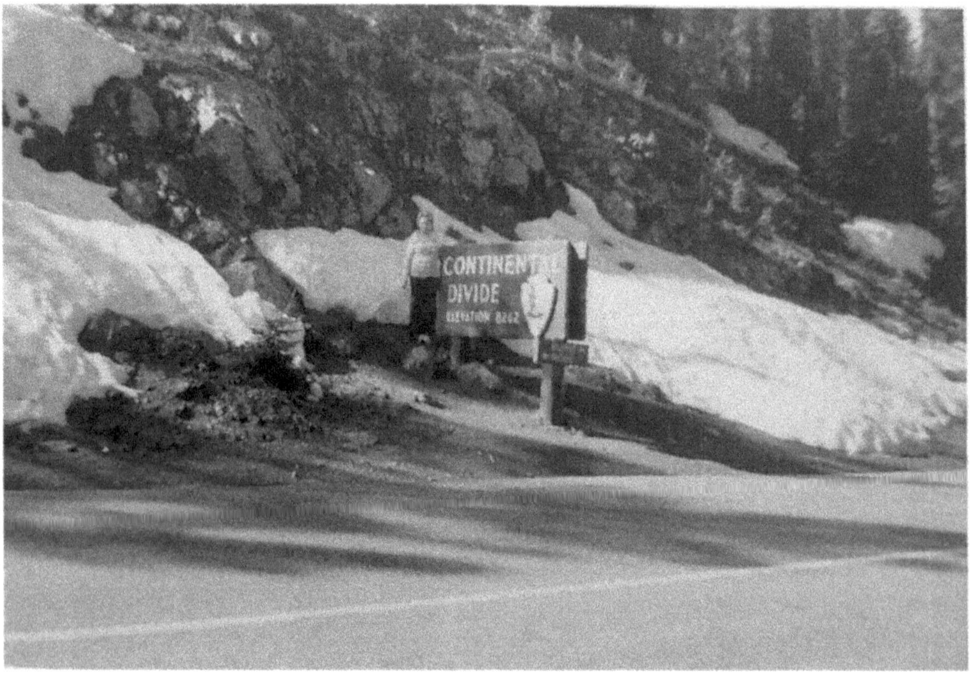
CONTINENT
DIVIDE

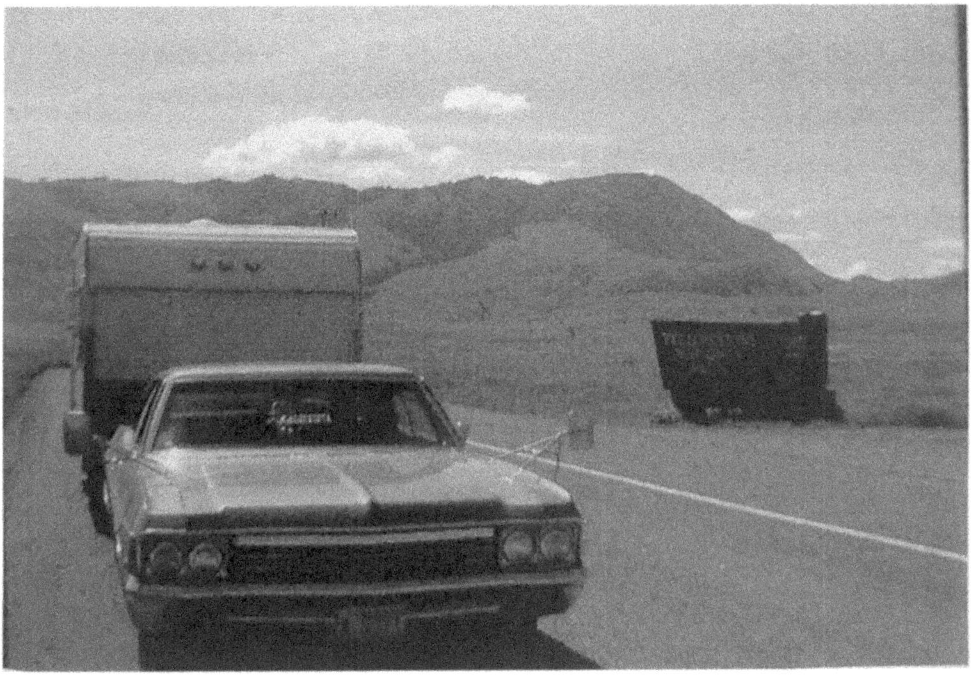

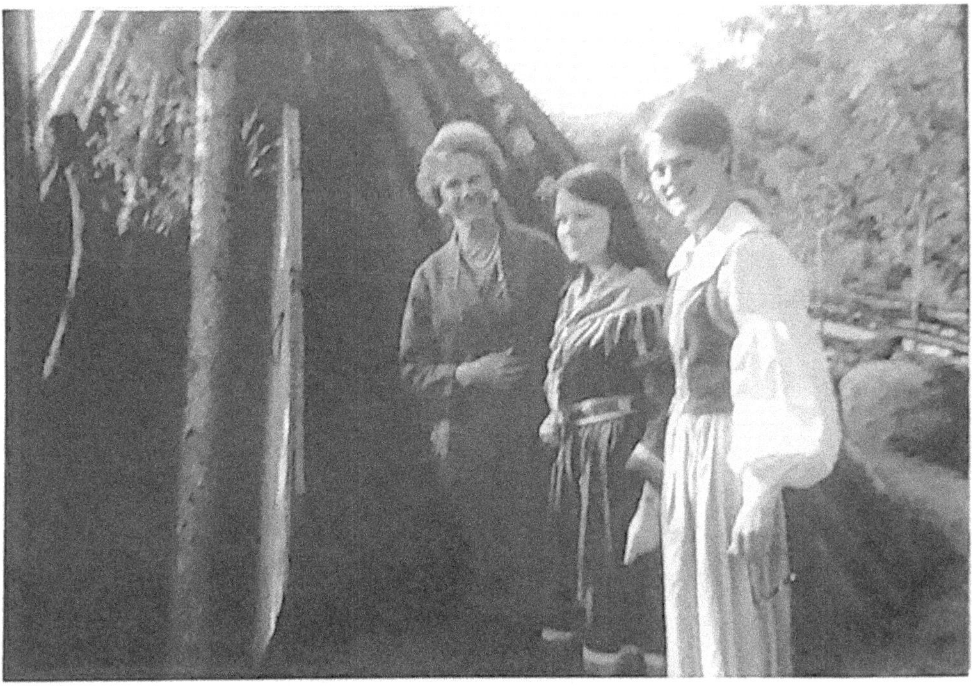

To Byrne L. Corbin,
Grandson extraordinaire, "a
beautiful human being who has
brought nothing but joy into the
lives of his family + especially into
the life of his Grandmother,

Elizabeth N. Metayer
Nov. 10, 1997